WM 425 FRE   £53.99

KU-286-063
369 0160281

LIBRARY
ACCESSION No.
This book is due for return on or before the last date shown below.
SUBJE

MONKLANDS HOSPITAL
AIRDRIE ML6 0JS

5/11/12

Clinical Applications
of Cognitive Therapy

Second Edition

Clinical Applications of Cognitive Therapy

Second Edition

ARTHUR FREEMAN

Dean, School of Counseling, Education, Psychology,
and Social Work, University of St. Francis,
Fort Wayne, Indiana

JAMES PRETZER

Cleveland Center for Cognitive Therapy and
Case Western Reserve University School of Medicine
Cleveland, Ohio

BARBARA FLEMING

Anxiety Treatment Center and
Case Western Reserve University School of Medicine
Cleveland, Ohio

KAREN M. SIMON

Cognitive Behavioral Therapy of Newport Beach
Newport Beach, California

Kluwer Academic/Plenum Publishers
New York • Boston • Dordrecht • London • Moscow

Library of Congress Cataloging-in-Publication Data

Clinical applications of cognitive therapy/Arthur Freeman . . . [et al.].—2nd ed.
    p.   ; cm.
    Includes bibliographical references and index.
    ISBN 0-306-48462-5
    1. Cognitive therapy.   2. Personality disorders—Treatment.   I. Freeman, Arthur, 1942–
    [DNLM: 1. Cognitive Therapy—methods.   2. Anxiety Disorders—therapy.   3. Mood
Disorders—therapy.   4. Personality Disorders—therapy.   5. Substance-Related
Disorders—therapy. WM 425.5.C6 C6409 2004]
    RC489.C63C576   2004
    616.89′142—dc22

                                                                            2004041845

ISBN 0-306-48462-5

© 2004 by Kluwer Academic/Plenum Publishers, New York
233 Spring Street, New York, New York 10013

http://www.kluweronline.com

10 9 8 7 6 5 4 3 2 1

A C.I.P. record for this book is available from the Library of Congress.

All rights reserved

No part of this work may be reproduced, stored in a retrieval system, or transmitted in any form or by
any means, electronic, mechanical, photocopying, microfilming, recording, or otherwise, without
written permission from the Publisher, with the exception of any material supplied specifically for the
purpose of being entered and executed on a computer system, for exclusive use by the purchaser of
the work.

Permissions for books published in Europe: permissions@wkap.nl
Permissions for books published in the United States of America: permissions@wkap.com

Printed in the United States of America

Foreword

When the first edition of *Clinical Applications of Cognitive Therapy* was published in 1990, it provided a valuable resource for practitioners, researchers, and advanced students of Cognitive Therapy. At that time, a large body of research supported the cognitive view of psychopathology and showed that Cognitive Therapy was an effective treatment approach. However, as practitioners went forth to apply Cognitive Therapy in real-life clinical practice, they faced significant challenges. In controlled outcome studies, standardized treatment protocols for treating one specific problem had been applied with carefully selected research subjects. In clinical practice, individuals seeking treatment typically had more than one problem at a time, had a variety of factors which complicated treatment, or had problems for which no standardized treatment protocol had yet been developed.

Clinical Applications of Cognitive Therapy was a volume written by practitioners, for practitioners, which provided an integrated, step-wise approach to understanding the principles and practice of Cognitive Therapy. Its clear, practical approach was rich in clinical vignettes that demonstrated how the principles and strategies of Cognitive Therapy are applied. In addition to discussing the treatment of depression, suicidality, and anxiety disorders, it discussed the complications that arise when applying Cognitive Therapy's apparently straightforward approach in the consulting room. In particular, it included an extensive discussion of the interpersonal complexities encountered when applying Cognitive Therapy with clients who have personality disorders.

In this second edition, the authors have updated their discussion to reflect fifteen years of additional research and experience. They have expanded their coverage to include important topics such as the treatment of substance abuse, intervention with marital and family problems, Cognitive Therapy with children and adolescents, Cognitive Therapy in groups, and ways to maintain and enhance one's skill in Cognitive Therapy. The result is a volume which is assessible to readers who are new to Cognitive Therapy, but which has the depth to be valuable to seasoned cognitive therapists as well. I am confident that the Second Edition will prove to be as valuable a resource as its precursor was.

When I look back, it is amazing how far Cognitive Therapy has come in the past 40 years. When I started my career, I had no idea of where my investigations into the psychopathology of depression would lead. At the time I hoped to provide empirical support for the psychoanalytic theory of depression. However, the results of my early research failed to support the psychoanalytic hypothesis that depression was hostility turned inward. Instead, my clinical observations and empirical research suggested that there was a thinking disorder at the core of depression. Depressed patients showed a systematic bias in the way that they interpreted experiences. When I pointed out these biased interpretations and proposed less biased alternatives to the patients. I could produce an almost immediate lessening of symptoms. These discoveries led me away from psychoanalysis and provided the foundation for a very different system of psychotherapy.

Cognitive Therapy was developed as a short-term, here-and-now treatment for unipolar depression. Early clinical trials and controlled outcome studies found Cognitive Therapy for depression to be quite effective. From there, Cognitive Therapy has grown into a system of psychotherapy that consists of a theory of personality and psychopathology with solid empirical support for its basic postulates, a model of psychotherapy with basic principles and strategies that apply to a wide range of problems. Outcome research over the past several decades shows that it is just as effective when applied under "real-life" conditions as it is in carefully controlled research conditions. Exciting new research provides evidence that, in addition to being effective with depression and anxiety disorders, Cognitive Therapy can provide effective treatment for refractory conditions such as schizophrenia and personality disorders.

Join four seasoned cognitive therapists in taking on the challenge of providing sensitive, effective treatment for the wide range of problems encountered in clinical practice.

Aaron T. Beck, M.D.
Wynnewood, PA

Contents

I

Clinical Practice of Cognitive Therapy

More than four decades ago, a young psychoanalytically trained psychiatrist embarked on a program of research that was to transform the practice of psychotherapy. Aaron T. Beck was determined to conduct research that would provide empirical support for psychoanalytic theory (Weishaar, 1993). To test the psychoanalytic view that depression was due to hostility turned inwards, he collected the dreams of depressed patients and interpreted these dreams. In his initial study, Beck found that the dreams of depressed individuals depicted the dreamer as a loser and this seemed to support psychoanalytic theory. However, follow-up studies contradicted psychoanalytic theory by showing that the dreams of depressed clients mirrored their conscious thought instead of revealing signs of inward hostility. Rather than discarding his research and going on with a career as a psychoanalyst, Beck embarked on systematic research into the nature of depression that eventually led to the development of Cognitive Therapy[1] and to his being one of the most influential psychotherapists of the twentieth century.

Extensive research has provided support both for the theoretical propositions on which Cognitive Therapy is based and for the efficacy of Cognitive Therapy as a treatment for a broad range of problems. Recently, the American Psychological Association's Division of Clinical Psychology convened a panel to review the empirical status of various approaches to psychotherapy. The panel concluded that there is strong empirical support for Cognitive Therapy (DeRubeis & Crits-Cristoph, 1998). Cognitive Therapy was selected as an "empirically supported" treatment approach for Major Depressive Disorder, Generalized Anxiety Disorder, and Panic Disorder and closely related treatment approaches were selected as empirically supported treatments for Social Phobia, Obsessive–Compulsive Disorder, Agoraphobia, and Posttraumatic Stress Disorder. Research is currently under way for testing the effectiveness of Cognitive Therapy with an even broader range of problems.

---

[1] A wide variety of "cognitive" and "cognitive-behavioral" therapies have been developed in recent years. To minimize confusion without creating the illusion that all cognitive therapies are equivalent, only Aaron Beck's approach will be referred to as Cognitive Therapy. The broader range of cognitive-behavioral and cognitive therapies in general will be referred to as cognitive-behavioral therapies.

When the principles of Cognitive Therapy are presented in workshops and training programs, they strike many therapists as straightforward and reasonable. This leads some to conclude that using Cognitive Therapy in clinical practice is simply a matter of learning a few new techniques. Unfortunately, neither life nor therapy is this simple. The effective application of Cognitive Therapy requires: (1) a clinical assessment that provides a basis for developing an understanding of the client and his or her problems, (2) a strategic intervention plan based on this conceptualization, and (3) a wide range of cognitive and behavioral interventions that can be used flexibly in executing the intervention plan.

The initial section of this book will introduce the theoretical and practical foundations of Cognitive Therapy. It is designed to provide readers who are not experienced cognitive-behavioral therapists with a solid foundation and orient experienced cognitive-behavioral therapists to the particular approach that we advocate. We recommend that all readers review Section 1 before moving on to more advanced topics.

1

Cognitive Therapy in the Real World
Establishing a Foundation for Effective Treatment

In recent years, treatment protocols have been tested for disorders ranging from depression to agoraphobia and to obsessive–compulsive disorder. Given the recent emphasis on empirically supported treatment approaches (DeRubeis & Crits-Cristoph, 1998) and the number of treatment manuals that have been published, it might seem that all one needs to do is to choose the treatment protocol that matches the individual's diagnosis and follow the directions. Unfortunately, clients rarely present with a single problem for which there is a well-validated treatment protocol. Consider this situation:

> It is Monday morning and a therapist looks at his schedule: "Let's see . . . at 9 a.m. I have a couple stuck in an on-again, off-again relationship; then I have a young executive recovering from depression complicated by alcohol abuse. Next I go to the Family Practice Center to see a client with somatic symptoms of stress, a young father obsessed with the thought of harming his child, and a family with chronic conflict among adolescent children. Later I return to my office to see a dentist with chronic social anxiety, an agoraphobic housewife, and a CPA troubled by anxiety, depression, and outbursts of anger."

Although this monologue is imaginary, the caseload on that particular Monday was real and it illustrates one problem in the practice of Cognitive Therapy. Typically, clients enter treatment with multiple problems, with a variety of factors complicating therapy, or with problems for which empirically tested treatment approaches are not yet available. The practicing clinician must try to bridge the gap between controlled outcome studies and the complexities encountered in clinical practice. This volume is written for that practitioner.

A COGNITIVE VIEW OF PSYCHOPATHOLOGY

The first task a practicing clinician faces is that of finding a way to understand the wide range of individual, interpersonal, and family problems that he or she encounters. Cognitive Therapy is based on a straightforward, commonsense model

3

of the relationships among cognition, emotion, and behavior in human functioning in general and in psychopathology in particular. Three aspects of cognition are emphasized: automatic thoughts, schemas, and cognitive distortions.

In Cognitive Therapy, an individual's immediate, unpremeditated interpretations of events are referred to as "automatic thoughts" because they occur spontaneously and without apparent volition. One major premise of the cognitive view is the idea that automatic thoughts shape both individuals' emotions and their actions in response to events. For example, when Al, a secretary in his late 20s, was summoned to his superior's office, his immediate thoughts were, "Oh God, I must have really blown it! I'm really in trouble now." According to the cognitive view, we would expect him to feel and act as though he was in serious trouble as long as he maintained this interpretation of the situation. If his interpretation of the situation is accurate, his responses are likely to be reasonably appropriate. However, if he is overestimating the extent to which he is in trouble or is completely mistaken, his emotions and actions are not likely to be appropriate to the situation. The cognitive approach is based on the observation that automatic thoughts that are exaggerated, distorted, mistaken, or unrealistic play a major role in psychopathology. If it is possible to identify the automatic thoughts that the client experiences in problem situations, this often provides a simple explanation for apparently incomprehensible reactions.

Often the thoughts that clients report are so extreme that it is hard to believe that intelligent, capable, well-educated individuals could believe such things without there being some "deep" reason behind it. For example, Al was certain that he was going to be vigorously criticized and possibly fired even though he was not aware of having committed any major infractions and had never received hostile criticism or unfair treatment from his supervisor in the past. How could Al be convinced that he was "in big trouble" despite the lack of evidence to support this conviction? An individual's beliefs, assumptions, and "schemas" shape the perception and interpretation of events. Al had grown up in a family in which he received many punitive reprimands, deserved and undeserved, while receiving little positive feedback. As an adult, he presumed that attention from authority figures was almost certain to be hostile and punitive. This preconception shaped his response to being summoned to his supervisor's office.

In the Cognitive Therapy literature, the terms "schema," "irrational belief," "underlying assumption," "dysfunctional belief," and so on, have sometimes been used interchangeably and, at other times, distinctions have been drawn among these closely related terms. In the hope of making this a bit less confusing, we will use these terms as discussed by Padesky (1994) and Pretzer and Beck (1996): *Schemas* are unconditional core beliefs which serve as a basis for screening, categorizing, and interpreting experiences (i.e., "I'm no good." "Others can't be trusted." "Effort does not pay off."). Schemas often operate outside of the individual's awareness and often are not clearly verbalized. *Underlying Assumptions* (or Dysfunctional Beliefs) are conditional beliefs that shape one's response to experiences and situations (i.e., "If someone gets close to me, they will discover the 'real me' and reject me."). These assumptions may operate outside of the individual's awareness and may not be clearly verbalized or the individual may be aware of these assumptions.

Interpersonal Strategies are underlying assumptions that focus specifically on ways of influencing others (i.e., "The way to get children to be good is to punish them for being bad." or, "If I want someone to like me, I should be nice to them."). Often the individual is aware of these assumptions/beliefs or finds them fairly easy to recognize. *Automatic Thoughts* are cognitions that spontaneously flow through one's mind in the moment (i.e., "Oh My God! Now I'm in big trouble!"). Individuals may or may not be aware of their automatic thoughts but most people can easily learn to be more aware of their automatic thoughts.

In addition, human thought is subject to a number of errors in logic termed as "cognitive distortions" by Beck (1976) and shown in Table 1.1. These cognitive distortions can lead individuals to erroneous conclusions even if their perception of the situation is accurate. If the situation is perceived erroneously, these distortions can amplify the impact of the misperceptions. For example, Al tended to view others as either completely benevolent or completely hostile (dichotomous thinking,

TABLE 1.1. Commonly Observed Cognitive Distortions[a]

Dichotomous thinking—Things are seen in terms of two mutually exclusive categories with no "shades of gray" in between. For example, believing that one is *either* a success *or* a failure and that anything short of a perfect performance is a total failure.

Overgeneralization—A specific event is seen as being characteristic of life in general rather than as being one event among many. For example, concluding that an inconsiderate response from one's spouse shows that she doesn't care despite her having shown consideration on other occasions.

Selective abstraction—A single aspect of a complex situation is the focus of attention and other relevant aspects of the situation are ignored. For example, focusing on the one negative comment in a performance evaluation received at work and overlooking a number of positive comments.

Disqualifying the positive—Positive experiences, which would conflict with the individual's negative views are discounted by declaring that they "don't count." For example, disbelieving positive feedback from friends and colleagues and thinking, "They're only saying that to be nice."

Mind reading—The individual assumes that others are reacting negatively without evidence that this is the case. For example, thinking "I just *know* he thought I was an idiot!", despite the other person's having behaved politely.

Fortune-telling—The individual reacts as though his or her negative expectations about future events are established facts. For example, thinking "He's leaving me, I just know it!" and acting as though this is definitely true.

Catastrophizing—Negative events that might occur are treated as intolerable catastrophes rather than being seen in perspective. For example, thinking "Oh my God, what if I faint!" without considering that, while fainting may be unpleasant and embarrassing, it is not terribly dangerous.

Minimization—Positive characteristics or experiences are treated as real but insignificant. For example, thinking "Sure, I'm good at my job, but so what, my parents don't respect me."

Emotional reasoning—Assuming that emotional reactions necessarily reflect the true situation. For example, deciding that since one feels hopeless, the situation must really be hopeless.

"Should" Statements—The use of "should" and "have to" statements to provide motivation or control behavior. For example, thinking "I shouldn't feel aggravated. She's my mother, I *have* to listen to her."

Labeling— Attaching a global label to oneself rather than referring to specific events or actions. For example, thinking, "I'm a failure!" rather than, "Boy, I blew that one!"

Personalization—Assuming that one is the cause of a particular external event when, in fact, other factors are responsible. For example, assuming that a supervisor's lack of friendliness is a reflection of her feelings about the client rather than realizing that she is upset over a death in the family.

[a] Adapted from Burns (1999a)

see Table 1.1). Because his supervisor was not *always* kind and considerate, Al un-thinkingly categorized her as hostile. This, in combination with his assumptions about authority figures, contributed to his anticipation of punishment.

The cognitive model is not simply that "thoughts cause feelings and actions." It also recognizes that emotions can influence cognitive processes and that behaviors can influence the evaluation of a situation by modifying the situation or by eliciting responses from others. In fact, the impact of mood on cognitions is an important part of the cognitive understanding of psychopathology. A number of studies have produced evidence that an individual's mood can significantly bias recall and perception (Ingram & Wisnicki, 1991). For example, Bower (1981) found that sadness facilitated recall of sad events whereas happiness facilitated recall of happy events. Moods other than sadness and happiness have not been the subject of extensive empirical research, but clinical observation suggests that other moods such as anxiety and anger also bias perception and recall in mood-congruent ways. Because both biased recall and biased perception of events would tend to elicit more of the same mood, it appears that the tendency of mood to bias cognition in a mood-congruent way could easily perpetuate a mood regardless of its initial cause.

Automatic thoughts, underlying assumptions, cognitive distortions, and the impact of mood on cognition set the stage for a self-perpetuating cycle (presented graphically in Figure 1.1) that is observed in many disorders. An individual may hold assumptions that predispose him or her to psychopathology without having any noticeable effect until a situation relevant to the assumptions arises. However, when a relevant situation does occur, the dysfunctional assumptions, in combination with any cognitive distortions, contribute to problematic automatic thoughts. These automatic thoughts elicit a corresponding mood, the nature of which depends on the content of the automatic thoughts. This mood then biases recall and perception in such a way that the individual is likely to experience additional dysfunctional automatic thoughts, intensifying his or her mood. As the mood intensifies, recall and perception are biased further and the cycle easily becomes self-perpetuating. In Al's case, his negative preconceptions about authority figures

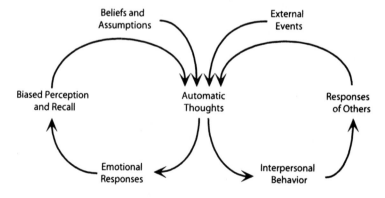

FIGURE 1.1. The Role of Cognition in Psychopathology.

and his tendency toward dichotomous thinking caused no problems except when he interacted with authority figures. When he received the summons discussed above, he quickly became both depressed and anxious in response to his antici-pation of punishment. Once he became depressed and anxious, he began to focus selectively on past transgressions that might be grounds for disciplinary action and he overlooked his overall work record. By the time he met with his supervisor, Al was convinced that he would be fired and was quite upset. He was amazed to discover that his supervisor only wanted to change some of his assignments.

Automatic thoughts directly influence the individual's behavior as well as his or her mood. In addition, interpersonal behavior is strongly influenced by interpersonal strategies, the individual's assumptions about interpersonal interac-tions. For example, some individuals believe that the thing to do when one is in trouble is to blame someone else; some believe that the thing to do is to apologize; still others believe that the thing to do is to accept responsibility and resolve to do better in the future. Al assumed that the thing to do when one is in trouble is to passively accept the inevitable punishment when it comes. Thus, his anticipation of hostility and punishment from his supervisor resulted in considerable anxiety and depression before his meeting with his supervisor but he quietly went in to "take his medicine" when the time came.

The responses of others can either aggravate the problem or alleviate it. Had Al's supervisor noticed nonverbal indications of his anxiety and depression, she might have suspected that this was because "he had something to feel guilty about" and, therefore, have been more critical than usual. This, of course, would have seemed to confirm his fears and would have intensified his reaction. On the other hand, she might have recognized his reactions as a manifestation of his insecurity and expressed sympathy and concern. This would have been incompatible with his preconceptions about her and would have decreased his anxiety. As it happened, on this occasion his subjective distress elicited no apparent response from her and the interpersonal aspects of the problem were negligible.

It is important to note that the cycle presented in Figure 1.1 need not start with the combined effects of dysfunctional beliefs and an event relevant to those beliefs. If dysfunctional automatic thoughts are elicited by objectively negative events or if a particular mood is elicited by biochemical changes, the same cycle could result. Regardless of the point at which the cycle starts, cognition plays an important role in the cycle and often is a productive point for intervention.

A Strategic Approach to Cognitive Therapy

The cognitive view of psychopathology suggests a variety of possible inter-vention points. Usually the initial goal of therapy would be to break the cycles that perpetuate and amplify the client's problems. This could be done by modifying the client's automatic thoughts, improving the client's mood, working to eliminate the biasing impact of mood on recall and perception, changing the client's behavior, or significantly changing the way others respond to the client. A combination of these interventions could break the cycles that perpetuate the problems and alleviate the client's immediate distress. However, if the therapist only worked to break these cycles, the client would be at risk for a relapse whenever he or she experienced events similar to those that precipitated the current episode. To achieve lasting results, it would also be important to modify the beliefs and assumptions that pre-dispose the client to his or her problems and to help plan effective ways to handle situations that might precipitate a relapse.

Because there are many possible intervention points and clients' problems are often quite complex, Cognitive Therapy is most effective when the therapist thinks strategically about intervention. This involves conducting an initial assessment and forming a provisional understanding of the client and his or her problems at the outset of therapy. This initial conceptualization is then used as a basis for selecting targets for intervention and for choosing intervention techniques. The results of the initial interventions then provide feedback that the therapist can use to refine his or her understanding of the client. If the initial interventions produce the expected results, it confirms that the therapist's understanding is "on target." If the interventions produce unexpected results, it highlights inadequacies in the therapist's understanding of the client and his or her problems. The importance of intervening on the basis of an understanding of the client and his or her problems rather than using a "cookbook" approach has been emphasized repeatedly in re-cent years (e.g., J. Beck, 1995; Freeman, Pretzer, Fleming, & Simon, 1990; Persons, 1989; Pretzer & Beck, 1996). Nezu (1998) has proposed a simple acronym that high-lights the importance of assessment and conceptualization in cognitive–behavioral therapy. This acronym, **FACT**, stands for First Assess, Conceptualize, and then Treat.

This straightforward, practical approach to therapy makes sense, but it is not simple. A therapist meeting a new client for the first time is faced with a complex task. Somehow, the therapist must form an initial understanding of the client, figure out how to be helpful, develop a good working relationship, and, at the same time, handle the practical details of working together. The task of understanding an individual and his or her problems is a difficult one. After all, the client is not likely to be able to provide a clear and concise analysis of his or her problems and may well be unable or unwilling to provide the detailed information that the therapist needs. The task facing the therapist in Cognitive Therapy is further complicated by the need to go beyond behavioral assessment and the collection of historical information to the assessment of the client's thoughts, feelings, beliefs, and schemas.

Although the task of assessment can be difficult, it plays a crucial role throughout the course of Cognitive Therapy. The initial assessment of the client's symptomatology, history, current functioning, and goals for therapy forms the foundation for the understanding of the processes that produce and maintain the client's difficulties and thus is the basis for the initial treatment strategy. Through-out treatment, the therapist constantly tests and refines his or her understanding of the client, revises this conceptualization as the client changes (and as flaws in the conceptualization are discovered), tests the effectiveness of interventions, and monitors the progress of therapy. The continuing need for assessment does not end even when therapy ends. The client will need to develop the ability to monitor his or her own progress to maintain and build upon the gains made in therapy.

The Initial Assessment

The challenge for the therapist during an initial evaluation is to obtain enough information to permit the development of an early treatment plan without taking an unreasonable amount of time or sacrificing attention to the development of a good therapeutic relationship. This is most easily done through a semistructured interview supplemented by questionnaire data. Table 1.2 lists the topics ideally

TABLE 1.2. Topics to be Covered in an Initial Evaluation

Presenting problem
  Nature of problem(s), precipitants, course, client's understanding of problem, previous attempts at dealing with problem
Current life situation
  Living situation, work, interests and activities, use of leisure time, family relationships, level of satisfaction with current life
Developmental history
  Family history: descriptions of parents, relationships with parents, relationships with siblings, major events during childhood
  School/occupational history: level of achievement, satisfaction, enjoyment, interests, career choices, problems (including legal problems)
  Social history: peer relationships in childhood, adolescence, adulthood; sexual relationships, sexual identity and preferences, dating, serious relationships, and marriage including description of partners and any relationship problems
  Legal history: problems with school authorities and legal system
Traumatic experiences
  Disruptions of family relationships; medical, psychological, or substance abuse problems within the family; physical or sexual abuse
Medical history
  Current health, time since last checkup, current medications, known allergies to medications, previous medical problems, substance abuse
  Family history of medical problems, psychological problems, and/or substance abuse
Psychiatric history
  Previous therapy or counseling (when? with whom? why? what was helpful/unhelpful? were there any problems with therapy?)
  Previous and current psychiatric medication (who prescribed? results? side effects? If discontinued, why?)
  Previous occurrences of current problems; their course and outcome
Mental status
  Appearance, attitude, behavior, mood and affect, speech and thought, perception, intellectual and cognitive functioning
Client's goals for therapy
  State clearly and specifically, prioritize
Client's questions and concerns

---

covered in an initial evaluation. This list of topics may appear both exhaustive and exhausting, but it is important to remember that the clinician's task is to obtain an overview of each area and to go into detail only when detailed information is needed. With practice, it is possible to cover these topics in about an hour and a half while remaining emotionally responsive and beginning to develop a therapeutic relationship.

Many traditional approaches to therapy rely on an informal assessment process of simply observing whatever information emerges in the course of therapy and interpreting it in terms of the therapist's own experience instead of starting therapy with an explicit assessment phase. The informal observations of experienced clinicians may be quite rich and remarkably accurate; however, informal assessment has several major drawbacks. First, because the information is not collected systematically, important information may be overlooked or a biased picture may be created. Second, informally collected information can easily be influenced by a variety of factors, such as the therapist's verbal and nonverbal cues or the client's concerns and inhibitions, without the biases being apparent. Third, it is difficult to compare informally collected information from one client with similar information from another client or with information collected from the same client on another occasion. (For example, is a client who is "bummed out" more depressed than one who is feeling "pretty down"? Is a shift from feeling "bummed out" to feeling "not too good" an improvement or not?) Finally, it takes an extended period of time to develop a reasonably complete conceptualization of a client on the basis of informal assessment. This may not be a problem with undirected long-term therapies but a directed, strategic therapy such as Cognitive Therapy requires a clear conceptualization of the client early in treatment to form a basis for early intervention. A more systematic approach to assessment[1] can overcome these problems without interfering with the process of therapy.

A balance between structure and flexibility is needed to be both efficient and sensitive in the initial interview. Without the therapist actively structuring the interview, an extremely verbal client could easily spend weeks telling his or her story. On the other hand, a less verbal client might finish quickly but fail to mention important information. However, a therapist who rigidly adheres to a preconceived structure risks appearing insensitive and alienating the client. The therapist's task can be simplified if he or she uses an initial evaluation form (see Appendix A) which

---

[1] Much of what has been written on the topic of cognitive assessment or on assessment in cognitive-behavioral therapy has been written from a research-oriented perspective (e.g., Arnkoff & Glass, 1982; Glass & Arnkoff, 1982; Kendall & Korgeski, 1979; Merluzzi, Glass, & Genest, 1981). These authors have much to contribute. However, there are important differences between assessment for use in research and assessment for use in clinical practice. In particular, the psychometric characteristics of measures are of great importance in research due to the requirements of statistical analyses, the need to be able to reach firm conclusions on the basis of a limited amount of data, and the desire to generalize findings beyond the individuals being assessed. Reliability and validity are of obvious value in clinical assessment as well; however, the most crucial question is whether the assessment procedure proves useful and practical in treatment. Assessment techniques which provide rich data that is difficult to quantify may be quite valuable in clinical assessment but may not be acceptable for research use. Conversely, techniques which provide reliable, valid numerical scores may be ideal for use in research but of limited value in clinical practice.

outlines the major points to be covered and provides sufficient space for recording the client's responses. By using such a form the therapist is freed from the task of remembering both the topics to be covered and the client's responses and thus can be more sensitive and responsive. With the outline to aid in maintaining structure, the therapist is free to cover topics whenever they fit naturally with the client's story without fear of forgetting to cover other important topics.

Using a semistructured approach to the initial evaluation also reduces the risk of overlooking important issues such as substance abuse, a history of physical or sexual abuse, or medical conditions that may be relevant to treatment. It is useful to recognize such issues early in treatment because they can have a major impact on the course of treatment. For suggestions regarding methods for assessing substance abuse and responding to clients who resist acknowledging a substance abuse problem, see Chapter 6.

Forming an Initial Conceptualization as a Basis for Intervention

Once the initial evaluation has been completed, the therapist is faced with the task of making sense of a large amount of information and developing an initial understanding of the client and his or her problems. This will serve as the basis for choosing initial interventions. Several authors have attempted to devise forms to help therapists organize the information they have obtained for simplifying the task of developing an individualized conceptualization. Figures 1.2 and 1.3 show how conceptualization forms developed by J. Beck (1995) and J. Persons (1989) would be used to organize the information obtained in Al's initial evaluation. (For explanations on how to use these forms, see Beck, 1995, and Persons, 1989.)

One thing that is apparent from these two examples is that the information obtained in the initial evaluation is necessarily incomplete and leads to hypotheses about the client which may or may not prove to be true. These initial hypotheses are tested and refined over the course of treatment as the therapist collects more detailed information and observes the results of interventions.

With most clients, the initial stage in therapy includes significant amounts of time and effort that are devoted to "filling in the blanks" and testing some of the therapist's initial hypotheses. When doing this, it is more productive for the therapist to focus on specific incidents that occur and the specific thoughts, feelings, and actions that occur at that time than for therapist and client to discuss the issues in more general terms. Thus, in trying to understand Al's problems with authority figures, a cognitive therapist might start by saying, "Al, I'll need to understand your problems with your boss and other authority figures to be able to help you with them. Can you think of a recent example of a situation where these problems came up?" Then the therapist would focus on understanding Al's thoughts, feelings, and actions *in that specific incident*. After exploring several specific examples of the problems in question, the therapist may well have the information he or she needs to understand the problem. If the therapist were to encourage the client to discuss

Cognitive Conceptualization Diagram

Client: __Al_____   Date: _____

Diagnosis: __pending_____

Relevant Childhood Data

Parents were critical and demanding. They punished assertion and reinforced submission. Parochial school reinforced this pattern.

Core Belief(s)

?

Conditional Assumptions/Beliefs/Rules

If [an authority figure] is dissatisfied I'll be punished? If I'm criticized it's my fault? If I stand up for myself I'll be punished?

Compensatory Strategy(ies)

Tries to anticipate criticism & avoid it. Vigilant for criticism. Avoids being focus of attention. Avoids challenges. Passively accepts criticism, blames self.

Situation	Situation	Situation
Boss calls me in to his office.	Boss left me a note asking me to re-type a letter.	
Automatic Thought	**Automatic Thought**	**Automatic Thought**
Oh God, I must have really blown it! I'm really in trouble now.	I'm in big trouble now!	
Meaning of AT	**Meaning of AT**	**Meaning of AT**
I'm in trouble, I must have done something wrong.	I'm going to be punished.	
Emotion	**Emotion**	**Emotion**
Anxiety, Panic	Anxiety, Depression	
Behavior	**Behavior**	**Behavior**
I just went on in to take my medicine.	Slowly type letter and wait for boss to return.	

FIGURE 1.2. Example of Using Judith Beck's Conceptualization Form.

Identifying information:

> *Al, 28 year-old unmarried male, employed as a secretary*

Chief complaint:

> *Recurrent, brief episodes of intense anxiety and depression.*

Problem list:

> *1. Sensitivity to criticism*
>
> *2. Anxiety when anticipating criticism, avoidance of criticism*
>
> *3. Depression and self-blame following criticism*
>
> *4. Lack of appropriate assertion*
>
> *5. Reluctance to pursue career advancement*

Hypothesized mechanism:

> *Some, as yet unknown, belief or beliefs results in excessive fear of criticism and self-blame following criticism.*

Relation of mechanism to problems:

> *Fear of criticism leads to vigilance for signs of criticism and anticipation of criticism. This elicits anxiety and avoidance. Avoidance perpetuates fears. When criticism is received, this leads to self-blame which contributes to depression. Self-blame reinforces avoidance.*

FIGURE 1.3. Example of Using Jacqueline Persons's Case Formulation Form.

the problem in more general terms, it is likely to take much longer for the therapist and client to develop an understanding of the problem.

Many of the subsequent chapters in this volume present cognitive conceptualizations of specific disorders. It might appear that a therapist could simply take this "standard" conceptualization and use it as the basis for intervention without going to the trouble of developing an individualized conceptualization. This would work if all clients with a given diagnosis were identical. However, this is not at all the case. We hope that the conceptualizations presented in this book are useful as starting points for developing individualized conceptualizations but we would not advocate simply using them "off-the-shelf" as a basis for intervention.

Precipitants of current problems:

Authority figures are seen as sources of criticism. When Al was in college he felt he was "just one of the crowd" and usually did not fear being singled out for criticism. Once he began working, he felt exposed to the scrutiny of his boss. At present, interactions with his boss are the primary precipitant.

Origins of the central problem:

Parents were critical and demanding. As a child Al tried to avoid their criticism. Parents punished assertion and rewarded submission. Parochial school reinforced these patterns.

Treatment plan:

Identify and challenge the automatic thoughts which occur when anticipating criticism.

Identify and challenge the automatic thoughts which occur when criticized, especially ones involving self-blame.

Identify fears about the consequences of criticism and address them.

In vivo desensitization to criticism (by decreasing avoidance of criticism and tolerating criticism when it occurs). .

Assertion training.

Identify any beliefs and assumptions which contribute to these problems and modify them.

Predicted obstacles to treatment:

He may well fear being criticized by the therapist and avoid it. This could well result in "I forgot," "I didn't have time," and other problems with homework. He may be reluctant to be assertive in therapy or may be overly submissive.

FIGURE 1.3. (cont.)

The Therapeutic Relationship

It is important for the therapist to use the initial therapy sessions to establish a solid foundation for therapy before plunging into interventions. The effectiveness of any form of psychotherapy depends on a relationship of confidence, openness, caring, and trust established between client and therapist, and this is certainly true of Cognitive Therapy. The cognitive therapist takes an active, directive role in treatment and thus can intentionally work to develop the therapeutic relationship rather than waiting for it to spontaneously unfold over time. With many clients, the process of establishing a good working relationship is quite straightforward, but with other clients, it is much more complicated. Discussions of the complexities and difficulties encountered in the therapeutic relationship are found in many of the treatment chapters, particularly in those discussing treatment of personality disorders.

In Cognitive Therapy, the therapist attempts to establish a collaborative relationship in which therapist and client work together toward the client's goals. This maximizes the client's involvement in therapy and minimizes resistance and noncompliance, yet still allows the therapist to structure each session as well as the overall course of therapy so as to be as efficient and effective as possible. To collaborate effectively, the therapist and client must reach an agreement on the goals of therapy. Therefore, following the initial evaluation, the therapist works with the client to specify goals for therapy and prioritize them. These goals include both the problems that the client wishes to overcome and the positive changes he or she wants to work toward. They should be operationalized clearly and specifically enough so that both therapist and client can tell if progress is being made. For example: Frank, a depressed salesman, initially stated his goal for therapy as, "to become the best I can be." When stated in that way, the goal was overly vague and abstract. It was also clearly unmanageable considering that Frank was so depressed that he could not manage to revise his resume or do household chores. After some discussion, Frank and his therapist agreed on more specific goals including, "feel less depressed and anxious," "decrease amount of time spent worrying," and "actively hunt for a job (i.e., revise resume, actively search for job openings, complete applications for appropriate openings, and so on)." With clearer, more concrete goals, it is much easier for the therapist to select appropriate interventions and for both therapist and client to tell if they are making progress toward achieving the goals.

It is also necessary for therapist and client to decide which goal or goals to focus on first. This generally requires little additional effort if it is done when the goals of therapy are being clarified. The therapist will consider the client's priorities, the therapist's conceptualization, which problems seem most likely to respond to early interventions, and any practical considerations that may be relevant. There is an advantage to working initially on a goal that appears manageable, even if it is not the client's highest priority. If it is possible to make demonstrable progress toward a valued goal early in therapy, the client will be encouraged and his or her motivation to persist with therapy will increase.

The process of jointly agreeing on goals and priorities maximizes the likelihood that therapy will accomplish what the client is seeking. At the same time, it establishes the precedent of the therapist's soliciting and respecting the client's input while being open regarding his or her own views. Thus, it lays the foundation for therapist and client to work together collaboratively, and makes it clear to the client that his or her concerns are understood and respected. The time and effort spent on establishing mutually agreed on goals and priorities are more than compensated for by the resulting increase in client involvement, decrease in resistance, and decrease in time wasted on peripheral topics.

Maintaining a collaborative approach to therapy is facilitated by introducing the client to the therapist's conceptualization of the problems and to his or her approach to therapy. Although this could be done as a "minilecture" about psychopathology and psychotherapy, it is much more effective to base the explanation on the thoughts and feelings the client reports experiencing on a particular occasion when his or her problems were occurring. For example:

THERAPIST: (Summarizing the previous discussion) So, from what you've said, as you were walking into your boss's office you were thinking, "Oh God, I must have really blown it! I'm really in trouble now." and you felt intense dread and anxiety. After the meeting you were thinking "It's OK after all" and instead of feeling anxious, you felt relieved. Do you see a connection between your thoughts and how you felt?

AL: Of course, when I thought I was in trouble, I was scared and when I found out I wasn't, I felt a lot better.

THERAPIST: This is one of the principles that Cognitive Therapy is based on, the idea that what a person is thinking at the moment has a big impact on how they feel and what they do.

AL: Okay.

THERAPIST: One of the things that strikes me is that here we've got a situation where your thoughts were unrealistic and they led to much stronger feelings than fit the situation. Suppose you'd have been able to notice that you were jumping to conclusions and that you'd actually done a good job. Do you think that would have made a difference in how you felt when you were on your way to the boss's office?

AL: Well yeah, it would have.

THERAPIST: That's something we may want to try. A lot of people find that if they can learn to notice when they're jumping to conclusions and to talk sense to themselves, that can be useful in dealing with some of their problems. Let's take another situation where you ran into strong feelings and see if we can work out how to put that approach into practice. Can you think of another good example of a time where you found yourself reacting as though you were in trouble? . . . .

If the client does not have a clear memory of his or her thoughts and feelings in a problem situation, it often is possible to use the thoughts and feelings experienced at some other time, such as while waiting for the session to begin or at a particularly emotional point during the session. It is wise to reserve more didactic explanations for occasions where the client is not able to report his or her thoughts and feelings clearly enough for this to form the basis of the explanation.

When a more didactic explanation is necessary, explanations based on concrete examples can be quite useful. For example:

> Imagine that you're walking through the woods on a pleasant spring morning, and you go around a bend in the trail and see a bear standing there. Obviously you're going to have an emotional reaction and you're going to do something. What isn't obvious to many people is that your emotions and your actions are based on your interpretation of the situation.
>
> Suppose that before you left camp you heard that Joe drove into town to rent a bear costume. Your reaction when you see the bear is going to be very different than if you didn't know that. But just because Joe has a bear costume doesn't mean that's him on the trail ahead of you. Until you're close enough to see if this bear has a zipper down the front, your reactions are going to depend on whether you think it's Joe or you think it's a real bear on the trail ahead of you. If you're wrong you may be in for a big surprise.

As people go through their day-to-day lives, they're constantly interpreting the situations they run into. When people have problems, sometimes it's because they're misinterpreting events and reacting in ways that don't fit the situation and sometimes because they see the situation clearly but don't have a good way to handle it.

In Cognitive Therapy we find that it can be useful to look at the thoughts that run through people's heads at the times when their problems flare up and to figure out whether their interpretations of what's going on are useful or not. If the person is misinterpreting events, it can be useful to help him or her learn to recognize when the interpretations are off target and learn to see events more clearly. If it turns out that he or she is seeing things clearly but doesn't have good ways of handling the problems that come up, then it's useful to help find better ways of dealing with the problems. How does that sound to you?

The Process of Cognitive Therapy

A wide variety of approaches ranging from empathic support to hypnotic suggestion, philosophical debate, or operant conditioning can be used in psychotherapy. The approach used in Cognitive Therapy has been described as "collaborative empiricism" (Beck, Rush, Shaw, & Emery, 1979). The therapist endeavors to work with the client to identify the cognitions, behaviors, emotions, and other factors that contribute to the client's problems. Then, rather than simply relying on rational analysis or on the therapist's wisdom, therapist and client observe the actual results of the client's actions and test the validity of the thoughts, beliefs, and assumptions that prove to be important. As dysfunctional cognitions and behaviors are identified, therapist and client then work to identify more adaptive alternatives and work together to make the needed changes in both cognition and behavior.

This process can be facilitated by making use of "guided discovery" as an alternative to direct confrontation or didactic instruction. By asking a series of questions, the therapist can guide the client through the process of developing an understanding of his or her problems, exploring possible solutions, and developing a plan for dealing with the problems. For example, in a situation where Al once again thought he was "in big trouble" the therapist could ask a series of questions such as: "What convinces you that you're in big trouble?"; "Do you see any evidence that would contradict the idea that you are in big trouble?"; "The last time you thought you were in big trouble, how did it turn out? Were you in trouble?"; "Overall, is the feeling that you are in trouble a good guide to whether you are in trouble or not?"; "Suppose it turns out that you are in trouble, how serious would it be?"; "How would you usually handle being in trouble?"; "How well does that way of handling it work out for you?"; "Can you think of any other ways that people handle being in trouble?"; and "Do any of those other options seem promising?"

Guided discovery maximizes client involvement in therapy sessions and minimizes the possibility of the client's feeling that the therapist is attempting to impose his or her own ideas on the client. In addition, this approach provides the client with an opportunity to learn a more effective method for understanding and solving his or her own problems. Approaches to therapy in which the therapist simply provides the solutions and persuades the client to adopt them are less likely to equip the client with the skills needed to deal independently with new problems as they arise in the future.

The Structure of a Cognitive Therapy Session

Since Cognitive Therapy aspires to be a short-term therapy that accomplishes lasting change, it is important to structure sessions so as to use the time productively. Figure 1.4 shows the way in which a Cognitive Therapy session is typically structured. This structure is designed to maximize the collaboration between therapist and client while working efficiently toward the client's goals.

Note that the session begins with "agenda setting". "This brief step makes it much easier for therapist and client to use the session efficiently. If the therapist

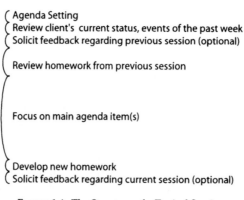

FIGURE 1.4. The Structure of a Typical Session.

follows the client's lead and simply responds to the topics the client brings up, the session may or may not address the issues that are most productive on that day. If the therapist unilaterally directs the session onto the topics he or she thinks are most important, the client may well perceive the therapist as controlling or unresponsive. If the therapist and client invest a few minutes at the beginning of each session to agree on an agenda for that session, they are much more likely to use the available time productively and the therapist is likely to be perceived as responsive to the client's wants and preferences.

Agreeing on an agenda does not automatically prevent the client from digressing onto other topics. However, it makes it easier for the therapist to gently but firmly limit the digressions and return the discussion to more productive topics without seeming authoritarian or controlling. The use of a mutually agreed on agenda also minimizes the occurrence of the "hand on the doorknob phenomenon" when, in the closing seconds of the session, the client raises an important topic when there is no time to address it (i.e., "Oh, by the way, I think I'm gay."). With many clients, an explicit discussion of "what we want to be sure to get to today" will identify the important issues so that therapist and client can decide how to best allocate the time. If a client introduces an important topic at the close of the session anyway, the therapist can respond to non-emergency topics with a statement such as, "That sounds really important to you. It's a shame we don't have time to do it justice. Let's be sure to get it on the agenda next time." The client will quickly get in the habit of thinking ahead about how he or she wants to use the session.

It is usually simplest for therapist and client to agree on the agenda before the client updates the therapist on the events of the week and his or her current status. A quick review of major events since the last session obviously is valuable in enabling the therapist to monitor progress and identify any pressing problems that may have been overlooked in agenda setting. A review of homework from the previous session is important because most clients will do homework only if it is reviewed during the session and also because even a brief amount of time spent reviewing the homework can help the client get more out of it. Each of these "housekeeping" functions is typically completed in a few minutes, and most of the session then may be devoted to one particular issue or may be divided among several issues. The final work of the session consists of collaboratively developing a new homework assignment and then getting feedback from the client about the therapy session.

It may seem unusual to solicit the client's feedback on two points during the therapy session and soliciting feedback on both of these points in every session would probably amount to overkill. However, it is important for the therapist to solicit the client's feedback on a regular basis so that interpersonal problems or client dissatisfactions can be identified in time to address them before they disrupt therapy. The therapist can choose to ask for feedback about the previous session toward the beginning of a session, or to ask for feedback about the current session at the end of the session, or both. It takes little time to solicit feedback unless there is a significant problem that needs to be discussed; if there is a problem, the time needed to resolve it is well spent.

ASSESSMENT THROUGHOUT THE COURSE OF THERAPY

Cognitive Therapy typically starts with an initial assessment but this does not eliminate the need for clinical assessment throughout the course of therapy. Cognition, emotion, and behavior are the three aspects of human functioning that are of prime importance in Cognitive Therapy and they are the targets of assessment in ongoing therapy. The therapist's goal is to assess the client's cognitive, emotional, and behavioral responses in problem situations in enough detail to permit clear conceptualization of the problems and strategic planning of interventions. This is not a simple task.

Many different aspects of cognition are potentially of interest including self-statements, attributions, expectations, self-efficacy expectations, irrational beliefs, basic assumptions, schemas, mental images, and current concerns. To further complicate the picture, these categories are not mutually exclusive. For example, the thought, "He's going to be mad at me because I'm so dumb" is a self-statement that includes an expectation ("He's going to be mad at me..."), an attribution ("...because I'm so dumb"), is suggestive of an efficacy expectation ("I'm dumb, therefore I won't do well at tasks requiring intelligence."), and a current concern ("I don't want him to be mad at me."). Fortunately, it is not necessary for the therapist to draw fine distinctions among different categories of cognitions in clinical practice. The focus is on the client's immediate, spontaneous cognitive response in a particular situation, not on specific categories of cognitions. The questions being addressed are "What is the client's immediate cognitive response in the problem situation?" and "What cognitions coincide with intensification of the client's symptoms?"

The focus in assessing emotion is determined largely by the client's goals for therapy. Those emotions which play an important role in the client's problem or which occur in problem situations are the emotions that we need to understand. The therapist's goal is to develop a clear understanding of the emotions that the client experiences and of their intensity. It is generally most productive to focus on changes in the intensity of emotion or changes in the type of feeling rather than to attempt to assess the client's overall mood. Clients may initially report a general mood that they describe as unchanging or as fluctuating only randomly, but a careful assessment often provides a very different picture. For example:

> A middle-aged history professor complained of a chronic depressed mood, which he described as stable and unchanging. He reported that he felt no pleasure or sense of accomplishment in any activities and said that this had been the case for years. The therapist asked him to collect additional data concerning the relationship between his activities and his mood by recording the activity he was engaged in and rating both his level of enjoyment and the level of his feeling of accomplishment during each waking hour. To the surprise of both therapist and client, this self-monitoring exercise revealed a number of activities that the client actually found to be quite enjoyable and satisfying at the time when he engaged in them. The client tended to overlook or devalue these events when discussing his activities in retrospect.

As with cognition and emotion, the focus in assessing behavior in Cognitive Therapy is on the client's actions in problem situations. The therapist's goal is to understand clearly what the client did, when, and in what context. The importance of clear, specific information cannot be overemphasized. A client's verbal description of behavior may be misleading if the therapist is not careful about obtaining specific information. For example:

> A timid bookkeeper who was working toward being more assertive opened the session by expressing strong concerns over the possible repercussions of his having "told off" a colleague at work. When he was asked to describe his actual behavior in detail it turned out that he had actually said, "Isn't that rushing things a bit?" in a very appropriate way. In his anxiety about assertion, he mislabeled his behavior as inappropriately aggressive.

Assessment Techniques

Clinical Interview

In assessing cognition, emotion, and, to a lesser extent, behavior, we are forced to rely primarily on the client's self-reports despite knowing that these reports can easily be inaccurate, biased, censored, or fabricated. These problems with self-report measures have generated considerable discussion (Ericsson & Simon, 1980). There has been controversy over whether it is at all possible for individuals' self-reported cognitions to be useful (Ericsson & Simon, 1980; Nisbett & Wilson, 1977; White, 1980). Although there is evidence that clients who are appropriately motivated and trained can provide useful data about behavior (Linehan, 1977), it has been argued that many important cognitions are not accessible to self-monitoring and that reports by individuals concerning their own cognitions are often no more accurate than are inferences made by naive observers (Nisbett & Wilson, 1977).

Ericsson and Simon (1980) have reviewed the empirical literature bearing on these points and their analysis supports the conclusion that properly obtained reports can be quite useful. However, the way in which therapists obtain clients' reports of cognitions has a strong influence on their validity and usefulness. Table 1.3 presents guidelines for obtaining useful self-reports in the course of Cognitive Therapy. In clinical practice, the ultimate test of the value of self-reports is their utility in predicting or controlling behavior (Kendall & Hollon, 1981). If interventions based on the reports are effective, it demonstrates that the client's reports are useful whether or not their accuracy can be confirmed.

Some have argued that open-ended questions may not provide cues of sufficient strength to attain recall of all available information and suggest that assessment techniques that provide clients with possible cognitions (or emotions, or behaviors) to endorse or reject may facilitate a more complete recall of information (Kendall, 1981). Although it is true that providing more detailed retrieval cues can facilitate recall, questions that suggest possible cognitions, emotions, or behaviors are more likely to bias clients' responses than do open-ended questions. If increased recall is gained at the cost of decreased accuracy, this strategy for improving recall may be counterproductive. In general, techniques for improving recall that do not suggest possible responses are preferable. Out of the techniques included in the guidelines above, the most effective ways of enhancing recall while minimizing

Table 1.3. Guidelines for Obtaining Useful Self-Reports in Psychotherapy

1. *Motivate the client to be open and forthright.* Make sure that it is clear that providing full, honest, detailed reports is in the client's interest by: (a) providing a clear rationale for seeking the information, (b) demonstrating the relevance of the information being requested to the client's goals, and (c) demonstrating the value of clear, specific information by explicitly making use of the information.

2. *Minimize the delay between event and report.* This will result in more detailed information and reduce the amount of distortion due to imperfect recall. For events occurring outside of the therapist's office, use an *in vivo* interview or self-monitoring techniques when possible.

3. *Provide retrieval cues.* Review the setting and the events leading up to the event of interest either verbally or by using imagery to improve recall.

4. *Avoid possible biases.* Begin with open-ended questions that ask the client to describe his or her experience without suggesting possible answers or requiring inference. Focus on, "What happened?" not on, "Why?" or, "What did it mean?". Do not ask clients to infer experiences they cannot remember. Wait until after the entire experience has been described to test your hypotheses or ask for specific details.

5. *Encourage and reinforce attention to thoughts and feelings.* Clients who initially have difficulty monitoring their own cognitive processes are more likely to gradually develop increased skill if they are reinforced for accomplishments than if they are criticized for failures. Some clients may need explicit training in differentiating between thoughts and emotions, in attending to cognitions, or in reporting observations rather than inferences.

6. *Encourage and reinforce acknowledgment of limitations in recall.* If the therapist accepts only long, detailed reports, it increases the risk of the client's inventing data to satisfy the therapist. It is important for the therapist to appreciate the information the client can provide and to encourage the client to acknowledge his or her limits in recalling details. Incomplete but accurate information is much more useful than detailed reports fabricated to please the therapist.

7. *Watch for indications of invalidity.* Be alert for inconsistency within the client's report, inconsistency between the verbal report and nonverbal cues, and inconsistency between the report and data obtained previously. If apparent inconsistencies are observed, explore them collaboratively with the client without being accusatory or judgmental.

8. *Watch for factors that may interfere.* Be alert for indications of beliefs, assumptions, expectancies, and misunderstandings that may interfere with the client's providing accurate self-reports. Common problems include: (a) the fear that the therapist will be unable to accept the truth and will become angry, shocked, disgusted, or rejected if the client reports his or her experiences accurately, (b) the belief that the client must do a perfect job of observing and reporting the experiences and that he or she is a failure if the reports are not perfect from the beginning, (c) the fear that the information revealed in therapy may be used against the client or may give the therapist power over him or her, and (d) the belief that it is dangerous to closely examine experiences involving strong or "crazy" feelings for fear that the feelings will be intolerable or will "get out of control."

possible biases include:

1. reducing the delay before obtaining the report,
2. providing recall cues by reviewing the stimuli that elicited the event of interest,
3. using self-monitoring techniques,
4. planning *in vivo* experiences for the specific purpose of collecting data.

The task of assessing emotional responses through clinical interview can be particularly complex. Clients may have difficulty labeling emotions, may label emotions idiosyncratically, or may have difficulty noticing mild emotions.

Inconsistencies among reported emotions and nonverbal cues, actions, or reported cognitions make it possible to detect these difficulties and take remedial action. It is not unusual for the therapist to help clients develop greater skill at detecting and expressing emotions or to help clients differentiate between thoughts and emotions. If the therapist provides feedback regarding nonverbal indications of emotion in facial expression, voice tone, or action, most clients learn to identify and describe emotions fairly quickly.

Self-Monitoring

Self-monitoring is an excellent method for reducing reliance on client recall regarding cognitions, emotions, and behavior occurring outside the therapist's office. A variety of methods have been developed for recording events as they occur. These include maintaining a diary or journal (Mahoney, 1977), making audiotape recordings (Craighead, Kimball, & Rehak, 1979), and completing structured questionnaires (Schwartz & Gottman, 1976) among others.

The thought record (TR), often referred to as a "thought sheet," is the most frequently used approach to self-monitoring in Cognitive Therapy and appears in a variety of formats (Beck, Rush, et al., 1979; Beck, Wright, Newman & Liese, 1993; Burns, 1999a; Greenberger & Padesky, 1995). The "three-column" TR (see Figure 1.5) is a chart that provides a simple, open-ended framework to aid clients in recording information regarding the stimulus situation, emotional responses, and cognitions. Its simplicity renders it quite versatile, and the instructions can easily be tailored to suit virtually any clinical situation. For example:

Situation Briefly describe the situation	Emotion(s) Rate 0-100%	Automatic Thought(s) Try to quote the thoughts then rate your belief in each thought 0-100%
I had just taken my trash out monday nite - I realized I had forgotten something so I took another bag out later and set the bag in the back. I ran into my landlord there & we were talking about the animals going out there at nite. When I went upstairs he put the trash in the cans. I saw this from my kitchen window.	Depression 50%	Why was I so stupid not to think to put the trash in the cans & close them tight so the animals couldn't get at it. He probably thinks I'm so stupid. I'm always doing stupid things around him. He might not want me for a tennant anymore since I think he has the idea I've been sick with my nerves.

FIGURE 1.5. Sample Thought Record.

Dianne was a young woman who entered treatment complaining of problems with both depression and anxiety. Initially, she was not able to specify the situations that elicited her depression or anxiety and was unable to describe her thoughts and feelings in sufficient detail to be useful. Since the need for more detailed information was already clear to the client, the TR was introduced to her with a dialogue similar to the following:

THERAPIST: Well, it seems clear that our first step will need to be getting a better picture of just when your problems flare up and what's going on then, so that we can figure out how to deal with them. How does that sound to you?

DIANNE: That makes sense.

THERAPIST: The problem with trying to figure things out here in the office is that it's hard for you to remember all the detailed information we need. (Client nods) Now, it would have been easier to remember the details if you had known ahead of time that we were going to talk about these things, but you'd still be stuck relying on memory and it would be easy to lose track of the details.

DIANNE: Yeah.

THERAPIST: The obvious solution would be to write down the stuff you want to remember, then you don't have to worry about forgetting. What do you think about that?

DIANNE: I'll try it.

THERAPIST: There's one particular format I generally recommend to people because it makes keeping track of the information we need easier. How about if I show it to you and see what you think?

DIANNE: Sure.

THERAPIST: (Showing Dianne a blank three-column TR form) This is really just three columns on a sheet of paper. In the first column you'd briefly describe what the situation is, just the facts without any commentary on it, such as "in bed after alarm clock goes off Monday morning." Does that make sense?

DIANNE: Yeah, that's pretty straightforward.

THERAPIST: In the next column you'd write down what you're feeling . . . sad, happy, anxious, whatever. You might just feel depressed, for example, or you might feel depressed, anxious, and discouraged all at once, so you'd write all three down. Also, it turns out that it's useful to have an idea how strong these feelings are. That's not an easy thing to put down on paper. The best way we've been able to come up with is to rate each feeling on a scale from 0 to 100% where 100% is the strongest you've ever felt that particular feeling and a 1 is a feeling that's just barely noticeable.

For example, if you woke up Monday morning feeling discouraged, you'd write down "discouraged"; then you'd think of the most discouraged you've ever felt (which would be 100%) and compare how you're feeling Monday morning with that. Fifty percent would be about half that discouraged, 80% or 90% would be feeling pretty intensely discouraged, and 20% or 30% would be feeling mildly discouraged. It's not precise but it gives us a clear enough idea to be useful. Does that sound like something you could try?

DIANNE: I guess I can do that.

THERAPIST: Most people find it's a bit awkward at first but that they get used to it pretty quickly.

DIANNE: Okay.

THERAPIST: In the third column you'd write down what we call your "automatic thoughts." Those are the thoughts that just pop into your head without any particular line of reasoning leading up to it, without you particularly intending to think about it. It turns out that the immediate thoughts are most useful for understanding people's problems and figuring out how to deal with them. Just pay attention to the thoughts that come to you right away and write them down whether or not there's an obvious connection between the thoughts and your problem.

It's most helpful if you can write down the thoughts just the way they ran through your head, quoting them as much as possible. If the thought you notice Monday morning is, "God, I don't want to get up! The day's gonna be a drag," it will be more useful to write it down just like that than to paraphrase it as "I didn't want to get up because it seemed like a bad day." Does that make sense?

DIANNE: Yeah, I think so.

THERAPIST: Most people find it takes a little practice to get smooth at noticing the thoughts running through their heads and writing them down. That's not the sort of thing people usually do very often.

The final thing that would be useful to know would be how much you believe each of the thoughts you write down. You've probably noticed that a lot of the thoughts that run through your head are real believable but that there are some thoughts that you've got doubts about or don't believe at all even as you think them. So, the last thing is to rate how much you believe each thought right as you think it from 0 to 100%, where 100 means you're absolutely certain it's true and 0 means you don't believe it at all.

DIANNE: Do I try to write down everything that happens?

THERAPIST: That's a good question. Since we're trying to understand your periods of anxiety and depression, what would probably be most useful would be to watch for times when you start feeling noticeably more anxious or depressed and record this information then. Since there's a limit to how much we can discuss in a session, writing down two or three events a day would end up being plenty. How does that sound?

DIANNE: I'll try it.

> Dianne returned with the TR seen in Figure 1.5. She and her therapist were then able to review the incident in more detail using the interview techniques discussed above to obtain additional information. At the same time, the therapist was able to provide constructive feedback that improved Dianne's subsequent use of the TR. The data from this and other situations she monitored made it possible for Dianne's therapist to develop a clear understanding of her problems quickly.

In the example above, a hypothetical example was used to explain the use of the TR to Dianne. It can be particularly effective for the therapist to use an actual incident that the client has already described during the session when explaining the TR. When the therapist anticipates asking the client to complete the TR as a homework assignment, he or she can make a point of recording a situation being discussed during the session in the "three column" format. Then, when the TR is explained the therapist can easily show how the TR was used as a simple way for recording the information the client provided.

Clients typically find the TR easy to use once they have an opportunity to practice using it, and they typically use it effectively once it is clear to them that the TRs prove useful. Some individuals need training in differentiating between thoughts and feelings or in rating the intensity of feelings or the degree of belief in automatic thoughts. In such cases, jointly completing TRs during a therapy session and providing nonpunitive feedback on clients' attempts to use the TR is generally sufficient. Sometimes clients have difficulty completing their initial TR because of a fear that "I won't do it right." Usually, all the therapist needs to do is to make it clear that the client need not complete the form perfectly or "right" for it to be useful and to encourage the client to "give it a try."

In Vivo Interview and Observation

As discussed above, most events of interest to the therapist occur outside of the therapist's office. One possible solution to the problems inherent in client recall is for the therapist to accompany his or her client into the problem situation, both to conduct an interview and to observe carefully as the events of interest occur. This approach effectively eliminates the limitations imposed by extensive reliance on memory and can quickly provide much valuable information. However, the therapist's presence in the problem situation may have an important impact on the situation or the client's response. In addition, in vivo expeditions may entail a substantial investment of the therapist's time (and thus the client's money). When it is feasible, in vivo interviewing and observation can be quite productive.

Questionnaires and Other Assessment Instruments

A broad range of questionnaires and other "paper and pencil" measures have been developed to measure emotions, cognitions, and behaviors. These include the Beck Depression Inventory (BDI; Beck, 1972), the Dysfunctional Attitude Scale (Weissman, 1979; Weissman & Beck, 1978), and the Fear Survey Schedule (Wolpe & Lang, 1969). These can be invaluable to researchers looking for a simple way of quantifying a few specific variables for statistical analysis.

Paper and pencil measures can be useful in therapy but it is more practical to use these measures selectively when there is a need to quantify specific emotions, cognitions, or behaviors than to use them routinely. After all, a wide range of different cognitions, emotions, and behaviors are of interest in clinical practice but each questionnaire measures only a small sampling of these. It is not practical to stockpile a large assortment of questionnaires and have clients fill out questionnaire after questionnaire. The most common way in which brief questionnaires are used in Cognitive Therapy is to monitor progress in therapy. For example, weekly administrations of a scale relevant to the goals of therapy, such as the Beck Depression Inventory or the Beck Hopelessness Scale, can provide a useful way of monitoring progress.

Overall, the clinical interview and self-monitoring techniques appear to be the most generally useful assessment strategies for the cognitive therapist. These techniques are practical and, when done skillfully, can provide a wealth of useful data. Ideally, clinical assessment is a self-correcting process: If therapist and client work together to collect and interpret needed information and then implement therapeutic interventions based on their resulting conceptualizations, the results of their interventions serve as a source of corrective feedback. Successful interventions both produce desired changes and provide evidence of the clinical utility of the conceptualizations on which the interventions were based. Unsuccessful or partially successful interventions highlight areas in which the current conceptualizations may be inadequate. Observation of the actual effects of the unsuccessful interventions and of the factors that influence this outcome can serve as a basis for a revised conceptualization that can again be tested in practice. When clinical assessment is integrated with intervention, this self-correcting process can make the most of rich data, even if the reliability and validity of a particular observation or self-report are uncertain. For this process to function effectively, the therapist and client must remember that their conceptualizations are hypotheses and be alert for data that is inconsistent with their hypotheses.

The Role of Cognitive and Behavioral Interventions in Cognitive Therapy

Some therapists mistakenly think of Cognitive Therapy as a collection of specific techniques and assume that effective treatment is simply a matter of matching techniques to symptoms. Although it is true that cognitive therapists make use of a wide range of intervention techniques when appropriate (see Chapter 2), these are used in the context of a collaborative therapeutic relationship and are used flexibly on the basis of the therapist's conceptualization. Specific therapeutic techniques are a useful part of Cognitive Therapy but they are only one aspect of it. With many presenting problems, one can do effective Cognitive Therapy without needing to use advanced techniques.

Early in treatment, the cognitive therapist often helps the client identify the specific automatic thoughts that occur in problem situations, recognize the effects these thoughts have on his or her emotions and behavior, and respond effectively to those thoughts that prove problematic. This can often be done through fairly straightforward questioning. For example, in an early session with a client who had serious problems with procrastination.

THERAPIST: Do you remember what was running through your head while you were trying to get started on that?

CLIENT: I was thinking, "I'm not going to be able to do it. I'm not going to do it right."

THERAPIST: Do you think that had anything to do with your difficulty getting started?

CLIENT: I guess it's not very positive, is it?

THERAPIST: You were saying earlier that you avoid situations where you might make a mistake, or be criticized, or fail. It sounds like you were thinking that this was a time when you were going to fail or make a mistake and that made it harder to go ahead and try.

CLIENT: Yeah, it did!

THERAPIST: Does this fit for the other times when you found yourself procrastinating?

Clients often find their negative automatic thoughts to be quite believable, even after their detrimental impact is clear. Thus, the therapist's next task is to help their clients look critically at their automatic thoughts. This can be done through guided discovery, as in the following example from a depressed client:

THERAPIST: One of the thoughts you said ran through your head when you were sitting at home yesterday was, "I'm a failure." A total failure?

CLIENT: Yeah. I can't seem to do nothing right.

THERAPIST: I can see how sitting at home and thinking that would be pretty depressing. Not only do you feel bad about what you've done with your life so far, but it doesn't seem like that would give you much hope for the future.

CLIENT: It don't seem like there's nothing I can do.

THERAPIST: What is it that convinces you that you're a total failure?

CLIENT: Just look at me . . . I didn't finish school. I got two kids on welfare and I can hardly keep them fed.

THERAPIST: Yeah, things are really tough for you and being stuck with no job and no money sure isn't success, but I'm wondering if that means you're a total failure . . . One thing you mentioned when you were telling me what your day was like was that you make a point of giving your kids three square meals a day. Does that count as a failure?

CLIENT: No, I guess that's something good.

THERAPIST: It sounds pretty worthwhile to me. I know there are plenty of mothers in your neighborhood who don't manage to do that. Is there a chance that there are other worthwhile things about you that you're not giving yourself credit for?

CLIENT: I guess so. The neighbor kids sure like to come over to see me.

THERAPIST: When you're sitting at home and thinking, "I'm a failure" you feel pretty depressed. How do you think you would feel if you were thinking something like, "I've failed at some things, but I do some good things too."

CLIENT: (smiling slightly) I wouldn't feel nearly so bad.

THERAPIST: And which is closer to the truth?

CLIENT: What you said.

As can be seen from the examples above, questions that guide the client through the process of identifying automatic thoughts and looking critically at them often leads naturally to effective interventions. The specific techniques discussed in Chapter 2 can be very useful in facilitating this process but it is important to remember that the techniques are tools used in therapy, they are not the therapy itself.

HOMEWORK ASSIGNMENTS

From the beginning of treatment, cognitive therapists think in terms of finding ways in which clients can continue to make progress toward overcoming their problems between sessions; thus, "homework assignments" are used extensively throughout Cognitive Therapy. Clients who continue the work of therapy between sessions get faster results and accomplish more than those who simply wait for their weekly hour with the therapist (Persons, Burns, & Perloff, 1988). The client can collect data and test the effects of cognitive and behavioral changes in the course of daily life in a way that would be difficult to do within the therapy session.

Often therapists respond to this concept with, "Sure, the idea of homework makes sense, but how do you get them to do it?" The manner in which homework

Table 1.4. Structuring Assignments to Maximize Compliance

Establish a precedent of consistently using assignments between sessions.

Develop assignments collaboratively:
  Maximize the client's input
  Use assignments that are clearly connected to the client's goals
  Keep the assignments practical, manageable, simple
  Check to see if the rationale for the assignment is clear
  Check to see if the client has a clear understanding of what he or she is to do
  Try to anticipate likely problems or impediments
  Teach any skills the client needs to master to complete the task successfully
  Get the client's feedback regarding the assignment; encourage the client to express any
    reservations or objections he or she has (and take them seriously)

Follow up at the next encounter:
  Check to see how it went, what the results were, what conclusions the client is drawing
    If possible, make use of the results in today's encounter
  Appreciate the client's efforts regardless of the results
  Avoid critical or punitive responses
  Rely primarily on positive feedback when trying to improve the client's performance on
    the task
  Address any problems or impediments that the client encountered. Plan how to deal
    with them if they arise again
  Help the client recognize that he or she can take concrete steps to overcome problems
    and help the client take credit for the benefits that result from these actions

---

assignments are developed and presented to the client make an enormous difference. If the therapist simply says "I want you to _____ by next week" only a small proportion of clients will complete the assignment. Compliance is much less of a problem if the therapist works with the client to develop an assignment which makes sense to the client, which is a useful step toward accomplishing the client's goals, and which the client is willing to do. Table 1.4 provides some practical guidelines for improving adherence with homework assignments.

Note that there is no requirement that the word "homework" be used in discussing assignments with the client. Some clients relate well to the idea of "homework assignments," while others have a negative reaction to the term. One way to introduce the concept is to raise the issue toward the end of the initial therapy session by saying, "One of the things I like to do is to think in terms of what the people I work with can do between sessions to make headway, that way you can get results more quickly. How does that sound to you?" Then the therapist can work collaboratively with the client ("Do you have any idea of what would be useful to do between now and the next time we meet?") to develop and refine a simple assignment. Whether the therapist refers to this as a "homework assignment" in discussing it with the client is optional.

Despite these efforts, noncompliance sometimes occurs when homework assignments are used. However, this need not be a problem. Episodes of noncompliance can be quite useful in identifying the factors that block the client from making the desired changes and in identifying problems in the therapist–client relationship. For example:

Doug, a young accountant, experienced chronic problems with procrastination that were so severe that he had lost three jobs because he was unable to complete his work on schedule. Early in therapy it became clear that part of the problem stemmed from his reluctance to perform any task less than perfectly. Doug and his therapist agreed that it would be very helpful if he could become more comfortable with performing tasks imperfectly when appropriate.

Since Doug was unemployed at the time, it was not possible to use his job as an arena for working on this issue, so it was agreed that Doug's hobby of model plane building would be a good starting place. After some discussion, it was agreed that he would begin by starting to assemble a new model, intentionally doing it less perfectly than he normally would and monitoring his thoughts and feelings while doing so. When he returned for the next therapy session Doug reported that (even though he was unemployed) he had been "too busy" to begin working on the model. When he and the therapist explored this, he explained that to work on the model he would need to completely unpack the boxes in his workroom (having moved recently), set up his workbench, carefully arrange the lighting, and arrange all of his tools in their proper places. He was trying to arrange everything perfectly so that he could assemble a model imperfectly!

This made it easy for the therapist to point out how pervasive Doug's perfectionism was and the way in which it transformed simple tasks into major projects. Doug responded with increased motivation for working on his perfectionism and was able to make steady progress thereafter.

One of the most effective ways of responding to noncompliance is to choose a specific moment when the client thought of attempting the task but did not do so, and then to identify the thoughts and feelings which the client experienced at that time. Often this proves quite enlightening and highlights fears, concerns, or other issues that need to be addressed.

The therapeutic relationship has an important impact on noncompliance. Research in medical settings has identified a number of aspects of the physician–patient relationship that can have a substantial impact on compliance (Meichenbaum & Turk, 1987). Pause for a minute and think of your last visit to your physician. Now consider the points listed in Table 1.5. Often, well-intentioned caregivers provide care in ways that needlessly contribute to compliance problems. One might assume that psychotherapists would be aware enough of the impact of

TABLE 1.5. How to Encourage NonCompliance

Act unfriendly, distant, unapproachable
Look and act busy
See the client in a chaotic setting with many interruptions
Use jargon. Never ask if the client understands
Cut the client off. Interrupt. Don't allow clients to tell their story in their own words
Ignore the client's questions or react as though the questions are "dumb"
Don't bother to understand the client's ideas about his or her illness. Don't ask about his or her concerns or expectations
Don't bother with a clear explanation of the diagnosis and the causes of the illness
State the treatment regimen vaguely or in technical terms. Don't explain the rationale for the treatment regimen
Don't ask for feedback. Ignore any objections the client expresses
Terminate the interview abruptly
Provide little encouragement or support

the therapeutic relationship that this would not be a problem in psychotherapy. However, after training psychotherapists in many settings, we have learned that it is often a significant problem. Something as simple as consistently being late for appointments, frequently needing to reschedule appointments, or answering the telephone during therapy sessions can have a noticeable impact. If noncompliance is an on-going problem, it may be useful to examine the way in which care is being delivered and consider it from the client's point of view.

TERMINATION AND RELAPSE PREVENTION

In theory, once we have interrupted the problematic cognitive/interpersonal cycles and have modified the client's beliefs, assumptions, or dysfunctional inter-action patterns, he or she should be no more prone to future problems than anyone else. However, even if these interventions were completely effective, they would not render the client immune to future difficulties. Therefore, Cognitive Therapy ends with explicitly working to prepare the client to deal with future setbacks. This work, based on Marlatt and Gordon's (1985) research on relapse prevention, con-sists of helping the client become aware of high-risk situations, identify early signs of impending relapse, and develop explicit plans for handling high-risk situations and heading off potential relapse (see Chapter 3).

It is particularly valuable to watch for signs of unrealistic expectations re-garding the long-term results of therapy. Clients who expect their problems to be completely gone forever may overreact when they encounter similar problems in the future. When clients adopt the more realistic view that all people encounter problems from time to time but that Cognitive Therapy has equipped them with the skills needed to cope effectively with problems, the risk of their overreacting to future setbacks and relapsing should be decreased.

Preferably, the decision to terminate therapy is made when (1) the client has attained his or her goals for therapy, (2) work on relapse prevention has been completed, and (3) the client's progress has been maintained long enough for him or her to have a reasonable amount of confidence that he or she will be able to cope with problems as they arise. In the typical case, the therapist and client agree to "taper off" therapy sessions by shifting from weekly sessions to biweekly and, possibly, monthly sessions when the time for termination is near. This not only makes the ending of therapy less abrupt but also provides therapist and client an opportunity to discover how well the client handles problems without the therapist's help. It also allows time for the client to discover whether any additional issues need to be addressed. Finally, the client is usually offered the opportunity to return for "booster sessions" in the hope that early intervention with future problems may forestall major difficulties.

COMMON MISCONCEPTIONS ABOUT COGNITIVE THERAPY

A number of myths and misconceptions about Cognitive Therapy are encoun-tered frequently. The following are among the most common ones:

1. *Cognitive Therapy is "the power of positive thinking".* If anything, Cognitive Therapy is "the power of realistic thinking," or "the power of adaptive thinking". Although "affirmations" can cheer one up for the time being, unrealistic positive thinking has a number of limitations. First, it is often difficult to convince people of things that are not true. Second, the results tend to be temporary since reality is likely to confront the individual sooner or later. Also, actions based on views that are unrealistically optimistic can be just as maladaptive as actions that are based on unrealistically negative views. Although viewing problem situations realistically may be less cheery than a "Pollyanna" approach, it is almost always less negative than the client's view and lays a good foundation for effective coping.

2. *Cognitive Therapy claims that negative thoughts cause psychopathology.* From Figure 1.1 it should be obvious that negative thoughts are seen as only one part of a problematic cycle. Life events, social interactions, and any biochemical abnormalities play important parts in clients' problems as well. The cycles which perpetuate clients' disorders can be initiated at any point in the cycle. However, once a cycle has begun, cognition plays an important role and provides a promising point for intervention.

3. *Cognitive Therapy is simple.* While the theory behind Cognitive Therapy is one that many people find quite reasonable and easy to understand, the practice of Cognitive Therapy is anything but simple. Humans are complex and, as the chapters on personality disorders show, intervening effectively can be quite complicated despite the simplicity of the theory.

4. *Cognitive Therapy is talking people out of their problems.* Many therapists are aware of Albert Ellis' disputational approach to challenging clients' irrational beliefs (e.g., Ellis & Greiger, 1977) and assume that Cognitive Therapy uses a similar approach. However, despite the theoretical similarities between the two approaches, Cognitive Therapy relies on guided discovery and collaborative empiricism rather than debate (Dryden, 1984; Ellis, Young, & Lockwood, 1987). When the therapist works with the client to help him or her look critically at his or her views, the client is likely to be less resistant and is more likely to develop the skills needed to analyze future problems on his or her own.

5. *Cognitive Therapy ignores emotion and behavior.* Although the therapy's name is Cognitive Therapy, it might be more accurately called "Cognitive-Behavioral-Emotive Therapy." Although cognitions often are the direct targets in Cognitive Therapy, therapeutic success is measured by corresponding change in emotion and behavior.

6. *Cognitive Therapy ignores the past.* It would be more accurate to say that Cognitive Therapy pays only as much attention to the past as is necessary for therapeutic success. We find that although the client's previous experiences may be the foundation of his or her current problems, it is often possible to resolve the problems by focusing primarily on the present. If "here and now" interventions are effective, there is no need to use the client's time and money to explore the past. When "here and now"

interventions prove insufficient, there is no need to abandon Cognitive Therapy. Cognitive Therapy can be applied effectively with "family of origin" problems and other problems where the past is an important focus of attention (Bedrosian & Bozicas, 1994). When working to challenge strongly held dysfunctional beliefs that resist "here and now" interventions, exploration of the origins of the beliefs can be both enlightening and effective.

7. *Cognitive Therapy is superficial.* It is true that Cognitive Therapy focuses on achieving the client's specific goals for therapy rather than automatically working for major personality changes. However, this does not necessarily mean that the resulting changes are limited or trivial. For example, a depressed engineer received 19 sessions of Cognitive Therapy that focused on his depression, perfectionism, and procrastination. At the close of treatment he not only had experienced substantial improvement with his presenting problem, but also was more emotionally expressive, more able to empathize with others, and more comfortable with intimacy in relationships. Cognitive Therapy can be superficial or deep depending on the client's goals and the nature of the problems being addressed.

8. *The therapeutic relationship is unimportant in Cognitive Therapy.* Actually, a good therapeutic relationship is essential for collaborating effectively with a client. In addition, the interpersonal relationship between therapist and client can be very powerful for challenging the client's dysfunctional beliefs and assumptions regarding interpersonal relationships. In some works on Cognitive Therapy, only limited attention is devoted to the therapeutic relationship because the type of collaborative relationship advocated is frequently straightforward. The therapeutic relationship generally receives more extensive attention in volumes devoted to the treatment of problems such as personality disorders, where the therapeutic relationship tends to be more problematic.

9. *Cognitive Therapy is finished in 15 sessions or less.* A number of outcome studies of Cognitive Therapy have limited the duration of therapy to 12–20 sessions for methodological reasons. As a result, some readers have mistakenly concluded that Cognitive Therapy always lasts 12–20 sessions. Cognitive Therapy tends to accomplish results relatively quickly, but the duration of therapy depends on the nature of the client's problems, his or her level of motivation, and the degree to which the client's life situation complicates therapy. It can range from a few sessions to several years.

10. *Cognitive Therapy means no medication.* Although Cognitive Therapy alone has been found to be as effective as pharmacotherapy in the treatment of unipolar depression (see Butler & Beck, 2000; DeRubeis & Crits-Christoph, 1998; Simon & Fleming, 1985), it has also been found to work well in combination with psychotropic medication (Wright, 1987). Medication is definitely recommended in combination with Cognitive Therapy for clients with bipolar disorder or psychosis, and for clients who are so depressed that they are unresponsive to verbal interventions. With other clients, the decision needs to be made on a case-by-case basis.

11. *Cognitive Therapy is just a collection of techniques.* Cognitive Therapy has developed a wide variety of specific techniques and has also borrowed freely from other therapies (for example, see McMullin, 1986). However, the therapist who focuses solely on applying techniques will encounter many situations where "cookbook" application of techniques proves ineffective. It is important to base interventions on an understanding of the client and his or her problems and to use interventions strategically rather than becoming preoccupied with techniques.

12. *The goal of Cognitive Therapy is to eliminate emotion.* Actually, the goal of Cognitive Therapy is to have emotion proportional to the situation and to have the client handle the emotion adaptively. In many situations, one goal of therapy is to "tone down" emotional overreactions; however, working to help the client recognize and understand his or her emotional reactions is often an important part of doing this. On the other hand, overcontrolled, inexpressive clients often become more "in touch" with their feelings as a side-effect of Cognitive Therapy even when this is not one of their major goals.

13. *Cognitive Therapy is only appropriate for bright, intellectually oriented clients.* It is sometimes assumed that only bright, middle-class clients can benefit from interventions based on looking critically at dysfunctional thoughts. This is not at all the case. Cognitive Therapy has been used effectively with disadvantaged clients including clients who have had little formal education or who are illiterate. It is true that it is easiest to work with bright, well-educated, psychologically minded, highly motivated clients, but this is true for all therapies. With clients who have difficulty with abstract thinking, it is simply necessary to rely less on purely verbal interventions and more on using behavioral interventions to achieve cognitive change.

14. *Cognitive Therapy is not useful for seriously disturbed clients who need inpatient treatment.* Since Cognitive Therapy was developed primarily in outpatient settings and has been studied most extensively in outpatient settings, some have assumed that it is not appropriate for seriously disturbed clients. Although inpatient treatment typically consists of medication, supportive counseling, and occupational and expressive therapies, Cognitive Therapy can be used quite effectively in inpatient settings even in acute care with seriously disturbed clients. Various clinicians around the world have begun a literature regarding the application of Cognitive Therapy in inpatient settings and report promising results. The interested reader is referred to Perris and McGorry (1998) and Wright, Thase, Beck and Ludgate (1993).

Clinical Applications of Cognitive Therapy

When reading through a summary of the principles of Cognitive Therapy, it can seem fairly straightforward. However, when one is faced by the realities of day-to-day practice, Cognitive Therapy is not at all simple. This book is intended to help the practicing clinician deal effectively with the complex problems encountered in clinical practice. Cognitive Therapy can provide an effective and comprehensible approach to working with the full range of clients encountered in clinical practice. However, to achieve this, the therapist needs to understand the basic principles of Cognitive Therapy, develop a comprehensive conceptualization of each client, incorporate cognitive principles into the structure of therapy sessions, and not be misled by myths and misconceptions.

2

The Mid-Stage
Cognitive and Behavioral Interventions

Once the therapist and client have jointly agreed on treatment goals, the therapist will need a range of skills and techniques to implement the overall treatment strategy. The goal of this chapter is to describe the wide range of techniques that are used in Cognitive Therapy. The techniques will be broadly categorized as "cognitive" and "behavioral." However, it is important to remember that a "behavioral" technique, such as assertion training, can be used to accomplish cognitive changes (i.e., changes in expectancies regarding the consequences of assertion), as well as changes in interpersonal behavior. Similarly, cognitive techniques are often intended to produce changes in behavior as well as cognition. Therefore, in our descriptions of these techniques, we will distinguish between those that primarily produce changes in cognition and those that primarily produce changes in behavior.

COGNITIVE TECHNIQUES

Not surprisingly, cognitive interventions play a central role in Cognitive Therapy. Early in therapy, the therapist and client work to identify and modify dysfunctional automatic thoughts and cognitive distortions. Later in therapy, the client's maladaptive beliefs and assumptions become the focus of attention. A wide range of specific techniques has been developed for use in modifying these cognitions. Although many of these techniques can be used effectively to change automatic thoughts, cognitive distortions, and underlying beliefs, the techniques in this chapter are categorized according to the type of cognition they are most commonly used to modify. Strategies for changing underlying assumptions and schemas are given in Chapter 3.

Techniques for Challenging Automatic Thoughts

As was discussed in the last chapter, the process of identifying and challenging automatic thoughts is central to Cognitive Therapy. The use of thought records

Situation	Emotion(s)	Automatic Thought(s)	Rational Response	Outcome
Briefly describe the situation	Rate 0-100%	Rate degree of belief 0-100%	Rate degree of belief 0-100%	Re-rate emotions 0-100%

FIGURE 2.1. Five-Column Thought Record.

(TRs), or "thought sheets," in monitoring and recording automatic thoughts was discussed in Chapter 1 (Figure 1.5). With the addition of columns in which clients can record their "rational responses" and re-rate their emotions after developing these responses to the automatic thoughts, thought sheets can be used as a format for challenging the automatic thoughts as well as being used for self-monitoring. See Figure 2.1 for a complete "five column" thought record.

The guidelines for using TRs effectively proposed by Judith Beck (1995) are shown in Table 2.1. Typically, after the client has learned to use thought sheets to record the automatic thoughts that occur in problem situations, the therapist and client work together to look at them critically, and to develop more adaptive alternatives to those thoughts that are found to be unrealistic or unhelpful. These are then listed on the thought sheet as rational responses. Although the goal is for the client to develop the ability to identify problematic automatic thoughts as they occur and to generate effective responses quickly, most clients find this task difficult enough, which makes it necessary to approach this goal in a series of steps. At first, many clients are able to look critically at their automatic thoughts only with the therapist's assistance. With practice, clients become able to review their automatic thoughts and develop written rational responses soon after problem situations have passed, needing limited help from the therapist. Next, clients find that they are able to look critically at their automatic thoughts even when they are quite upset, as long as they do so in writing. Finally, clients reach the point where they can develop effective responses to automatic thoughts "in their heads" and only need to write out the thoughts and responses when particularly difficult problems arise.

TABLE 2.1. Using the TR Effectively*

1. The therapist should have mastered the use of the TR personally (recording and challenging his or her own automatic thoughts) before presenting it to a client.
2. The TR should be introduced after the client understands the relevance of automatic thoughts to his or her problems and after the client has demonstrated the ability to recognize automatic thoughts and emotions that occur in specific situations.
3. The therapist should demonstrate how to use the TR to record the situation, automatic thoughts, and emotions before asking the client to do this as homework.
4. The therapist should (a) make sure that the client has mastered the process of recording automatic thoughts on the TR, (b) help the client to generate rational responses during the session, and (c) demonstrate how to record those rational responses on the TR before asking the client to try doing this as homework.
5. If the client fails to complete this homework assignment, the therapist should elicit the client's automatic thoughts about doing the TR itself and address those thoughts.

*adapted from J. Beck (1995)

Once the client becomes able to generate rational responses soon after the problem has arisen, an immediate index of the effectiveness of the responses is provided by the client's re-rating of the intensity of his or her emotions. If the intensity of the problematic emotions has dropped substantially, the responses have been effective. Whereas, if the intensity has changed little, the responses have been ineffective. It is important for the client to be able to generate rational responses that are convincing and which address each of the major points raised in the automatic thoughts.

There are a wide variety of thought records available in the literature. Some of these forms are designed to make the process of challenging automatic thoughts easier for clients. For example, see Figure 2.2 from Greenberger and Padesky (1995). A more portable form of thought record is shown in Figure 2.3 and is called a "Pocket Thought Record" (Hale, 1998). However, most of the alternative forms of TRs are targeted toward the specific needs of particular populations. For an example of a thought record adapted to the specific clinical needs of clients dealing with substance abuse, see Chapter 6.

A wide variety of techniques for challenging automatic thoughts have been developed and, because no single technique is universally effective, the therapist needs to master a wide range of these techniques. A number of the most widely used techniques are discussed below.

Understanding Idiosyncratic Meaning. It is not advisable for the therapist to assume that he or she completely understands the terms used by the client without asking for clarification. For example, if a group of 100 professionals were asked to indicate what they meant by "depression," they would not give identical responses. Similarly, one cannot be sure exactly what a client means when he or she uses words such as "depressed," "suicidal," "anxious," or "upset." To be able to intervene effectively, it is important for the therapist to make sure that he or she is not merely in the right neighborhood in understanding the client's terminology, but that the

Thought Record

Situation	Moods	Automatic Thoughts (Images)	Evidence That Supports the Hot Thought	Evidence That Does Not Support the Hot Thought
Who were you with? What were you doing? When was it? Where were you?	Describe each mood in one word. Rate intensity of mood. (0-100%)	What was going through my mind just before I started to feel this way? What does this say about me? What does this mean about me? my life? my future? What am I afraid might happen? What is the worst thing that could happen if this is true? What does this mean about how the other person(s) feel(s)/think(s) about me? What does this mean about the other person(s) or people in general? What images or memories do I have in this situation?	Circle hot thought in previous column for which you are looking for evidence. Write factual evidence to support this conclusion. (Try to avoid mind-reading and interpretation of facts)	Ask yourself the questions in the Hint Box (p. 70) to help discover evidence which does not support your hot thought.

FIGURE 2.2. Greenberger and Padesky's Version of the Thought Record.

DAILY THOUGHT RECORD

Date _____ Time_____

Situation/Event Leading To Negative Feelings
_____
_____
_____

Automatic Thought(s) About Situation/Self/Others
_____
_____
_____
_____

How Strongly Do I Believe This? (0-100%) ___

Resulting Emotions/Physical Sensations
_____
_____
_____

How Strongly Do I Feel This? (0-100%) ___

(Over)

Rational Response To The Situation/Event
_____
_____
_____
_____
_____
_____
_____
_____
_____
_____

How Strongly Do I Believe This? (0-100%) ___

Now, How Strongly Do I Believe my Original Thoughts
About this Situation/Event? (0-100%)

Outcome (How Do I Feel Using This Rational Response?)
_____
_____
_____

How Strongly Do I Feel This? (0-100%) ___

Now, How Strong Are Those Original Feelings About This
Situation/Event? (0-100%) ___

TIPS FOR RESPONDING RATIONALLY

- What is the EVIDENCE that my automatic thoughts are true? not true?
- What are the alternative explanations for this situation?
- What's the worst that could happen? Could I survive?
- What's the best that could happen?

(Over)

- What is the MOST REALISTIC outcome of this situation?
- What can I do to change the situation and/or outcome positively, rather than just reacting?
- If (a friend) were in the same situation and thought like I am thinking, what would I tell him/her?
- What effect does holding onto these automatic thoughts have on my well-being? What effect might changing them have?

FIGURE 2.3. Hale's Pocket Thought Record.

therapist is right on target. This process requires the therapist to assume that there may be a great deal that he or she does not know about the client's world view and requires a willingness to ask what might appear to be obvious or even "dumb" questions. For example:

CLIENT: I'm stupid, really dumb!

THERAPIST: You call yourself stupid and dumb. Just what does it mean to be dumb? What does being stupid mean to you?

CLIENT: You know D-U-M-B. You know what dumb is, don't you? I'm stupid, really stupid.

THERAPIST: I know what I mean when I use the term dumb, but it would be important to know what YOU mean by the term.

CLIENT: Someone stupid screws everything up, they don't do anything right, nothing works out for them.

THERAPIST: And how does that fit you?

CLIENT: Well, maybe I don't screw everything up but nothing much has been working out for me lately.

THERAPIST: So is that being dumb or having a run of bad luck?

Guided Discovery.   Guided discovery, also known as "Socratic questioning," is one of the techniques that is used most widely in Cognitive Therapy. Through a series of simple questions such as, "Then what?", "What would that mean?", "What would happen then?", the therapist can help the client explore the significance he or she sees in events, review the available evidence, and draw realistic conclusions. This collaborative, therapist-guided technique stands in opposition to the technique of free association basic to psychoanalysis, which involves unguided speech that, it is assumed, will eventually get to areas of conflict and concern. The guided discovery technique involves the therapist working with the client to understand the connections between the client's ideas, thoughts, and images. For example:

THERAPIST: What would happen if you gave her a call?

CLIENT: I can't do that!

THERAPIST: Do you have an image of what would happen if you did call?

CLIENT: She'd laugh.

THERAPIST: And then what would happen?

CLIENT: I'd feel like a fool.

THERAPIST: And then what?

CLIENT: I'd be embarrassed, terribly embarrassed.

THERAPIST: If you were to call, and she laughed and you felt embarrassed, what would that indicate to you?

CLIENT: I'm a complete idiot. What girl in her right mind would want to go out with me?

THERAPIST: So, if I've got it right, you anticipate that, if you give her a call, she'll laugh because you're a complete idiot and no girl would want to go out with you. Therefore you don't call.

CLIENT: Right.

Examining the Evidence.   One of the most effective ways of challenging a dysfunctional thought is to examine both the extent to which the thought is supported by the available evidence and the extent to which it is disconfirmed by the evidence. This can be followed by considering whether other interpretations would better fit the evidence. This process not only involves examining the evidence but also involves considering the source of the data and the validity of the client's conclusions, as well as considering whether the client is overlooking available data. Many clients begin with a conclusion such as, "I'm no good," and then selectively focus on evidence that supports their conclusion. By examining the evidence, the client's conclusion can be more easily challenged and altered. For example:

CLIENT: It's hopeless. I'll never get better. I'm going to live the rest of my life in this awful state of depression.

THERAPIST: You say that you'll never get any better; that you'll always be this way. Have you ever felt better, less depressed?

CLIENT: Yeah, but that was long ago. I spoke to someone who really knows this stuff, and he said that I can expect to be this way forever.

THERAPIST: Who was that person? Was this person one of your previous therapists?

CLIENT: Not exactly, but he really knows.

THERAPIST: Who was this?

CLIENT: One of the guys on the psych unit. He told me that he knew lots of guys like me and they never got better.

THERAPIST: Was this someone on the staff or a patient?

CLIENT: One of the patients.

THERAPIST: It sounds like you're taking his opinion pretty seriously. Have you heard any other opinions about your depression?

CLIENT: The doctor who referred me to you said Cognitive Therapy could help me.

THERAPIST: Who do you think knows more about your odds of getting out of this depression?

CLIENT: I guess it's obvious now that you point it out.

Challenging Absolutes.   By taking an idea literally, or to its full extreme, the therapist can often help the client to move to a more moderate statement of his or her views. A corresponding moderation in the intensity of emotional responses typically follows. Absolutes such as "never," "always," "no one," "everyone," and so on, are often easy targets. Clients often complain initially that the therapist is only drawing semantic distinctions; however, "I've got some real problems at work, but I'm good at some of what I do," has a very different impact from, "I'm totally incompetent." For example:

CLIENT: No one would help me, no one cares.

THERAPIST: No one? No one in the whole world?

CLIENT: Well, maybe my parents would care, but no one else.

THERAPIST: Let's start with that. It's not true that no one would care, someone would, your parents would, anyone else?

CLIENT: Well, maybe my younger sisters would care—Sue and Jan. I helped to raise them and we are pretty close.

THERAPIST: So it sounds like it would be pretty realistic to say, "My parents and Sue and Jan care and will help me if I need it, but I can't count on most other people." How do you feel when you look at things that way?

CLIENT: That is not nearly as bad.

Considering the Odds.   Clients often focus on the outcome they fear most and react as though this worst possible outcome is certain. It can be quite useful to examine the likelihood of the events they fear. For example:

THERAPIST: So, the thought that is most frightening to you is, "He'll never come back." Do you have any idea how likely it is that he'll never come back?

CLIENT: After the fight last night he probably won't.

THERAPIST: Have the two of you had fights like last night before?

CLIENT: Yeah, I guess we fight a lot.

THERAPIST: And has there been a time so far when he's gone away angry and never come back?

CLIENT: No, either he comes back to me or I go to him.

THERAPIST: Do you see any reason why last night's fight should be different from the others?

CLIENT: No, I guess not.

THERAPIST: So what does that tell you about the chances of his never coming back?

CLIENT: I guess it's not too likely, is it?

Re-attribution. A common statement made by clients is, "It is all my fault" (or "It is all his/her fault"). Although one cannot dismiss this out of hand, it is unlikely that a single person is totally responsible for everything that happens in a particular situation. Some clients take responsibility for events and situations that are only minimally attributable to them whereas others tend to blame someone else and take no responsibility. The therapist can help the client distribute responsibility more accurately among the relevant parties, often the result being substantial reductions in guilt or anger. For example:

CLIENT: It's all my fault. I really screwed things up this time. If I could only have handled things differently the relationship could have worked. If only I hadn't been so demanding. It could have been good; I blew it. What's left?

THERAPIST: There's much that you did both good and bad in the relationship. Is it ALL your fault that things didn't work out?

CLIENT: Yeah. Who else?

THERAPIST: What part did Alicia play in the break-up? Did she do anything to contribute to the difficulty? I know that you feel that it was all your fault. I think it would be helpful to examine just what you contributed and what Alicia contributed to the ending of this relationship.

CLIENT: No, it is my fault.

THERAPIST: Did Alicia do anything at all to contribute to the problem?

CLIENT: You mean besides being a bitch?

THERAPIST: Let's start with that...

Turning Adversity to Advantage. Clients are often quicker to identify the disadvantages resulting from life changes than to recognize their advantages. Explicitly checking to see whether an event has good as well as bad aspects can have a major impact. There are times that even a seeming disaster can be used to advantage. Losing one's job may seem like a tragedy but may, in some cases, be the entry point to a new job or even a new career. Having a deadline imposed may be seen as oppressive and unfair, but may be used as a motivator. This technique involves asking the client to look to see if there is a silver lining to the cloud. Given that the depressed individual often does the opposite and finds a dark lining to every silver cloud, looking for the kernel of positive in a situation can be very difficult for many clients. They may simply not see the positive aspect, and if the therapist points out positive aspects, they may react with greater negativity. It is important for the therapist to make a point of identifying only realistically positive sides to negative events and to avoid the tendency to become overly optimistic in response to the client's negativity. For example:

CLIENT: Now that I've lost him, what do I do?

THERAPIST: With him gone, what keeps you in Philadelphia? You've thought of other cities, in fact we've spoken of you wanting to move. You disliked living here but stayed here because of Larry.

CLIENT: That's true, now I don't have to sweat leaving. There's no guy to leave. It is freeing. I hate living in the city. But I don't know whether I am ready to do something new at this point.

THERAPIST: Let's look at that . . . .

Direct Disputation. As explained in Chapter 1, Cognitive Therapy generally advocates guided discovery rather than directly challenging the client's views. However, there are times when direct confrontation is necessary. This is most likely to arise when a client is seriously suicidal and the therapist must directly and quickly work to challenge his or her hopelessness. Direct confrontation also can be useful in other situations in which the therapist must intervene quickly and the client is not willing or able to participate actively in the process. Disputation and debate are potentially dangerous tools because it can be difficult to present a convincing argument without seeming to demean, nag, or browbeat the client, and without the discussion simply becoming an intellectual debate.

It is generally a good idea to encourage as much collaboration as possible, to emphasize data rather than abstract logic or philosophical principles, and to switch back to guided discovery as soon as is feasible. For example:

CLIENT: I'm going crazy. My mind is going. What am I going to do? I've got to do something before my mind is totally gone. I feel that I need to just run away. Maybe that will help.

THERAPIST: I understand that you are terrified of going crazy, but obviously I'm not as concerned as you are. Would you like to know why?

CLIENT: I guess so.

THERAPIST: The reason that I'm not afraid of your going crazy is that this isn't the way craziness starts. You're anxious and very scared but those are not signs of craziness. Being afraid of craziness is very different from being crazy.

CLIENT: You mean I'm not crazy?

THERAPIST: No, you're not crazy!

Externalization of Voices. The client can get very effective practice in responding adaptively to dysfunctional thoughts by having the therapist role-play the part of the client's dysfunctional thoughts and having the client practice more adaptive responding (see Burns, 1999a). A necessary foundation for this exercise is a thorough discussion of ways of responding effectively to the particular dysfunctional thoughts in question. It may help to have the therapist first model responding to

Situation Briefly describe the situation	Emotion(s) Rate 0-100%	Automatic Thought(s) Rate degree of belief 0-100%	Rational Response Rate degree of belief 0-100%	Outcome Re-rate emotions 0-100%
Driving home from appointment in the rain. I almost hit the car ahead of me.	Anxiety 90	It was a miracle that I survived. You only get one chance to screw up. If I were in another accident it would be the end of me.	I did survive. I didn't screw up. The road was wet. I'm no more likely to die in another accident.	Anxiety 90

FIGURE 2.4. When Rational Responses "Don't Work".

dysfunctional thoughts that the client presents. After this, the therapist can express a series of the client's dysfunctional thoughts for the client to respond to. It is usually most effective to start with dysfunctional thoughts that the client finds relatively easy to handle and then build up to more problematic ones presented powerfully and dramatically. For example:

THERAPIST: I'd like to be your negative voice. I'd like you to be a more positive and functional voice.

CLIENT: I'll try.

THERAPIST: Okay. Let's begin. "You really don't know what you're talking about!"

CLIENT: That's not true. There are times that I may be over my head, but overall, I really do know my stuff.

THERAPIST: "If you're so smart, what are you doing in this dead end job?"

The clinician may encounter occasions when responses to automatic thoughts "don't work." For example, consider the TR in Figure 2.4. The client has generated responses to her dysfunctional thoughts but her mood has not improved. What is wrong? The "rational responses" on a TR can be ineffective for a variety of reasons. If important dysfunctional thoughts have been overlooked and are not recorded on the TR, the client may not respond effectively to those thoughts and the emotions they elicit may persist. If the client generates plausible responses but does not believe them, the responses are likely to have little impact. Or, as in this case, the client may come up with responses that sound good on the surface but miss the point.

In this example, the client responds to the thought, "It was a miracle that I survived," with the response, "I did survive." This response does not challenge the view that, "It was a miracle that I survived." In actuality, the client had been driving on a city street at low speed when the car ahead of her stopped unexpectedly. She was startled but reacted quickly enough to stop safely and avoid an accident. It was *not* a miracle that she survived. The situation presented the risk of a "fender-bender," but it was not a life and death situation. Furthermore, the client had demonstrated that she was a good enough driver to handle such situations safely. Responses such as, "It wasn't a miracle that I survived, it was an unexpected situation that I could handle safely.", "It won't be the end of me if it happens again. I will probably handle it as safely as I handled it this time.", and "It's not true that you only get to screw up once. Besides I didn't screw up, I handled the situation." would be more effective.

It is important to note that responding to dysfunctional thoughts is not equally effective with all emotions. With some emotions, such as depression, effective responses usually produce an immediate change in mood. With other emotions, such as anxiety and guilt, effective responses reduce the individual's belief in the dysfunctional thoughts but do not necessarily produce an immediate improvement in mood. Usually, the individual working to overcome anxiety or guilt must put his or her adaptive responses to the dysfunctional thoughts into practice in real life to reduce the problematic emotions.

Techniques for Changing Cognitive Distortions

Techniques that can be used to change cognitive distortions can obviously be used to challenge automatic thoughts, as well. However, these techniques are especially good at reducing the client's belief in the value or truthfulness of specific distortions. They, therefore, have a specialized value that we would like to emphasize.

Labeling of Distortions.   Many clients find it useful to label the particular cognitive distortions that they notice among their automatic thoughts and find that simply doing this weakens the emotional impact of the thoughts. A list of distortions such as the one in Chapter 1 can be provided to the client. *Feeling Good* (Burns, 1999a) is also an excellent self-help book that can be useful in educating clients about cognitive distortions. Once the client understands what each distortion is, he or she can watch for examples of "personalizing," "mind-reading," and so on, among his or her automatic thoughts. For example:

CLIENT: He really doesn't care. I can tell. If he cared he would call. He probably thinks that I'm not worth it.
THERAPIST: What are you doing?
CLIENT: What do you mean?
THERAPIST: What are you doing right now as you think about him?
CLIENT: You mean like in the book?
THERAPIST: Yes. Like in the book.
CLIENT: Mind-reading?
THERAPIST: Mind-reading!
CLIENT: I guess I am.
THERAPIST: Can you really read his mind and know exactly what he is thinking?
CLIENT: (Laughing) Hey, I am depressed, not crazy!

De-catastrophizing.   Even an outcome that is extremely unlikely can be quite upsetting if it is so negative that it would be intolerable were it to happen. For example, if you were to hear your physician say, "There is only a five percent chance that you have a brain tumor," you probably would not be very reassured. If the client is reacting as though the outcome he or she fears would be completely devastating, the therapist can work to help the client see whether he or she is overestimating the catastrophic nature of the situation. Questions that might be asked of the client include, "What is the worst that could happen?", or "If it does happen, how would your life be different three months after that point?". It is important to seriously look at the likely consequences of the events the client fears rather than asking these questions rhetorically and it is important that this technique be used with gentleness and care so that the client does not feel ridiculed or demeaned by the therapist. For example:

CLIENT: She'll think I'm an idiot. A moron. A loser.

THERAPIST: And if she does, how bad would that be?

CLIENT: It WOULD be awful.

THERAPIST: I understand that it would be embarrassing and you would feel bad but what would be awful about it?

CLIENT: It just would be.

THERAPIST: Let's think that through. Other than embarrassment, what consequences would it have if she were to think you were an idiot?

CLIENT: I guess it would be mostly embarrassing.

THERAPIST: And being embarrassed is really unpleasant for you. Does it have any lasting effects?

CLIENT: I guess not.

Challenging Dichotomous Thinking.   With clients who see things as "all or nothing", a technique for breaking down the dichotomy can be quite useful. Abstract discussions of whether things are ever really black and white often have little emotional impact. However, two techniques can be quite useful in reducing dichotomous thinking.

When dichotomous thinking is relatively mild, the simple process of scaling can be used. In this process, the client rates the intensity of emotions or the validity of automatic thoughts relative to the extreme ends of the continuum. This can help the client both to recognize the "in between" levels and to reduce habitual dichotomous thinking. Because the client has been manifesting extreme thoughts and extreme behaviors, any movement toward moderation is usually quite helpful. For example:

THERAPIST: If you put your sadness on a scale of 1–100, how sad are you?

CLIENT: 90 to 95.

THERAPIST: That's a lot. Can you think of the saddest you've ever been in your life? When was that?

CLIENT: That's easy. When my mother died.

THERAPIST: How sad were you then?

CLIENT: 100!

THERAPIST: Can you remember a time that you were not sad at all?

CLIENT: Not really.

THERAPIST: No time at all?

CLIENT: Well, on my fifth birthday, I got a train set.

THERAPIST: Good. Let's label that 0 for sadness. Use those two events, your fifth birthday party as 0 sadness and your mom's death as 100 sadness. Compared to those events, how sad are you now?

CLIENT: Well, compared to that, this is a 50, maybe 45.

When dichotomous thinking is more firmly entrenched, a more powerful intervention is needed. This involves first confirming that the client sees the issue in question dichotomously and then developing an operational definition, in the client's own words, of each pole of the dichotomy. Once this has been done it is possible to examine the available data to determine if the topic in question is truly dichotomous or not. For example:

THERAPIST: It sounds as though you see people as being either completely trustworthy or not trustworthy at all, with nothing in between.

CLIENT: Sure, you can either trust somebody or you can't.

THERAPIST: As you see it, what are the characteristics of a completely trustworthy person? For example, if a Martian came down knowing nothing of humans, what should he look for to decide who could be trusted?

CLIENT: Well, trustworthy people follow through on what they say.

THERAPIST: Some of the time? All of the time?

CLIENT: All of the time. They never lie. They don't let anything interfere with doing what they say they will. They don't let you down or hurt you.

THERAPIST: Does that cover it or is there more than that to trustworthiness?

CLIENT: That's about it.

THERAPIST: What would be a good label for the other extreme, the people who aren't trustworthy?

CLIENT: Treacherous.

THERAPIST: And what would the characteristics of treacherous people be?

CLIENT: They don't follow through on what they say.

THERAPIST: From what you said about the characteristics of untrustworthy people, it sounds like they'd lie and deceive a lot. Am I right?

CLIENT: Yeah, all the time. They try to take advantage of you when there's a chance. They try to hurt you then come up with excuses. They get your hopes up then let you down.

THERAPIST: Does that pretty much cover it?

CLIENT: Yeah.

THERAPIST: Let's see how this works in practice. Let's take your sister-in-law. Which category would she fall in?

CLIENT: Oh, I can trust her.

THERAPIST: Does she meet the full criteria for trustworthiness? Don't I remember you being really upset last week that she hadn't called when she said she would?

CLIENT: I guess she doesn't follow through on everything she says.

THERAPIST: So does that mean she's "treacherous", lying and deceiving all the time and so on.

CLIENT: No, she's pretty nice.

THERAPIST: Hmm. She does not seem to fall one hundred percent in either category. Suppose we imagine a zero to ten scale where zero means completely treacherous and ten means absolutely, completely trustworthy. Where would you rate her?

CLIENT: She'd be about an eight.

THERAPIST: How about your mother?

CLIENT: She's not as reliable. She'd be about a six.

Mental Imagery Techniques

Not all automatic thoughts are verbal in nature. It can be important to assess the content of any mental images that occur in problem situations and to deal with any dysfunctional images that occur. Whether or not mental images play an important role in the client's problems, mental imagery can be used in responding to dysfunctional thoughts, as a way of practicing new behaviors, or as a way of reducing problematic emotional responses.

Replacement Imagery. If the client experiences dysfunctional images in problem situations, one option is to help him or her to generate more adaptive alternative images to replace the dysfunctional ones. For example:

THERAPIST: When you anticipate going into the grocery store, do you get any images or pictures in your mind?

CLIENT: I see myself having a panic attack, screaming at the top of my lungs, and running out of the store, leaving all the groceries in the cart and pushing people aside as I rush out. Everyone is staring at me, saying that I must be a lunatic.

THERAPIST: Has that ever actually happened?

CLIENT: No. I get real anxious but even if I have a panic attack I'm able to leave quietly without attracting much attention.

THERAPIST: Do you have any idea what effect it would have if you were able to replace the image of running out screaming with the image of leaving quietly?

CLIENT: I guess I'd be a heck of a lot more comfortable with that and it would be more realistic too.

Cognitive Rehearsal. By visualizing an event in the mind's eye, the client can covertly practice particular behaviors without encountering the practical problems or risks that sometimes make it difficult to practice new behaviors in real-life situations. By realistically imagining himself or herself in a scene, the client can explore a range of possible responses, select the most promising one, and practice it to some extent. For example:

THERAPIST: I'd like you to close your eyes and picture speaking with your girlfriend. Can you picture that?

CLIENT: Yeah. I don't like it.

THERAPIST: Like what?

CLIENT: What I'm seeing.

THERAPIST: What do you see? Describe it.

CLIENT: I see her listening to me and then turning away. I start crying and begging her to stay and then I start feeling embarrassed and want to die.

THERAPIST: How does she react when you start crying and begging?

CLIENT: It just turns her off more.

THERAPIST: Let's try to construct a picture of a way that you'd like to be able to react. What would you like to see happen?

CLIENT: I'd like her to listen and understand.

THERAPIST: Yeah, if she listens and understands there's no problem. How would you like to handle it if she turns away?

CLIENT: I don't want to beg, I need to stand up for myself.

THERAPIST: Do you think that would go better?

CLIENT: Yeah. She'd respect that more and I'd feel a lot better about it.

THERAPIST: So what would you actually say to her?

CLIENT: (after further developing the imaginary scene) That sounds pretty good to me but I'm not sure I could pull it off in real life.

THERAPIST: What if you were to practice it in imagination several times? Would that help you remember the things you want to say?

CLIENT: I bet it would.

Desensitization and Flooding Imagery. Ever since Wolpe's pioneering work (1958), mental imagery has been used in a variety of ways to reduce or eliminate problematic emotional responses, especially anxiety. In systematic desensitization (St. Onge, 1995; Wilson, 1996), the client proceeds through a hierarchy of imagined scenes starting with a situation that elicits only mild levels of anxiety. The client imagines the scene repeatedly, while practicing relaxation techniques, until he or she is comfortable while imagining the situation. The client then proceeds in a step-wise fashion until he or she is comfortable imagining the situations that initially would have been most frightening. Flooding in imagery (Jones & River, 1997; Stampfl & Levis, 1967) is a similar approach in which the hierarchy of scenes is dispensed with and the client imagines being in the situations which would be most intensely frightening to him or her for an extended period until the anxiety gradually subsides. Both of these techniques have been widely used clinically and have been demonstrated to be effective with a range of problems.

Coping Imagery. It is possible to combine the desensitization or flooding approaches discussed above with cognitive rehearsal by having the client imagine a problem situation, imagine that the problems which he or she fears occur, and then imagine tolerating the anxiety and coping effectively with the situation. This combined approach makes it possible to "decondition" the emotional responses and improve coping skills at the same time. For example:

THERAPIST: Now close your eyes and relax and I'll start to guide you through the scene.

CLIENT: Okay.

Therapist: The professor has just started passing out the math exam and you are sitting there in your usual seat waiting to get your copy of the exam. Do you have a clear image of that?

Client: Yeah, I can see the room real clear. Everybody's sort of quiet and tense.

Therapist: How do you feel?

Client: I'm pretty tense.

Therapist: Remind yourself to use the relaxation exercise you've been practicing and go ahead and do it, then continue imagining and signal when the exam gets to you by raising your finger the way we discussed. Now you look at the exam and you realize you don't have the foggiest idea how to solve the first problem. It's something you should know how to do but you can't remember anything about it.

Client: Oh God!

Therapist: How do you feel?

Client: I'm really tense. I'm starting to break into a sweat and my stomach doesn't feel too good.

Therapist: Okay, stay with those feelings. Do you remember how you want to handle this situation?

Client: Yeah, remind myself there's no need to panic, I can come back to that one later, then try to stay calm and go on to the next one.

Therapist: Try that as you imagine the exam. . . . How are you feeling?

Client: It's working. I'm not nearly as tense and I can think a lot clearer. Maybe one of the other questions will remind me how to do that first one.

Therapist: Great! Let's go on with that second question. Imagine that you pretty much remember how to do it but can't remember all the details. How do you want to handle that?

When using coping imagery, it is important to remember that effective coping does not guarantee success. Therapist and client should prepare for failure as well as success. In the case illustrated above, the client found it quite useful to imagine discovering both that he had done well in the exam and that he had failed the course despite his efforts. He found that both situations elicited problematic emotions (imagining success initially evoked anticipation of future, even harder, exams; imagining failure initially elicited harsh self-criticism), which he could then prepare to cope with.

Techniques for Coping with Recurrent Thoughts

Clients are often troubled by recurrent dysfunctional thoughts such as chronic worries and ruminations. When this is the case it is often useful to help them find ways of coping with the recurrent thoughts.

Thought-Stopping. Dysfunctional thoughts often have a snowball effect. One dysfunctional thought may elicit another and, if the process continues unimpeded, the client may be unable to respond to the thoughts effectively, simply because dysfunctional thoughts occur faster than he or she can develop responses. When this is the case, the client can be taught how to interrupt the flow of thoughts to deal more effectively with both the thoughts and the situation. The process is actually quite simple: the client simply interrupts the stream of thoughts with a sudden stimulus, imagined or real, then switches to other thoughts before the stream of dysfunctional thoughts resumes. However, because most clients have been advised repeatedly, "Don't worry about it!" and have been unable to do so, a simple explanation of the technique is generally not credible and thus is ineffective. The technique is much more effective when demonstrated to the client.

THERAPIST: It sounds like these thoughts are really upsetting to you and if there was some way to stop them you'd feel a lot better.

CLIENT: I know, Doc, but I've tried to get them out of my head and I just can't.

THERAPIST: I'd like to try something. Can you get those thoughts started now?

CLIENT: I guess so. I just keep thinking about the plane crashing. God, I'm sweating just thinking about it. I'm really getting upset...

THERAPIST: (Slapping the desk loudly) STOP!

CLIENT: I...I....Okay.

THERAPIST: Take a second to catch your breath...How are you feeling?

CLIENT: Boy, that got intense fast.

THERAPIST: Are the thoughts still running now?

CLIENT: No, they're gone.

THERAPIST: What just happened? What allowed you to stop?

CLIENT: The noise, I guess. You startled me.

THERAPIST: So it's hard to just stop the thoughts but a dramatic enough stimulus can break the flow...How do you think it would work if you were to be the one shouting, "stop"?

CLIENT: I don't know. I guess it might work.

THERAPIST: Let's try it.

After the client has seen that the technique works, the explanation of the technique becomes credible and the client can learn to use more versatile stimuli such as imagining a shouted "Stop!" or snapping a sturdy rubber band worn around his or her wrist. Thought-stopping is easiest to use when the stream of thoughts is just beginning, and clients often find that they may need to do it periodically and to combine it with the following technique.

Refocusing. Although clients often find that it is very hard to stop thinking about their pressing concerns, there is a limit to how many things a person can think about at once. By completely occupying his or her mind with neutral or pleasant thoughts, it is possible for the client to block dysfunctional thoughts for a period of time. Any cognitive activity with which the client can occupy his or her mind will have this effect whether it involves counting, focusing on calming and pleasant images, focusing on external stimuli, or engaging in some activity that requires concentration. Although this technique excludes the dysfunctional thoughts only for a limited period of time, it can be very useful in allowing the client to establish some control over his or her thinking and in allowing him or her to "take a break" from the dysfunctional thoughts. Also, if used conscientiously, it seems to have the effect of reducing the frequency of rumination in general. Increased compliance may be gained by emphasizing this to ruminative clients.

This technique can be particularly useful in several different contexts. When thought-stopping is effective in disrupting the stream of dysfunctional thoughts, but the client finds that the thoughts resume quickly, refocusing can be used to keep the dysfunctional thoughts from resuming immediately. When worries or dysfunctional thoughts make it difficult for the client to get to sleep, imagining a pleasant, relaxing scene can block the thoughts or worries long enough for the client to get to sleep. Finally, when the client's symptom is maintained by the stream of dysfunctional thoughts, a refocusing technique such as the "outward focus" technique used in coping with panic attacks (see Chapter 5) can disrupt the stream of thoughts long enough for the symptom to subside.

Scheduling Worries. When a client's concentration or mood is negatively affected by recurrent thoughts or worries which are frequent but do not form an unbroken stream, it is often possible to gain a sense of control over the worries by scheduling specific time periods for the thoughts or worries and using the focusing technique discussed above to postpone these thoughts until the allotted time. For example:

THERAPIST: It may sound strange, but one approach that often works well when people are bothered by their worries interfering with accomplishing their work and enjoying their free time is to schedule times to worry when it won't interfere too much. Then they can postpone their worries until that time.

CLIENT: What do you mean?

THERAPIST: Well, rather than getting immersed in your worries whenever your mind happens to drift onto an upsetting subject, you decide that you are only going to get immersed at a particular time during the day. You make an agreement with yourself that you will set aside a specific time for your worries and that you will stop them and refocus your thinking any time you start to worry other than in the time period you have decided on. For some people, it's not as big a struggle to stop thinking about something when they know that they will be getting a chance to think about them soon. How does that sound to you?

CLIENT: That makes sense.

THERAPIST: What we'd need to do is figure out a reasonable schedule to start with, then try it out to see how it works for you. Do you have any ideas what sort of schedule would be good to try?

CLIENT: I don't know, I don't seem to go very long without worrying.

THERAPIST: It can take a certain amount of trial and error to find a good schedule. Often scheduling 10 or 15 minutes every few hours is a good starting place.

CLIENT: That sounds good. I could use my breaks and lunch.

THERAPIST: Let's try that and see how it works, then you can adjust it if you need to. The important thing is to have a clear agreement with yourself about when you'll plan to worry next and then to follow through on it. It's normal, particularly at first, to have the worries pop up and have to intentionally set them aside until the right time. If you find it really hard to postpone the worries, you may be trying to go too long between worry sessions and you might need to schedule more frequent times to worry.

If it has been established that the thoughts or worries are completely unnecessary, it should be possible to gradually lengthen the interval between worry periods and simultaneously shorten their duration, eventually eliminating them. If the thoughts or worries involve topics about which the client does need to think to make decisions, plan a course of action or resolve conflicting thoughts and feelings, it may be possible to replace time spent worrying with time spent on effective problem solving.

Cognitive Techniques for Changing and Controlling Behavior

When maladaptive behavior is an important component of the client's problem, it might seem that interventions would need to be primarily behavioral. However, a number of cognitive interventions are used primarily for their impact on behavior.

Anticipating the Consequences of One's Actions. Many clients handle problem situations much less effectively than possible because they fail to accurately anticipate the consequences of their actions. Despite the obvious disadvantages of acting without forethought, many otherwise capable and effective clients either act out of habit, act on impulse, or otherwise fail to think clearly in problem situations. If a client shows a generalized inability to plan effectively, a comprehensive intervention such as problem-solving training may be required. However, many clients are able to think effectively in most areas of life. With such individuals, simply clarifying their goals in problem situations and directing their attention to the likely consequences of alternative courses of action will produce quick improvement in means-ends thinking and subsequent changes in behavior. For example:

> Joan, a graduate student in art history, complained of being chronically overwhelmed by her work load. After all, when a paper was due she "had" to read all relevant books and journals so that she could write a "truly comprehensive" paper.
> When asked if being comprehensive was a more important goal than getting a good grade, preparing for a career in academia, or reducing her workload to manageable proportions, she responded, "I never thought of it that way." She concluded that her top priorities were mastering her field and preparing for an academic career. Her therapist then asked for her observations regarding the consequences of attempts to write "truly comprehensive" papers. She quickly concluded that such attempts were invariably counterproductive and willingly agreed to try approaching her assignments differently.

Inducing Dissonance. When what one thinks and what one feels are in conflict, anxiety is the result (Elliot & Devine, 1994; Festinger, 1957). This anxiety drives the individual to reduce the conflict, or dissonance, by changing what he or she thinks. There are several theoretical explanations for this cognitive dissonance phenomenon, but it is sufficient to recognize that it exists and can be used therapeutically. Actions, feelings, or beliefs cause dissonance when they conflict with personal, family, cultural, or religious values. A therapist can induce dissonance by highlighting these conflicts and then can help the client to resolve the dissonance in an adaptive way. For example, a client who believes that his or her death will be meaningless or go unnoticed is likely to experience little dissonance as he or she contemplates suicide. If the therapist draws the client's attention to the likely effects of his or her death on children or family, the therapist can induce dissonance. This may deter the client from making a suicide attempt and motivate the client to look for another solution. For example:

THERAPIST: What effect will this have on your kids?

CLIENT: They'll survive.

THERAPIST: I'm sure that they will survive, but with what effect? How will what you do influence how they think, feel, or behave in the future?

CLIENT: I don't want to think of it.

THERAPIST: I know, but it is something that's there, that you've got to at least look at.

CLIENT: Why? Why do I have to look at it? Once I'm gone. . . .

THERAPIST: Once you're gone the effects will linger.

Considering the Pros and Cons.   When an informal look at the consequences of the client's actions is ineffective, helping the client explicitly list the advantages and disadvantages of maintaining a particular belief, behavior pattern, or course of action, as well as those of some promising alternatives can be quite useful. This can help clients make more adaptive choices, improve motivation for change, identify impediments to change, and help the client to achieve a broader perspective. For example:

CLIENT: I can't stay in this marriage. If I stay, I'll die.

THERAPIST: There are many parts to the relationship from what you've described in the past, both good and bad. So far you've been pretty uncertain about what you want to do.

CLIENT: You're right. I just can't make up my mind.

THERAPIST: Let's explore the possibilities. We can work at making two lists; the first can be the advantages and the disadvantages of staying with Steve. The second can look at the advantages and disadvantages of leaving.

CLIENT: Aren't they the same?

THERAPIST: We'll see. There will be some overlap, but I think the lists will show some very different ideas too. It sounds like right now you see lot of disadvantages in staying with Steve. What disadvantages come to mind?

The client may argue initially that there is no point in considering the pros and cons of changing feelings, actions, or thoughts that he or she cannot control. However, there is considerable value in weighing the pros and cons of proposed change before investing time and energy in attempting to achieve it. If the client concludes that the change would be a good idea, then the therapist and client can work together to develop whatever control over feelings, actions, or thoughts is needed.

Self-Instructional Training.   Meichenbaum (Meichenbaum, 1977; Meichenbaum & Fong, 1993) has developed an extensive model for understanding the role of self-instruction in controlling impulses and behavior. According to Meichenbaum's view, children normally develop the ability to use self-instruction to control impulses and behavior by following certain steps. Children are seen as moving from overt repetition of instructions to overt verbalization of self-instructions to subvocalization of self-instruction and finally to the use of self-instruction without verbalization. However, some individuals have either failed to master the use of self-instruction or failed to use it effectively. When a client has problems with impulse control, explicit training in self-instruction may help him or her to develop better self-control. First, the therapist and client develop a set of instructions which, if followed, will result in more adaptive behavior. Then the client can start by repeating out loud the self-instructions. With practice, the client can learn to use the instructions without needing to say them out loud and eventually the instructions can become automatic. For example:

THERAPIST: How can you deal more effectively with Jon (the son) when he starts to act up?

CLIENT: What do you expect me to do? I just act this way.

THERAPIST: Would you like to be able to act differently?

CLIENT: Sure, but I just respond. I need some space. I want to throw him out of the window.

THERAPIST: What would happen if you could tell yourself the following: "I need to just walk away and not respond. I need to walk away and not respond."

CLIENT: Well, if I listened to myself I would probably be in far better shape.

THERAPIST: That's interesting! If you could tell yourself, very directly, very forcefully to leave the situation, both you and Jon would do better. Is that so?

CLIENT: I suppose. But how can I talk rationally to myself when I'm so angry?

THERAPIST: Let's practice and see if you can get to where you can do that.

Self-Motivation.   Clients often present a lack of motivation as one of their primary problems or attribute their failure to take necessary actions to a lack of motivation. Often this problem is actually due to fears about the consequences of the actions or is due to indirectly expressed anger and resentment (see Chapter 3). However, many clients, particularly depressed ones, experience problems that are largely due to a lack of motivation. When this is the case, it is possible to help the client learn to develop greater motivation.

When individuals can see that their actions can lead to valued goals and they are reasonably confident that their attempts at attaining the goal can be successful, they typically feel enthusiastic and motivated. Individuals who lack motivation typically do not have clear goals in mind, have not identified a course of action that will result in their attaining the goals, or doubt their ability to succeed at the endeavor. If the therapist can help clarify the client's goals, help him or her to develop a plausible plan for attaining the goals, and increase his or her expectancy of success, the client's motivation will be enhanced. For example:

CLIENT: I know I should be working on the project, but I just can't get myself to start.

THERAPIST: You said a few minutes ago that one thought that runs through your head when you're procrastinating is, "Why bother?" Do you have an answer for that? Is there any point to "bothering" with the project?

CLIENT: I'm supposed to do it; they've assigned me to it.

THERAPIST: And you've tried to get started on it by telling yourself that you have to, you're supposed to. How well has that worked so far?

CLIENT: Obviously, it hasn't worked at all.

THERAPIST: Suppose there were some legitimate reasons why this project was worth bothering with. Do you think that might make a difference?

CLIENT: Like what?

THERAPIST: Are there any good reasons for bothering with it that you see right now?

CLIENT: I'll get in trouble if I don't.

THERAPIST: That sounds like a possible reason to bother with it. Do you see any other reasons?

CLIENT: Not really.

THERAPIST: How do you feel while you're in the office procrastinating?

CLIENT: I'm usually pretty bored and afraid of getting caught.

THERAPIST: Do you have any idea how you'd feel if you were working away on the project and making headway on it?

CLIENT: I certainly wouldn't be afraid of getting caught. I usually get wrapped up in my work pretty quickly and sometimes enjoy it.

THERAPIST: Suppose that tomorrow when you want to get to work, you remind yourself, "Even though I'd rather not have this project, I'll probably feel better working on it than killing time," "The sooner I get started, the sooner I'll be done with it," "If I do a good job, maybe they'll give me something more interesting to do next," and so on. What effect do you think that would have?

CLIENT: It should make it a heck of a lot easier to get started.

Of course, any fears or unexpressed resentments, which play a role in the client's failure to act may need to be addressed as well.

BEHAVIORAL TECHNIQUES

Behavioral techniques can be used in several ways within Cognitive Therapy. They can be used straightforwardly to achieve behavior change; they may be needed to teach the skills necessary for the client to reach his or her goals; or they may be used primarily to achieve cognitive change. It is beyond the scope of the present volume to describe the full range of behavioral techniques available to the clinician (see Bellack & Hersen, 1985; Hersen, 2002). We will instead discuss a number of techniques that most frequently prove useful in Cognitive Therapy.

The relative proportion of cognitive techniques to behavioral techniques in Cognitive Therapy depends on the particular symptom being addressed and on the client's overall goals for therapy. A useful heuristic for estimating the cognitive versus behavioral focus of the therapy is for the therapist to make a subjective estimate of the degree of the client's pathology or lack of effective coping skills. In general, the more severe the pathology, the greater the emphasis on behavioral strategies (see Figure 2.5). Note that even with the least severe problems, some of the work will be behavioral; and that even with the most severe problems, some of the work will be cognitive. Other factors that influence the balance between

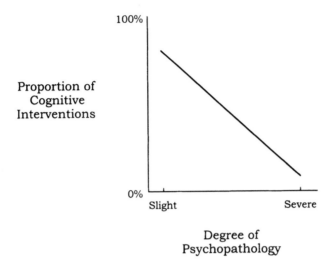

FIGURE 2.5. The Typical Balance between Cognitive and Behavioral Interventions.

cognitive and behavioral techniques include the client's responsiveness to verbal interventions and the extent to which anxiety plays an important role in the client's problems. Clients who do not respond well to verbal interventions because of intellectual limitations or communication difficulties may require greater reliance on behavioral interventions. When anxiety is a significant component of the client's problems, *in vivo* exposure to the situations that elicit the anxiety is often essential for effective treatment.

Techniques Used Primarily for Behavior Change

Graded Task Assignments. Many clients feel overwhelmed by the tasks that face them and see themselves as powerless to change their behavior or the situations in which they find themselves. The tasks can be made less overwhelming and more manageable by helping clients approach them systematically and to break large tasks into manageable subtasks. By utilizing a "shaping" strategy, with each small step moving the client closer to the eventual goal, the therapist can often help the client who has been immobilized by anxiety or depression begin to expand his or her activities in a gradual manner. For example:

> Raoul, a married man in his late 60s, had been quite inactive for some time. He reported that whenever he considered trying any activity his immediate thought was, "I can't do that; that's too much for me," and that he invariably decided not to attempt the activity. When his therapist asked for a specific example of this, Raoul reported that for some time he had wanted to clean out the basement and that several times in the past week he had considered starting on it but had given up. In describing the amount of effort that it would require to complete the task, Raoul said, "It's an incredible mess. It must be about 30 by 60 and it's literally packed to the ceiling. We've just been storing odds and ends down there for years. There's no way I could clean that place out." However, when asked how hard it would be to take one box from the basement, sort out the things that were worth saving,

and discard the rest, Raoul's response was, "That wouldn't be too hard as long as I took my time." The therapist then asked, "Suppose you took care of just one box a day... What would happen?" and Raoul responded, "Sooner or later I'd get it cleaned up. But I could do more than one box a day and I could get my son to help."

At the close of the session he agreed to try working on the basement one box at a time and to be careful not to overload himself. Over the next several weeks he found that he was able to make steady progress on cleaning the basement and that he was able to successfully use the same approach with other tasks as well.

With many clients, progress on the small steps is quite reinforcing and results in substantial improvement in mood and motivation. However, for some clients, especially those who are demanding and perfectionist, their response to small sequential steps is often "so what?", "big deal", or "it is not enough." Often this can be addressed by reminding the client that the small steps they have completed are steps toward a larger, worthwhile goal.

Activity Scheduling. Clients can also feel overwhelmed and helpless when they have not planned ahead sufficiently to use their time effectively, to choose among conflicting priorities, or to allocate time for relaxation and enjoyment as well as work. When the problem is mild, an unstructured discussion of these issues may suffice; but it often is valuable to address these issues more systematically by using the Activity Schedule (Figure 2.6). This form provides a simple way for clients to record how they use their time as well as relevant information regarding mood. A detailed assessment of the client's use of his or her time can be used to identify inefficiencies and to re-evaluate his or her choices among conflicting priorities. Once the client has developed some ideas of how to better utilize his or her time, the Activity Schedule form can be used prospectively to write out a plan and to monitor the effectiveness of this intervention.

Clients often find that by reviewing their use of time, it is possible to both be more productive and have more free time. For example:

> Tom was a retired classical pianist who complained that there was simply not enough time in his day for some of the activities that would help in alleviating his depression, such as exercising and playing his piano. When he completed an Activity Schedule at his therapist's request, the therapist noticed that over 3 hours of each day were occupied by activities which Tom labeled "morning ritual" and "after-dinner ritual". This very orderly, meticulous man had developed a ritualized sequence of household chores, personal hygiene activities, and meditation exercises that he performed methodically twice a day. As the therapist and client reviewed these activities, their value to the client, and the negative impact of devoting so much time to the activities, the client chose to drop some of his rituals and streamline the rest. As a result he was able to find time to exercise and practice the piano each day and had additional free time to spend with his wife and on his hobbies.

Social Skills Training. When a client describes having social difficulty, the therapist cannot assume that the client is being unrealistic in anticipating negative reactions from others. He or she may lack important social skills that must be learned for interpersonal interactions to go well. The therapist can work to help clients gain social skills that they have not mastered in the course of their development. These skills might include dressing appropriately, learning how to shake hands and make

Instructions:

	Mon	Tues	Wed	Thurs	Fri	Sat	Sun
6 a.m.							
7 a.m.							
8 a.m.							
9 a.m.							
10 a.m.							
11 a.m.							
12 noon							
1 p.m.							
2 p.m.							
3 p.m.							
4 p.m.							
5 p.m.							
6 p.m.							
7 p.m.							
8 p.m.							
9 p.m.							
10 p.m.							
11 p.m.							
12 midnight							
1-6 a.m.							

FIGURE 2.6. The Activity Schedule.

eye contact, learning how to start a conversation and be a good listener, and so on. In addition to directly teaching the needed skills, the therapist can facilitate their development through audiotaped or videotaped feedback, through role-playing, and then through graded task assignment. When it is feasible, a group setting can be particularly useful for social skills training. For a more detailed discussion of social skills training methods see Franklin, Jaycox, and Foa (1999).

Assertiveness Training. Many unassertive individuals are inhibited from becoming more assertive by their expectancies regarding the reactions of others rather than by actual skill deficits. However, assertion training can be quite useful for two reasons. First, many unassertive individuals are relatively unskilled at assertion and can benefit from polishing their skills. Second, assertion training can be an effective way to challenge the client's expectancies regarding the consequences of assertion. One can discuss the advantages of assertive behavior at length, but if it is possible to induce the client to try acting assertively and observe the consequences,

this will produce cognitive change much more quickly than will verbal intervention alone. For a detailed description of assertion training techniques, see Alberti
and Emmons (2001), Peterson (2000), or Rakos (1991).

Behavior Rehearsal. It can often be useful to help clients develop or polish
a variety of skills in addition to social skills and assertion. Session time can be
used to practice behaviors such as discussing a problem with a significant other,
disciplining a child, or saying farewell to a friend. This practice allows the therapist
to give feedback and coach the client on more effective responses. This strategy
may be used for skill building, to practice existing skills, or to increase the client's
comfort in dealing with certain situations. In individual therapy, this is usually
done by role-playing the interaction, with the therapist either taking the client's
role to model the desired behavior or taking the role of the person with whom the
client is interacting. It is not easy to simultaneously play a role realistically and
provide useful feedback; therefore, when an appropriate individual is available to
assist with the role-play or when group therapy is feasible, it may be advisable
for the therapist to coach the client without enacting a role himself or herself. For
many clients, learning to rehearse behaviors as a way of preparing for situations
with which they expect to have difficulty is extremely helpful (Bower & Bower,
1976).

Techniques Used Primarily to Change Mood or Emotion

Activity Scheduling. Activity scheduling was discussed previously as a way of
helping clients manage their time more effectively. The same technique can also be
used for another purpose. Initial interventions with seriously depressed clients can
be quite difficult if they respond slowly (or not at all) to the therapist's questions and
are quite inactive outside of therapy. If it is possible to improve the client's mood
somewhat, he or she will usually become more responsive to verbal interventions
and will be easier to engage in therapy. It is obvious that the use of antidepressant
medication is one possible way to improve the client's mood. Another strategy
is to increase the client's activity level, because an increase in activity level often
produces an immediate improvement in mood. The main problem with this option
is that seriously depressed clients are usually quite apathetic and inactive and can
be quite difficult to motivate. When working with inpatients, the staff can actively
intervene to increase the client's activity level. Therapists working with outpatients
must find some way to induce clients to voluntarily increase their activity level
unless family members can be recruited to help.

The "self-motivation" strategy discussed earlier in this chapter can be quite
useful for this purpose. As long as the rationale for becoming more active is presented convincingly, the client can increase his or her chances of successfully increasing his or her activity level by reminding himself or herself of the purpose of
increased activity and the evidence that this will prove helpful.

THERAPIST: Have you noticed any times when you've felt particularly depressed during the
    past week?

CLIENT: . . . Yesterday I felt really lousy.

THERAPIST: At the time when you were feeling particularly lousy, what were you doing?

CLIENT: Nothing, just sitting and thinking about my daughter.

THERAPIST: I understand that you've been feeling depressed constantly for months now. Do you remember any times in the past week when you've been a bit less depressed?

CLIENT: Not really.

THERAPIST: Were there any times when you ended up doing something active despite your depression?

CLIENT: Monday my sister talked me into going shopping.

THERAPIST: How did you feel while you were out shopping?

CLIENT: I was still depressed.

THERAPIST: How did your level of depression then compare with the way you were feeling yesterday when you were particularly depressed?

CLIENT: It wasn't nearly that bad.

THERAPIST: So one of the times when you've felt the worst this week was when you were just sitting and thinking. At another time when you were more active, you felt depressed but a bit less depressed. A lot of people find that when they're depressed, if they can be more active it helps them feel less depressed. Does that seem to be true for you?

CLIENT: I guess so, but I can't get myself to do anything.

THERAPIST: That is often part of the problem. When people are depressed they usually don't feel like doing anything and find it hard to get themselves to be active even if they're sure it will help. Would you like to learn a simple way to make it easier to motivate yourself to take action?

CLIENT: What is it?

THERAPIST: One way to motivate a person to take action is for them to see something they want and the steps that will get it. When people are depressed they often find it hard to be clear on the specific things they want in a particular situation. They also find it hard to believe that their actions will accomplish anything, so they don't see any point in taking action. But there's something we can do about that. Suppose you're sitting at home and thinking. One thing we know is that you'd like to feel less depressed. Right?

CLIENT: Yeah.

THERAPIST: And you know from your own experience as well as from what I've told you that being more active is likely to result in your feeling less depressed. . . What effect do you think it would have if while sitting at home you were to say to yourself, "Boy, I sure don't feel like doing anything but I'd like to feel less depressed and I know that if I get up and get involved in doing something I'll end up feeling better."?

CLIENT: I guess it would make it a lot easier to get in gear.

THERAPIST: What do you think of trying this out to see how it works for you? (client nods) Do you have any ideas what activities would be good to try?

The therapist would then proceed to identify a range of activities in which the client could engage. Obviously it is important for the activities to be practical for the client to engage in, not overly ambitious, and which the client would be willing to try. The activities that tend to have the most beneficial impact on mood seem to be those which occupy the client's mind, involve some exertion or exercise, are potentially enjoyable, or are seen as "worthwhile." Once a range of appropriate activities has been identified, the Activity Schedule can be used to develop a plan for the client to follow and to monitor the client's activities and their impact on his or her mood.

It is important for the client to realize that increased activity is not intended to be "fun" or to eliminate his or her depression completely. The goal of this intervention is to improve the client's mood so that he or she will be more able to participate actively in therapy and to become more responsive to verbal interventions. If the client expects more than this, he or she will be disappointed and may erroneously conclude that the intervention was a failure.

In vivo Exposure.   For many problems, the most effective manner of intervention may involve therapist and client working together in the actual situations in which the client's problems arise. The advantages of *in vivo* observation for collecting data are discussed in Chapter 1; intervention *in vivo* makes it possible for the therapist to tailor treatment to the demands of the situation and to obtain immediate feedback regarding the effects of the intervention. As will be seen in Chapter 5, *in vivo* interventions are particularly useful for reducing excessive anxiety. Agoraphobia, social phobia, and social anxiety difficulties respond well to the therapist working with the client in the very situations where the client is most anxious.

Relaxation and Breathing Exercises.   The use of progressive relaxation, focused breathing, or meditation can be helpful as a way for clients to gain a sense of control over their anxiety and to lower their anxiety level. However, clients with clinically significant levels of anxiety typically require additional interventions that address the cognitive and behavioral aspects of their excessive anxiety (see Chapter 5). Bernstein and Borkovec (1976); Bourne (1995); and Davis, Eshelman, and McKay (2000) provide good primers for those who are not familiar with these widely used techniques. Relaxation techniques can include the use of imagery (Jones & River, 1997), progressive muscle relaxation (Benson, 1975; Carlson & Bernstein, 1995; Wolpe, 1958), autohypnosis (Brown, 1998; Haber, 1995), and patterned breathing, as well as a variety of other strategies.

Mindfulness Techniques.   A somewhat different approach to coping with anxiety, stress, and aversive physical sensations involves the use of mindfulness meditation and related techniques borrowed from Buddhist practices. This approach focuses on non-judgmental awareness and acceptance of bodily sensations rather than focusing directly on relaxation, though it generally results in increased relaxation and decreased reactivity as well as increased awareness and self-control. For a concise discussion of mindfulness skills see Linehan (1993a, pp. 144–147).

Shame Attack Exercises.   Many clients worry a great deal about what other people will think of them and go to great lengths to avoid situations that might prove embarrassing. Shame attack exercises that are favored by Ellis (2002) and his colleagues (Grieger & Boyd, 1980; Wessler & Wessler, 1980) are a method for reducing excessive sensitivity to the reactions of others. This technique involves having clients intentionally perform activities that are likely to attract unfavorable attention from others to test the client's catastrophic thinking about the importance of what other will think. For example, if a client tries loudly calling out each stop while riding on the subway or leading a banana down the street on a leash, he or she generally discovers that most people do not respond in extreme ways and that if someone does notice and think poorly of him or her, the consequences are minimal. The shame attack experiences that offer the greatest value are exaggerations of experiences that are similar to ones that the client may actually wish to perform, because this is likely to enhance generalization. After all, there is limited value in becoming comfortable doing ape imitations in public if one is still uncomfortable eating at nice restaurants for fear of using the wrong fork. Grieger and Boyd (1980, p. 153) outline four conditions for the optimal use of the shame attack:

1. The exercises should be used regularly after the identification of the irrational ideas.
2. The client should generate the exercise rather than the therapist concocting the most absurd or bizarre experiences.
3. The therapist must closely monitor the client's experience so that the client does not engage in dangerous or life-threatening behaviors.
4. The therapist needs to follow-up on the results of the exercise and review the results or insights gained by the homework.

Behavioral Techniques Used Primarily to Achieve Cognitive Change

Behavioral Experiments. One of the most powerful ways to achieve cognitive change is to obtain evidence from personal experience that is incompatible with the target cognition. In Cognitive Therapy, this is most often done through designing a behavioral experiment in which the client intentionally tests the validity of his or her views. To do this, it is necessary to specify the belief or expectancy being tested and then to operationalize it so that it can be tested unequivocally in a way that is both practical and likely to be successful. For example:

THERAPIST: It sounds like your basic idea is, " I've got to do what is socially expected or people will get upset with me." What do you think, is that true?

CLIENT: I don't know. I've always done what I was supposed to.

THERAPIST: How could you find out if this idea is true or not?

CLIENT: I guess I could try doing something that's not expected and see what happens.

THERAPIST: That sounds like a reasonable idea. What would be a good thing to try?

CLIENT: I guess I could do somersaults down the hallway at work.

THERAPIST: Could you actually get yourself to do that in real life?

CLIENT: God, no! I'd be too scared.

THERAPIST: How about starting with something more trivial that you could actually get yourself to try?

(after some discussion)

THERAPIST: So we're agreed, you're going to try wearing a tie that clashes with your suit and see if people at work get upset... How will you know whether they're upset or not?

A well-designed behavioral experiment can be very effective, particularly when the client accepts the therapist's point of view intellectually but is not yet convinced "on a gut level." However, it is important for the therapist to explore the conclusions the client draws on the basis of the behavioral experiment as well as the results of the experiment, since clients frequently fail to draw conclusions that seem obvious to the therapist or draw conclusions that do not follow logically from the results of the experiment.

Fixed Role Therapy.   Often clients want to wait until their emotions or their beliefs change before changing their behavior. For example, an unemployed client might prefer to apply for jobs only after he or she feels confident about succeeding. Unfortunately, this could mean a long wait. Often it is easier to feel differently or believe differently as a result of acting differently than it is to change feelings and beliefs without first changing behavior. One application of this principle is Fixed Role Therapy, a technique usually associated with Kelley's (1955) Personal Construct Theory. As practiced in Cognitive Therapy, this technique consists of the therapist and client identifying the ways in which the client would behave differently if the desired feeling or belief were present. The client then agrees to try acting "as if" the desired feeling or belief was present (Wessler & Hankin-Wessler, 1989). For example:

> Carrie, a college freshman, complained of low self-esteem, which inhibited her academically and in her personal life. After cognitive interventions were only partially effective, she and her therapist identified number of ways in which she thought she would act differently if she had higher self-esteem. These included asking more questions in class, being more assertive with roommates, and dressing more dramatically. With some hesitation she agreed to try acting in those ways despite her low self-esteem. When she returned to therapy the following week, she reported proudly that not only had these behaviors proven successful but that she was also feeling much less insecure and more able to fully believe that she was a likable and capable person.

Role Reversal.   When the client's extreme reactions are based on a lack of understanding or a misunderstanding of the other person's point of view, it can be quite useful to reverse the roles so that the client is required to try to take on the other person's role within the session. This can be done verbally (e.g., "How do you think you'd feel if your boyfriend just said 'Okay' in that situation?") or in imagination. However, with clients who are willing to try role-playing, it can have a particularly strong impact if the client attempts to act out the other person's side of the interaction while the therapist, having been coached by the client, acts out the client's role. One of two outcomes is common. Often the client obtains a new and more accurate understanding of the other person's point of view, which he or she is then able to use both in responding to dysfunctional thoughts and in dealing with the other person more effectively. On other occasions, the client's misunderstandings and misperceptions persist. If this is the case, it is possible for the therapist to point out the differences between the client's enactment of the other person's role and the other person's actual behavior as evidence that the person reacts very differently from the client's expectations. Then the therapist and client can try to develop a more accurate understanding of the other person.

Bibliotherapy. Reading appropriate books in conjunction with therapy can be very helpful for certain clients. Books that are frequently helpful adjuncts to Cognitive Therapy are *The Feeling Good Handbook* (Burns, 1999b), *Mind Over Mood* (Greenberger & Padesky, 1995), *Anxiety and Phobia Workbook* (Bourne, 1995), *Thoughts and Feelings: Taking Control of your Moods and your Life* (McKay, Davis, & Fanning, 1999), *Love Is Never Enough* (Beck, 1988), and many of the books published by New Harbinger Publications of Oakland, California.

Books such as these can consolidate points made in therapy sessions and help the client do much of the therapy work on his or her own. It should be stressed that bibliotherapy should be used as only one part of the overall psychotherapy and not as an alternative to effective intervention on the part of the therapist. It is important for the therapist to monitor the client's understanding of the material he or she has read, to correct misconceptions, and to help the client implement the changes discussed in the readings. No matter how eloquent an author may be, his or her words have no effect until they are put into practice.

CONCLUSIONS

A review of the full range of therapeutic techniques that can prove useful in Cognitive Therapy is far beyond the scope of this chapter. However, some of the more frequently used techniques are described here. In addition to the references cited above in connection with specific techniques, several volumes may be useful to clinicians. Even though the books noted in the bibliotherapy section above were written as self-help books, they include a wealth of specific interventions and can be a useful resource for therapists as well as being useful as a reading for clients. Additional excellent resources for ideas regarding cognitive interventions include *Cognitive Therapy: Basics and Beyond* (Beck, 1995), *Clinician's Guide to Mind Over Mood* (Padesky & Greenberger, 1995), the *Handbook of Cognitive Therapy Techniques* (McMullin, 1986), and *Cognitive Therapy Techniques: A Practitioner's Guide* (Leahy, 2003).

The wide range of therapeutic techniques that can be used within Cognitive Therapy provides the therapist with a valuable resource. However, it is important for the therapist not to become preoccupied with techniques and attempt to apply them without a clear conceptualization of the client's problems and a strategic plan for intervention. A therapist who is able to develop an accurate understanding of his or her client and then think strategically will be able to develop effective interventions even if he or she knows few established techniques. On the other hand, a therapist who has mastered many techniques but applies them without a conceptualization of the client to guide his or her intervention will often find that ostensibly powerful techniques prove ineffective.

3

The Final Stage
Overcoming Impediments, Schema Change, Relapse Prevention, and Termination

The cognitive and behavioral interventions introduced in Chapter 2 and applied throughout the remainder of this volume are quite useful in helping clients overcome their problems and work toward their goals. However, there is much more to effective treatment than simply applying an assortment of therapeutic techniques. This chapter will discuss how to handle times when progress in therapy slows or stalls, how to accomplish the "deep" changes often needed to produce lasting change, and how to end therapy in a way that maximizes the likelihood that improvements will persist.

Overcoming Impediments to Therapeutic Progress

In an old joke the question is asked, "How many therapists does it take to change a light bulb?" The answer is: "One. But only if the bulb really wants to change," or alternatively, "None. If the bulb really wanted to change, it would change itself." It is tempting to blame a lack of progress in therapy on the client's noncompliance or "resistance," and many therapists are quick to assume that when progress lags it is because the client does not want to change or "get well," for either conscious or unconscious reasons. However, there are many different problems that can slow or block progress in therapy and few of them are due to the client's wanting to retain his or her problems. To illustrate this point, think of a "self-improvement" task such as losing weight, exercising regularly, or completing unfinished paperwork that you have been slow to get to work on. Next, complete, "Possible Reasons for Not Completing Self-help Assignments" (Table 3.1). To what extent is your lack of follow-through due to a secret desire to remain heavy, out of shape, or behind in your paperwork, and to what extent is it due to a number of more mundane factors?

The first step in overcoming stumbling blocks encountered during therapy is for therapist and client to identify specific points at which (1) homework

TABLE 3.1. Possible Reasons for Not Completing Self-Help Assignments[a]

The following is a list of reasons that various clients have given for not doing their self-help assignments during the course of therapy. Because the speed of improvement depends primarily on the self-help assignments that you are willing to do, it is of crucial importance to pinpoint any reasons that you may have for not doing this work. As you read the following statements about the self-help assignments, rate each of them with a number between 0 and 5 to indicate how accurately the statement reflects feelings or attitudes you may have. A 5 would indicate that you agree very much with the statement, whereas a 0 would indicate that it does not apply to you at all. Return this to the therapist so that he or she can review the results with you. This might help the two of you understand more clearly why you have difficulty completing the self-help assignments. If you feel you might have difficulty filling out this form and returning it to the therapist, it might be best to do it together during a therapy session.

(Rate each statement with a number between 0 and 5. The higher the number the more you agree with the statement.)

1. I feel totally hopeless. I am convinced that nothing could help me so there is no point in trying. __
2. The purpose of these assignments has not been sufficiently explained to me and I really can't see the point of what the therapist has asked me to do. __
3. I feel that the particular method the therapist has suggested will not be helpful. It really doesn't make good sense to me. __
4. I tend to label myself. I say "I'm a procrastinator, therefore I can't do this." Then I end up not doing it. __
5. I am willing to do some self-help assignments but I keep forgetting. __
6. I do not have enough time. I am too busy. __
7. I feel resentful toward the therapist. He or she doesn't seem to have a sense of mutual teamwork. __
8. I have a strong desire to be independent and do things on my own. I feel that if I do something the therapist suggests it's not as good as if I come up with my own ideas. __
9. If I do the assignments it will mean I'm just a typical patient. This will mean that I am a weak person or that something is wrong with me. __
10. The therapist has not made it clear to me that the speed of improvement depends on the amount of self-help that I do between therapy sessions. __
11. I feel helpless. I don't really believe that I can do the assignments if I choose to. __
12. I have the feeling that the therapist is trying to boss me around or control me. __
13. I don't feel like cooperating with the therapist. He or she seems pushy, arrogant, insensitive, mechanical, _____. (fill in) __
14. I fear the therapist's disapproval or criticism of my work. I believe that what I do just won't be good enough for him or her. __
15. I feel that to a certain extent the therapist is missing the point in therapy and he or she is not focusing on what is most important to me. __
16. I have no desire or motivation to do self-help assignments or anything else. Because I don't feel like doing these assignments, it follows that I can't do them. __
17. Change seems dangerous. The status quo is uncomfortable, but at least it is familiar. __
18. If I try something new like what the therapist is suggesting, I might make a mistake. __
19. Because I'm feeling better now there is no point in doing systematic self-help exercises. I've got my problems licked. __
20. Because I'm feeling worse now there is no point in doing the systematic self-help exercises. Cognitive therapy just won't work for me. __
21. Because I'm feeling about the same now it shows that the self-help exercises cannot help me. __
22. I have done some things to try to help myself but they just didn't seem to work. Therefore there's no point in trying anything else. __
23. I don't trust my therapist. I'm not convinced he or she is the type of individual I want to make a commitment to work with. __
24. It's up to the therapist to make me feel better. __

Table 3.1. (*Cont.*)

---

25. If I start doing something then I will have to continue to produce and I couldn't do that. It's safer to be a spectator. __

26. I notice that when I don't do homework the therapist gets frustrated. This makes me feel even less like participating. __

27. I thought all you had to do in therapy is go to sessions and talk about your past and express your feelings. So why should I have to *work* in between sessions? __

28. I want a good personal relationship with a therapist who cares about me and who understands me. That's what I need to get better. All this focus on techniques to control my mood is a lot of hokum. __

29. These homework assignments are too complicated. The work is just too much for me. __

30. I don't have the patience to do these self-help assignments. __

31. It's not in the cards for me to feel good. I am bound to feel miserable all my life, no matter how hard I try. __

32. I don't want to feel happy. I want to be miserable. __

33. I can't think of anything to do between sessions which would be enjoyable or satisfying or which would have some growth potential. __

34. This therapy seems too simplistic. It's too much like the power of positive thinking. __

35. It's embarrassing to write down my negative thoughts because someone might see what I'm doing. __

36. The therapist hasn't given me adequate training. I don't really know how to do it. __

---

a Adapted from Burns (1999b)

assignments are not done; (2) interventions fail to work or backfire; or (3) problematic reactions occur. The therapist can then use guided discovery to explore these events and to identify automatic thoughts with the goal of developing an understanding of how things went awry. Understanding this may lead to a simple solution to the problem or reveal an important issue that has not yet been addressed. In many ways, instances in which the client is noncompliant or where interventions do not have the desired outcome can be even more useful than instances where the client does the homework as agreed and everything goes smoothly. When everything goes smoothly and an intervention has the desired result, this confirms the therapist's conceptualization of the client's problems and is a step toward overcoming them. However, when noncompliance or unexpected results occur, the therapist and client have an opportunity to discover a barrier to overcoming the client's problems that they had not yet recognized and can work to overcome this obstacle. By using "failures" as an opportunity for discovery, the therapist can revise and fine-tune his or her conceptualization and treatment plan and develop more effective interventions.

Commonly encountered problems that may create stumbling blocks in Cognitive Therapy include the following:

Lack of Collaboration

The client is likely to follow through on tasks willingly if the client and therapist have a good working alliance, if the "homework assignment" is clearly related to mutually agreed on goals, and if both therapist and client have had a voice in developing the assignment. If there is no apparent connection between the issues the therapist is working on and the client's goals, or if the therapist is pursuing his or her own goals rather than the client's, active or passive resistance can be expected. For example:

> A therapist in training asked for advice in handling a client's noncompliance with behavioral experiments that were designed to reduce the client's perfectionism. The client's goals for therapy were to resolve some relatively minor marital problems, but the therapist saw the client's perfectionism and the stress and job dissatisfaction that resulted from it as more significant problems. Rather than discussing this issue with the client and reaching an agreement on the goals of therapy, the therapist had unilaterally begun working on perfectionism and this led to the noncompliance.

Collaboration involves both the therapist and the client and either of them can disrupt it. If the client feels that he or she has no voice in how therapy proceeds, either because this is indeed the case or because of his or her beliefs and expectations, this is likely to interfere with collaboration and produce problems with compliance. It is important for the therapist to actively solicit and value the client's input in setting agendas, determining the focus of therapy, and developing homework assignments, particularly with clients who tend to be unassertive. It is also important to be alert for any cognitions on the part of the client that could block collaboration.

> Mary was a 31-year-old married woman who was severely depressed (BDI = 49). Any attempt to establish collaboration was met with, "This won't work, so why bother?" Each homework assignment was received with the same comment. Discussions of options or alternatives were met with a smile and a "Yes, but..." She would often inquire as to whether the therapist thought that she was hard to work with and said that her previous therapists had told her that directly prior to transferring her to other therapists. Repeated attempts at working collaboratively were stymied until exploration of the client's cognitions during incidents of noncompliance produced the statement, "I have no power anywhere in my life. At least here I can assert my power and win." Once this issue was recognized, the therapist was able to help her find ways of exerting power and "winning" within therapy (and in day-to-day life) that did not block collaboration.

Obviously, the client who does not understand and agree to what is expected of him or her will have difficulty complying with the therapeutic regimen. However, it is easy for therapists to overlook the possibility that their instructions and explanations may not be understood or accepted by the client. It is important for the therapist to repeatedly solicit feedback from the client and to encourage the client to raise any concerns and objections. In so doing, the therapist and client can develop a shared understanding of the client's problems, which forms a basis for collaboration. This also helps to ensure that the client understands and accepts the homework assignments. This generally proves to be sufficient, but when the client holds strong preconceptions about therapy, the therapist may need to compromise to some extent to facilitate collaboration. For example:

> Ed was a 42-year-old physician referred for Cognitive Therapy after his analyst died. He had been in psychoanalysis three times a week for 15 years and valued his experience in analysis. Ed would come into each session and begin to speak immediately, bringing in dreams and fantasies and generally discussing everything that came to mind despite the therapist's attempts to set an agenda and keep the session focused. Explicit discussions of

the value of a more focused, structured approach and constant redirection by the therapist did not resolve this problem. Eventually, however, the therapist found that scheduling 10 to 15 minutes of free association at the beginning of the session helped to keep the rest of the hour directed and focused, with good therapeutic results.

Anticipation of Failure

Clients' expectations regarding the likelihood of failure and the consequences of failure can have a strong influence on compliance. For example:

> Mitch was a 29-year-old college junior with very limited dating experience. When he was encouraged to try asking a particular girl out, his thoughts included, "How can I ask her out? There's no way in the world she would go out with me. And if I were able to ask her out, what would happen? She'd go out with me once, and never again. So what would I gain? A single date and then if I like her and ask her out again, I'd get turned down. She would tell others what a jerk I am and the entire school would know that I was a loser. I'm better off not opening myself up to failure and ridicule. In fact, I'm better off dead. No one would even miss me."

Given his conviction that the consequences of his making any attempt to begin dating would be failure and humiliation, it is not surprising that Mitch was noncompliant until he was able to respond effectively to his negative cognitions. The effects of fear of failure can be reduced by choosing a task that is not overly difficult or complex, being sure that the client understands the instructions, and helping the client look objectively at both the likelihood of failure and the potential consequences of failure. If it turns out that failure would indeed entail serious consequences, it may be necessary to reevaluate the assignment.

One aspect of "failure" that inhibits many clients is their anticipation of the therapist's reaction if homework assignments are not done "right." If the client anticipates receiving harsh criticism, anger, expressions of disappointment, or other aversive responses from the therapist when the homework is discussed, this can easily result in his or her avoiding the homework and producing excuses for not having done it. It is obviously important for the therapist to respond to noncompliance without being punitive or authoritarian and instead to work with the client to understand what blocked compliance. However, it is also important for the therapist to be alert for negative expectations based on the client's previous experience with parents and teachers and to address these explicitly if they impede therapy. In particular, perfectionistic clients often anticipate extreme reactions if homework is not done perfectly, and it can be quite useful to address these expectations early in therapy.

It is usually possible to present the client's task honestly as a "no-lose" situation by pointing out that occasions of noncompliance or unexpected results provide opportunities for making valuable discoveries. For example, the therapist might follow the first homework assignment with, "One of the nice things about this sort of approach is that whatever happens, we come out ahead. If you go ahead and do [the assignment] and it goes the way we expect, great! We're making progress toward your goals. If you unexpectedly cannot get yourself to do it or if it does not work out the way we expect, then we have an opportunity to look at what happened and at your thoughts and feelings to discover more about what blocks you from your goals. If it goes smoothly we're making progress and if it doesn't, we're making a discovery." For many clients this greatly reduces the fear of failure.

Client's Lack of Skill

One major source of a fear of failure is the client's belief that he or she is not capable of performing the task that has been assigned. If the client is accurate in believing that he or she cannot handle the situation, the therapist may need to help the client master the necessary skills. If the client is underestimating his or her capabilities, the therapist needs to boost the client's confidence. For example:

> Leo was a 39-year-old lawyer who had recently been divorced after his wife had an affair and bore her lover's child. He entered therapy because of depression due to his conviction that he would never find another woman and, therefore, life was not worth living. A homework assignment given during the fourth session involved his calling a woman whose number had been given to him by a colleague. By the seventh session, the call had still not been made. Leo had many excuses for this: he was busy, he left the number at home when he was at work, he left the number at work when he was home, and so on. In trying to understand the noncompliance, the therapist asked Leo to role-play the phone call, and it immediately became clear that he had no idea of how to make such a call or what to say. The therapist then remembered that Leo had not dated throughout college or law school and that his ex-wife had initiated their courtship. Despite having adequate social skills in professional interactions, Leo was quite inexperienced at dating and had not developed the necessary skills. After role-playing several different approaches to the phone call, Leo was willing to attempt the call and was able to do so without additional delay.

Client's Lack of Motivation

When a client enters therapy because of family pressure, the demands of a spouse, or a court order, he or she may well lack any personal motivation for change and thus fail to participate during therapy sessions or to comply with homework assignments. If this is the case, it is essential to devote effort early in therapy to identifying goals or incentives that can provide the individual with motivation for actively engaging in therapy. If no personally relevant reasons for participating in therapy can be identified, therapy is likely to accomplish little.

> Lisa was a 14-year-old girl who was brought in for therapy by her parents after recurrent discipline problems at home and at school and an unsuccessful attempt at family therapy. Her initial stance was quite defiant and she apparently expected the therapist to take an authoritarian approach and to try to force her to "behave." She relaxed considerably when the therapist explained his understanding of the situation and asked, "Given that you're stuck being here, is there anything you'd like to get out of this?" However, she did not identify any personal goals for therapy until the therapist suggested that they could possibly work on how to get her parents "off her back." When she expressed tentative interest in this goal, the therapist responded, "Obviously you could get them off your back by giving in and doing what they want, but you've made it clear that that's not something you're willing to do. It sounds like the question is whether there's any way to get them off your back without giving in to them." This agreement formed a basis for a very productive course of therapy that resulted in Lisa's learning how to be appropriately independent without having to be rebellious.

Problems in therapy resulting from a lack of motivation are also common with severely depressed clients because a general lack of motivation is a common symptom of depression. This can present a substantial problem because the interventions used in Cognitive Therapy for depression require substantial client participation. Fortunately, activity scheduling accompanied by self-motivation training and graded task assignment (all discussed in Chapter 2) is usually quite effective in overcoming this problem. For example:

> Sam was a 59-year-old jeweler who had been severely depressed and suicidal for several years as a result of business problems. Though he went to work consistently, he saw no way of regaining the income, customers, and status that he once had and, therefore, had little motivation to attempt to overcome his business problems. He allowed the store to become piled up with boxes of what he described as "junk" and sought no new business. He came to therapy because his wife, son, and daughter made frequent demands that he seek help; however, he approached therapy in the same way he approached his business, going through the motions but doing little to address the problems. As the therapist helped Sam to identify small but manageable subgoals and to motivate himself to attempt them, Sam discovered that he was not as helpless as he had believed. He was gradually able to take steps that soon helped him feel better, think of suicide less, and work more energetically to overcome his depression and his business problems.

Antidepressant medication can also be useful in overcoming a serious lack of motivation in a depressed client, but activity scheduling and related interventions are often effective more quickly than pharmacological interventions because medications often take several weeks to have full effect.

Trying to Move Too Fast

The timing and pacing of interventions can be quite important. If the therapist tries to push or rush the client, the result may be the loss of collaboration, poor compliance, poor attendance, or premature termination of therapy.

> Bonnie was a predoctoral intern who typically set high standards for herself and worked hard to achieve them. As a result of her desire to succeed as a therapist and to help her clients quickly, she tended to suggest homework assignments that clients found difficult. In addition, she often attempted to challenge clients' beliefs and assumptions without gathering enough data to support her interventions. As a result, her clients saw her as being quite demanding and as not understanding them. Her immediate reaction to client noncompliance was to assume that she had to work even harder to get her clients to change. However, after meeting with her supervisor, she was persuaded to try a slower pace in therapy, to come up with relatively easy homework assignments, and to collect extensive data before attempting to change beliefs and assumptions. To her surprise, she found that not only did her clients perceive her more positively, but she also had fewer problems with noncompliance and therapy actually proceeded more quickly.

An overly eager client can rush the pace of therapy just as much as an overly eager therapist. Often it is possible to obtain useful feedback about the pacing of therapy by assessing the client's level of anxiety either while discussing the proposed assignment or while attempting it. If the client is completely comfortable, the assignment is probably not breaking any new ground. If the client is extremely anxious, the assignment may be too big a step. For example:

Linda, a 51-year-old woman, entered therapy for the purpose of overcoming her fear of driving freeways. Although fearful, she was resolved to overcome her decades long avoidance. Early in therapy, she was compliant with the gradual pace of the exposure homework and increased her confidence and enjoyment in driving. This confidence led her to impulsively attempt significant jumps in exposure, even though she had been warned to resist such urges. The result of some of these spur-of-the-moment exposures was high anxiety, approaching panic. After such an experience, she would avoid even driving assignments that she had been facing successfully. She would then have to backtrack to an earlier level of exposure and work her way forward again. After several of these experiences, she recognized the pattern and was willing to consistently moderate her pace.

Concerns about the Consequences of Change

Compliance with homework assignments and active participation during therapy sessions can also be inhibited by the client's concerns about the consequences of successfully making the changes that are the goal of therapy. The concern may be about the effects the changes will have on others. For example:

Marta, a 42-year-old single woman, was employed as a secretary and lived with her mother. By Marta's description, her mother was hypochondriacal and was constantly going to doctors at Marta's expense. When Marta refused to pay for the doctor's appointments any longer, her mother launched into a diatribe about what a bad daughter Marta was. Marta's expressed goals for therapy included being able to assert herself with her mother and being able to move out and live a life of her own. However, she was reluctant to take any steps toward doing so, in part because she believed that if she stayed at home and catered to her mother, her mother would live much longer than if she did not. She feared that if she were to succeed in becoming more assertive and independent, her mother would quickly sicken and die because of Marta's spending less time and energy taking care of her. She was able to take steps toward greater autonomy only after these concerns had been addressed.

The concern may also be about the effects the client expects the change to have in his or her own life.

Tony was a hard-driving businessman who came into therapy saying that he had read a number of books by Burns and Ellis and had decided to reduce his perfectionism but was unable to do so. He had an accurate understanding of the cognitions supporting his perfectionism, could produce good "rational responses," and could list many good reasons for reducing his perfectionism but still was unable to put his understanding into practice. When asked what risks there would be in relaxing his perfectionism he initially said, "None at all!" With additional probing, he went on to describe fears of becoming lazy and unmotivated, of becoming "mediocre," of becoming a "short-term hedonist," of hurting those he cared about, and of eventually losing family and friends. Once these concerns were addressed, he was able to begin changing.

As long as the client believes that he or she risks disaster for self or others by attempting to attain a goal, he or she is likely to hesitate, procrastinate, or even drop out of treatment (see Turkat & Maisto, 1985). It can be quite useful to explore the client's anticipations and expectations about the negative consequences of desired changes before attempting to make the change, because it is often possible to address the client's concerns effectively and forestall problems with noncompliance.

Some clients manifest a fear of change itself rather than fearing particular consequences of change. This can often be overcome by acknowledging the client's concerns, giving the client increased control over the pace of change, and pointing out that trying a change does not commit one to persisting with it regardless of the consequences. For a more detailed discussion of this issue, see Chapter 8.

Environmental Impediments to Change

Interactions with family members, the policies of the client's employer, and other environmental factors may work actively against the client making the changes that are the goals of therapy. In many cases, this happens without malice or intent on the part of others. This can take many forms from family members, overtly criticizing the client for talking of "private family matters with a stranger" to trying to be helpful in ways that encourage passivity and dependency. Sometimes these problems can be resolved by working individually with the client, but often marital or family intervention is indicated. The concerns of family members may inadvertently reinforce the client's fears of change.

> LeVar was a 30-year-old single male who lived at home with his parents. He was a college graduate employed as a customer service representative for a large corporation. Even though he made ample money to support himself, his parents continued to press him to continue living at home. Their concern was that if he lived on his own, he would not take care of himself, and would begin to eat and gain weight, going up to his previous weight of 290 lb. Although he presently weighed 225 lb, was in therapy, and was committed to losing weight, their concern and fears frightened him and kept him from taking steps to live on his own until these fears had been addressed in therapy.

Significant others may resist the changes the client wishes to make because of the impact the changes would have on their own lives.

> Ann had never learned to drive, and at the close of Cognitive Therapy for depression she wanted to work on overcoming her anxiety so that she could take driving lessons. Her husband somehow kept "forgetting" to take her to get her learner's permit, started questioning whether her learning to drive was really "necessary," and began having angry outbursts at times when he felt she was being "disobedient." As a result, she was unable to carry out the behavioral experiments needed to effectively challenge her belief that driving safely was beyond her abilities. Marital therapy calmed her husband's insecurities and increased his tolerance for her growing assertion as well as having other benefits. As a result, Ann's husband started actively encouraging her to learn to drive and her progress in therapy resumed.

Finally, others may resist the changes the client seeks due to their own psychopathology.

> After he successfully completed an inpatient treatment program for his alcohol abuse, Roger experienced recurrent difficulty resisting relapse. Several family members had drinking problems of their own and not only insisted on drinking in his presence but actively pressured him to drink at a family Christmas party and became offended when he refused. Because his family refused family therapy, it was necessary to devote considerable time to helping him figure out how to best handle pressure from them. This required a serious examination of the pros and cons of continuing to attend family functions as well as a realistic appraisal of what he would need to do in those situations to stay sober.

When the client's dysfunctional behavior results in significant interpersonal benefits for the client, this "secondary gain" can greatly impede progress in therapy. This can be overcome by helping the client consider whether the benefits outweigh the costs of maintaining the dysfunctional behavior, identifying more adaptive ways to attain the same benefits, and by intervening with the family to eliminate the payoffs to maintaining dysfunctional behavior. For example:

> Guy was a 38-year-old unemployed carpenter who had not worked regularly in 5 years due to a fear that if he exerted himself he would have a heart attack or stroke. His time was spent at home, watching television and doing minimal housework. Even though he had never had any major medical problems, his wife and two children were so concerned about his health that they never asked him to do anything at home. Although Guy's anxiety was genuine, his family members' response enabled him to avoid doing any work or tolerating any anxiety and that established a powerful disincentive to change. It was only when he realized the extent of the actual personal, marital, and family costs of maintaining his life of leisure that he was willing to work in therapy.

Unrecognized Problems

No matter how thorough the initial evaluation, the therapist will sometimes be unable to detect important problems until they are manifested in therapy. When therapy seems "stuck," a reevaluation may be indicated. Problems such as substance abuse and certain of the personality disorders are often missed in the initial evaluation and may be discovered only when they begin to disrupt therapy. For example, a client's Paranoid Personality Disorder was only recognized after he began complaining of times when his progressive relaxation exercises "didn't work" (see Chapter 7). If his personality disorder had not been recognized, therapy would have soon reached an impasse and his problems with anxiety would have persisted.

Therapist Blind Spots

When the therapist shares the client's dysfunctional beliefs to some extent, it naturally is very difficult for him or her to help the client challenge them. In fact, unless a supervisor or colleague is available to help the therapist recognize this problem, he or she is likely to have difficulty even identifying the problem. For example:

> Dr. Mason's work was very careful and precise; she believed that when she was under stress, exerting extra care, effort, and worry would help reduce the stress. This approach had resulted in excellent academic achievement but it often took much longer than she would have liked to complete her work and she tended to worry about its completeness and quality. In presenting a client for the first time in supervision, she described the client as a "perfectionistic, obsessive, and internally demanding" person who despaired of ever living up to his standards. When her supervisor questioned her as to her goals for this client, Dr. Mason responded, "I would like to help him get rid of all the perfectionism that makes him feel so hopeless." When her supervisor suggested that by trying to get rid of all the client's perfectionism, rather than simply modifying it, she was revealing her own perfectionism, the therapist began to argue that it was necessary for her to be perfectionistic to succeed at anything.

Obviously, it would have been difficult for this therapist to help the client give up his perfectionism as long as she was convinced herself that becoming less perfectionistic would lead to failure.

Therapist Emotional Reactions

Therapists, being human, can themselves experience the full range of emotions in the course of doing therapy. Although emotional reactions can be quite useful if they are recognized and are handled well, they can also impede therapy at times. In addition to emotions that are largely elicited by the client's behavior, therapists experience emotions that are a product of their own beliefs and assumptions. Ellis (1990) gives examples of a number of automatic thoughts regarding therapy and clients that therapists are subject to (see Table 3.2).

When therapists' automatic thoughts and schemas are responsible for problematic reactions, it can take some time and effort to resolve the problem. It may be useful for the therapist to actually write out thought records (TRs) regarding his or her own thoughts and feelings (see Figure 3.1) or to seek the help of a colleague or supervisor. In looking at Figure 3.1 note that only the most problematic of the automatic thoughts (Numbers 3 and 4) were challenged. Padesky and Greenberger (1995) call these the "hot thoughts." They are the automatic thoughts associated with the most distressing emotions. Frequently, once these hot thoughts have been challenged successfully, the level of distress has reduced sufficiently such that any remaining thoughts do not need further attention.

Therapist reactions to a lack of progress in therapy can be particularly problematic. Many therapists learning Cognitive Therapy and seeing the promising results reported in outcome research begin to believe that they should be able to vanquish all psychopathology quickly and easily. The result can be frustration and anger at the "resistant" client when therapy proceeds slowly, and guilt and self-condemnation when it goes badly. However, effective techniques and polished skills do not make one all-powerful and, as can be seen from the foregoing discussion, a lack of progress in therapy is not necessarily the fault of either therapist or client. When a therapist can acknowledge his or her limitations and take them into account without lapsing into blaming the client or excessive self-criticism, this results in better service to clients and less wear and tear on the therapist. When sessions with a "problem" client produce strong feelings of frustration, discouragement, guilt, or anxiety, even the most seasoned therapist can benefit from consultation with a trusted colleague.

The process of working to overcome impediments to progress in therapy is not merely a necessary evil, it is also the opportunity to learn a great deal about the client's belief system. Through identifying, illuminating, and overcoming obstacles to treatment, internal obstacles in day-to-day healthy functioning may also come to light. For example, Mary's belief that "cooperating means losing" might show up in other spheres of her life beside therapy. To the extent that this gets in the way of her attaining her goals, she may choose to work to change it. Recurring beliefs, or schema, are frequently found to be responsible for recurring life problems. Identifying these underlying beliefs can lead to changing important problematic schema and to improved functioning and quality of life for clients.

TABLE 3.2. Dysfunctional Thoughts and Beliefs Commonly Encountered by Therapists[a]

1. I must be successful with virtually all of my clients all of the time.
    (a) I must continually make brilliant statements/interpretations.
    (b) I must always show excellent judgment.
    (c) I must continually help to move my clients along.
    (d) If I fail, it's all my fault.
    (e) If I fail, I am a lousy therapist and person.
    (f) If I fail, my successes don't count.
2. I must be an outstanding therapist, better than all others.
    (a) I must succeed with impossible clients where others have failed.
    (b) I must have all good sessions.
    (c) I must use a therapy model that is universally accepted.
    (d) I must be well known and recognized as a therapist.
    (e) I must not have any problems of my own.
3. I must be greatly respected and loved by all of my clients.
    (a) I cannot dislike my clients or ever show annoyance.
    (b) I must not push clients too hard or they will dislike me.
    (c) I must be very careful to not deal with ticklish issues.
    (d) My clients should stay in therapy forever.
    (e) I am thoroughly responsible for any client discomfort in the session.
    (f) Clients should not disapprove of me.
4. Because I'm doing my best, clients should work as hard.
    (a) My clients should not be too difficult.
    (b) They should do what I advise them to do.
    (c) Clients should do their homework.
    (d) I should be blessed with young, bright, attractive, motivated, good-smelling clients.
5. I should enjoy therapy sessions.
    (a) I should use the therapeutic techniques that I enjoy the most.
    (b) I should only have to use techniques that are easy and don't wear me out.
    (c) I should be able to make money easily.
    (d) I shouldn't have to do any work, reading, thinking, or preparation outside of the therapy session.
    (e) I can be late for sessions, cancel sessions, or even miss sessions because I'm the therapist.

And for students and trainees:

6. I must be the best student/trainee ever seen in this setting.
    (a) I must be conversant with the most obscure literature.
    (b) I cannot do anything in therapy that may be criticized.
    (c) I must be better than all of my peers.
    (d) My supervisors should all see me as special and brilliant.
    (e) My errors or problems should never be pointed out to me.
    (f) My supervisors should love me as a person.

[a] Adapted from Ellis (1990)

SCHEMAS AND SCHEMA CHANGE

We all have a great number of automatic thoughts in the course of a single day. They come and go through our conscious mind almost continuously. For the depressed individual, this represents thousands of occasions each day in which he or she runs the risk of a downward spiral into increasingly severe depression. For the anxious individual, this represents thousands of occasions for catastrophizing

Situation <small>Briefly describe the situation</small>	Emotion(s) <small>Rate 0-100%</small>	Automatic Thought(s) <small>Rate degree of belief 0-100%</small>	Rational Response <small>Rate degree of belief 0-100%</small>	Outcome <small>Re-rate emotions 0-100%</small>
Wednesday 7:45 p.m., I looked at my appointment book and noticed that M. is coming in the morning.	Annoyance 25% Tension 35% Frustration 40%	1. Oh, no, it can't be two weeks already. 2. Not again. 3. I don't know what to do with her. 4. Nothing will work. 75%* 5. She'll find fault with any suggestion I make. 85%* 6. Maybe she'll cancel. * hot thoughts	4. Now wait a minute. She has made some definite improvements since intake: She is hopeless less frequently and less of the time. She is more social and more productive at work. Change does seem to be slower than with most clients, however. Perhaps a review of my case conceptualization would be helpful. I could also get a peer consultation. 95% 5. She is very afraid of being hurt again and is very leery of new ideas. However, when I have backed off and tried alternative, low-keyed approaches, she has eventually come around. It just takes more time and care than usual to make progress	Annoyance 5% Tension 10% Frustration 10%

FIGURE 3.1. Example of a Therapist's Thought Record.

and panic. Where do these automatic thoughts come from? What can be done to change the nature and frequency of problematic automatic thoughts beyond challenging each one as it appears?

According to Beck's cognitive model, there are relatively stable cognitive structures that give rise to automatic thoughts. These structures are called schemas, and they integrate and attach meaning to the events in our lives (Beck *et al.*, 2003). Schemas consist of our beliefs regarding ourselves (e.g., "I am weak"), other people (e.g., "People only look out for themselves"), and our world (e.g., "It's a dog-eat-dog world"). Much has been written regarding the etiology of schemas, but it is generally agreed that the majority of our central, or core, schemas originate in childhood.

Some writers have referred to the core schemas of individuals with personality disorders as maladaptive (e.g., Young, 1994; Young & Lindemann, 2002). There is no question that many of these schemas lead to dysfunction and are certainly maladaptive in day-to-day adult functioning. However, most schemas can be seen as having been adaptive to the (frequently dysfunctional) circumstances existing in the client's family of origin. For example:

Kevin was a 39-year-old accountant, who was married with three children. He presented with complaints of depression, chronic anxiety and worry, and increasingly frequent panic attacks. During Kevin's childhood, his father had been severely alcoholic and abusive. One of the ways in which his father would terrorize the family was especially disturbing. On occasion, he would come home late at night after everyone was asleep, drag them out of bed, force them to strip and stand in a row, while he pointed a gun at them and screamed, threatening to murder them all. The core beliefs that Kevin developed as a child included, "It is essential that I always be on guard," "You can never know what monster may lie beneath the surface," and, "Expect the worst." Although these beliefs were clearly maladaptive in Kevin's adult life, generating chronic symptoms and distress, they were adaptive and reasonable conclusions during his early life.

The position that we take in this book and in our therapy practice is that people develop schemas in childhood that may well have been functional or have been perceived as functional in their family of origin. Although a schema may be dysfunctional currently, and may have been so for many years, the schema may have been adaptive within a dysfunctional home environment.

As was discussed in Chapter 1, distinctions can be drawn between schemas, core beliefs, underlying assumptions, conditional assumptions, interpersonal strategies, and so on (e.g., Beck *et al.*, 2003; Padesky, 1994). However, in discussing intervention there is no need to draw fine distinctions between these concepts. The same interventions can be used with all of these.

Identifying Schemas

Schemas are the substrate from which automatic thoughts arise. When a situation activates a schema, the individual will have thoughts or images based on the schema. For example, when a neighbor acts unusually friendly, the individual who holds the belief that, "People can't be trusted," might have automatic thoughts such as "He wants something. What is it? He has some ulterior motive. Get away now." Dysfunctional automatic thoughts often can be identified simply by having the client monitor his or her thoughts in problem situations. However, dysfunctional schemas are not necessarily manifested directly in the individual's automatic thoughts and may not be easy to identify.

Schema are most likely to be revealed directly in the individual's automatic thoughts and spontaneous verbalizations when the individual is experiencing an intense personal crisis. This can often be seen with nonpsychotic individuals recently admitted to inpatient psychiatric treatment. Their automatic thoughts often reflect their schemas directly, for example, "I'm worthless," "I'm a total failure," "I'm defective." Persons and Miranda (2002) propose that core problematic schemas of depressed clients are most accessible early in treatment, before they start to feel better. Their theory is that access to problematic schema is mood dependent, with depression-enhancing schema being easiest to access during depressed mood.

In a very real sense, the search for schemas begins the first time the therapist asks the client to report what was going through his or her mind at a particular time when his or her mood took a turn for the worse. These initial listings of the client's automatic thoughts may provide clues to the problematic schemas. The therapist is not likely to have a clear enough understanding of the client to identify underlying beliefs with any certainty but he or she can generate hypotheses based on the information that is being revealed.

As therapy proceeds, some hypotheses will be disconfirmed and some will continue to be supported. The therapist will gradually develop a more comprehensive conceptualization of the client. In addition, as the evidence mounts, the clients also become more familiar with their automatic thoughts. If certain thoughts keep reappearing under various circumstances, they are likely to be important subjects for therapy and may well reflect important schemas.

> Trevor was a 43-year-old engineer with generalized anxiety disorder and panic. He had certain automatic thoughts that recurred when he was in distress, even though the situations in which they occurred varied widely. These thoughts were, "I'm going to have a panic attack; I need to get home; I'm out of control; I'm not safe here." Guided discovery regarding the assumptions implicit in all four thoughts revealed the schema, "The world is a dangerous place."

One useful technique for identifying problematic schemas is the use of the downward arrow. When using this technique, the therapist focuses on a disturbing or recurring automatic thought and asks, "If that were true, what would it mean to you?" This often leads to another disturbing automatic thought, which can also be addressed in the same way. After a series of queries, the underlying belief or schema may be revealed. For example:

> Christopher was a 57-year-old chef who was accustomed to excelling at his profession. He lost his job when a downturn in the economy caused his restaurant to fail. He became so depressed and hopeless that he required a brief psychiatric hospitalization. While participating in cognitive group therapy, Christopher produced a number of TRs. The downward arrow technique was applied to a number of these thoughts. Across situations and automatic thoughts, one underlying belief emerged. See Figure 3.2 for a summary of the results of this process.

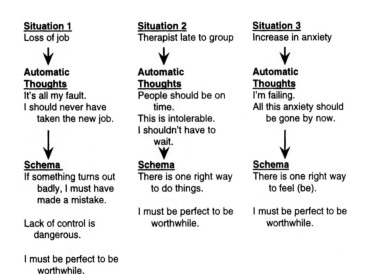

FIGURE 3.2. Summary of the Results of the Downward Arrow Technique with Christopher.

Padesky (1994) endorses Beck's advice (1972) to "follow the affect" to discover schemas. She recommends focusing on "hot thoughts" (i.e., the automatic thoughts that trigger the strongest emotional responses) and asking the client, "What does this say about you?" to access self-schema; "What does this say about other people?" to access other-schema; and "What does this say about your life or about how the world operates?" to access world-schemas. She also uses sentence completion to accomplish this: "I am _____," "People are _____," and, "The world is _____." These techniques have the advantage of expressing schemas in the clients' idiosyncratic language, using examples from their own lives and using their own words, images, or memories.

There are also questionnaires that are useful in identifying core beliefs. These include the Dysfunctional Attitude Scale (Weissman, 1979); the Schema Checklist (Beck et al., 1990), and the Schema Questionnaire (Young, 1994). There are also some excellent forms for assisting in identifying schemas as well as for case conceptualization in general. The conceptualization forms developed by J. Persons (1989) and J. Beck (1995) were discussed in Chapter 1 (Figures 1.2 and 1.3). Needleman (1999) has selected information from both of these conceptualization forms and integrated them into one form (see Figure 3.3). Although all three of these forms are useful in case conceptualization, the latter two place more emphasis on identification of schemas and are probably more useful after the early stages of Cognitive Therapy.

Choosing Whether to Address Schemas and Which Schemas to Address

Some clients simply seek symptomatic relief and are eager to terminate therapy as soon as they feel better whereas other clients are aware of persistent dysfunctional patterns in their life and wish to achieve more than simple relief from distress. Schema change is not a mandatory part of Cognitive Therapy. When a client seeks help with a situational problem or a problem that has not been persistent or recurrent, it is possible that dysfunctional schemas do not play a major role in the problem and do not need to be addressed. However, dysfunctional schemas are likely to play a role in problems that are persistent, are recurrent, or are not strongly influenced by situational factors. When this is the case, work on schema change may reduce the likelihood of the problem's recurring. It is important to explore the pros and cons of working on schema change with clients so they are able to make an informed decision. Ultimately, this is the client's choice and it is important to convey respect for whichever option they choose. It is not uncommon for clients who choose not to work on schema change to return to therapy when problems recur and then to express increased interest in addressing their schemas.

The choice of whether to work on schema change is followed by the choice of which schemas to address. We all have a large number of schemas comprising our belief system. When a number of schemas are identified, it is useful to think strategically and decide which schemas to address rather than proceeding haphazardly. In keeping with Cognitive Therapy's collaborative approach, it is important to consider the client's goals and priorities in deciding whether to work toward schema change and in deciding which schemas to address.

Identifying Information:
Presenting Problem:
  Precipitant(s):
Exhaustive List of Problems, Issues, and Therapy-Relevant Behaviors:

1.	5.
2.	6.
3.	7.
4.	8.

Diagnoses (Axis I):
Personality Characteristics:
Relevant Beliefs:

1.	5.
2.	6.
3.	7.
4.	8.

Origins of Key Core Beliefs:

WORKING MODEL

VICIOUS CYCLES/MAINTAINING FACTORS:

TREATMENT:

GOALS:
1.
2.
3.

Possible Obstacles to Treatment:

Plan:
1.
2.
3.
4.

FIGURE 3.3. Needleman's Conceptualization Form.

If one schema is be found to underlie many of the most distressing or most common of the client's dysfunctional thoughts, this would be the logical place to start. Some schemas are at the core of our belief system and permeate most of our experiences, whereas others are more peripheral. Our core schemas are the ones that are most basic to who we are, that are activated frequently and apply to a wide variety of situations. Unconditional beliefs such as "I am unacceptable," or "People can't be trusted," may be core beliefs for certain individuals. Attempts to modify core beliefs can have broad impacts if therapeutic interventions are successful. However, core beliefs can be more difficult to identify and address than more superficial beliefs and assumptions. It can also be quite useful for the therapist to address the specific dysfunctional belief, assumption, or interpersonal strategy that plays a role in a particular problem. The decision on whether to try to identify and modify core beliefs or whether to focus narrowly on specific beliefs that play a role in problem situations needs to be made collaboratively by therapist and client on the basis of their shared understanding of the problem.

Strategies for Schema Change

There are three basic conceptual approaches to schema change in therapy (Beck *et al.*, 2003): "Schema replacement" is the most ambitious approach and is the most difficult to attain. This approach seeks to deconstruct an individual's unhelpful schemas and construct new, fully functional schemas in their place. An example would be to take an individual with severe social phobia who believes, "Saying the wrong thing would be terrible! I must avoid it at all costs," and through therapy transform her into someone who believes, "If I say the wrong thing I can just apologize and people will understand."

"Schema modification" involves smaller changes in the individual's basic philosophy of life rather than complete schema replacement. The schemas remain basically the same but are modified so as to be more moderate and more flexible. An example of this would be changing our social phobic's belief to "Saying the wrong thing is serious but it is not a disaster, if I'm reasonably careful I'll do OK."

"Schema reinterpretation" involves helping the individual understand and express his or her schema in more helpful ways without changing the schema significantly. For example, our social phobic might conclude "Saying the wrong thing would be terrible but worrying about just makes the problem worse, when I go ahead and participate despite my fears I have a better time and I don't end up saying anything terrible."

Techniques for Changing Schemas

The first step in effectively modifying problematic beliefs and assumptions is to identify these cognitions and to help the client recognize their negative effects. Once this has been done, the techniques for challenging automatic thoughts described in Chapter 2 can also be used to challenge problematic beliefs and assumptions. As is the case with automatic thoughts, schemas can be challenged through "reality testing" by reviewing the available evidence that seems to support or contradict them.

In addition to the techniques for challenging dysfunctional thoughts that have been discussed previously, a number of techniques have been developed specifically for modifying dysfunctional schemas. In using these techniques, it is important to remember that Cognitive Therapy emphasizes the use of believable specific evidence rather then philosophical debate to counter cognitions. Abstract logic alone often is ineffective.

Byers, Morse, and Nackoul (1992) described the use of a *life history time line* in their inpatient treatment manual. Once the client's schemas have been identified, he or she is asked to identify early life experiences that contributed to the schemas. For example:

> Kyle, a 38-year-old single man, described his home life as "perfect" until he was 11 years old and his parents separated. Using the life history time line, he attributed the development of his current problematic belief, "I cannot trust my own senses and judgment," to that life-changing experience.

Often, significant life events appear to be associated with the development of dysfunctional beliefs. When this is the case, the therapist can help the client reevaluate whether the client's experiences do indeed show that the belief is valid. Dysfunctional beliefs may stem from childhood misinterpretations of significant events or from beliefs that were realistic when the client was a child but which are no longer valid.

The life history time line may be followed by the use of an *historical test of schema* (Greenberger & Padesky, 1995; Young, 1994). Using this technique, clients question the validity of their childhood conclusions or beliefs based on their adult knowledge. In the above example, for instance, Kyle may explore additional evidence that bears on the belief that he cannot trust his own senses or judgment. His prediction might be that if the schema were true, he would find few instances in which his judgment was accurate, and many in which it was inaccurate. He would then identify experiences that were inconsistent with his schema at each of several age ranges (i.e., birth to 2 years, 3–5 years, 6–12 years, and so on). Finally, he would make a summary of these experiences and compare the results to his prediction.

Even after a client recognizes the assumptions that have been shaping his or her behavior and understands they are not valid, he or she may have difficulty finding an adaptive alternative view. The client may simply "draw a blank" when trying to think of a more adaptive belief or may assume that the only alternative is to go to the opposite extreme. It can be quite useful for the therapist to help the client write an alternative belief and test it against the available evidence (Beck *et al.*, 2003; Padesky, 1994). For example:

THERAPIST: So it's pretty clear that you've been operating on the assumption, "I've got to be truly outstanding and nothing short of that is worthwhile." and that has been causing a lot of your problems with motivation. If that view is unrealistic and causes problems, what would be a better view to live by?

CLIENT: I'm just mediocre and that's it. I may as well quit trying for more than that.

THERAPIST: What effect do you think it would have on your motivation if you were to assume that?

CLIENT: Hmm, I guess there wouldn't be much point to trying anything.

THERAPIST: So that view doesn't sound like much of an improvement. Do any other alternatives come to mind?

CLIENT: What else is there?

THERAPIST: Let's try to think that through. Is it true that nothing short of outstanding is worth doing? For example, when I play softball I'm not outstanding but I have a good time. Is that worth doing?

CLIENT: I guess it is if you want to have a good time.

THERAPIST: What does that suggest to you?

CLIENT: That some things are worth doing even if you aren't great at them?

THERAPIST: Let's see if we can work this out clearly enough to put down on paper. What sorts of things might be worth doing even if you aren't outstanding?

Once a more adaptive alternative has been identified, it is important to test the validity of the alternative belief. The core belief worksheet (J. Beck, 1995, see Figure 3.4) provides a useful format for doing this. This form asks clients to write their old as well as their new, alternative schemas and rate the believability (0–100%) of each. The client then records evidence that supports the new belief. In addition, the client lists evidence that seems to support the old belief, but that can be seen as consistent with the new belief, given an alternative explanation.

It is one thing for the client and therapist to discuss and develop alternative schema; and another for the client to make the new schema a part of his or her life. Behavioral experiments can be the means of transition from abstract to concrete. The use of behavioral experiments was discussed in Chapter 2 as a means of testing automatic thoughts as well as practicing new skills. It is also extremely useful for

Old core belief: _____

How much do you believe the old core belief right now? (0-100) _____

   *What's the most you've believed it this week? (0-100) _____

   *What's the least you've believed it this week? (0-100) _____

New belief: _____

How much do you believe the new belief right now? (0-100) _____

Evidence that contradicts old core belief and supports new belief	Evidence that supports old core belief with reframe
1.	1.
2.	2.
3.	3.
etc.	etc.

* Should situations related to an increase or decrease in the strength of the belief be topics for the agenda?

FIGURE 3.4. Core Belief Worksheet.

testing new schemas. For example:

> Brittany was a 22-year-old graduate student who had previously been treated with Cognitive Therapy for depression. She returned to treatment about 15 months later to address the perfectionism schema that had been previously identified, but not treated. Although she was highly motivated to change the perfectionism because she believed that it predisposed her to depression, she was also terrified at becoming an outcast if she became less perfectionistic. She feared that if she did not get herself perfectly coifed and made up each day, no one would even speak to her. As a result, she took at least 2 hours to get ready to leave the house in the morning. Brittany and her therapist designed a behavioral experiment to test her fear in a tolerable way. Initially, she compared the number of people who spoke to her on days when she wore mascara with the number of people who spoke to her on days when she chose not to wear mascara. The experiment was designed for six consecutive days: during the first day and the last two days, she would refrain from using mascara, but otherwise would use her usual cosmetics; during the middle three days she would wear mascara. Brittany was truly amazed when the experiment showed that going without mascara did not make people shun her. She, thereafter, went on to allow herself to be increasingly "imperfect" through a series of behavioral experiments involving appearance, work, and housekeeping that gradually became more challenging. At the same time Brittany's therapist worked to help Brittany decide how "perfect" to be in a range of day-to-day situations.

The positive data log is a simple but useful and versatile cognitive technique that can be used to increase the individual's belief in an alternative schema. It simply involves having the client maintain a running list of any evidence they encounter that supports the new belief. For example, Brittany would record occasions when others responded in a positive or neutral way despite her being "imperfect." If the client is actively looking for experiences that are consistent with the new belief, they are likely to be less focused on the day-to-day experiences that maintained their old belief.

Another extremely useful technique for helping the client move away from absolutist beliefs is rating the concept being discussed on a continuum (see Chapter 2, also see Pretzer, 1983; J. Beck, 1995). The therapist may construct a continuum of almost any quality that triggers a client's all or nothing thinking. For example, an avoidant individual may hold the belief that others will never accept her. To help this client see the possibility of being accepted to some extent by others, the therapist may find it useful to have the client rate the degree of acceptance–rejection on a continuum (see Figure 3.5).

As can be seen, the anchor points are 0% acceptance–100% rejection and 100% acceptance–0% rejection, with all the possible gradations between. The therapist would usually translate the concept to positive terms, if possible. Thus, rather than

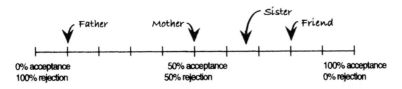

FIGURE 3.5. Rating Degree of Acceptance/Rejection.

considering whether there are different degrees of rejection, he or she will help the client consider whether there are differing degrees of acceptance. The avoidant individual may not recognize acceptance unless it is 100%, and therefore ignore evidence that might be encouraging to her. However, if asked to identify significant people from her life and then rate where they actually fall on the continuum of acceptance, this individual might see that many people have been somewhat accepting and that a few people have been very accepting of her. This might be the beginning of moving the client off the most extreme and depressing belief that she is totally unacceptable to all. Belief continua are also frequently useful in therapy when applied to trustworthiness, lovability, competence, and so on. See Padesky (1994) for a discussion regarding two-dimensional continua.

For clients who cannot imagine themselves as being any different, the fixed role or "as if" technique (Kelley, 1955) can be powerful in changing schemas. The individual is asked to try the experiment of acting as if they held some new, specific alternative schema for a period of time and to record the results. Because the client is not asked to hold any degree of belief in the plausibility of the new schema, resistance can often be avoided. For example:

> Brian, a young man with paranoid personality disorder, was extremely uncomfortable using public transportation because of fear of others' thoughts and intentions regarding him. As this was his only way to travel, other than by foot, he wanted to work on being more comfortable on the bus. After a number of relaxation, distraction, and thought challenging strategies failed, Brian's therapist asked him to ride the bus acting as if he were Humphrey Bogart, and therefore too cool to care what anyone was thinking of him. Although Brian could not be convinced to ignore the possibly judgmental thoughts of his fellow riders on his own behalf, he reported that he could do this as Bogie. When he did this, he discovered that no serious consequences came from being less concerned about what others thought and that he could travel in greater (although not absolute) comfort.

There are probably as many variations on these techniques as there are therapists to apply them. There are also other useful techniques for schema change. The interested reader is referred to the following excellent resources: Beck *et al.* (2003), Beck (1995), Padesky (1994), and Padesky and Greenberger (1995).

RELAPSE PREVENTION AND TERMINATION

The cognitive therapist begins to prepare for the termination of therapy almost from the earliest stages of treatment. As the sessions progress, responsibility for guiding treatment shifts gradually from falling mostly on the therapist at intake, through equal collaboration, to the client's taking a large share of the responsibility. Many aspects of Cognitive Therapy prepare the client to maintain gains and continue progress outside of therapy. These include educating the client about his or her problems and strategies for addressing them, the use of guided discovery, practice with behavioral and cognitive homework, and frequent summaries of what has been learned. As therapy progresses, frequency of therapy sessions typically is gradually reduced from weekly sessions to bimonthly sessions to meeting less frequently or meeting as needed. This blurs the distinction between being in therapy and being out of therapy and provides the client with an opportunity to gain experience handling problems on his or her own. Therefore, by the time treatment actually ends, the client will have had most of the responsibility for managing his or her own care for some time. In addition, termination is not seen as an absolute end to treatment. Clients are typically encouraged to return for booster sessions and tune-ups as the need arises.

The basic principles of relapse prevention were summarized in Chapter 1. At the close of treatment, the therapist helps the client identify high-risk situations and early warning signs to watch for. The therapist helps the client plan ways to deal effectively with high-risk situations and to respond to warning signs. There are many ways to put these principles into action. A simple format for summarizing a relapse prevention plan is shown in Figure 3.6.

Relapse Prevention Plan

High-Risk Situation(s) What situations have been hard to handle in the past? What situations are hard to handle currently? What situations are likely to be hard to handle in the future?	Plan How do I want to deal with it?

Early Warning Signs What feelings, thoughts, or actions would be early noticeable signs that I'm having difficulty?	Plan What would be good for me to do if I see these warning signs?

If this doesn't work, then what?

FIGURE 3.6. Relapse Prevention Plan Form.

Simon has developed a technique called the personalized treatment manual (PTM) (Beck *et al.*, 2003) for maximizing generalization of therapy progress. As a course of therapy is starting to wind down because most of the goals have been met, the focus includes work on maintaining gains and preventing relapse and preparing for termination. At that point, therapist and client review the course of therapy and summarize what the client has learned. First, the client's initial goals and presenting problems are reviewed and the client lists the techniques that have been helpful in attaining those goals. Then, the client writes the list of effective techniques in order of their application. This process is begun in the session and continued as homework with the therapist adding any information that the client has overlooked. Finally, the client puts this information in a form that is organized enough to be referred to later. Some clients use a flow-chart; some use a list of "if . . . then" statements; some put the information in the form of a letter to themselves. In any case, the terminating client produces a personalized treatment manual for future reference. An example of a very detailed PTM developed by a previously depressed client is shown in Table 3.3.

TABLE 3.3. "Personal Therapy Manual" Developed by a Previously Depressed Client

I. If experiencing no particular problem:
   A. Read, refine, and edit PTM at least monthly at regular therapy time.
   B. Complete BDI and compare score to previous scores.
   C. Monitor early warning signs, such as frequency of pleasurable and social activities, self-care, and exercise.
   D. Attend booster sessions as planned.
   E. Identify areas of procrastination and set goals.
   F. Anticipate potentially difficult occasions over the next month, e.g., family holidays, and make an action plan to avoid pitfalls or handle any that may occur.
II. If mood has slipped slightly since last BDI:
   A. Administer scales weekly at regular therapy time.
   B. List stressors and make an action plan for each.
   C. Set specific goals from action plan.
   D. Perform at least one action right now.
   E. Schedule at least one action goal from the plan for each of the next several days.
   F. Complete Thought Record daily.
   G. Do at least one pleasurable activity daily.
   H. If score and mood improve by the following week, continue plan for each of the next several days.
   I. Monitor mood at 2 week intervals
      1. If normal for the next month, resume monthly monitoring.
      2. If mood slips again, go to IIA. and repeat to IIH.
         (a) If mood continues to deteriorate, call therapist for appointment.
         (b) Call psychiatrist regarding a possible adjustment of medication.
III. If mood suddenly spirals downward:
   A. Get therapy materials from notebook, i.e., PTM, Thought Records, and pen.
   B. Leave the house immediately and go to beach, movie, library, etc.
   C. After distracting activity, find a place to sit and complete a Thought Record.
      1. If feeling better, go to IIB and follow instructions.
      2. If not feeling better, look for characteristic distortions, double standards, personalization, etc., and incorporate into balanced response.
         (a) If feeling better, go to IIB.
         (b) If not feeling better, call spouse or friend for help; if this does not work, call therapist.

Conclusions

This chapter summarizes some of the more challenging and powerful methods in Cognitive Therapy. Noncompliance and other problems encountered in the course of therapy can disrupt treatment if they are not resolved successfully but they also provide opportunities for developing more accurate and helpful case conceptualizations if they are successfully overcome. The process of identifying dysfunctional schemas and modifying them is not simple but schema change can have broad, lasting benefits. Finally, working explicitly to prepare for termination and to minimize the risk of relapse can greatly improve the likelihood that gains achieved through therapy will persist.

II

Cognitive Therapy with Axis I Disorders

The general principles of Cognitive Therapy (summarized in Table II.1) apply across a broad range of disorders and a wide range of clients. However, this does not mean that the practice of Cognitive Therapy is the same no matter who the client is, who the therapist is, or what problems are being worked on. Cognitive Therapy is a flexible, integrative approach that encompasses a broad range of therapeutic interventions and can be tailored to meet the needs of the client, the therapist's personal style, and the goals of therapy.

This section begins with a discussion of the application of Cognitive Therapy to the treatment of depression and suicidality, the area in which the approach was initially developed. It then details the adjustments necessary to apply Cognitive Therapy effectively with the anxiety disorders and with substance abuse. Further recommendations and resources for applying Cognitive Therapy with a wide range of Axis I disorders are found in Appendix B.

Although this information is organized by diagnosis, it is important to remember that the diagnosis does not equal the individual. This volume presents conceptualizations and treatment recommendations for many diagnostic categories; however, these are intended as a guide, not as a prescription or a cookbook. Interventions must be based on individualized conceptualizations and on a collaborative relationship.

TABLE II.1. General Principles of Cognitive Therapy

Therapist and client work collaboratively toward clear goals
The therapist takes an active, directive role
Interventions are based on an individualized conceptualization
The focus is on specific problem situations and on specific thoughts, feelings, and actions
Therapist and client focus on modifying thoughts, coping with emotions, and/or changing behavior as needed
The client continues the work of therapy between sessions
Interventions later in therapy focus on identifying and modifying predisposing factors including schemas and core beliefs
At the close of treatment therapist and client work explicitly on relapse prevention

---

4

The Treatment of Depression

A discussion of the treatment of depression has a special place in any book on Cognitive Therapy. Depression was, after all, the first problem area to which A. T. Beck (1972, 1976) applied Cognitive Therapy. It is also the clinical problem that has been most extensively studied in terms of the efficacy of Cognitive Therapy (Butler & Beck, 2000; DeRubeis & Crits-Christoph, 1998; Simon & Fleming, 1985). Finally, depression, by itself and in combination with other disorders, is one of the most common problems seen in clinical practice (Seligman, 1975).

The term depression encompasses a broad range of mood disorders. Rather than being a unitary phenomenon, it is a highly complex, multidimensional clinical syndrome. Depression may be mild or severe, obvious or masked, episodic or chronic. Depression has emotional and behavioral manifestations, as well as distinctive cognitive patterns and neurochemical changes. Depression can exist as a chronic, low-level dysthymia with very subtle symptoms, or as an acute, severe depression with definite and extremely problematic symptoms. Depression manifests itself both interpersonally and intrapersonally and can have major impact on the individual, the couple, and the family (Freeman, Epstein, & Simon, 1986).

This chapter seeks to achieve two goals. For readers who are familiar with Cognitive Therapy of depression, this chapter will refresh the reader's knowledge while also discussing aspects of treatment that have not been emphasized in previous discussions of this subject. For readers who are not familiar with Beck's approach to depression (Beck, Rush, *et al.*, 1979), this chapter will provide an overview and will introduce many of the concepts, strategies, and interventions that will be adapted in subsequent chapters for use with other disorders.

ASSESSMENT

Because depression is such a complex phenomenon, the clinician is faced with the task of discriminating among a number of related disorders ranging from Adjustment Disorder with Depressed Mood through Dysthymic Disorder and Bipolar II Disorder, Depressed type to Bipolar I Disorder, Depressed type, and Major Depressive Disorder. The assessment process is further complicated by the fact that complaints of depression can be secondary to other disorders and those

Table 4.1. *DSM-IV-TR* Diagnostic Criteria for Adjustment Disorder with Depressed Mood

A. The development of emotional or behavioral symptoms in response to an identifiable stressor(s) occurring within 3 months of the onset of the stressor(s).
B. These symptoms or behaviors are clinically significant as evidenced by either of the following:
    (1) marked distress that is in excess of what would be expected from exposure to the stressor
    (2) significant impairment in social or occupational (academic) functioning
C. The stress-related disturbance does not meet the criteria for another specific, Axis I disorder and is not merely an exacerbation of a preexisting Axis I or Axis II disorder.
D. The symptoms do not represent Bereavement.
E. Once the stressor (or its consequences) has terminated, the symptoms do not persist for more than an additional 6 months.

Specify if:
    Acute: if the disturbance lasts less than 6 months
    Chronic: if the disturbance lasts for 6 months or longer
Adjustment Disorders are coded based on the subtype, which is selected according to the predominant symptoms. The specific stressor(s) can be specified on Axis IV.
    309.0   With Depressed Mood

depressed individuals may present for therapy with symptoms of disorders other than depression. The distinctions among these various disorders are not academic; they can have important implications for intervention. Fortunately, the detailed information provided by the type of initial evaluation described in Chapter 2 provides the information needed to draw these distinctions.

Consider the following case example:

> Frank was a 45-year-old, married man with three children who had been employed as a machine tool salesman. At the time he sought treatment, Frank had been unemployed for several months and was feeling quite depressed and hopeless over his career difficulties and the prospect of not being able to provide well for his family. He had become increasingly withdrawn and inactive, was unable to job-hunt effectively, and spent most of his time sitting around the house brooding about his problems and feeling miserable.

The mildest of the various forms of depression is Adjustment Disorder with Depressed Mood (see Table 4.1). In this form of depression, an individual whose premorbid functioning has been unremarkable experiences an identifiable stressor and becomes depressed; however, his or her depression does not satisfy the diagnostic criteria for other disorders. It is sometimes assumed that no intervention is needed with adjustment disorders because they tend to resolve without treatment. However, treatment could be quite valuable if it can decrease the client's distress, speed recovery, improve the outcome, and decrease the risk of the client's problems progressing to the point where they qualify for a more serious diagnosis. In Frank's case, his initial reaction to being fired would have satisfied the diagnostic criteria for Adjustment Disorder with Depressed Mood but his depression soon progressed further.

Dysthymic Disorder (Table 4.2) and Cyclothymic Disorder (Table 4.3) are characterized by more chronic and persistent problems than result from an adjustment disorder but milder symptomatology than either Major Depression or Bipolar Disorder. It would be natural to assume that Dysthymic Disorder and Cyclothymic

TABLE 4.2. *DSM-IV-TR* Diagnostic Criteria for Dysthymic Disorder

---

A. Depressed mood for most of the day, more days than not, as indicated either by subjective account or observation by others, for at least 2 years.
Note: In children and adolescents, mood can be irritable and duration must be at least 1 year.
B. Presence, while depressed, of at least two of the following:
     (1) poor appetite or overeating
     (2) insomnia or hypersomnia
     (3) low energy or fatigue
     (4) low self-esteem
     (5) poor concentration or difficulty making decisions
     (6) feelings of hopelessness
C. During the 2-year period (1 year for children or adolescents) of the disturbance, the person has never been without the symptoms in Criteria A and B for more then 2 months at a time.
D. No Major Depressive Episode (see p. 356) has been present during the first 2 years of the disturbance (1 year for children and adolescents); i.e., the disturbance is not better accounted for by chronic Major Depressive Disorder, or Major Depressive Disorder, in Partial Remission.
Note: There may have been a previous Major Depressive Episode provided there was a full remission (no significant signs or symptoms for 2 months) before development of the Dysthymic Disorder. In addition, after the initial 2 years (1 year in children or adolescents) of Dysthymic Disorder, there may be superimposed episodes of Major Depressive Disorder, in which case both diagnoses may be given when the criteria are met for a Major Depressive Episode.
E. There has never been a Manic Episode (see p. 362), a Mixed Episode (see p. 365), or a Hypomanic Episode (see p. 368), and criteria have never been met for Cyclothymic Disorder.
F. The disturbance does not occur exclusively during the course of a chronic Psychotic Disorder, such as Schizophrenia or Delusional Disorder.
G. The symptoms are not due to the direct physiological effects of a substance (e.g., a drug of abuse, a medication) or a general medical condition (e.g., hypothyroidism).
H. The symptoms cause clinically significant distress or impairment in social, occupational, or other important areas of functioning.

Disorder would respond to treatment more quickly than Major Depression and Bipolar Disorder because the symptoms are milder and result in less impairment. However, the high instance of substance abuse among clients with Cyclothymic Disorder and the high incidence of personality disorders among clients with Dysthymic Disorder greatly complicate and slow treatment.

In fact, the individual with Dysthymic Disorder may be the most difficult depressed client to treat. This client gains little pleasure from life without being severely debilitated and often without having obvious precipitants for his or her depressed moods. Severely depressed clients are powerfully motivated to change by the intensity of their distress, although the severity of their depression may initially mask this motivation to change. However, the individual with dysthymia experiences a much more tolerable level of distress and thus is less motivated to change. Furthermore, initial interventions with seriously depressed clients often produce noticeable changes early in therapy. The client feels better, does more, thinks differently, and is therefore motivated to persist in therapy because it obviously is helping. With dysthymic clients, initial changes usually are slower and less obvious. When the changes produced by therapy are barely noticeable and the client sees little indication that therapy is accomplishing anything, whatever motivation for treatment the client had initially tends to disappear altogether.

TABLE 4.3. *DSM-IV-TR* Diagnostic Criteria for Cyclothymic Disorder

A. For at least 2 years, presence of numerous periods with hypomanic symptoms (see p. 368) and numerous periods with depressive symptoms that do not meet criteria for a Major Depressive Episode.

Note: In children and adolescents, the duration must be at least 1 year.

B. During the above 2-year period (1 year in children and adolescents), the person has not been without the symptoms in Criterion A for more than 2 months at a time.

C. No Major Depressive Episode (p. 356), Manic Episode p. 362), or Mixed Episode (see p. 365) has been present during the first 2 years of the disturbance.

Note: After the initial 2 years (1 year in children and adolescents) of Cyclothymic Disorder, there may be superimposed Manic or Mixed Episodes (in which case both Bipolar I Disorder and Cyclothymic Disorder may be diagnosed) or Major Depression Episodes (in which case both Bipolar II Disorder and Cyclothymic Disorder may be diagnosed).

D. The symptoms in Criterion A are not better accounted for by Schizoaffective Disorder and are not superimposed on Schizophrenia, Schizophreniform Disorder, Delusional Disorder, or Psychotic Disorder Not Otherwise Specified.

E. The symptoms are not due to the direct physiological effects of a substance (e.g., a drug of abuse, a medication) or a general medical condition (e.g., hyperthyroidism).

F. The symptoms cause clinically significant distress or impairment in social, occupational, or other important areas of functioning.

The *DSM-IV-TR* (American Psychiatric Association, 2000) criteria for Major Depressive Episode are given in Table 4.4. As can be seen, this is the diagnosis given for severe, episodic depressions that are extremely incapacitating for the individual. It is sometimes assumed that clients who are this severely depressed need antidepressant medication or hospitalization or some more "powerful" intervention rather than "talking therapy." In fact, Cognitive Therapy works well even with clients who are quite severely depressed and it has been found to be at least as "powerful" as the other treatment options (see Butler & Beck, 2000 for a recent review of research on the effectiveness of Cognitive Therapy). At the time of his initial evaluation, Frank clearly met the diagnostic criteria for Major Depressive Episode. He reported a constant depressed mood and indeed appeared quite depressed. He reported that he no longer felt any interest in or enjoyment from his usual activities. He also reported a chronic problem with waking in the early morning hours and being unable to get back to sleep, with resulting fatigue. Frank also complained of feeling completely worthless.

Bipolar I Disorder is more widely known by the older term, Manic–Depressive Disorder. Many persons assume that this disorder is characterized by a regular alternation between manic and depressive episodes but, in actuality, the essential feature of Bipolar I Disorder is simply a history of one or more manic episodes accompanied by one or more Major Depressive Episodes. The presence of manic episodes complicates treatment of depressed clients who have a Bipolar I Disorder in several ways. First, many bipolar individuals are not good at recognizing their mania or underestimate the extent to which it is dysfunctional; therefore it can be hard to get accurate self-report information. Second, depressed individuals typically feel miserable and want to change whereas manic individuals often enjoy their mania and are not necessarily motivated to change. Also, bipolar individuals

Table 4.4. *DSM-IV-TR* Diagnostic Criteria for Major Depressive Episode

---

A. Five (or more) of the following symptoms have been present during the same 2-week period and represent a change from previous functioning; at least one of the symptoms is either (1) depressed mood, or (2) loss of interest or pleasure.
Note: Do not include symptoms that are clearly due to a general medical condition, or mood-incongruent delusions or hallucinations.
  (1) Depressed mood most of the day, nearly every day, as indicated by either subjective report (e.g., feels sad or empty) or observation made by others (e.g., appears tearful).
  Note: In children and adolescents, can be irritable mood.
  (2) Markedly diminished interest or pleasure in all, or almost all, activities most of the day, nearly every day (as indicated by either subjective account or observation made by others).
  (3) Significant weight loss when not dieting or weight gain (e.g., a change of more than 5% of body weight in a month), or decrease or increase in appetite nearly every day.
  Note: In children, consider failure to make expected weight gains.
  (4) Insomnia or hypersomnia nearly every day.
  (5) Psychomotor agitation or retardation nearly every day (observable by others, not merely subjective feelings of restlessness or being slowed down)
  (6) Fatigue or loss of energy nearly every day.
  (7) Feelings of worthlessness or excessive or inappropriate guilt (that may be delusional) nearly every day (not merely self-reproach or guilt about being sick)
  (8) Diminished ability to think or concentrate, or indecisiveness, nearly every day (either by subjective account or as observed by others)
  (9) Recurrent thoughts of death (not just fear of dying), recurrent suicidal ideation without a specific plan, or a suicide attempt or a specific plan for committing suicide.
B. The symptoms do not meet criteria for a Mixed Episode (see p. 365).
C. The symptoms cause clinically significant distress or impairment in social, occupational, or other important areas of functioning.
D. The symptoms are not due to the direct physiological effects of a substance (e.g., a drug of abuse, a medication) or a general medical condition (e.g., hypothyroidism).
E. The symptoms are not better accounted for by Bereavement, i.e., after the loss of a loved one, the symptoms persist for longer than 2 months or are characterized by marked functional impairment, morbid preoccupation with worthlessness, suicidal ideation, psychotic symptoms, or psychomotor retardation.

---

often fail to show up for their appointments and abandon homework assignments during manic episodes, making it difficult to intervene effectively. Finally, mania seems to impair critical thinking, making it almost impossible to challenge dysfunctional thinking during manic episodes.

Cognitive Therapy is an appropriate treatment for depressive episodes in clients with Bipolar I Disorder as long as appropriate medication is used to control the manic episodes (Zaretsky, Segal, & Gemar, 1999). Mood stabilizing medication can be quite useful in relapse prevention with Bipolar I Disorder (Lam *et al.*, 2000). However, the consensus is that it is important to combine Cognitive Therapy with appropriate medication when treating Bipolar Disorder. For more information about applying Cognitive Therapy with Bipolar Disorder see Appendix B.

It is important to note that both Cyclothymic Disorder and Dysthymic Disorder can co-occur with Bipolar Disorder or Major Depression. When a sufficiently detailed history of the client's symptoms is available, it is possible to diagnose both disorders by examining the pattern of symptomatology over time. However, often a detailed history is not available and the Cyclothymic or Dysthymic Disorder may not be apparent until the client's Major Depressive Episode has been at least partly treated.

Although the term "masked depression" is not a diagnostic label, it still is a concept that the clinician needs to consider. When a client complains of being "blue," "down," or "sad," his or her depression is easy to recognize. However, individuals differ widely in the extent to which they are able to recognize and express their emotions and in the extent to which they are willing to acknowledge having psychological problems. Depressed individuals may seek help either without recognizing their depressed mood or without being willing to admit that they are depressed. When this is the case they are likely to present "nonpsychological" symptoms such as insomnia, loss of appetite, loss of libido, or a lack of motivation without mentioning feelings of sadness or depression. If these individuals are asked directly about depressed mood, periods of tearfulness, and so on, it may be possible to determine if they are indeed depressed. In addition, the Beck Depression Inventory (BDI) (see Chapter 1) can be useful in determining the extent to which a client's complaints correspond to symptoms of depression. Obviously, when a client's "medical" complaints are symptoms of depression, effective treatment of the depression should alleviate the symptoms.

Conversely, a client's depressed mood may reflect a "secondary depression," in which the depressed mood is a response to some other medical or psychiatric problem (Shaw, Vallis, & McCabe, 1985). Problems ranging from cardiac surgery to agoraphobia can elicit a depressed mood or a full depressive disorder in a susceptible person. Whether the depression is primary or secondary, Cognitive Therapy techniques can be used to treat the depression. However, when depression is a response to another psychiatric disorder, it may be more appropriate for therapist and client to focus most of their efforts on treating the primary disorder.

Cognitive Therapy can also be applied to helping clients deal with objectively tragic or saddening life problems. Many life situations cause realistic sadness, frustration, or grief. For example, Holmes and Rahe (1967) found the death of a loved one to be one of the most powerful stressors that most persons experience. Assessment of the client who is responding to a life crisis does not differ from that of any other client. The therapist must assess the degree to which the client's response is realistic as well as any distortions in the client's thinking that aggravate the situation. When dysfunctional beliefs and cognitive distortions do not impair the individual's ability to cope with difficult situations, support and reassurance from the therapist may be sufficient. However, when dysfunctional cognitions (such as "I can't live without him" or "No one will ever love me again") intensify the individual's reactions or impair effective coping, Cognitive Therapy can be quite useful. It is important to differentiate between grief and depression when treating individuals who are coping with significant losses. Grief is a normal response to loss and is likely to remit without professional intervention unless it is complicated by other factors. Depression, on the other hand, is a pathological state that is likely to persist or recur without effective intervention.

Even when a client presents with classic symptoms of depression, it is important for the therapist to be certain that depression is, in fact, the problem. A wide range of medical problems can contribute to depression or produce symptoms that mimic depression. Therefore, any clients who have not had a complete physical exam in the past year should be directed to get one early in treatment to rule out the possibility that a medical disorder is involved. Obviously, treating a low thyroid level or congestive heart failure with Cognitive Therapy or with any other psychotherapy will be ineffective.

CONCEPTUALIZATION

The cognitive view is that depression is characterized by the "cognitive triad" of a negative view of the self, a negative view of the world[1], and a negative view of the future (Beck, 1976; Beck, Rush, et al., 1979). This cognitive triad is manifested in the content of the individual's "automatic thoughts," his or her immediate, involuntary, nonreflective cognitive response to a situation. Frank, for example, made many negative statements reflecting these automatic thoughts such as, "I'm not good enough," "I've never really been successful," "I'll never get anywhere," and, "I'll fail." Furthermore, he believed these statements implicitly. These thoughts contributed to Frank's depressed mood, his low motivation for job-hunting ("I'm not good enough. I'll fail. Why bother?"), and to his pervasive sense of hopelessness and dissatisfaction.

If Frank's negative views had been accurate, his mood and his actions would have been easy to understand. However, when the situation was examined in detail, it turned out that Frank lost his job as part of a major work-force reduction resulting from a recession. Not only had the lay-off been based on seniority rather than on any lack on Frank's part, but instead he actually had received very positive evaluations on the job and had been promoted regularly before the firm's economic difficulties. Frank's former supervisor had a high opinion of his abilities and expressed confidence that Frank would be able to get a good job and do well in it. By all accounts (except Frank's), his view of himself as a failure, his pessimistic outlook, and his subsequent lack of motivation were completely unrealistic. How could an intelligent, well-educated man develop such an unrealistically negative view of himself?

The cognitive view argues that an individual's schemas, beliefs, and assumptions constantly and automatically shape his or her perceptions and interpretations of events. In the course of growing up, Frank had been taught, both explicitly and implicitly, that success was essential for one to be worthwhile, to be liked, and to enjoy life. In addition, he had been taught that the way to succeed was to set very high standards and to push hard in trying to meet those standards. Consequently, he viewed most situations in terms of success and failure, had a lifelong pattern of setting unrealistically high standards for himself, and tried to do things perfectly. These beliefs and assumptions predisposed him to be unreasonably self-critical and to react strongly to perceived failures.

Frank's cognitive distortions intensified the impact of his dysfunctional beliefs. He was particularly prone to the distortions of "dichotomous thinking" and "labeling". For example, he viewed success and failure in absolute terms. As he

---

[1] It is important to note that Beck uses the phrase "negative view of the world" to refer to the depressed individual's negative view of his or her personal experience, not a negative view of the world in general.

saw it, anything that was not a complete success was clearly a total failure and if he failed at a task then he was a failure. Because being laid off, whatever the reason, was not success, then by definition he was a failure. This view of himself had a broad impact. After all, what prospective employer would choose to hire a failure? Frank's view was that even if he were able to fool someone into hiring him, it would lead inevitably to disaster because he was a failure. Thus it was not surprising that Frank was unable to motivate himself to actively apply for another job. From his point of view, job hunting seemed futile at best and potentially disastrous at the worst.

The combination of his unrealistically high standards for himself and his dichotomous thinking about success and failure was particularly devastating for Frank. Because his standards for judging his performance were excessively severe, he was doomed to frequently fall short of his standards. When the "failure" was relatively minor, Frank simply became quite upset with himself and redoubled his efforts; but each time a significant "failure" occurred, Frank would consider himself a complete failure. He would then expect to fail at anything he tried and would lapse into a depression. This pattern of cognitions had been responsible for his history of recurrent episodes of depression.

The third factor, which completed the picture of Frank's depression, was the impact his mood had on his cognition. As discussed in Chapter 1, perception and evaluation of personally relevant events are negatively biased during depression. Thus, Frank showed a tendency to selectively recall previous failures and shortcomings and to be biased toward interpreting ambiguous situations negatively. Because both recall of sad events and biased perception of events would tend to elicit a depressed mood, the tendency of moods to bias cognition in a mood-congruent way perpetuated and amplified Frank's depressed mood.

These three factors set the stage for the "downward spiral of depression" (Figure 4.1). In Frank's case, his schemas and basic assumptions about failure and self-worth predisposed him to depressive reactions when confronted by "failure." When he was laid off, these beliefs about the significance of failure were activated and a stream of negative automatic thoughts about himself, his situation,

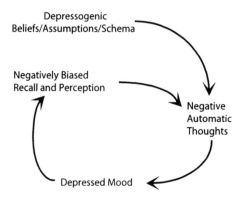

Figure 4.1. The Downward Spiral of Depression.

and his future prospects resulted. Given his proclivity for dichotomous thinking, these negative thoughts were quite extreme and seemed completely plausible to him. These negative thoughts then elicited depressed mood, which further biased Frank's perception and recall in a depression-congruent way. This resulted in his selectively remembering past failures while overlooking experiences that were inconsistent with his negative views. Thus, his thoughts became increasingly negative, his mood increasingly depressed, and so on. As a result, it was possible for Frank's reaction to being laid off to spiral from shock and disappointment to significant depression over a short period of time.

A number of additional factors commonly tend to perpetuate depressions once they occur. The depressed individual's lack of motivation often results in a decrease in activity that has several effects: First, the unoccupied time provides additional opportunity for depressing ruminations. Second, the depressed individual may become concerned or self-critical about his or her decreased productivity. Third, the individual has fewer experiences that he or she might possibly enjoy or find worthwhile. Fourth, changes in the depressed individual's behavior, as well as his or her expressions of depressed mood, may affect interpersonal interactions in a way that is likely to perpetuate the depression.

STRATEGIES FOR INTERVENTION

The cognitive conceptualization of depression in terms of the "downward spiral of depression" suggests that it is important to break the self-perpetuating cycle of negative automatic thoughts, depressed mood, and biased recall and perception to alleviate the depression. Frank's therapist hypothesized that the cycle that perpetuated his depression could be broken at a number of points. The therapist believed that his depression should subside if Frank could be induced to take a more balanced view of himself, his experiences, and his future prospects, or if his mood could be improved, or if the biasing impact of his depressed mood on perception and recall could be counteracted. However, Figure 4.1 shows that if Frank and his therapist accomplished only this without modifying his dysfunctional beliefs, Frank would still be at risk for a relapse whenever he experienced a setback or failure. To achieve lasting results, it would be necessary to modify the beliefs and assumptions that predisposed Frank to depression and to help him plan effective ways to handle situations that might precipitate a relapse.

The general strategy for treatment of a depressed individual who is not suicidal consists of first attempting to disrupt the cycles that perpetuate the client's depression. The therapist then attempts to modify the beliefs and assumptions predisposing the individual to depression through any of the means outlined in Chapter 3. A wide variety of techniques for modifying automatic thoughts, dysfunctional beliefs and assumptions, dysphoric moods, and maladaptive behavior are available to the therapist. If it is possible to develop a clear individualized understanding of each client and use this as a foundation for a unique treatment plan, the therapist can intervene more effectively than if he or she uses a "standard" approach for all depressed clients.

Cognitive and Behavioral Techniques

After working to establish a collaborative therapeutic relationship with the depressed client, the cognitive therapist often begins either with behavioral interventions designed to improve the client's mood or with cognitive interventions focused on identifying and challenging dysfunctional automatic thoughts. In Frank's case, his depression was so intense that he was largely inactive at home and was lethargic during the session. Frank's answers to the therapist's questions were slow and terse and he was not able to participate actively in a collaborative approach to dealing with his problems. This led the therapist to focus initially on improving Frank's mood in the hope that this would increase his responsiveness to verbal interventions and his motivation to take an active part in therapy. Despite Frank's lethargy, it was possible to use guided discovery to analyze the differences between times when Frank's depression was intense and times when it was less intense and to demonstrate that his level of activity had an important impact on his mood. This made it possible to introduce Frank to Activity Scheduling (Chapter 2) in such a way that he was willing to try it as a "homework assignment."

When Frank tried to intentionally be more active despite his depression, he quickly discovered that by simply increasing the number of things he did each day he was able to improve his mood substantially. Although this intervention did not eliminate Frank's depression or his procrastination, it resulted in his being more responsive and motivated during sessions. It also provided him with clear evidence that he was not helpless in the face of his depression. At this point it was possible to engage Frank more actively in collaboration and to clarify his goals for therapy.

Interventions that challenge negative automatic thoughts typically play a major part in Cognitive Therapy with depressed clients. In working with Frank, the therapist's next goal was to demonstrate the connection between automatic thoughts and mood to Frank and to work to help him learn to challenge his negative automatic thoughts. This was done by asking Frank to identify a recent time when he had experienced a noticeable increase in his depressed mood and then pinpointing the automatic thoughts that occurred in that situation as follows:

THERAPIST: Can you think of a particular point in the past week when you became noticeably more depressed? A time when your mood took a turn for the worse?

CLIENT: Um . . . I guess I got pretty depressed Thursday morning.

THERAPIST: What was the situation at the time when your mood shifted?

CLIENT: Let me think. . . . The mail had just come and I was sitting on the couch flipping through it.

THERAPIST: Do you remember what thoughts were running through your mind as you sat there flipping through the mail?

CLIENT: No, I don't think anything was on my mind.

THERAPIST: Let's try something that should make it easier to remember whatever you might have been thinking. What I'm going to ask you to do is imagine that situation over again as realistically as you can. People often find that that makes it easier to remember the details. How does that sound?

Client: OK.

Therapist: So settle back in a comfortable position, close your eyes to shut out distractions, and let yourself relax.... Now I'd like you to imagine being back in that situation as realistically as you can. It's Thursday morning, the mail has just come, and you're flipping through it. Imagine the room just the way it was on Thursday, the mail in your hands, the whole situation.... How do you feel as you imagine that?

Client: I'm starting to feel depressed like I did then.

Therapist: What thoughts are running through your head?

Client: I'm thinking about the bills.

Therapist: What I'd like you to do is try to quote the thoughts as much as possible in the same words as when they ran through your head. Sometimes the wording can make a big difference.

Client: "Look at all these bills! I'll never be able to pay them off. How's Jack ever going to go to college?"

Therapist: OK. Stop imagining and open your eyes. Do you think those thoughts might have something to do with your getting more depressed right then?

The therapist was then able to explain the cognitive view of the impact of automatic thoughts on mood using Frank's reactions to illustrate his points. He then introduced the idea of challenging negative automatic thoughts as follows:

Therapist: When you went ahead and opened the mail, how did it turn out?

Client: Well, they weren't all bills and it wasn't as bad as I expected.

Therapist: Are you going to be able to pay them off?

Client: Yeah. I'm getting unemployment and my wife works part time so we haven't had to dip into our savings yet.

Therapist: How do you think you would have felt if instead of thinking "I'll never be able to pay them off" you'd been thinking, "These damn bills are a pain. It's a good thing I've got unemployment and some money in the bank"?

Client: I'd probably have felt better.

Therapist: Which would have been closer to the truth?

Client: That they're a pain.

The therapist first discussed the merits of looking critically at automatic thoughts and "talking back" to those that are exaggerated or distorted. He was then able to demonstrate the use of the thought record (TR) (Chapter 2) by showing Frank his thoughts on a TR. Frank's next homework assignment was to use the TR to record his automatic thoughts at times when his mood worsened and to begin reading Feeling Good (Burns, 1999a) in addition to maintaining his increased activity level.

One of the most frequently used strategies in Cognitive Therapy is that of developing adaptive responses to dysfunctional thoughts (see Chapter 2). In Frank's case, negative thoughts relating to his self-worth, judgments of his performance, and the futility of trying to find another job frequently occurred at the times when he became more depressed. Most of Frank's negative thoughts were not completely true (as is the case with most depressives), and therefore could be challenged with specific disconfirming evidence from his life. By correcting exaggerations and distortions in his automatic thoughts, Frank was able to improve his mood considerably. However, as Frank examined his automatic thoughts, he discovered some of them to be "true, but not useful." For example, Frank experienced periods during which he ruminated over the possibility that his savings might eventually be exhausted. Although such an eventuality was possible and would have posed serious problems were it to occur, Frank's periods of ruminating about this were very depressing to him and did nothing to forestall the problem. Dysfunctional thoughts of this type can be handled adaptively by the client's learning to control the occurrence of these thoughts through techniques such as "thought stopping" and "scheduling worries," through replacing them with more adaptive thoughts, or through developing effective plans for preventing or handling the anticipated problem. In Frank's case, he found that when he took active steps to find a new job these worries subsided.

Often the themes that occur in a person's automatic thoughts most frequently are the most important ones to address. Frank's conviction that he was "a complete failure" was a recurrent theme among the thoughts he recorded on his TRs and thus was selected as the next target for intervention. This view of himself could have been addressed in the abstract through a philosophical analysis; however, it was simpler and more powerful for the therapist to guide Frank to examine the evidence regarding whether he was indeed a complete failure. The therapist discovered that Frank had been laid off purely on the basis of seniority after years of being one of the better salesmen at his firm and of providing well for his family. Once this evidence had been made explicit, Frank no longer accepted the view that he was "a complete failure" and instead endorsed the view that he had failed at some things and succeeded at others.

The discussion of success and failure highlighted Frank's long-standing tendency to set unrealistically high standards for himself and the negative consequences this had for him. The therapist chose to intervene here by examining the pros and cons of holding very high standards for oneself. Frank initially expressed a strong conviction that it was necessary to do his work perfectly to be successful. However, as he and his therapist considered the available evidence he quickly realized that this resulted in considerable stress and pressure. Beyond this, it often resulted in his becoming preoccupied with trivial imperfections in his work and in interpreting his performance as inadequate, even when his superiors were complimentary. In addition to continuing to use TRs, he agreed to try a behavioral experiment (Chapter 2) of doing a "good but not perfect" job on several household tasks to test whether setting more moderate standards for himself was actually a good idea.

Noncompliance with homework assignments can be very useful in identifying important issues that have not yet been addressed. It was at this point in therapy that Frank suddenly found himself unable to follow through on therapy homework despite having been quite reliable previously. At the same time, he began experiencing upsetting visual images and disturbing dreams of himself ending up as a vagrant. When he and his therapist examined the thoughts that occurred when he tried to do his homework and when the images occurred, they discovered that Frank had an intense fear that if he relaxed his perfectionism at all, the consequences would be disastrous. Once the fear was identified, Frank and his therapist were able to challenge it successfully and Frank's work on reducing his perfectionism was able to proceed.

At this point in therapy Frank's depression had subsided to nonclinical levels and he had begun to actively search for a job. When the previously depressed client's goals for therapy have been attained, it may seem that the time for termination has arrived. However, therapy should not end before identifying and challenging the client's dysfunctional assumptions and preparing him or her to handle future setbacks. Without this, the client will continue to have a predisposition toward depression. The middle stage of Frank's therapy began with helping him look for patterns among the automatic thoughts recorded thus far in therapy through the "downward arrow" technique (Chapter 3) for identifying his problematic beliefs and assumptions. Once his assumptions were identified, it was possible to help Frank look at them critically. His therapist also helped him develop more adaptive alternative beliefs and test them through behavioral experiments (Chapter 3). For example, one of the basic assumptions that had previously been uncovered in examining Frank's difficulty with homework was the idea that he must always set very high standards for himself and work as hard as possible. Otherwise, he believed, "If I quit pushing I might end up there [as a vagrant on a street corner]." When asked whether he had any evidence that supported this view, Frank pointed to his poor performance when depressed. However, the therapist was able to remind Frank that he did not lower his standards for himself or quit trying to force himself to work hard when he was depressed. Rather, the problem was that this approach to motivating himself was ineffective when he was depressed. In fact, the approach to self-motivation that had proven effective in overcoming his inactivity and procrastination included setting moderate, clearly manageable goals rather than high standards for himself. Furthermore, focusing on what he hoped to accomplish through the activity worked much better than pushing himself or dwelling on the disasters that would occur if he did not act. After reviewing his experiences in several other situations, Frank concluded that the available evidence was incompatible with his initial assumption.

This review of the evidence did not completely eliminate Frank's belief that a more positive, less pressured approach to work would lead to disaster. However, it did prepare Frank to test the assumption through a "behavioral experiment" in which he tried his new approach to self-motivation with job-hunting tasks and compared the results with the results he had achieved previously by setting high standards and pressuring himself. He was surprised to discover that his new approach not only was much more pleasant but also resulted in his completing more applications and being able to present himself more confidently in interviews. After this experience, he no longer accepted his former assumption that it was necessary to set high standards for himself and constantly push himself to achieve.

Work on relapse prevention generally begins by clearly identifying situations that would be likely to present a risk of relapse and pinpointing early warning signs of relapse. The following step is to then develop plans for coping with those situations should they arise. In Frank's case, it was already clear that work-related "failures" were the primary situation in which there would be a risk of another depression. From a review of Frank's responses to earlier work-related setbacks, he and his therapist learned that a reliable early sign that he was heading toward depression was when he began to feel increasingly pressured and began to focus solely on work. Knowing this, he and his therapist formulated a plan for handling setbacks that included a number of steps: (1) to intentionally resist his tendency to withdraw and become inactive, (2) to use adaptive self-statements, such as "Failing at one task doesn't make me a failure in general," and, "The thing to do is to plan ahead rather than dwelling on this setback", (3) to take active steps to deal with the situation, (4) to re-read the portions of Feeling Good (Burns, 1999a) that he had found particularly useful, and (5) to return to therapy for a "booster session" when necessary.

Particular attention was paid to Frank's expectations regarding future problems. He initially expected never to feel depressed again and was at risk for reacting to a future period of sadness or depression with thoughts such as, "Oh my God, I'm depressed again! Cognitive Therapy didn't work, it really is hopeless." Unrealistically optimistic expectations regarding the long-term effects of therapy might be encouraging initially, but could predispose him to relapse when he encountered future problems. His adoption of a more realistic view (that Cognitive Therapy had equipped him with the skills he needed to cope effectively with depression and to prevent depressed moods from becoming major problems) decreased the risk of his overreacting to future setbacks and should decrease the risk of relapse.

The final stage of therapy is termination. This is usually a collaborative process during which therapy sessions are gradually scheduled less frequently. This provides the therapist and client with an opportunity to see whether the gains achieved in therapy persist without frequent intervention by the therapist. In Frank's case, termination was more abrupt than usual because soon after he and his therapist began discussing termination he began a new job some distance away and was unable to get to his therapist's office during the hours his therapist had available. It was, therefore, necessary to handle the final steps of work on relapse prevention and termination by telephone. At the close of therapy Frank had achieved a number of important goals beyond being completely free of depression for 3 weeks. He had been able to actively pursue job-hunting without procrastination and had resumed his normal family and social activities. He had also begun a new job about which he was enthusiastic, and was experiencing much less stress and pressure than he had experienced when starting previous jobs. Because termination had been more abrupt than usual, there had not been an opportunity to observe how Frank coped with significant setbacks or failures; however, he did have a clear plan for handling failures adaptively, was confident that he would be able to do so, and was comfortable with the idea of returning for booster sessions if necessary.

Intervening with Suicidal Clients

The preceding discussion has focused on the treatment of depression in individuals who are not suicidal. However, when a depressed individual is also suicidal it is important to address the suicidality effectively before proceeding with the treatment of depression. It may appear that suicidal ideation is a product of depression and would therefore disappear if the depression was treated effectively. However, it is not safe to simply proceed with the treatment of depression and assume that the suicidal thoughts and wishes will disappear as the depression improves. Treatment of depression takes time and there is no guarantee that the individual will survive to complete treatment for his or her depression unless the risk of suicide is addressed promptly.

Cognitive Therapy with a suicidal client differs in important ways from therapy with a nonsuicidal depressed client. Even the most experienced therapist reacts with a surge of emotion when it becomes clear that a client is seriously considering taking his or her own life. The suicidal client presents the therapist with a life and death crisis that demands an immediate response and in which the possible consequences of ineffective interventions are obvious and final. At the same time, Cognitive Therapy's collaborative approach can be difficult to implement when the client is seriously considering suicide and the therapist has the conflicting goal of keeping the client alive. It can also be difficult to use guided discovery when the client's motivation for therapy is questionable and the therapist feels realistic pressure to intervene quickly.

Myths and Misconceptions Regarding Suicide

Given the pressure the therapist is under and the potential seriousness of the situation, it is essential for the therapist to have a clear understanding of suicidal thinking and behavior to guide effective intervention. A body of clinical lore about suicide has been developed over the years (Freeman & White, 1989). Unfortunately, some of these beliefs are valid and useful whereas others are myths that may put clients at risk. Some of these myths can contribute to the therapist's underestimating the risk of suicide, having difficulty in developing a conceptualization of the problem, or having difficulty in developing and implementing effective treatment strategies. Some beliefs about suicide that are common among clinicians include the following:

1. *Suicide is a "cry for help."* It certainly is true that some clients threaten suicide or make suicide attempts in an attempt to demonstrate the magnitude of their distress and obtain the help they feel they need. However, if this were generally true for suicidal individuals, few of them would make lethal suicide attempts, because one can not receive help after death. It is more useful to view a suicide attempt as a statement that the individual sees few or no other options left to effect a change in his or her life. The strong relationship between hopelessness and suicide that has been found in a number of studies (Beck, Kovacs, & Weissman, 1975) suggests that suicidality is often an indication that the client has concluded that he or she is beyond help rather than being a "cry for help."

2. *Suicide is hostility turned inward.* The traditional psychodynamic conceptualization of suicide is that the suicidal individual is so enraged and furious

at some significant other that he or she wishes to kill them. However, rather than turning the rage and murderous intent on the object of the anger, the suicidal individual is forced, by virtue of socialization, to kill himself or herself. Little evidence has been found to support this view. Although anger plays a role in some suicide attempts, the available evidence suggests that hopelessness usually plays a much more important role.

3. *Suicidal risk can be determined from history and demographic characteristics.* Most clinicians are aware that suicide rates vary with sex, age, social support, and other factors; and attempts have been made to use factors such as these to develop criteria for estimating suicidal risk (e.g., Patterson, Dohn, Bird, & Patterson, 1983). Although criteria based on these factors can improve judgments about suicidal risk made by relatively unsophisticated assessors (Patterson *et al.*, 1983), this approach is of limited value when used on a case-by-case basis. These factors are relatively stable over time although suicidal risk can fluctuate widely. Therefore, overreliance on these factors will lead to overestimation of suicidal risk with some clients and underestimation with others. In clinical practice, therapists need to be able to determine whether an individual is at significant risk for suicide *today*, not whether he or she is in a generally high-risk group.

4. *Clients are more likely to make suicide attempts as they get less depressed.* It is true that the client who is so severely depressed that he or she cannot get out of bed is not likely to have the energy to plan and carry out a suicide attempt. As this client becomes less depressed, he or she will have more energy and may make a suicide attempt if his or her hopelessness persists when the depression lifts. The more typical depressed individual, however, does not become more suicidal as his or her depression lifts; instead he or she becomes increasingly hopeful and commensurately less suicidal as problems are overcome.

5. *The risk of suicide is higher at holiday times.* The popular media have, over the years, focused on Christmas and New Year's as times of increased depression and suicide. There is, in fact, no evidence that there are higher rates of suicide, psychiatric hospitalization, or depression during the holiday season. In fact, the suicide rate and rate of suicide attempts are higher in the Spring (Lester, 1983).

6. *If you talk openly about the topic of suicide with clients, you might "put the idea in their heads."* Novice therapists often fear that talking explicitly about suicide may give the client an idea that he or she had not considered previously. As a result, they hesitate to ask about suicidal ideation and intent to avoid responsibility for any negative consequences. This fear might make sense if clients were generally unaware of suicide. However, the possibility of suicide is not a closely held secret. Any client who is even remotely at risk for attempting suicide will have considered this option long before the therapist raises the topic. Abundant clinical experience shows that explicit discussions of suicide in therapy make it possible to address the issues directly and therefore are much more likely to reduce the risk of suicide than to increase it.

7. *Talking about suicide decreases the risk.* The old "hydraulic" model of psychological functioning assumed that talking about an impulse dissipates the energy. This has led some to assume that simply talking about suicide will automatically reduce the risk of an actual suicide attempt. However, simply talking about an impulse does not necessarily make it disappear. A discussion of suicide may decrease the risk of a suicide attempt, increase the risk, or have no effect depending on the content of the discussion and the client's reaction to it. Simply discussing suicide is not an effective intervention; it is important to address the client's motivation for suicide and develop viable alternatives to suicide.

8. *If the client were serious about suicide he or she would not bring it up in therapy.* It certainly is natural to assume that a client who is serious about suicide will not bring it up in therapy as the therapist is likely to interfere. Some assume that if a client is willing to talk about suicide, this shows that the client isn't "really" serious. However, a high proportion of persons who go on to commit suicide do, in fact, directly or indirectly communicate their intent to significant others (Robins, Gassner, Kayes, Wilkinson, & Murphy, 1959). Although evasiveness in talking about suicide is a bad sign, willingness to talk openly about suicide does not necessarily mean that the risk of suicide is low.

9. *If someone is serious about suicide you cannot stop him or her.* It is true that even hospitalization cannot prevent a person who is determined to commit suicide from finding an opportunity to do so. However, this does not mean that the therapist is helpless when confronted by a seriously suicidal client. For one thing, episodes of serious suicidal intent tend to be time-limited; thus, simply delaying a suicide attempt may allow time for the immediate crisis to pass. The key to intervening effectively with a seriously suicidal client is to challenge the client's conclusion that suicide is the most promising option he or she has rather than trying to make suicide impossible. If the client who seriously intends to take his or her own life realizes that he or she has better options than suicide, the situation becomes much easier to deal with.

10. *Suicidal "gestures" need not be taken seriously.* Often, suicide attempts are labeled as "gestures" when it appears to the clinician that the client's intent was not to die but rather to elicit some sort of reaction from significant others. The individual who makes a suicide attempt and then immediately calls a hospital, who carefully times his or her attempt so as to be discovered in time, or who "attempts suicide" using a nonlethal method may well intend to achieve some desired effect rather than intending to die. However, even if the client's intent has been carefully assessed, there are two good reasons not to simply dismiss the act as a "gesture." First, a client can miscalculate and die even if this was not his or her intent. Second, if the "gesture" does not achieve the desired response from others and the therapist does not intervene effectively, the client may progress to more extreme actions. The fact that a client's last suicide attempt was nonlethal does not guarantee that the next one will be as well.

11. *Suicidal clients must immediately be started on medication.* Many nonmedi-
    cal therapists react to suicidality by immediately referring the client to a
    psychiatrist for antidepressant medication. However, most antidepressants
    require as long as 3 or 4 weeks before they have a substantial antidepres-
    sant effect. If a client is imminently suicidal, the medication may well be
    too late, even though it might be useful as a part of long-term treatment
    plan. Also, some antidepressants can be quite lethal in overdose and may
    provide a convenient means for suicide. Antidepressant medication can be
    useful, but it is neither necessary nor sufficient in the treatment of suicidal
    risk.
12. *Suicidal clients must be hospitalized.* Related to the medication myth is the no-
    tion that the suicidal client must be immediately hospitalized. It is obvious
    that hospitalization will be required if the therapist is not able to intervene
    effectively enough to eliminate the immediate danger to the client. How-
    ever, if hospitalization is the therapist's primary response to suicidal risk
    and other interventions are not tried first, clients will often be hospitalized
    when less drastic interventions could have been effective. Also, more than
    one suicidal inpatient has feigned improvement to be discharged and has
    then gone home to kill himself or herself.

Assessing Suicide Risk

An immediate and complete clinical assessment of suicidal risk is important
both as a part of the initial evaluation and whenever indications of possible suicidal ideation or intent appear. The therapist needs considerable sensitivity to subtle
distinctions in meaning to detect early signs of increasing suicidality. For one client,
the statement, "I would like to die" may mean that he or she finds the idea of death
attractive as an escape from his or her problems but would not do anything to
hasten his or her demise. For another client, the same statement may indicate that
he or she intends to take active steps toward suicide or even has started implementing his or her plan. The client who updates his or her will, begins wrapping
up the unfinished details of life, or begins giving away possessions may well be in
the process of implementing a suicide plan and merits an immediate evaluation.
Likewise, expressions of increasing hopelessness or vague comments such as, "If
I'm still around next month, I'll . . ." can be important warning signs. If the clinician
can recognize early indications of increasing suicidal risk, he or she may be able to
intervene before the crisis arises. However, even the most sensitive clinician cannot
assume that he or she understands the significance of possible indications of risk
without directly asking the client about them and discussing his or her intentions.
When in doubt, assess.

In assessing suicidal risk, it is important for the clinician to obtain information
regarding the client's thoughts and intentions regarding suicide, any plan that the
client has formed, and relevant background information. Table 4.5, adapted from
the Scale of Suicidal Ideation (Beck, Kovacs, & Weissman, 1979), provides a useful
framework for assessing these content areas. The risk of suicide increases when
the client's wish to die is stronger than his or her wish to live; it increases when

TABLE 4.5. Information Useful in Assessing Suicidality[a]

Assess the following, both at the time of the assessment and at the most severe point of the crisis:

1. The strength of the client's wish to live. (*The stronger the wish to live, the lower the risk of suicide completion*)
2. The strength of the client's wish to die. (*The higher the wish to die, the higher the risk*)
3. The degree to which client believes that the reasons for living outweigh the reasons for dying. (*The more the reasons to live outweigh the reasons to die, the lower the risk*)
4. The client's desire to make a suicide attempt. (*The stronger the wish to make an attempt, the higher the risk*)
5. The client's willingness to take steps necessary to stay safe, such as taking necessary medication, taking usual safety precautions, etc. (*If the client is being less careful, this indicates an increased risk*)
6. When the client has thoughts of suicide, how long do the thoughts last? (*as the duration of thoughts of suicide increases, the risk increases*)
7. How frequently does the client think of suicide? (*as the frequency of thoughts of suicide increases, the risk increases*)
8. What is the client's attitude toward these thoughts of suicide? (*rejecting the thoughts of suicide suggests lower risk; as the response to thoughts of suicide becomes more positive, risk increases*)
9. Does the client feel he or she has control over whether he or she acts on these thoughts? (*as the sense of not having control over suicidal impulses increases, risk increases*)
10. Does the client see important reasons *not* to kill himself or herself? (*the fewer deterrents to suicide the client sees, the higher the risk*)
11. Would the reason for suicide be to have an impact on others or to escape problems? (*the risk of suicide completion is higher if the goal is to escape one's problems and misery*)
12. Has the client chosen a suicide method? (*the risk is higher the farther the client has progressed through choosing a method and working out the details*)
13. Is the method easily available? (*the more easily available the method, the higher the risk*)
14. Does the client feel capable of carrying out a suicide attempt if he or she decides to? (*clients who are confident of their ability to follow through on a suicide attempt are at higher risk*)
15. Does the client expect to make a suicide attempt? (*clients who expect to make a suicide attempt are higher risk*)
16. Has the client made preparations for a suicide attempt? (*the farther the client has progressed in preparing for suicide, the higher the risk*)
17. Has he or she written a suicide note? (*if the client has written a suicide note this suggests imminent risk*)
18. Has he or she made any final acts in preparation for death such as getting affairs in order or giving mementos to friends and family? (*likewise, acts that appear to be preparations for death suggest imminent risk*)
19. How deceptive has the client been in responding to this assessment? (*attempts at deception and concealment suggest more imminent risk than if the client is open and genuine in his or her responses*)
20. Is there a history of previous suicide attempts? (*individuals with a history of previous suicide attempts are at increased risk*)
21. If there were previous suicide attempts, how strong was the intent to die associated with the most recent attempt? (*if the client intended to die in the most recent suicide attempt, he or she is at increased risk*)

[a] Adapted from Beck, Kovacs, & Weissman, 1979.

the client's reasons for dying outweigh the reasons for living; it increases when the client strongly wants to attempt suicide and when he or she sees no significant deterrents to suicide. The risk increases substantially when the individual has chosen a means of suicide, has developed a plan, and has made the necessary preparations. A history of previous "serious" suicide attempts also increases the risk of another serious attempt. It is useful to assess these factors both at the time of the intake interview and at the client's worst point during the current episode. A client who is feeling somewhat better at the time of the assessment may become substantially more suicidal if his or her mood deteriorates again.

It is important to distinguish clearly between thoughts of suicide, suicidal intent, and lethality of method in assessing suicidal risk because the three can be quite independent of each other. For example:

> A young woman presented for therapy tearfully saying, "Help me, I'm suicidal." A careful assessment revealed that she experienced nearly constant thoughts of suicide but found these thoughts distressing and repugnant rather than appealing. She did not wish to die and in fact was terrified by the thought that she might attempt suicide even though she did not want to do so. Despite her fear that she was suicidal, this young woman actually suffered from obsessions regarding suicide and was not at all suicidal (for further discussion of Obsessive–Compulsive Disorder see Chapter 5).

The use of a nonlethal method in a suicide attempt can create the impression that the attempt was "manipulative" and not serious, but it is important to assess the client's intention rather than jumping to conclusions. For example:

> A young woman despondent over a lost love planned to die by asphyxiation. She closed the kitchen window tightly and stuffed kitchen towels around the door to make it airtight. She then turned on the oven and put her head in. Her oven, however, was electric and all she did was singe her hair.

Because her intent was to die, the situation is quite serious even though the method she chose for her suicide attempt was not lethal. Without effective intervention, she may well choose a more lethal method for her next attempt.

Similarly, an action that is intended as a suicide gesture can still be fatal if the client miscalculates. For example:

> Gina, a 17-year-old girl, who had a history of chronic conflict with her mother, took an overdose in the hope of making the extent of her distress clear to family and caregivers. She had no intention of dying, so she chose a method that she thought was harmless, an overdose of Tylenol. Unfortunately, a Tylenol overdose is not at all harmless. She spent a week in the Intensive Care Unit and nearly died from severe liver damage.

It is important to take "manipulative" suicide attempts seriously, not only because they can prove fatal despite the client's intentions, but also because there is no guarantee that "serious" attempts will not follow. Some months after her near-death, Gina took another Tylenol overdose knowing full well that it was potentially lethal.

An evaluation of the client's overall level of depression can provide information useful in assessing suicidal risk. The Beck Depression Inventory can be used to measure overall level of depression, while also providing information regarding specific symptoms of depression indicated by particular items endorsed by the client. The client's responses to items 2 (hopelessness) and 9 (suicidality) are of particular value.

As emphasized previously, it is important to assess the client's level of hopelessness. This often can be done simply by asking the client directly how much hope he or she has that his or her problems will be overcome. When a more structured assessment of suicidality is desired, Beck's Hopelessness Scale is a useful measure of hopelessness and a good predictor of suicidal risk (Beck, Steer, Kovacs, & Garrison, 1985).

Understanding Suicidality

Many clinicians assume that suicide is directly linked to depression because the majority of persons who attempt suicide or commit suicide show signs of depression. However, recent research has made it increasingly clear that hopelessness is a major factor in suicide (Beck *et al.*, 1985). In fact, when the relationship between hopelessness and suicide is taken into account statistically, no relationship between depression and suicide remains. The apparent relationship between depression and suicide is primarily due to the high incidence of hopelessness among depressed individuals.

The finding of a strong association between suicide and hopelessness makes suicide quite understandable. If a person is suffering but is hopeful that tomorrow things will improve, whether through one's own actions or merely through the passage of time, the suffering becomes more tolerable. However, if an individual believes that there is no hope of the situation improving and that he or she faces a choice between never ending misery and quick death, death may seem the obvious choice. This is true if the drawbacks of making a suicide attempt are not apparent. For example:

> Carmen, a divorced mother of one, arrived at her therapist's office in tears, without an appointment. She told the receptionist that she would wait as long as necessary but that she had to see her therapist; she couldn't go home. When her therapist met with her, Carmen revealed that she was sure that if she had gone home she would have started her car in a closed garage and have killed herself by inhaling carbon monoxide.
>
> As Carmen saw it, problems at work had gotten so bad that, "I can't go back!" However, without a job she would be unable to provide for herself and her son. She had not thought carefully about what would happen if she quit her job but was convinced that it would be so intolerable that death would be preferable. She was certain that there was no other way to resolve her dilemma and that suicide was the only viable option open to her.

By far the majority of suicidal individuals hold the belief that there is no hope of things improving and therefore no longer any reason for continuing life. They see suicide as the only way of obtaining relief from intolerable misery. Although suicide is an option for any person, few individuals exercise this option because they see more promising options for dealing with their problems. Suicide is at the bottom of most people's list of options and only becomes an issue as they exhaust other options and get closer to the bottom of their list. When people feel that they have no further options, suicide is likely unless they are inhibited by powerful deterrents such as religious beliefs, concern about the effects that suicide would have on family members, or fear of death.

Hopelessness is not the only factor that can lead to suicidal risk. Some individuals who are intensely angry but who are unskilled at handling anger think of suicide as a way of punishing the object of their anger. For example:

> Melissa, a 32-year-old mother of two, came into therapy one day talking of suicide but appearing more angry than depressed. When asked if any event had precipitated her thoughts of suicide, she described a series of slights by her husband and her in-laws. When asked what suicide would accomplish, she talked of how her family would finally realize how badly they had mistreated her and would be overcome with guilt and regret.

This type of suicidality bears a superficial resemblance to the traditional view that suicide is hostility turned inwards. However, hopelessness plays an important role here as well. The session with Melissa made it clear that she saw no other way to vent her anger with her family or to induce them to treat her better in the future. If she had seen viable alternatives, she would not have seriously considered suicide.

Suicidal command hallucinations (voices from within that command the individual to commit suicide) are another factor that can contribute to suicide attempts. The voices are usually experienced as compelling, and rather than expressing a desire to die, the client feels that he or she must obey the voices. Although Cognitive Therapy can be quite helpful in the treatment of psychotic individuals, individuals experiencing command hallucinations may need to be hospitalized until they have been stabilized on appropriate medication.

Strategies for Intervention

With all suicidal clients, it is imperative to take whatever steps are needed to prevent a suicide attempt. However, this does not necessarily mean that hospitalization is necessary. If initial interventions are effective, it may be possible to continue working with the client on an outpatient basis and to take precautions that are sufficient to forestall suicide, but that are less disruptive of therapy than hospitalization can be. Cognitive Therapy's typical approach to intervention with suicidal clients is summarized in Table 4.6.

The approach to assessing suicide risk discussed in this chapter provides a good foundation for intervention with suicidal clients. It provides an assessment of suicidality and also provides most of the information needed for effective

TABLE 4.6. Typical Interventions with Suicidal Individuals

Assess suicidality
Adopt a collaborative stance
Address hopelessness
Examine pros and cons of suicide, maximize deterrents
Consider alternatives to suicide
Propose testing the promising alternatives before considering suicide
Negotiate an agreement to "put suicide on hold" until the alternatives have been tested
Explicitly instruct client not to attempt suicide and to follow through on plan instead
Dismantle any preparations for suicide
Anticipate likely crises and develop plans for managing them (include guidelines for when and how to contact therapist or professional providing emergency coverage)
Reassess suicidality
Proceed with outpatient treatment only if the client is not a danger to self or others, consider more frequent appointments until the crisis is resolved
Document assessment and treatment plan

---

intervention. After identifying the client's motivation for suicide, it is necessary to help him or her consider whether suicide is the most promising method for attaining his or her goals. This is done by helping the client consider whether there are disadvantages to suicide that outweigh its perceived advantages, and whether there are better alternatives for attaining his or her goals. When the client becomes a willing participant in a serious discussion regarding whether suicide is in his or her interest, it is possible for the therapist to challenge the distortions and misconceptions that have led the client to conclude that suicide is his or her best (or only) option. This straightforward approach results in the therapist and client discovering that suicide is not the most promising approach to the client's problems, and it is usually possible to persuade the client to make a firm commitment to refrain from suicide at least long enough to explore the other alternatives.

Outpatient treatment is viable if it is possible to reach a point where the client makes a believable commitment to refrain from suicide attempts while the therapist and client try other approaches to overcoming the client's problems. Then the therapist and client can take steps to minimize the risks of a suicide attempt should a crisis arise and begin working on the client's problems using the usual Cognitive Therapy approach. If the client will not make a believable commitment to refrain from suicide, is not willing to take steps to dismantle his or her suicide plan, or if the client makes it clear that he or she is still planning to attempt suicide, the therapist must take decisive action. The options at that point include voluntary or involuntary hospitalization and contacting the client's significant others to involve them in intervention. It is the therapist's responsibility to do all that is within his or her power to minimize the risk of suicide.

When hospitalization proves necessary, the therapist may face several problems as a result. First, hospitalization can be difficult to arrange if the client is not willing to agree to a voluntary admission. In most states, if it cannot be clearly demonstrated that the client is an imminent danger to him or herself or to others, the client cannot be hospitalized involuntarily. Nonmedical therapists who are not able to admit clients themselves are sometimes frustrated by having clients whom they consider in need of involuntary hospitalization being refused admission because the admitting physician does not agree with their assessment. Also, clients who wish to leave the hospital can often manage to be discharged within a few days simply by acting as if they are no longer suicidal. Furthermore, being hospitalized has a number of effects on the suicidal client, some positive, and some negative. Among the potentially positive effects of hospitalization are:

(1) it will place the seriously suicidal client in a generally safe environment where he or she can be closely observed (although clients can, and do, make suicide attempts in hospitals);
(2) placing a client in the hospital allows the outpatient therapist to share responsibility for the client's survival with other professionals;
(3) the hospitalized client can be stabilized on medication more easily; and
(4) the client in the hospital may be taken out of an overwhelmingly stressful home, job, or general life situation.

Some of the potentially negative effects of hospitalization are:

(1) the client in the hospital is often removed from family and other available support systems;

(2) the client may be stigmatized by a psychiatric hospitalization;

(3) the client may be upset with the therapist over involuntary hospitalization (although, of course, it is better to have an upset client than a dead one); and

(4) the therapist may have difficulty continuing his or her work with the client unless the admitting physician is cooperative.

The therapist needs to carefully consider the setting in which the client will be placed, the long-term effect of the hospitalization, and his or her responsibility to the client and the client's family. Adverse reactions can be minimized by obtaining the client's consent when possible and by pointing out the ways that the therapist's actions are in the client's best interest. However, these strong actions risk offending some clients to the point that they will terminate therapy. This should not deter the therapist from taking necessary action. After all, a live client will have the opportunity to see another therapist.

Considering whether to involve a suicidal client's significant others in intervention raises difficult questions that must be decided on a case by case basis. Although the legal aspects of this situation may vary somewhat from state to state, confidentiality allows sharing this information if the client presents a danger to himself or others and the therapist is not able to intervene in a way that eliminates the danger. In fact, the therapist is likely to discover that he or she is legally obligated to notify significant others rather than simply notifying authorities if a substantial danger to self or others persists.

No matter how effective the initial interventions with a potentially suicidal client may appear, the therapist cannot assume that the client will remain hopeful. It is essential for the therapist to reassess the client's suicidal risk following the interventions and to develop a plan of action to which the client is willing to make a commitment. It is also important for the therapist to take steps to minimize the possibility of an impulsive suicide attempt and, to arrange timely follow-up assessments, until it is clear that the crisis has passed.

Cognitive and Behavioral Techniques

It is important for the therapist not to overlook the therapist–client relationship in his or her hurry to respond quickly to a client's increased suicidality. Assessment and intervention will proceed more smoothly if the therapist is perceived as an individual who can be trusted, who is supportive, resourceful, and available, and who is allied with the client. The therapist's openness and lack of self-consciousness in asking directly about the client's thoughts of suicide and in utilizing the data from relevant measures, from the client's history, and from clinical observation can serve to build confidence in the therapist and put the client at ease. One client reported, after the initial crisis intervention interview, "I really felt uncomfortable when you asked all those questions. But you touched on all the thoughts I was having but that I was afraid to say, thinking that you would think that I was crazy for having those thoughts. When you asked me those questions so directly, I knew that you must of asked them before and that maybe I wasn't so crazy, just really upset."

Initially, the suicidal client and his or her therapist are likely to have conflicting goals because the client is at least considering suicide and the therapist's primary goal is to keep the client alive. This makes collaboration difficult unless therapist and client can identify a goal toward which both are willing to work. The goal of trying to determine whether suicide is a good idea or not is one good place to start. For example:

> "It sounds like you're pretty certain that suicide's the best option you have in this situation. This is something that is important to take seriously. With most decisions, people have the option of changing their minds if it turns out that they've made a poor choice. However, with suicide you don't get to try something else if it turns out that you weren't thinking clearly. Would you be willing to take a look at whether suicide is really the best option you have?"

With this rationale it is usually possible to take a collaborative approach with even seriously suicidal clients.

The therapist is then in a position to clarify the client's motivation for suicide and his or her expectations regarding the likely consequences of suicide. The full range of interventions that are used in challenging automatic thoughts can be used in looking critically at the client's views regarding suicide. Whatever the motivation for suicide, it can be quite valuable to help the client look carefully at the evidence supporting his or her conclusion that suicide is necessary and will accomplish the desired ends, as well as looking at the alternatives to suicide.

Intervening with the Hopeless Suicidal Client. When hopelessness is a significant part of the client's motivation for suicide, it is important to help the client verbalize his or her hopelessness and then examine his or her conviction that the situation is hopeless. What specific evidence convinces the client that the situation is hopeless? Will the hopeless situation last forever? Is it unchangeable? Might there be options for dealing with his or her problems that the client has overlooked? When clients are helped to examine their situation, they are often able to see the distortions in their logic and discover that the situation is not nearly as hopeless as it appeared. For example:

> When Carmen, the divorced mother of one mentioned above, first described her dilemma to her therapist, she was convinced that the situation was truly hopeless because she could not return to her job but could not support herself and her son without doing so. However, when she and her therapist examined the situation in detail, it became clear that Carmen and her son would not perish immediately if she quit her job. Actually she had a number of alternatives: she could live off her savings for a few months and look for a new job, her parents would help her out financially if she really needed it, and if all else failed, she could go on welfare.

Once it was clear that the situation was difficult rather than hopeless, her suicidal intent subsided and her mood improved considerably. Other assumptions such as, "They'll be better off without me," "Nobody will miss me," or "I'd be better off dead" can often be handled in a similar way.

In addition to questioning what would be accomplished by suicide, it is important for the therapist to help the client identify significant reasons not to commit suicide. It is obvious that one of the major drawbacks to suicide is that the individual forfeits the rest of his or her life. However, this is seen as a good reason to refrain from suicide only if the individual has a significant amount of hope that life can be worth living. With hopeless individuals in particular, it is important to identify reasons to refrain from suicide that do not rely on hope for the future. These deterrents to suicide may include the likely effects of the client's suicide on family and friends, religious prohibitions regarding suicide, fear of surviving an attempt but being seriously injured, concern about what others will think, and so on. It is usually necessary for the therapist to take an active role in generating possible deterrents; but this can be done most effectively if the therapist engages the client in the process rather than simply listing reasons for the client not to commit suicide.

Explicitly listing the advantages and disadvantages of suicide and separately listing the advantages and disadvantages of continuing to live can be an effective way of integrating the results of the above interventions. This will have the additional benefit of providing the client with a concise summary of the conclusions reached during the session. This becomes a document to which the client can refer if suicide should again start to seem like a promising option. For example, the thought, "I would be better off dead," can have an enormous impact as long as it is accepted without critical examination. Furthermore, clients may have difficulty challenging such thoughts on their own, especially if they have not been in treatment long. A concise summary of the major conclusions reached in therapy can be quite useful to clients when suicidal thinking re-emerges between sessions.

In intervening with hopeless clients, it is not necessary for the therapist to convince the client that all problems will be overcome, that the alternatives to suicide will definitely be successful, or even that suicide is always unacceptable as an option. All that is necessary is:

(1) to raise sufficient doubt regarding the merits of suicide;
(2) to identify sufficiently promising alternatives to suicide; so that,
(3) the client is willing to make a commitment to refrain from suicide attempts; while
(4) the therapist and client explore other options.

It is important for the therapist to accept the client's skepticism and not to encourage unrealistic expectations that are likely to lead to sudden disappointment. Reluctant clients are often more willing to agree to refrain from suicide for a reasonable period of time if the therapist points out that by agreeing to this approach the client is not giving up suicide as an option. For better or worse, the client will always have the option of choosing to commit suicide later should it ever turn out that suicide is the best option available to him or her.

Cognitive Therapy generally emphasizes guided discovery rather than confrontation or disputation. However, when the therapist is faced with a hopeless client who is not willing to participate actively in the process described above, it is important to actively dispute the client's distortions and misconceptions. It is also essential for the therapist to present possible alternatives to suicide even if the client participates very little in this process. Of course, there are important advantages to involving the client in this as much as possible; however, if guided discovery is not feasible, direct disputation may prove effective. If it is, the therapist should be able to shift to greater collaboration as the client becomes more willing to look at alternatives to suicide.

Once it is clear that suicide is not a good option and that there are important reasons not to commit suicide, the client may still see no viable alternatives to suicide. It is the therapist's next task to help the client to do so. However, if the therapist only takes the approach of trying to elicit options from the client, a rather limited list is likely to be generated. If the therapist takes a brainstorming approach and raises a wide variety of possibilities, encouraging the client to consider options that at first glance seem absurd or unworkable, it is possible to generate a much larger pool of alternatives to choose from. Options that strike the client as unworkable may well prove to have more potential than was immediately apparent or may suggest other, more feasible options.

Having explored the perceived advantages and disadvantages of suicide as well as having identified alternatives to suicide, the stage is set for the therapist and client to agree on a course of action and pursue it. An important part of this agreement is the client's making a credible commitment to refrain from suicide for a reasonable period of time during which therapist and client will work to overcome his or her problems. The agreement should also include the client's commitment to call and talk with the therapist (not just leave a message) before actually doing anything to harm him or herself. Some therapists make a practice of having the client sign a written contract containing these and other provisions; doing so would have an advantage with clients who take written agreements more seriously than verbal agreements. However, the key element is the agreement, and the clinician's judgment as to whether the client's commitment is genuine, rather than the contract itself. This point is emphasized by one client's response to the therapist's suggestion that he sign a written contract, "So what are you going to do if I kill myself, sue me?" The contract, whether spoken or written, is not intended to be enforceable, but is one step in a collaborative approach to dealing with suicidality.

The therapist and client should try to anticipate any situations that would be likely to produce a sudden increase in suicidal risk and plan how the client can best cope with these should they arise. An important early intervention is to help the client dispose of any available means for suicide that the client may have considered. This might include asking an individual who collects guns and who had planned to shoot himself to turn the guns over to the police or to place the guns in the custody of a reliable significant other. The purpose of such precautions is not to make suicide impossible but to decrease the risk of an impulsive suicide attempt by making the means of suicide less accessible. It is best to design precautions that can be confirmed because otherwise the therapist may face some difficult decisions. For example:

> One client reported that he had three handguns loaded and available to use in a planned
> suicide attempt. After a rather lengthy discussion, he agreed to turn the guns over to his
> brother, who would keep them indefinitely. The client was asked to call the therapist that
> evening to confirm that the guns had indeed been turned over to his brother. Instead,
> what the client reported was that he had changed his mind; rather than turning the guns
> over to his brother, he had gone down to the river, tossed the guns, in a paper bag, over
> the side and watched them sink beneath the waves.

The therapist had no way of confirming whether the guns had actually been disposed of and therefore had to decide whether the client's assertions were true on the basis of little or no data.

If the preceding interventions have been effective, and hospitalization is not needed, the recently suicidal client is likely to need closer follow-up than most clients. It is not unusual for cognitive therapists to meet with such a client two or three times per week during times of crisis or to arrange scheduled telephone contacts between sessions. It is important for the therapist or a colleague to be accessible to handle crises as they arise, even if that means the client calls late at night or on weekends. If sufficient therapist–client contact is scheduled throughout the week, emergency phone calls should be held to a minimum.

With the above foundation, Cognitive Therapy can then proceed much as it would if the client had not been suicidal. It is usually best for therapist and client to work first on issues that are related to the motivation for suicide, which are important to the client, and on which there is a good chance of making progress quickly. In addition, it is important for the therapist to be alert to any indications of increasing suicidal risk and to repeat the above interventions if a setback or crisis should produce a renewed risk.

When suicidal impulses are a product of intense anger and a desire to punish oneself or others, the optimal solution is to help the client develop more adaptive ways of handling intense anger. However, because it is likely to take considerably more than a single session to accomplish this, it is important to deal effectively with the immediate crisis first.

Once it is clear that suicide would be an attempt to punish oneself or others, therapist and client are in a good position to consider whether suicide is likely to be the best option for doing so. This would include an examination of the client's expectations about the consequences of a suicide attempt, the degree to which he or she is certain that suicide will have the desired impact, the deterrents to suicide, and alternative ways to accomplish the desired results. It is also important to question whether the desired results are important enough to be worth the client's risking his or her life. The client may not have considered that suicide attempts that are not intended to be fatal can still be lethal.

If it is possible to identify acceptable alternatives to suicide, these can be substituted for suicidal behavior as a way of "buying time" so that the client can be helped to develop more adaptive ways of handling anger. Even alternatives that the therapist would not normally suggest are worth considering. These include strategies such as throwing a tempter tantrum, writing a nasty letter to the object of his or her anger, or marking his or her wrists with a pen rather than slitting them. Although these are not very appropriate ways of handling anger, they are much better than suicide. Once the client has agreed to refrain from suicide for a certain period of time, it is important to proceed with a mutually acceptable treatment plan, dismantling any preparations for suicide, and periodically monitoring suicidal risk, as discussed above.

Many clients who consider suicide out of anger rather than hopelessness manifest characteristics of Borderline Personality Disorder. The treatment ideas discussed in Chapter 8 may prove useful in working with these clients even if they do not completely meet the criteria for Borderline Personality Disorder. In particular, these clients are likely to have problems with impulse control; and the methods for increasing impulse control discussed in Chapter 8 are likely to be helpful.

As with the angry suicidal client, in working with the histrionic suicidal client it is important to identify the functions that would be served by a suicide attempt and to consider whether suicide is really the best means for accomplishing those ends. Whether the goal of a suicide attempt is to reduce anxiety, to achieve a desired response from significant others, or simply to obtain stimulation and excitement, the process of exploring the pros and cons of a suicide attempt, the deterrents to suicide, and alternatives to suicide that have been discussed above can be quite useful.

In working with histrionic suicidal clients, it is important for the therapist to be aware of his or her reactions to them. When the client's talk of suicide seems manipulative, it is easy to conclude that he or she is not "really" suicidal. This is particularly true if there is a history of apparently manipulative suicide attempts. However, if these clients feel that their threats of suicide are not being taken seriously, they may take more extreme steps in the hopes of being taken seriously. On the other hand, histrionic clients can sometimes be quite skilled at inducing others to come to their aid; and the therapist can easily slip into trying to "rescue" them rather than working to get them to take an active part in therapy. To be effective, the therapist needs to avoid both extremes. Additional suggestions for working with histrionic clients can be found in Chapter 9.

Intervention with clients who are suicidal due to command hallucinations is quite different from intervening with other suicidal clients in that the primary intervention is pharmacological, that is, antipsychotic medication. Often, medication alone is effective in reducing or eliminating command hallucinations, and cognitive interventions are primarily directed toward increasing the client's compliance with the medication regimen. In addition, it is possible to work cognitively to increase the client's ability to cope with the voices once the medication has reduced the florid psychotic symptoms.

Therapists working with clients who have command hallucinations need to know the precise nature of the commands. Thus, these clients must be questioned directly about the content and nature of the commands as well as their ability to resist them. Once the nature of the commands is understood, it is important to help the client examine whether obeying the commands is a good idea. Individuals suffering from command hallucinations usually have never stopped to consider what would be accomplished by obeying the voices and what would happen if they refused. By raising this question the therapist can start to lay a foundation for the client's choosing not to obey the voices rather than feeling compelled to obey.

Sometimes, an approach as simple as, "What evidence do you have that it is a good idea to obey the voices? Have they given you good advice in the past?" can be quite effective in clearly establishing that resisting the commands is a good policy.

Next, the therapist and client need to develop a plan for coping with the command hallucinations. If the client has already discovered some partially effective strategies such as staying active or keeping his or her mind occupied, these can be incorporated into the plan. Clients often find it useful to minimize the amount of unstructured time in their day, to explicitly remind themselves that they do not have to do what the voices say, and to remind themselves that the voices give poor advice. It also can be useful to help these clients "talk back" to the commands. They can learn to refuse directly (for example, "I don't have to. I won't, I won't, I won't.") They may also be able to learn more sophisticated responses (such as, "I'm not going to. Suicide is sinful and it would hurt my family. And besides, if I can hold on till my new job starts, money won't be so tight and I'll be able to get my own apartment again.") It can be particularly useful to have the client write a summary of the most convincing arguments for resisting the voices and of the most promising coping strategies to aid him or her in remembering the plan for coping with the voices. It is also important to take steps to reduce the risk of an impulsive suicide attempt as discussed above.

If the client is chronically psychotic, then Cognitive Therapy is likely to be of greatest value in increasing the client's compliance with his or her medication regimen and in helping the client deal more effectively with problem situations that arise. If the psychotic symptoms are acute and subside once the immediate crisis is over, then the usual cognitive approach to the client's remaining problems should prove effective.

A seriously suicidal client presents even the most seasoned therapist with a crisis situation to which he or she must respond quickly and effectively while under considerable pressure. If it is possible to understand the client's motivation for suicide and to help the client consider promising alternatives to suicide, the immediate crisis is usually averted and the therapist and client have an opportunity to work on the on-going issues. It is important to remember, however, that obtaining knowledge, mastering effective techniques, and gaining clinical experience do not render a therapist omnipotent or infallible.

Therapists often have considerable difficulty coping with the suicide of one of their clients, in part due to the intensity of their own reactions and in part because of the reactions of colleagues. Certainly, some degree of self-examination as well as a wide range of emotional reactions on the therapist's part is both inevitable and healthy following any negative outcome in therapy. However, therapists are not immune to dysfunctional beliefs and cognitive distortions. Many go from thinking, "There must have been something I could have done! What did I miss?" to thinking, "How can I call myself a therapist? I can't help anybody." Distorted thinking prevents them from giving the same attention to their successes as to their failures and prevents them from acknowledging factors outside their control that complicated intervention. At times like these, a therapist can benefit from a dose of his or her own medicine, whether self-administered or provided by a consultant, supervisor, colleague, or his or her own therapist.

The uninitiated might assume that therapists would automatically be sensitive, supportive, and caring when a colleague has a crisis. In actuality, responses can vary from sympathy and support to completely ignoring the event, criticizing the therapist, acting as though the therapist should not find a client's suicide upsetting, or even ostracizing the therapist. A suicide leaves many victims, and all those who have been involved with the client who has died are likely to be in need of support and an opportunity to share their thoughts and feelings. It would serve us well to be as humane in responding to colleagues as we are in responding to clients.

CONCLUSIONS

Because Beck originally developed Cognitive Therapy specifically for the treatment of depression, it is not surprising that the majority of outcome studies of Cognitive Therapy have involved the treatment of depression. In controlled outcome studies, Cognitive Therapy has been found to be an effective treatment for depression. It has been found to be at least as effective as treatment with antidepressant medication and often to be superior. Furthermore, it seems to have a lower dropout rate and a lower relapse rate than treatment with antidepressant medication (see Butler & Beck, 2000; DeRubeis & Crits-Christoph, 1998; Simon & Fleming, 1985). In almost all comparisons between Cognitive Therapy and an alternative treatment, Cognitive Therapy has been found to be at least as effective as the alternatives and often more so.

Cognitive Therapy of depression is not only a well-developed, well-validated approach to effectively treating an important problem, it is also the "standard" Cognitive Therapy approach. As such, it serves as a foundation for the cognitive approach to other, more complex disorders. Thus, a solid understanding of Cognitive Therapy of depression is strongly recommended.

5

Anxiety Disorders

Although anxiety is one of the most common of emotional responses, it is not necessarily problematic. When experienced in moderate intensity, anxiety can serve to motivate, energize, and mobilize the individual to heights of performance and spectacular deeds. Many people claim to "work best under pressure", i.e., when their anxiety level is high enough to motivate them to exert additional effort. It is only when the anxiety level is so high that it debilitates the individual or causes emotional or physical discomfort that anxiety becomes a problem. Despite this, anxiety disorders are among the most prevalent psychiatric conditions in the United States (Stein & Hollander, 2002). Research on anxiety disorders has mushroomed so quickly that a review of the literature can easily be overwhelming to the clinician. An excellent summary of recent research can be found in Barlow (2002).

ASSESSMENT

At first glance, it seems that differential diagnosis of anxiety disorders would be a simple, straightforward task: If people report a fear of flying, they must have Specific Phobia; if they cannot leave home, they must have Agoraphobia; if they are afraid in social situations, they must have Social Phobia. In actuality, however, the distinctions are much more complex, and a simple checklist of symptoms is insufficient to adequately diagnose anxiety disorders or to determine the most useful type of treatment. Upon careful assessment, for example, fear of flying may turn out to be part of a broader agoraphobic syndrome; staying at home may turn out to be due to depression rather than agoraphobia; and fear in social situations could be part of a personality disorder rather than a Social Phobia.

A thorough assessment, including assessment of cognitions, is an important part of effective treatment. This is true because the same outward behavior patterns and reported fears may reflect very different disorders depending on the personal meaning of the situations to the client. Any given phobic stimulus may be part of a Specific Phobia, Social Phobia, or Panic Disorder, depending upon the cognitions behind the fear. Two clients seeking treatment for driving phobia, for example, may have different disorders depending on their cognitions. One client may report only such thoughts as, "I could have an accident and die," "People drive like maniacs," and "This is too dangerous," indicating a Specific Phobia. The second client may report thoughts such as, "What if I have a panic attack and can't get home?" "I'll be stuck on the highway all alone," and "No one will be there to help me," which indicates the possibility that the client may be agoraphobic and possibly have other areas of avoidance as well.

Cognitive assessment with anxiety clients can be challenging because they frequently focus their attention on the object or situation that they fear and pay little attention to their thoughts about the object or situation. Thus they typically are unaware of the thoughts related to their anxiety and avoidance. When initially asked what they are afraid of, the most common response is "I don't know, I just feel afraid," or, "I don't have any particular thoughts, I just feel bad." Given the frequent lack of awareness of cognitions, it may be necessary to be creative in eliciting automatic thoughts from anxious clients. For example:

> Lawanna was a young woman who sought treatment complaining of a fear of bridges. Initially, she insisted that she had no thoughts whatsoever about bridges, that she knew there was nothing to be afraid of, and that she just got an intense physical feeling of fear any time she approached a bridge. Her therapist began by simply asking what thoughts ran through her mind as she approached a bridge and Lawanna reiterated her assertion that no thoughts ran through her mind. When that was ineffective, the therapist decided to try using imagery to recreate the phobic stimulus and observe cognitions this elicited. She asked Lawanna to close her eyes and picture herself driving toward one particular bridge while the therapist described the scene in detail. As Lawanna vividly imagined herself approaching the bridge, she reported all of the physical sensations of fear that she experienced when approaching bridges in real life. In the midst of her descriptions of the sensations she spontaneously said, "What if I fall off the edge?" When her therapist asked, she confirmed that this was a thought that had spontaneously run through her head. She was then able to report several other thoughts including "It's so narrow," and "The railing's so low." When Lawanna subsequently monitored her thoughts as she faced phobic situations, she confirmed that these were indeed thoughts that played an important role in her fear and phobic avoidance.

If imagery is not vivid enough to elicit automatic thoughts, it may be useful to use *in vivo* exposure (actually going into the feared situation with the client) for the purpose of collecting automatic thoughts. With the therapist along to help focus the client's attention on thoughts and with the level of anxiety rising as the object or situation becomes closer, most clients are able to report some of their cognitions. In some cases, role-playing can be useful in eliciting automatic thoughts, especially those occurring in interpersonal situations. Because many clients have been told by family and friends that their fears are silly, they may be inhibited from disclosing their automatic thoughts. They know the thoughts are irrational and are often concerned about being rejected by the therapist. The therapist can reassure the client that although thoughts may sound silly on the surface, those fears can be very intense and just as strong as if a gun were put to his or her head.

Cognitive assessment is generally discussed in terms of assessing verbal thought. In one study of anxiety, however, 90% of clients reported visual images of being in danger prior to and concomitant with their anxiety (Beck, Laude, & Bohnert, 1974). Many clients who have difficulty pinpointing specific verbal automatic thoughts will be able to graphically describe images of disaster when asked whether they get any pictures, images, or scenes that flash through their mind when they are anxious. Therefore, assessment of imagery should always be a part of cognitive assessment of anxiety. Just as imagining a scene in systematic desensitization evokes emotional reactions similar to those that would be experienced if exposed to the actual stimulus, so too does imagining a catastrophe evoke emotional responses similar to those that would occur in reaction to an actual catastrophe. Therefore, in treating anxiety disorders, it is just as important to identify and modify mental imagery as it is to identify and modify verbal automatic thoughts.

Given the wide variety of physical symptoms experienced by clients with anxiety disorders, it is crucial to have the client receive a complete physical examination to rule out physiological disorders that may require medical treatment. Certain endocrine disorders can cause symptoms similar to anxiety disorders, as can some medications, withdrawal from substances such as sedatives or alcohol, and intoxication from caffeine or amphetamines. The practice of requiring a physical examination as part of treating anxiety disorders has many important advantages. For example, many anxious clients have catastrophic thoughts about their symptoms, thinking they are dying or having a stroke or heart attack. It is crucial for both the client and the therapist to know whether there is a rational basis for the fears or not. Thus, having a thorough physical examination can be the first step in challenging the catastrophic thoughts.

It is also important to pay careful attention to symptoms of depression when dealing with clients with anxiety disorders. Depressive symptoms are quite common in anxiety clients, especially those with Panic Disorder or Obsessive–Compulsive Disorder (OCD). Frequently the symptoms are severe enough to fit the *DSM-IV-TR* (2000) criteria for Major Depression. In fact, when attempting to conduct a study that required subjects with agoraphobia without symptoms of depression, one of the authors found it almost impossible to find such subjects even among a sample of hundreds of agoraphobics.

The crucial distinction to make when a person shows symptoms of both an anxiety disorder and depression is whether the depression is primary or secondary. If the client has no history of depression prior to the onset of the anxiety disorder, if the anxiety disorder clearly preceded the depression, or if the client reports that the depression is due to the limitations imposed by their anxiety and avoidance, then the person might well meet criteria both for an anxiety disorder and depression. However, the depression would be considered secondary to the anxiety disorder. In such cases, treatment primarily focusing on anxiety would be appropriate, although it may be necessary to address some aspects of the depression early in the treatment. When the depression is secondary to the anxiety disorder, it is likely to remit as progress is made in overcoming the anxiety disorder.

However, if the depression predated the agoraphobia or is clearly independent of it, the depression would not be considered secondary to the anxiety disorder and successful treatment of the anxiety would not necessarily alleviate the depression. When this is the case, the client is likely to need treatmer*: for both their anxiety and their depression. If the client is so severely depressed that he or she cannot deal with the stresses involved in working to overcome an anxiety disorder, then treatment for depression may need to precede treatment for the anxiety disorder. When an individual presents with an anxiety disorder and clinically significant depression that is not secondary to the anxiety disorder, there is an increased risk that a personality disorder may be present as well (see Section 3 of this volume for a discussion of Cognitive Therapy with personality disorders).

Many clients use alcohol or other substances to reduce their anxiety, often to the point of abuse or dependence. Because these clients often under-report their use of these substances, it is crucial to get a careful and detailed history of their use of alcohol and other substances and to ask specific questions about their current use. Research has consistently provided evidence of state-dependent learning (e.g., Eich, 1977), and it appears that any type of desensitization procedure administered under the influence of alcohol may not generalize to a dry state. Thus, any alcohol or substance abuse is likely to need to be treated before the anxiety disorder is treated. Even clients who do not actually abuse alcohol may count on its availability as a coping strategy. If so, they will need to stop using alcohol in this way and learn alternative coping strategies for treatment to be effective.

DIFFERENTIAL DIAGNOSIS

Although the same basic principles apply to Cognitive Therapy with each of the anxiety disorders, there are important differences among disorders in the way in which these principles are applied. Therefore it is important to be able to distinguish the various anxiety disorders from one another.

Panic and Agoraphobia

One difference between *DSM-III-R* (1987) and *DSM-IV-TR* (2000) is that *DSM-IV-TR* is more explicit regarding the definition and criteria for panic attacks (see Table 5.1). Because panic attacks occur as one component of several different anxiety disorders, *DSM-IV-TR* discusses and describes panic attacks in a section separate

TABLE 5.1. *DSM-IV-TR* Criteria for Panic Attack

Note: A Panic Attack is not a codable disorder. Code the specific diagnosis in which the Panic Attack occurs (e.g., 300.21 Panic Disorder With Agoraphobia [p. 441]).

A discrete period of intense fear or discomfort, in which four (or more) of the following symptoms developed abruptly and reached a peak within 10 minutes:
(1) palpitations, pounding heart, or accelerated heart rate
(2) sweating
(3) trembling or shaking
(4) sensations of shortness of breath or smothering
(5) feeling of choking
(6) chest pain or discomfort
(7) nausea or abdominal distress
(8) feeling dizzy, unsteady, lightheaded, or faint
(9) derealization (feelings of unreality) or depersonalization (being detached from oneself)
(10) fear of losing control or going crazy
(11) fear of dying
(12) paresthesias (numbness or tingling sensations)
(13) chills or hot flushes

---

from any of the specific anxiety disorders. A panic attack is described as "a discrete period of intense fear or discomfort, in which four (or more) symptoms developed abruptly and reached a peak within 10 minutes" (2000, p. 395). The presence of panic attacks alone is not sufficient evidence to conclude that a client has an anxiety disorder, much less Panic Disorder. One study found that 34% of normal young adults had experienced at least one panic attack in the previous year (Norton, Harrison, Hauch, & Rhodes, 1985); and panic attacks have been found to be present in varying degrees in a wide range of disorders (Boyd, 1986). When the panic attacks are due to another disorder, such as Schizophrenia or Somatization Disorder, the diagnosis of Panic Disorder is not made. Also, the presence or absence of panic attacks is insufficient to distinguish among the anxiety disorders. In Specific Phobia or Social Phobia, the person may have panic attacks, but these occur only in the presence of specific phobic stimuli. The diagnosis of Panic Disorder is made only when attacks are unexpected and do not occur immediately before or during exposure to a specific situation that almost always causes anxiety.

DSM-IV-TR also has a separate section devoted to the definition and diagnostic criteria for Agoraphobia, although Agoraphobia itself is not a codable disorder (see Table 5.2). Agoraphobia is defined as anxiety about being in a situation where escape might be difficult or where help may not be available in case of a panic attack. These places are then avoided, endured with marked distress, or require the presence of a companion. As with Panic Attacks, Agoraphobia can occur in the context of more than one anxiety disorder.

Another change with DSM-IV-TR (2000) is that simply having frequent panic attacks is no longer sufficient for the diagnosis of Panic Disorder. In DSM-III-R (1987), having four attacks within a four-week period was one criterion for the diagnosis of Panic Disorder. In DSM-IV-TR, however, frequency is not sufficient.

TABLE 5.2. *DSM-IV-TR* Criteria for Agoraphobia

Note: Agoraphobia is not a codable disorder. Code the specific diagnosis in which the Agoraphobia occurs (e.g., 300.21 Panic Disorder With Agoraphobia [p. 441] or 300.22 Agoraphobia Without History of Panic Disorder [p. 441]).

A. Anxiety about being in places or situations from which escape might be difficult (or embarrassing) or in which help may not be available in the event of having an unexpected or situationally predisposed Panic Attack or panic-like symptoms. Agoraphobic fears typically involve characteristic clusters of situations that include being outside the home alone; being in a crowd or standing in line; being on a bridge; and traveling in a bus, train, or automobile.
   Note: Consider the diagnosis of Specific phobia if the avoidance is limited to one or only a few specific situations, or Social phobia if the avoidance is limited to social situations.

B. The situations are avoided (e.g., travel is restricted) or else are endured with marked distress or with anxiety about having a Panic Attack or panic-like symptoms, or require the presence of a companion.

C. The anxiety or phobic avoidance is not better accounted for by another mental disorder, such as Social phobia (e.g., avoidance limited to social situations because of fear of embarrassment), Specific phobia (e.g., avoidance limited to a single situation such as elevators), Obsessive–Compulsive Disorder (e.g., avoidance of dirt in someone with an obsession about contamination), Posttraumatic Stress Disorder (e.g., avoidance of stimuli associated with a severe stressor), or Separation Anxiety Disorder (e.g., avoidance of leaving home or relatives).

Table 5.3. DSM-IV-TR Criteria for Panic Disorder With and Without Agoraphobia

A. Both (1) and (2):
    (1) recurrent unexpected Panic Attacks
    (2) at least one of the attacks has been followed by 1 month (or more) of one (or more) of the following:
        (a) persistent concern about having additional attacks
        (b) worry about the implications of the attack or its consequences (e.g., losing control, having a heart attack, 'going crazy')
        (c) a significant change in behavior related to the attacks
B. The presence of Agoraphobia
C. The Panic Attacks are not due to the direct physiological effects of a substance (e.g., a drug of abuse, a medication) or a general medical condition (e.g., hyperthyroidism).
D. The Panic Attacks are not better accounted for by another mental disorder, such as Social Phobia (e.g., occurring on exposure to feared social situations), Specific Phobia (e.g., on exposure to a specific phobic situation), Obsessive–Compulsive Disorder (e.g., on exposure to dirt in someone with an obsession about contamination), Posttraumatic Stress Disorder (e.g., in response to stimuli associated with a severe stressor), or Separation Anxiety Disorder (e.g., in response to being away from home or close relatives).

Note: The DSM-IV-TR criteria for Panic Disorder without Agoraphobia are the same as above, except that criterion B is "Absence of Agoraphobia."

To qualify for the diagnosis, one needs to have at least one panic attack followed by one month or more of persistent concern, worry, or a behavioral change. The distinction between Panic Disorder with and without Agoraphobia (Table 5.3) can be a difficult one if the agoraphobic avoidance is mild. When asked if they avoid many situations, clients with panic attacks may answer "No," leading one to conclude that they have Panic Disorder without Agoraphobia. However, patterns of avoidance may be subtle or may have continued for so long that the client does not recognize the avoidance. It may be necessary to specifically ask about the frequency of their involvement in commonplace activities such as driving on freeways, flying, traveling far away from home, and attending group activities such as religious services, concerts, plays, and sporting events. It is not unusual to discover that the individual habitually avoids a number of these activities due to their fear of panic attacks or faces them only when accompanied by a trusted companion. One must also ask about any special conditions needed to enable them to face feared situations, such as, having a glass of water available when speaking in public, or sitting near the door in large meetings, to accurately ascertain the extent of the Agoraphobia.

The category of Agoraphobia without History of Panic Disorder shares the essential features of Panic Disorder with Agoraphobia except that there is no history of panic attacks. The focus of the fear typically is on incapacitating or embarrassing symptoms other than panic attacks or on limited symptom attacks, rather than full Panic Attacks.

Social Phobia

Social Phobia (which is also called Social Anxiety Disorder in *DSM-IV-TR*) involves a fear of exposure to the scrutiny of others, particularly the fear of

TABLE 5.4. *DSM-IV-TR* Criteria for Social Phobia

A. A marked and persistent fear of one or more social or performance situations in which the person is exposed to unfamiliar people or to possible scrutiny by others. The individual fears that he or she will act in a way (or show anxiety symptoms) that will be humiliating or embarrassing. **Note:** In children, there must be evidence of the capacity for age-appropriate social relationships with familiar people and the anxiety must occur in peer settings, not just in interactions with adults.

B. Exposure to the feared social situation almost invariably provokes anxiety, which may take the form of a situationally bound or situationally predisposed Panic Attack. **Note:** In children, the anxiety may be expressed by crying, tantrums, freezing, or shrinking from social situations with unfamiliar people.

C. The person recognizes that the fear is excessive or unreasonable. **Note:** In children, this feature may be absent.

D. The feared social or performance situations are avoided or else are endured with intense anxiety or distress.

E. The avoidance, anxious anticipation, or distress in the feared social or performance situation(s) interferes significantly with the person's normal routine, occupational (academic) functioning, or social activities or relationships, or there is marked distress about having the phobia.

F. In individuals under age 18 years, the duration is at least 6 months.

G. The fear or avoidance is not due to the direct physiological effects of a substance (e.g., a drug of abuse, a medication) or a general medical condition and is not better accounted for by another mental disorder (e.g., Panic Disorder With or Without Agoraphobia, Separation Anxiety Disorder, Body Dysmorphic Disorder, a Pervasive Developmental Disorder, or Schizoid Personality Disorder).

H. If a general medical condition or another mental disorder is present, the fear in Criterion A is unrelated to it, e.g., the fear is not of Stuttering, trembling in Parkinson's disease, or exhibiting abnormal eating behavior in Anorexia Nervosa or Bulimia Nervosa.

Specify if:

Generalized: If the fears include most social situations (also consider the additional diagnosis of Avoidant Personality Disorder).

---

embarrassment or humiliation due to one's actions while others are watching (see Table 5.4). Although seemingly straightforward, the diagnosis of Social Phobia can be a complex one to make. The presence of social anxiety in and of itself is not sufficient to warrant the diagnosis of Social Phobia. For example, social anxiety resulting from intense fear of intimacy in a person with Borderline Personality Disorder or from hypersensitivity to potential rejection in a person with Avoidant Personality Disorder would not lead to a separate diagnosis of Social Phobia. There must be a persistent fear of one or more situations in which the person is exposed to scrutiny by others and fears that he or she may act in a way that will be humiliating or embarrassing. Social Phobias often include fear that one's anxiety will be noticed by others. Thus, a social phobic may be unwilling to write in the view of others for fear that his or her hand will tremble or may avoid social situations for fear of being so nervous that he or she will perspire excessively.

One important but difficult differential diagnosis is that between Social Phobia and Paranoia. Social phobics are often concerned that people are watching them and talking about them, and thus might be misdiagnosed as paranoid. However, individuals with Social Phobia are acutely self-conscious rather than paranoid. These clients are often so worried about people noticing their anxiety that they feel

Table 5.5. DSM-IV-TR Criteria for Specific Phobia

A. Marked and persistent fear that is excessive or unreasonable, cued by the presence or anticipation of a specific object or situation (e.g., flying, heights, animals, receiving an injection, seeing blood).
B. Exposure to the phobic stimulus almost invariably provokes an immediate anxiety response, which may take the form of a situationally bound or situationally predisposed Panic Attack. **Note:** In children, the anxiety may be expressed by crying, tantrums, freezing, or clinging.
C. The person recognizes that the fear is excessive or unreasonable. **Note:** In children, this feature may be absent.
D. The phobic situation(s) is avoided or else is endured with intense anxiety or distress.
E. The avoidance, anxious anticipation, or distress in the feared situation(s) interferes significantly with the person's normal routine, occupational (academic) functioning, or social activities or relationships, or there is marked distress about having the phobia.
F. In individuals under age 18 years, the duration is at least 6 months.

as if they are the center of attention. Unlike individuals with true Paranoia, they do not ascribe malicious intentions to other people and do not feel that they are in danger of anything worse than embarrassment or humiliation.

Both agoraphobics and social phobics can become anxious in public, but in different ways and for different reasons. Social phobics are not primarily concerned with the risk having panic attacks, as agoraphobics are, but are primarily concerned with the risk of embarrassment and humiliation. They generally do not feel a need to be accompanied by a friend or family member. Although agoraphobics may worry about embarrassing themselves in public by having a panic attack, they are primarily concerned about the risk of having a panic attack and can be distinguished from social phobics by the fact that they also worry about being unable to escape from the situation or unable to get help if they do panic.

Specific Phobia

With *DSM-IV-TR*, the term Simple Phobia has, quite appropriately, been replaced with Specific Phobia. A Specific Phobia is characterized by a marked and persistent fear that is triggered by the presence or the anticipation of a specific object or situation (see Table 5.5). Fears of specific stimuli such as heights, insects, snakes, and so on are quite common but would be considered to be Specific Phobias only if the fear or avoidance results in significant impairment or distress. Specific Phobias encountered in clinical practice range from the commonplace, such as fear of flying, to the idiosyncratic, such as fear of the wind. It is important to remember that if the consequence that the individual fears is embarrassment or humiliation, a diagnosis of Social Phobia is likely to be more appropriate than a diagnosis of Specific Phobia. For example, most clients who enter therapy complaining of a fear of breaking into a sweat in social situations would not be diagnosed with a Specific Phobia (fear of sweat) but, rather, with Social Phobia. They are actually less concerned about sweat itself than they are about the risk that others will notice their excessive perspiration and that this will lead to humiliation and embarrassment.

Obsessive–Compulsive Disorder

When a client seeks therapy for what appears to be a fear or phobia, it is important to ascertain whether the symptoms involve compulsive rituals or not. For example, many clients who report a fear of germs or dirt have developed elaborate handwashing or cleaning rituals as a result of their fears. It is often necessary to explore this area carefully, because clients may be so used to their extensive strategies for preventing harm that they no longer view them as rituals and may not think to mention them. Even if fears and phobias do exist, if a person also has significant obsessions or compulsions, he or she would be diagnosed as having an OCD (see Table 5.6), rather than a phobia. Treatment for the rituals would generally need to precede any treatment of the fears or phobias.

TABLE 5.6. DSM-IV-TR Criteria for Obsessive–Compulsive Disorder

---

A. Either obsessions or compulsions:
   Obsessions as defined by (1), (2), (3), and (4):
   (1) recurrent and persistent thoughts, impulses, or images that are experienced, at some time during the disturbance, as intrusive and inappropriate and that cause marked anxiety or distress
   (2) the thoughts, impulses, or images are not simply excessive worries about real-life problems
   (3) the person attempts to ignore or suppress such thoughts, impulses, or images, or to neutralize them with some other thought or action
   (4) the person recognizes that the obsessional thoughts, impulses, or images are a product of his or her own mind (not imposed from without as in thought insertion).
   Compulsions as defined by (1) and (2):
   (1) repetitive behaviors (e.g., hand washing, ordering, checking) or mental acts (e.g., praying, counting, repeating words silently) that the person feels driven to perform in response to an obsession, or according to rules that must be applied rigidly
   (2) the behaviors or mental acts are aimed at preventing or reducing distress or preventing some dreaded event or situation; however, these behaviors or mental acts either are not connected in a realistic way with what they are designed to neutralize or prevent or are clearly excessive.
B. At some point during the course of the disorder, the person has recognized that the obsessions or compulsions are excessive or unreasonable. **Note:** This does not apply to children.
C. The obsessions or compulsions cause marked distress, are time consuming (take more than 1 hour a day), or significantly interfere with the person's normal routine, occupational (or academic) functioning, or usual social activities or relationships.
D. If another Axis I disorder is present, the content of the obsessions or compulsions is not restricted to it (e.g., preoccupation with food in the presence of an Eating Disorder; hair pulling in the presence of Trichotillomania; concern with appearance in the presence of Body Dysmorphic Disorder; preoccupation with drugs in the presence of a Substance Use Disorder; preoccupation with having a serious illness in the presence of Hypochondriasis; preoccupation with sexual urges or fantasies in the presence of a Paraphilia; or guilty ruminations in the presence of Major Depressive Disorder).
E. The disturbance is not due to the direct physiological effects of a substance (e.g., a drug of abuse, a medication) or a general medical condition.
Specify if:
   With Poor Insight: if, for most of the time during the current episode, the person does not recognize that the obsessions and compulsions are excessive or unreasonable.

TABLE 5.7. DSM-IV-TR Criteria for Generalized Anxiety Disorder

---

A. Excessive anxiety and worry (apprehensive expectation), occurring more days than not for at least 6 months, about a number of events or activities (such as work or school performance).

B. The person finds it difficult to control the worry.

C. The anxiety and worry are associated with three (or more) of the following six symptoms (with at least some symptoms present for more days than not for the past 6 months). **Note:** Only one item is required in children.
   (1) restlessness or feeling keyed up or on edge
   (2) being easily fatigued
   (3) difficulty concentrating or mind going blank
   (4) irritability
   (5) muscle tension
   (6) sleep disturbance (difficulty falling or staying asleep, or restless unsatisfying sleep).

D. The focus of the anxiety is not confined to features of an Axis I disorder, e.g., the anxiety or worry is not about having a Panic Attack (as in Panic Disorder), being embarrassed public (as in Social Phobia), being contaminated (as in Obsessive–Compulsive Disorder), being away from home or close relatives (as in Separation Anxiety Disorder), gaining weight (as in Anorexia Nervosa), having multiple physical complaints (as in Somatization Disorder), or having a serious illness (as in Hypochondriasis), and the anxiety and worry do not occur exclusively during Posttraumatic Stress Disorder.

E. The anxiety, worry, or physical symptoms cause clinically significant distress or impairment in social, occupational, or other important areas of functioning.

F. The disturbance is not due to the direct physiological effects of a substance (e.g., a drug of abuse, a medication) or a general medical condition (e.g., hyperthyroidism) and does not occur exclusively during a Mood Disorder, a Psychotic Disorder, or a Pervasive Developmental Disorder.

DSM-IV-TR clarifies that obsessions are not simply excessive worries about real-life problems and that compulsions can be either repetitive behaviors or mental acts.

Generalized Anxiety Disorder

The criteria for Generalized Anxiety Disorder (GAD) are much more specific in *DSM-IV-TR* than they were in previous diagnostic systems (see Table 5.7); however, fewer specific symptoms are required than in *DSM-III-R* (3 out of 6 symptoms as opposed to the previous 6 out of 18). Despite the more detailed criteria, the use of the term "generalized" still leads many to mistakenly assume that the anxiety in GAD is continuous, pervasive, and "free-floating." Careful cognitive and behavioral assessment of individuals with GAD makes it clear that there are definite variations in the intensity of anxiety, depending on the situation and cognitions of the client at the time. Even though it is common for clients to initially experience their anxiety as occurring spontaneously for no apparent reason, the concept of free-floating anxiety (i.e., anxiety which occurs "out of the blue" for no reason) does not seem to be borne out when careful assessment takes place. With systematic monitoring of both behavior and cognition, it becomes apparent that the anxiety is indeed triggered by particular stimuli (often by thoughts or by interoceptive cues) that may not be obvious to the external observer.

TABLE 5.8. DSM-IV-TR Criteria for Post-Traumatic Stress Disorder

A. The person has been exposed to a traumatic event in which both of the following were present:
   (1) the person experienced, witnessed, or was confronted with an event or events that involved actual or threatened death or serious injury, or a threat to the physical integrity of self or others
   (2) The person's response involved intense fear, helplessness, or horror. **Note**: In children, this may be expressed instead by disorganized or agitated behavior
B. The traumatic event is persistently reexperienced in one (or more) of the following ways:
   (1) recurrent and intrusive distressing recollections of the event, including images, thoughts, or perceptions. **Note**: In young children, repetitive play may occur in which themes or aspects of the trauma are expressed.
   (2) recurrent distressing dreams of the event. **Note**: In children, there may be frightening dreams without recognizable content.
   (3) acting or feeling as if the traumatic event were recurring (includes a sense of reliving the experience, illusions, hallucinations, and dissociative flashback episodes, including those that occur on awakening or when intoxicated). **Note**: In young children, trauma-specific reenactment may occur.
   (4) intense psychological distress at exposure to internal or external cues that symbolize or resemble an aspect of the traumatic event.
   (5) physiological reactivity on exposure to internal or external cues that symbolize or resemble an aspect of the traumatic event.
C. Persistent avoidance of stimuli associated with the trauma and numbing of general responsiveness (not present before the trauma), as indicated by three (or more) of the following:
   (1) efforts to avoid thoughts, feelings, or conversations associated with the trauma
   (2) efforts to avoid activities, places, or people that arouse recollections of the trauma
   (3) inability to recall an important aspect of the trauma
   (4) markedly diminished interest or participation in significant activities
   (5) feeling of detachment or estrangement from others
   (6) restricted range of affect (e.g., unable to have loving feelings)
   (7) sense of a foreshortened future (e.g., does not expect to have a career, marriage, children, or a normal life span).
D. Persistent symptoms of increased arousal (not present before the trauma), as indicated by two (or more) of the following:
   (1) difficulty falling or staying asleep
   (2) irritability or outbursts of anger
   (3) difficulty concentrating
   (4) hypervigilance
   (5) exaggerated startle response.
E. Duration of the disturbance (symptoms in Criteria B, C, and D) is more than 1 month.
F. The disturbance causes clinically significant distress or impairment in social, occupational, or other important areas of functioning.
Specify if:
   Acute: if duration of symptoms is less than 3 months
   Chronic: if duration of symptoms is 3 months or more
   Specify if:
   With Delayed Onset: if onset of symptoms is at least 6 months after the stressor.

Stress Disorders

Post-Traumatic Stress Disorder (PTSD) has received much attention in recent years due to the high incidence of PTSD among combat veterans. However, it should be noted that PTSD can occur following any traumatic event, such as a natural disaster, a major accident, or a victimization (see Table 5.8). In fact, *DSM-IV-TR* no longer requires that the event be outside the range of usual human experience. Instead, the event needs to involve actual or threatened death or serious injury, or a threat to the physical integrity of self or others, and the person's response needs to involve intense fear, helplessness, or horror. Whereas PTSD often develops in response to events that objectively do involve risk of serious injury or death, it is also possible to develop PTSD in response to events that the individual misperceives as presenting a threat of injury or death.

The category of Acute Stress Disorder appeared for the first time with *DSM-IV* (1994). This category is similar to PTSD, but involves a reaction within 1 month after exposure to an extreme traumatic stressor. This diagnosis should only be considered if the symptoms last at least 2 days up to a maximum of 4 weeks and occur within 4 weeks of the traumatic event. If the symptoms persist longer than 4 weeks, then the diagnosis of PTSD should be considered.

Note that the impact of anxiety is not limited to individuals who meet criteria for one of the *DSM-IV-TR* anxiety disorders. As noted earlier, panic attacks and anxiety can occur in a wide variety of disorders. In addition, other disorders appear to be related to anxiety disorders. For example, Body Dysmorphic Disorder and Trichotillomania appear to be related to OCD. The conceptualizations and treatment approaches discussed in this chapter can also be applied with individuals who have problems which involve anxiety but who do not meet criteria for an anxiety disorder.

CONCEPTUALIZATION

If anxiety is a part of everyday life and can be functional in many situations, how do anxiety disorders develop? It is clear that there are non-cognitive contributions to the etiology of anxiety disorders. For example, research has shown that individuals with OCD differ from those who do not have OCD in a number of biological features, including brain morphology and chemistry, and that there is some degree of genetic transmission of OCD within families. Whereas one can inherit a tendency to develop OCD, it is also clear that this genetic predisposition is just one of many components of OCD (for a detailed discussion of the biological aspects of OCD, see Zohar, Insel, and Rasmussen, 1991). It is likely that biological factors play a role in many anxiety disorders but it is also clear that anxiety disorders are more than a biological problem.

According to Beck's cognitive theory of psychopathology (Beck, 1976), the thinking of the anxious client is dominated by themes of danger. The client anticipates threats to self and family, which can be physical, psychological, or social in nature. In phobias, the anticipation of physical or psychological harm is confined to specific situations. The fears are based on the client's exaggerated conception of specific harmful attributes of these situations. The phobic is not afraid of the situation or object in and of itself, but rather is afraid of the consequences of being in the situation or in contact with the object. In Generalized Anxiety Disorder and Panic Disorder, the client anticipates danger in situations that are less specific and therefore more difficult to avoid. Thus, the thinking of the anxious client is characterized by repetitive thoughts about danger. These take the form of continuous verbal or pictorial cognitions about the occurrence of harmful events.

A number of cognitive distortions are particularly common in anxious clients and tend to amplify their anxiety:

1. Catastrophizing. Anxious clients tend to dwell on the most extreme negative consequences conceivable, assuming that a situation in which there is any possibility of harm constitutes a highly probable danger. Specific phobics tend to expect disaster in the form of physical harm when faced with a specific situation or object, social phobics expect more personal disaster in the form of humiliation and embarrassment, and agoraphobics expect disaster as the consequence of their own internal experience of anxiety or panic attacks.
2. Personalization. Anxious individuals often react as though external events are personally relevant and are indications of a potential danger to themselves. Thus, an anxious client who hears about a car accident may decide that he or she is likely to have a car accident as well.
3. Magnification and minimization. When anxious, individuals tend to focus on signs of danger or potential threat to the exclusion of other aspects of the situation. Thus the anxious client tends to emphasize any aspects of a situation that might be seen as dangerous, and minimize or ignore the non-threatening or rescue factors in a situation.
4. Selective abstraction. The anxious person often focuses on the threatening elements of a situation and ignores remainder of the context.
5. Arbitrary inference. The anxious client frequently jumps to dire conclusions on the basis of little or no data. For example, a client may assume that any unusual feeling in his or her chest must be a heart attack or that any turbulence means the airplane will crash.
6. Overgeneralization. The client may view a time-limited situation as lasting forever, i.e., "This panic attack will never end". The anxious individual may assume that because a particular problem has occurred previously it is bound to recur frequently, or may assume that if he or she had any fear in a particular situation, the situation must be dangerous.

Research has also demonstrated that certain beliefs are characteristic of anxious individuals (Deffenbacher, Zwemer, Whisman, Hill, & Sloan, 1986; Zwemer & Deffenbacher, 1984). In a nonclinical population, these authors found that anxious individuals tended to share the following beliefs:

1. Anxious overconcern. If something is or may be dangerous or fearsome, one should be terribly upset about it and continually think and worry about it.
2. Personal perfection. One has to be thoroughly competent, adequate and achieving for it to be worthwhile.
3. Catastrophizing. It is horrible when things are not the way one would like them to be.
4. Problem avoidance. It is easier to avoid than to face life's difficulties.

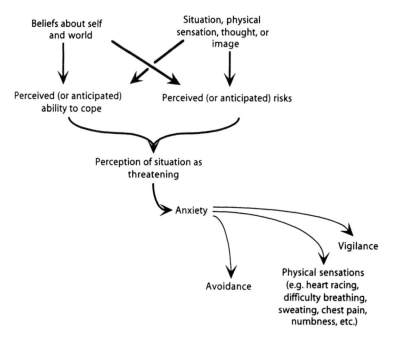

FIGURE 5.1. Cognitive Model of Anxiety.

In a clinical study of the beliefs of phobics, Mizes, Landolf-Fritsche, and Grossman-McKee (1987) found that in addition to anxious overconcern and problem avoidance discussed above, phobics also endorsed the belief that it is essential to be loved and approved by all significant others (demand for approval). Significant, but weaker, correlations were found between level of phobic avoidance and both the idea that the past determines present feelings and behaviors that cannot be changed (helplessness) and the idea that one must do well at everything to be worthwhile (high self-expectations). Although research is not yet available on clinical populations of different types of phobics, clinical observations suggest that social phobics are ruled by the belief that it is a dire necessity to be loved by everyone for everything they do. They also seem to hold the underlying assumption that it is essential to appear strong and in control at all times, and that any demonstration of weakness or anxiety is disastrous. Agoraphobics seem to be especially concerned with the issue of control and to hold the underlying assumption that one must have certain and perfect control at all times. They also tend to hold a generalized belief that the world is threatening if confronted independently and that security from danger must be ensured either through the availability of a loved one or by being extremely cautious.

A cognitive model of anxiety (Figure 5.1) demonstrates how a number of cognitive factors work together in the development and maintenance of anxiety. An individual's perception of the situations he or she encounters is shaped by his or her beliefs and assumptions and can be biased by any cognitive distortions that occur. When approaching any situation, an individual automatically evaluates the degree of risk present as well as his or her capacity for handling the situation satisfactorily. If the person does not perceive any particular risk in the situation, or if the person feels capable of coping effectively with the risk, the situation would not be perceived as threatening and the person would not experience anxiety. When an individual does perceive risk in a situation, belief in one's own self-efficacy (Bandura, 1977) moderates the perception of threat and hence the anxiety. Self-efficacy is defined by Bandura (1977, p. 79) as the conviction that one can successfully execute the behavior required to produce the desired outcome. Thus, if an individual perceives a situation as dangerous but is convinced that he or she will be able to deal safely with the danger, the stimulus is seen as less of a threat and causes less anxiety. If one has a low sense of self-efficacy and feels incapable of dealing with the potential danger, the anxiety is increased.

Take the example of two people looking down from a steep cliff. One person is an experienced mountain climber. She can see that there is the risk of falling and that it would be dangerous to fall. However, she knows from her experience that she has the skills needed to cope with the situation, so she experiences a sense of challenge, excitement, and enthusiasm. The other person has never done any mountain climbing before. He sees the threat of falling and, in addition, perceives that he does not have the ability to cope with the risk. Instead of a sense of challenge, he is overwhelmed with the sense of danger and experiences intense anxiety. A person's sense of self-efficacy is shaped by one's experience. If one perceives a situation as dangerous and is able to cope successfully with the situation, one's sense of self-efficacy is increased. The next time a similar situation is approached, that person is likely to feel less anxious and more able to handle it. If, however, one experiences intense anxiety and is not able to handle it effectively, one's sense of self-efficacy is decreased and similar situations are likely to be viewed as even more dangerous in the future.

The experience of anxiety leads to a number of reactions. Anxious feelings tend to lead to vigilance for signs of danger and, if any indications of danger are perceived, the individual's attention focuses on these danger signs. When one is objectively in danger, it is only natural to focus one's attention on the danger until a solution has been found. However, the client with an anxiety disorder is unrealistically anxious and thus is vigilant for signs of danger or is preoccupied with perceived dangers when this is not adaptive. As a result, the amount of attention available for focusing on specific tasks, recalling information, or self-reflection can be greatly restricted and the client may well complain of inability to concentrate or of forgetfulness.

The experience of intense anxiety tends to lead to a variety of physical symptoms, which can be upsetting in themselves. Different individuals experience different physical sensations of anxiety, which can include a wide variety of symptoms such as heart racing, difficulty in breathing, dizziness, sweating, feelings of unreality, chest pain, and numbness. If the person in turn becomes worried or frightened by the physical symptoms of anxiety, this can serve to reduce self-efficacy and increase the perception of risk, leading to a spiral of increasing anxiety.

When faced with the experience of intense anxiety, an individual may choose to avoid or escape from the stimulus seen as dangerous. This can be a very effective short-term strategy, successfully reducing anxiety for the moment. However, it has its cost. Because avoidance does nothing to change the perception of the stimulus as dangerous, the appraisal of threat is unmodified and the stimulus continues to be seen as dangerous. In addition, avoidance does not help to increase self-efficacy. The client learns that the anxiety-provoking stimulus can be avoided, but has no evidence that he or she is capable of handling it in any other, more direct way. Thus, when again faced with the stimulus, the person may believe that he or she has no alternative but to avoid or escape the situation once again. Thus, avoidance increases the likelihood of future avoidance of the same and similar situations. Over time, consistent avoidance of problem situations can lower self-efficacy and increase the individual's anxiety.

This general cognitive model of anxiety points out specific areas where cognitive and behavioral interventions can be useful. They can be used to challenge the perception that the situation is dangerous, the perception that one is unable to cope, or both. They can also be used to decrease vigilance for signs of danger, to reduce the physical sensations of anxiety and the fear of such sensations, as well as to reduce avoidance of anxiety-provoking situations. Changing any one of these factors through cognitive and behavioral interventions can help to reduce the overall anxiety.

The patterns of avoidance in anxiety can lead to any of the phobic disorders; the types of phobias differ primarily in the situations that elicit the anxiety and in the consequences that are feared. In Specific Phobia, the avoidance is of a specific object or situation. If the person avoids the possibility of embarrassment or humiliation, they may develop Social Phobia. In Panic Disorder, the individual is afraid of having panic attacks and develops catastrophic misinterpretations of the frightening bodily sensations (Clark, 1986). If the person then begins to avoid the situations in which he or she has experienced panic attacks, they develop Panic Disorder with Agoraphobia. For example:

> Mary Lou was a 28-year-old married woman with a $3^{1}/_{2}$-year-old son. Her husband was the pastor of a church in a small southern town. Mary Lou sought treatment because she had been having severe panic attacks for the past two years and her life had become increasingly restricted. She was afraid of any situation where she felt she might be trapped and unable to get home. She avoided stores, church, restaurants, waiting in line, theaters, and traveling alone. This avoidance had severely limited her life; she felt depressed, and had gained 20 pounds in the previous two years.
>
> Mary Lou described herself as always having been "high-strung", but said that this had never been a problem for her in the past. As she saw it, her problems had begun about two years previously during a church service when she suddenly felt light-headed and dizzy, her heart pounded, her hands became cold and clammy, she felt terrified, and she felt she had to leave. She left in the middle of her husband's sermon and was very embarrassed. This was the first in a series of panic attacks that occurred when Mary Lou was out in public.
>
> The first panic attack occurred at a time when Mary Lou had just moved from a large city to a small town. She was a homemaker with a toddler, and her husband had a new parish and was spending much less time at home. However, Mary Lou did not attribute her physical symptoms to the stress she was experiencing. Instead, she saw them as coming totally out of the blue and thought that she must have a physical problem. She sought

medical attention, was diagnosed as having mitral valve prolapse, and her physician prescribed 150 mg of Imiprimine per day. She felt somewhat better on the medication, but still had panic attacks and avoided a range of situations.

If, instead of avoiding situations that he or she perceives as dangerous, the individual attempts to cope with the perceived danger through vigilance and worry and no catastrophe follows, he or she may conclude that the vigilance and worry proved effective. This pattern of response to perceived or anticipated threats can easily become habitual and result in frequent periods of stress and anxiety due to rumination about such threats. If such a pattern becomes sufficiently ingrained and the resulting anxiety becomes sufficiently intense, Generalized Anxiety Disorder could develop.

Obsessions go far beyond the distressing worries and ruminations characteristic of individuals with GAD and are associated with a somewhat different pattern of cognitions. All individuals occasionally experience thoughts, images, or impulses that they find repugnant. If the individual accepts that this experience is just a part of being human, no problem arises. However, some individuals believe that certain thoughts, feelings, or impulses are totally unacceptable, perhaps because they are a sign of insanity or moral depravity. When these individuals have such a thought, feeling, or impulse, it is likely to be followed by catastrophic cognitions such as, "God! How could I think such a thing? Only a freak would think that!" These cognitions elicit strong emotional reactions, including anxiety, and because anxiety produces an involuntary fixation of attention on signs of danger and vigilance for signs of danger (i.e., unacceptable thoughts), the individual can quickly become preoccupied with his or her unacceptable thoughts. This preoccupation tends to generate additional thoughts, images, or impulses on the same theme and the flow of unacceptable cognitions can quickly become quite intense.

Salkovskis (1985) proposed that five assumptions are specifically characteristic of OCD:

1. Thinking of an action is tantamount to its performance.
2. Failing to prevent (or failing to try to prevent) harm to self or others is morally equivalent to causing the harm.
3. Responsibility for harm is not diminished by extenuating circumstances.
4. Failing to ritualize in response to an idea about harm constitutes an intention to harm.
5. One should exercise control over one's thoughts.

Compulsions arise when the individual engages in a behavioral or cognitive response that reduces his or her anxiety in the short-run without dealing with the situation effectively. The anxiety soon returns and the individual can become involved in a pattern of repeating the behavior or thought to obtain short-term anxiety relief, but which worsens the problem over time. For example, a young mother may believe that a fleeting thoughts of harming her infant means that she is evil and is likely to harm him, rather than recognizing that it simply shows that she is tired, overwhelmed, and frustrated. As a result of her fear, she may avoid being alone with the baby, rather than addressing her increased stress and difficult situation. If she is able to avoid being alone with her baby for the time being, this will reduce her anxiety for the moment. Unfortunately, the next time she is alone with her baby she is likely to fear that her "evil" thoughts will return and her vigilance for such thoughts increases the likelihood that the thoughts will reoccur. Over time, her fears are likely to grow stronger and her avoidance is likely to become more and more compulsive.

Clients with compulsions are frequently unwilling to acknowledge thoughts or feelings that they find unacceptable. Such an individual is unable to deal with the thoughts and feelings directly and can easily become dependent on any strategy that provides temporary relief. In the example above, the young mother dealt with her fear that she would harm her child by trying to avoid being alone with her child. Mental rituals such as compulsive counting or compulsively repeating a particular prayer can develop as a way of blocking unacceptable thoughts, images, or impulses from awareness and then become "addictive" in the same way as compulsive acts do.

PTSD can be conceptualized in terms of the individual's partially effective, but partially dysfunctional, attempts to avoid recalling his or her traumatic experiences. Individuals with PTSD attempt to avoid stimuli which might arouse recollections of the traumatic event(s) and attempt to avoid thoughts and feelings associated with the trauma, yet they are plagued by very distressing intrusive memories of the event(s). It is quite understandable that an individual who has undergone traumatic experiences would fear memories of the event and attempt to avoid them, because these recollections are intensely distressing. However, he or she encounters the same problem as the person who is plagued by obsessions. The fear of memories, images, thoughts, and feelings associated with the traumatic event(s) results in a focus of attention on these cognitions and vigilance for stimuli which might elicit them. At the same time, the individual's determined avoidance of these cognitions blocks him or her from realizing that they are not dangerous, simply quite distressing.

In the more traditional, psychodynamic theory of anxiety, anxiety is a manifestation of underlying conflict. It is presumed that, if the underlying conflict is not dealt with in treatment, another anxiety problem will take its place. However, there is no evidence that a client successfully treated through a direct, focused cognitive behavioral treatment will develop another problem to take its place. In fact, the opposite has often been found: when individuals have resolved anxiety problems through straightforward cognitive and behavioral interventions, their overall psychological functioning tends to improve and they show increased self-efficacy. In cognitive behavioral treatment, generalization of improvement is much more likely to occur than symptom substitution.

Strategies for Intervention

The primary goal in treating clients with anxiety disorders is to eliminate both their disproportionate fears and any maladaptive patterns of avoiding, preventing, or escaping anxiety that the individual may have developed. However, this is not easily done because the fears and the dysfunctional behaviors tend to perpetuate each other. The task is further complicated by the fact that rational responses do not have the same impact on anxiety as on other problematic emotions. It is quite common for a client to understand intellectually that he or she is in no danger but to continue to feel quite anxious and to avoid the feared situation.

The conceptualization of anxiety disorders presented above in Figure 5.1 suggests a variety of points where useful intervention can occur. The client's overall level of anxiety can be reduced by training him or her in anxiety-reduction skills. The client's catastrophic cognitions regarding the feared situation, the anxiety symptoms, memories, thoughts, and images, can all be challenged through cognitive restructuring. Avoidance, whether behavioral or cognitive, can be modified through intentionally exposing the client to the stimuli he or she fears (in collaboration with the client, of course). Finally, the client's sense of self-efficacy and self-sufficiency can be increased through cognitively challenging any unrealistically harsh appraisals of his or her capacities and through training in coping skills such as assertion. Each of these points of possible intervention can have an impact on the entire process of the anxiety disorder, but a more powerful impact is achieved when several aspects of the anxiety process are modified at the same time.

In general, individuals with anxiety disorders have allowed anxiety to take over their lives and invest a great deal of time and energy trying to fight, control, or avoid the anxiety. One important treatment tactic is to ask clients to give up their "control" of anxiety and instead to accept the experience of anxiety and expose themselves to situations in which their anxiety would be heightened. As they do so and discover that the consequences are not as catastrophic as they initially expected, the anxiety gradually fades away. However, to enable clients to face the situations they fear, it is necessary to first challenge their appraisal of threat cognitively. As long as clients truly believe that exposing themselves to the feared situation will result in serious consequences such as dying, "going crazy", being humiliated, and so forth, they will not expose themselves to the situation, no matter how hard the therapist tries to encourage them. Only when their belief that disaster is inevitable has been effectively challenged will clients be willing to face the situations they fear.

Exposure to the phobic stimulus, whether it is exposure to a single situation, a wide range of situations, or a range of internal cues, is an essential part of the treatment of anxiety disorders. This exposure can be done in imagery or in the actual situations the client fears; it can be done in gradual steps or all at once; and it can be done as homework or with the therapist's assistance; the coping skills used to reduce the client's general level of stress may be used to help reduce his or her anxiety during exposure to feared situations or exposure can be done without the use of anxiety reduction techniques. It is the experience of encountering the feared situations in such a way that disaster does not follow which is crucial.

Training in coping skills and exposure to phobic situations are useful in reversing avoidance and weakening the connection between the situation and the experience of anxiety. These interventions also serve to increase the client's sense of self-efficacy, leaving clients with a new sense that they can indeed cope with frightening situations. These interventions are especially powerful because they provide the client with concrete accomplishments which provide particularly convincing evidence of self-efficacy (Bandura, 1977). An increase in self-efficacy should not only lower the client's anxiety level and contribute to improved confidence in dealing with similar situations, but also should help reduce the client's likelihood of developing further anxiety reactions.

The process of monitoring and challenging dysfunctional thoughts can be used to help the client face his or her fears and to enhance acceptance of symptoms in the situations where the client becomes anxious. Cognitive restructuring can help the client learn to take the time to look critically at the thoughts and feelings generated in various situations, thus reducing the automatic tendency to avoid. This can also facilitate more effective problem solving and reduces the likelihood of similar problems occurring in the future. However, it is important to remember that cognitive restructuring alone is not likely to be effective with anxiety disorders.

Cognitive and Behavioral Techniques

Table 5.9 illustrates some of the key ingredients of the treatment of anxiety disorders. Many clients with anxiety disorders are frightened in part because their problems seem incomprehensible to them. Therefore, it can be quite valuable to begin treatment by educating the client about anxiety. After the initial evaluation, the therapist can use guided discovery to explain the symptoms of anxiety to the client in detail, basing the explanation on the client's personal experience as much as possible. This brief discussion helps the client to feel understood and to have confidence in the therapist; it also begins the process of establishing a rationale for the interventions that will follow. Most clients with anxiety symptoms have been to many different medical and mental health professionals without receiving clear explanations and without feeling that anyone understands their problems. They often feel that their problems are unique and are reassured to discover that other people have had similar problems and have been successfully treated. A clear explanation can also be the first step in decatastrophizing the presence of the symptoms and helping clients become less excessively terrified of them.

TABLE 5.9. Key Ingredients in the Treatment of Anxiety

- Education and accurate information about the nature of anxiety and panic
- Development of the proper attitude—Acceptance
- Acquisition of physiological coping skills (i.e. breathing retraining and/or relaxation training) to increase self-efficacy and reduce helplessness
- Modification of dysfunctional thoughts and beliefs that obstruct acceptance
- Repeated, intentional exposure to anxiety-provoking sensations and situations
- Modification of underlying issues (e.g., marital problems, dependency, perfectionism, and so on) that support the development and maintenance of anxiety and panic.

Development of an Attitude of Acceptance

Developing the attitude of acceptance is one of the most crucial elements in the treatment of anxiety disorders. As long as the individual is fighting their anxiety or running from the feeling of anxiety, he or she inadvertently makes the feelings stronger and more powerful. The idea of actually accepting the feelings of anxiety rather than fighting them is a foreign concept to most clients and one that can be quite difficult for them to grasp. Typically, the client's primary goal at the beginning of therapy is to make the anxiety go away totally, once and for all. The idea of learning to accept the feelings of anxiety and cope with them is generally the furthest thing from the client's mind. Therefore, simply explaining the importance of acceptance at the beginning of treatment is not sufficient. The concepts of acceptance need to be revisited throughout the treatment and reinforced in each and every treatment session.

The emphasis on acceptance starts with goal setting. Once the concept of setting goals for therapy is explained to the client, the therapist needs to help the client to change goals such as, "Never feel anxious again," to goals such as, "Learn to cope with anxiety better," or, "Reduce the intensity and frequency of anxiety." Because this concept is so difficult for clients to truly understand, this is an area where bibliotherapy can be quite useful. Giving the client copies of handouts such as, "The Consequences of Fighting Panic," (Table 5.10) and, "The Consequences of Accepting Panic," (Table 5.11) can be useful. The therapist can review such handouts in the session, have the client take them home and consult them in situations where he or she feels anxious, and return to therapy with any questions and concerns about the idea of acceptance. DuPont and colleagues summarized this process by saying, "The universal antidote for all anxiety disorders is acceptance. Acceptance as a cure for anxiety disorders means acceptance of the feelings and the thoughts that are automatically produced in the anxious, sensitized brain. But acceptance does not mean accepting the limitations in your life that anxiety is trying to force on you." (DuPont, Spencer, & DuPont, 1998).

TABLE 5.10. The Consequences of Fighting Panic

- People often fight panic, so, they believe, it won't "get the better of them." Since they already feel bad enough, they reason that if they suspend the fight something *really bad* might happen.
- Consequently, fighting panic reinforces fear . . . in other words, you will continually wonder what awful things would happen if you *didn't* fight it.
- Perhaps you believe that if you let panic happen, or work on developing a more accepting attitude, you have somehow "given in." But, in reality, the harder you try to control a part of yourself, the more that part controls you.
- A fight requires an enemy. You think of panic as the enemy. If there's an enemy, then you must be vigilant and on guard. But if you are vigilant and on guard then you increase your tension and anxiety level. This contributes to maintenance of sensitization, thereby maintaining the panic cycle.
- Every time you react to panic by trying to fight it, you are essentially giving the panic more strength. Fighting the panic adds *second fear*, keeping the first fear alive.
- By fighting panic you are likely to sustain unpleasant feelings for a very long period of time, instead of the much shorter burst of panic that peaks and passes when you suspend the fight.

TABLE 5.11. The Consequences of Acceptance

- Acceptance does not mean "do nothing." It means working to develop a particular attitude. With acceptance you will build in a new attitude to take the place of all the negative, catastrophic thoughts that make up *second fear*. All these negative thoughts unnecessarily amplify the intensify of the anxiety.
- By giving up a need to control anxiety, you will eventually increase your feelings of being in control.
- With acceptance, anxiety feelings can peak and pass in a relatively brief period of time. Anxiety is self-limiting: it will end.
- With acceptance, you can get to the other side of anxiety and experience all it has to offer. You will discover that the worst isn't so bad, and that your catastrophic fears do not materialize. This discovery will carry much more weight than my words—experience is always the most valuable teacher.
- As you practice acceptance, you will learn to have greater trust in your body and your mind. You'll develop a more solid sense of self-support, no matter where you are at or who you are with.
- Anxiety feelings depend on your dislike of them for their very existence. Acceptance is the antidote to anxiety. Of course, you'll need multiple administrations of this antidote. Each time you experience anxiety, and each time you face a situation that you fear, you can practice 100% acceptance.
- Remember that anxiety is perpetuated by the "fear of the fear." With acceptance, you will not be adding the "second fear," and thereby lessen the flow of adrenaline. *It's the second fear that keeps the first fear alive.* You will break the fear-adrenaline-fear cycle.

The idea of acceptance in the treatment of Panic Disorder was introduced beautifully by Claire Weekes back in the 1960s (e.g., Weekes, 1969). Although that volume may seem somewhat dated today, her books still speak clearly to clients and help them to grasp the usefulness of acceptance. Beck and Emery (1985) outline a five-step A-W-A-R-E strategy for accepting and coping with anxiety:

1. Accept the feelings of anxiety;
2. Watch your anxiety. Look at it without judgment;
3. Act with the anxiety. Behave as you would if you weren't anxious;
4. Repeat Steps 1–3;
5. Expect the best.

Instead of anticipating disaster, clients need to remember that what they fear the most rarely happens and that they can cope both with anxiety and with the situations in which they encounter anxiety. They need to accept that they will have anxiety in the future and realize that having future anxiety will help them to get additional practice in accepting anxiety and coping with it.

Physiologic Interventions

One way to give anxious clients some initial relief, to improve their coping skills, and also to begin to challenge the belief that they are powerless in the face of anxiety is to increase their self-efficacy by teaching them specific anxiety-reduction skills. Learning coping skills provides convincing evidence that the client can, in fact, handle the feeling of anxiety. Thus, training in coping skills can serve two distinct purposes: (a) to actually help the person reduce his or her baseline level of anxiety, and (b) to build the person's self-efficacy and make him or her more willing to confront his or her fears.

Relaxation training can be an especially useful coping skill for reducing mild to moderate anxiety. A wide variety of relaxation training methods are useful clinically, ranging from simple deep breathing techniques to elaborate, highly technical biofeedback procedures (see Bernstein, Borkovec & Hazlett-Stevens, 2000, and Bourne, 1995, for good introductions to relaxation techniques). Many different methods of teaching relaxation have been shown to be effective, rather than trying to find the "best" technique it is more useful to try to find a relaxation technique which the client will practice consistently and have faith in. Any relaxation method that is practiced regularly with confidence will help the client achieve deeper levels of relaxation. It is important, however, to choose a method which will engage the client and which is likely to maintain their interest and cooperation. A review of their previous attempts at relaxation, if any, and an understanding of their current cognitions about relaxation are useful in choosing a relaxation method that is likely to be effective for a particular client. An individual who finds a simple deep breathing method too boring or has difficulty keeping his or her mind from wandering may need a somewhat more complex method, possibly with a tape recording to help to focus their attention. If the individual experiences physical pain which is aggravated by muscle tension, progressive muscle relaxation, which involves tensing various muscle groups, may not be a good choice. If the individual's tension tends to build in one area of the body that is particularly difficult to relax, biofeedback focused on that particular muscle group may be worth considering. One simple way to determine the relaxation method most likely to appeal to the client is to do a brief trial of several different methods in the session, having the client rate his or her anxiety level before and after trying each method. Generally, even brief trials of a few methods will give the client enough of a sample so that he or she will be able to express a preference. For example:

> Mary Lou was initially taught several ways of lowering her general level of anxiety. She found that breathing exercises were not helpful because, if she focused her attention on her breathing, she started to worry about whether she was breathing "right" or not. However, she found that autogenic relaxation where she learned to systematically relax various muscle groups was quite helpful. In addition to helping her relax, it diverted her from focusing exclusively on her anxiety symptoms.

Relaxation can be helpful for clients with the full range of anxiety disorders and serves to reduce general anxiety, increase self-efficacy, and provide a coping tool for use when facing particularly stressful or anxiety-provoking situations. It also tends to increase clients' awareness of early stages of anxiety, so that they may be able to deal with their anxiety while it is still reasonably low. It is important for the client to have realistic expectations about the likely effects of relaxation training. Clients with Generalized Anxiety Disorder may find that relaxation methods alone bring about a significant change in their symptoms; but for clients with phobias, relaxation is only a first step in the treatment and cannot be expected to have a major impact on the symptoms by itself. In particular, although relaxation can be useful in reducing the frequency of panic attacks by lowering the client's overall

Table 5.12. Proper and Improper Application of Relaxation Training

Proper Application of Relaxation
  To reduce baseline level of tension and anxiety.
  To reduce muscle tension so the client suspends the "fight" response and permits the anxiety to pass.
  At times, as a way of increasing tolerance of "letting go."
  To decrease maladaptive efforts to maintain tension as a way of maintaining control.
  To help increase confidence so that the client is more likely to engage in exposure practice, and
    recover rapidly between exposure trials.

Improper Application of Relaxation
  As an aid for suppressing anxiety, its sensations, and other emotions.
  As a last ditch effort to "fight off" anxiety.
  To keep anxiety within a safe and comfortable limit.

level of anxiety, once a panic attack has started, clients do not find relaxation helpful in coping with the panic attack itself.

The therapist must be careful that relaxation techniques (and other coping techniques as well) are used as a tool for coping with anxiety rather than being used as a weapon to fight off anxiety. Table 5.12 shows the difference between the proper and improper applications of relaxation. Even if the therapist has been careful to explain the concept of acceptance in great detail, clients often still hope that they will find a magic technique that will make the anxiety go away forever. If the client is hoping that relaxation will be an automatic cure, or tries to use relaxation to fight the anxiety, the technique can backfire and actually make the anxiety worse in the long run. Although relaxation can be useful to increase self-efficacy and lower the baseline level of anxiety, it is not essential to the treatment of anxiety disorders. Accepting the feelings of anxiety is a more important element to the treatment of anxiety than is relaxation. Therefore, if the client persists in trying to use relaxation as a weapon to fight anxiety, rather than as a tool to facilitate the acceptance of anxiety, it should not be used in the treatment.

Another physiologic intervention that has received much attention in recent years is the use of medication, especially for reducing or eliminating panic attacks. The use of medication is often compatible with Cognitive Therapy. In fact, there is some research which indicates that medications may facilitate the process of exposure by helping the client be more willing to approach anxiety-provoking situations (summarized in Barlow & Waddell, 1985). It has sometimes been assumed that if cognitive behavioral therapy is helpful and medications are helpful, then the combination of the two must be even more effective. However, this has not yet been clearly demonstrated empirically and may turn out to be an oversimplification. In fact, there are some studies that indicate that adding medication to Cognitive Therapy can have a deleterious effect, especially on the long-term maintenance of positive outcomes achieved in Cognitive Therapy (i.e., Otto, Pollack & Sabatino, 1996). The relationship between Cognitive Therapy and medication is complex and needs further study.

Medication can be quite useful if the client is in such distress at the beginning of therapy that he or she cannot concentrate enough to understand the basic principles of Cognitive Therapy. It also can be useful in reducing the intensity of anxiety so that the client is more able to cope with their anxiety and more willing to face their fears. However, because the relapse rates for medication treatment alone are alarmingly high and since many anti-anxiety medications are potentially addicting, the use of medication alone is not likely to be sufficient treatment for any of the anxiety disorders. In addition, some anxiety medications have side effects which anxious clients (who are particularly sensitive to physical reactions) may find troubling.

Just as relaxation can interfere with Cognitive Therapy if it is used as a weapon to fight anxiety, medications can also interfere with Cognitive Therapy, particularly if the client relies on medication as a means of escaping or avoiding anxiety (Westra & Stewart, 1998; Westra, Stewart & Conrad, 2002). For this reason, it is not recommended to use anti-anxiety medications on an "as needed" basis (PRN). The idea of waiting until one get too anxious and then taking a medicine in a desperate attempt to feel better is counter to the idea of accepting the feelings of anxiety and coping with them. Whereas further research is needed, it is likely that medications that are used on a regular schedule, rather than being taken in response to an increase in anxiety are more likely to be compatible with Cognitive Therapy. It is also important to explore the client's cognitions regarding medication. Clients who attribute all of their improvement to the medication may be less motivated to do the work involved in Cognitive Therapy. They will therefore find it especially difficult to maintain their gains once they are taken off the medication.

When medication is used in conjunction with Cognitive Therapy, it is important either for the client accept the idea of staying on the medication indefinitely or for the medication to gradually be withdrawn while the client is still in Cognitive Therapy. Otherwise, there is a significant risk that the client will have a short-term increase in their anxiety when medication is withdrawn, will revert to avoidance of previously feared situations, and will gradually relapse. If the client is still in Cognitive Therapy at the time when the medication is discontinued, the therapist can help the client recognize the importance of tolerating the anxiety without reverting to avoidance and can address any cognitions that might otherwise contribute to relapse.

Cognitive Interventions

The process of educating the client about anxiety and learning an attitude of acceptance can be seen as the initial cognitive interventions in the treatment of anxiety disorders. In addition, while the therapist is educating the client about anxiety and teaching coping skills, he or she will be collecting data about the client's automatic thoughts and images. Learning to identify automatic thoughts is a crucial early step in Cognitive Therapy with anxiety. It is very important to understand the idiosyncratic nature of the client's cognitive misinterpretations, because even clients with patterns of anxiety that seem identical may be experiencing anxiety for very different reasons.

Identifying automatic thoughts is more difficult with anxiety than with depression. Anxious clients often are focused on their physical symptoms or stimuli associated with their fears rather than on their thoughts. In addition, the experience of

Table 5.13. Examples of Specific Links Between Sensations and Thoughts

Sensation	Thought (Interpretation)
Breathlessness	I am about to suffocate to death
Palpitations/heart racing	I am about to have a heart attack
Feeling unreal	I am going insane
Numbness in head	I'm having a stroke
Giddiness	I'm about to pass out and faint

anxiety itself interferes with concentration. Therefore, the client often is not aware of any thoughts at all, just feelings of anxiety. As discussed at the beginning of this chapter, imagery can be helpful in helping clients to pinpoint their automatic thoughts. By vividly imagining being in an anxiety-provoking situation, the client may be better able to notice the thoughts running though his or her mind. In addition, encouraging clients to report the types of pictures that run through their minds allows them to report the full range of cognitive experience.

The therapist needs to be sure to validate the client's feelings, so the client feels understood, and only then to challenge the client's interpretations. Rather than jumping to catastrophic conclusions about the physical symptoms that accompany anxiety, the client needs to develop an alternative, more benign explanation for the intense, diverse sensations he or she is experiencing. For this reason, asking clients to identify thoughts about their symptoms can be especially useful. Table 5.13 shows some examples of typical links between anxiety sensations and automatic thoughts. Charts such as these can be used to demonstrate to clients how to make sense of their symptoms without drawing inaccurate, catastrophic conclusions regarding on their symptoms.

> In the case of Mary Lou, treatment quickly moved to address her catastrophic cognitions about panic attacks. Her main fear was that she would have a panic attack and either pass out or embarrassing herself in public. She began to write Thought Records between sessions whenever she attempted to face situations she feared and at any other times when she felt particularly anxious. An example of an early TR is shown in Figure 5.2. She reported that the most helpful thing in challenging her automatic thoughts was learning to distinguish specific symptoms of anxiety and other, normal feelings of discomfort from a full panic attack. In the past, whenever she noticed that she was feeling dizzy, for example, she would immediately conclude that she was going to have a panic attack, pass out, and humiliate herself. As she became more skilled at identifying and challenging her automatic thoughts, however, she was able to "do a stress check." When she noticed a symptom, she would check to see if she could understand why she might be having that symptom by identifying recent stressors (e.g., stress from rushing around too fast, son cranky, fight with husband, expecting her period, and so on). Often, her sensations were symptoms of ordinary stress rather than being a sign of an impending panic attack. Once Mary Lou realized that a panic attack was not imminent, she could practice using coping skills to reduce the symptoms.

One useful experience that occurred coincidentally after her sixth therapy session was that Mary Lou was driving alone with her son when her car broke down far from home. Despite her previous fears regarding what would happen if she were trapped away from home, she handled the situation appropriately. Later, as she looked back on that experience, she could see that she had been realistically

Daily Record of Automatic Thoughts				
Situation Briefly describe the situation	Emotions Rate 0-100%	Automatic Thoughts Try to quote thoughts then rate your belief in each thought 1-100%	Rational Response Rate degree of belief 0-100%	Outcome re-rate emotions
Before shopping at Jacobson's	Anxious 65	I haven't been here since I had a panic attack here. What if I panic again?	There's no reason to believe I'll panic again. besides, if I get anxious, I can do relaxation and concentrate on my shopping and I'll survive.	Anxious 20
While shopping at Jacobson's	Anxious 25	I feel a bit disoriented and wobbly. Am i starting to panic?	The floor is made of plank and uneven. This may just be a natural response.	Anxious 0
At church, sitting in the middle in a crowded service	Anxious 50	My heart is pounding Without Joey here with me, I have no excuse to leave.	I'll be all right even if my heart pounds a great deal. (it didn't) If i want to leave, i can even if Joey isn't here.	Anxious 0

FIGURE 5.2. An early TR from Mary Lou.

anxious but had not panicked; and she was able to refer back to that experience throughout treatment whenever she began to confuse feelings of anxiety with panic.

Once the client has been able to pinpoint specific automatic thoughts, possibly using TRs, the methods of challenging thoughts discussed earlier in this book can be used. Clients often react as though the events they fear would be truly intolerable. It can be quite useful to help them look realistically at the likely consequences:

THERAPIST: Suppose you decided to stay even thought you felt dizzy . . . What would your concerns be?

CLIENT: Oh my God, what if I pass out?

THERAPIST: (writing it down) What if I pass out . . . . any other concerns?

CLIENT: No, I'm just afraid I'll pass out.

THERAPIST: So, "What if I pass out?" That's a good question. What would really happen if you passed out? Do you have an image of what would happen?

CLIENT: It would be terrible. Everybody would gather around. They'd have to call an ambulance. I'd never live it down.

THERAPIST: What convinces you that that's what would happen? Have you ever passed out before?

CLIENT: No, it often feels like I'm going to pass out but it's never happened.

THERAPIST: So you don't know from first-hand experience what happens if you pass out. Have you ever been around when someone else has passed out?

CLIENT: When I was in grade school a girl fainted one day.

THERAPIST: What happened that time?

CLIENT: Her friend called the teacher and everybody gathered around. She woke up in a few minutes and had to go to the nurses office. She didn't come back till the next day and was real embarrassed about it.

THERAPIST: Did anything more come of it?

CLIENT: Not that I remember.

THERAPIST: A week or two later was it a big topic of conversation? Did anything serious come of it medically? Did it make a big difference in who were her friends?

CLIENT: Not really.

THERAPIST: So it sounds as though it was embarrassing to her at the moment but it wasn't a medical emergency and didn't make a lasting difference in her life.

CLIENT: Yeah.

THERAPIST: Do you see any reasons why it would turn out differently if you were the one who passed out?

CLIENT: I guess not.

THERAPIST: What do you think of the idea that you'd never live it down? Would the people at church hold it against you?

CLIENT: No, they'd want to be helpful. It probably would be talked about for a few days but it wouldn't be a big deal.

When challenging the thoughts of anxious clients, it is important that the Socratic questions not sound rhetorical to the clients, but clearly be genuine attempts to clarify and understand the client's experience. Clients with anxiety often use distorted logic that can be challenged. This may include overgeneralization (seeing danger in more and more situations), minimization (overlooking times when things turned out fine), probability overestimation (assuming that because something bad could possibly happen, it will happen), and all or nothing thinking. The therapist can also help the client challenge his or her thoughts by providing factual information that the client does not have. This may include, for example, facts about the physical consequences of physical symptoms or statistics about the odds of being killed in an airplane crash, as well as helping the client explore sources of support and assistance in the situation.

Because it is natural for clients to lose their concentration when they become particularly anxious, it can be useful to give them a list of coping self-statements to read when they get anxious between sessions. The most useful types of self-statements are those that emphasize acceptance. Just as with relaxation training, the therapist needs to be careful that cognitive restructuring is used as a tool and not a weapon. The goal of changing thoughts is not to make the dreaded anxiety disappear, but rather to help the client to accept the symptoms and cope with them. It is important to remember that rational responses alone will not eliminate the anxiety.

In the past, one of the major cognitive techniques used for the reduction of anxiety was "diversion" or "distraction." This involves having clients learn methods of focusing their attention on some neutral aspect of the environment to stop the flow of dysfunctional thoughts. Although this can actually be quite effective at reducing anxiety in the short-run, in practice it is very difficult for clients to do this without using it to fight the anxiety. Clients are relieved when distraction makes the anxiety go away for a moment, but this generally serves only as a brief avoidance of the symptoms; clients are then even more upset when the anxiety returns. The exercise of distraction tends to feel like running away from the anxiety. Therefore, the use of distraction can be much like the use of benzodiazepines on an as needed basis: It is virtually impossible to practice true acceptance while holding on to some special technique or medicine to take to make the anxiety go away if it gets "too bad." Because one of the primary goals of Cognitive Therapy with anxiety is to de-catastrophize what actually does happen when the anxiety gets as bad as possible, methods such as distraction can easily backfire and cannot be recommended.

Because catastrophizing is one of the major cognitive distortions in anxiety disorders, decatastrophizing is one of the major cognitive interventions. Through Socratic questioning, the therapist helps the client explore what could actually happen in the situation. In the treatment of anxiety disorders, the most commonly asked question is, "What is the worst that could happen?" The therapist has the client describe in detail what he or she sees as the ultimate consequences so that the therapist and client can consider whether it would be possible to cope with the situation even if the worst were to happen.

> Keisha was a 23-year-old single, unemployed female. She presented for therapy as being uncomfortable in a wide variety of social situations, in which her heart beat "too fast," she felt shaky, had dry mouth, and felt extremely nervous. This had been a problem for her since age 17. She was a recovering alcoholic who had been sober for one year, and she had a history of Major Depression, with one long inpatient stay at age 20. When she came for Cognitive Therapy, she was avoiding restaurants, parties, eating or drinking in public, writing in public, and job interviews. Keisha came into treatment with the specific goal of being able to eat and drink comfortably in public.
>
> As she was planning to go out for coffee with some friends (including Sarah, a woman she did not know well), she was able to identify the thought, "What if I get upset and really start shaking?" She and the therapist explored the likelihood of that happening and concluded that it was possible (because it had happened before) but not very likely (because she had been quite anxious in a number of situations but had not had a severe shaking episode in a long time). The therapist then moved on to explore the worst possible scenario.

THERAPIST: Well, let's just say that you did get so upset that you did shake harder than you ever have before. What's the worst that could happen?

KEISHA: Sarah might notice and ask what's the matter with me.

THERAPIST: And if she did notice and ask you, what's the worst that could happen?

KEISHA: I could be so nervous that I couldn't even answer her!

THERAPIST: And if that did happen, what is the worst that would happen next?

KEISHA: (pause) Well, I'd be terribly embarrassed and Sarah would probably think I was weird.

THERAPIST: And what's the worst that could happen then?

KEISHA: (another pause) Well, Sarah might not want to have any more to do with me, but the other people there are my friends and probably would understand.

THERAPIST: And if that did happen?

KEISHA: I'd feel embarrassed, but I do have plenty of good friends, so I'd live without Sarah as a friend. Besides, if she's that narrow-minded, who needs her anyway?

In addition to challenging and modifying the verbal automatic thoughts, clients may need to learn how to modify images, because images often have a strong effect on their anxiety. One client learned to stop cringing in the face of her anxiety by imagining her anxiety as a blue box and herself as a green box. As she imagined herself developing more self-efficacy, she imagined her own green box getting larger and larger, whereas the blue anxiety box became smaller and smaller. Clients with OCD often find it helpful to imagine their obsessions as entities separate from themselves (such as small imps) and to use imagery to imagine talking back to the imps, which they visualize as annoying, but not dangerous. Other techniques that can be helpful in modifying imagery include using time projection (imagining the situation 6 months, a year, or several years from the present), developing a positive image to substitute for the dysfunctional one, and using imagery to practice coping skills.

> As Keisha's thoughts in the above social situation were discussed further, she was able to describe in detail an image she had of looking like one of the schizophrenic clients she had seen when she was in a psychiatric hospital. The therapist was then able to use several techniques to begin to challenge that image. Keisha was asked to practice acting very anxious in front of a mirror, and she was able to see the difference between looking anxious and looking "crazy". She was also asked to re-imagine that picture of herself, but this time to give the image a different ending. This time, she imagined herself using her coping skills and ending up looking and feeling much more relaxed. She and her therapist also worked on decatastrophizing her "schizophrenia" image, exploring what would happen in the unlikely event that she did end up looking that "crazy" and she came to a similar conclusion: Sarah might not want anything to do with her, she might even make some disparaging remarks, but that would have little lasting effect on Keisha's life. Challenging that image also helped to identify another one of Keisha's fears: that if she became extremely anxious, she would, in fact, go crazy. This fear could then be challenged as well.

Once the client has learned to successfully challenge his or her automatic thoughts and is actively confronting feared situations, the focus of treatment shifts to the underlying assumptions, which predispose that person to anxiety. After having collected several weeks of automatic thoughts in a variety of situations, basic themes can generally be identified. In addition, the "downward arrow" technique (discussed in Chapter 3) can be used to pinpoint the specific underlying assumptions that seem most prominent for that client. Even though many anxious clients may share similar underlying assumptions, it is important not to assume that a given client holds a particular belief. It is important to identify the client's central idiosyncratic assumptions and to specify these assumptions in the client's own words, so that challenging the assumptions will have maximal impact.

Another way to challenge dysfunctional beliefs is to examine the advantages and disadvantages of maintaining those beliefs. It is particularly useful to examine the price the client pays for holding the beliefs that one should worry about anything that could go wrong, that one should anticipate the worst that could happen, that one should avoid anxiety, and that one is helpless in the face of worry. Once the client can see that there is a choice regarding whether to continue to pay that price, it can be useful to write out a new, more adaptive underlying assumption. For example, a socially anxious client may decide that he no longer wants to maintain the belief that it is essential to be loved and approved of by everyone at all times. He could write a new belief such as, "It feels good to be loved and approved of, but it's even more important that I approve of what I'm doing". Then, without assuming that the client can change his or her belief immediately, the therapist can help the client outline how he or she would behave differently if he or she did endorse the new belief. Once the changes are elaborated sufficiently, the client could practice acting for one week as if he or she believed the new belief (Fixed-Role Therapy, Chapter 3) and observe the consequences.

> As treatment went on, it became clear that Mary Lou strongly held the belief that being the minister's wife and a pillar of the community meant she should be perfect at whatever she did. This included not having any strong negative emotions. The prohibition against strong emotions included not only anxiety, but also anger and sadness as well. She had already begun to see how fighting anxiety only made it worse and how accepting it worked much better. This was used as evidence that accepting strong emotions in general might be a more useful strategy than prohibiting them. She realized that she tended to hold her feelings in and pout when she was angry with her husband. This was not very useful because he was so busy he generally did not notice. Instead, she decided to accept her anger and work on assertive ways of expressing it. While working on assertion, she was able to pinpoint another underlying assumption: She felt she needed approval from everyone and that other people's reactions were extremely important. Assertion training served as a continuing, and powerful, challenge to that assumption.
>
> Later in Mary Lou's treatment, she wanted to discontinue her medication, so it was necessary to address attributions about her medications and gradually discontinue the medication (with the full cooperation of her physician). Because she was concerned that all her improvement might be due to the medication, she and her therapist conducted a behavioral experiment, having her redo all her hierarchy items once she was off medication. She also did Thought Records whenever she felt concerned about being medication-free. Except for some initial anxiety when she first went off the medication, she was able to go through her hierarchy very quickly and successfully without medication.

Behavioral Interventions

Exposure techniques are an essential component of Cognitive Therapy with anxiety disorders. Purely verbal interventions have only a limited effect on problems involving significant anxiety. For treatment to be effective, the client must repeatedly confront the situation he or she fears, tolerate the anxiety, and cope effectively with both the situation and the anxiety (see Table 5.14). This exposure can be gradual, following a graded hierarchy, or massed, as in flooding, but it is an essential component of treatment. Although cognitive therapists do exposure both through imagery in the office and through *in vivo* assignments, the rationale for the use of these assignments is different from that presented by the strict behaviorists using similar techniques. These homework assignments are not simply used to "decondition" the connection between the stimulus and anxiety, but, rather, as a powerful way of challenging the client's thoughts and beliefs. Exposure homework

Table 5.14. Sample Instructions for Applying Acceptance and Coping with Panic Attacks

Coping Strategies

- **Practice Slow Paced Breathing.** Gently and slowly inhale a normal amount of air through your nose. Exhale easily. And continue this slow, gentle, paced breathing with your diaphragm.
- **Relax your muscles.** Just notice where you feel tense and let the muscles relax . . . release your muscle tension.
- **Slow your thoughts.** Focus your attention on the activity at hand.
- **Practice acceptance.** Work on total and complete acceptance. Welcome the anxiety so you can practice coping with it.

Why Acceptance?

- You will strengthen and prolong the symptoms if you attempt to stop or fight them.
- Anxiety requires resistance to live. By accepting your feelings you will eventually starve the anxiety.
- Acceptance allows you to rise above a situation . . . and adopt a new perspective.
- When you practice acceptance, the feelings will peak and pass; accept the feelings and the fear will break and sweep past you.
- If you successfully practice acceptance, you will eliminate the "second fear," and your body will release less adrenaline.

Coping Self-Statements

I'll just let the feelings peak and pass. No need to fight them. Fighting only strengthens anxiety. Instead I'll go *with* the feelings, without resistance.

I'll trust my body. Just let go. My body and mind will take care of me.

I feel my fear and I accept that. I won't run away from the fear. I'll look at it and see it as no more than a physical feeling.

My anxiety is harmless. I won't be bluffed by physical feelings. I'll practice acceptance.

First fear always comes in a wave and it will die down. I'll avoid stoking it with second fear. *This is an opportunity to practice dealing with the fear of fear.*

I'll practice rational thinking.

I will practice, practice, practice acceptance until anxiety means so little—seems to unimportant—that it eventually turns itself off before it even starts.

What other coping self-statements can help you deal with this episode?

(1) _____

(2) _____

(3) _____

assignments constitute behavioral experiments for the client to use to ascertain experientially the difference between his or her catastrophic expectations and the events as they actually occur.

> One early part of Mary Lou's treatment involved reversing avoidance using graded exposure. She developed a hierarchy of anxiety-provoking situations, ranging from driving one block away from home alone (anxiety rating of 5) to driving alone and being caught in rush hour traffic (100). She began practicing doing at least one of the lower level hierarchy items each day. She was very eager to get better and worked hard at her hierarchy items, so she was able to drive alone to her therapy sessions by the third session and was very proud of herself. This experience was then used to challenge her belief that, "If I drive alone, I'll panic and crash."

The distinction between using behavioral experiments to test cognitions and using desensitization to decondition anxiety is more than a semantic one. It has definite implications for treatment. In classic systematic desensitization, the goal is to break any possible connection between the stimulus and anxiety. It is therefore crucial to proceed through the hierarchy slowly and systematically, making sure that the client does not at any point experience high levels of anxiety. In the cognitive approach to graded exposure, however, it is not considered crucial to protect the client from any anxiety. In fact, with agoraphobics, the belief that they cannot tolerate anxiety must be challenged, so it is important that clients do experience anxiety and even panic attacks during the course of treatment to learn that they can indeed tolerate and cope with them.

The therapist needs to be careful that the client is being exposed to the aspect of the situation which he or she fears the most. With Specific Phobia, this is usually straightforward: If the person is afraid of elevators, he or she needs exposure to riding elevators. With some of the other anxiety disorders, however, it becomes more complicated. With Panic Disorder, for example, exposure to the places the client is avoiding is necessary but not sufficient. Because clients with Panic Disorder are primarily afraid of panic attacks, they also need to be exposed to the experience of having panic attacks. Similarly, because clients with Social Phobia are afraid of embarrassment, they need to be exposed to embarrassment; and because clients with PTSD are afraid of their flashbacks, they need to be exposed to the memories and flashbacks.

Before attempting any behavioral experiments, it is useful to go through a process of cognitive review in the office. Using imagery or verbal discussion to plan the behavioral experiment step by step can begin to desensitize the client to the situation, but it can also be helpful in identifying the automatic thoughts that are the most likely to occur in the actual situation. Once these have been identified, the therapist and the client can work together to develop an active coping plan and practice ways that the client can challenge the thoughts as they occur. It is particularly useful to attempt to identify and address all of the client's major fears about the particular situation before attempting a behavioral experiment to improve the chances that the client will prove willing to follow through with it. If the client changes his or her mind about doing exposure at the last minute, it is likely that this indicates that an important fear has not been addressed sufficiently.

The therapist needs to be careful that the exposure serves the true purpose of the Cognitive Therapy and is not just a repeat of other, useless attempts the client may have made to just "force myself to do it". Careful study of the General Guidelines for Exposure (Table 5.15) suggests specific areas to watch for when preparing for an exposure exercise.

In planning an exposure, the therapist needs to decide whether to do the exposure *in vivo* (in real life) with the client or as a self-directed exposure done by the client as a homework assignment. Because people do not process information as well when anxious, they often retain only part of the instructions and often miss the crucial part about staying in the situation until the anxiety peaks and passes. If the therapist does an *in vivo* exposure with the client first, then he or she is present to make sure that the client remembers the instructions. The therapist can also encourage the client to follow through, and to address the cognitions as they arise. The client can then follow-up with self-directed exposure on a regular basis

Table 5.15. General Guidelines for Exposure

It is more useful to...	Rather than...
Think of exposure as "practice" to enhance coping skills and acceptance, and reduce sense of helplessness.	Look at it as a test in which there's something at stake (one's self-worth or whether or not one will get anxious).
Let anxiety peak and pass.	Fight the anxiety.
Pace breathing, relax muscles, and engage in rational self-talk.	Hang on to tension and try to suppress anxiety.
Experience anxiety.	Experience no anxiety.
Let the "worst" occur.	Try at all costs to prevent anticipated events from occurring.
Focus on rating beliefs (e.g., "I'll faint"; "I'll make a fool of myself.")	Emphasize rating of anxiety.
Focus on behavioral performance and competence.	Focus on whether or not symptoms are experienced.
Actively engage oneself in the exposure.	Distract self from the experience.
Stay in the anxiety-provoking situation until reasonably comfortable.	Leave while in a state of high anxiety.
Engage in prolonged, repeated exposures.	Engage in brief, single exposures.
Repeat successes numerous times.	Expose oneself to a situation just a few times.
Welcome anxiety should it occur.	Avoid anxiety at all costs.
Systematically withdraw safety signals.	Keep using safety signals.
Intentionally produce sensations associated with anxiety.	Try to avoid unpleasant sensations.

as homework. It is not always practical for the therapist to accompany the client on *in vivo* exposures, however. Fortunately, self-directed exposures conducted by the client on his or her own often work well.

Many of the behavioral experiments used to test automatic thoughts will also serve as tests of some of the client's underlying assumptions, but it cannot be assumed that the client will draw those connections on his or her own. It is necessary to repeatedly restate the underlying assumption and discuss explicitly how a given behavioral experiment could be used as a challenge to that assumption. For example, an agoraphobic client may be practicing hierarchy items that involve being alone, but may not spontaneously draw the connection that each successfully completed hierarchy item is further evidence to challenge the belief that he or she is incapable of functioning independently in the world.

In addition to consistently pointing out the steps the client is already taking to challenge his or her underlying assumptions, specific new behavioral assignments can be set up to directly test out these beliefs. For example, if a client has the belief that he or she must always be competent in all respects, an experiment could be set up where he or she deliberately does a task imperfectly and observes the consequences. If the individual believes that total control over emotions is necessary at all times, he or she could practice being out of control (either by having a panic attack or allowing him or herself to have other strong emotions). The person who believes that it is necessary to get approval from everyone could deliberately do something that will clearly be disapproved of by someone else to test out that assumption.

Relapse Prevention

The final stage in therapy is work on relapse prevention. In addition to the usual process of identifying high-risk situations and planning how to handle them if they arise, it is important for clients recovering from anxiety disorders to understand the risks inherent in avoidance. The tendency to avoid situations that evoke anxiety is a very natural one; in fact, the client can expect that following treatment, if he or she goes without confronting a previously feared situation for some time, anxiety will return. This is not a sign of relapse. All the client needs to do is to confront the situation again and the anxiety will fade quickly.

> As Mary Lou and her therapist reviewed her goals and realized that she had made significant headway toward them, they decided to increase the time between sessions so that she could build up her confidence that she could continue her progress on her own. In the final sessions, treatment focused on getting some time away from her son, increasing her involvement in activities she found rewarding without her husband, and scheduling enjoyable activities alone with her husband to improve their marriage. The therapy was terminated by mutual agreement after a total of 20 sessions; contact two years later showed that she had maintained her progress and continued to improve further. During this time, she had dealt with a number of serious stressors including the birth of a second child and her husband's having a serious illness. She had found it difficult to resume her normal activities after long periods at home with a new baby and sick husband, but she had managed to get through it all without a recurrence of the agoraphobia.

Adapting Therapy for Specific Anxiety Disorders

Although the same basic components are used in the Cognitive Therapy of all the anxiety disorders, there are specific considerations to be given depending on the anxiety disorder being treated.

Specific Phobia

There appears to be general agreement among researchers and clinicians that exposure is the essential component to the treatment of Specific Phobia. This appears to be the one anxiety disorder for which there is no particular advantage to one type of exposure over another: Specific Phobias can be treated equally effectively using either gradual exposure or flooding. This can often be left to the client's choice, because both are effective. For gradual exposure, relaxation training can be useful but is not required.

Gradual exposure has the advantage of not requiring the client to experience high levels of anxiety, but it can take a long period of repeated and often monotonous work. If the person has a medical condition for which intense anxiety presents an unacceptable risk, flooding may not be an option. On the other hand, if there is time pressure, or if the client is unlikely to persistently practice exposure, flooding may be the better choice.

The primary role of cognitive procedures in the treatment of Specific Phobia is in pinpointing cognitions so that the exposure can be designed to precisely target the aspects of the object or situation that lead to the most fear. A full understanding of the cognitions involved in the fear can also be helpful in refining a graded hierarchy or in maximizing the effectiveness of a flooding procedure.

There has been much excitement about the use of virtual reality technology as a means of exposure in the treatment of Specific Phobias. In this approach, computer-generated representations of anxiety-provoking situations are viewed through a head-mounted display. Outcome studies by Rothbaum and her colleagues (Rothbaum & Hodges, 1999; Rothbaum et al., 1995) have shown that virtual reality can be used as an effective method of exposure in the treatment of various specific phobias. These procedures, however, have not yet been demonstrated to be more effective than either *in vivo* exposure or exposure using imagery. Thus far, virtual reality appears to be a more expensive way to accomplish the same changes as can be accomplished through conventional cognitive–behavioral therapy. Because *in vivo* exposure and imaginal exposure are both effective in treating Specific Phobia, clinicians may want to wait until there is evidence of clinical advantages to virtual reality technology before making the significant financial investment involved in using these procedures.

Cognitive–behavioral treatment for specific phobias can be conducted in short-term, focused group sessions. Specific Phobias often treated in groups include fear of flying and fear of highway driving. Group treatment is efficient and can add to the cost-effectiveness of treatment; however, there does not seem to be any clear clinical advantage to conducting Cognitive Therapy for Specific Phobia in a group format.

Panic Disorder

Because the defining feature of Panic Disorder is the fear of panic attacks, it is ultimately necessary for the client to practice experiencing and accepting full-fledged panic attacks as part of the exposure process. Claire Weekes (1969), in her pioneering work on Panic Disorder, presented a simple yet very effective model for acceptance of the feelings of anxiety, especially for Panic Disorder. Clients find her model to be extremely helpful due to its simplicity and the eloquent way that her writings capture the inner experience of panic. Simply stated, Weekes' model includes: 1. Facing; 2. Accepting; 3. Floating; 4. Letting time pass.

> To address Mary Lou's fear of fear, it was necessary to have her experience panic attacks and deal with them rather than always working to keep her anxiety down. She was initially resistant to the idea of deliberately inducing panic, because she had been able to cope well and had not been having spontaneous panic attacks. Unfortunately, there was no panic disorder group available for her to join so that she could see how useful this type of exposure had been to other clients. She decided to go ahead and try exposure to panic attacks after she spontaneously did have another panic attack, and realized that she could not count on never panicking again no matter how skilled she was at coping. Because her main fear was of getting dizzy and fainting, she chose to go into a situation that was high on her hierarchy (going to a restaurant where she had a particularly bad panic attack two years before) and deliberately trying to get dizzy and faint. She did get quite anxious, but as she tried to make it worse, she found that the symptoms decreased and that she was even able to enjoy her lunch. Encouraged by the success of her attempt at accepting the panic, she tried panic exposure in a variety of situations, especially when she felt that a panic attack was coming on.

One of the most useful procedures for the treatment of Panic Disorder has been interoceptive exposure, or exposure to internal cues associated with panic (Barlow & Craske, 2000). Because many clients are afraid of the sensations of anxiety or panic, interoceptive exposure deliberately and systematically exposes the client to the specific symptoms of his or her anxiety. Not only does this type of exposure challenge the client's most basic fears, it often is convenient to do in the office and can be practiced daily at home. The best target for interoceptive exposure is the symptom that is the most frightening to the client. Clients can usually identify the symptom they fear the most. If this is not clear, however, the therapist can use Barlow's symptom assessment approach in which a series of symptoms are induced and rated (Barlow & Craske, 2000, p. 118–123). It is important to remember that the goal of this procedure is to discover which symptoms frighten the client the most, not which ones they experience most strongly. If the symptoms on this assessment form do not happen to capture the particular symptom that is most upsetting to a client, the therapist may need to be creative in thinking of other ways of inducing the symptom. For example, clients frightened by feelings of unreality may find it helpful to stand with their face very close to a mirror and stare into their own eyes intensely for as long as possible. Another example is the client who could only describe the feeling of suffocation she found most frightening as being similar to when her grandmother had her inhale steam from a hot bowl of water with a towel covering her head to treat congestion from a cold. This, then, was the method necessary to induce those feelings of suffocation in her interoceptive exposure.

Behavioral experiments, such as exposure, are some of the most powerful ways to challenge cognitions. First, interoceptive exposure can be used to demonstrate the true cause of symptoms. For example, if voluntary hyperventilation in the office can serve to replicate many of the symptoms of a panic attack, clients can see firsthand how something as simple as rapid, shallow breathing can actually be the cause of their symptoms. Second, exposure can be used to test the client's catastrophic predictions about the consequences of the symptoms. If a client practices spinning around until he or she gets extremely dizzy, but still does not faint, this can be seen as convincing evidence that dizziness does not automatically lead to fainting.

Group treatment can be particularly useful with Panic Disorder. The concept of accepting panic attacks is difficult for many clients to grasp, and clients often complain that therapists simply do not understand how difficult this can be. Watching other group members do exposure to panic attacks can inspire clients to try what might have otherwise seemed impossible or foolhardy to attempt.

There are too many outcome studies of cognitive behavioral treatment of Panic Disorder to summarize here, but excellent reviews are available (for example, Antony & Swinson, 2000). Several controlled studies by Barlow's group at the State University of New York at Albany have found approximately 85% of clients were panic-free by the end of the 12-session treatment program. These gains were maintained up to two years later, which is the longest follow-up period used. In general, outcome studies have found cognitive behavioral treatments to be as effective as medication and, in some cases, to show some advantages in terms of durability of results (Barlow, Gorman, Shear, & Woods, 2000).

Cognitive behavioral treatments for Panic Disorder tend to include *in vivo* exposure to the feared situation, interoceptive exposure to the upsetting symptoms of panic, cognitive restructuring, and relaxation training. These combination treatments have been found to be quite effective. Attempts to isolate the various components of treatments have produced less consistent results, with some studies showing few differences among treatment strategies and other studies showing significant differences in the efficacy of particular strategies. Relaxation training alone does not appear to be a promising treatment for Panic Disorder, and several studies have found that Cognitive Therapy is more effective than relaxation training, especially for reducing the frequency of panic attacks and agoraphobic fear. Including spouses in the treatment for Panic Disorder can be helpful; but, here again, studies have been inconsistent, with some studies showing more improvement when the spouse was included in the treatment and other studies failing to show these differences.

Social Phobia

With Social Phobia, the defining fear is of being negatively evaluated by others. Individuals with this disorder are afraid that they will be embarrassed or humiliated in public. Social Phobia can be very specific (such as a fear of eating or drinking in public) or generalized to include many social interactions. Clients may have social skills deficits or they may have appropriate social skills but be too anxious to apply them in the situations they find stressful. Consider the following examples:

> Emily was a 38-year-old married business manager with two school-aged children. She presented for therapy with a specific fear of public speaking, which dated from college (she had successfully avoided public speaking before that). She had one bad experience with public speaking in college where her voice shook the entire time, and another public speaking experience in which she lost her train of thought. She had taken Inderol with some success initially, but then her fear started to generalize to the point that it had even begun to occur in stressful one-on-one situations. When she became anxious, her heart started pounding, her mouth became dry, her head started buzzing, she felt as if she had to force words to come out, her mind went blank, her whole body started shaking, and she felt as if she could not stand it. Thus, Emily had a fairly specific Social Phobia that was beginning to generalize.
>
> Jose was a 30-year-old, married man in intensive training to become an X-ray technician. He had a long-standing and very specific Social Phobia regarding being unable to urinate in public restrooms. He had simply avoided public restrooms in the past or waited until he was alone in the bathroom. However, this was no longer an option because his training required him to be present in the X-ray suite for an entire eight-hour shift and, as a result, he only had access to the public restroom. He was afraid that he would become so anxious that he would be unable to pee and that others would notice. Before going in to work each day, he anticipated having a problem, and consequently became so anxious that he was, in fact, unable to urinate.
>
> Keisha, discussed earlier in this chapter, had a more generalized Social Phobia. Her concerns about whether people would notice her being anxious in public had led to a pervasive avoidance of various social situations, a pattern which was increasingly limiting both her social and work life.

If the individual has significant social skills deficits, training in social skills may be needed before exposure would be recommended (i.e., Liberman, De Risis, &

Mueser, 1989). Role-playing can be useful in the assessment of Social Phobia as well as in social skills training. However, because the defining fear in Social Phobia is that of embarrassment, it is not sufficient for the client to improve his or her social skills and become more adept in social situations. In addition, it is crucial that the client eventually practice exposure to, and acceptance of, the experience of being embarrassed. This can be done gradually, using an embarrassment hierarchy with items ranging from dropping keys or change in a store to making mistakes in a public speaking situation. Exposure could also be done through flooding, where the client practices an extreme, highly anxiety-provoking embarrassment situation. Ellis recommends several challenging embarrassment exposure exercises, which he calls "shame-attack" exercises (Ellis & Becker, 1982; Grieger & Boyd, 1980). These include activities such as loudly announcing each floor in a crowded elevator or leading a banana down the street on a leash.

In the treatment of Social Phobia, "decentering" is the process of having the client challenge the basic belief that she or he is the focal point of all events. This can be a useful cognitive intervention. The client is asked to collect concrete evidence to determine how often he or she actually is the focus of attention and which behaviors are being noticed by others. Thus, for example, a client may be asked to go to a mall or restaurant and count how many people actually are watching him or her sitting there. This exercise in itself requires a shift in focus because the person is required to adopt the perspective of other people.

There have been many outcome studies of cognitive behavioral therapy of Social Phobia conducted by Heimberg and his colleagues (Heimberg, Liebowitz, Hope & Schneier, 1995; Hope & Heimberg, 1993). These studies are usually conducted in groups of 5–7 participants, 2 hours per session, meeting weekly for 12 weeks. They demonstrate high efficacy for *in vivo* exposure in the treatment of Social Phobia. Some studies also show that "enriched" exposure (with cognitive restructuring) was superior to the use of exposure alone. Group therapy can be particularly useful with this population, because the group provides a natural arena for practicing social skills and for practicing exposure. After 12 weeks of treatment, cognitive behavioral therapy produced response rates equivalent to that produced by medication (MAO-inhibitors), but after 6 months of maintenance treatment and 6 months of follow-up, there were more relapses among medication subjects than among CBT subjects, especially among subjects with generalized Social Phobia. Here, as with Panic Disorder, there are early indications that cognitive behavioral approaches may have advantages over the use of medications, especially in terms of relapse prevention.

Obsessive–Compulsive Disorder

Although many of the anxiety disorders cause tremendous suffering and may seem overwhelming to the individual, OCD is arguably among the more complex and difficult to treat. The research literature regarding OCD indicates that it has genetic, neurological, chemical, infectious, cognitive, and behavioral components. In fact, there is some controversy as to whether OCD is better categorized as an anxiety disorder or as a neurological disorder. However, whatever the cause of OCD,

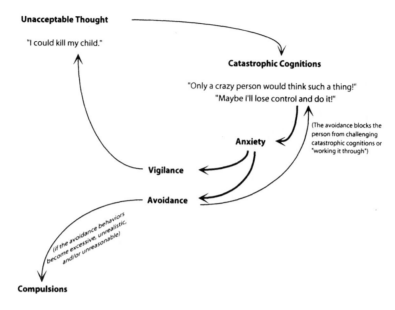

Figure 5.3. Cognitive Model of Obsession.

effective treatment can be achieved through behavioral and cognitive strategies, often in combination with medication.

The cognitive conceptualization of OCD (see Figure 5.3) starts with the proposition that obsessional thinking has its origins in normal intrusive cognitions. Intrusive cognitions are ideas, thoughts, images, or impulses that intrude in the sense that they interrupt the person's current stream of consciousness and the person also finds them upsetting, unacceptable, or otherwise unpleasant. The difference between normal intrusive cognitions and obsessional intrusive cognitions lies not in the occurrence or even the uncontrollability of the intrusions themselves, but in the interpretation made by the individuals about the occurrence or content of the intrusions. The client may happen to notice an unacceptable thought when under stress or angry, then become very frightened of the thought and become convinced that he or she is going crazy and will lose control and act on the thoughts. When one is frightened of something, it is only natural to focus increased attention on it. For example, when you spot a bear in the woods, you are likely to focus on the bear and not on the flowers and trees as long as you see the bear as a threat. Similarly, the client who is frightened by unacceptable thoughts is likely to focus more attention on them and hence think such thoughts more frequently. Some clients (often referred to as "pure obsessionals") are tormented by their thoughts but do not develop rituals to reduce the anxiety. Other individuals, try to avoid the thoughts by avoiding situations that elicit the thoughts, by trying to stop the thoughts, and/or by doing something to compensate for them through ritualistic behaviors.

In keeping with the attitude of acceptance discussed earlier, the goal of treatment for OCD is not to eliminate intrusive thoughts, images, or impulses. Instead, the goal is for the client to be able to accept and cope with them effectively and not make them worse than necessary by struggling to fight them. The most commonly discussed and researched behavioral treatment for Obsessive–Compulsive Disorder is exposure and response prevention. This can be seen in cognitive terms as the behavioral experiment of refraining from the obsessive–compulsive behavior as a test of whether or not the feared consequences occur. Treatment generally involves repeated, prolonged confrontation with the situations that cause anxiety. In addition, the client must refrain from performing any of the rituals that have served in the past to reduce the anxiety. Exposure can be conducted in reality (*in vivo* exposure) or in imagery. It can be conducted gradually or all at once (flooding).

This intervention approach is appropriate and useful for both cognitive as well as behavioral rituals that are anxiety reducing in nature. When the individual is using rituals to avoid anxiety, preventing the rituals serves to help the client confront his or her fears. For example, if a compulsive hand-washer is prevented from washing his or her hands even though he or she feels contaminated, the anxiety will initially increase substantially, then peak, and begin to subside with no catastrophe following. In this manner, the client has challenged his or her idea that the germs and feelings of contamination are dangerous and that the only way to make these feelings go away is to repeatedly wash his or her hands. The client thus discovers that the hand washing is unnecessary and that his or her anxiety can be reduced more effectively by confronting the fears.

Numerous studies of exposure and response prevention have found that approximately 75% of clients have responded to treatment at follow-up (Foa & Kozak, 1996). For a detailed discussion of how to implement these procedures, see Steketee and Foa (1985).

Although the initial exposure and response prevention session may be done in the presence of the therapist, a single exposure session is not sufficient to constitute the entire treatment. The procedure needs to be repeated regularly between sessions as homework and prevention of the subtler rituals, as well as the more obvious ones, needs to be incorporated into the treatment. Clients may also need to be taught basic rules for "normal" behavior, because they may not have a clear idea what is normal in terms of hand washing or checking. Relapse prevention is especially important with OCD, because stressful situations often lead to anxiety and urges to ritualize in the future. Acceptance of OCD as a chronic disease that can be managed effectively is crucial. It may be helpful to include some sessions with significant others present so that they can also understand this illness and learn how to be helpful and not inadvertently enable obsessive–compulsive behavior.

Despite the effectiveness of exposure and response prevention with compulsions that are anxiety reducing in nature, these same methods would not be appropriate for obsessions that are anxiety-evoking (such as, "I could hurt my baby!"). For the treatment of anxiety-evoking obsessions, flooding with feared cognitions is necessary. These thoughts are maintained by the individual's fears and horror at the thoughts, and attempts at preventing these thoughts through procedures such as thought-stopping could serve to reinforce the view that the thoughts are indeed terrible and such procedures could inadvertently make the disorder worse. If the client is induced repeatedly to confront the feared thoughts, images, or impulses and sufficient time is allowed for his or her anxiety to come to a peak and then subside, he or she discovers that they are unpleasant but not dangerous. This helps to break the cycle that perpetuates them.

When obsessions are not accompanied by compulsions, the exposure focuses less on overt response prevention and more on exposure to the obsessional thoughts. This can be implemented by scheduling a daily "obsession time," when the client deliberately focuses on the obsessive thoughts without any attempt at avoidance. The therapist will need to be vigilant for any mental rituals, which could defeat the value of the exposure. Making a loop tape of the obsessions that plays over and over again without stopping can be useful. Another strategy is to teach the client to make the conscious choice to obsess, but to change the way in which he or she obsesses. First, the client needs to recognize that he or she has started to obsess, but instead of fighting the obsession, the client practices acceptance rather than avoidance. The client can learn to apply a variety of strategies to change the process of the obsessing: write the obsession down, sing it, change the image, and so on. Once the scheduled obsession time is ended, clients are taught to temporarily put the obsessions away until the scheduled time the next day, becoming more mindful of their current life in the meantime. For clients to successfully postpone their obsessions until the next scheduled obsession time, it is necessary to teach them to be mindfully present in the reality of the moment.

Cognitive interventions can also be used to address such issues as faulty estimation of danger or the exaggerated sense of personal responsibility often seen in OCD clients. Other useful foci for intervention include their perfectionistic attempts to control thoughts and actions, their closely related need for certainty, their unwillingness to tolerate ambiguity, their belief that all questions must have an all-or-nothing answer, and their belief that there is one 'right' choice in a situation. Three of the beliefs that are useful to challenge with OCD clients are:

1. I have to avoid the distressing situation or else my intense distress will continue forever;
2. The rituals will keep me (or others) safe;
3. I must ritualize to keep myself from going crazy.

Studies by Foa and her colleagues (Foa, Steketee, Grayson, Turner, & Latimer, 1984; Foa, Steketee, & Milby, 1980; Steketee, Foa, & Grayson, 1982) have shown that a combination of response prevention and prolonged exposure to obsessional cues was clearly superior to either component used alone for the treatment of OCD. In recent years, Consensus Guidelines for the Treatment of Obsessive–Compulsive Disorder have been published which conclude that these methods are the treatment of choice for OCD (March, Frances, Carpenter, & Kahn, 1997). The experts prefer to begin the treatment of OCD with either cognitive behavioral therapy alone or with a combination of cognitive–behavioral therapy and medication. The likelihood that medication will be included in the recommendation varies with the severity of the OCD and the age of the client. In mild levels of OCD, cognitive behavioral therapy alone is the initial preferred choice. As severity increases, the experts are more likely to add medications to cognitive behavioral therapy or to use medication alone. In younger clients, the experts are more likely to use cognitive behavioral therapy alone.

Outcome studies regarding OCD have been reviewed by Steketee, Pigott, and Schemmel (1999). Their conclusion is that both serotonin re-uptake inhibitor (SRI) medication and exposure and response prevention are effective within six months or less. Exposure and response prevention studies have found that 90 percent of clients were at least moderately improved after treatment, and at follow-up 76 percent remained improved. SRI medication was found to be similarly effective with 65 to 80 percent of clients improving with treatment. However, follow-ups of treatment with medication are not as promising as those with behavioral therapy. Research shows that as many as 90 percent of clients relapse within four weeks of discontinuing SRI medication.

Although most of the outcome studies regarding OCD have investigated treatment protocols focusing purely on exposure and response prevention, cognitive interventions have shown some success as well. One study (van Oppen, de Haan, van Balkom, Spinohoven, Hoogduin, & van Dyck, 1995) showed that challenging negative automatic thoughts was as effective as exposure and response prevention. Another study (Freeston et al., 1997) found an 84 percent success rate when Cognitive Therapy was combined with exposure and response prevention. In actual clinical practice, most therapists combine cognitive and behavioral techniques, and in the Expert Consensus Guidelines (March, Frances, Carpenter, & Kahn, 1997), the cognitive behavioral treatment recommended includes a combination of exposure, response prevention, and cognitive restructuring. Kozak and Foa (1997) acknowledge that published descriptions of exposure procedures often fail to elucidate the cognitive elements in the procedures, and they conclude that, "there is ample justification for construing much of the exposure-based therapy as cognitive–behavioral" (p. 27).

The efficacy of this treatment approach was initially tested in intensive inpatient programs where exposure and response prevention were conducted for many hours per day, every day of the week. More recently, intensive outpatient treatment has become an alternative treatment of OCD that can make intensive, prolonged exposure and response prevention available without the expense of a full inpatient treatment program. Less research has been conducted on outpatient treatment conducted once or twice a week. However, clinical experience suggests that low-intensity outpatient treatment can be effective when clients follow through consistently on homework assignments.

Post-Traumatic Stress Disorder

Cognitive behavioral treatment for PTSD generally involves imaginal exposure to the traumatic stimuli plus *in vivo* exposure to the actual scene of the traumatic event (or the places avoided following the event), if practical. Foa and Rothbaum (1998) theorize that several mechanisms are involved in the therapeutic effects of cognitive behavioral treatment of PTSD:

1. Repeated imaginal reliving of trauma leads to habituation and the reduction of the anxiety;
2. Deliberate confrontation of the feared memories blocks the negative reinforcement related to the fear reduction following cognitive avoidance of trauma-related thoughts and feelings;

3. Reliving the trauma in a supportive setting leads to the incorporation of safety information into the trauma memory, teaching the client that remembering the trauma is not itself dangerous;

4. Focusing on the trauma for prolonged periods of time helps the client to differentiate the trauma event from daily reality, making the trauma into one specific occurrence rather than a symbol of a dangerous world in general;

5. Imaginal reliving helps change the meaning of PTSD symptoms from a sign of personal failure and weakness into a sign of mastery and courage; and

6. Prolonged exposure to the traumatic memories gives the opportunity to identify and challenge negative evaluations of the clients.

Exposure to PTSD stimuli can be done in a variety of ways, but all share the common feature of confronting the client with anxiety-provoking stimuli and persisting until the anxiety is reduced. Exposure can be done gradually, moving up an anxiety hierarchy, or it can be done through flooding (beginning with the most anxiety-provoking images). Some imaginal methods involve clients providing their own narrative by discussing the trauma in detail in the present tense for prolonged periods of time. In other forms of imaginal exposure, the therapist presents a scene to the client to imagine based on information gathered from the client prior to the exposure session. Most exposure treatments do not consist exclusively of exposure, but also include other components such as psychoeducation, relaxation training, or cognitive restructuring.

One variation of the cognitive behavioral treatment for PTSD is Resick's Cognitive Processing Therapy (Resick & Schnicke, 1992) for rape victims. In this treatment, an information-processing formulation is presented to the client and the exposure component of the treatment involves writing an account of the trauma including all the sensory details, emotions, and thoughts the client can remember. The clients are also encouraged to experience their emotions fully while writing and reading over the account. This approach was designed specifically for female sexual assault survivors, and would need modification to be used with other PTSD populations.

Eye Movement Desensitization and Reprocessing (EMDR) has been a controversial cognitive behavioral treatment approach for over a decade. Originally developed by Francine Shapiro as a treatment for PTSD, it combines "standard" cognitive behavioral interventions such as cognitive restructuring and imaginal exposure with therapist-guided eye movements (Shapiro, 1995). Many have questioned the relevance of the eye movements, although these are emphasized in Shapiro's rationale for the treatment approach. Early reports by EMDR proponents portrayed the approach as producing dramatic results, often in a single session. Unfortunately, these claims are not supported by the available evidence and Shapiro and her colleagues have retreated from making such extreme claims. A study by Devilly and Spence (1999) found that cognitive behavioral therapy was statistically and clinically more efficacious than EMDR at both posttreatment and follow-up. In a recent meta-analysis, Davidson and Parker (2001) analyzed the results of 28 published outcome studies and conclude that EMDR appears to be an effective treatment when compared to no-treatment control groups or non-specific treatments. However, EMDR was found to be no more effective than treatments that included *in vivo* exposure or that included more traditional cognitive behavioral interventions. In fact, there was a non-significant trend for EMDR to be less effective than exposure/cognitive behavioral treatment.

In a recent summary of effective treatments for PTSD, Rothbaum, Meadows, Resick and Foy (2000) concluded that exposure is the treatment modality with the strongest empirical evidence for its efficacy. There are many well-controlled studies of exposure with a wide variety of traumatized populations, and the authors recommend that some form of exposure be included in the treatment of PTSD unless otherwise indicated. Cognitive interventions have been found to be effective in reducing PTSD symptoms in some studies; but most investigators recommend using cognitive interventions in combination with exposure-based interventions. The cognitive components of a treatment that combines exposure and Cognitive Therapy can be helpful in overcoming some trauma survivor's reluctance to confront trauma reminders and in motivating them to tolerate the high anxiety and temporarily increased symptoms that can accompany exposure.

Generalized Anxiety Disorder

The first step in treating GAD is to understand the basis for the anxiety. Even when clients say that their anxiety is free-floating and constant, self-monitoring is very helpful in the early stages of treatment. Careful data collection usually reveals that specific stimuli elicit the anxiety. These stimuli may be totally cognitive, so cognitive assessment is crucial.

Ladouceur and colleagues (Ladouceur, Dugas, Freeston, Leger, Gagnon, & Thibodeau, 2000) have proposed a cognitive model of worry in GAD that includes intolerance of uncertainty, erroneous beliefs about worry, poor problem orientation, and cognitive avoidance. This model helps clients separate worries into two categories: those worries that are amenable to problem solving; and worries about situations (such as situations that do not yet exist) that are not amenable to problem solving. For some clients who are worrying about a current problem or crisis, it might be necessary to teach specific problem-solving skills. Other clients may have problem-solving skills but lack an effective problem orientation. They may see the problem as a threat to be avoided rather than a challenge to overcome or may have little confidence in their problem-solving skills. For these clients, a focus using their problem-solving skills effectively can be very useful.

For those clients who worry about situations not amenable to problem solving, cognitive restructuring methods can be used. Some of the erroneous beliefs to be challenged include the idea that worry serves a crucial purpose such as preventing negative outcomes and minimizing the negative effects if these outcomes should occur. Other beliefs that encourage worry include the ideas that worry motivates one to overcome adversity, that it prepares one for the worst, that it is the responsible thing to do, and that it helps analytical thinking. Cognitive restructuring may require decatastrophizing, working toward more accurate risk assessments, and education. It may be important to address both the likelihood of the feared event and its true seriousness should the event occur. Fear of food poisoning is a good example: with a client who worries excessively about food poisoning, the therapist will help the client to have an accurate understanding of the likelihood of food poisoning and to develop reasonable precautions to minimize the risk. In addition, the therapist will want to help the client to understand that, in the vast majority of cases, food poisoning results in a brief, unpleasant illness not in death or permanent damage.

When anxious, humans naturally experience two conflicting tendencies: a tendency to focus on the fear-related stimuli as well as a tendency to avoid stimuli that elicit anxiety (including thoughts about the feared events). Cognitive avoidance, as other phobic avoidance, may temporarily lead to a reduction of anxiety, but unfortunately leads to increased anxiety over time. Cognitive avoidance interferes with effective problem solving and is ultimately unsuccessful because the fears and worries eventually intrude anyway. In addition, cognitive avoidance may reduce fear-related mental imagery, which may interfere with the emotional processing needed to let go of the issues and move on with life. If cognitive avoidance is a prominent part of the GAD, the client can be taught to systematically expose himself or herself to the avoided cognitions by scheduling worry time, just as scheduling of obsession time is used in the treatment of OCD. Clients can be taught to focus for a set period of time on their worries, possibly using a loop-tape to expose them to their thoughts. After the worry time, clients are taught to use mindfulness skills to get back to a focus on their actual daily life.

For individuals who have a low tolerance for uncertainty, the goal of cognitive interventions is not to eliminate uncertainty for the client. On the contrary, the goal is to help them recognize that uncertainty is inevitable, to accept it, and to develop coping strategies to can use in facing upsetting, uncertain situations. Work on the other key cognitive aspects of worry can also help to increase tolerance of uncertainty. For example, helping to improve problem orientation can also serve to reduce intolerance of uncertainty. The therapist can help clients stay focused on the problem and identify all the key elements of the problem situation, without paying undue attention to minor details. Cognitive exposure can also help to reduce intolerance of uncertainty by changing the meaning given to threatening future events.

If reassurance-seeking is prominent, the therapist needs to establish a program of gradually reducing the reassurance-seeking, possibly by instituting a delay before asking for reassurance, and gradually building up to preventing reassurance-seeking entirely. In such an instance, it may be helpful to include the primary reassurance-giver in a session, so that he or she can be trained to withhold reassurance.

Instruction in coping skills, such as applied relaxation, can be useful in increasing the client's self-efficacy in coping with anxiety-provoking situations as well as the feelings of anxiety. When clients are feeling overwhelmed and stressed in general, it can also be helpful to guide them to improve their self-care in general (i.e., increasing exercise, healthy eating, sufficient sleep, assertion, doing positive activities, and so on.)

Medications are less useful with GAD than with some of the other anxiety disorders. Some clients see Benzodiazepines as the answer, yet these medications have a limited therapeutic effect and are intended for brief, temporary usage. Usage over a longer period of time can lead to problems with physical addiction, psychological dependence, sedation, or impairment in concentration or performance. There can also be a rebound of anxiety upon withdrawal from the medication.

There have been many controlled outcome studies of cognitive behavioral treatment for GAD that have included relaxation training, anxiety management, and cognitive interventions (summarized by Borkovec & Costello, 1993). These treatments have generally been found to produce greater improvement than no-treatment controls, with treatment gains maintained up to 2 years later, despite the previous duration of the illness. Ladouceur and colleagues (2000) evaluated their specific cognitive model of worry and found that their treatment was effective for treating GAD and that these treatment gains were maintained at 6- and 12-month follow-ups.

CONCLUSIONS

Although Cognitive Therapy is effective for the full range of anxiety disorders, Cognitive Therapy of anxiety appears to be somewhat more time-consuming than Cognitive Therapy of depression. Whereas for depression the treatment is often effective within 10 to 12 weeks, Cognitive Therapy for anxiety often can take between six months and one year to complete. This may be because individuals with anxiety disorders to have less access to their dysfunctional cognitions and also because avoidance behaviors can become so comfortable that they are difficult to change.

Research evidence for the efficacy of cognitive behavioral therapies for anxiety has been accumulating over the years, and several meta-analytic reviews have shown promising results (Barrios & Shigatomi, 1980; Dushe, Hurt, & Schroeder, 1983; Miller & Berman, 1983). In comparisons between behavioral and cognitive behavioral treatments, some studies show an advantage to cognitive behavioral approaches over purely behavioral treatments, other studies show the two approaches to be equivalent, and yet other studies demonstrate a superiority of purely behavioral treatments over the cognitive behavioral approaches (summarized in Michelson, 1987). Although further research is clearly needed, Michelson (referring to agoraphobics) concludes that, "A multimodal treatment approach would represent a more state-of-the-art treatment of this complex anxiety disorder by simultaneously addressing the three dimensions of the disorder (behavior, cognition, and physiology). Treatment integration of this nature is likely to result in improved outcome, synchrony, and maintenance and generalization effects" (1987, pg. 264). Cognitive Therapy can provide such a multimodal, integrated approach.

6

Substance Abuse

Substance abuse is widely recognized as a critical public health problem. Substance abuse takes a major toll on the lives of both those who abuse drugs and alcohol and those who care about them. It has serious health consequences, plays a significant role in criminal activity, and imposes substantial costs on our economy. Despite receiving considerable attention over many years, substance abuse has proved to be difficult to treat effectively. Moral exhortation, prohibition, and an expensive "War On Drugs" have not eliminated the problem. Fortunately, recent advances have the potential for helping us understand substance abuse, treat it effectively, and reduce the risk of relapse.

Substance abuse is a problem that extends far beyond the individual. Cultural, historical, and economic factors are relevant to understanding the prevalence of substance abuse in our society. Understanding the development and persistence of the problem requires the consideration of genetic, physiological, personality, and interpersonal factors. Approaches to treating individuals with substance abuse problems have been affected by cultural, political, and economic factors as well. These broad, theoretical issues are beyond the scope of this chapter. Here, we will focus on understanding and treating individuals with substance abuse problems.

ASSESSMENT

The assessment of substance abuse problems would be simple if use of drugs or alcohol automatically demonstrated the presence of a substance abuse problem. This is clearly not the case. Although roughly two third of U.S. adults drink alcoholic beverages (Institute of Medicine, 1987), most are light to moderate drinkers who have few problems as a result. About half of the alcohol consumed in this country is consumed by the 10% or so who are heavy drinkers and who encounter many problems as a result of their alcohol abuse. The clinician is faced with the problem of distinguishing between moderate substance use and substance abuse. This task is complicated by the tendency of individuals with substance abuse problems to deny the extent of their substance use and of the problems resulting from it, both to themselves and to others.

TABLE 6.1. *DSM-IV-TR* Diagnostic Criteria for Substance Abuse

---

A. A maladaptive pattern of substance use leading to clinically significant impairment or distress, as manifested by one (or more) of the following occurring within a 12-month period:
  1. Recurrent substance use resulting in a failure to fulfill major role obligations at work, school, or home (e.g., repeated absences or poor work performance related to substance use; substance-related absences, suspensions, or expulsions from school; neglect of children or household)
  2. Recurrent substance use in situations in which it is physically hazardous (e.g., driving an automobile or operating a machine when impaired by substance use)
  3. Recurrent substance-related legal problems (e.g., arrests for substance-related disorderly conduct
  4. Continued substance use despite having persistent or recurrent social or interpersonal problems caused or exacerbated by the effects of the substance (e.g., arguments with spouse about consequences of intoxication, physical fights)
B. The symptoms have never met the criteria for Substance Dependence for this class of substance

---

TABLE 6.2. *DSM-IV-TR* Diagnostic Criteria for Substance Dependence

---

A maladaptive pattern of substance use, leading to clinically significant impairment or distress, as manifested by three (or more) of the following, occurring at any time in the same 12-month period:

1. Tolerance, as defined by either of the following:
  (a) A need for markedly increased amounts of the substance to achieve intoxication or desired effect
  (b) Markedly diminished effect with continued use of the same amount of the substance
2. Withdrawal as manifested by either of the following:
  (a) The characteristic withdrawal syndrome for the substance
  (b) The same (or a closely related) substance is taken to relieve or avoid withdrawal symptoms
3. The substance is often taken in larger amounts or over a longer period than was intended
4. There is a persistent desire or unsuccessful efforts to cut down or control substance use
5. A great deal of time is spent in activities necessary for obtaining the substance (e.g., visiting multiple doctors or driving long distances), using the substance (e.g., chain smoking), or recovering from its effects
6. Important social, occupational, or recreational activities are given up or reduced because of substance use
7. The substance use is continued despite knowledge of having a persistent or recurrent physical or psychological problem that is likely to have been caused or exacerbated by the substance (e.g., current cocaine use despite recognition of cocaine-induced depression, or continued drinking despite recognition that an ulcer was made worse by alcohol consumption).

Fortunately, *DSM-IV-TR* (2000) provides clear diagnostic criteria for Substance Abuse and Substance Dependence (see Tables 6.1 and 6.2). The essential feature of Substance Abuse is a persistent pattern of use despite recurrent adverse consequences. Substance Dependence is characterized by this pattern of pathological use in combination with indications of physiological addiction. Thus, Substance Dependence involves repeated use of the substance over time resulting in increasing amounts being needed to achieve the desired effect (tolerance). It also involves unpleasant physical and subjective changes that occur if the substance is discontinued (withdrawal). Furthermore, with dependence, the time and effort needed to obtain the substance, use it, and recover from its use becomes a larger and larger part of the individual's life. The degree to which tolerance and withdrawal symptoms develop varies to some extent from substance to substance, but the diagnostic criteria for Substance Abuse and Substance Dependence are designed to be applicable across the range of substances that humans abuse.

These diagnoses are not difficult to make if it is possible to obtain accurate information. However, individuals with substance abuse problems are notorious for evasiveness, deception, and denial. Substance abusing clients present for therapy by a variety of routes. When they recognize their substance use as being a problem and voluntarily seek help, they are likely to cooperate and try to provide accurate information. For example:

> Ellen came to therapy stating, "I need to get my drinking under control." An executive with a large advertising firm, Ellen had continued to have three martini lunches even after this was no longer considered acceptable and even after her job performance began to suffer. Having been called in for "counseling" by her boss, Ellen recognized that unless she did something quickly, her job and career would be jeopardized. She was motivated to cooperate with assessment and treatment.

However, individuals with substance abuse problems frequently come into treatment under duress because significant others, employers, or the criminal justice system believe that they need treatment. When this is the case, the individuals may do their best to prove that they do not need treatment rather than cooperating with an unbiased assessment. For example:

> George was "brought" to therapy by his wife who insisted on sitting in on the initial session and telling the therapist about George's drinking and subsequent irresponsible behavior regarding childcare, household chores, and financial matters. When interviewed without his wife in the room, George admitted to "having a few too many" at times, but pointed out that he never missed a day of work. George was willing to come to therapy to get his wife off of his back but was not enthusiastic about looking realistically at his drinking and the resulting problems.
>
> Alex was referred to therapy by his attorney. The avowed goal was to help Alex with his drinking "problem." During the initial interview it became clear that Alex's referral was an attempt to help him to present a case to the court that he was remorseful and seeking help. In fact, he was facing one more in a series of drunk driving arrests that Alex had experienced over a period of 5 years. In each of the previous arrests, entering therapy had been an alternative to going to jail. Alex was not at all motivated to cooperate with an objective assessment.

It is easiest to assess and treat substance abuse when a collaborative relationship between therapist and client has been established. With individuals who seek treatment voluntarily, it usually is not difficult to do this and to help the client realize that it is to his or her advantage to be open and honest. Unfortunately, it can be difficult to establish a collaborative relationship with individuals who are in treatment at the insistence of others. One good starting place is to acknowledge the client's feelings about being in treatment against his or her will and then to explore whether he or she sees any value to treatment. For example:

THERAPIST: My understanding is that you're here because your wife thinks that you need to be here, not because you see a point to it. Do I have that right?

George: Damn straight!

Therapist: How do you feel about being dragged in to see me?

George: Seems like a total waste of time.

Therapist: I can see that. I imagine it's pretty frustrating.

George: Hmpf.

Therapist: Given that you're stuck spending some time with me, is there anything you'd like to get out of this? Do you see any way I can be useful to you?

George: Well, she may have a point. I wouldn't admit it to her face, you know, but I guess my drinking has been getting a little out of hand.

If the reluctant client can identify goals that he or she wants to work toward, this provides a basis for a collaborative relationship and effective treatment. However, many individuals enter therapy at a point where they do not see their substance use as a problem and are not motivated to work collaboratively with the therapist. When this is the case, the Motivational Interviewing approach discussed later in this chapter can be a powerful way to help these individuals recognize the impact that substance abuse is having in their life and to generate motivation for change.

Even if a collaborative relationship has been established and the client seems motivated and open, it may be important to use some care in seeking information. If the therapist simply asks, "How much do you drink?" and "Do you see this as a problem?" many clients will deny having any problem. Table 6.3 lists some "warning signs" that are often present in individuals who are trying to deny a substance abuse problem and Table 6.4 gives some examples of questions that often provide useful information in assessing substance abuse. For example:

> Even after George acknowledged that his wife "may have a point" in being concerned about his drinking, he continued to minimize the problem. Questions such as, "What's the most you can put away in an evening?", "Do you ever end up drinking more than you intended?, and, "What have you tried to do about your drinking?", produced an account of increasing tolerance, episodes of excessive drinking that had serious consequences, and failed attempts to control or limit drinking. Questions such as, "What concerns *you* the most about your drinking?", "How has your drinking changed over the years?", and, "Suppose this keeps happening, what do you think will come of it?" resulted in George expressing genuine concern about his own drinking and showing increased motivation for treatment.

Table 6.3. "Warning Signs" Suggestive of a Substance Abuse Problem

Defensiveness, evasiveness, or hostility in response to routine questions about substance use

Attempts to justify substance use by comparing self to others who use larger amounts or who have larger problems as a result of substance use

Pressure from others to reduce use or abstain

Attempts to control substance use through limiting time or place of use. (i.e., "I never drink alone.")

A history of recurrent attempts to reduce or eliminate substance use followed by resumption (i.e., "I can quit any time I want, I've quit lots of times before.")

Persistent substance use despite significant problems resulting from substance use

Ability to consume large quantities of substance before effect is felt. (i.e., "I can put away a fifth before I even feel it.")

TABLE 6.4. Examples of Questions Useful in Assessing Substance Abuse

Personal concerns
    Do you ever feel bad about your drinking?
    Have you ever tried to cut back on your drinking? (If so, Why? What happened? Did you resume? If
    so, why?)
Interpersonal problems
    Does your (wife/husband/partner) ever complain about your drinking? (If so, What do they say?)
    Have you ever lost friends because of drinking?
Work/Financial/Legal problems
    Have you ever gotten into trouble at work because of drinking?
    Have you ever been arrested for things you did while drinking?
Loss of control
    Do you ever end up drinking more than you intended?
    Can you stop drinking without a struggle after one or two drinks?
Indications of tolerance or withdrawal
    How much does it take for you to get drunk?
    How much do you need to drink before you start to feel it?
    What's the most you ever have to drink?
    Do you ever go a few days without drinking? How do you feel then?

When information is available from significant others, previous therapists, physicians, or others, this can be quite useful in determining whether the client is being open and honest or not.

A wide range of questionnaires, structured interviews, and other instruments have been developed for assessing substance abuse. These can be useful for screening or diagnosing substance abuse, treatment planning, assessing of treatment process and outcome. However, a discussion of the many measures that are available is beyond the scope of this chapter. Interested readers will find that the *NIAAA* handbook edited by Allen and Columbus (1995) provides a detailed review focusing on measures for assessing alcohol problems.

CONCEPTUALIZATION

Why do people start using mind- or mood-altering substances, increase their use to problematic levels, and then persist with substance use once it causes problems? A cognitive analysis of the development and maintenance of substance abuse is presented by Beck *et al.* (1993). Many factors such as the physiological effects of the substance, the neuronal reward systems in the brain, and the social context in which the substance use occur are involved in the development of substance abuse. Beck and his colleagues (1993) focus on the role that cognition plays. They argue that often individuals first try a substance because they expect to enjoy it and because they are in a social context that supports or encourages substance use. Once a particular substance has been tried, substance use often persists because the individual likes the effects the substance produces and because he or she believes that substance use helps him or her cope with real-life problems or aversive emotional states.

Over time, the individual begins to develop a tolerance for the substance and advances to higher and higher doses to achieve the desired effects. At the same time, he or she may rely increasingly on using the substance to deal with life problems and aversive emotions. This often results in an increasing belief that he or she needs the substance to cope. Eventually, the individual encounters more and more problems due to the direct effects of the substance on health, personal life, and job performance and due to indirect effects such as the time and expense needed to obtain the substance. Although it might seem that these problems would dissuade the individual from persisting with substance use, if the individual's accustomed way of dealing with problems is to ingest the substance, these problems may actually trigger additional substance abuse.

Once an individual has been using a substance (or substances) for some time, a cycle evolves which may be triggered by internal cues (e.g., feeling sad) or by external cues (e.g., going to a party). This activating stimulus elicits beliefs and automatic thoughts that encourage substance use such as, "If get high I'll feel better," or "If I have a drink I'll relax and have a better time." The activating stimuli and the thoughts and beliefs may also elicit cravings and urges that the individual believes that substance use will relieve. Facilitating thoughts such as, "It's OK, everybody else is drinking," or, "It won't do any harm this one time," may also reduce any inhibitions regarding substance use. At this point, the individual typically becomes preoccupied with the actions needed to obtain and ingest the substance. These factors can produce episodic substance abuse, which only occurs when the eliciting stimuli are encountered. However, if either the subjective effects of withdrawal or the real-life consequences of the substance abuse provide additional activating stimuli, this can result in on-going substance abuse. In other words, individuals may begin to use their substance to avoid withdrawal symptoms, cope with distress over the vocational and interpersonal problems that result from their substance abuse, or cope with guilty feelings regarding their substance abuse or their actions while intoxicated. When any of these occur, substance abuse can easily become chronic.

Beck and his colleagues (1993) argue that unrealistic expectations and dysfunctional beliefs about substance use (e.g., "I can't be happy unless I use," or "I'm more creative when I have a few drinks.") play an important role in maintaining substance abuse. They also note that when substance-abusing individuals do try to quit, their thoughts and beliefs about withdrawal and cravings (e.g., "I can't stand feeling like this." "I don't have the strength to stop.") as well as their anticipations regarding life without substance use (e.g., "I won't be able to stand the boredom." "The guys won't have anything to do with me any more.") make it difficult for individuals to quit on their own.

INTERVENTION STRATEGY

Many of the factors that play important roles in substance abuse (such as broad cultural influences, genetic predisposition, the physiological effects of substances, and so forth) are beyond the reach of an individual therapist or an organized treatment program. However, cognitive analysis of substance abuse (Beck *et al.*, 1993) suggests a number of points where therapeutic interventions may be effective. Cognitive Therapy can be used to identify and alter situations, activities, and other cues that trigger substance abuse. It can also be used to help the individual develop adaptive ways of coping with life problems and emotional distress. Beyond this, cognitive-behavioral interventions can be used to reduce the frequency and intensity of cravings and urges, as well as to modify dysfunctional thoughts and beliefs that contribute to substance abuse. As with any difficult problem, Cognitive Therapy can also be useful in generating motivation for change in individuals who are ambivalent or resistant. Finally, the full complement of cognitive-behavioral strategies may be needed to reduce the risk of relapse following treatment.

One important issue in choosing an intervention strategy is the question of whether total abstinence must be the goal of treatment or whether some form of "moderate" or "controlled" use is an option as well. The traditional view has been that total, lifetime abstinence is the only acceptable goal of substance abuse treatment. The idea that controlled use might be a viable option with some substances has generated intense controversy (see Marlatt, 1983). Traditionally, the idea that total abstinence is the only acceptable goal of treatment is often rooted in the assumption that the consumption of any amount of a previously abused substance will lead immediately and directly to relapse. However, the evidence available does not support this assumption and instead shows that some individuals show an extended period of moderate substance use following even abstinence-based treatment programs (see Marlatt, 1983, p. 1101). In fact, the evidence available suggests that moderate use is a viable treatment goal for at least some problem drinkers (see Sobell & Sobell, 1993, pp. 32–36).

The fact that there is little empirical basis for asserting that abstinence must be the goal of treatment and that there is evidence that moderate use can be attained by some individuals with substance abuse problems does not necessarily mean that one should endorse moderate use as a treatment goal. Sobell and Sobell (1993) suggest allowing clients to choose between abstinence and controlled use (with advice from the therapist). However, it is important to develop an understanding of the individual's reasons for choosing moderate use or abstinence, both to address any misconceptions and to evaluate whether the client seems to be exercising good judgment. In general, it seems reasonable to consider moderate use as a possible treatment goal for those who show lower levels of physiological dependence and have a less chronic pattern of substance abuse. Abstinence would seem to be a more appropriate goal with individuals who show higher levels of physical dependence, have a more chronic pattern of substance abuse, have a strong family history of substance abuse, or who are abusing a substance that is illegal and/or highly addictive. If an individual is unsuccessful after an adequate trial of working toward moderate use, abstinence may be a more appropriate treatment goal.

COGNITIVE AND BEHAVIORAL TECHNIQUES

The full range of cognitive and behavioral techniques can be useful in the treatment of substance abuse. However, a number of specific interventions are particularly useful.

Generating Motivation for Change

One of the first tasks a therapist faces in treating an individual with a substance abuse problem is that of generating persistent motivation for change. Individuals who seek treatment on their own may be ambivalent about the changes that treatment requires or their motivation may wane as treatment progresses. Individuals who enter treatment at the behest of others may have little motivation for change or may actively resist change. A large body of research has examined how and why people change, either on their own or with the help of a therapist (see Prochaska, DiClemente, & Norcross, 1992), and has provided a foundation for a promising approach to increasing motivation for change.

Prochaska and DiClemente (1982) have developed a model of how change occurs that presents the stages of the change process as a cycle (Figure 6.1). Individuals typically progress from not even thinking about changing (Precontemplation) to considering whether to make a change (Contemplation), deciding to make a change (Determination), making the change (Action), and maintaining the change (Maintenance). Frequently, individuals trying to overcome a substance abuse problem resume substance abuse (Relapse) and, when this is the case, they typically return to the Precontemplation, Contemplation, or Determination stage and progress through the cycle again. With substance use problems, many individuals proceed through this cycle several times before they achieve a stable change.

Although this model of the stages of change may seem like commonsense, it is based on extensive research (see Prochaska et al., 1992) and it has two important implications for clinical practice. First, interventions that are matched to the individual's stage in the change process are likely to be most effective (see Table 6.5). Second, if most individuals who succeed in making lasting change progress through this cycle a number of times, then relapse represents one more step in the process of change rather than representing failure. If relapse can be followed by a resumption of the change process, it provides an opportunity to identify the factors that led to relapse and to learn how to achieve a more lasting change.

Miller, Rollnick, Conforti, and Miller (2002) have used the Stages of Change model as a foundation for Motivational Interviewing, an effective method for

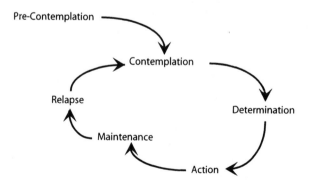

Figure 6.1. Prochaska and DiClemente's Stages of Change.

TABLE 6.5. The Therapist's Task at Each Stage of Change

Stage	Task
Precontemplation	Raise the issue, get the person to start thinking about the drawbacks of his or her current behavior
Contemplation	Tip the balance, help the person see the reasons for changing, the risks in not changing, and his or her potential for change
Determination	Help him or her choose a promising course of action
Action	Help him or her follow through on steps toward change
Maintenance	Help him or her plan and use strategies to prevent relapse
Relapse	Help him or her renew the process of contemplation, determination, and action without becoming demoralized because of the relapse

increasing motivation for change in individuals with substance abuse problems (as well as for people with other problems). Motivational Interviewing is a brief intervention approach that spells out methods for establishing a collaborative relationship, minimizing resistance, and increasing motivation for change. In Motivational Interviewing a series of questions are used first to increase the individual's recognition of the problems that substance use presents for him or her. Next, additional questions are used to increase the individual's awareness regarding the adverse consequences of substance abuse and to increase his or her awareness of the advantages of change. Finally, questions are used to increase the client's confidence that change is possible (see Table 6.6). The Motivational Interviewing approach is completely compatible with Cognitive Therapy and has proved to be quite effective (see Miller *et al.*, 2002).

Functional Analysis of Episodes of Substance Use

Effective treatment of substance abuse relies on an accurate understanding of the role of the substance in the client's life. To develop this understanding, the client and therapist can discuss specific episodes of abuse one at a time and identify the specific situations, thoughts, and feelings that lead to the client's use of the substance (Stasiewicz, Carey, Bradizza, & Maisto, 1996). Either standard thought records (TRs) can be used for this purpose (see Chapter 2), or a specialized format, such as that presented by Stasiewicz and his colleagues (Stasiewicz *et al.*, 1996; see Figure 6.2), can be used. Once adaptive alternatives to substance abuse have been developed, a second form provides a simple way of highlighting both the drawbacks of substance abuse and the advantages of adaptive alternatives (Figure 6.3, adapted from Stasiewicz *et al.*, 1996).

Modifying Dysfunctional Thoughts and Beliefs

Interventions that focus on modifying dysfunctional thoughts and beliefs (Chapter 3) can be useful in the treatment of substance abuse in two major ways. First, when emotions play a role in triggering episodes of substance abuse and

TABLE 6.6. Examples of Questions Used to Elicit Self-Motivational Statements[a]

Problem recognition
What makes you think that this is a problem?
What difficulties have you had in relation to your drug use?
In what ways do you think you or others have been harmed by your drinking?
In what ways has this been a problem for you?
How has your use of tranquilizers stopped you from doing what you want to do?

Concern
What is there about your drinking that you or others might see as reasons for concern?
What worries you about your drug use? What can you imagine happening to you?
How do you feel about your gambling?
In what ways does this concern you?
What do you think will happen if you don't make a change?

Intention to change (advantages of change)
Your coming in today shows that at least a part of you thinks it's time to do something. What are the reasons you see for making a change?
What makes you think that you may need to make a change?
If you were 100% successful and things worked out exactly as you would like, what would be different?
What would be the advantages of making a change?

Optimism (self-efficacy)
What makes you think that if you decide to make a change, you can do it?
What encourages you to think that you can change if you want to?
What do you think would work for you, if you decided to change?

[a] Adapted from Miller & Rollnick, 1991

Trigger	Thought	Feeling	Behavior	Consequence

FIGURE 6.2. One Possible Format for Functional Analysis of Episodes of Substance Abuse. *Source:* Adapted from Stasiewicz *et al.*, 1996

dysfunctional cognitions contribute to those emotions, then interventions that modify those cognitions can be useful in helping the client to cope more effectively. Second, when cognitions such as, "I've had a rough day, I deserve a drink," or "One more drink won't do any harm this time," contribute to episodes of substance abuse, it can be very important to address those cognitions. However, it is important to note that cognitive interventions alone are not likely to be adequate. They are just one component of Cognitive Therapy with substance abuse.

Trigger	Thought	Feeling	Old Behavior		New Behavior	
			Behavior	Consequence	Behavior	Consequence
Alone in new apartment	How did I get into this mess?	Depressed	Drink	Reduce Depression. Feel worse tomorrow.	Play with children.	Reduce depression. Increase Self-esteem.
	I'm all alone.	Lonely	Drink	Reduce Lonliness. Stay Isolated.	Call a friend.	Reduce Lonliness. Improve social life.

FIGURE 6.3. Functional Analysis of Alternatives to Substance Abuse.
Source: Adapted from Stasiewicz *et al.*, 1996

Managing Withdrawal

Many individuals with substance abuse problems face the prospect of experiencing significant withdrawal symptoms when they discontinue their substance use. On the one hand, withdrawal from many commonly abused substances including alcohol, anxiolytics, and opioids may entail a risk of serious medical complications, including death. On the other hand, unrealistic fears of withdrawal often interfere with clients following through on treatment for substance abuse. In fact, some individuals go through withdrawal on a regular basis to avoid a positive drug test or to increase the effectiveness of a drug to which they have developed tolerance.

Readers who are not familiar with the medical aspects of withdrawal will want to consult the client's physician or a knowledgeable medical consultant if the client has developed a significant tolerance to the substance(s) he or she is abusing or if there is a history of significant withdrawal symptoms. It is important to note that many prescription medications can have substantial withdrawal symptoms. The fact that an individual is abusing prescription medication does not mean that withdrawal is harmless. Signs that a medically supervised detoxification may be needed include hallucinations, disorientation, signs of delirium tremens, severely elevated blood pressure, severe emotional crisis, concurrent medical problems, or exacerbation of concurrent psychiatric problems (Hoffman, Halikas, Mee-Lee, & Weedman, 1991; Pattison, 1979, pp. 184–186; Schuckit, 1979, pp. 241–242). The Federal Bureau of Prisons has a set of clinical practice guidelines regarding the detoxification of chemically dependent inmates (2000) that provide a concise summary of many aspects of withdrawal, including handouts regarding withdrawal which are designed to be given to substance abusing individuals.

Developing Adaptive Alternatives to Substance Abuse

It is important for therapy to focus on helping clients develop strategies for replacing the function of the substance in their lives rather than simply focusing on avoidance of substance use. Unless the individual has adaptive alternatives to substance use, it will be difficult for him or her to keep from returning to substance abuse. For example:

> Nat was an unmarried man in his late 30s undergoing assessment in an alcohol treatment program. He explained that 5 years previously he had begun having panic attacks. He had discovered that having a few drinks reduced his anxiety, and he had quickly become dependent on drinking as his primary strategy for managing anxiety. It was clear that if he stopped drinking without also learning how to deal with anxiety and panic, his panic attacks would likely return, leading to a return of alcohol abuse. However, because efforts to treat his Panic Disorder while he continued abusing alcohol were likely to be unsuccessful (see Chapter 5), it was necessary to treat the two problems concurrently.

The functional analysis of episodes of substance abuse discussed above can be quite useful in identifying the role that substance abuse plays in the client's life and identifying the areas in which adaptive alternatives are needed. The volume by Monti, Abrams, Kadden, and Cooney (1989) includes specific suggestions regarding many areas in which substance-abusing individuals often need to develop adaptive alternatives. Many individuals with substance abuse problems benefit significantly from time spent on helping them to think ahead about the consequences of their actions and working to improve their problem-solving skills.

Intervening within the Family Context

Peer and family relationships are strongly affected by substance abuse and can have an important impact on substance abuse. Work with family and peer relationship systems may well be a necessary part of treatment. For example:

> John, a 22-year-old male, referred himself for treatment of his heroin addiction. He stated during the intake evaluation that he wanted to stop using heroin because he wanted to go to a community college and major in Criminal Justice. His goal was to become a police officer. His statement was that, "I can't do that as a junkie." John had been using heroin almost daily. He reported that he had, on his own, stopped using on several occasions but went back to active use. He lived at home with his mother and two brothers. He had a third brother who lived in a city about 400 miles away from the family, who had been "clean" for many years. All the other members of his family were heroin addicted. He reported that his mother would wash and boil their "works" each night before use, and lay the paraphernalia out on paper towels in the kitchen to prevent transmission of disease. Each time that John tried to quit, family members invited him back to "take a taste." It was clear that to quit, John would either need to deal effectively with his family or leave them.

Couple therapy and family therapy (see Chapter 11) can often be quite useful in modifying family interactions that contribute to substance abuse and in repairing the damage done by the individual's substance abuse. When helping individuals cope effectively with their family and peer group, it often is important to help them master drink refusal skills, assertion, stress management techniques, and so on. Monti and his colleagues (Monti *et al.*, 1989) have provided a treatment manual that includes skill training guidelines for a broad range of interpersonal and intrapersonal skills.

Integrating Psychotherapeutic Treatment with Alcoholics Anonymous

Treatment options for individuals with substance abuse problems include referral to Alcoholics Anonymous (AA), to another of the "12-Step" programs such as Narcotics Anonymous (NA), or to one of the alternative groups, such as Rational Recovery. Although cognitive therapists might not agree with all of the premises underlying 12-Step programs, these groups offer support that most therapists cannot offer. This support includes meetings that are widely available and free of charge, a sponsor who can be called any hour of the day or night, and a social activity that is an alternative to drinking. Many aspects of 12-Step programs are quite compatible with Cognitive Therapy, such as their emphasis on avoiding "stinking thinking."

Despite these advantages, such programs are not a good match for all clients. Some AA groups can be quite rigid, insisting that abstinence is the only way, asserting that stepwise reduction in substance use is inappropriate, and demanding that the client yield control to a higher power. As a self-help organization with meetings led by nonprofessionals, the quality of AA meetings can vary widely, with some AA groups taking extreme stances such as exhorting members to discontinue all medications regardless of their medical or psychiatric condition. AA and other self-help programs are a resource that many substance-abusing clients find useful; however, participation in AA is not necessary for treatment to be effective.

When it appears that participation in AA would be a useful part of an individual's treatment but he or she is reluctant to attend AA meetings, it can be useful to develop an understanding of the client's objections. Sometimes these objections are based on misconceptions that can easily be corrected. For example:

> Joe was a newly abstaining individual with a long history of alcohol abuse. He had few friends and few activities aside from work, and he needed more support than his therapist could easily provide. However, when his therapist suggested that AA might be worth considering, Joe's reaction was quite negative. When his therapist inquired about Joe's objections to AA, he explained that he didn't want to sit in a room full of smelly skid-row bums. The therapist was then able to explain that AA members were mostly working guys who had a lot in common with Joe, not skid-row bums. After a little more discussion of the possible advantages of trying AA, Joe endorsed the plan of attending a few meetings to find out what they were like and then deciding whether to continue attending or not.

When clients are willing to try AA or are already active in AA, it can be important to explain that AA's terminology differs from that of Cognitive Therapy and encourage clients to speak up if the things the therapist is saying seem to contradict AA's assertions. Many of the apparent contradictions between AA and Cognitive Therapy are semantic differences that can be resolved with a brief discussion.

Relapse Prevention

In some ways, getting the individual with a substance abuse problem to stop using is the easy part of treatment. After all, most individuals with substance abuse problems have quit many times. Helping the client to refrain from substance abuse in the long run is more of a challenge. Working explicitly on relapse prevention is an important part of Cognitive Therapy with most problems. With problems such as substance abuse where relapse is quite common, work on relapse prevention is even more critical. The first step is to help the client realize that, in order for the changes he or she has made to persist, the changes need to be actively maintained. Then therapist and client can work together to identify high-risk situations and to prepare to cope with them when they arise.

The process of identifying situations that pose a high risk for relapse and then preparing the client to deal effectively with those situations is valuable. Often, high-risk situations can be identified by examining situations in which previous relapses have occurred, situations that currently elicit urges and cravings, and situations that the client thinks would be difficult to handle. Situations in which the client has to cope with temptation, with negative affect, with interpersonal conflict, or cues associated with previous substance abuse often pose a high risk of relapse.

Preparing the client to cope with such high-risk situations includes both identifying appropriate coping strategies and making sure that the individual can successfully implement those strategies. Thus, if a recovering alcoholic realizes that encountering a beer vendor at a baseball game is a high-risk situation and plans to buy a soft drink instead, we need to be confident that the client will be able to follow through on this plan. The more it is possible for the client to actually practice coping with high-risk situations under controlled conditions, the more grounds the therapist has for confidence that the client is ready to deal with those situations in real life. When practice in real-life situations is not feasible, the use of imagery or role-play can provide good ways to practice coping with high-risk situations.

Often, cues that have been repeatedly associated with substance abuse trigger strong urges or cravings which present a challenge to clients (see Somers & Marlatt, 1992). Repeated, prolonged exposure to such cues under controlled circumstances can be useful for decreasing the intensity of the urges and cravings. If it is not feasible to conduct cue exposure under controlled real-life conditions, cue exposure can be conducted in the therapist's office. Mental imagery, videotaped stimuli, and objects that can be brought into the therapist's office can provide useful alternatives.

One important aspect of relapse prevention is working to equip the client to prevent a "slip" from becoming a full-blown relapse. Clients who have been abstinent for some time and who then have a drink in response to temptation, social pressure, or an emotional crisis, may well find themselves thinking, "Oh, hell! Now I've blown it. Well, I may as well have another one." Obviously, it is not helpful for abstinent clients to take a drink, but if they can catch themselves, deal with the situation, and resume abstinence, little harm is done. Much more harm results if the lapse leads them to abandon abstinence and resume alcohol abuse. It can be quite useful to help the client realize that he or she may have a lapse some day and plan how to deal with it. It is not that lapses are trivial, but that a lapse that is handled well does much less damage than a full relapse does.

There often is a risk of relapse if the client starts to think, " I've got my drug problem licked now. I can go back to using drugs occasionally." It is important to help the client realize that success in overcoming a drug problem does not mean that one can safely resume drug use.

The client's sense of self-efficacy regarding coping with high-risk situations has been found to be strongly predictive of drinking behavior following treatment (Alsop & Saunders, 1989; Solomon & Annis, 1990) and therefore this is another important focus of treatment. Although the experience of coping effectively with problem situations is likely to result in an increased sense of self-efficacy, it is important for the therapist to address cognitions that undercut the client's sense of self-efficacy as vigorously as he or she addresses cognitions that lead to overconfidence.

CONCLUSIONS

Although individuals with substance abuse problems have the reputation of being difficult to treat and having a high rate of relapse, a large body of research shows that cognitive-behavioral interventions are effective with this population (see Miller & Brown, 1997, for a concise overview). Many mental health professionals believe that individuals with substance abuse problems should automatically be referred to a substance abuse treatment program or to a 12-Step program. Although we would agree that mental health professionals should not practice outside of their areas of competence, this does not mean that mental health professionals should not provide treatment for drug and alcohol problems.

Many drug and alcohol treatment programs are strongly influenced by tradition and have been slow to adopt empirically supported treatment approaches. There is little reason to presume that those specialized drug and alcohol treatment programs provide more effective treatment than those provided by mental health professionals who are knowledgeable about substance abuse and other mental health problems (Miller & Brown, 1997). Given the prevalence of substance abuse problems and their comorbidity with other mental health problems, it is fortunate that cognitive-behavioral interventions provide a useful way of increasing motivation for change, facilitate change, and reduce the risk of relapse.

III

Cognitive Therapy of Personality Disorders

Clients with personality disorders are among the most challenging clients we encounter in clinical practice. By definition (*DSM-IV-TR*, 2000), personality disorders are long-standing, inflexible patterns of perceiving and responding to one's environment and to oneself that are characteristic of the individual across a wide range of situations. Therapy with clients diagnosed as having personality disorders often is complex, intense, and difficult. In addition, personality disorders often co-occur with Axis I disorders. When this is the case, the presence of an Axis II disorder can have a significant effect on the clinical presentation, development, and course of the Axis I disorder. Clearly, the development of effective approaches to understanding and treating individuals with personality disorders is of great importance.

Behavioral and cognitive-behavioral theorists have had a long tradition of rejecting explanations of psychopathological behavior based on the idea of enduring personality traits, favoring instead explanations based on the stimuli, consequences, and cognitions experienced in the particular situations in which the problems occur. As a result, cognitive behaviorists were slow to turn their attention to the treatment of personality disorders. However, following an interval during which personality disorders received little attention, a number of cognitive-behavioral approaches to personality disorders have been developed (see Pretzer, 1998).

Cognitive Therapy proves to be well suited to the treatment of clients with personality disorders when appropriate adjustments are made. The inclusion of clients' core beliefs and their interpersonal behavior as well as their immediate cognitions permits a clear conceptualization of these complex disorders that can facilitate intervention. The use of a collaborative approach to therapy based on guided discovery aids in addressing the interpersonal complexities of psychotherapy with these clients. Also, despite the clients' complexity, cognitive-behavioral interventions often prove effective both for achieving symptomatic relief and making lasting changes.

Current cognitive-behavioral approaches to treating personality disorders are based largely on clinical experience, but a growing body of empirical research provides reason to believe that Cognitive Therapy and related approaches can provide effective treatment for these complex disorders. Initially there were many uncontrolled clinical reports that asserted that cognitive-behavioral therapy could provide effective treatment for personality disorders (many of which propose specific treatment approaches) but only a limited number of controlled outcome studies to provide support for those assertions. This led some to be concerned about the risks associated with a rapid expansion of theory and practice that outstripped the empirical research (Dobson & Pusch, 1993). Fortunately, the body of empirical research supporting cognitive-behavioral approaches to the treatment of personality disorder is growing.

A full review of this literature is beyond the scope of this volume (for a recent review, see Pretzer, 1998). However, two studies are particularly worth mentioning. Persons and her colleagues (Persons *et al.*, 1988) conducted an empirical study of the effectiveness of Cognitive Therapy under "real world" conditions. The participants were 70 clients receiving Cognitive Therapy for depression in David Burns' and Persons' own private practices. Treatment was open-ended and individualized rather than standardized, and both medication and inpatient treatment were used as needed. The study focused on identifying predictors of dropout and treatment outcome in Cognitive Therapy for depression and considered the presence of a personality disorder diagnosis as a potential predictor both of premature termination of therapy and of therapy outcome. Participants meeting *DSM-III* (1980) criteria for a personality disorder diagnosis were 54.3%.

Not surprisingly, this study found that patients with personality disorders were significantly more likely to drop out of therapy prematurely than patients without personality disorders. However, it also found that those patients with personality disorder diagnoses who persisted in therapy through the completion of treatment showed substantial improvement and did not differ significantly in degree of improvement from patients without personality disorders. Similar findings have been reported by Sanderson, Beck, and McGinn (1994) in a study of Cognitive Therapy for Generalized Anxiety Disorder. Participants diagnosed with a comorbid personality disorder were more likely to drop out of treatment than others, but treatment was effective in reducing both anxiety and depression for those who completed a minimum course of treatment. Although there is clearly a need for much more research, these studies provide empirical support for clinically based assertions that Cognitive Therapy can provide effective treatment for individuals with personality disorders.

General guidelines for applying Cognitive Therapy to clients diagnosed as having personality disorders have been proposed in recent years, most recently by Pretzer (1998, presented in Table III.1). The following chapters present specific cognitive approaches to conceptualizing and treating each of the currently recognized personality disorders. This section is organized according to *DSM-IV-TR's* division of personality disorders into three clusters (2000). Chapter 7 (Cluster A) includes Paranoid, Schizoid, and Schizotypal Personality Disorders, which comprise

Table iii.1. Proposed Guidelines for Cognitive Therapy with Personality Disorders

1. *Interventions are most effective when based on an individualized conceptualization of the client's problems.* In working with clients who have personality disorders, the therapist is often faced with choosing among many possible targets for intervention and a variety of possible intervention techniques. A clear treatment plan that is based on a thorough evaluation, clinical observation, and the results of clinical interventions, minimizes the risk of the therapist being confused by the complexity of the client's problems.

2. *It is important for therapist and client to work collaboratively toward clearly identified, shared goals.* Clear, consistent goals for therapy are necessary to avoid skipping from problem to problem without making any lasting progress. However, it is important for these goals to be mutually agreed upon so as to minimize the noncompliance and power struggles that often impede treatment of clients with personality disorders. The time and effort spent developing mutually acceptable goals can be a good investment.

3. *It is important to focus more than the usual amount of attention on the therapist–client relationship.* A good therapeutic relationship is as necessary for effective intervention in cognitive therapy as in any other approach to therapy. Behavioral and cognitive-behavioral therapists are generally accustomed to being able to establish a fairly straightforward therapeutic relationship at the outset of therapy and then to proceed without paying much attention to the interpersonal aspects of therapy. However, this is not usually the case when working with clients who have personality disorders. The client's perception of the therapist may be biased at times, and the dysfunctional interpersonal behaviors that clients manifest in relationships outside of therapy are likely to be manifested in the therapist–client relationship as well. Although the interpersonal difficulties that occur in the therapist–client relationship can disrupt therapy if they are not addressed effectively, they also provide the therapist with the opportunity to do *in vivo* observation and intervention.

4. *Consider beginning with interventions that do not require extensive self-disclosure.* Clients with personality disorders often are quite uncomfortable with self-disclosure due to a lack of trust in the therapist, discomfort with intimacy, fear of rejection, etc. Although it is sometimes necessary to begin treatment with interventions that require discussion of deeply personal thoughts and feelings, it can be useful to begin treatment by working on a problem that does not require extensive self-disclosure. This allows time for the client to gradually become more comfortable with therapy and for the therapist to gradually address the client's discomfort with self-disclosure.

5. *Interventions that increase the client's sense of self-efficacy often reduce the intensity of the client's symptomatology and facilitate other interventions.* The intensity of the emotional and behavioral responses manifested by individuals with personality disorders is often exacerbated by the individual's doubting his or her ability to cope effectively with particular problem situations. If it is possible to increase the individual's confidence that he or she will be able to handle problem situations if they arise, this often lowers the client's level of anxiety, moderates his or her symptomatology, enables him or her to react more deliberately, and makes it easier to implement other interventions. The individual's sense of self-efficacy can be increased through interventions that correct any exaggerations of the demands of the situation or minimization of the individual's capabilities, through helping the individual to improve his or her coping skills, or through a combination of the two.

6. *Do not rely primarily on verbal interventions.* The more severe a client's problems, the more important it is to use behavioral interventions to accomplish cognitive as well as behavioral change. A gradual hierarchy of "behavioral experiments" not only provides an opportunity for desensitization to happen and for the client to master new skills but also can be quite effective in challenging unrealistic beliefs and expectations.

7. *Try to identify and address the client's fears before implementing changes.* Clients with personality disorders often have strong, unexpressed fears about the changes they seek or are asked to make in the course of therapy. Attempts to induce the client to implement changes without first addressing these fears are often unsuccessful (Mays, 1985). If the therapist makes a practice of discussing the client's expectations and concerns before each change is attempted, it is likely to reduce the client's level of anxiety regarding therapy and improve compliance.

Table III.1. *(cont.)*

8. *Help the client deal adaptively with aversive emotions.* Clients with personality disorders often experience very intense aversive emotional reactions in specific situations. These intense reactions can be a significant problem in their own right but, in addition, the individual's attempts to avoid experiencing these emotions, his or her attempts to escape the emotions, and his or her cognitive and behavioral response to the emotions often play an important role in the client's problems in living. Often, the individual's unwillingness to tolerate aversive affect blocks him or her from handling the emotions adaptively and perpetuates fears about the consequences of experiencing the emotions. Individuals with personality disorders may need to acquire some of the cognitive and/or behavioral skills needed to handle the emotions effectively.

9. *Anticipate problems with compliance.* Many factors contribute to a high rate of noncompliance among clients with personality disorders. In addition to the complexities in the therapist–client relationship and the fears regarding change that were discussed above, the dysfunctional behaviors of individuals with personality disorders are strongly ingrained and often are reinforced by aspects of the client's environment. However, rather than simply being an impediment to progress, episodes of noncompliance can provide an opportunity for effective intervention. When noncompliance is anticipated, one can improve compliance by identifying and addressing the issues beforehand. When non-compliance arises unexpectedly, it provides an opportunity to identify issues that are impeding progress in therapy so that they can be addressed.

10. *Do not presume that the client exists in a reasonable environment.* Some behaviors, such as assertion, are so generally adaptive that it is easy to assume that they are always a good idea. However, clients with personality disorders are often the product of seriously atypical families and live in atypical environments. When implementing changes, it is important to assess the likely responses of significant others in the client's environment rather than presuming that they will respond in a reasonable way.

11. *Attend to your own emotional reactions during the course of therapy.* Interactions with clients with personality disorders can elicit emotional reactions from the therapist ranging from empathic feelings of depression to strong anger, discouragement, fear, or sexual attraction. It is important for the therapist to be aware of these responses so they do not unduly influence or disrupt the therapist's work with the client and so they can be used as a source of potentially useful data. Therapists may benefit from using cognitive techniques themselves (see Layden *et al.*, 1993, Chapter 6) and/or seeking consultation with an objective colleague.

12. *Be realistic regarding the length of therapy, goals for therapy, and standards for therapist self-evaluation.* Many therapists using behavioral and cognitive-behavioral approaches to therapy are accustomed to accomplishing substantial results relatively quickly. One can easily become frustrated and angry with the "resistant" client when therapy proceeds slowly or become self-critical and discouraged when therapy goes badly. Behavioral and cognitive-behavioral interventions can accomplish substantial, apparently lasting changes in some clients with personality disorders, but more modest results are achieved in other cases, and little is accomplished in others. When therapy proceeds slowly, it is important to neither give up prematurely nor perseverate with an unsuccessful treatment approach. When treatment is unsuccessful, it is important to remember that therapist competence is not the only factor influencing the outcome of therapy.

persons who are often seen as odd or eccentric. Chapter 8 (Cluster B), includes Antisocial, Borderline, Histrionic, and Narcissistic Personality Disorders, which comprise persons who are seen as dramatic, emotional, or erratic. Chapter 9 (Cluster C) includes Avoidant, Dependent, and Obsessive–Compulsive Personality Disorders, which comprise persons who often appear anxious or fearful.

7

Paranoid, Schizoid, and Schizotypal Personality Disorders
The Eccentric Cluster

In *DSM-IV-TR* (2000), Paranoid, Schizoid, and Schizotypal Personality Disorders are collectively categorized as "Cluster A" on the basis of the rationale that individuals with these disorders often appear odd or eccentric. This is a plausible reason for grouping these disorders together and it is consistent with the long-standing idea that these disorders are "schizophrenic spectrum disorders" that are closely related to Schizophrenia. However, current empirical research suggests that the three disorders are distinct from each other (Nestadt, Hanfelt, Liang, Lamacz, Wolyniec, & Pulver, 1994) and does not necessarily support the hypothesis that all three disorders are related to Schizophrenia (e.g., Maier, Lichtermann, Minges & Heun, 1994). In this chapter, these will be treated as three distinct disorders.

PARANOID PERSONALITY DISORDER

In many ways, Paranoid Personality Disorder is primarily a cognitive disorder. It is characterized by a set of extreme and unrealistic beliefs regarding the motivations and likely actions of other persons. The paranoid individual is certain that people in general have malicious intentions and will take advantage of any opportunity to deceive, attack, or take advantage of him or her. This "paranoid" world-view is firmly held and is not substantially changed by interactions in which the client is treated well by others. However, these unrealistically suspicious views are not accompanied by a thought disorder or by systematized delusions as in Paranoid Schizophrenia or Paranoid Disorder, respectively. Individuals with Paranoid Personality Disorder are prone to a variety of intrapersonal and interpersonal problems that stem from their paranoid world-view. The beliefs of these individuals about the nature of other persons and their interpretations of the actions of others are responsible for most of the problems they encounter.

It might appear that a disorder such as this, where cognition plays such a central role, would be ideally suited to cognitive interventions. However, simply

197

establishing a working relationship with these clients can be difficult and, as most therapists can attest, attempts to directly challenge the paranoid individual's view of others typically prove ineffective or counterproductive. Psychodynamically oriented writers have concluded that modest gains achieved slowly over extended periods of time are the best that can be expected with Paranoid Personality Disorder (Weintraub, 1981). Cognitive Therapy's more active, collaborative approach offers some advantages in working with paranoid clients, but for cognitive-behavioral techniques to be effective they must be used strategically.

Assessment

Persons with Paranoid Personality Disorder are reputed to rarely enter therapy because they do not see their suspiciousness as a problem, are reluctant to accept help, and rarely function so poorly that they require hospitalization (Weintraub, 1981). However, it may be the case that individuals with Paranoid Personality Disorder often enter therapy without the disorder being diagnosed. Although it is true that these individuals rarely seek therapy for their paranoia, they may well seek therapy due to difficulty handling job stress, conflicts with superiors or colleagues, problems with anxiety, depression, marital problems, and substance abuse, perhaps without their underlying suspiciousness being recognized.

These clients have a strong tendency to blame others for interpersonal problems (Kinderman & Bental, 1997). Thus, when the assessment is based on the clients' self-report, an impression may be created that their problems are due to mistreatment by others and that their suspicions are justified. In addition, the client may well realize that a paranoid worldview is not socially acceptable and actively conceal his or her paranoia. When this is the case, indications of paranoia may emerge only gradually over the course of therapy and may easily be missed.

The *DSM-IV-TR* diagnostic criteria for Paranoid Personality Disorder are shown in Table 7.1. Sometimes Paranoid Personality Disorder is obvious. For example:

> Ann was a married administrative assistant in her mid-30s who sought help with stress management because of problems with tension, fatigue, insomnia, and being short-tempered. She attributed these problems to job stress. When asked what the main sources of stress were she said, "People at work are constantly dropping things and making noise just to get me." and, "They keep trying to turn my supervisor against me." She was unwilling to consider alternative explanations for their actions and described herself as typically sensitive, jealous, easily offended, and quick to anger.

However, the diagnosis can be much more difficult to make:

> Gary was a radiologist in his late 20s, who was single with a steady girlfriend. He was working while going to graduate school part-time and living with his parents to afford tuition. He described himself as chronically nervous and reported problems with worry, anxiety attacks, and insomnia. He was seeking therapy because his symptoms had intensified due to school pressures. He talked openly and seemed forthright. The initial interview was remarkable only for his not wanting his family to know he was in therapy, because they did not believe in seeking help for problems, and his not wanting to use his health insurance because of concerns about confidentiality.

TABLE 7.1. *DSM-IV-TR* Diagnostic Criteria for Paranoid Personality Disorder

---

A. A pervasive distrust and suspiciousness of others such that their motives are interpreted as malevolent, beginning by early adulthood and present in a variety of contexts, as indicated by four or more of the following:
1. Suspects, without sufficient basis, that others are exploiting, harming, or deceiving him or her
2. Is preoccupied with unjustified doubts about the loyalty or trustworthiness of friends or associates
3. Is reluctant to confide in others because of unwarranted fear that the information will be used maliciously against him or her
4. Reads hidden demeaning or threatening meanings into benign remarks or events
5. Persistently bears grudges, i.e., is unforgiving of insults, injuries, or slights
6. Perceives attacks on his or her character or reputation that are not apparent to others and is quick to react angrily or to counterattack
7. Has recurrent suspicions, without justification, regarding fidelity of spouse or sexual partner
B. Does not occur exclusively during the course of Schizophrenia, a Mood Disorder With Psychotic Features, or another Psychotic Disorder and is not due to the direct physiological effects of a general medical condition.

Note: If criteria are met prior to the onset of Schizophrenia, add "Premorbid," e.g., "Paranoid Personality Disorder (Premorbid)."

> Cognitive Therapy with Gary focused both on learning skills for coping more effectively with stress and anxiety and on examining his fears. Treatment proceeded unremarkably and effectively for six sessions. At the beginning of the seventh session he described a number of occasions on which progressive relaxation techniques "didn't work." In discussing these episodes he said, "It's like I don't want to relax," "Maybe I'm afraid of people just taking from me," "I don't want him stealing my idea," "Every little thing you say is used against you," and finally that people are "...out to take you for what they can get." Further discussion made it clear that a suspicious, defensive approach to interpersonal situations was characteristic of his long-term functioning and played a central role both in his problems with stress and anxiety and in his difficulty using relaxation techniques effectively.

The distinctive feature of Paranoid Personality Disorder is a long-standing, pervasive, and unwarranted suspiciousness and mistrust of others. Although guardedness, mistrust, or suspicion may be both justified and adaptive in a variety of difficult situations, well-functioning individuals are willing to look critically at their suspicions and are able to abandon them in the face of contradictory evidence. The individual with Paranoid Personality Disorder overlooks or rejects evidence that conflicts with his or her suspicions and may become suspicious of persons who challenge his or her beliefs. This suspiciousness is not confined to situations in which there are grounds for vigilance or suspicion but is characteristic of the individual's overall functioning.

Individuals with this disorder are typically hypervigilant, quick to interpret ambiguous situations as threatening, and quick to take precautions against perceived threats. They expect others to be devious, deceptive, disloyal, and hostile, and they act on the assumption that these expectations are accurate. As a result, they frequently are perceived by others as devious, deceptive, disloyal, and hostile and also are often seen as stubborn, defensive, and unwilling to compromise. They often have little recognition of the impact their behavior has on others' perception

TABLE 7.2. Possible Indications of Paranoid Personality Disorder

Constant vigilance, possibly manifested as a tendency to scan the therapist's office during the
  interview or to frequently glance out the window
Greater than normal concern about confidentiality, possibly including reluctance to allow the therapist
  to maintain progress notes or requests that the therapist take special steps to assure confidentiality
  when returning telephone calls from the client
A tendency to attribute all blame for problems to others and to perceive himself or herself as
  frequently mistreated and abused
Recurrent conflict with figures of authority
Unusually strong convictions regarding the motives of others and difficulty considering alternative
  explanations for their actions
A tendency to interpret small events as having great significance and thus react strongly, apparently
  "making mountains out of molehills"
A tendency to counterattack quickly in response to a perceived threat or slight and to be contentious
  and litigious
A tendency to receive more than his or her share of bad treatment from others or to provoke hostility
  from others
A tendency to search intensely and narrowly for evidence which confirms his or her negative
  expectations regarding others, ignoring the context and reading (plausible) special meanings and
  hidden motives into ordinary events
Inability to relax, particularly when in the presence of others, possibly including unwillingness or
  inability to close his or her eyes in the presence of the therapist for relaxation training
Inability to see the humor in situations
An unusually strong need for self-sufficiency and independence
Disdain for those he or she sees as weak, soft, sickly, or defective
Difficulty expressing warm, tender feelings or expressing doubts and insecurities
Pathological jealousy

of them, blaming others for all interpersonal problems and refusing to accept their
share of responsibility for the problems. Table 7.2 presents a number of possible
indications of a paranoid personality style that may warn the clinician to be alert
for other indications of Paranoid Personality Disorder.

It is important to note that the discussion in this chapter applies to Paranoid
Personality Disorder, not to Delusional Disorder, Persecutory Type or Paranoid
Schizophrenia. Paranoia is also a symptom of these other disorders; however, in
these disorders there are persistent psychotic symptoms such as delusions and hallucinations. According to the *DSM-IV-TR* diagnostic criteria, psychotic symptoms
are never part of Paranoid Personality Disorder except for brief periods at times of
extreme stress. Although many of the principles discussed in this chapter may apply with Delusional Disorder or Paranoid Schizophrenia, it is not clear what impact
the presence of thought disorder or a formalized delusional system would have on
treatment. The principles often do apply well to individuals who abruptly develop
paranoid symptomatology without thought disorder in response to a stressor such
as an illness or an unexpected failure.

Conceptualization

The topic of paranoia in general has received extensive attention from psychodynamic writers from Freud to the present. A lucid discussion of the traditional

view of paranoia is presented by Shapiro (1965, pp. 54–107). Following a clear and extensive discussion of the paranoid cognitive style, he argues that the disorder is a result of "projection" of unacceptable feelings and impulses onto others. A similar view of paranoia has been presented in the cognitive-behavioral literature by Colby and his colleagues (Colby, 1981; Colby, Faught, & Parkinson, 1979). These investigators have developed a computer simulation of a paranoid client's responses in a psychiatric interview based on their model of paranoia. This computer simulation is sufficiently realistic so that experienced interviewers are unable to distinguish the responses of the computer model from the responses of an actual client (as long as the domain of the interview is sufficiently restricted). Colby's model is based on the assumption that the paranoid individual strongly believes that he or she is inadequate, imperfect, and insufficient. It is proposed that these beliefs are activated when relevant events or thoughts occur and that, at that time, the individual experiences distress due to the resulting "shame–humiliation." Colby and his colleagues suggest that paranoid individuals are able to reduce their shame–humiliation by attributing the distress to the inadequacy of others rather than of themselves. Thus, the paranoid cognitive style is seen as being motivated and perpetuated by its distress-reducing effects. On the basis of this model, the authors speculate that the most effective interventions might focus on: (1) challenging the client's belief that he or she is inadequate or insufficient; (2) restricting the scope of events that are accepted as evidence of inadequacy; and (3) counteracting the client's external attributions regarding the sources of his or her distress. The Colby model argues that directly challenging specific suspicions and allegations will prove ineffective as well as difficult because it has little effect on the factors producing the disorder. The authors make it clear that these suggestions are based purely on their computer simulation and have not been clinically validated. Furthermore, Colby's theoretical model is of paranoia in general and it is not clear to what extent it provides a comprehensive understanding of Paranoid Personality Disorder.

Paranoid Personality Disorder *per se* has received less attention from cognitive-behavioral authors. In a discussion of personality disorders in general, Marshall and Barbaree (1984) commented briefly that the paranoid client's suspiciousness plays a central role in the disorder through its dual impact on cognition and on social interaction, but they go no further in discussing the disorder or in proposing interventions. Turkat and Maisto (1985) discussed a case example of treatment in progress with Mr. E, a client with Paranoid Personality Disorder, in a paper presenting their experimentally based behavioral approach to the treatment of personality disorders. The core of the conceptualization of Mr. E proposed by Turkat and Maisto is that, as a result of childhood learning, he had developed a hypersensitivity to others' evaluations of him but did not acquire good social skills. This was seen as resulting in a self-perpetuating cycle in which the client was concerned about the opinions of others, attempted to gain their approval and/or to avoid their disapproval, but did so in a way that instead elicited criticism. In response, he withdrew and ruminated about his failures and his mistreatment by others. Mr. E's cognitions about persecution at the hands of others were seen as a rationalization used to cope with his recurrent failures and his ruminations about failures. On the basis of this conceptualization, Turkat and Maisto (1985) selected interventions focused on

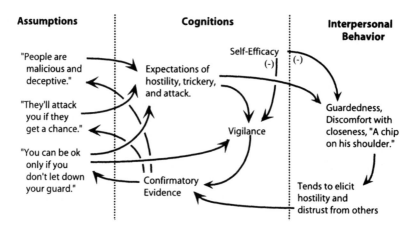

FIGURE 7.1. Cognitive Model of Paranoid Personality Disorder.

decreasing the client's anxiety regarding evaluation by others and on improving his social skills, paying only limited attention to his paranoid thought style. Although treatment had not been completed at the time of publication, the authors documented considerable progress that had been made after 7 months of twice-weekly therapy.

Clinical observations made in the course of Cognitive Therapy with clients with Paranoid Personality Disorder suggest conclusions that are somewhat different from those of Colby (1981) or of Turkat and Maisto (1985). For example, Figure 7.1 summarizes the cognitive and interpersonal components of Gary's paranoid approach to life, which were uncovered in the course of his therapy. He held three basic assumptions quite strongly: "People are malevolent and deceptive," "They'll attack you if they get the chance," and "You can be OK only if you stay on your toes." Obviously these assumptions led to the expectation of deception, trickery, and harm in interpersonal interactions and to the conclusion that vigilance for signs of deception, trickery, and malicious intentions was necessary. However, this vigilance produced an unintended side effect. If one is vigilant for subtle indications that others are untrustworthy (and not equally vigilant for signs of trustworthiness and benign intentions) one quickly accumulates considerable evidence to support the view that people cannot be trusted. After all, people are not uniformly trustworthy and many interactions are ambiguous enough to leave room for them to be interpreted as revealing malicious intentions even if such is actually not the case. Thus, Gary's vigilance produced substantial evidence to support his assumptions about human nature and tended to perpetuate his paranoid approach to life.

Also, Gary's negative expectations about interpersonal interactions had a major impact on his interactions with colleagues and acquaintances. He avoided closeness in relationships for fear that the emotional involvement and greater openness involved in close relationships would make him more vulnerable to being hurt. In addition, he was generally guarded and defensive, tended to react strongly to small slights, and was quick to respond to perceived provocation with hostility. Naturally, these characteristics did not endear him to others or establish the types of relationships that would encourage others to be kind and generous toward him. Instead, he tended to provoke distrust and hostility from others. His beliefs regarding human nature led Gary to interact with people in a way that provided him with the repeated experience of being badly treated and these experiences supported his negative view of human nature.

As noted in the previous discussion of anxiety disorders (Chapter 5), self-efficacy expectations, the individual's estimate of his or her ability to handle a particular situation effectively, play a major role in individuals' responses to situations perceived as risky or dangerous. If one is faced with a dangerous situation but is confident that he or she can handle it effectively, the emotional and behavioral responses will be quite different from those experienced by a person in the same situation who has serious doubts about his or her ability to handle it. If Gary had been confident that he could see through the deceptions of others and thwart their attacks, he would have felt less need to be constantly on guard. However, he doubted his ability to deal effectively with others and felt that it would be quite dangerous to lower his guard.

Many aspects of paranoia follow naturally from the pattern of cognition and behavior observed in Paranoid Personality Disorder. The assumptions that people are malevolent and deceptive and that one can be safe only through vigilance lead the individual to be alert for signs of danger and result in selective attention to experiences that support the paranoid world-view. However, these assumptions also contribute to paranoid interpretations of experiences that would otherwise be incompatible with the assumption that others are malicious. If one assumes that people cannot be trusted, then interactions in which other people seem benign or helpful can easily be interpreted as revealing deception on their part, as being an attempt to trick one into trusting them. If this interpretation of benign acts as deceptive occurs, the "fact" that people are trying to deceive the client by acting nice is seen as clear evidence that their intentions are malicious. This pattern leads to the commonly observed tendency to reject "obvious" interpretations of the actions of others and to search for the "real" underlying meaning, a search that continues until an interpretation consistent with the paranoid individual's preconceptions is found.

In many ways the paranoid reacts as anyone would in a dangerous situation that is confronted rather than avoided. Vigilant for signs of danger, he or she acts cautiously and purposefully, avoiding carelessness and unnecessary risks. Because the most important danger is seen as coming from others and others are seen as potentially deceptive, the paranoid is alert for signs of danger or deception during interactions, constantly scanning for subtle cues of the individual's true intentions. In such a "dog eat dog" world, to show any weakness is to court attack so the paranoid carefully conceals his or her insecurities and shortcomings through deception, denial, excuses, or blaming others. Believing that what others know about you may be used against you, the paranoid carefully guards his or her privacy, striving to suppress even trivial information and, in particular, suppressing signs of his or her own emotions and intentions.

When one is facing a hostile situation such as the paranoid believes he or she faces, any restrictions on one's freedom can leave one trapped and vulnerable.

Thus, the paranoid has a low tolerance for rules and regulations unless they serve his or her plans. The more powerful an individual is, the more of a threat he or she is seen as posing. As a result, the paranoid is keenly aware of power hierarchies, both admiring and fearing persons in positions of authority, hoping for a powerful ally but fearing betrayal or attack. He or she is typically unwilling to "give in" because the appearance of weakness might encourage attack, yet is reluctant to challenge powerful individuals and risk-provoking retaliation.

When one is vigilant for signs of threat or attack and presumes malicious intentions, any slights or mistreatments seem to be intentional and malicious. When others protest that their actions were unintentional, accidental, or justified, their protestations are seen as evidence of deception. Because attention is focused on mistreatment by others, although any apparently good treatment by others is discounted and any mistreatment of others is justified, situations constantly seem unfair and unjust. The perception that others are making unjustified intrusions on the client's personal domain elicits anger that is expressed aggressively, passive-aggressively, or explosively rather than assertively.

This view of Paranoid Personality Disorder is substantially different from those presented by Colby (1981) and by Turkat and Maisto (1985). It differs from Colby's view in that there is no need to make the traditional psychodynamic assumption that the paranoid individual's suspicions of others are due to "projection" of unacceptable impulses (Colby, 1981). Neither does it assume that paranoia is a rationalization used to cope with recurrent failures (Turkat & Maisto, 1985). Both of these views argue that the paranoid individuals' suspicions, which seem central to the disorder, are actually complex side effects of other, more important processes. However, the model of Paranoid Personality Disorder presented here provides a more parsimonious explanation of the paranoid's suspicions and assigns them a more central role. Both the "expectation of malevolence–vigilance–perception of malevolence" cycle and the "expectation of malevolence–defensiveness–hostility from others" cycle discussed above can easily result in a "self-fulfilling prophecy" and thus be self-perpetuating. Furthermore, these cycles are largely impervious to experiences that would conflict with the assumptions that others have malicious intentions and that they are deceptive as well. These assumptions result in a strong tendency for the paranoid individual to assume that apparently benign or benevolent actions on the part of others are deceptive rather than genuine. As a result, the paranoid searches for concealed meanings in apparently benign events. This view suggests that rather than being peripheral, the paranoid client's suspicions are an important component of the cognitive and interpersonal cycles that perpetuate the disorder and should be considered as potential targets for intervention.

Any conclusions regarding the etiology of Paranoid Personality Disorder are purely speculative because it is difficult to collect reliable data regarding the developmental histories from people with Paranoid Personality Disorder. This is true not only because of their reluctance to self-disclose, but also because their recollections of previous events tend to be distorted in a paranoia-congruent way. However, it is interesting to consider that a paranoid stance would actually be adaptive if one were faced by a truly dangerous situation where others were likely to prove to be overtly or covertly hostile. Many paranoid clients describe growing up in families that they experienced as quite dangerous. For example, Gary described a long history of being ridiculed by family members for any sign of sensitivity or weakness, of being lied to and cheated by parents and siblings, and of verbal and physical assaults by family members. In addition, he reported being explicitly taught by his parents that the world was a "dog eat dog" place where one must be tough to survive. Such accounts give the impression that growing up in a generally hostile or paranoid family where vigilance is truly necessary could contribute substantially to the development of Paranoid Personality Disorder. Such a hypothesis is appealing but it will remain speculative until it is possible to obtain more objective data regarding the histories of these individuals.

A comprehensive theoretical treatment of the etiology of Paranoid Personality Disorder would also need to account for studies that find an unusually high incidence of "schizophrenic spectrum" disorders among relatives of individuals diagnosed with Paranoid Personality Disorder (Kendler & Gruenberg, 1982). Such findings raise the possibility of a genetic link; but it is important to note that other studies have produced results that are not consistent with the hypothesis that Paranoid Personality Disorder is linked with Schizophrenia (Nestadt *et al.*, 1994).

Intervention Strategies and Techniques

The model of Paranoid Personality Disorder presented above may appear to provide little opportunity for effective intervention. It is obvious that one goal of intervention would be to modify the core beliefs which are the foundation of the disorder. But how can one hope to challenge these assumptions effectively when the client's vigilance and paranoid approach to interactions constantly produce experiences that seem to confirm them? On the other hand, how can the therapist hope to induce the client to relax his or her vigilance or to treat others more appropriately as long as the client is convinced that others have malicious intentions? If these two self-perpetuating cycles were the entire cognitive model of Paranoid Personality Disorder, there would be little prospect for effective cognitive-behavioral intervention with these clients.

Fortunately, the client's self-efficacy has an important role in Paranoid Personality Disorder. The paranoid individual's intense vigilance and defensiveness is a product of the belief that constant vigilance and defensiveness is necessary to preserve his or her safety. If it is possible to increase the client's sense of self efficacy, he or she will be more confident of being able to handle problems as they arise, and the intense vigilance and defensiveness will seem less necessary. This might make it possible for the client to relax his or her vigilance and defensiveness to some extent. This relaxation in vigilance and defensiveness would reduce the intensity of the client's symptomatology substantially. It would also make it much easier to address the client's cognitions through conventional cognitive techniques. Reducing vigilance would also make it easier to persuade the client to try alternative ways of handling interpersonal conflicts. Therefore, the primary strategy in the cognitive treatment of Paranoid Personality Disorder is to increase the client's sense of self-efficacy before attempting to modify other aspects of the client's automatic thoughts, interpersonal behavior, and basic assumptions.

The first task in Cognitive Therapy with Paranoid Personality Disorder, as with any other problem, is establishing a working relationship. This is not an easy task when working with someone who assumes that others are likely to prove malevolent and deceptive. The paranoid is certain that it can be very dangerous to trust other people and quickly realizes that the therapist–client relationship is a relationship in which he or she will be quite vulnerable at times. It rarely is productive to try to establish trust through persuasion, argument, or pointing to one's credentials. The paranoid is not foolish enough to trust people simply because they say they can be trusted or because they have a diploma. Trust is most effectively established through explicitly acknowledging and accepting the client's difficulty in trusting the therapist (once this becomes evident) and being careful to behave in a trustworthy manner to provide the evidence on which trust can be based. It is important to exercise more than the usual amount of care in communicating clearly, assertively, and honestly, avoiding misunderstandings, maintaining congruence between verbal statements and nonverbal cues, and following through on agreements. It is important not to press the client to take risks in therapy until a sufficient level of trust has been established and to make it clear that the client has the right to not talk about sensitive topics until ready to do so.

Collaboration is always important in Cognitive Therapy; but it is especially important in working with paranoid individuals because they are likely to become intensely anxious or angry if they feel coerced, treated unfairly, or placed in a "one-down" position. Because these clients rarely present their paranoia as a problem they wish to work on, it is important to focus on the client's stated goals for therapy. There is no need to worry that by focusing on their stress, marital problems, or whatever they bring into therapy, the "real problem" of their paranoia will be missed. A guided discovery approach to pursuing the clients' goals will quickly reveal the ways in which paranoia contributes to their other problems. Ideally, this will create the opportunity to work collaboratively on their distrust of others, feelings of vulnerability, and so on, rather than the therapist insisting that these issues be addressed.

The initial phase of therapy can be quite stressful to paranoid clients even when it seems to the therapist that the focus is on superficial topics that should not be very threatening. It is important to remember that simply participating in therapy requires the client to engage in a number of activities that he or she experiences as being quite dangerous. These include self-disclosure, acknowledging weakness, and trusting another person, among others. The stress that results from simply participating in therapy can be reduced by focusing initially on the least sensitive topics and by starting with primarily behavioral interventions. Stress can also be reduced by discussing issues indirectly (i.e., through the use of analogies or through talking about how "some people" react in such situations) rather than pressing for direct self-disclosure. One of the more effective ways to increase a paranoid client's comfort with therapy is to give the client even more than the usual amount of control over the content of sessions, homework assignments, and the scheduling of sessions. These clients may be much more comfortable and progress more quickly if sessions are scheduled less frequently than usual. With a number of paranoid clients, scheduling sessions about once every 3 weeks has seemed optimal.

As therapy shifts from establishing a working relationship to working toward the client's initial goals, it is generally most productive for the therapist to focus on increasing the client's sense of self-efficacy in problem situations. There are two main ways in which this can be done. If the client overestimates the threat posed by the situation or underestimates his or her capacity for handling the situation, a more realistic appraisal of his or her ability to cope with the situation will increase self-efficacy expectations. If there is room for improvement in the client's coping skills, interventions that improve his or her skills will increase self-efficacy. In practice, it often works best to use the two approaches in combination.

With Ann (the administrative assistant mentioned above), it would have been ineffective to challenge her paranoid ideation, e.g., "They are making noise just to get me." It did, however, prove quite useful for the therapist to help her reevaluate how much danger such actions would pose if her co-workers were indeed trying to provoke her as well as to reevaluate her capacity for coping with the situation:

THERAPIST: You're reacting as though this is a very dangerous situation. What are the risks you see?

ANN: They'll keep dropping things and making noise to annoy me.

THERAPIST: Are you sure nothing worse is a risk?

ANN: (After a moment of thought) Yeah.

THERAPIST: So you don't think there's much chance of them attacking you or anything?

ANN: Nah, they wouldn't do that.

THERAPIST: If they do keep dropping things and making noises how bad will that be?

ANN: Like I told you it's real aggravating. It really bugs me.

THERAPIST: So it would continue pretty much as it has been going for years now.

ANN: Yeah, it bugs me but I can take it.

THERAPIST: And you know that if it keeps happening, at the very least you can keep handling it the way you have been, holding the aggravation in then taking it out on your husband when you get home. . . . Suppose we could come up with some ways to handle the aggravation even better or have them get to you less, is that something you'd be interested in?

ANN: Yeah, that sounds good.

THERAPIST: Another risk you mentioned earlier was that they might talk to your supervisor and turn her against you. As you see it, how long have they been trying to do this?

ANN: Ever since I've been there.

THERAPIST: How much luck have they had so far in doing that?

ANN: Not much.

THERAPIST: Do you see any indications that they're going to have any more success now than they have so far?

ANN: No, I don't guess so.

THERAPIST: So your gut reaction is as though the situation at work is really dangerous. But when you stop and think it through, you conclude that the worst they're going to do is to be really aggravating and that even if we don't come up with anything new, you can handle it well enough to get by. Does that sound right?

ANN: Yeah, I guess so!

THERAPIST: And if we can come up with some ways to handle the stress better or handle them better, there will be even less they can do to you.

Obviously, this interchange alone was not sufficient to transform Ann dramatically, but following this session she reported a noticeable decrease in vigilance and stress at work. Additional interventions, which focused on reevaluating perceived threats, on stress management and assertion, and on improving marital communication, resulted in rapid improvement. According to her husband's report as well as her own, she continued to be somewhat guarded and vigilant but no longer overreacted to minor provocations. Furthermore, she became assertive rather than hostile, and no longer exploded at her husband as a result of aggravations at work.

Gary's Paranoid Personality Disorder was not recognized until the seventh session of Cognitive Therapy which, up to that point, had focused on coping with chronic stress and anxiety. By that time, successful stress-management interventions had already raised his self-efficacy expectations substantially. It was possible to further boost his sense of self-efficacy by helping him to reevaluate his perfectionistic, dichotomous standards for himself. He had previously assumed that if one were truly competent, one would handle situations without any stress or difficulty. Therefore, he assumed that if he experienced any distress this showed that he was incompetent. A reevaluation of these beliefs led him to conclude that his ability to handle difficult situations well despite considerable stress and anxiety was actually a sign of his capabilities rather than being a sign of incompetence. His shift from a dichotomous view of competence to a more continuous one enabled him to set more manageable standards for himself and thus experience more frequent successes. Following these increases in his sense of self-efficacy, he was much more willing to disclose thoughts and feelings, to look critically at his beliefs and assumptions, and to test new approaches to problem situations. This made it possible to use standard cognitive techniques with greater effectiveness.

One intervention that had a particularly strong impact on Gary was the continuum technique (Chapter 2); this was used to challenge his dichotomous view of trustworthiness. First, he delineated the behaviors that he saw as being characteristic of completely trustworthy and completely untrustworthy individuals. When he considered whether his acquaintances completely fit into one category or the other, it became clear to him that few people actually fell at either extreme. However, Gary still did not know how to gauge a particular individual's trustworthiness or how to deal with persons who were at intermediate levels of trustworthiness. It was necessary to introduce the idea that he could learn which persons were likely to prove trustworthy by noticing how well they followed through when trusted on trivial issues and that he could then decide whether to risk trusting them on more important issues. The therapist also helped Gary consider the evidence regarding whether his family's malevolence was typical of people in general. As a result, Gary was able to gradually risk trusting colleagues and acquaintances in small things and was pleasantly surprised to discover that the world at large was much less malevolent than he had believed.

Because the paranoid individual tends to provoke hostile reactions from others that could interfere with progress, it is important to also work behaviorally to modify the client's dysfunctional interpersonal interactions. This helps to avoid situations that would tend to confirm the paranoid views regarding other people. In Gary's case this required focusing on specific problem situations that arose, addressing the cognitions that blocked appropriate assertion, and helping him develop adequate skills in assertion and clear communication. The resulting improvements in his relationships with colleagues and with his girlfriend helped him recognize the ways in which his previous interaction style had inadvertently provoked hostility from others. The improvements in his interpersonal interactions also supported his new belief that the world contained benevolent and indifferent people as well as malevolent ones.

Toward the close of therapy it was possible to "fine-tune" Gary's new perspective on people and new interpersonal skills by working to help him develop an increased ability to understand the perspectives of others and to empathize with them. This was done by asking questions that focused on anticipating the impact of his actions on others and considering how he would feel if the roles were reversed. He was also asked to infer the thoughts and feelings of others from their actions and then to examine the correspondence between his answers and the available data. Initially Gary found these questions difficult to answer and he was often off the mark. As he received feedback both from the therapist and through subsequent interactions, his ability to accurately understand other people's perspectives increased steadily. He found that aggravating actions by others were not necessarily motivated by malicious intentions and that these actions were less aggravating when he could understand the other person's point of view.

At the close of therapy Gary was noticeably more relaxed and was bothered by mild symptoms of stress and anxiety only at times when many people experience mild symptoms, such as immediately before major examinations. He reported being much more comfortable with friends and colleagues, was socializing more actively, and seemed to feel no particular need to be vigilant. When he and his girlfriend began having difficulties, which were due in part to her discomfort with the increasing closeness in their relationship, he was able to suspend his initial feelings of rejection and desire to retaliate long enough to consider her point of view. Then he was able to take a major role in resolving their difficulties by clearly communicating his understanding of her concerns, his own fears and doubts, and his commitment to their relationship.

Conclusions

The authors' clinical experience in working with individuals with Paranoid Personality Disorder has been quite promising. The proposed interventions (increasing self-efficacy, seeing trustworthiness as a continuum, learning a more assertive approach to interpersonal conflicts, and developing an increased awareness of the other person's point of view) are all changes that would be expected to have broad intrapersonal and interpersonal impact. It appears that significant personality change can occur as a result of Cognitive Therapy with these clients. However, we do not yet have the follow-up data that would be needed to determine how well the improvements generalize and persist.

SCHIZOID PERSONALITY DISORDER

The diagnosis of Schizoid Personality Disorder is probably one of the most confusing of the Axis II diagnoses. The label "schizoid" has been a diagnostic category that has been in transition for almost 100 years. The original use of the term schizoid can be traced to Manfred Bleuler of the Swiss Burgholzi Clinic (Siever, 1981). It is composed of the prefix "schizo" from the Greek word meaning cleaving or splitting and the suffix "oid" which means "like or representing." Traditionally, the schizoid was seen as an individual who was quiet, shy, reserved, and "schizophrenic like" (Kraepelin, 1913). In reviewing historical conceptions of schizoid individuals, Siever (1981) cites several authors who saw schizoid behavior as part of the schizophrenic process as well as being a precursor to schizophrenia. Alternately, Campbell (1981) argues that schizoid behavior can represent either a chronic vulnerability to a schizophrenic process that may be genetically dictated or can be due to a partial recovery from schizophrenia. He utilizes the traditional definition when he states that the schizoid personality disorder resembles, "....the division, separation, or split of the personality that is characteristic of schizophrenia" (p. 563).

Kretschmer (1936) described several subtypes of schizoid personality. Some were stiff, formal, and correct in social situations, indicating a keen awareness of social requirements. Others were isolated and eccentric, either not caring about social conventions or unaware of them. Still others appeared fragile, delicate, and hypersensitive. In Kretchmer's view, the schizoid diagnosis was not necessarily synonymous with disability. The schizoid personality could be very creative in occupations that allowed solitary work. More frequently, the schizoid was employed at simple jobs that were below his or her level of ability. A number of early studies examined the premorbid adjustment of schizophrenics. They found that a premorbid schizoid adjustment was prognostically related to the severity of the schizophrenic illness, predicting a poorer outcome. However, it was not necessarily a precursor to schizophrenia (Frazee, 1953; Gittleman-Klein & Klein, 1969; Longabaugh & Eldred, 1973; Mellsop, 1972, 1973; Morris, Soroker, & Burruss, 1954; Roff, Knight, & Wertheim, 1976).

The view of schizoid individuals presented in *DSM-IV-TR* differs markedly from the traditional view. Here, Schizoid Personality Disorder is not seen as a precursor to Schizophrenia, but rather the schizoid individual is seen as chronically reclusive and isolated. The schizoid diagnosis has been separated from another diagnostic group, the schizotypal group, which is seen as more closely related to the schizophrenic disorders (Baron, Gruen, Asnis, & Kane, 1983; Kendler, Gruenberg, & Strauss, 1981; Kety, Rosenthal, Wender, & Schulsinger, 1968) and that will be discussed later in this chapter.

Assessment

The *DSM-IV-TR* criteria for Schizoid Personality Disorder can be seen in Table 7.3. Schizoid individuals often appear odd or eccentric and their isolation in the midst of a generally sociable milieu stands out in sharp relief. However, although these individuals may be noticed by their neighbors and labeled as

Table 7.3. *DSM-IV-TR* Criteria for Schizoid Personality Disorder

A. A pervasive pattern of detachment from social relationships and a restricted range of expression or emotions in interpersonal settings, beginning by early adulthood and present in a variety of contexts, as indicated by four (or more) of the following:
1. Neither desires nor enjoys close relationships, including being part of a family
2. Almost always chooses solitary activities
3. Has little, if any, interest in having sexual experiences with another person
4. Takes pleasure in few, if any, activities
5. Lacks close friends or confidants other than first-degree relatives
6. Appears indifferent to the praise or criticism of others
7. Shows emotional coldness, detachment, or flattened affectivity

B. Does not occur exclusively during the course of Schizophrenia, a Mood Disorder With Psychotic Features, another Psychotic Disorder, or a Pervasive Developmental Disorder and is not due to the direct physiological effects of a general medical condition.

Note: If criteria are met prior to the onset of Schizophrenia, add "Premorbid," e.g., "Schizoid Personality Disorder (Premorbid)."

"strange," the clinician who is assessing a client often will not have access to data about the client's social behavior other than that that he or she observes within the session. Schizoid individuals fall into two broad groups. The first group generally does not seek treatment of their own volition and often does not describe substantial problems when interviewed. Often these individuals come to the attention of mental health professionals when their behavior is noticed by physicians, employers, or family members. Others are likely to be concerned because, to them, the client seems unusual, avoids interactions with staff, co-workers, and others, avoids relating personal information, and generally is nonresponsive in group settings. The second group does not experience distress from their isolation or constriction, but they seek help for their depression, anxiety, somatic problems, or vague, general dysphoria when their Axis I disorders become intolerable.

Individuals with Schizoid Personality Disorder may function well in settings where a preference for social isolation is acceptable or is actually an asset. In occupational settings that encourage or require working in isolation, such as computer work, typing, or research, these individuals may be very successful. For example:

> Evan, aged 37, was a graduate of a prestigious law school and a partner in a large law firm. He sought therapy for mild depression after his medical doctor recommended doing so. His position in his law firm was that of a research expert and drafter of briefs for the other partners. He would be given a complex legal problem to deal with, would utilize library and computer search facilities to investigate the relevant cases, and then write a brief for other attorneys to use. He would send the brief to the other attorney via interoffice mail or e-mail.
>
> Evan rarely attended office parties, had no friends in the office, and could generally be counted on to work evenings and weekends. He was aware that others in his office saw him as "strange" because of his isolation. He had on several occasions overheard himself being referred to as "the turtle" by staff members. Neither his work nor this title upset him.

As can be seen from Table 7.3, one of the key factors in assessing Schizoid Personality Disorder is the individual's isolated life style. The diagnostician is often faced with the question of whether a client is schizoid or avoidant, because both share difficulty in interpersonal relationships and an avoidance of contact with others. In both disorders, the problems begin by the early adult years, and are pervasive in a variety of life contexts. A lively debate regarding the similarities and differences between these diagnoses has been conducted (Akhtar, 1986; Livesley, West, & Tanney, 1985, 1986a, b; Millon, 1986a, b; Reich & Noyes, 1986; Scott, 1986). The *DSM IV-TR* criteria agree with the view advocated by Millon, treating the disorders as quite distinct. Millon (1981, 1996) distinguishes between the two based on the basis of the reasons for the individual's avoidance of interpersonal relationships. When the schizoid individual observes others in social situations, he or she can acknowledge that other people choose to affiliate with each other, but cannot understand why they do so and personally feels no desire to socialize. The avoidant individual, on the other hand, sees others in social situations and would very much like to join them, but fears rejection. The following clinical vignette illustrates the schizoid response:

> Austin, a 38-year-old draftsman, came for therapy because of his depression. He had worked in the same company for the past 7 years and shared a workspace with six other men. When asked whether he had friends at work, he said, "No, I'm not friends with them. We work together." In fact, he did not even speak with them during the day. The other men shared a coffeepot and would contribute periodically for coffee, sugar, etc. Austin had his own pot. His drafting table faced a wall, and he insisted that the other men call him by his family name. When asked why he insisted on the title "Mr.", he responded, "We're not friends, we just work together." In point of fact, Austin had no friends. One of the therapeutic recommendations was for Austin to participate in group therapy. He asked why, and the therapist explained about the advantages of getting feedback from others, practicing social skills, and simply being social. Austin looked quite bewildered and asked, "Why would I want to do those things?"

Conceptualization

The social isolation and emotional constriction of the schizoid individual seem to follow directly from a lack of positive thoughts about closeness coupled with positive thoughts about being alone. Typical views expressed by schizoid clients include: "There are few reasons to be close to people;" "I am my own best friend;" "Stay calm, displays of emotion are unnecessary and embarrassing," "What others say is of little interest or importance to me;" and, "Sex is okay, but just for release." For example:

> Dante, a 66-year-old retired chemist, came for therapy reporting a high level of anxiety. He had never married, but had been dating one woman for the past 8 years. He would typically see her once a week on a Saturday night. They would have dinner in a restaurant, see a movie, and then go to her home and have sex. Dante would then go home. When asked why he did not ever have dinner at her home, stay over at her home after sex, or stay at her home and watch television, he said, "Why stay over? I did what I came for. That's pretty funny, what I *came* for".

Dante described himself as "low key" and stated, "I never get angry." Dante's therapeutic goals were first to lower his anxiety and then to explore his avoidance, or ignorance as to why people spend time together. He came for weekly therapy sessions, and seemed to respond positively to the sessions but did not show much emotional involvement. When the therapist informed Dante of the therapist's impending vacation, in a month, Dante replied, "So what! You deserve a vacation. Why tell me at all? We just won't schedule any appointments for those days." The therapist said that he wanted to tell Dante early enough so that any reactions to the therapist's absence could be talked over. Dante replied, "I don't understand. If you're away, you're away. What is that to me?"

The schizoid client's expressed view is that there is no point to social interaction. This lack of motivation for social interaction, in combination with the subsequent low frequency of social interaction, is sufficient to explain the primary characteristics of the disorder. The schizoid individual typically denies having any desire for close relationships and denies having any significant fears of close relationships. Despite this, it is tempting to hypothesize that both a desire for closeness and fear regarding closeness are present but are being suppressed. However, it is not at all clear whether this is the case or not.

Although it is difficult to judge the accuracy of clients' reports of their history, it is interesting to note that, when historical information can be obtained, schizoid clients often report experiences that could contribute to a neutral or negative view of interpersonal closeness and a positive view of social isolation. In Dante's case:

> Dante reported that when he was 2-years old, his mother became quite ill with tuberculosis and was sent to a sanitarium for 2 years. She returned home for several months and then had to return to the sanitarium, where she died a year later. During his mother's illness, he lived with his maternal grandmother. After his mother's death, he continued to live with his grandmother until age six or seven. At that time his father remarried and Dante had to return to live with his father and stepmother. He did not want to leave his grandmother and barely knew his father. Through childhood, adolescence, and his young adult years, he avoided relationships. In Dante's case, a major assumption was, "Getting attached to people is not a good idea. They'll probably leave me."

Intervention Strategies and Techniques

The schizoid individual may not enter therapy with any strong interest in altering his or her manner of relating to other people. Therefore, the initial goals of treatment need to focus on the client's presenting problems. As the client and therapist work on the explicit presenting problems, the therapist can begin to make the nature of the schizoid adjustment pattern explicit, pointing out some of the advantages and disadvantages of this pattern and showing how this adaptation effects the presenting problems.

Schizoid clients typically show little understanding of interpersonal relationships and may have quite poor social skills. Therapists working with these clients may find themselves explaining very basic patterns of human interaction that the client has apparently managed not to observe or experience. At times it is as though the therapist were explaining human interactions to a Martian, newly arrived on our planet and completely naive about humans. Therapist–client interactions within the session can provide valuable opportunities for the therapist to point out characteristic interaction patterns and to provide the client with feedback regarding his or her impact on others. As the client gradually develops a greater understanding of interpersonal relationships, it is important to also help him or her to master any social skills in which he or she is deficient. Then the client can begin to test his or her new understanding and new skills both in interactions with the therapist and with others.

It is important not to rely primarily on verbal interventions to increase positive views of social interaction and closeness and to reduce positive views of social isolation. The therapist can use the therapeutic relationship as a prototype for other interpersonal relationships and can work to increase the client's range and frequency of interpersonal interactions outside the session. In using the therapist–client relationship to establish a more positive view of interpersonal relationships and in attempting to broaden the client's social interactions, the therapist must work carefully so as to not have the client's anxiety increase to a point where he or she would choose to leave therapy. Because schizoid clients are usually quite inexpressive, it is particularly important for the therapist to make a point of soliciting feedback from the client on a regular basis as well as being sensitive to nonverbal indications of stress or anxiety.

Although the therapeutic relationship can be very useful in working with schizoid clients, it can also present problems. The therapist may find it difficult to maintain a warm, supportive, empathic stance with an individual who, because of his or her lack of interpersonal involvement, can often be frustrating. Most therapists are accustomed to having considerable leverage for influencing clients, due to the close personal relationship that develops between therapist and client, the client's desire to "get better," the client's desire to please the therapist, and the client's responsiveness to even mild praise or criticism from the therapist. However, with the schizoid client much of this leverage is unavailable. Fortunately, reason is still available as a tool for motivating change. If the therapist clearly presents the rationale for the therapy, the reasons for acting differently, the pros and cons of changing behavior, and the concrete gains that are possible, the schizoid client can be induced to make the necessary changes. However, this can be a slow and tedious process and it is important for the therapist to be alert for annoyance, resentment, or resignation on his or her part that could impede therapy.

> From the beginning, therapy with Dante focused on increasing his interactions with others. He eventually began to spend weekends with his girlfriend, attend her family's functions (weddings, Thanksgiving dinner, Christmas, and funerals) and went away on a 2-week vacation with her. Dante was not opposed to spending time with others, it was just never something that he ever really understood. Although it was not his first thought or choice, he was able to use self-instructional strategies to help him to be with others. His self-instruction was, "When in doubt, don't be alone." In an attempt to increase Dante's motivation for social interaction, his therapist argued that spending time with his girlfriend would make her happier, and she might then want to make him happier. In discussing the pros and cons of spending more time with his girlfriend, the therapist observed that among other things there was an opportunity for increased sex. Dante did not see the need for the increase. "After all, I can use sex once a week. Why push it?"
>
> At that point, Dante's behavior had been altered, although the underlying assumptions remained the same. With continued interpersonal contacts, the older schema were gradually modified to include the idea of pleasing others because this could lead to more positive responses from them and the idea of pleasing others simply because it is a nice thing to do.

Conclusions

Our experience with Schizoid Personality Disorder has been less encouraging than our experience with Paranoid Personality Disorder. With persistence it is possible to improve the client's social skills, increase his or her frequency of social interaction, and decrease his or her "strangeness." However, these individuals typically continue to be relatively distant and passive in interpersonal relationships and they seem to develop little capacity for warmth and intimacy.

SCHIZOTYPAL PERSONALITY DISORDER

Individuals with Schizotypal Personality Disorder are definitely "eccentric." As described in *DSM IV-TR* (2000), "The essential feature of this disorder is a pervasive pattern of social and interpersonal deficits marked by an acute discomfort with, and reduced capacity for, close relationships as well as by cognitive or perceptual distortions and eccentricities of behavior." (p. 697). These are individuals who would be diagnosed as "borderline" if one were using the term to refer to persons who seem to lie on the border between neurosis and psychosis; however, they do not manifest the characteristics of Borderline Personality Disorder. Other diagnostic labels which have been used to refer to these individuals have included "pseudoneurotic schizophrenia" (Hoch & Polatin, 1949) and "psychotic personality" (Frosch, 1964).

Assessment

The differential diagnosis between Schizotypal Personality Disorder and Schizophrenia is determined by the severity of the disorder rather than by symptoms that clearly differentiate between the two disorders. As can be seen from Table 7.4, comparison of the diagnostic criteria for the two disorders reveals broad areas of overlap, once the acute psychotic episode has passed. The distinction between the two disorders seems to depend on subjective judgments regarding the severity of symptoms. It is possible that attempts to clearly differentiate between Schizotypal Personality Disorder and schizophrenia are unnecessary. Millon writes that, "Since schizotypals...experience transient psychotic episodes, usually those of a schizophrenic nature, then it would appear that they [Schizotypal Personality Disorder and Schizophrenia: Residual Type] must always coexist...except before the schizotypal's first schizophrenic episode" (Millon, 1981, p. 422).

Conceptualization

It has often been assumed that Schizotypal Personality Disorder has much in common with Schizophrenia. In particular, the term "schizotypal" is derived from "schizotype," an abbreviation of "schizophrenic genotype" coined by Sandor Rado (1956), and the theory that this disorder is genetically related to schizophrenia has been popular. Millon (1981, 1996) presents a conceptualization of the development

TABLE 7.4. Comparison of *DSM-IV-TR* Criteria for Schizotypal Personality Disorder and Schizophrenia

Schizotypal Personality Disorder

A. A pervasive pattern of social and interpersonal deficits marked by acute discomfort with, and reduced capacity for, close relationships as well as by cognitive or perceptual distortions and eccentricities of behavior, beginning by early adulthood and present in a variety of contexts, as indicated by five (or more) of the following:
  1. Ideas of reference (excluding delusions of reference)
  2. Odd beliefs or magical thinking that influences behavior and is inconsistent with subcultural norms (e.g., superstitiousness, belief in clairvoyance, telepathy, or "sixth sense"; in children and adolescents, bizarre fantasies or preoccupations)
  3. Unusual perceptual experiences including bodily illusions
  4. Odd thinking and speech (e.g., vague, circumstantial, metaphorical, overelaborate, or stereotyped)
  5. Suspiciousness or paranoid ideation
  6. Inappropriate or constricted affect
  7. Behavior or appearance that is odd or eccentric, or peculiar
  8. Lack of close friends or confidants other than first-degree relatives
  9. Excessive social anxiety that does not diminish with familiarity and tends to be associated with paranoid fears rather than negative judgments about self

Schizophrenia

A. Characteristic symptoms: Two (or more) of the following, each present for a significant portion of time during a 1-month period (or less if successfully treated):
  1. Delusions
  2. Hallucinations
  3. Disorganized speech (e.g., frequent derailment or incoherence)
  4. Grossly disorganized or catatonic behavior
  5. Negative symptoms, i.e., affective flattening, alogia, or avolition
     Note: Only one Criterion A symptom is required if delusions are bizarre or hallucinations consist of a voice keeping up a running commentary of the person's behavior or thoughts, or two or more voices conversing with each other.
B. Social/occupational dysfunction: For a significant portion of the time since the onset of the disturbance, one or more major areas of functioning such as work, interpersonal relations, or self-care are markedly below the level achieved prior to the onset (or when the onset is in childhood or adolescence, failure to achieve expected level of interpersonal, academic, or occupational achievement).
C. Duration: Continuous signs of the disturbance persist for at least 6 months. This 6-month period must include at least 1 month of symptoms (or less if successfully treated) that meet Criterion A (i.e., active-phase symptoms) and may include periods of prodromal or residual symptoms. During these prodromal or residual periods, the signs of the disturbance may be manifested by only negative symptoms or two or more symptoms listed in Criterion A present in an attenuated form (e.g., odd beliefs, unusual perceptual experiences).
D. Schizoaffective and Mood Disorder exclusion: Schizoaffective Disorder and Mood Disorder with Psychotic Features have been ruled out because either (1) no Major Depressive, Manic, or Mixed Episodes have occurred concurrently with the active-phase symptoms; or (2) if mood episodes have occurred during active-phase symptoms, their total duration has been brief relative to the duration of the active and residual periods.
E. Substance/general medical condition exclusion: The disturbance is not due to the direct physiological effects of a substance (e.g., a drug of abuse, a medication) or a general medical condition.

TABLE 7.4. (cont.)

F. Relationship to a Pervasive Developmental Disorder: If there is a history of Autistic Disorder or another Pervasive Developmental Disorder, the additional diagnosis of Schizophrenia is made only if prominent delusions or hallucinations are also present for at least a month (or less if successfully treated).

of this disorder that integrates genetic, social-learning, and cognitive factors. He suggests that Schizotypal Personality Disorder can be viewed as an extreme form of either Schizoid or Avoidant Personality Disorder. This may be due to a learning history that would predispose the individual to the development of one of these two disorders interacting with biological vulnerabilities that further impair development and functioning.

Millon (1981) suggests that, in the subtype of Schizotypal Personality Disorder he refers to as "schizoid schizotypals," a relative insensitivity to social stimuli, deficient learning of social attachment behaviors, and learning of a disjointed, unfocused thought style result in an extremely passive, unresponsive interpersonal style. This disengaged interpersonal style is hypothesized to contribute to increasing social isolation that perpetuates the lack of social skills and social attachments. He suggests that these individuals then become increasingly preoccupied with personal fantasy "unchecked by the logic and control of reciprocal social communication and activity" (Millon, 1981, p. 424) and eventually present the full schizotypal picture.

Millon (1981) refers to another subgroup, as "schizotypal avoidants,". These individuals may be genetically predisposed to "muddled" thinking and thus may initially be fearful and easily overwhelmed by stimulation. If this elicits deprecation and humiliation from parents, siblings, and peers, the resulting low self-esteem and avoidance of social interaction results in deficiencies in social skills and continuing avoidance of social interaction. Withdrawal into idiosyncratic thought and fantasy is seen as a consequence of this cycle. Then, when the individual's tendency toward "muddled" thinking is combined with the lack of corrective feedback from interpersonal interactions, the individual's functioning can easily deteriorate into a schizotypal rather than avoidant pattern.

In his 1996 volume, Millon divides Schizotypal Personality Disorder into two somewhat different subtypes. The "insipid" subtype is characterized as an individual who is insensitive both to his or her own feelings and to interpersonal emotional experiences. As a result, the individual tends to "drift on the periphery of life," interacting with others only minimally and being detached from his or her own emotional experiences. The "timorous" subtype is seen as actively trying to "kill" his or her feelings and desires to avoid the pain and anguish experienced in interpersonal relationships.

These conceptualizations are certainly plausible and compatible with a cognitive point of view. Unfortunately, it is not possible to elaborate further on the cognitive aspects of this disorder with any confidence. The combination of extreme difficulty relating to others coherently and the bizarre thought processes characterizing this disorder greatly complicates the process of identifying specific automatic thoughts and underlying assumptions in the course of therapy.

Intervention Strategies and Techniques

Millon's (1981) view that Schizotypal Personality Disorder can be viewed as an extreme form of Schizoid or Avoidant Personality Disorders suggests that the intervention approaches recommended for use with each of those disorders might be useful with schizotypal clients. However, the preponderance of illogical, "magical" thinking requires a somewhat different approach, at least initially. The major goals in working with these clients are similar to those in working with Schizophrenics, i.e., improving social skills (including grooming, interpersonal skills, and generally appearing less peculiar), anxiety reduction, and improving social problem solving (see Perris and McGorry (1998) for a recent overview of Cognitive Therapy with Schizophrenia). The interventions used in working toward these goals are typically more behavioral than cognitive, focusing on teaching skills rather than monitoring thoughts and developing responses to them (Goldsmith & McFall, 1975). Over time, as the client becomes somewhat less peculiar and as interactions with the therapist provide "the logic and control of reciprocal social communication and activity" to which Millon refers, the intervention strategies suggested for use with schizoid and avoidant clients may be quite appropriate.

Conclusions

The bizarre thinking of individuals with Schizotypal Personality Disorder greatly complicates intervention and particularly interferes with the use of purely cognitive interventions. Our experience is that the outcome of treatment is similar to that observed with clients with Schizoid Personality Disorder. If the therapist is persistent and active, schizotypal clients can learn to behave in more socially appropriate ways and their vocational functioning and ability to cope with day-to-day problems can improve substantially. However, they are likely to remain somewhat withdrawn and eccentric.

8

Antisocial and Borderline Personality Disorders
The Dramatic Cluster—Part 1

DSM-IV-TR (2000) categorizes Antisocial, Borderline, Histrionic, and Narcissistic Personality Disorders together as Cluster B, the "dramatic cluster." Certainly, individuals who meet diagnostic criteria for these disorders can be quite dramatic. Interventions directed toward improving impulse control, increasing emotional stability, and replacing maladaptive interpersonal behavior with more adaptive alternatives can be useful with each of these disorders. However, there are important differences among these disorders as well. Therefore, each of these disorders will be discussed separately. To keep the chapter to a manageable size, Antisocial and Borderline Personality Disorders will be discussed in this chapter and Histrionic and Narcissistic Personality Disorders will be discussed in Chapter 9.

ANTISOCIAL PERSONALITY DISORDER

Perhaps because of the societal impact of its symptoms, its refractoriness to traditional treatment, and the easy availability of imprisoned participants for research, Antisocial Personality Disorder is distinguished from other personality disorders by the large volume of empirical research that it has inspired. Unfortunately, the voluminous research has resulted in neither a consensus on how to best conceptualize the disorder nor in an effective approach to outpatient treatment. Frosch (1983, pp. 98–99) expresses a widely held view when he writes, "The person with antisocial personality is the least popular of patients. Many would question whether these people should be considered patients at all, rather than criminals. The common view is that they are unable to experience guilt, incapable of empathy, and unresponsive to treatment.... Almost everybody does agree that outpatient therapy, when it is the sole treatment, is of little benefit, no matter what the approach."

TABLE 8.1. *DSM-IV-TR* Diagnostic Criteria for Antisocial Personality Disorder

---

A. There is a pervasive pattern of disregard for and violation of the rights of others occurring since age 15 years, as indicated by three (or more) of the following:
   1. Failure to conform to social norms with respect to lawful behaviors as indicated by repeatedly performing acts that are grounds for arrest
   2. Deceitfulness, as indicated by repeated lying, use of aliases, or conning others for personal profit or pleasure
   3. Impulsivity or failure to plan ahead
   4. Irritability and aggressiveness, as indicated by repeated physical fights or assaults
   5. Reckless disregard for safety of self and others
   6. Consistent irresponsibility, as indicated by repeated failure to sustain consistent work behavior or honor financial obligations
   7. Lack of remorse, as indicated by being indifferent to or rationalizing having hurt, mistreated, or stolen from another
B. The individual is at least age 18 years
C. There is evidence of Conduct Disorder (see p. 98) with onset before age 15 years
D. The occurrence of antisocial behavior is not exclusively during the course of Schizophrenia or a Manic Episode

---

This pessimism presents a dilemma for the clinician practicing in an outpatient setting[1]. When a client with Antisocial Personality Disorder enters therapy, whether voluntarily or involuntarily, what is the therapist to do? Frosch's view cited above suggests that it is fruitless to offer outpatient therapy and some would argue that it is unethical to offer a treatment known to be ineffective. However, is it reasonable or ethical for the therapist to refuse treatment in the hope that the person will eventually be arrested and sentenced to one of the few inpatient treatment programs that have been reported to be effective (for example, see Carney, 1986; Matthews & Reid, 1986; Reid & Solomon, 1986)? Fortunately, there are recent indications that short-term outpatient cognitive behavioral therapy (CBT) can be effective for at least some clients with Antisocial Personality Disorder (Davidson & Tyrer, 1996; Kristiansson, 1995; Woody, McLellan, Luborsky, & O'Brien, 1985). This chapter will present a treatment approach that may offer a viable option for therapists attempting outpatient therapy with clients with Antisocial Personality Disorder or with significant antisocial features.

Assessment

The diagnosis of Antisocial Personality Disorder is not simply a matter of the individual having engaged in criminal behavior (see Table 8.1). The disorder is characterized by a pattern of irresponsible and antisocial behavior beginning in childhood or early adolescence and continuing through adulthood. However, it

---

[1] Obviously, treatment of Antisocial Personality Disorder in a correctional setting involves somewhat different considerations given the restricted social environment that the individual faces, the greater environmental control that is possible, and legal considerations. Because this volume is designed primarily for practitioners in "ordinary" outpatient settings, this section does not discuss considerations specific to correctional settings.

also includes problems that extend beyond criminal behavior. These individuals are typically irritable and impulsive to an extent that makes it difficult for them to succeed in prosocial activities if they do make an attempt to conform to social norms. Also, despite the common impression that "sociopaths" or "psychopaths" are free of guilt and subjective distress, they typically complain of tension, inability to tolerate boredom, and depression as well as problems in relationships with family, friends, and sexual partners. These emotional and interpersonal problems tend to persist even if flagrant antisocial activity declines later in adulthood.

Consider this example:

> Rex was a deeply tanned man of average build who appeared for his first appointment dressed in skin-tight pants, a bold print shirt unbuttoned far down his chest, several gold chains, and alligator shoes. His physician had referred him for evaluation because the pain and impairment that Rex reported as resulting from his rheumatoid arthritis was out of proportion to the physical findings and because Rex repeatedly referred to himself as a "cripple" and as "decrepit." The physician suspected that this "negative thinking" might amplify the pain produced by Rex's medical problems and result in increased impairment. Rex rejected this suggestion but accepted referral for an evaluation anyway.
>
> Rex was cooperative but vague in the initial interview and managed to provide little information without seeming closemouthed. For example, in describing a typical day he said, "Well, ya know, I see some people, run some errands, make a couple'a deals...Ya know how it is." Later in the interview he seemed to relax and begin to enjoy telling tales of his exploits. As a child he had "hung around" with older kids "on the street" and he described himself as quite streetwise, making sharp deals, exploiting loopholes, and taking advantage of the rules. As a boy he had become involved with illegal gambling operations, first as an errand boy and then increasing in involvement to the point where he was nearly indicted by the Grand Jury and "had to leave town for a while." He had earned his living as a bookie at one time and later had a lucrative position about which he was quite vague but that involved frequent trips to exotic locations. By that point in the interview, the therapist had decided not to ask for more detailed information than Rex volunteered.
>
> When asked about stressors, Rex acknowledged that a recent problem was constantly on this mind and that his physician was probably right in suspecting that emotional factors were affecting his health. Shortly before his arthritis had started "acting up," Rex had learned through unofficial channels that an associate whom he had befriended was informing on him. He felt that he should "snuff the bastard" but did not want to do so. He found himself unable to stop ruminating about this situation despite fearing that the resulting stress would have a lasting impact on his health. He concluded, "This bastard is crippling me!" This view of the situation led to additional anger and intensified Rex's conflict over what action to take.

Rex fits the common stereotypes regarding Antisocial Personality Disorder in many ways, including his apparent freedom from guilt and remorse. However, this did not mean that he was free from distress. He was greatly distressed by his physical symptoms and the impact they had on his life. In addition, he was experiencing considerable stress as a result of his indecision and was experiencing sadness as well as anger in response to his betrayal by a man whom he had considered a close friend.

The diagnosis of Antisocial Personality Disorder is not difficult to make if the necessary information can be obtained. However, in clinical practice it may take some time to determine if the individual meets full criteria for Antisocial

Personality Disorder or simply manifests some antisocial features. Individuals involved in criminal activity may be reluctant to provide detailed information about such activity or they may enjoy boasting about their exploits to such an extent that the therapist may doubt their truthfulness. Some therapists may be cautious about seeking detailed information for fear of "knowing too much" or of angering the client; others may be intrigued by the client's lifestyle and seek more information than is needed simply because the stories are fascinating. Clearly, neither extreme is productive. Ideally, the therapist would pursue the information that is needed for assessment and treatment without undue timidity but would not be distracted by anecdotes that are interesting but unnecessary.

Individuals with Antisocial Personality Disorder typically are quick to deny personal problems and blame difficulties on mistreatment by others. As a result, it is important for the therapist to be alert for data that is inconsistent with such denials and to explore apparent inconsistencies. When information is available from sources such as family members, employers, or probation officers, the therapist has a better opportunity to evaluate the accuracy of the client's report of events.

A number of authors have drawn a distinction between "criminal" or "unsuccessful" sociopaths (persons with Antisocial Personality Disorder who get caught) and "creative" or "successful" sociopaths, who are clever enough to profit from their freedom from socially imposed limitations on behavior without being imprisoned. It is difficult to imagine an empirical test of the hypothesis that there are many persons with Antisocial Personality Disorder who elude detection. After all, how can one locate participants who, by definition, escape detection? *DSM-III* (1980) asserts that individuals who engage in antisocial or "shady" acts with the forethought and planning required for them to consistently profit from such acts rarely meet the full criteria for Antisocial Personality Disorder. Although this assertion is not repeated in *DSM-IV-TR*, it is clear that individuals with Antisocial Personality Disorder typically manifest levels of impulsivity, irresponsibility, and lack of forethought that would preclude long-term success in business or politics.

Other authors (for example, Cleckley, 1976; Hare, 1970; 1991) have drawn a distinction between individuals who meet diagnostic criteria for Antisocial Personality Disorder and a more severe subgroup who are usually referred to as "psychopaths" (see Table 8.2 for Hare's list of the characteristics of "psychopaths"). The literature on psychopathy is quite extensive and is beyond the scope of this chapter (see Millon, Simonsen, Birket-Smith, & Davis, 1998, for a recent overview). It is frequently assumed that the characteristics of psychopathy are biologically based and that these individuals are untreatable. However, a recent report (Kristiansson, 1995) asserts that psychopaths can be treated effectively with CBT when they receive appropriate pharmacotherapy as well. Although further research is needed, Kristiansson's report provides grounds for hoping that psychopaths may not be as untreatable as many have believed.

The discussion that follows applies both to persons who meet the full diagnostic criteria for Antisocial Personality Disorder and to persons who manifest some of the features of this disorder without meeting the full diagnostic criteria. Kristiansson (1995) argues that, to use this type of approach effectively with the psychopathic subgroup, appropriate pharmacotherapy is needed as well.

Table 8.2. Characteristics of Psychopaths[a]

Glibness/Superficial charm
Grandiose sense of self-worth
Need for stimulation/Proneness to boredom
Pathological lying
Conning/Manipulativeness
Lack of remorse or guilt
Shallow affect
Callousness/Lack of empathy
Parasitic lifestyle
Poor behavioral controls
Promiscuous sexual behavior
Early behavioral problems
Lack of realistic, long-term goals
Impulsivity
Irresponsibility
Failure to accept responsibility for own actions
Many short-term marital relationships
Juvenile delinquency
Revocation of conditional release
Criminal versatility

---

[a] From Hare, 1991

Conceptualization

The traditional view of Antisocial Personality Disorder is that these individuals have failed to internalize family and societal standards for behavior and consequently have no conscience and feel no guilt. It is typically assumed that without a conscience to inhibit unacceptable behavior and without guilt to serve as punishment for such behavior, people would act on their aggressive, self-centered, antisocial impulses. The various authors who adopt this view disagree as to whether this failure to develop conscience and guilt is a result of genetic factors, family factors, or the interaction of the two[2]. Whatever the cause, this view implies that treatment would need to somehow instill a conscience to be effective. Unfortunately, no effective way to do so has yet been developed.

Is it true that Antisocial Personality Disorder is due to a lack of conscience? Pause for a moment and consider whether one must feel guilt to refrain from antisocial behavior. What stops you from robbing banks for obtaining extra spending money? Is it primarily because you would feel guilty if you did so, or is it for other reasons? Even without guilt, the allure of antisocial behavior is low as long as one believes that prosocial behavior is an effective way of achieving goals, believes that the risks of antisocial behavior outweigh the benefits, or appreciates the negative impact that antisocial behavior will have on others.

It is possible to explain much antisocial behavior without reference to the individual's conscience or to the amount of guilt he or she experiences. To a large extent,

---

[2] See Rutter, 1997 for a recent discussion of the complex interactions between genes and environment in producing antisocial behavior.

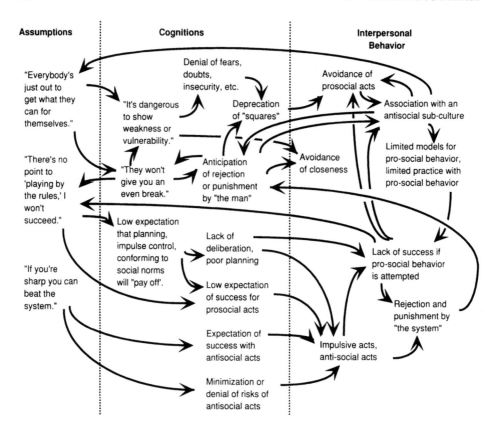

Figure 8.1. Cognitive model of Antisocial Personality Disorder.

the constellation of behaviors that constitutes Antisocial Personality Disorder can be accounted for by inadequate impulse control, poor means–ends thinking, a lack of adaptive control over anger, low-frustration tolerance, and a belief that antisocial behavior is more effective than prosocial behavior. In fact, a lack of guilt alone would not explain the behavior of a person with Antisocial Personality Disorder. Antisocial behavior is counterproductive for the individual as well as for society. Even the minority of persons with Antisocial Personality Disorder who manage to avoid jail and who are financially successful pay a heavy price in terms of the disorder's impact on interpersonal relationships. An individual who simply was not inhibited by conscience and acted purely out of self-interest would be more of a hedonist than a criminal and could lead a far happier, more successful life than that resulting from Antisocial Personality Disorder.

A cognitive model of Antisocial Personality Disorder is presented graphically in Figure 8.1. The reader may note similarities to the cognitive model of Paranoid Personality Disorder (Chapter 7) in that the individual sees others as being "out to get what they can for themselves" and thus sees the world as a hostile place where one must look out for oneself. As a consequence, persons with Antisocial Personality Disorder present themselves as strong and tough, anticipate mistreatment by others, avoid revealing any vulnerabilities, and tend to avoid closeness. However, although the paranoid individual attempts to cope with perceived dangers through carefully analyzing situations and planning his or her actions, the antisocial individual typically assumes that planning ahead will prove ineffective and that instead one must quickly seize opportunities. As a result the individual tends to act on the basis of momentary impulses or on the basis of short-term consequences of actions. This results in erratic behavior, contributes to impulsive, self-defeating acts, and makes it difficult for the individual to work consistently toward long-term goals. As a result, such individuals are generally unsuccessful when they do try to plan ahead or "play by the rules," and these experiences support their view that there is no point in trying to do so.

The self-defeating nature of the antisocial style and the frequency of antisocial acts are greatly increased by the individual's tendency to overestimate the likelihood of being able to "get away with it" and the tendency to minimize the likelihood and significance of negative consequences. This strongly biases the individual toward acting on each impulse as it occurs unless there are obvious and undeniable reasons not to do so. This results in impulsive behavior that is not governed by conventional ideas regarding appropriate behavior. The combination of a lack of success at prosocial behavior and impulsive antisocial behavior provides the individual with recurrent experiences of rejection and punishment at the hands of "the system." This provides the individual with grounds for anticipating similar experiences in the future and results in generalized anger at society as well as anger over specific incidents. The anger contributes to the antisocial, destructive nature of the individual's impulses whereas the anticipation of rejection or punishment by mainstream society encourages the individual to associate with an antisocial or criminal subculture.

This selective association provides the individual with many experiences that support the view that, "Everybody's just out to get what they can for themselves." It also provides him or her with few models of effective prosocial behavior, and strongly reinforces antisocial attitudes and behaviors. The antisocial subculture also presents a disparaging view of those who "play by the rules." This can result in reluctance to engage in prosocial behavior even if the client's ability to control impulses and anticipate the consequences of his or her actions have improved to the point that he or she could be successful in doing so. This is particularly true when previous attempts at prosocial activities have been unsuccessful and when the individual wants to maintain links with criminal friends and associates.

Intervention Strategies and Techniques

The view of Antisocial Personality Disorder presented above provides the therapist with more viable treatment options than that of trying to instill a conscience. These clients need to develop a more enlightened view of their self-interest and recognize the value of anticipating the long-term consequences of their actions. If they can do this, they may find that they have an incentive to control their impulsivity long enough to consider the consequences of possible actions. Because the long-term consequences of prosocial behavior are often better than those of antisocial behavior, a client who is able to realistically anticipate the consequences of his or her actions is likely to engage in less antisocial activity. In working to more effectively pursue long-term self-interest, the antisocial client will find that it is also necessary to develop more adaptive ways of handling anger, to develop the ability to tolerate frustration, and to make a number of other changes. Cognitive-behavioral interventions can be used to good effect, but only once the therapist and client are working collaboratively and the client can see that it is in his or her self-interest to work to make such changes. Such interventions are typically ineffective when the client does not clearly realize "what's in it for me?"

It might seem risky to help an antisocial client more effectively pursue his or her long-term self-interest, in that it might help him or her become a more successful criminal. However, in practice this does not usually become a problem. The cliché, "Crime doesn't pay," may seem false when only the immediate consequences of antisocial acts are considered. However, when the long-term effects of antisocial behavior on relationships, lifestyle, and self-esteem are considered along with the risk of being apprehended, antisocial behavior "pays" less well than does prosocial behavior.

The idea of intervening with clients with Antisocial Personality Disorder by helping them take a more realistic, long-term view of their self-interest seems deceptively simple. The actual implementation of this strategy can be considerably more complex. Simply establishing a working relationship can be a major undertaking. These clients are a difficult population to work with in several ways: first, they tend to distrust therapists and to be uncomfortable accepting help; second, motivation for therapy is usually a problem, particularly if treatment is involuntary; and, finally, the therapist's reactions to the client often are a problem.

A collaborative approach to therapy with these clients is essential, but is a challenge to achieve. One major advantage of the treatment strategy discussed above is that it provides a general goal toward which therapist and client can work collaboratively, i.e., overcoming impediments to the client's successfully pursuing his or her self-interest. A client with Antisocial Personality Disorder is not going to be willing to work to become less impulsive simply because the therapist thinks it would be a good idea or because doing so would be socially acceptable. However, he or she may be quite willing to work on impulse control and other issues if it is clear that doing so will lead to greater success in dealing with others. Antisocial clients are strongly motivated to pursue their own self-interest and it is possible to use this tendency to develop motivation for therapy. If guided discovery is used to identify the ways in which impulsive actions, inappropriate expression of anger, failure to anticipate the consequences of actions, and so on, block the client from attaining goals he or she desires, the client may become motivated to change. Given the difficulty these clients typically have in recognizing the long-term consequences of their actions, the connection between interventions made in therapy and the client's goals will probably need to be pointed out frequently. However, by doing so it is possible to maintain a collaborative relationship.

Antisocial clients enter therapy with a long history of punishment and rejection at the hands of authority figures and upstanding members of society and with extensive practice in devising alibis, resisting coercion, and concealing their true intentions. This, of course, greatly complicates therapy. It is important for the therapist to avoid taking an authoritarian approach to the client and to anticipate that the client will repeatedly test whether the therapist is genuine in presenting a collaborative approach. It is also important to avoid appearing nonauthoritarian in a way that makes the therapist appear weak and easily deceived. Although it requires some delicacy to establish oneself as strong but not authoritarian, this can be done by emphasizing collaboration, setting clear, firm limits, and being alert for attempts at deception or manipulation. When confronted by inconsistencies in the client's statements, it is generally most productive for the therapist to work non-punitively to clarify the apparent inconsistencies. The therapist can then make it clear that attempts at deceit are counterproductive because they make it more difficult for the therapist to help the client work toward their shared goals. Attempts to "crossexamine" the client to determine the truth, get the client to confess that he or she was lying, or punish the client are usually counterproductive.

It is particularly important for the therapist to monitor his or her own responses to the client because disgust, impulses to punish the client, fear of the client, and anger at the client's attempts at deception are common and can easily disrupt therapy. Because the client expects punishment or rejection from the therapist (as a representative of society), he or she is likely to be vigilant for indications of such reactions and may be quick to perceive and react to unacknowledged reactions on the therapist's part. It would be ideal not to have problematic emotional reactions in the first place. However, if the therapist openly acknowledges any reactions, he or she can reduce the risk of being misinterpreted or exploited as well as providing the client with a model for being open without being weak or vulnerable.

Antisocial clients typically adopt a "tough guy" role and refuse to acknowledge fears, doubts, and insecurities, as well as tenderness and caring, for fear of revealing vulnerabilities that others could exploit. Although this often makes it difficult for the therapist to obtain needed information, it is important to minimize the need for the client to acknowledge weaknesses early in therapy to reduce the risk of premature termination. If the therapist works gradually to establish trust, handles confidences sensitively, and explicitly acknowledges the client's strengths and capabilities, the client's discomfort with self-disclosure and with accepting help will gradually decrease.

In the initial phase of therapy, once the goals have been agreed upon, it is most productive to focus on specific problem situations and use a Problem-Solving Training (Coche', 1987) type of approach. This approach begins by clarifying the nature of the situation, the desired outcomes, and the problems encountered achieving them. The focus then moves to identifying possible solutions, anticipating the likely outcome of each alternative, working to overcome impediments to potentially adaptive responses, and testing the most promising alternatives in practice. If this process is conducted collaboratively through guided discovery, resistance is minimized and the client gradually masters the skills needed for effective problem-solving. For example:

Rex's primary goal for therapy was to minimize the degree to which his medical symptoms interfered with his life. By helping him identify the situations, thoughts, and feelings that coincided with exacerbations of his arthritis, it was possible to demonstrate a clear relationship between subjective stress and amount of pain. A treatment plan was developed that included mastering stress management techniques, dealing more effectively with situations that were recurrent sources of stress, and developing more adaptive responses to pain.

Rex and his therapist examined the consequences of staying in bed when he was in pain versus going on with his activities despite the pain. Staying in bed resulted in less pain at the moment; but on days when he remained in bed his pain persisted for much of the day, he became increasingly depressed, and he tended to ruminate about having been betrayed by his friend. However, on days when he got out of bed and went on with his activities despite the pain, he experienced substantially more pain at first but the pain passed fairly quickly and he felt much better for the remainder of the day. This analysis helped Rex find a better way to handle his physical symptoms and demonstrated the value of considering more than just the immediate consequences of his actions.

It is important to persistently focus the individual's attention on the actual consequences of his or her actions. However, there is evidence suggesting that antisocial clients are less affected by aversive consequences than others are (see Marshall and Barbaree, 1984). Therefore, it may be most productive to focus on pursuing desired outcomes rather than on avoiding negative outcomes while working on problem solving.

The individual's thoughts, beliefs, and attitudes may interfere with his or her choosing courses of action that are likely to produce the desired consequences. It can be important to help the individual identify and challenge cognitions such as, "Don't let anybody push you around", "A man has to fight to gain respect", or "If I do what he says, I'm not in charge of my life any more." Such challenges may enable the client to use more adaptive ways of dealing with problem situations (Nauth, 1998) and decrease the frequency of angry outbursts (Beck, 1999). When poor impulse control or inappropriate expression of anger are major problems, the intervention approaches described in the discussion of Borderline Personality Disorder later in this chapter may be useful.

As the client begins to control impulses and attempts to anticipate the consequences of his or her actions, the therapist can watch for situations where an accurate understanding of the motivations and feelings of others will be useful. This provides an opportunity to work toward "empathy induction." Questions such as, "How do you think he felt when you said that?" and, "How would you feel if you were in her place?" can be used to focus the client's attention on the other person's perspective and to encourage the development of understanding and possibly even empathy[3]. When the client's perception of the motivations, intentions, and likely responses of others seem accurate, this information can be used in planning how to deal with the situation more effectively. If the advantages

---

[3] It is important to note that some reports suggest that empathy training is effective with most members of forensic populations but actually results in a worse outcome with the minority who meet criteria for psychopathy (see Rice, 1997, p. 415; Ruegg & Frances, 1995, p. 17). Caution should be used in considering this intervention with individuals who manifest characteristics of psychopathy.

of considering the other person's point of view are clear, the client will be motivated to consider the other person's perspective and improve his or her skill at doing so. This not only enables the individual to interact with others more effectively, it may also result in his or her being less inclined to abuse and exploit others.

When working to increase empathy, situations often will arise where the client is confident that he or she accurately understands the motivations of others although it seems to the therapist that the client is mistaken. When this occurs, it is more useful for the therapist to treat the client's view as a hypothesis, to be tested through a review of the available evidence or through behavioral experiments, rather than to attempt to convince the client that he or she is wrong.

It is important to be realistic in looking critically at the client's understanding of others' motivation. If the client attributes selfish or malicious intentions to virtually everyone, this negative view of others may turn out to be accurate for those with whom the client interacts regularly. In this case, it may be necessary to devote substantial time to help the client develop new relationships or to repair damaged relationships.

Over the course of therapy, there is likely to be a gradual transition from a largely behavioral focus, which does not require the client to disclose his or her own thoughts and feelings in detail, to a more cognitive focus where the client's cognitions and emotions receive considerable attention. As the client becomes more willing to acknowledge doubts, fears, and longings, it becomes easier to identify the beliefs and assumptions that underlie the client's responses in various situations and to address these beliefs and assumptions as well.

With outpatient treatment, premature termination is likely to be a major problem. Even when the therapist is able to establish a collaborative relationship with the client and intervene effectively, there is a substantial risk of the client's terminating therapy when his or her distress is alleviated. For example:

> Rex hesitantly agreed to a treatment plan directed toward alleviating the stress that aggravated his medical symptoms and was making good progress toward recognizing the consequences of his typical ways of responding to stressful situations and exploring his alternatives. Then he learned that the former friend who had betrayed him had also offended important crime figures elsewhere in the country and that they planned to have the former friend killed. This resolved Rex's dilemma regarding whether to take direct action himself, and the stress and physical symptoms that brought him into therapy quickly subsided. Not surprisingly, he immediately decided to terminate therapy and insisted that similar problems would never occur in the future.

When faced with this situation, the therapist can best handle it by pointing out, as clearly as possible, the ways in which continuing in therapy is in the client's best interest and by identifying any remaining distress that the client may be minimizing or denying. In a study of the effectiveness of psychotherapy with clients in a methadone maintenance program, Woody *et al.* (1985) found that depressed antisocial clients benefited substantially from short-term CBT whereas nondepressed antisocial clients did not. If the client is truly free of distress, he or she is likely to invest little effort in therapy or is likely to terminate prematurely despite the therapist's efforts. However, if some distress remains, this may provide sufficient motivation for continued treatment.

Before the close of therapy, it is important to pay special attention to the social pressure to continue engaging in antisocial behavior that the individual may experience from friends and associates. The obvious solution would be for the client to establish new friendships with persons who are not associated with his or her previous lifestyle. However, to do this the client may need to work on the social skills needed to fit in with prosocial groups, to face his or her anticipation of rejection, and modify his or her derogatory attitudes toward prosocial individuals.

In working on relapse prevention, it is particularly important to prepare for situations in which the client is treated unfairly, rejected, or punished despite having tried to "play by the rules." Obviously, "playing by the rules" does not guarantee success; but a client who has recently adopted a prosocial approach can easily misinterpret unfair treatment or rejection as an indication that it does not work at all.

The interventions described above can be conducted in individual, group, or family therapy. Group and family therapy are likely to have substantial advantages and prove superior to individual intervention when they are feasible. Family intervention presents the possibility of obtaining information from family members as well as the client. There is also the opportunity of using feedback from family members to help the antisocial individual recognize the consequences of his or her actions. Beyond this, family therapy provides the possibility of modifying the family system that otherwise may tend to perpetuate antisocial behavior. Therapy with a group of antisocial clients presents an opportunity for group members to give each other feedback about the impact of their behavior within the session as well as presenting an opportunity to use role-playing to develop problem-solving skills (see Coche', 1987). In addition, group members may be particularly perceptive in confronting other group members' attempts at evasion or manipulation and may be especially credible in pointing out the ways in which antisocial behavior is counterproductive.

Conclusions

If the antisocial client stays in therapy long enough to complete this treatment approach, much can be accomplished, not only in decreasing antisocial behavior but also in enabling the client to adopt a lifestyle that is more rewarding both to the client and to his or her acquaintances. In fact, both case studies (Davidson & Tyrer, 1996; Kristiansson, 1995) and controlled outcome studies (Woody et al., 1985) have demonstrated that CBT can be effective with Antisocial Personality Disorder. However, clients with Antisocial Personality Disorder often discontinue therapy prematurely unless treatment is involuntary or the client is experiencing continued distress. Therefore, the impact of outpatient Cognitive Therapy on clients with Antisocial Personality Disorder is likely to be limited unless the client suffers from problems in addition to his or her personality disorder that provide an incentive for persistent work in therapy.

Borderline Personality Disorder

Borderline Personality Disorder (BPD) is a significant mental health problem. It is relatively common (*DSM-IV-TR*, 2000, p. 708), it typically produces substantial impairment, and it has been cited as a major cause of negative outcome in psychotherapy (Mays & Franks, 1985). It is a disorder that many psychotherapists find difficult to understand and treat and has motivated an extensive literature regarding many different approaches to treatment. Much of the early literature on psychotherapy with BPD was based on object-relations theory or other psychoanalytic approaches, and some have argued that psychoanalytic psychotherapy is the treatment of choice for borderline clients (Kernberg, 1977). At one time, even some cognitive therapists asserted that Cognitive Therapy was not effective with this complex, long-standing problem (Rush & Shaw, 1983). However, recent evidence suggests that, when properly applied, CBT can be effective with BPD and may have advantages over alternative treatment approaches.

Assessment

Over the years, the term "borderline" has been used in a wide variety of ways. It was originally used to refer to clients who presented both "neurotic" and "psychotic" types of symptoms and who were thus seen as falling on the "borderline" between neurotic and psychotic. In common usage this term often meant "nearly psychotic" or "somewhat psychotic." This usage might make sense if there were, indeed, a "borderline" between neurosis and psychosis. However, this is not the case. If an individual becomes more and more neurotic, they do not reach a point where they become psychotic. If a psychotic individual receives effective treatment, they do not cross some sort of boundary and become neurotic instead.

With the rise of object-relations theory, many authors began to use the term borderline to refer to a particular type of personality organization rather than as a diagnostic category *per se* (e.g., Kernberg, 1975). With this usage of "borderline," an individual could be considered to be borderline if a particular personality structure was judged to be present, independent of the pattern of symptoms present at the time. Conversely, an individual presenting a mixture of neurotic and psychotic symptoms would not be considered borderline if his or her personality organization did not correspond to the expected pattern of "poorly integrated identity," "primitive defensive operations," "relatively firm self-object boundaries," and "reasonably intact reality testing" (Bauer, Hunt, Gould, & Goldstein, 1980).

As with many other poorly understood diagnostic categories, the term borderline has often been used simply to refer to individuals who do not seem to belong to other diagnostic categories and has therefore functioned as an "unspecified" or "miscellaneous" category. This often results in "borderline" being used to refer to a heterogeneous group of individuals who differ from each other in significant ways. For example, when Grinker, Werble, and Drye (1968) performed a cluster analysis on data from 51 participants who had been labeled "borderline," they found four distinct subgroups rather than one group of individuals sharing a core of common characteristics.

Table 8.3. *DSM-IV-TR* Diagnostic Criteria for Borderline Personality Disorder

A pervasive pattern of instability of interpersonal relationships, self-image, and affects, and marked impulsivity beginning by early adulthood and present in a variety of contexts, as indicated by five (or more) of the following:

1. Frantic efforts to avoid real or imagined abandonment
   Note: Do not include suicidal or self-mutilating behavior covered in Criterion 5.
2. A pattern of unstable and intense interpersonal relationships characterized by alternating between extremes of idealization and devaluation
3. Identity disturbance: markedly and persistently unstable self-image or sense of self
4. Impulsivity in at least two areas that are potentially self-damaging (e.g., spending, sex, substance use, reckless driving, binge eating)
   Note: Do not include suicidal or self-mutilating behavior covered in Criterion 5.
5. Recurrent suicidal behaviors, gestures, threats, or self-mutilating behavior
6. Affective instability due to a marked reactivity of mood (e.g., intense episodic dysphoria, irritability, or anxiety, usually lasting a few hours and only rarely more than a few days)
7. Chronic feelings of emptiness
8. Inappropriate, intense anger or difficulty controlling anger (e.g., frequent displays of temper, constant anger, recurrent physical fights)
9. Transient, stress-related paranoid ideation or severe dissociative symptoms

Given this mixture of conflicting and overlapping meanings for "borderline," it is not surprising that some of the authors of *DSM-III* (1980) argued that it would be best to drop the term and choose a more descriptive label. Millon suggested alternatives such as "ambivalent," "erratic," "impulsive," or "quixotic" personality disorder (1996, p. 645). Although this idea has not been adopted, *DSM-IV-TR* (2000) provides a clear definition of "borderline" in its diagnostic criteria for BPD. When the term borderline is used in this discussion it will refer to BPD as defined in *DSM-IV-TR* unless otherwise noted. In comparing the present chapter with other literature regarding psychotherapy with clients with BPD, it is important to remember that other authors may be referring to quite different groups of clients unless they are explicitly using *DSM* criteria. For example, one study found that in a sample previously diagnosed as "Personality Disorder with a Borderline Personality Organization" using criteria based on psychoanalytic theory, only 44% met *DSM-III* criteria for BPD (Hamilton, Green, Mech, Brand, Wong, & Coyne, 1984).

In *DSM-IV-TR*, BPD is defined as an enduring pattern of perceiving, relating to, and thinking about the environment and oneself in which there are problems in a variety of areas including interpersonal behavior, mood, and self-image. No single feature is invariably present and variability is one of the hallmarks of BPD. Therefore, assessment and diagnosis is more complex than with many of the other diagnostic categories. Diagnosis is based on the presence of at least five of nine categories of problems (shown in Table 8.3) as a part of the individual's long-term functioning, not simply their presence during a period of acute disturbance.

An empirical study of diagnostic criteria for BPD (Clarkin, Widiger, Frances, Hurt, & Gilmore, 1983) examined the diagnostic efficiency of each of the criteria used in *DSM-III*. The study showed that when the symptoms of identity disturbance and unstable/intense relationships were both present, or when impulsivity, unstable/intense relationships, and intense/uncontrolled anger appeared together, the probability of the individual meeting diagnostic criteria for BPD was quite high. These two patterns were characteristic of approximately 80% of their borderline sample.

Clinically, the most striking features of borderlines are the intensity of their reactions, their lability, and the great variety of symptoms they present. They may abruptly shift from a pervasive depressed mood to anxious agitation or intense anger. They may impulsively engage in actions that they later recognize as irrational and counterproductive. They may present a problem with obsessive ruminations in one therapy session, depression in the next, and a specific phobia in the third. They typically present an erratic, inconsistent, unpredictable pattern of problems that can include their functioning effectively and competently in some areas of life while encountering dramatic problems in other areas.

Individuals with BPD are not necessarily in constant turmoil and may experience extended periods of stability. However, they typically seek therapy at times of crisis and present a complex and chaotic clinical picture. The unstable pattern of symptoms can make diagnosis of BPD complex. The task is further complicated by the fact that borderline individuals often present with other disorders as well. Millon (1996) reports that borderline clients often manifest Generalized Anxiety Disorder, Panic Disorder, Somatoform Disorders, Psychogenic Fugue states, Major Depression, Bipolar Disorder, Schizoaffective Disorder, Brief Psychotic Disorder, Substance Abuse, or additional personality disorders. Clarkin *et al.* (1983) found that even when consensus of three raters on the presence or absence of each of the *DSM-III-R* criteria (1987) was required for diagnosis, 60% of their borderline sample met the criteria for other personality disorders as well. These diagnoses included Paranoid, Schizotypal, Histrionic, Narcissistic, Avoidant, and Dependent Personality Disorders.

The diagnosis of BPD need not be difficult, however. *DSM-IV-TR* diagnostic criteria are sufficiently clear to permit reliable diagnosis if the clinician considers a diagnosis of BPD and obtains the necessary information. For many clinicians, the primary difficulty lies in recognizing when it might be appropriate consider a diagnosis of BPD. Clients rarely enter therapy saying, "Doc, I think I'm borderline. Can you help me?" Table 8.4 lists a number of characteristics that often serve as indications of BPD. These are not intended as additional diagnostic criteria, but may be useful as cues to the clinician to consider the possibility of an undiagnosed personality disorder.

A clinical example may illustrate the complexities involved in correctly diagnosing BPD:

> Mika, a 30-year-old mother of two, requested treatment for chronic problems with depression, anxiety, isolation, and alienation. She said that she had been depressed her whole life but had first realized that she was depressed about 10 years previously. During the period following her realization that she was depressed, she had sought treatment from five different therapists. She had not been helped by psychoanalytic psychotherapy and was frightened of psychotrophic medication. As a part of the intake procedure, she was asked to complete the Beck Depression Inventory, the Beck Anxiety Checklist, and the Minnesota Multiphasic Personality Inventory. Her responses indicated that she was

TABLE 8.4. Possible Indications of Borderline Personality Disorder

In presenting problems and symptoms

1. A diverse assortment of problems and symptoms that may shift from week to week
2. Unusual symptoms or unusual combinations of symptoms
3. Intense emotional reactions that are out of proportion to the situation
4. Self-punitive or self-destructive behavior
5. Impulsive, poorly planned behavior that is later recognized as foolish, "crazy," or counterproductive
6. Brief periods of psychotic symptoms in response to stressful life events (that may have been misdiagnosed as Schizophrenia)
7. Confusion regarding goals, priorities, feelings, sexual orientation, etc.
8. Feelings of emptiness or void, possibly localized in the solar plexus

In interpersonal relationships

1. Lack of stable intimate relationships (possibly masked by stable nonintimate relationships or relationships that are stable as long as full intimacy is not possible)
2. Tendency to either idealize or denigrate others, perhaps switching abruptly from idealization to denigration
3. A tendency to confuse intimacy and sexuality

In therapy

1. Frequent crises, frequent telephone calls to the therapist, or demands for special treatment
2. Extreme or frequent misinterpretations of therapist's statements, intentions, or feelings
3. Unusually strong reactions to changes in appointment time, room changes, vacations, or termination of therapy
4. Low tolerance for direct eye contact, physical contact, or close proximity
5. Unusually strong ambivalence on many issues
6. Fear of change or unusually strong resistance to change

In psychological testing

1. Good performance on structured tests such as the WAIS combined with poor performance or indications of thought disorder on projective tests
2. Elevation of both "neurotic" and "psychotic" MMPI scales or indications of an unusually wide variety of problems

---

severely depressed, that she experienced frequent periods of intense anxiety, and that she was uncomfortable in social situations. The psychological testing results alone indicated that she was likely to have a strongly negative self-image, unrealistically high standards for herself, and difficulty expressing anger or acting assertively, and suggested a diagnosis of Major Depression.

In the initial therapy session her goals and priorities for therapy were discussed and Mika developed the list of goals and priorities shown in Table 8.5 as her homework for the second session. This list reveals several types of anxiety disorder (Agoraphobia, possible Social Phobia, possible Obsessive–Compulsive Disorder) as well as difficulty trusting others, low-stress tolerance, difficulty handling anger adaptively, and confusion over her sexual orientation. In the second session she reported serious suicidal impulses resulting from a complex marital conflict. In the third session she was extremely confused over whether to leave her husband, whether to return to her previous therapist, and whether to ask for medication and was pleading for someone to take care of her. Within 2 months these issues had largely been resolved and she was preoccupied with panic attacks elicited by a planned trip to Jamaica.

Table 8.5. Mika's Problem/Goal List (In order of priority)

The anxiety symptoms are driving me nuts. I want them gone before the problems have been solved!

1. I feel my mental/emotional problems are so severe they will never be resolved ... I fear and believe I'm beyond help.
2. There's nobody I trust completely to help me if I'm ever unable to help myself ... this causes me terrible anxiety and hostility.
3. I'd like to feel less isolated, alienated, alone and unique ...
4. I'm very ambivalent about having a third child ... I'd like to resolve this dilemma once and for all.
5. I'm terrified of the idea of being "out of control." I'd like to be able to ... risk lessening control.
6. I suffer from agoraphobic symptoms at times ... I'd like ... to put an end to them.
7. I want to be able to display hurt and anger better instead of withdrawing into a shell. The only people in the world to whom I can express affection freely ... are my children. I'd like to feel more comfortable being demonstrative.
8. I want to find better ways of dealing with my negative feelings about my mother ...
9. I feel the majority of my life's energies & talents are going to waste because I spend so much time worrying ...
10. I'd like to examine my "God/shit" complex—sometimes feeling superior to others, other times feeling so inferior ...
11. ... the more I respect, admire, or care about a particular couple the more anxious I get going out socially with them.
12. I'm really obsessive/compulsive. As soon as one obsession disappears, I must immediately have something else to obsess about.
13. I have this nagging fear that something awful will happen to one of my children.
14. I want to define what I can realistically expect of myself as a parent and become comfortable with that.
15. I worry, if I begin to feel close to another female, that my feelings could be sexual.
16. I'm so perfectionistic that I'm perpetually frustrated, disappointed, or afraid to risk failure. But I'm also afraid of success beyond a certain point.
17. I become overwhelmed by tight, demanding schedules—getting almost unbearably hyper.

Mika's intake interview and her MMPI scores suggested a diagnosis of Major Depression. However, it was clear within the first few sessions that she also manifested many features of BPD. She presented a wide range of problems, had difficulty choosing her goals, and her problems varied dramatically from week to week. Her emotional reactions were intense, changeable, and tended to switch from one extreme to another. She described a very difficult childhood, periods of impulsive behavior, and an apparent psychotic period following recreational drug use. She had a long history of uneven performance and continued to do well in graduate school despite periods of personal and marital crisis.

It is common for symptoms of a BPD to become apparent only gradually. In a problem-focused therapy approach such as Cognitive Therapy, it is possible for such a personality disorder to go unrecognized for an extended period of time. This is because the individual's relationship history, his or her characteristic ways of handling anger, or whether he or she has a clear sense of identity may not be discussed in detail unless these issues are related to the treatment goals. Mika was unusual in that her intelligence, verbal fluency, and insights gained through years of psychoanalytic therapy allowing her to present the salient issues much more clearly and concisely than is often the case.

Conceptualization

The most widely known conceptualizations of BPD have been based on object-relations theory and other contemporary psychoanalytic approaches (e.g., Guntrip, 1969; Kernberg, 1977; Masterson, 1978). Unfortunately, the vocabulary used in these analyses renders them inaccessible to the many clinicians who are not fluent in psychoanalytic terminology. When translated into cognitive-behavioral terminology, it appears that the core of the object-relations view is: The borderline individual holds extreme, poorly integrated views of relationships with early caregivers and, as a result, holds extreme, unrealistic expectancies regarding interpersonal relationships. These expectancies are seen as consistently shaping both behavior and emotional responses. These traditional approaches assume that the most appropriate way to resolve this situation is to conduct therapy in such a way that these expectancies will be manifested in an intensely emotional relationship with the therapist. Then these issues can be resolved through the application of psychoanalytic techniques.

Millon (1981) provided a competing view based on Social Learning Theory in which he attributed a central role to the borderline individual's lack of a clear, consistent sense of his or her own identity. He argued that a lack of clear, consistent goals results in poorly coordinated actions, poorly controlled impulses, and a lack of consistent accomplishment. In addition, he suggested that as a result of unstable or unsure identities, borderlines became dependent on others for protection and reassurance and became vulnerable to separation from these sources of support. He asserted that this situation is complicated by intense conflicts regarding dependency and assertion and by the realization that anger over being trapped by dependency could result in their losing the security they gain from dependency.

In his more recent work, Millon (1996) argues that BPD is a more extreme variant of other personality disorders and therefore is a less homogenous category than many others. He presents a more complex model in which he separately discusses several subtypes of BPD. He describes different patterns of interactions between a child's temperament and the characteristic of the family environment that he sees as contributing to excessive dependency on others, conflicts overdependency, and extreme interpersonal behavior. Millon argues that dysfunctional interpersonal behaviors are maintained because they often produce short-term rewards by eliciting attention, releasing tension, obtaining revenge, and, at the same time, avoiding permanent rejection. Unfortunately, despite these short-term benefits, the borderline's extreme interpersonal behavior proves to be seriously dysfunctional in the long run and ends up reinforcing dysfunctional attitudes and strategies.

Linehan (1993a) has developed a cognitive-behavioral approach to conceptualizing and treating BPD that has received considerable attention. Her approach, termed Dialectical Behavior Therapy (DBT), integrates behavioral and cognitive behavioral perspectives with concepts adapted from Dialectical Materialism and Buddhism. DBT views BPD as resulting from the interaction between biologically based problems with the regulation of emotion and an environment that is emotionally invalidating, reinforces intense expressions of emotion, or punishes moderate expressions of emotion. As a result the individual fails to develop adequate skills in the regulation of emotion, experiences intensely painful, intolerable emotions, and engages in extreme actions in an attempt to reduce the intolerable emotions. These extreme attempts to reduce or escape intolerable emotions can include dramatic outbursts, self-mutilation, and recurrent suicide attempts. DBT takes a transactional view that focuses on the interaction between the individual and his or her environment. It presumes that, at each moment, the individual is doing the best that he or she can but lacks the skills and perspective needed to handle the situation in more adaptive ways.

A number of investigators have used Cognitive Therapy as a framework for understanding and treating BPD (Beck *et al.*, 1990, 2003; Freeman *et al.*, 1990; Layden, Newman, Freeman, & Morse, 1993; Pretzer, 1983). A cognitive perspective can make important contributions to the treatment of BPD. An examination of the content of clients' thoughts in specific situations makes apparently extreme responses much more comprehensible. More importantly, an understanding of the cognitive distortions, assumptions, and interpersonal strategies common among borderlines can form a basis for a conceptualization that permits a strategic approach to intervention.

Borderlines are notorious for their intense emotional reactions and abrupt mood swings. Mika, the depressed mother of two discussed above, initially did well in therapy but when her depression had subsided substantially and she had been doing reasonably well for several weeks, she arrived for her weekly appointment having suddenly become quite agitated and suicidal. It turned out that when her husband had suggested that they take a vacation to Jamaica, she became filled with hopelessness and despair. Fortunately she had completed a thought record (TR) regarding her reaction to the proposed vacation, seen in Figure 8.2. As you can see, knowledge of her thoughts while anticipating the trip provides a simple explanation of her apparently strange reaction. Further exploration of her expectations regarding the trip made it clear that she was certain that recurrent, inescapable panic attacks would ruin the vacation, alienate her husband, and inevitably lead to his divorcing her and seeking custody of their children. Because she was also certain that refusing to go to Jamaica would alienate her husband and also result in divorce and the loss of her children, she saw the trip to Jamaica as presenting an inescapable catastrophe rather than a pleasant vacation.

Although an understanding of Mika's automatic thoughts regarding the proposed trip to Jamaica clears up some of the mystery regarding her intense reaction, we are still left with the question of how she comes to have such extreme thoughts. Cognitive accounts of BPD emphasize the role played by strongly held core beliefs (Arntz, Roos, & Dreessen, 1999; Fossel & Wright, 1999). Four key assumptions are frequently uncovered in the course of therapy with borderline clients. Although the exact phrasing varies from individual to individual, these assumptions typically are: "The world is dangerous and malevolent"; "I am powerless and vulnerable"; "I am unacceptable"; and, "No one will take my feelings seriously." These assumptions have an important impact on the borderline's cognition and behavior.

Viewing the world as a dangerous place in which one is relatively powerless has important consequences. It leads directly to the conclusion that it is dangerous to relax vigilance, to take risks, to reveal one's weakness, to be "out of control," to be in a situation from which one cannot escape easily, and so on. Not only

Daily Record of Automatic Thoughts

Situation Briefly describe the situation	Emotion(s) Rate 0-100%	Automatic Thoughts Try to quote then rate belief in each thought 0-100%
Thinking about trip to Jamaica	Scared 100% Anxious 100% Guilty 100% Pessimistic 75% Inadequate 75% Hopeless 75%	It will be just like it always is; I'll spend all the time till we go away being afraid of "freaking out", when we actually go, my fears will become a self-fulfilling prophecy, & I'll ruin the vacation for both of us. 100% I'm scared to death of the incapacitating, all-consuming panic attacks I've always had before on vacations. I want to avert them but I don't think I'll be able to. 100% I'm tired of being an emotional cripple, but I don't think I'll ever be better. 100% I feel so guilty about going away - first because we can have this vacation & others can't; second, because I'm going some place other than to visit my parents. 100%

FIGURE 8.2. A Thought Record Completed by Mika.

does this result in chronic tension and anxiety, but vigilance for signs of danger results in the individual's noticing many apparent signs of danger, which tends to perpetuate the view of the world as a dangerous place. Thus, as Mika anticipated the trip to Jamaica she focused on the risks the trip presented, including the risk of having panic attacks as she had on some previous trips. As she thought about the possibility of having panic attacks, her anxiety increased, and she interpreted her increasing anxiety as evidence that she would, indeed, experience panic attacks.

Some persons who view the world as a dangerous, malevolent place believe that the thing to do is for them to be vigilant and on guard and to rely on their own capabilities in dealing with the dangers that life presents (and thus develop a paranoid pattern). However, Mika's belief that she is weak and powerless blocks this alternative. Other persons who see themselves as not being capable of dealing effectively with the risks presented by daily life are able to resolve this dilemma by becoming dependent on someone whom they see as capable of taking care of them (and develop a dependent or histrionic pattern). However, Mika's belief that she is inherently unacceptable leads to the conclusion that dependence entails a high risk of eventual rejection, abandonment, or attack. Thus Mika, like other borderline individuals, faces a serious dilemma, convinced that she is relatively helpless in a hostile world with no safe source of security.

The weak or unstable sense of identity that Millon emphasizes also appears to play an important role in BPD. Confusion regarding goals and priorities makes it difficult to work consistently toward long-term goals, especially in the face of abrupt emotional shifts. A low sense of self-efficacy leads to low motivation and persistence and thus to limited success in the face of adversity. The lack of a clear sense of self makes it difficult to decide what to do in ambiguous situations. It also makes it difficult to maintain a clear sense of oneself as separate from the other person in an intimate relationship.

In addition, the interpersonal strategies used by individuals have a big impact on their interactions with others. Many borderline individuals hold the conviction that others will not see their wants, preferences, and feelings as valid. They, therefore, believe that a straightforward, assertive approach to dealing with others entails an unacceptable risk of provoking rejection or retaliation. Often they believe that the only safe, effective ways of influencing others are to covertly manipulate the situation or to react intensely. Mika vacillated among passively tolerating situations that did not meet her needs, attempting to indirectly manipulate the situation to get what she wanted, and exploding in anger. She was certain that asking directly for what she wanted would be ineffective or dangerous.

Borderline individuals' interpersonal problems often are greatly aggravated by an intense fear of abandonment or rejection and an inability to tolerate being alone. The fear of rejection results in vigilance for signs of rejection, intense reactions to perceived signs of rejection, and desperate attempts to avoid rejection. These attempts to avoid rejection can include excessive attention seeking, a constant demand for signs of caring, and dramatic displays of emotional distress in response to rejection, such as dramatic outbursts or threats of suicide. This often results in recurrent crises and great difficulty maintaining stable, supportive relationships.

Cognitive distortions also play an important role in BPD. Dichotomous thinking is a particularly common distortion among borderlines and contributes substantially to the extreme reactions and mood shifts characteristic of these clients (Veen & Arntz, 2000). As discussed earlier, dichotomous thinking is the tendency to evaluate experiences in terms of mutually exclusive categories (e.g., good or bad, flawless or defective, love or hate) rather than seeing experiences as falling along continua or dimensions. The end result of this "black or white" thinking is to force extreme interpretations of relatively neutral events. There is no neutral category, only a choice between two extreme categorizations. As a result, persons and events are necessarily evaluated in extreme terms. These extreme evaluations are then accompanied by extreme emotional responses and actions. In addition, dichotomous thinking leads to abrupt shifts in mood and behavior because the absence of intermediate categories means that when the individual's perception of a situation changes, it necessarily changes from one extreme to another. In dichotomous thinking, a person who is believed to be trustworthy is seen as completely trustworthy until the first time he or she falls at all short of expectations. Then the person suddenly is seen as completely untrustworthy. The idea that a person might be trustworthy most of the time or might be fairly trustworthy would be incompatible with dichotomous thinking.

The combination of dichotomous thinking coupled with the borderline's basic assumptions is particularly potent. We all recognize that the world presents risks and threats, but dichotomous thinking results in the world's being seen as deadly. We all have our faults and shortcomings but the borderline's dichotomous categorization of people as either "okay" or "not okay" leads to the conclusion that he or she is irrevocably "not okay" and must hide this fact from others to be accepted. A desire for closeness and security conflicts with this world-view and self-concept, and dichotomous thinking leads easily to the conclusion, "I'll never get what I want. Everything is pointless."

Dichotomous thinking also creates and perpetuates some of the borderline's conflicts. For example, frustration (or anticipated frustration) of the borderline's desire for closeness and dependency often leads to intense anger. This anger is seen by the borderline as being so devastating that it would destroy any chance of a close relationship if expressed. However, satisfaction of the desire for closeness and dependency is also seen as being intolerably dangerous because, in a hostile world, to be dependent is to be helpless and vulnerable. This intense conflict over dependency and anger would vanish if it were possible for the borderline to take a more moderate view and say: "It would be good to be diplomatic in expressing my dissatisfactions so that this doesn't cause additional problems"; or, "Depending on someone opens me to the possibility of being hurt or disappointed, so I should try to use good judgment about whom to depend on and how dependent to be." However, without help, borderline individuals seem to have great difficulty shifting from dichotomous thinking to dimensional thinking.

The basic assumptions, dichotomous thinking, and weak sense of identity each do not simply contribute separately to BPD. They form a mutually reinforcing and self-perpetuating system that is quite complex. For example, viewing a situation as dangerous may encourage dichotomous thinking; dichotomous thinking can encourage the idea that one is inadequate; and the belief that one is inadequate supports the idea that the situation is dangerous. Similarly, viewing the situation as dangerous discourages risk-taking; avoidance of risk-taking deprives the individual of the experiences that could serve as a basis for a positive sense of self-efficacy; and a low sense of self-efficacy supports the idea that risk-taking should be avoided. The complexity of the resulting pattern can be seen easily when an attempt is made to present it graphically as in Figure 8.3.

Intervention Strategies

When the "standard" Cognitive Therapy described in Chapters 1 through 3 is used with borderline clients, problems soon arise. Establishing a collaborative working relationship requires some degree of trust and intimacy. However, trust and intimacy are major issues for most borderline individuals. Strategic, problem-focused psychotherapeutic approaches such as Cognitive Therapy require the therapist and client to agree on specific goals and maintain a consistent focus on those goals. However, many borderline individuals have difficulty determining what

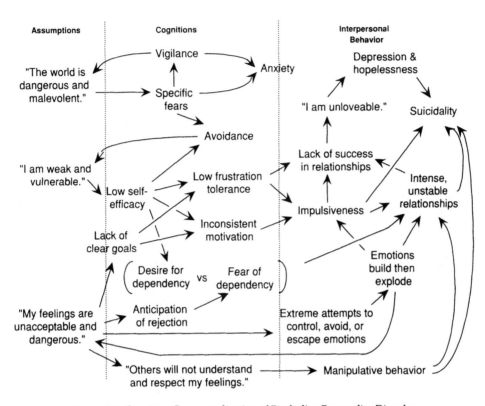

FIGURE 8.3. Cognitive Conceptualization of Borderline Personality Disorder.

their goals are and their priorities may change from week to week. Cognitive behavioral therapists are generally accustomed to establishing straightforward, business-like relationships with their clients, minimizing transference and other interpersonal complications. However, therapy with borderline individuals necessarily involves working with intense emotional interactions within the therapy session. Cognitive therapists are oriented toward helping clients change quickly and efficiently, but borderline individuals often fear and resist sudden change. Cognitive Therapy is often seen as a short-term therapy; but borderline individuals often need much more than 10 or 20 weeks of treatment. Therapists who attempt to work with borderline individuals without taking these features into account run the risk of providing ineffective treatment, having the client terminate therapy prematurely, or precipitating a serious crisis (Mays & Franks, 1985; Rush & Shaw, 1983).

Dialectical Behavior Therapy. Linehan's (1993a) response to these challenges has been to develop a comprehensive treatment approach tailored specifically to BPD. Dialectical Behavior Therapy combines standard cognitive behavioral interventions, an increased emphasis on the therapeutic relationship, concepts adapted from Dialectical Materialism, and contemplative practices and teaching methods used by eastern and western meditative approaches. Dialectical Behavior Therapy combines the following:

1. Weekly individual psychotherapy focused on increasing motivation to change dysfunctional behaviors and apply new behavioral skills;
2. Weekly skills-training groups that teach skills in mindfulness, emotion regulation, distress tolerance, and interpersonal effectiveness;
3. Telephone consultation with the individual therapist for skills coaching and relationship repair, as needed; and
4. Weekly team consultation meetings, which provide emotional support for therapists and help therapists remain within the DBT model.

With treatment structured in this way, the individual psychotherapist can focus wholeheartedly on important psychotherapeutic issues without needing to devote time to teaching the self-management skills that are taught in the skills-training groups. At the same time, the skills-training groups can focus totally on teaching skills because complex emotional issues and crises can be deferred to the individual psychotherapist. By encouraging telephone contact as needed between sessions, the individual therapist can actively deal with crises as they arise and has many opportunities to remind the client to apply the strategies learned in the skills-training group. Regular consultation meetings are seen as an essential component of DBT (Linehan, 1993a) because, without regular consultation, supervision, and support, therapists are likely to gradually diverge from the treatment protocol.

Dialectical Behavior Therapy envisions treatment progressing through a series of stages. Borderline clients typically enter treatment at a time of crisis and the initial focus of treatment is to help clients gain control over their lives. This involves decreasing life-threatening behaviors, increasing connections to helping individuals, and reinforcing stability and control. Once the client's actions are under a reasonable degree of control, he or she typically is still "leading a life of quiet desperation." The focus of treatment then is on reducing the traumatic effects of emotional experiences, understanding and reducing the sequelae of early traumas, and increasing connections to people, places, and activities such as work. As clients complete the first two stages of treatment, the focus shifts to addressing residual problems that interfere with the client's achieving important goals and on increasing self-respect and self-trust. At the close of treatment, a residual sense of incompleteness often remains and the final stage of DBT works to resolve this, develop a capacity for sustained joy, and expand awareness, spiritual fulfillment, and peak experiences.

Dialectical Behavior Therapy addresses problematic behaviors and problematic therapy situations in a systematic, problem-solving manner, validating the client's experiences and attending to the therapeutic relationship. Interventions directed toward change are balanced with interventions directed toward acceptance, and an "irreverent" communication style is balanced with a warmly responsive communication style. The types of interventions emphasized in DBT are summarized in Table 8.6.

Dialectical Behavior Therapy is designed as an integrated approach that necessarily includes individual psychotherapy, skills-training groups, telephone contact

Table 8.6. Interventions Emphasized in Dialectical Behavior Therapy

The skills-training group teaches cognitive-behavioral and mindfulness skills for coping with intense affect, increasing interpersonal effectiveness, improving regulation of emotion, and increasing distress tolerance.

The individual therapist conducts functional analyses of problem behaviors and helps the client find more adaptive alternatives. The therapist addresses motivational issues, deals with the emotional complexities of treatment, and provides consultation about applying the skills learned in the skills-training group.

A consultation group for therapists provides support and guidance while maintaining fidelity to the treatment approach.

with the individual therapist, and consultation meetings for the therapists. It is not a treatment that can be delivered by a single therapist who is not part of an organized treatment program. Although it is a very promising approach and is supported by controlled outcome studies, it is not a practical approach for solo practitioners or small group practices. A major investment of resources is needed to support a program that involves weekly individual psychotherapy and skills-training groups, telephone contact as needed, and regular consultation for therapists. Although it seems like an excellent approach for large mental health systems with adequate financial resources, the cost of DBT is likely to be a major issue in settings where health insurance coverage and the client's own resources must fund treatment.

Marsha Linehan is skeptical about whether individual psychotherapy alone can be effective as a treatment for BPD (M. Linehan, personal communication, January 26, 1995). However, a number of authors assert that it is indeed possible to treat BPD effectively through individual CBT (Beck *et al.*, 1990, 2003; Freeman *et al.*, 1990; Layden *et al.*, 1993). The remaining portion of this chapter will focus on treating BPD through individual psychotherapy, since most readers are not in a position to implement the full DBT treatment program. We would recommend that readers who are part of a mental health system that has the resources to offer a comprehensive program consider DBT as well as considering the treatment approach presented in this chapter.

Individual Cognitive Behavioral Therapy. A variety of different approaches have been proposed for treating BPD through individual CBT (for example, Beck *et al.*, 1990, 2003; Farrell & Shaw, 1994; Fossel & Wright, 1999; Freeman *et al.*, 1990; Kuyken, 1999; Layden *et al.*, 1993; Newman, 1999; Pretzer, 1983; Ramsay, 1999; Ratto & Capitano, 1999). Although each author emphasizes different points, there is consensus on the basic approach.

It is generally agreed that the basic principles of Cognitive Therapy are important in treating BPD. Thus the therapist first endeavors to establish a strong collaborative relationship, to base initial interventions on a careful assessment and an individualized conceptualization, and modify the treatment plan over the course of therapy as the therapist fine-tunes his or her understanding of the client. Borderline clients often enter treatment at a time of crisis; therefore beginning interventions often focus on improving the client's coping skills. Once the initial crisis has been stabilized, it is easier to work toward mutually agreed upon goals. Early interventions typically include carefully assessing problem situations, addressing dysfunctional thoughts and dichotomous thinking through cognitive techniques, helping the client deal with interpersonal problems more effectively, increasing his or her ability to cope with intense emotions, and using homework assignments consistently between sessions.

A number of authors emphasize the importance of maintaining clear, consistent limits and boundaries, which are balanced by empathy, concern, and understanding. The therapist-client relationship is an arena in which the client's interpersonal problems may well be manifested. Thus, it is important for the therapist to be alert to misunderstandings and dysfunctional behavior and to address them before they disrupt therapy or precipitate a crisis. Therapists are encouraged to be as consistent and predictable as possible, to avoid recapitulating dysfunctional interaction patterns, and to respond calmly under pressure.

Later in therapy, the emphasis shifts to identifying and addressing deeply held dysfunctional beliefs or schemas and helping the client develop more adaptive beliefs and put them into practice in daily life. The client's fears of rejection and the ways in which he or she avoids openness and intimacy in relationships may be addressed as a step toward helping the client develop more rewarding interpersonal relationships. As the conclusion of therapy approaches, attention is paid to the "ripple effects" of the changes the client is making and the client's thoughts and feelings about the termination of therapy. "Tapering off" at the close of therapy, by gradually reducing the frequency of therapy sessions, is recommended. During the termination sessions, therapist and client work actively on relapse prevention, anticipating high-risk situations, identifying early warning signs, and planning how to cope with problems that may arise in the future.

Cognitive and Behavioral Techniques

The treatment strategy outlined above is not simple to put it into practice because of complexities that often arise in the therapeutic relationship. Therapeutic techniques cannot be applied effectively without a good therapeutic relationship. Thus the first step in Cognitive Therapy with borderline individuals is establishing a collaborative working relationship.

Consider therapy from the client's perspective. Although clients with BPD want both help and acceptance, they typically see the world as a dangerous place in which they are relatively weak and vulnerable and in which they face the risk of being rejected or abandoned. This fear of vulnerability and anticipation of rejection results in a strong ambivalence about forming a close relationship with other persons and this can greatly complicate their relationship with a therapist. Often the borderline has had many negative experiences with mental health professionals, physicians, and other authority figures and has good reason not to trust the therapist initially. The client is likely to be on the lookout for signs of rejection and to react intensely when he or she spots them. In addition, the borderline is likely to have learned dysfunctional ways of relating to people that are manifested in their interactions within therapy. Although it can be quite difficult to establish a good therapeutic relationship and maintain it, if the therapist can accomplish this, the therapeutic relationship itself challenges the borderline's worldview.

The borderline is not foolish enough to trust others simply because they say they can be trusted or because they have a diploma. Trust is most effectively established by using the approach discussed in Chapter 7. This involves acknowledging and accepting the client's difficulty in trusting the therapist once this becomes evident and thereafter being careful to behave in a trustworthy manner so as to provide evidence on which trust can be based. It is important for the therapist to exercise more than the usual amount of care in communicating clearly, assertively, and honestly, avoiding misunderstandings, maintaining congruence between verbal statements and nonverbal cues, and following through on agreements.

Given the borderline's vigilance for signs of rejection, he or she can be quite sensitive to seemingly critical comments by the therapist. This can make it difficult to confront the client with the consequences of dysfunctional behavior without precipitating an overreaction. One option is to make a point of combining clear expressions of concern and caring with confrontation. For example, if a depressed client has been increasingly inactive and the therapist is concerned that the inactivity may contribute to a worsening of the depression, it would be natural to say, "When you are depressed and you don't stay active, your depression gets worse." However, borderline clients might well react as though the therapist is blaming them for their depression. The therapist might be less likely to provoke an overreaction by saying, instead, "I'm concerned, your depression seems much worse and you're being less active. When you've been depressed before, being inactive has led to your depression getting worse. Do you think that staying active would help with your depression?"

The interpersonal aspects of Cognitive Therapy are much more important with clients who have personality disorders than is usually the case, and this is particularly true with borderlines. Not only does the borderline client have problems involving interpersonal relationships that are manifested in the relationship of clients with his or her therapist, but also these problems can arise abruptly and change suddenly and unexpectedly. In addition, the client's strong emotional responses to the therapist, the complexity of the client's problems, and the intensity of the client's responses may elicit strong emotional responses in the therapist that can have an important impact on therapy.

Psychodynamic therapists spend much time discussing the phenomenon of transference, in which the client responds to the therapist on the basis of experiences in previous relationships rather than responding to the therapist's behavior. This is a phenomenon that is not prominent in Cognitive Therapy with many clients but is quite likely with borderline clients. This can present difficulties for therapists who are not used to dealing with strong emotional responses from their clients. For example:

> A 38-year-old medical technician consulted her physician regarding difficulties handling stress. The physician began providing biofeedback training. Treatment proceeded uneventfully until the patient suddenly began to experience a strong sexual attraction to her physician and decided she was in love with him. The physician decided he could not continue to work with her given these feelings. He had his secretary call the patient to tell her

that he could no longer treat her but that his wife, who also was a physician, would be able to continue the biofeedback training. The patient became increasingly preoccupied with the physician, her behavior became increasingly inappropriate, and she was eventually hospitalized with a Brief Reactive Psychosis.

"Transference" can be understood in cognitive terms as the client's responding to the therapist on the basis of generalized beliefs and expectancies rather than responding to the therapist as an individual. In an ambiguous interpersonal situation, such as traditional psychoanalytic psychotherapy where the therapist tries to be a "blank screen," many of the individual's responses are based on his or her beliefs and expectancies because the therapist's behavior is difficult to interpret. An active, directive therapeutic approach such as that used in Cognitive Therapy can often avoid this because the therapist takes a straightforward, unambiguous role. However, an active therapeutic approach does not completely eliminate these intense emotional responses. This is especially the case with clients, such as borderlines, who are vigilant for any indication that their hopes or fears may be realized. When intense emotional responses do occur it is essential to deal with them promptly and directly. This is done, first, by developing a clear understanding of what the client is thinking and feeling and then clearing up the misconceptions and misunderstandings directly and explicitly. It is particularly important to make it clear to the client that he or she will be neither exploited nor rejected in therapy.

Therapists working with borderline clients are likely to discover that, from time to time, interactions with clients elicit strong emotional reactions within the therapist that can range from empathic feelings of depression to strong anger, hopelessness, or attraction. It is important for the therapist to be aware of these responses and to look at them critically so that they do not unduly bias his or her responses. However, far from being an impediment, these feelings can be quite useful if the therapist is able to understand his or her responses to the client.

Emotional responses do not occur randomly. If a therapist experiences an unusually strong response to a client, this is likely to be a response to some aspect of the client's behavior and it may provide valuable information if it can be understood. It is not unusual for a therapist to respond emotionally to a pattern in the client's behavior long before that pattern has been recognized intellectually. Accurate interpretation of emotional responses can speed recognition of these patterns. However, judgment must be exercised in deciding whether to express these emotional reactions. Self-disclosure by the therapist increases the level of intimacy in the relationship and may be threatening to the client. On the other hand, denial of an emotional response that is apparent to the client from nonverbal cues may decrease trust and encourage the client's fears. Whenever a therapist is having difficulty understanding his or her responses to a client or is uncertain about how to handle them, he or she should consult an unbiased colleague.

It is advisable for the therapist to strive for a calm, methodical approach throughout therapy and to resist the tendency to respond to each new symptom or crisis as an emergency. Many new symptoms and crises will turn out to be transitory problems, which vanish as quickly as they appear. For those problems that do become the focus of therapy for a period of time, it is important to evaluate the situation in detail before intervening rather than reflexively trying "standard" interventions that may be off the mark. In particular, if the borderline client begins to manifest extreme agitation, signs of thought disorder, or other indications of a Brief Psychotic Disorder, a calm, measured response from the therapist may be sufficient to calm the client and avert the psychotic episode. If it is not possible to prevent the psychosis from developing, this need not be tragic. Although a brief hospitalization may be necessary and psychotropic medication may be useful, these psychotic reactions rarely produce lasting effects as long as the client and therapist do not decide that this is a sign of "craziness" and give up. Although the symptoms manifested during a Brief Reactive Psychosis may resemble Schizophrenia, a duration of at least 6 months is required for the diagnosis of Schizophrenia, whereas a Brief Psychotic Disorder often lasts only a few days (*DSM-IV-TR*, 2000).

In short, when working with borderline clients, it is particularly important to "stay close to the data" rather than relying on clinical or theoretical preconceptions, to pay close attention to the therapist–client relationship, and to think strategically rather than slipping into a "cookbook" approach. The intensity of the client's emotions (and the therapist's responses) calls for a calm, measured approach and for sufficient therapist self-understanding so that the therapist's responses can be used to facilitate therapy rather than serving as impediments.

Linehan (1993a) has made an important contribution by emphasizing the importance of effectively addressing the wide range of behaviors that interfere with effective treatment of borderline clients. These "therapy interfering behaviors" range from simple problems such as inconsistent attendance and noncompliance with homework to complex problems such as angry outbursts during therapy sessions or recurrent suicidal crises. Although the client usually does not intend to render therapy ineffective, these behaviors can easily have that effect unless they are addressed promptly and effectively.

Borderline clients are often quite sensitive to issues of control; and in an active, directive therapy it is quite easy for therapist and client to become locked in a power struggle over agenda setting or homework assignments. It is important to remember that it is very difficult for a client to stage a power struggle if the therapist does not participate actively in it. If the therapist adheres to the collaborative model underlying Cognitive Therapy, allows the client to have a part in developing agendas and homework assignments, and is responsive to his or her requests, power struggles are less likely. It is important to remember that there is no need to adhere rigidly to one particular format for monitoring and challenging thoughts, learning to relax, and so on. The therapist may need to use some flexibility in tailoring standard techniques to the individual client's needs and preferences.

However, although it is important for the therapist to be flexible and collaborative, it is also important for the therapist to have well-established clinical policies that are clearly communicated and are followed consistently (Newman, 1999). These typically would include policies regarding appointment times, fees, telephone calls between sessions, and so on. If the therapist is too flexible, it is easy for situations to develop that create practical problems and impose an undue burden on the therapist. Being too flexible can result in special arrangements that the therapist eventually resents, or that gradually evolve into seriously dysfunctional relationships that are problematic for both therapist and client.

Crises, emergency telephone calls, and requests for special arrangements are common during the early stages of therapy with many borderline clients. This behavior typically has been viewed as a "test" of the therapist's reliability and caring. Although it is not clear that crises early in therapy are intentionally staged as tests of the therapist, they often function as such. It is, therefore, crucial for the therapist to handle emergency phone calls and requests for special treatment effectively if he or she wishes the client to continue in treatment. However, it is not necessarily important (or helpful) for the therapist to agree to the client's requests or encourage midnight telephone calls. The therapist needs to consider how far he or she is willing to go in being responsive to the client while setting clear, consistent limits. If the therapist is unresponsive, or is inconsistent in setting limits, the client is likely to become angry, terminate therapy abruptly, or become increasingly demanding. If the therapist fails to set suitable limits and begins to resent the client's demands, this resentment is likely to interfere with therapy. It often works well to set a policy of keeping emergency telephone sessions brief and limiting them to crisis intervention, and then offering to schedule a therapy session as soon as possible as an alternative to lengthy phone contacts. Also, it is generally advisable for the therapist to make no special arrangements for one client that he or she would not be willing to extend to other clients. Most borderline clients adapt to clear, consistent guidelines. If a client is not willing or able to accept reasonable limits, he or she is not likely to be able to benefit from the collaborative approach inherent in Cognitive Therapy.

It is not unusual for therapists to be faced with the question of whether to consider inpatient rather than continuing outpatient treatment at times of crisis. Table 8.7 summarizes the American Psychiatric Association's treatment guidelines for BPD (American Psychiatric Association, 2003). Although these guidelines regarding level of treatment are based on clinical experience rather than empirical research, they seem both reasonable and practical.

At times, borderline clients (and others) may seek hospitalization even though hospitalization is unnecessary and may actually be counterproductive. For example, clients may feel safe and nurtured while they are in the hospital; or they may like the attention they receive and may use hospitalization to escape loneliness or other aversive moods. Some individuals will go to great lengths to be admitted to the hospital even though inpatient treatment is not necessary. When this occurs, it is important to understand the individual's reasons for seeking hospitalization and to help them look realistically at the pros and cons. If inpatient treatment proves not to be in the client's best interest, then the therapist can help him or her to find healthier alternatives to unnecessary hospitalizations.

When working with borderline clients, there may be a conflict between being responsive to the client's immediate concerns and maintaining a focused strategic approach. If each session deals with a different issue as the concerns of clients shift from week to week, little will be accomplished toward achieving the client's overall goals. However, if the therapist unilaterally insists on sticking to a fixed set of goals and priorities, the therapist has abandoned Cognitive Therapy's collaborative approach and risks alienating the client. As mentioned previously, Cognitive Therapy with borderline individuals calls for greater flexibility than conventional Cognitive

Table 8.7. APA Recommendations Regarding Determination of Treatment Setting

---

Indications for partial hospitalization
Dangerous, impulsive behavior that cannot be managed effectively with outpatient treatment
Nonadherence with outpatient treatment in combination with deterioration in day-to-day functioning
Complex comorbid conditions that need intensive assessment and management
Symptoms that interfere significantly with functioning, work, and/or family life that do not respond
   to outpatient treatment

Indications for brief inpatient hospitalization
Imminent danger to others
Loss of control over suicidal impulses or a serious suicide attempt
Transient psychotic episodes accompanied by a loss of impulse control or impaired judgment
Symptoms that interfere significantly with functioning, work, and/or family life which do not
   respond to outpatient treatment and partial hospitalization.
Indications for partial hospitalization but partial hospitalization is not available

Indications for extended inpatient hospitalization
Persistent, severe suicidality, self-destructiveness, or nonadherence to outpatient treatment and partial
   hospitalization
Comorbid Axis I disorder (e.g., eating disorder, mood disorder) that is refractory and presents a
   potential threat to life
Comorbid substance abuse or substance dependence that is severe and is unresponsive to outpatient
   treatment or partial hospitalization
Continued risk of assaultive behavior toward others despite brief hospitalization
Symptoms that interfere significantly with functioning, work, and/or family life that do not respond
   to outpatient treatment, partial hospitalization, and brief hospitalization

---

Therapy. It may be possible to maintain a consistent focus either by discussing the pros and cons of doing so or by agreeing to set aside part of the session for the current crises and then use the remainder of the session to address ongoing goals. However, with some clients it is necessary to focus on a different immediate crisis each week and to maintain continuity by addressing the issues underlying the various crises. For example, a problem such as failure to anticipate the consequences of one's actions may be manifested in many different problem situations. As a result, it is possible to maintain a consistent focus on anticipating the consequences of one's actions while responding to a series of different problems. However, the therapist must draw attention to the underlying issue while addressing each problem.

Noncompliance with homework assignments is a common problem in therapy with borderline individuals. Often the problem can be reduced to some extent by making a point of developing assignments collaboratively, making sure that the rationale for the assignment is clear, and maximizing the client's control over the selection of assignments. When problems with noncompliance do occur, it is rarely productive for the therapist to take a parental role and simply insist that the client do the assignments. It is often more productive to explicitly acknowledge that the client has the power to refuse to do whatever he or she wishes but then to also explore the pros and cons of choosing to do homework versus choosing not to do it. If the rationale behind the assignment is clear and the client recognizes that he or she is choosing to do the task, not being forced to do it, then there is less risk of noncompliance. If noncompliance persists, exploration of the client's thoughts at moments when he or she decides not to do the homework should be useful in identifying additional issues that need to be addressed.

Fear of change often contributes to noncompliance, increased distress during therapy, or premature termination. Because borderlines typically assume that the world is a dangerous place and often have a low tolerance for ambiguity, it is not surprising that they often find change, even change for the better, to be quite threatening. When persons are in a dangerous situation (or one they view as dangerous), they have a tendency to rely on their usual coping responses. The borderline client's usual coping responses may be quite unsatisfactory, but at least they are familiar and the outcomes are predictable. Trying a new response involves taking a step into the unknown; and even if the client is intellectually convinced that the proposed change will be a change for the better, he or she is likely to experience a significant amount of anxiety. If the fear of change is not recognized and discussed, the client may interpret this anxiety as a sign that the change really is dangerous and become quite opposed to it.

The borderline client's fear of change can be reduced to some extent by addressing it openly when it becomes apparent and by realistically examining the risks involved in trying new responses in specific situations. However, it is generally necessary to make changes in a series of small steps and not to press for change too quickly. Therapists often experience a desire to "go for the kill" when they see an opportunity to make a dramatic intervention that could produce a sudden change. However, with borderline clients, it is generally better to err on the side of caution. It is much easier to work with clients who see gradual change and are eager to continue, than it is to work with clients who are terrified by sudden changes and are reluctant to continue therapy. Clients can be valuable guides in pacing therapy if the therapist solicits their feedback and is attentive to signs of increased distress or reluctance. Fear of change can be intensified if the client assumes that therapy will end as soon as the problems are overcome. When such fears are present, it is important to make it clear that therapy will not be terminated abruptly and that termination will be a mutual decision, not a unilateral decision on the part of the therapist.

Often the borderline client's discomfort with intimacy will make certain subtle aspects of the interpersonal interaction intensely anxiety provoking to the client. For example:

> After several weeks of therapy, a client hesitantly mentioned that several times in each session she would become intensely anxious for no apparent reason and would have to resist a strong desire to run from the room. As this problem was explored, it gradually became clear that whenever the therapist leaned forward in his chair and made direct eye contact, the level of intimacy became higher than the client could tolerate at that point in therapy.

With clients who find it hard to tolerate even mild levels of intimacy, it may be necessary to make a number of accommodations to avoid excessive discomfort that could impede therapy or lead to premature termination. These could include limiting the amount of direct eye contact, increasing the distance between chairs, and avoiding handshakes, familiarity, or therapist self-disclosure. It can be helpful to explicitly involve clients in this process by soliciting their feedback and making it clear that you will seriously consider suggestions they have for making therapy more comfortable for them. The client's realization that he or she has some control over the seating arrangement, the topics discussed, and so on, in itself renders the intimacy of the therapeutic relationship less threatening by making it clear that the intimacy is escapable.

An initial focus on concrete behavioral goals can be very useful in reducing the impact of the difficulties of borderlines with intimacy and trust. Most borderline individuals find it less threatening to work on problems for which little introspection is required, and where the focus is on behavior rather than on thoughts and feelings. However, this provides an opportunity to build trust and increase their tolerance for intimacy, while making demonstrable progress toward their goals and thereby increasing their motivation to persist in therapy.

"Therapy interfering behaviors" can occur on the therapist's part as well. Psychotherapy with borderline clients often elicits strong emotional reactions on the part of the therapist that, over time, can result in the therapist's engaging in actions that interfere with the effectiveness of therapy. Our desire to help, to comfort, and to demonstrate that we care, can motivate us to remain engaged in the therapeutic relationship and make our best efforts to provide effective therapy. On the other hand, it can motivate us to cross therapeutic boundaries in misguided attempts to be helpful, which may create problems for both therapist and client. Well-intended therapists have been known to end up hiring borderline clients, moving borderline clients into their homes, or becoming embroiled in personal relationships with borderline clients. Even when the therapist's intentions are good, such dual relationships often prove seriously detrimental to both the client and the therapist (not to mention the risk of losing one's license or being sued for malpractice). Conversely, our understandable attempts to avoid such entanglements, resist manipulation and coercion, and rebuff verbal attacks can lead us to be defensive, rigid, and strict in a way that gives the client the impression that we are cold and uncaring. This typically elicits an intense reaction from the borderline client and can seriously disrupt therapy.

How can a therapist handle this? Table 8.8 provides some guidelines adapted from Welch (2000) and Newman (1999). It obviously is important to maintain a clear awareness of the boundaries of the therapeutic relationship and not to cross those boundaries by trying to personally meet the client's needs, whether these are needs for love, for employment, or for shelter. This does not mean that one is indifferent to these needs, but the therapist's role is to help the client get his or her needs met in day-to-day life, not to meet those needs personally. Although it is important to maintain clear boundaries to the therapeutic relationship, it is also important to avoid defensiveness, rigidity, or excessive caution. As was emphasized previously, it is important to balance concern and caring with clearly communicated limits and boundaries.

Borderline clients are likely to experience strong emotional reactions and potential crises at the termination of therapy, especially if it is necessary to terminate therapy before treatment is completed. It is important for the therapist to initiate discussion of the client's expectations, fears, and feelings well in advance of

Table 8.8. Guidelines for Minimizing "Therapy Interfering Behavior"

1. Set clear limits and discuss them with your clients in a straightforward, empathic manner. Counterbalance limit-setting with genuine expressions of caring and concern.
2. If the client responds negatively to the limits you set, respond empathically and explain the reason for the limits. Make it clear that these are general limits of the therapeutic relationship, not a personal rejection of the client.
3. Promptly address any violations of these limits, any misperceptions or misinterpretations of you, and any therapy-interfering behaviors. Communicate empathy and respect for the client but, at the same time, demonstrate a healthy respect for your own feelings and limits.
4. Be aware of your emotional reactions. Do not allow your desire to help or your desire to avoid the client's anger to pull you into crossing the boundaries of the therapeutic relationship. Do not allow your desire to resist coercion or to defend yourself against attack to induce you to be rigid, defensive, or rejecting.
5. Practice what you preach. Use techniques such as rational responses, imaginal rehearsal, and appropriate assertion to manage your own responses in therapy.
6. Seek periodic consultation from colleagues who understand the complexity of working with borderline clients.
7. If you anticipate problems with a borderline client, take the situation seriously and get help early—from a colleague, from an expert consultant, from an attorney, and/or your malpractice insurance carrier, as needed.

the termination date and to return to this discussion on several occasions even if the client initially insists that termination is not a major concern. Clinical experience suggests that it is often advisable to initiate this process 3 months or more in advance of the anticipated termination date. When terminating therapy because the client's goals have been achieved, it is often quite helpful to taper treatment gradually, moving from weekly to biweekly sessions and then to monthly sessions.

Cognitive and Behavioral Interventions

If a good working relationship can be established and maintained, the full range of cognitive and behavioral interventions can be used productively with borderline clients. However, it is especially important for the therapist to be alert to the client's reactions to any interventions and address them promptly. A number of techniques that are particularly useful in working with borderline clients are discussed below.

It can be argued that emotional instability plays a major role in a number of borderlines problems and in the difficulties therapists encounter in therapy with them (Farrell & Shaw, 1994; Linehan, 1993a). Sudden swings from one intense emotion to another tend to disrupt interpersonal relationships, contribute to an unstable, negative sense of self, and often lead to dysfunctional attempts to escape emotional distress. Farrell and Shaw (1994) argue that increasing the borderline individual's ability to recognize his or her emotional states and cope with them effectively is a prerequisite to effective intervention. They propose a treatment approach that includes experiential exercises and self-monitoring to increase the individual's ability to recognize emotional states at intermediate levels of intensity. They also recommend training in distress-reduction skills, developing a personalized distress-reduction plan, and *in vivo* desensitization to emotions that the individual tends to fear and avoid.

Many borderline individuals attempt to avoid or ignore problematic emotions when they are mild (and manageable) and then are suddenly overwhelmed by the emotions once they become intense. It is frequently important to help the client see the value of recognizing and dealing with emotions while they are mild to moderate in intensity. It is also important to help the client tolerate painful emotions at times rather than engaging in desperate attempts to escape them. Identifying the client's fears regarding intense emotions (such as, "I'll go crazy!" or, "It will go on and on forever!") and helping him or her to challenge the fears cognitively are often important precursors to *in vivo* exposure. A treatment manual is available for Emotional Awareness Training (Farrell & Shaw, 1994); other useful resources on this topic are available in the manual used with DBT skills-training groups (Linehan, 1993b).

Dichotomous thinking contributes to the borderline individual's sudden, intense mood swings. It is often such a pervasive component of the borderline individual's cognitive functioning that it is difficult for him or her to conceive of thinking in dimensional terms. However, dichotomous thinking can be challenged by using the continuum technique that was discussed in Chapter 2. By identifying a clear example of dichotomous thinking, helping the client operationalize his or her definitions of the two extremes, and then testing to see whether the dichotomous view is really consistent with the available evidence, it is possible to demonstrate that dichotomous thinking is neither realistic nor adaptive. With practice, borderline clients can become skilled at challenging their own dichotomous thinking, leading to a gradual decline in the frequency of dichotomous thinking. Farrell and Shaw (1994) suggest that Emotional Awareness Training often reduces dichotomous thinking as well. This decrease in dichotomous thinking often results in a decrease in the frequency of sudden mood swings and in the intensity of emotional reactions as the client evaluates problem situations in more moderate terms.

In addition, the client can attain even greater control over emotional responses by increasing his or her ability to look critically at thoughts in problem situations, developing alternative ways to respond to problem situations, and learning adaptive ways to express emotional responses. The techniques used in monitoring and challenging thoughts and developing active, assertive responses to problem situations with borderline clients are no different from those used with other clinical groups (Chapter 2). However, it is particularly important not to rush the borderline client and to be alert for complications. For example, many borderline clients believe that if they express certain feelings, such as anger, they will be immediately rejected or attacked. As a result, they often attempt to suppress any expression of these emotions and are extremely reluctant to consider an active, assertive approach that might include expressing annoyance or mild levels of other problematic emotions. The therapeutic relationship may provide a context in which the client can experiment with expressing these emotions in safety. The therapist can facilitate this by gently asking how the client is feeling when situations occur that might produce annoyance or other unpleasant emotions in the average client. Then the therapist can make a point of explicitly acknowledging and accepting the emotional

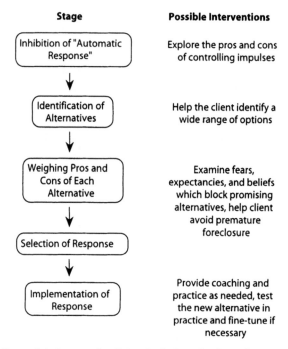

Stage   **Possible Interventions**

| Inhibition of "Automatic Response" | Explore the pros and cons of controlling impulses |

| Identification of Alternatives | Help the client identify a wide range of options |

| Weighing Pros and Cons of Each Alternative | Examine fears, expectancies, and beliefs which block promising alternatives, help client avoid premature foreclosure |

| Selection of Response |

| Implementation of Response | Provide coaching and practice as needed, test the new alternative in practice and fine-tune if necessary |

FIGURE 8.4. Intervention Points in the Impulse Control Process.

responses that the client is willing to express. To maintain trust in the therapist's genuineness and honesty, it is better to take advantage of naturally occurring situations than for the therapist to stage situations to elicit feelings.

Impulsive behavior is a very common problem with borderline clients. Figure 8.4 shows a series of possible interventions for helping clients develop better impulse control. The first step is to help the borderline client explore the advantages and disadvantages of impulse control to ensure sufficient motivation. Often these clients have had extensive experience with authority figures trying to force them to be less impulsive. They may well respond to the idea of increased impulse control with, "Why the hell should I?" This can be addressed by helping borderline clients recognize the ways in which it is in their interest to better control impulses. They can also be helped to realize that they retain the option of choosing to act on their impulses. The next step is to examine the cognitions preceding impulsive behavior and to use self-instructional training (Meichenbaum, 1977), if necessary, to enable these clients to inhibit their reactions long enough to choose an adaptive option. The therapist may also need to help clients identify adaptive options and master the skills needed to use them.

Self-destructive impulsive behavior may be a significant problem for the borderline and it may be necessary to eliminate this behavior quickly. First, it is important to understand the motivation for self-destructive behavior by examining the events leading to the self-destructive impulses or behavior (see Table 8.9). It is then possible to ask, "What do you want to accomplish through this action?" and, "Is there another way to accomplish this that is likely to be more effective

Table 8.9. Understanding the Motivation for Self-Mutilation

1. Ask about specific incidents one at a time rather than talking about it in general.
2. Find out about occasions on which clients have self-mutilated and occasions when they have been tempted but have not injured themselves.
3. Treat your preconceptions, intuitions, and hunches about the motivation for self-mutilation as hypotheses to be tested; do not assume that they are true.
4. Ask for specific information about specific events, *then* look for general patterns rather than starting off with generalities:

Precipitants
What led up to wanting to hurt yourself?
When did you start feeling like hurting yourself? What was going on before that?
How were you feeling beforehand? What other feelings went along with it?

Thoughts that precede impulses to self-mutilate
What was your immediate reaction when (the precipitating event) happened? What thoughts ran through your head?

"Goals"
What was the point to it? What did you hope to accomplish? How did you expect to feel afterwards?
How did you expect people to react to it? (If a particular individual precipitated the self-mutilation, ask specifically about him or her.)
Suppose you hadn't done it, what do you think would have happened? How would things have been different? How would you have felt then?

---

or have fewer bad side effects?" If it is possible to identify less destructive, effective responses, these can be substituted for the problem behaviors. As a temporary, stop-gap measure it is sometimes possible to substitute a minimally self-destructive behavior, such as marking oneself with a marking pen or snapping oneself with a rubber band, for a more damaging act, such as slashing oneself. This less destructive act can later be replaced with more adaptive alternatives. Because many of the adaptive alternatives to self-destructive behavior involve tolerating strong feelings rather than engaging in desperate attempts to escape painful feelings, additional work to increase affect tolerance (Farrell & Shaw, 1994, discussed previously) may be needed at this point.

Often, working toward more adaptive interpersonal behavior is a crucial part of dealing effectively with suicidality and self-mutilation. Borderline individuals often engage in desperate attempts to avoid abandonment or to have an impact on others. It is frequently useful to help clients recognize their interpersonal strategies ("If I want someone to care, I need to...."), to examine whether these strategies really are adaptive, and to find more effective alternatives. Often, strong fears (such as, "If I ask for what I want I'll be rejected!") block the client from trying promising strategies. It can be important to both address these fears cognitively during the session and to get the client to gradually test these preconceptions through behavioral experiments. Often, a good first step is to encourage the client to try strategies such as assertion in interactions with the therapist during the session, and discussing the thoughts and fears that emerge as he or she does so.

Choosing specific goals for therapy and working to adopt an active, assertive approach in dealing with problem situations can lead to a clearer sense of one's own goals, priorities, competencies, and accomplishments. However, it is possible to further facilitate the client's development of a clearer sense of identity by helping him or her to identify positive characteristics and accomplishments, providing positive feedback about good decisions and effective coping, and helping the client realistically evaluate his or her own actions. It is generally wise to provide feedback in moderation and to avoid effusiveness because borderline clients may be very uncomfortable with positive feedback at first. It is also important for feedback to be honest, because unrealistic positive feedback simply lowers the therapist's credibility.

The schema change methods discussed in Chapter 3 can be quite useful later in therapy with borderline individuals. Recall that borderline individuals tend to believe that the world is a dangerous place and that they are helpless. Both of these beliefs can be gradually challenged by helping clients test their expectancies against previous experience and by developing behavioral experiments that can be used to test expectancies. Beyond this, of course, the therapist can help these clients develop new competencies and coping skills. For example, when Mika developed her fear of vacationing in Jamaica, which was presented in Figure 8.1, it was possible for her therapist to approach this in much the same way as was recommended for working with other clients with Panic Disorder (see Chapter 5). Her therapist first helped her to examine her extensive experience with panic attacks and to realize that her panic attacks were not continuous and that even though she had experienced panic attacks on previous trips they did not ruin the whole trip. She was also helped to realize that although the attacks were intensely unpleasant, they were not dangerous. Over the course of the next several sessions she was able to learn to cope more effectively with anxiety and panic attacks through acceptance, progressive relaxation training, and related techniques (see Chapter 5). In addition, it was possible to challenge some of the thoughts that contributed to her anxiety, such as her conviction that her husband would leave her if her anxiety ruined the vacation. When the time for the vacation arrived, Mika's therapist used the vacation itself as a behavioral experiment by planning how to handle the situation, having her state her expectancies clearly before the trip, and then comparing these expectancies with her actual experience on the trip. Mika found that she was able to cope with intense anxiety well enough to prevent panic attacks, was able to have a very good time, and was able to cope effectively with unexpected problems as they arose. As a result, she began to look more skeptically at her tendency to anticipate that new challenges would always turn into disasters because of her incompetence.

Working with borderline clients is more complex than working with clients with isolated problems of depression or anxiety and it takes longer. However, clinical experience suggests that it is often possible to not only alleviate anxiety or depression, but also help them to gradually resolve long-standing problems such as identity confusion and inability to maintain stable intimate relationships. Because only limited outcome data is available, it is difficult to be certain how consistently these improvements can be achieved and how long they persist. However, many clients maintain these improvements well over the gradual "tapering-off" period at the close of therapy. It seems likely that clients who receive adequate preparation for dealing with future problems will be able to maintain the improvements achieved in therapy.

Conclusions

Given the complexity of psychotherapy with BPD and reports of poor outcome regardless of the treatment approach used (Mays, 1985), it is encouraging to find a growing body of evidence that cognitive-behavioral therapies can be effective with BPD. Dialectical Behavior Therapy is rare among approaches to treating BPD in that it has been subject to controlled outcome studies. Papers by Linehan and her colleagues (Linehan, Armstrong, Suarez, Allmon, & Heard, 1991; Linehan, Heard, & Armstrong, 1993; Linehan, Tutek, Heard, & Armstrong, 1994) have reported a controlled comparison of the effectiveness of DBT against that of "treatment-as-usual" (TAU) in a community mental health system with a sample of chronically parasuicidal borderline subjects.

Following 1 year of treatment, the clients in the DBT condition had a significantly lower drop-out rate and significantly less self-injurious behavior than TAU participants (Linehan et al., 1991). They also had significantly better scores on measures of interpersonal and social adjustment, anger, work performance, and anxious rumination (Linehan et al., 1994). However, the two groups showed only modest overall improvement in depression and other symptomatology and did not differ significantly from each other in these areas (Linehan et al., 1991). Throughout a 1-year follow-up, the DBT participants were found to have significantly higher global functioning than TAU participants. During the initial 6 months of the follow-up study they showed less parasuicidal behavior, less anger, and higher self-rated social adjustment. During the second 6 months, they had fewer days of hospitalization, and better interviewer-rated social adjustment (Linehan, et al., 1993). A subsequent replication by Koons and her colleagues (2001) using a sample with a less extreme history of self-mutilation showed significantly greater decreases in suicidal ideation, hopelessness, depression, and anger expression than a TAU control condition.

Dialectical Behavior Therapy and the approach to treating BPD through individual CBT discussed in this chapter not only have many elements in common but also have important differences. In particular, Linehan (1993a) emphasizes the importance of pairing individual psychotherapy with skills-training groups and has expressed serious doubts about the advisability of treating BPD through individual psychotherapy alone. The treatment approach discussed in this chapter has not yet been the subject of controlled outcome studies, though it has been supported by clinical reports, uncontrolled single-case investigations (Arntz, 1994; 1999; Turner, 1989), and an open-clinical trial (Brown, Newman, Charlesworth, Crits-Cristoph & Beck, in press). The results reported by these authors are encouraging. For example Arntz (1994) reports a case in which substantial improvement was achieved in depression, self-esteem, episodes of binge eating, and overall level of symptomatology despite the failure of four previous attempts at psychotherapy.

Brown and his colleagues (in press) conducted an open clinical trial in which 32 patients diagnosed with BPD received 1 year of weekly Cognitive Therapy for BPD

(Layden *et al.*, 1993). The year of treatment resulted in significant decreases in suicidal ideation, reports of self-injury, hopelessness, depression, number of borderline symptoms, and dysfunctional beliefs and these improvements were maintained over a 6-month follow-up. Ratings by independent diagnosticians showed that only 48% of the sample (14 of 29) still met *DSM-IV* criteria for BPD at the termination of treatment and, remarkable, only 16% (4 of 24) met criteria at the 6-month follow-up. Controlled outcome studies are definitely needed, but the data that has been reported thus far is quite encouraging.

Clinical reports suggest that Cognitive Therapy may have significant advantages over the leading treatment alternative, psychoanalytic psychotherapy. First, although psychoanalytic psychotherapy for BPD is a transference-based treatment that does not focus on treating specific symptoms (Kernberg, 1977), Cognitive Therapy typically produces improvement in important symptoms much more quickly. Second, psychoanalytic authorities on the treatment of BPD report that therapy typically is lengthy, with Masterson (1982) estimating that it typically takes 5 to 7 years. Cognitive therapists more commonly report completing treatment in $1\frac{1}{2}$ to $2\frac{1}{2}$ years. Cognitive Therapy with borderline clients is not at all quick and easy, but it shows potential for proving to be an effective treatment approach that is more efficient than the currently available alternatives.

9

Histrionic and Narcissistic Personality Disorders
The Dramatic Cluster—Part 2

HISTRIONIC PERSONALITY DISORDER

In keeping with the drama inherent in this personality disorder, Histrionic Personality Disorder, itself, has had a dramatic history. The use of the term "histrionic" is relatively recent. Originally, the term used to describe this disorder was "Hysterical Personality." The use of the term "hysteria" has varied widely over its 4000-year history and has often been a source of controversy (Vieth, 1977). Hysteria has at times been used to refer to conversion disorder, Briquet's Syndrome, a personality disorder, and a personality trait. Perhaps most commonly, it has been used pejoratively to describe hyperexcitable female clients who are difficult to treat. The concept of hysteria has been strongly rejected by feminists who view it as a sexist label due to the denigrating use of the term "hysterical" to discount the problems presented by the female client. Perhaps as an attempt to reduce the confusion regarding the use of the term "hysteria," the American Psychiatric Association did not include it in either *DSM-III-R* (1987) or *DSM-IV-TR* (2000). Instead, separate categories of Somatization Disorder, Conversion Disorder, Hypochondriasis, Dissociative Disorders, and Histrionic Personality Disorder have been designated. This chapter will focus on the treatment of people who fit the *DSM-IV-TR* criteria for Histrionic Personality Disorder (Table 9.1).

According to *DSM-IV-TR* (2000), the essential feature of this diagnosis is a pattern of pervasive and excessive emotionality and attention seeking behavior, which begins by early adulthood and is present in a variety of contexts. These clients are lively, dramatic, and, as the label implies, histrionic in style. They constantly draw attention to themselves and are prone to exaggeration. Their behavior is overly reactive and intense. They are emotionally excitable and crave stimulation, often responding to minor stimuli with irrational, angry outbursts or tantrums. Others perceive them as shallow, lacking in genuineness, demanding, and overly dependent. Although this chapter will focus on clients who meet the full criteria

Table 9.1. *DSM-IV-TR* Diagnostic Criteria for Histrionic Personality Disorder

---

A pervasive pattern of excessive emotionality and attention seeking, beginning by early adulthood and present in a variety of contexts, as indicated by five (or more) of the following:
  (1) is uncomfortable in situations in which he or she is not the center of attention
  (2) interaction with others is often characterized by inappropriate sexually seductive or provocative behavior
  (3) displays rapidly shifting and shallow expression of emotions
  (4) consistently uses physical appearance to draw attention to self
  (5) has a style of speech that is excessively impressionistic and lacking in detail
  (6) shows self-dramatization, theatricality, and exaggerated expression of emotion
  (7) is suggestible, i.e., easily influenced by others or circumstances
  (8) considers relationships to be more intimate than they actually are

---

of Histrionic Personality Disorder, many of the concepts may also be applied to clients who show a strong histrionic style without the depth of impairment of a full personality disorder.

As noted in *DSM-IV-TR*, the client with Histrionic Personality Disorder has been conceptualized as a caricature of what is defined as femininity in our culture—vain, shallow, self-dramatizing, immature, overly dependent, and selfish. This disorder is most frequently diagnosed in women, and when it is diagnosed in men it has been associated with homosexuality. This gender differential, however, may be more a product of our societal expectations than a true difference in occurrence. It has been suggested that Histrionic Personality Disorder is more appropriately seen as a caricature of sex roles in general, including extreme masculinity as well as extreme femininity (Kolb, 1968; MacKinnon & Michaels, 1971; Malmquist, 1971). The caricature of femininity is fairly commonly diagnosed as histrionic, yet a caricature of masculinity (an overly "macho" male who is dramatic, sensation-seeking, shallow, vain, and egocentric) is rarely recognized as Histrionic Personality Disorder and males may be less likely to seek treatment.

As is generally the case with personality disorders, people do not often seek treatment with Histrionic Personality Disorder as their presenting problem. Individuals with this disorder often experience periods of intense dissatisfaction and depression, sometimes making dramatic suicide attempts. Due to their dependence on the attention of other people, they are especially vulnerable to separation anxiety and may seek treatment when they become intensely upset over the breakup of a relationship. Anxiety disorders such as Panic Disorder with and without Agoraphobia are also common presenting problems in people with Histrionic Personality Disorder. Studies have shown that Histrionic Personality Disorder is one of the most commonly found personality disorders within Panic Disorder populations (Diaferia *et al.*, 1993; Sciuto, Diaferia, Battaglia, Perna, Gabriele, & Bellodi, 1991). In fact, Goldstein and Chambless (1978) suggest that one of the defining characteristics of the agoraphobic personality is a "hysterical response style," which they define as the inability to accurately connect feeling states with their eliciting stimuli and the inability to appropriately label current feeling states. Other common complications of Histrionic Personality Disorder that may lead to the seeking of treatment include alcoholism and substance abuse, Conversion Disorder, and Somatization Disorder.

Some changes to this diagnosis were made between *DSM-III-R* and *DSM-IV-TR* (discussed in Pfohl, 1991). The criteria "Constantly seeks or demands reassurance, approval, or praise," and, "Is self-centered, actions being directed toward obtaining immediate gratification; has no tolerance for the frustration of delayed gratification," were eliminated from *DSM-IV-TR* because these criteria were so frequently present in other personality disorders as well. A new criterion was added with *DSM-IV-TR*: "Considers relationships to be more intimate than they actually are." This new criterion was based on concepts in the historic literature and was added to maintain the same number of criteria as were present in *DSM-III-R*.

Assessment

The strongest indication of Histrionic Personality Disorder is an overly dramatic self-presentation. These clients express intense emotionality, but often do it in an exaggerated or unconvincing manner, as if they are playing a role. In fact, when talking with these clients, the clinician may have a sense of watching a performance rather than experiencing empathy for the individual. Histrionic clients can appear quite warm, charming, and even seductive; yet as the session goes on, their charm begins to seem superficial and to lack genuineness. They often present their symptoms, thoughts, and actions as if they were external entities involuntarily imposed upon them. They tend to throw up their hands (literally) and proclaim, "These things just always seem to be happening to me!" Histrionic clients often use strong, dramatic words, include much hyperbole in their speech, and seem to have a proclivity for meaningless generalizations. They use theatrical intonation with dramatic nonverbal gestures and facial expressions. They often dress in ways that are likely to attract attention, wearing striking and provocative styles in bright colors, and using cosmetics and hair dyes extensively.

Although these indications of a dramatic portrayal of the self can serve as useful cues to the presence of a Histrionic Personality Disorder, a dramatic style or unusual clothing alone certainly does not prove that the client has Histrionic Personality Disorder. Professionals in the past have seemed all too eager to label women "hysteric" whenever they presented complaints that were not easily explained or when they made demands that seemed excessive. If the term "Histrionic Personality Disorder" is going to be clinically useful rather than just being another term used to denigrate women, clinicians must be careful not to classify clients as histrionic merely on the basis of a dramatic flair. These characteristics, however, can serve as useful cues for the clinician to probe carefully for further information that will be useful in arriving at a diagnosis.

In the diagnosis of Histrionic Personality Disorder, it is crucial to explore interpersonal relationships in depth. Details should be obtained as to how previous relationships began, what happened, and how they ended. Indications to watch for would include an overly romantic view of relationships, with hopes or expectations of Prince Charming riding along on his white horse. Do their relationships start out as idyllic and end up as disasters? How stormy are their relationships and how dramatic are the endings? Another area to ask about is the way that they handle anger, fights, and disagreements. The clinician should ask for specific examples and look for signs of dramatic outbursts, temper tantrums, and the manipulative use of anger.

Many of the characteristics of histrionic personality are considered by our culture to be negative and most people would not readily acknowledge them. It is certainly not productive to ask people if they are shallow, egocentric, vain, and demanding; however, it may be possible to obtain some relevant information regarding these factors by asking them how other people tend to view them. One way to phrase this would be to ask what complaints the other person made about them, while exploring previous relationships that did not work out. With any client, details should be gathered about suicidal ideation, threats, and attempts to determine whether there is currently a risk of a suicide attempt. With a client who is potentially histrionic, this information is also useful to help determine whether or not there is a dramatic or manipulative quality to the threats or attempts. It can also be useful to ask for details of the types of activities the client most enjoys: Does he or she especially enjoy being the center of attention? Does he or she show a craving for activity and excitement?

Two brief clinical examples may help to illustrate the range of people who fit the criteria for Histrionic Personality Disorder:

> Sasha was a 31-year-old unmarried high school teacher with a master's degree in education. The reasons she gave for seeking therapy were vague and included phrases such as, "getting it all together." She was a recovering alcoholic who had not had a drink for the past 6 months but was worried that she would not be able to stay sober. She reported a variety of complaints including depression, anxiety, social isolation, procrastination, financial problems, and dissatisfaction with her job. She was overweight and sloppily dressed with long, frizzy hair and torn jeans with embroidered flowers. She looked somewhat like a burned-out hippie, out of place in the Midwest of the 1980s. She began the first therapy session with an angry outburst because she had been asked to fill out a variety of evaluation forms. She loudly expressed that this must mean that the therapist was more interested in the forms than in her. When the purpose of the forms was explained to her, however, her mood changed rapidly to one of eager compliance. In fact, her mood fluctuated wildly throughout the session. At times she had the voice of a little girl, and when she described situations involving other people she would imitate their voices, as if she were acting out their roles. She repeated her adjectives several times for emphasis, saying that she had a "real, real, real, real aversion to medications," and describing someone she barely knew as "just a beautiful, beautiful, beautiful person." She used dramatic, yet confusing statements such as, "It was as if all my synapses were thrown into the air and came down, I know not where." In describing her history, she said, "I killed myself in 1975," and only when she was asked to explain did she add, "Well, maybe not literally but that's how I look at it because so much of me died that day." She had recently broken up with her boyfriend and described that relationship saying, "I was madly in love with him ... He came along and I flipped out ... Then he turned into a real rat."

Sasha was fairly easy to diagnose as a case of Histrionic Personality Disorder, given her unconventional appearance, strongly dramatic style, labile mood, and attitudes toward relationships. Fred initially seemed to be completely different from Sasha, yet he also fits the diagnosis of Histrionic Personality Disorder.

> Fred was a 60-year-old married man who was very successful in sales. He looked businesslike in his three-piece suit when he sought treatment due to panic attacks, which led

him to avoid being alone at all and to avoid driving. His voice was powerful and dramatic and he began his first session by explaining (in hushed tones) how vital confidentiality was because he had so many prominent accounts and people would be appalled to learn he had these problems. He proceeded to regale the therapist at every opportunity with stories of his big business deals and even brought brochures describing his more successful accounts. He was disappointed to hear that his therapist was new in town and therefore could not appreciate the importance of his various clients. When it was possible to pin him down to discuss his reasons for seeking therapy, it became clear that whenever he had any physical symptom he immediately concluded that he was having a heart attack or going to die of suffocation. His wife was constantly at his beck and call and he actually demanded that she wear a beeper and drop everything whenever he became upset (which was quite frequent). He worked hard to maintain his businesslike image with other people, but had frequent angry outbursts toward his wife, throwing and breaking things when she displeased him in some small way.

Conceptualization

Most conceptualizations of Histrionic Personality Disorder have been psychodynamic in nature. Early dynamic descriptions emphasized unresolved Oedipal conflicts as the primary determinant of this disorder, whereas later dynamic theorists focused on the presence of a more pervasive and primitive disturbance arising during the oral stage of development (Halleck, 1967). Shapiro, although primarily psychodynamic in orientation, discusses many of the cognitive aspects of the "neurotic style" of the hysteric (1965). More recently, Millon (1996) has presented what he refers to as a bio-social learning theory view of personality disorders, including the Histrionic Personality Disorder. In his application of cognitive theory to a wide range of psychopathology, Beck (1976) discussed hysteria, but examined conversion hysteria rather than Histrionic Personality Disorder. However, the thoughts and beliefs of histrionic clients seem to indicate that a cognitive conceptualization (Figure 9.1) that combines some of the ideas of Millon and Shapiro with Beck's cognitive theory could clarify many of the aspects of the behavior of histrionic clients and suggest areas for useful clinical intervention.

As shown in this diagram, one of the basic beliefs of the person with this disorder seems to be, "I am inadequate and unable to handle life on my own." Individuals with a variety of disorders share this underlying assumption, but what distinguishes these various disorders is what conclusions follow from this assumption. For example, depressives with this underlying assumption might simply dwell on their shortcomings, feeling worthless and hopeless. Histrionic persons, however, seem to draw the conclusion, "Well, then, I need others to take care of me," and actively set about finding ways to insure that their needs are sufficiently met by others. As Millon (1996) observed, both the dependent and the histrionic personalities are dependent upon others for attention and affection. However, the dependent personality gets taken care of by emphasizing his or her helplessness and taking a passive role whereas the histrionic person takes the initiative in actively seeking attention and approval. The histrionic individual believes that, to be taken care of, "I *must* make them notice me and like me." Eventually, being noticed becomes more important than being liked.

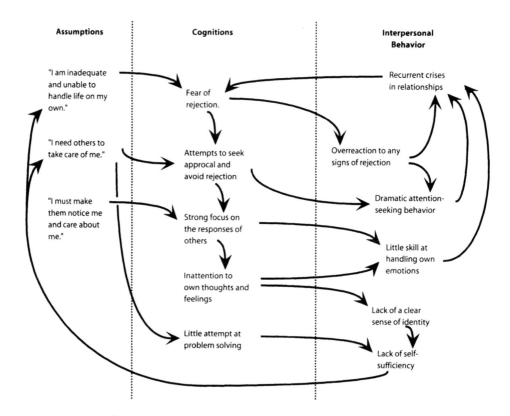

FIGURE 9.1. Cognitive Model of Histrionic Personality Disorder.

Because attention and approval are seen as the only way to survive in the world, histrionic clients tend to have a constant fear of rejection. When it is so important to be noticed and taken care of, having *anyone* not notice them is a frightening reminder that it is possible to be ignored and abandoned. Any rejection at all is seen as devastating, even when the person doing the rejecting was not previously important to the client. Just the idea that one can be rejected at all reminds the client of his or her tenuous position in the world. When someone is terrified of danger, it is natural to become vigilant to signs of that danger, so the histrionic person becomes hypervigilant to signs of rejection and abandonment. This can lead to over-reaction (e.g., temper tantrums) to any signs of rejection and recurrent crises in relationships.

Feeling basically inadequate yet desperate for approval as their only salvation, persons with Histrionic Personality Disorder are not willing to relax and leave the acquisition of approval to chance. Instead, they work diligently to seek approval and avoid rejection in the most effective ways they know—often through dramatic attention-seeking behavior, which generally means by fulfilling an extreme of their sex-role stereotype. Female histrionics (as well as some of the males) seem to have learned from an early age that they will be rewarded for cuteness, attractiveness, and charm rather than for competence or careful thought and planning. The more "macho" male histrionics have learned to play an extreme masculine role, being rewarded for the appearance of virility, toughness, and power rather than for actual competence or problem-solving ability. Understandably, then, both male and female histrionics learn to focus attention on the playing of roles, on "performing" for others, and on the responses of their intended "audience." Although winning approval from others is the primary goal, histrionics have not learned to systematically plan ways to please or impress others. Instead, they have been frequently rewarded for the global enactment of certain roles, so it is in the enactment of these roles that they learn to excel. This striving to please others is not necessarily dysfunctional in and of itself. Histrionic people, however, get so involved in this strategy that they take it beyond what is actually effective. They can get carried away with dramatics and attracting attention, losing sight of their actual goal and eventually seeking stimulation and drama for its own sake.

People with a Histrionic Personality Disorder view themselves as sociable, friendly, and agreeable and, in fact, they are often perceived that way at the beginning of relationships. Given their basic assumption that acceptance from others is essential, they tend to engage in a variety of subtle (and sometimes not so subtle) maneuvers to elicit favorable responses. As a relationship continues, they are gradually seen as overly demanding and in need of constant reassurance. They tend to overreact to anything they interpret as rejection and are prone to dramatic outbursts and tantrums. Because asking directly for what they want involves the risk of rejection, they often use manipulation to achieve their ends, but will resort to threats, coercion, temper tantrums, and suicide threats if their more subtle methods fail.

Histrionic individuals become so preoccupied with external approval that they learn to value external events over their own internal experience. They have learned to focus on cues and responses from others, paying little or no attention to their own thoughts and feelings. With so little focus on their own emotions, wants, and preferences, they are left without any clear sense of identity and see themselves primarily in relation to others. This lifelong focus on what others think and feel has prevented them from learning to deal with their own inner thoughts and feelings. In fact, their own internal experience can feel quite foreign and uncomfortable and at times they actively avoid self-knowledge, not knowing how to deal with it. Being somewhat aware of the superficial nature of their affections may also encourage them to shy away from true intimacy with another person for fear of being "found out." Because they have paid little attention to their own internal resources, histrionics individuals are at a loss when any depth is required in a relationship. Thus, their relationships tend to be stormy and shallow.

The histrionic's focus on the external and the dramatic may lead to the characteristic thought style that has been described by Shapiro (1965). The thinking of the histrionic client is seen as impressionistic, vivid, and interesting, but lacking detail or focus. This seems to result not only from the histrionic's lack of introspection, but also from the fact that he or she simply does not attend to details and specifics in the first place. What is not clearly perceived cannot be recalled in a specific manner, so histrionics' memories of events must necessarily remain global and diffuse. The resulting deficiency in knowledge of specific details and facts, along with a lack of experience in systematic problem solving, can lead to serious difficulty in coping constructively with conflicts or other problems. This serves to further reinforce the histrionic's sense that he or she is inadequate to cope with life alone and needs to rely on the help of others.

With this "vague" cognitive style, the histrionic individual's sense of self remains impressionistic rather than being based on specific characteristics and accomplishments. It is difficult to maintain a realistic impression of oneself if one does not view one's own actions and feelings in a sufficiently detailed fashion. In addition, if thoughts exert a strong influence on emotions (as is argued by cognitive theory), then it follows that global and exaggerated thoughts would lead to global and exaggerated emotions. Global emotions can be very intense and labile, so the client may get carried away by affect even though it does not feel totally connected to him or her. Without the availability of complex, cognitive integration, these undifferentiated emotions can be very difficult to control, leaving the person subject to explosive outbursts. Also, histrionic individuals typically lack skill at handling their own emotional reactions because they are not attending to them and often do not even notice them until they are extreme.

Because they have not been rewarded for active problem solving and carefully thinking situations through, many of these individuals never learned to value these skills and make little attempt to systematically solve problems. They end up with little self-sufficiency and a lack of self-efficacy. Automatic thoughts such as, "Oh, I couldn't possible handle that!" are common.

The histrionic client's characteristic style of thinking can manifest itself in several of the cognitive distortions. Because these clients tend to be struck by impressions rather than thinking things through, they are especially susceptible to all-or-no thinking. They react strongly and suddenly, jumping to extreme conclusions whether good or bad. Thus, one person is seen immediately as Mr. Wonderful whereas someone else is seen as a totally repulsive, evil figure. Due to the intensity of their felt emotions and lack of sharp attention to detail and logic, histrionic clients are also prone to the distortion of overgeneralization. If they are rejected once, they dramatically conclude that they always have been rejected and always will be. Unlike the depressive, however, they can be equally extreme in their positive conclusions about people and relationships, and can easily switch between the two extremes. Due to their inability to look at their responses critically, they are also subject to emotional reasoning—taking their emotions as evidence for the truth. Thus, histrionic individuals tend to assume that if they feel inadequate, they must truly be inadequate; if they feel stupid, they must be stupid; and conversely, if they feel charming, they must be irresistibly charming.

Strategies for Intervention

Since the days of Freud's work with Dora, psychoanalytic treatment has generally been seen as the treatment of choice for the various classes of hysteria. Little has been written about the treatment of hysteria from a behavioral point of view (summarized by Bird, 1979), and even less has been presented about behavioral treatment specifically for clients with Histrionic Personality Disorder. Given the problems that global, diffuse thinking causes for histrionic clients, it seems that a specific, focused approach to treatment might be useful, if they are able to accommodate to it.

Although admittedly an oversimplification, there is some truth to the statement that we need to "teach the hysteric to think and the obsessive to feel" (Allen, 1977, p. 317). Because the characteristic thought style of clients with Histrionic Personality Disorder is dysfunctional to them in many ways, Cognitive Therapy could be seen as a particularly appropriate treatment. Cognitive Therapy is a systematic and structured treatment, focusing on specific target problems and goals. The cognitive therapist tries to be well organized and comes to the session prepared to help the client work systematically toward the achievement of specific goals. The histrionic client, although perhaps cooperative and eager, comes to the session with an approach to life, which is diametrically opposed to the systematic, structured nature of Cognitive Therapy. With such different basic styles, both the therapist and the client may find Cognitive Therapy quite difficult and frustrating; however, if this conflict in styles can be gradually resolved, the cognitive changes facilitated by therapy can be particularly useful to the client. The therapist needs to maintain a steady, consistent effort and to be flexible if clients are to accept an approach that is so unnatural to them.

Teaching the histrionic client to use the techniques of Cognitive Therapy involves teaching an entirely new approach to the perception and processing of experience. Before the client can even begin to monitor thoughts and feelings, he or she needs to learn to focus attention on one issue at a time. Only then can details of events, thoughts, and feelings be identified. In treating many other disorders, cognitive techniques are basically tools used to help the client to change feelings and behavior. With Histrionic Personality Disorder, however, learning the process of Cognitive Therapy is more than just a means to an end; in fact, the skills acquired just by learning the process of Cognitive Therapy can constitute the most significant part of the treatment.

Because histrionic clients are generally dependent in relationships, the use of collaboration and guided discovery is particularly important. These clients are likely to view the therapist as the all-powerful rescuer who will make everything better, so the more active a role they are required to play in the treatment the less this image can be maintained. When they bring a series of problems to the therapist and ask for quick solutions, the therapist must be careful not to be seduced into the role of savior but rather to use questioning to help the clients arrive at their own solutions.

One aspect of teaching these clients is to focus their attention and to identify thoughts and feelings, and it is also important to reinforce them for competence and attention to specifics rather than for their more commonly reinforced emotionality and manipulation. If they can realize the ways that attention to details and assertion pays off in therapy sessions, they may also be able to learn that being assertive and doing active problem solving can pay off in everyday life. Thus, it is important for the therapist to be aware of attempts at manipulation within the therapy, so that they are not rewarded. Histrionic clients often maneuver to earn "special status" as clients by getting the therapist to agree to unusual fee arrangements or scheduling considerations. Their demands may seem insatiable and yet any refusal to comply may be seen by the client as rejection. These clients, therefore, need to learn that there are limits to the demands they can successfully make, and that limits are not necessarily a sign of rejection. Thus, the therapist needs to set clear limits early in therapy and be firm about enforcing them, while rewarding assertive requests within these limits and demonstrating caring in other ways.

An example of the importance of maintaining clear limits is seen in the case of Sasha (discussed above). She complained of financial hardship to her therapist and was concerned that she would be unable to pay the agreed upon fee. Rather than making special concessions for her, the standard fee arrangements were explained clearly and she was told that if she could not afford to be seen at this clinic, the therapist would be sorry but would help her try to find a therapist with a lower fee. It was also explained that letting her build up a large bill that she was unable to pay would not be useful to her or to the treatment; thus, if she fell two sessions behind in payments, she would need to wait until she was caught up before meeting again. She tested this arrangement once, and the therapist expressed regret that it would be necessary to postpone the next session but remained firm in the face of tears and pleas. From that point on, she kept up with her fee payments. Later it was discovered that in a previous therapy she had been given special fee considerations and abused them, racking up a substantial bill and not being able to pay it. When the consequences are clear, concrete, and immediate, the histrionic client finds it difficult to manipulate the situation and can learn to behave more adaptively.

Cognitive and Behavioral Techniques

An early step in Cognitive Therapy with any client involves learning to set an agenda. This generally straightforward and brief method of jointly making a plan for the session helps to enhance the collaborative relationship between the client and the therapist and structures the session to allow for focusing on goals. Because the inability to focus attention is one of the major problem areas for the client with Histrionic Personality Disorder, the process of learning to set an agenda takes on additional significance. Before any real problem solving can take place, the client needs to learn to focus attention on specific topics within the therapy session, and the setting of an agenda is an excellent place to begin working on this. Because setting a clear, specific agenda is likely to be a foreign concept to the histrionic client, it is necessary to use a graded task approach along with a great deal of patience. Getting the client to agree on even very broad, vague agenda items without going into extensive elaboration on each area can be quite an accomplishment. If the therapist remains flexible, however, and gradually works to impose more structure, even the most histrionic client can learn to cooperate with the setting of an adequate agenda.

Focusing attention on specific goals is difficult for histrionic clients. Their natural tendency is to want to come into the session and dramatically fill the therapist in on all the traumatic events of the week. Therefore, it may be necessary to schedule a part of each session expressly for that purpose. Thus, one agenda item could be to review how things went during the week (with a clear time limit) so the therapist can be empathic and the client can feel understood; then the rest of the session can be used to work toward goals. It is often most useful to schedule the unstructured review of the week for the end of the session, after the systematic work toward goals has taken place. That way, it is not necessary for the therapist to try to interrupt the client's dramatic portrayal of events to focus on other agenda items. Over time, the client may even be able to see that the goal-directed work is more useful and spontaneously ask to continue working on goals rather than move to the unstructured recitation of events.

Another early step in Cognitive Therapy is the setting of specific goals for the treatment. This is a challenging but crucial stage in the treatment of the histrionic client. One of the largest problems in the treatment of these clients is that they often do not stay in therapy long enough to make significant changes. This is because, as with other activities and relationships, they tend to lose interest and move on to something more exciting. The therapist is simply too boring! One key to keeping histrionic clients in treatment is to set goals which are genuinely meaningful and compelling, which are perceived as urgent to them, and which present the possibility of deriving some short-term benefit as well as longer term accomplishments. Initially, they may have a tendency to set broad, vague goals that sound "noble" and impressive and fit their image of what is expected from a therapy client. They may talk about "feeling better," "living a happier life," "being a better wife and mother," or "being more of a success."

It is crucial, however, that the goals be specific, concrete, and genuinely important to the client (and not just what they think they "should" want). The therapist can help clients to operationalize their goals by asking questions like, "How would you be able to tell if you had achieved your goal?", "What exactly would look and feel different, in what ways?", and "Why exactly would you want to accomplish that?" It may be useful to have clients fantasize in the session about how it would feel to have changed their lives, to help them begin to fit their ideas together into a tentative model of whom they would like to become. Because one of the main ways the therapist will be able to keep the client in treatment is by demonstrating actual progress toward the goals, the importance of setting goals cannot be overemphasized. In the treatment of a client with Panic Disorder as well as Histrionic Personality Disorder, her active work in therapy did not really begin until she moved from the "noble" but non-compelling goal of getting back to work and moved to a more engaging goal of being able to get to the mall to buy more shoes.

Goal-setting can also be a problem for histrionic clients who come to treatment focused on blaming other people for their problems and demanding that someone else "be fixed." The histrionic client needs to be taught that unless these significant others are present and involved in the therapy sessions, the therapist can only help the client to work on his or her own personal goals for change. Here again, it may be necessary to structure some time on the agenda for venting about other people, but the bulk of the session should be saved for working toward goals the individual can achieve.

Once the goals have been set, they can be enlisted as an aid to teach the client to focus attention. When an agenda has been set, but the client continually wanders off the subject (as he or she invariably will), the therapist can gently but persistently ask questions such as, "Now, that's very interesting, but how is that related to the goal we agreed to discuss?" If he or she continues to oppose efforts to focus on the agreed upon topic (despite having had time scheduled for ventilation), the therapist can introduce one of the primary cognitive techniques in the treatment of histrionic clients: the listing of advantages and disadvantages.

Helping the client to make conscious choices within the therapy session by examining the "pros and cons" of various courses of action is a useful antecedent to learning to make such choices in daily life. The histrionic client tends to react emotionally and dramatically to situations, rarely stopping to think or paying attention to the possible consequences. As a result, he or she tends to feel helpless and out of control over what happens. Exploration of the advantages and disadvantages of changing and working toward goals early in the treatment can help to minimize resistance and to make any resistance that does occur, obvious to both the client and the therapist. Often, when asked about the disadvantages of changing in the desired ways, the client will adamantly exclaim that it would be wonderful to change and there could not possibly be any disadvantages. With careful examination it will become clear that changing does have its consequences, including that of having to acknowledge some responsibility for actions rather than blaming external forces. If the therapist simply insists that the client focus attention on goals, the client can fight this and a power struggle may ensue with the client arguing that the therapist is "mean" and "doesn't understand." On the other hand, if the therapist consistently points out that the client may choose how to spend the therapy time but that achieving the desired goals will require some focus of attention, the client is left to make the decision. Furthermore, whatever the client chooses is experienced as coming more from the client than from the therapist.

After the initial stages of the treatment, the actual focus of therapy will depend on the client's particular presenting problem and goals. In general, the same Cognitive Therapy techniques would be used with histrionic clients as would be used to treat similar problems in other clients. The therapist, however, would need to be prepared to spend additional time in the initial stages of each technique, helping the client to adapt to the structure and to the focus of attention required.

In addition to working toward the specific, idiosyncratic goals of the client, it will be necessary to address each of the elements of the cognitive conceptualization of Histrionic Personality Disorder (Figure 9.1) to make a lasting change in the overall syndrome. To maintain collaboration, the specific elements of the conceptualization can be added to the client's goal list as necessary.

Given the hypothesis that histrionic clients' problems are exacerbated by their global, impressionistic thought style and their inability to attend to their own thoughts and feelings, it seems that teaching the client to monitor and pinpoint specific thoughts will be the crux of the treatment, regardless of the presenting problem. In teaching them to monitor thoughts using dysfunctional thought sheets, it is likely that a great deal of time will have to be spent on the first three columns; specifying events, thoughts, and feelings. It is unrealistic to expect histrionic clients to be able to go home and monitor thoughts accurately after a simple explanation and demonstration in the session, although this may be possible for many other types of clients. More commonly, histrionic clients will forget the point of monitoring thoughts and will instead bring unstructured pages of prose describing their stream of consciousness throughout the week. They should be praised for trying to do the homework. However, Thought Records will need to be explained again, reinforcing the idea that the goal is not just to communicate with the therapist but to learn the skill of identifying and challenging thoughts to change emotions. These clients often strongly feel the need to communicate all of their thoughts and feelings to the therapist in the hope that the therapist can understand them better and be able to help them more. If this is so, they can be encouraged to write unstructured prose in addition to the thought sheets, not as a substitute.

Figure 9.2 shows an example of a "thought sheet" written by a histrionic client early in her treatment. She had a driving phobia and had been asked to write her automatic thoughts and feelings when driving. Although she was writing on the appropriate form, she wrote a narrative of her experience rather than using the form to identify and challenge her thoughts. Figure 9.3 shows a thought sheet from later in her treatment, after she had learned to identify thoughts more specifically.

Once the clients have learned to identify their cognitions to some extent, they can begin to make gradual changes in their problematic thought style. The TRs can be used to help clients challenge any thoughts that prove to be dysfunctional

Daily Record of Automatic Thoughts

Situation Briefly describe the situation	Emotion(s) Rate 0-100%	Automatic Thoughts Try to quote then rate belief in each thought 0-100%
Drove to Chester to look at car, took son with me, had to get back to get Mary to swim class, drove Volvo, like it and salesman said make up your mind because this is last one. I said I'll buy it & signed paper. Then I said but I want to drive an Olds to make certain & I liked that too, so I said forget it & he said he would bring the car over that night to drive. I tried to talk my husband into signing papers, but he said we will sleep on it. Will probably buy it today. Was delighted to find car dealer near costume shop.	Couldn't make up mind & felt pressured, felt stupid for signing papers & then asking him to forget it.	

FIGURE 9.2. An Example Thought Record from Early in Therapy with a Histrionic Client.

Daily Record of Automatic Thoughts

Situation Briefly describe the situation	Emotion(s) Rate 0-100%	Automatic Thoughts Try to quote then rate belief in each thought 0-100%
Driving on Ventura Blvd., guy drives over yellow line.	Anxiety 50%	What if there was a car next to me? He would kill me. 50% What if lots of people get killed on this road and it just doesn't make the headlines? 50%
Drove on highway with husband	Anxious 50%	I will get stuck on the hill and my husband will get impatient and scream at me. 70%

FIGURE 9.3. An Example Thought Record from Later in Therapy with the Same Histrionic Client.

for them, cognitive distortions can be pinpointed and modified, and care can be taken to help histrionic clients to distinguish reality from their extreme fantasies. TRs can be especially useful in the process of reattribution. For example, Fred (discussed above) would attribute any slight change in his physical condition to a terrible disease and immediately conclude that he was going to have a heart attack and die. To him, it made no difference whether he became slightly lightheaded due to inhaling gasoline fumes from pumping his own gas, smelling ammonia in a restroom that had just been cleaned, or having a panic attack. Whatever the actual cause of his slight lightheadedness, he immediately concluded he was dying. Teaching him to stop and explore the possible alternative causes for his physical symptoms helped him to make more appropriate causal attributions and interrupt his cycle of panic.

Because histrionic clients have vivid imaginations, their cognitions often take the form of vivid imagery of disaster rather than verbal thoughts. Challenging cognitions is not restricted to verbal thoughts; in fact, imagery modification is an important aspect of Cognitive Therapy with histrionic clients. The therapist needs to specifically ask them what images go through their minds at upsetting times, because otherwise clients may not realize that imagery is important. Images can serve as powerful emotional stimuli; therefore, neglecting them in the treatment by focusing only on verbal thoughts can greatly decrease the effectiveness of treatment (Beck, 1970).

Simply challenging their immediate thoughts may not be sufficient, however, because histrionic individuals very often use emotional outbursts as a way of manipulating situations.

> Martha was a 42-year-old woman who was married to a man who worked long hours and did not pay as much attention to her as she wanted. Often when her husband came home late from work, Martha would have a temper tantrum with automatic thoughts such as, "How can he do this to me? He doesn't love me any more! I'll die if he leaves me!" As a

result of her tantrum, however, she got a great deal of attention from her husband and he would make clear statements of his love for her, which she found to be very reassuring. Thus, in addition to directly challenging her thoughts when she got emotionally upset, Martha also needed to learn to ask herself, "What do I really want now?" Only when she realized that what she really wanted at that point in time was reassurance from her husband, could she begin to explore alternative ways of achieving this.

Once clients can begin to stop and determine what they want from the situation, they can be taught to explore the various methods for achieving that goal and look at the advantages and disadvantages of each. Thus, they are presented with a choice between having a temper tantrum and trying other alternatives. Instead of asking them to make permanent changes in their behavior, the therapist can suggest that they set up brief behavioral experiments to test out which methods are the most effective with the least long-term cost. Setting up brief behavioral experiments can be much less threatening to clients than the idea of making long-term behavior changes and may help them to try out some behaviors which they might otherwise be unwilling to try.

In addition to helping clients challenge automatic thoughts, the self-monitoring of cognitions can be used to help them begin to control their impulsivity. As long as situations occur to which they automatically react in an emotional and manipulative manner, it is very difficult to make any change in their behavior. If they can learn to stop before they react (or, using a graded task approach, stop in the early stages of their reactions), long enough to note their thoughts, they have already taken a major step toward self-control. Thus, even before they learn to effectively challenge their cognitions, the simple pinpointing of cognitions may serve to reduce impulsivity and help them begin to develop skills for handling their own emotions. More information about improving impulse control can be found in Chapter 8.

Clients with Histrionic Personality Disorder may need to learn a variety of other skills to handle their own emotions. These include the skill of tolerating affect (see the Chapter 8), relaxation training (Bernstein *et al.*, 2000; Bourne, 1995), and empathy training (Turkat, 1990). As histrionic clients begin to learn to pause before reacting, they can also benefit from specific problem-solving training. Because they are rarely aware of the consequences before they act, it is helpful for them to learn to do what has been called "means-ends thinking" (Spivack & Shure, 1974). This problem-solving procedure involves teaching the client to generate a variety of suggested solutions (means) to a problem and then accurately evaluate the probable consequences (ends) of the various options.

For histrionic individuals to increase their sense of self-sufficiency, they first need to learn to value active problem solving and see how it may be useful to them. If the therapist can demonstrate how problem solving could help them to achieve important personal goals, they will be more likely to become interested in learning this process. Once they come to value the goal of self-sufficiency, they may need to be taught many of the skills of daily living, which they may have missed because they were not paying attention.

The treatment goals of histrionic clients often involve improving their inter-personal relationships. They are so concerned about maintaining attention and affection from others that they often attempt to dominate relationships in indirect ways that do not seem to carry the risk of rejection. The methods that they most generally use to manipulate relationships include inducing emotional crises, provoking jealousy, using their charm and seductiveness, withholding sex, nagging, scolding, and complaining. Although these behaviors seem sufficiently successful in the short term for the clients to maintain them, they have long-term costs that are not apparent to the clients. Once they are able to pause and examine their thoughts when they begin to have strong emotional reactions, histrionic individuals can begin to learn to challenge them.

One cognitive strategy that is useful in improving interpersonal relationships is the listing of advantages and disadvantages of dramatic attention-seeking behavior. This type of behavior feels very rewarding in the short term, so it is unlikely to change until the client can clearly see the negative consequences. Similarly, these individuals also need to learn to understand the consequences of their extreme reactions to perceived signs of rejection, and learn to make conscious choices as to whether these reactions are worth the negative results. Of course, interpersonal relationships, by definition, involve other people, so the client and the therapist do not have total control over changing these relationships. The client may have found relationships that reinforce the dramatic behavior; or the client's significant others may fail to reward, or even punish, increasing assertion and competence. When this appears to be the case, couple therapy may be indicated.

Once histrionic clients are able to explore various means of attempting to get what they want, the therapist can help them to consider the advantages of a method which may be quite new to them: assertiveness. The process of assertiveness training with histrionic clients involves more than just helping them learn to more directly communicate their wishes to others. Before they can communicate their wishes, they need to learn to identify those wishes and attend to them. Having spent so much time focusing on how to get attention and affection from others, these clients may have lost sight of what they want. Thus, effective assertiveness training with histrionic clients will involve using cognitive methods to help them pay attention to what they want, in addition to the behavioral methods of teaching them how to communicate assertively. This constitutes the beginnings of helping the client to develop a sense of his or her own identity.

The lack of a sense of identity is important to directly address in the treatment of Histrionic Personality Disorder. The goal of focusing on identity issues is to strengthen the sense of identity by clarifying goals, priorities, and opinions and helping the client to try to stick to them. Some of this work will already have been done in the early stages of Cognitive Therapy, because these issues are directly addressed as the client learns the processes of setting agendas and goals.

Phase 1 of identity work involves addressing the question of whether it is even acceptable for the client to have his or her own values, beliefs, and opinions. TRs can be used to challenge thoughts such as, "If I do have my own ideas, I'll have to confront people and risk being rejected." The therapist can help the client begin to explore what the consequences would be to having more of a sense of identify. Histrionic clients often believe that if they allow themselves to have their own opinions, they will need to then impose them on other people. It can be a major relief for them to realize that they can learn to hold strong opinions, but it is optional to confront other people with them.

Phase 2 of identity work involves helping clients learn to pay attention to their own wants and preferences instead of just focusing on other people. Learning to ask themselves, "What do *I* think?" can be quite helpful. Initially, when histrionic clients start looking at identity issues, they think of identity as a huge and mysterious entity, something other people seem to have and which they lack. The concrete task of collecting a list of preferences and opinions, without actually needing to act on them, makes the whole process of identity formation seem much more manageable. The homework assignment of starting a notebook and writing down preferences and opinions as they occur throughout the week is something that the client can generally understand and manage. This process can be started in the session, with the therapist pointing out every time the client expresses an opinion or preference and asking the client to write it down in the notebook. For example, if the client is talking about how angry she got when she was kept waiting, and says, "I hate it when people keep me waiting," the therapist can point out that this shows a strong preference for not being kept waiting and ask the client to jot it down right then and there.

Phase 3 of work on identity formation is to help clients to begin to put what they have learned about their goals, priorities, and opinions into practice and learn to stick to them, without being overly gullible and changing opinions whenever challenged by other people. By again examining pros and cons, clients can learn to make choices as to when and where they might want to practice expressing an opinion or acting on a preference or value. Rather than "trying to figure out who I am" in the abstract, clients can begin to do behavioral experiments to test out the validity of their opinions and ideas.

Of course, the experience of the client in the session needs to reinforce the idea that assertion and competence can be just as rewarding as manipulation and dramatics, if not more so. Thus, the therapist must be careful to reward attempts at clear communication and assertion, without falling into the patterns of so many of the client's previous relationships. This can be quite a challenge even to the experienced therapist, because the style of the histrionic client can be very appealing and attractive; and dramatic renditions of experience can be quite absorbing, entertaining, and amusing. The unwary therapist can easily be maneuvered into taking on the role of "rescuer," taking on too much of the blame if the client does not work toward change and giving in to too many demands. This may lead the therapist to feel manipulated, angered, and deceived by the histrionic client. A therapist who strongly wants to be helpful to others may inadvertently reinforce the client's feelings of helplessness and end up embroiled in a reenactment of the client's usual type of relationship. The methods of Cognitive Therapy can be useful for therapists as well as clients. The therapist may find himself or herself experiencing strong emotional reactions to the histrionic client and being less than consistent in reinforcing assertive and competent responses. If so, it may be time for the therapist to monitor his or her own cognitions and feelings for inconsistencies that might be interfering with the process of the treatment.

At the same time that clients work to improve their relationships, it is important that they also challenge their beliefs that the loss of a relationship would be disastrous. Even though their relationships may improve, as long as they still believe that they could not survive if the relationship ended, they will have difficulty continuing to take the risks of being assertive. Fantasizing about the reality of what would happen if their relationship should end and recalling how they survived before this relationship began are two ways to begin helping the client to "decatastrophize" the idea of rejection. Another useful method is to set up behavioral experiments that deliberately set up small "rejections" so the client can actually practice being rejected without being devastated.

Ultimately, clients need to learn to challenge their most basic assumption: the belief that, "I am inadequate and have to rely on others to survive." Many of the procedures discussed above (including assertion, problem solving, and behavioral experiments) can increase self-efficacy and help the client to feel some sense of competence. Given the difficulty these clients have in drawing connections, however, it is important to systematically point out to them how each task they accomplish challenges the idea that they cannot be competent. It can also be useful to set up small, specific behavioral experiments designed to test the idea that they cannot do things on their own.

Even clients who are able to see the advantages of thinking clearly and using assertion may become frightened by the idea that if they learn more "reasonable" ways of approaching life, they will lose all the excitement in their lives and become drab, dull people. Histrionic people can be lively, energetic, and fun to be with, and they stand to lose a lot if they give up their emotionality completely. It is therefore important to clarify throughout the treatment that the goal is not to eliminate emotions, but to use them more constructively. For example, clients can be encouraged to be dramatic when writing their rational responses, making the rational responses more powerful. Thus, when Sasha was challenging the automatic thought, "I'm too busy," while she was procrastinating about doing her homework, her most influential "rational response" was, "That's a pimply white lie and you know it!"

Clients may also need considerable help in finding effective alternatives to hystrionic behavior. For example:

> Paula was a 33-year-old cashier who had been married to an alcoholic and whose life had consisted of constant crises, including being beaten regularly by her husband and making frequent suicide attempts. After she divorced her alcoholic husband and became involved in a more stable relationship, she experienced feelings of loss for the stimulation and excitement she had experienced before. She had found the period of making up after a violent fight to be very reassuring and had not yet found equally intense ways of getting reassurance that she was loved. Through her work in therapy she was able to find assertive ways to ask for reassurance from her husband, and began to learn to recognize some of the less obvious signs of his affection. She also went back to school to add more challenge into her life. Other constructive avenues for sensation seeking can include involvement in theater and drama, participating in exciting activities and competitive sports, and occasional escape into dramatic literature, movies, and television.

For clients who feel reluctant to give up the emotional trauma in their lives and insist that they have no choice but to get terribly depressed and upset, it can be useful to help them gain at least some control by learning to "schedule a trauma." Clients can pick a specific time each day or week during which they will give in to their strong feelings (for example, depression, anger, a temper tantrum, and so on). However, rather than being overwhelmed whenever such feelings occur, they learn to postpone the feelings to a convenient time and keep them within an agreed upon time frame. This often has a paradoxical effect. When clients learn that they can indeed "schedule depression" and stick to the time limits without letting it interfere with their lives, they rarely feel the need to schedule such time on a regular basis. It always remains as an option for them, however. Thus, long after therapy has terminated, they will have a less destructive way to give in to such strong emotional experiences.

Because the histrionic client is so heavily invested in receiving approval and attention from others, structured cognitive group therapy can be a particularly effective mode of treatment. Kass, Silvers, and Abrams (1972) demonstrated that the help of group members could be enlisted to reinforce assertion and extinguish dysfunctional, overly emotional responses. One histrionic client continually focused on her physical symptoms of anxiety, complaining loudly, dramatically, and in graphic detail, despite the therapist's efforts. When she was placed in a Cognitive Therapy group, the feedback from the other group members, their consistent lack of reinforcement for physical complaints, and their positive reinforcement when she discussed other issues was much more successful at reducing her focus on her symptoms than her individual therapy had been. When Sasha entered a Cognitive Therapy group, her manipulative pattern of interacting with men became much more obvious than it had been when she was in therapy with a female therapist. If the client is involved in a significant relationship, couple therapy can also be especially useful. In couple therapy, both spouses can be helped to recognize the patterns in the relationship and the ways in which they each facilitate the maintenance of those patterns.

Conclusion

Most of the behavioral research that was conducted in the area of hysteria was confined to the treatment of conversion hysteria and somatization disorders (Bird, 1979). Woolson and Swanson (1972) presented an approach to the treatment of four "hysterical women" which included some behavioral components, and they report that all four clients made substantial gains toward all of their stated goals within four months of initiating therapy. Kass et al. (1972) described an inpatient behavioral group treatment of five women who had been admitted for suicidal intent and diagnosed as having a hysterical personality. Clients were required to adhere to a tight daily schedule, including therapeutic exercises to teach appropriate self-assertion. The clients were taught to identify their dysfunctional reactions to stress and systematically modify them. The group members were responsible for specifying each other's hysterical behaviors (which had been operationally defined) and providing the rewards and penalties that had been agreed upon. There was no control group, but multiple, concrete measures of progress were kept. Four of the five clients showed symptomatic improvement and more adaptive behavioral responses at the end of treatment and after an 18-month follow-up. Thus, fairly positive results were obtained in two studies of largely behavioral treatments with a population that is generally acknowledged to be very difficult to treat.

Although it has often been shown that clients with personality disorders have poorer outcomes in standardized treatments, this has sometimes been shown to be the opposite with Histrionic Personality Disorder. Both Turner (1987) and Chambless, Renneberg, Goldstein and Gracely (1992) found that in structured cognitive behavioral treatments for anxiety disorders, those participants with Histrionic Personality Disorder showed a better response than others on measures of panic frequency. It is hypothesized that the focus on relabeling affect may have been particularly useful for the histrionic clients.

The efficacy of Cognitive Therapy for the treatment of Histrionic Personality Disorders has not yet been tested empirically. However, it does show clinical promise in that several therapists have used these strategies over the past sixteen years with a variety of histrionic clients and report it to be an effective treatment. Furthermore, they report it to be a treatment that results in less frustration on the part of both therapist and client than more traditional approaches to treatment.

Narcissistic Personality Disorder

The concept of narcissism goes back to the earliest history of the psychoanalytic movement. The term itself is based on the Greek myth of Narcissus, the young boy who was so enamored of his own image that he ended up rooted in position, fascinated by his reflection. The earliest reference to the myth of Narcissus as a metaphor for psychological functioning was made by Havelock Ellis (1898). The term "narcissistic" and the use of this concept as a clinical description originated with Nacke (1899). This concept has been central to psychoanalytic thinking since then (Campbell, 1981; Millon, 1996). Despite this, Narcissistic Personality Disorder is relatively new as a diagnostic category, first appearing in *DSM-III* (1980).

Assessment

According to *DSM-IV-TR* (2000, p. 714), the individual with a Narcissistic Personality Disorder suffers from a "pervasive pattern of grandiosity, need for admiration, and lack of empathy" (see Table 9.2). This pattern of grandiosity occurs whether or not an objective evaluation of talent, accomplishment, physical prowess, intelligence, achievement, or beauty would validate the individual's high opinion of himself or herself. The self-focus inherent in this grandiosity is accompanied by a lack of empathy for others. For example, a young woman was "insulted" that, when she paid a condolence call on the parent of a co-worker who had died, no one noticed her new dress.

As with most personality disorders, clients with Narcissistic Personality Disorder usually seek treatment because of problems with depression or anxiety rather than because of narcissism itself. Their Axis II problems often become apparent quite quickly in therapy as they complain about not receiving the recognition or

TABLE 9.2. *DSM-IV-TR* Diagnostic Criteria for Narcissistic Personality Disorder

---

A pervasive pattern of grandiosity (in fantasy or behavior), need for admiration, and lack of empathy, beginning by early adulthood and present in a variety of contexts, as indicated by five (or more) of the following:

  (1) has a grandiose sense of self-importance (e.g., exaggerates achievements and talents, expects to be recognized as superior without commensurate achievements)
  (2) is preoccupied with fantasies of unlimited success, power, brilliance, beauty, or ideal love
  (3) believes that he or she is "special" and unique and can only be understood by, or should associate with, other special or high-status people (or institutions)
  (4) requires excessive admiration
  (5) has a sense of entitlement, i.e., unreasonable expectations of especially favorable treatment or automatic compliance with his or her expectations
  (6) is interpersonally exploitative, i.e., takes advantage of others to achieve his or her own ends
  (7) lacks empathy: is unwilling to recognize or identify with the feelings and needs of others
  (8) is often envious of others or believes that others are envious of him or her
  (9) shows arrogant, haughty behaviors or attitudes

---

approval that they deserve or as they indirectly reveal the lengths to which they go so as to assure receipt of this recognition and approval.

The constant pursuit of acknowledgment of his or her special status requires considerable effort and often leaves the narcissist feeling empty and depressed. The narcissistic individual may go beyond merely fantasizing about outstanding success and accomplishment and may be powerfully motivated to succeed so as to receive the recognition he or she desires. When the desired reactions from others are received, they often give the narcissist a brief period of happiness but are usually followed by a let down when the acknowledgment ends. This may result in what appears to be a driven and compulsive striving for wealth, fame, or recognition. For example:

> Sancho was a 64-year-old surgeon and Professor of Surgery at a major medical school. He had become internationally known after developing several new techniques for cardiac surgery over the years. Although acclaimed and invited to address medical groups around the world, he strove to receive awards that were actually meaningless in search of further proof of his skills and abilities. Each award would give him a transient sense of accomplishment but would be followed by a feeling of emptiness.

Narcissistic individuals will often go to considerable lengths to maintain their high opinion of themselves. Maintaining physical health may become exaggerated into fad dieting to maintain strength, health, or beauty. The need for academic success may result in a joyless, "educationless" school experience that centers on grades and recognition rather than on learning. For example:

> Jack, a 20-year-old male college student, was referred by the dean because of suicidal remarks. The student had asked the dean to investigate his grade in a course where he had received an "A". He requested a review because he had received an "A-" on the final exam, and he wanted an opportunity to retake the examination to achieve an "A" on the exam as well as in the course. He stated that he could not live his life knowing that his grade was "so poor," and not commensurate with his assessment of himself as "one of the finest students in the class."

There is, for the narcissist, little joy in succeeding, because any success is perceived as expected, rather than as an accomplishment worth savoring. In Jack's case, the achievement of attaining one of the highest grades in a course was undercut by the fact that it was not the highest and that others did equally well. When someone else has a greater accomplishment, the narcissistic individual often responds with envy and jealousy, rather than still being able to appreciate his or her achievements.

In some cases, the narcissistic behavior may be less problematic because it is consistent with societal expectations. A movie star is expected to be aware of his or her beauty and to demand special treatment because of it. Those who have become famous through achievement or through birth are often seen as deserving special treatment. Few are surprised when these individuals act as "prima donnas." However, even the "socially acceptable" narcissist may encounter problems in relationships with peers, when medicine and surgery can no longer stave off the aging process, or when the individual's career declines for other reasons.

Conceptualization

Freud's paper, "On Narcissism: An Introduction" (1914), was among his most important in that it first introduced the basic concepts of the ego ideal and the self-observing portion of the psyche that he was later to describe as the superego. The early, self-involved behavior of the infant was seen by Freud as a transitional state, eventually maturing into the ability to transfer this self-love to others. The basic psychoanalytic model of narcissism posits a disruption in the maturation process that fixates the individual's ability to love at the level of self-love.

The object relations theorists (Kernberg, 1967, 1970; Kohut, 1968, 1971) view narcissism as a paradoxical response to emotional deprivation during the early developmental stages. In effect, the exaggeration and over-valuation serve the defensive purpose of protecting the real self, which is threatened and weak. There is, however, little empirical research validating the notion that early deprivation will lead to an inflated sense of self. Studies of emotional deprivation have, in fact, presented evidence that emotional deprivation in infancy leads to apathy, withdrawal, poor social skills, and an avoidance of social interaction (Harlow, 1971).

Theories regarding the development of the "self-concept" provide another perspective on narcissism. During normal development, parents help a child develop a positive self-image and a strong self-concept or self-esteem (Hamner and Turner, 1985). This would ideally translate into a sense of personal efficacy and a feeling of satisfaction that is derived from successfully dealing with stressors and limitations imposed by one's environment as well as an acceptance of one's limitations and a striving to make use of one's abilities. Hamner and Turner (1985) make three assumptions about the development of self-concept. First, that it is learned; second, that this learning occurs early in the socialization process; and third, that the self-concept is a powerful determinant of behavior. This view implies that inappropriate early socialization could result in the individual's learning an unrealistically high appraisal of his or her capabilities and developing a pathological level of narcissism, but does not specify what problems in socialization would produce this problem.

Millon (1969, 1981, 1996) has proposed a social-learning hypothesis for the development of Narcissistic Personality Disorder that is compatible with this developmental view. He suggests that several elements may combine to establish an early over-valuation of self. In some cases, a narcissistic parent may model narcissistic behavior and a general narcissistic style for the child. Furthermore, narcissistic parents typically want to have special and wonderful children that enhance their own self-esteem and thus tend to exaggerate the accomplishments or abilities of their child. This modeling and reinforcement of exaggerated self-evaluation behavior could easily establish a narcissistic pattern for the child. In other cases, the parents may be unable or unwilling to assist the child in setting realistic boundaries within which to view him or herself. The parent who accepts the young child's grandiose visions of self, experience, or future possibilities, without offering realistic feedback and pointing out the child's limits and boundaries, reinforces this overinflated and eventually dysfunctional self-image. In either case, schools may further contribute to unrealistic self-evaluations and narcissistic behavior if they give in to demands for special treatment and give excessive positive feedback to children who are seen as special. For example:

> When Tyrone, a 15-year-old male, was referred because of school truancy, the therapist learned that he had been allowed to miss more than the usual number of classes before the school took action. The rationale offered by the teacher was that the boy was doing well, could easily catch up on the work, and was gifted so he deserved special consideration.

The same special attention may be offered to a child who appears to be gifted athletically or artistically. Such special attention would not be expected to establish a narcissistic pattern if it was the only such influence and if the child received sufficient reality-based feedback from other sources. However, if a narcissistic pattern has already been encouraged by family interactions, the child may interact with others in ways that tend to elicit special treatment and excessive attention from teachers and peers. This unintentionally perpetuates the pattern.

Narcissistic Personality Disorder is characterized by the cognitive distortions of selective abstraction and all-or-nothing thinking. Narcissistic individuals constantly scan the environment for evidence of their superiority and place great weight on the evidence they find. They may ignore any evidence that points to their being normal rather than exceptional or they may respond to any indications that they are "ordinary" with anger, anxiety, or overcompensatory words or actions. In either case, their view of the data is quite selective and leads to extreme conclusions. Poor problem-solving and reality-testing skills may exacerbate these problems.

It is no doubt obvious that the central dysfunctional belief underlying Narcissistic Personality Disorder is the assumption that the individual is, or must be, a "special" person. Their need to be admired for real or imagined achievement is an overriding factor. The nature of the attempt to impress others may depend on the degree to which the client has histrionic characteristics as well. The greater the hysteria, the more strange or bizarre the behavior. For example:

> Ralph, a 41-year-old attorney, was referred because of a number of somatic problems that his internist thought were psychogenic. In the initial session, the client announced that he

had been an assistant professor at a university medical school. When questioned further, he had to admit that he was not an assistant professor but had assisted a professor by giving two presentations as part of a lecture on medicine and the law. This same individual would meet women in a bar and speak in a very credible English accent. He would regale these women with stories of his work at Oxford and his law practice outside of London. Although many women found him intriguing, he could never go out with them again because, if he did, they would eventually find out that this was a charade.

A corollary to the client's belief in his or her specialness is the assumption that, as a result, he or she deserves special treatment. It is assumed that any deterrent or obstacle is not only to be avoided or destroyed but is also unfair and wrong. This view can generate considerable anger and frequent "temper tantrums" as well as behavior which can seem sociopathic. The narcissistic client often believes that no one should have more of anything than he or she has and shows an intense envy for any persons who seem to have more. This may be coupled with an insulting and denigrating attitude toward others and attempts to succeed by putting others down or actually destroying the productions of others. For example:

> Jaime, a 33-year-old insurance salesman, would take messages out of the mailboxes of other salesmen so that he could be the most successful salesman in his office and have his name on the "Salesman of the Month" plaque in the office corridor. When he was caught and was barred from winning for a year, he was incensed that such a big deal was being made of it and furious that he was not going to get the proper recognition for his work.

Obviously, the interpersonal patterns discussed above have a detrimental impact on relationships. Often the narcissistic individual will seek out kindred spirits who will participate in a "mutual admiration society" or individuals who will cater to their demands for special treatment. They may well believe that they should only have to relate to "special" people like themselves and see others as beneath them, socially, financially, or intellectually. They will tend to join only those clubs or organizations that offer them prestige, status, or the opportunity to associate with people who are seen as special, being very conscious of the trappings of status. For example:

> Marvin, a 42-year-old male accountant, was referred because of his anxiety about his dwindling practice. He would not have anything to do with his clients beyond doing their accounting work because he considered himself above them. He would avoid clients if he met them in a social situation, thinking, "Why should I have to mix with people I consider rabble?" Unfortunately for him, the usual response of his clients was to seek another accountant. The major concern he presented in therapy was that he could not keep up the payments on his Mercedes Benz. His goal was to have the therapist teach him ways of responding to his clients so that it would appear as if he cared, as long as that did not entail having drinks or lunch with them. When the therapist questioned that as a goal of therapy, the client responded by saying, "You are a consultant. I pay you to be whatever I want you to be."

These individuals may select spouses or partners who admire them greatly or who can be exploited. For example:

> Joel, a 32-year-old male client, prided himself on being what he called a "shark." He would attend dances or go to bars and pick up the women that he considered the least attractive or least socially skilled. He would almost always have sex with them and then never have any more contact with them. He said that he kept count of the number of sexual

experiences that he had. He justified his behavior saying, "I'm doing them a favor. I'm giving them what no one else will." He felt no remorse or guilt about his behavior and when questioned as to whether he felt uncomfortable with women that he considered so unattractive, his response was that he only thought about how wonderful these women would see him to be.

Intervention Strategies and Techniques

After the initial assessment, the building of a strong collaborative relationship is essential since participation in psychotherapy requires that narcissistic clients be asked to do things which they have great difficulty doing such as acknowledging shortcomings, tolerating frustration, coping with anxiety without their usual means of avoiding distress (such as alcohol, drug abuse, avoidance, abusing others, and so on), and talking seriously about thoughts, feelings, and ways of dealing with their problems. Unfortunately collaboration can be difficult both because of the characteristics of the client and the reactions the client elicits from the therapist.

One of the first steps in establishing collaboration is the task of agreeing on goals for therapy. Because the narcissistic client is not likely to present "becoming less narcissistic" or even "getting along with others better" as goals for therapy, it is important for the therapist to focus on clarifying and operationalizing the client's own goals for therapy. This provides a basis for working collaboratively in therapy and the client's narcissism can naturally become a focus of therapy when it impedes progress toward accomplishing the client's more concrete goals. With an individual such as Sancho who shows a long-standing, ingrained pattern of narcissistic behavior, it may be more realistic to work on changing specific behaviors than to plan to transforming him or her into a modest, sensitive, caring person. For example:

> Sancho, the surgeon mentioned earlier, came to therapy with great reluctance, as part of marital therapy. He had been married for 42 years to Anita. She had suffered a "nervous breakdown" (Major Depressive Episode), which required hospitalization and the treating psychiatrist strongly recommended marital therapy. As part of the assessment, Sancho was seen for two sessions. Although he made it quite clear that he did not like being in the therapist's office, he was smiling, pleasant, and collegial. He stated that he did not want to be part of the therapy ("I really don't think that I can offer anything useful"), was very busy ("You know how it is. We're all so busy"), and did not think that there was anything wrong with his wife which had anything to do with him ("This is her problem, it always was"). When his pleasant and charming manner did not work to convince the therapist that Sancho's involvement in therapy was unnecessary, he became brusque, bordering on rudeness. "Why," he inquired, "am I seeing a therapist who is only an Associate Professor, when I am a full Professor? If I have got to be part of this ridiculous business, I might as well have the best person."
>
> Sancho and Anita had been married for 40 years. The primary marital problem revolved around Sancho demanding that his wife wait on him, hand and foot. She had little more than servant status and was expected to provide for his every whim. She had graduated from college and immediately gotten married, becoming a housewife and mother. Over the last 10 years, Anita had become more and more "down" and finally ceased functioning and was admitted into the hospital. The beginning of her deterioration coincided with the last child marrying and leaving home. Sancho's view of Anita's problem was that she was just, "too moody, too weak, too spoiled, and too reluctant to do her job," which was, in his eyes, to do his bidding. Sancho considered his position in life as one that was well deserved. He described himself as a tyrant in the operating theater

because "I'm damn good." He described, with great relish, how he had his residents and nurses jump whenever he came into a room.

The goal of therapy, within the context of the agreed-upon marital work, was to have Sancho respond differently to his wife, the rationale being that this would help Anita return to full functioning. It was pointed out to Sancho that if he continued to create stress, his wife would continue to be depressed and would be unable to meet his needs. With this as rationale, he was willing to continue with the therapy and work on changing his behavior.

Once clear, manageable goals have been identified, the full range of cognitive and behavioral techniques is available for use. Because revealing one's flaws and shortcomings is incompatible with a narcissistic approach to life, behavioral interventions are often easier to implement because they require less self-disclosure than many of the cognitive interventions. Non-compliance with homework assignments is a common problem due to the belief that, "I must have my way in every interaction," the client's desire for special treatment, and power struggles with the therapist. The client may, in fact, attempt to bait the therapist into a power struggle in an attempt to demonstrate his or her superiority over the therapist. By pointing out what is happening, identifying the automatic thoughts and the underlying beliefs, and reminding the client that the point to the homework is to help the client achieve his or her goals, the therapist can deal with non-compliance without having to try to defeat the client. In time, the client may be able to see that there is no need to struggle and that, in fact, the struggle is counterproductive to reaching his or her goals.

Insofar as possible, the therapist must work with, rather than against, the narcissistic pattern to minimize unproductive conflict and to engage the client in therapy. The therapist who is not willing or able to tolerate the narcissistic client's behavior and accommodate to it will have difficulty inducing the client to persist in therapy. However, the therapist who is unwilling to confront the client because he or she is so easily offended is likely to end up having little impact.

The narcissistic client's sense of specialness complicates the therapeutic relationship. He or she is likely to expect special privileges and exemption from the standard rules followed by others and to demand special attention directly or indirectly. For example:

Marco, a 42-year-old salesman, would come early for sessions and ask for an empty office so that he could make phone calls and then would give the therapist's secretary photocopying to do, telling her it was okayed by the therapist. When it was pointed out that the client was impinging on the time of the staff, he responded by asking whether the therapist thought that his (Marco's) work was important.

It is essential for the therapist to establish and maintain firm guidelines and limits in therapy. This may as straightforward as in asking a client not to put muddy shoes on a couch in the office, or it may be more involved. Often the need to decide to which extent to accommodate the client's narcissism and to which extent to set limits or confront the client, presents itself from the beginning of therapy. For example:

When contacting her therapist to begin treatment, Noreen declared that she could be available on Tuesday at 3 P.M. When informed that that time was not available, the client became irritated and said, "Why must I make myself available only when you think it is best? My time and schedule are just as important as yours." When she was told that that time belonged to another client, she offered to call the other client and "persuade" him or her to come another time. When offered an appointment at 4 P.M., she quickly countered with, "How about 4:30?"

One area in which the client is likely to resist limit setting is in the therapist's attempts to agree on a clear agenda and stick to it, and this is an excellent point for beginning to set limits with the client. On this issue it is possible to turn the client's narcissism to the therapist's advantage by pointing out that the purpose of sticking to agreed-upon goals and a clear agenda is not to limit the client's freedom but rather to allow the therapist to most effectively pursue the client's goals and to be sure to address his or her important concerns. (There is no need to mention that all clients receive this form of "special treatment.") This issue of the agenda is also an ideal arena for limit setting because it is generally easy to demonstrate that it is in the client's interest to comply with the limits the therapist proposes. Having demonstrated that, in this one area, it is in the client's interest to comply with the limits the therapist sets, it may be easier to get the client to comply with limits in other areas as well.

Like the sociopath, narcissistic clients are not motivated by empathy for others, a desire to do what is right, or a desire to please the therapist. It is important to focus on the client's long-term self-interest in working to help him or her to choose the most adaptive courses of action and in trying to motivate him or her to take that action. As is the case with the sociopath, the client will discover that narcissistic behavior can be counterproductive and that it is in his or her self-interest to make substantial changes in his or her interpersonal behavior. The use of significant others in therapy can help to reinforce changes in the client's behavior and can help the significant others to cope more effectively with the client:

> In the treatment of Sancho and Anita, marital sessions were held weekly and Sancho was seen individually every other week. The therapy work with Sancho was limited, with much of the treatment consisting of direct instruction on more adaptive ways to behave with Anita. Sancho did, in fact, alter his response to Anita, not because he agreed with the changes, but because if he did not make those alterations he would get even less of what he wanted.
>
> Anita was a dependent individual who wanted to maintain the marriage. She stated that she loved Sancho and understood him "like no one in the whole world does." The focus of work with Anita was to help her be more assertive and to refuse doing things that she really did not want to do. Sancho and Anita concluded that if he wanted certain things done and she did not want to do them, they could hire someone or Sancho could do it himself. After 6 months of therapy Sancho and Anita terminated the therapy. She was less depressed and described Sancho as more responsive. She also pointed out that any response on Sancho's part was more than she had gotten in the past.

Conclusions

Therapy with narcissistic clients can be quite frustrating. These clients are not simply resistant to negative feedback. Any intimation that the therapist holds less than absolute positive regard (bordering on admiration or worship) toward the client may very quickly evoke either a dramatic over-reaction with strong anxiety or rage, or refusal to acknowledge the therapist's view. The, "Yes, but . . . ." nature of the client's typical response, an almost automatic dismissal of the therapist's statements, and a tendency to see the therapist as taking the side of all of the "others" who do not fully understand or appreciate the value and importance of the client, all serve to make it very difficult for the therapist to intervene effectively. It is essential that the therapist be aware of his or her emotional reactions to the client, not only to prevent the obvious frustration and annoyance from interfering with therapy, but also to avoid being inhibited by fear of the client's reactions. In particular, it is counterproductive to spend excessive time being angry with the narcissistic client for being narcissistic or to give in to his or her demands for special treatment, even though this may seem like less trouble than setting firm limits.

The cognitive-behavioral treatment of Narcissistic Personality Disorder has not been the focus of much empirical research. Clinical experience suggests that, despite the difficulties, narcissistic clients can be helped by Cognitive Therapy. It is less likely that the narcissistic patterns will be erased than it is that the patterns will be moderated to some extent. However, this limited improvement may have significant benefits for the client and his or her significant others. The best predictors of success seem to be the degree of narcissism and the therapist's ability to withstand the narcissistic individual's constant pressure for approval and special treatment.

10

Avoidant, Dependent, and Obsessive–Compulsive Personality Disorders
The Anxious Cluster

DSM-IV-TR (2000) categorizes Avoidant, Dependent, and Obsessive–Compulsive Personality Disorders together as Cluster C, the "anxious-fearful" cluster. However, although it is true that these individuals are often anxious and fearful, they differ markedly in their interpersonal behavior and present different challenges in treatment. We will discuss each of these disorders separately.

AVOIDANT PERSONALITY DISORDER

Withdrawal from other people is characteristic of a variety of disorders, including Avoidant Personality Disorder, Schizoid Personality Disorder, Social Phobia, Panic Disorder with Agoraphobia, Paranoia, Schizophrenia, Major Depression, and ordinary shyness. What distinguishes Avoidant Personality Disorder (APD) from these other disorders, according to *DSM-IV-TR* (2000), is that the social withdrawal of Avoidant Personality Disorder is due to "a pervasive pattern of social inhibition, feelings of inadequacy, and hypersensitivity to negative evaluation." (p. 718; see Table 10.1).

This withdrawal is a pattern that starts by early adulthood, if not before, and exists in a variety of situations. Individuals with Avoidant Personality Disorder are easily hurt by criticism or disapproval and are unwilling to get involved with people unless certain of being liked. They have at most one close friend other than immediate relatives and generally avoid activities that involve significant interpersonal contact. They are reticent in social situations and worry about being embarrassed in front of other people, exaggerating the potential difficulties and risks involved in ordinary activities which are outside their usual routine. This disorder is thought to be fairly common. Weissman (1993) reviewed epidemiological

Table 10.1. *DSM-IV-TR* Diagnostic Criteria for Avoidant Personality Disorder

---

A pervasive pattern of social inhibition, feelings of inadequacy, and hypersensitivity to negative evaluation, beginning by early adulthood and present in a variety of contexts, as indicated by four (or more) of the following:

    (1) avoids occupational activities that involve significant interpersonal contact, because of fear of criticism, disapproval, or rejection

    (2) is unwilling to get involved with people unless certain of being liked

    (3) shows restraint within intimate relationships because of the fear of being shamed or ridiculed

    (4) is preoccupied with being criticized or rejected in social situations

    (5) is inhibited in new interpersonal situations because of feelings of inadequacy

    (6) views self as socially inept, personally unappealing, or inferior to others

    (7) is unusually reluctant to take personal risks or to engage in any new activities because they may prove embarrassing

---

surveys conducted using a range of standardized interview schedules and found that prevalence rates for Avoidant Personality Disorder were between 1.1% and 1.4%. However, many such individuals avoid seeking treatment because therapy itself involves interpersonal contact, which is outside of their normal routine and is perceived as having a great risk of embarrassment.

In *DSM-IV-TR*, the criteria for APD place greater emphasis on social inhibition and feelings of inadequacy within interpersonal relationships than did the criteria in *DSM-III-R* (1987). Seemingly subtle differences in the wording of criteria in *DSM-IV-TR* convey a different emphasis. For example, *DSM-III-R* discussed "fear of negative evaluation" that has been changed in *DSM-IV-TR* to "hypersensitivity to negative evaluation." This indicates that the individual is not only afraid of criticism but is so sensitive to negativity that he or she could easily perceive negative evaluation where none was intended. Similarly, the wording "is easily hurt by criticism or disapproval" in *DSM-III-R* has been changed to "is preoccupied with being criticized or rejected in social situations" in *DSM-IV-TR*, emphasizing how pervasive these concerns are for the individual.

When people with Avoidant Personality Disorders seek treatment, they tend to do so because of depression, anxiety, alcoholism, or anger at themselves for their lack of relationships. Stravynski, Lamontagne, and Lavellee (1986) found that 35.1% of their sample of alcoholics met the criteria for Avoidant Personality Disorder, with 89% of these participants reporting that the abuse of alcohol developed after the onset of Avoidant Personality Disorder.

Assessment

To determine whether an individual may have an Avoidant Personality Disorder, it is important to explore the client's interpersonal relationships in depth. The therapist needs to pay attention to any tendency on the part of the client to interpret ambiguous actions as rejection or any pattern of leaving or avoiding relationships rather than facing the possibility of rejection. These people will often state that they wish they could have relationships, if only they could be certain that the relationships would work out, but that they are not willing to risk any possibility of rejection or humiliation.

In differentiating among the disorders characterized by social withdrawal and isolation, it is important to understand the client's reason for the avoidance of other people. In many cases, the distinction is fairly straightforward. Individuals with Avoidant Personality Disorder avoid others due to the fact that they are extremely uncomfortable with people, timid, and afraid of being viewed negatively. Unlike those with an Avoidant Personality Disorder, individuals in a Major Depressive Episode withdraw from others because of a loss of interest or pleasure in almost all activities, including social activities. In Panic Disorder with Agoraphobia, the individual may avoid social situations due to a fear of having a panic attack and finding it difficult or embarrassing to leave or to get home. Schizophrenics withdraw because of a preoccupation with egocentric and illogical ideas and fantasies. In Paranoid Personality Disorder, individuals may avoid other people based on a belief that other people have malicious intentions. In common shyness, the individual may be reluctant to enter social situations, but the pattern is less pervasive and less severe than in Avoidant Personality Disorder.

A more difficult differential diagnosis is that between Avoidant Personality Disorder and Schizoid Personality Disorder. The distinction between these two disorders was originally proposed by Millon (1969) and has been the source of some controversy (Akhtar, 1986; Livesley et al., 1985, 1986a, b; Millon, 1986a, b; Reich & Noyes, 1986; Scott, 1986). Clinically, however, the distinction seems to be crucial, because different interventions would be recommended for individuals with these two diagnoses. People with either disorder are socially isolated and avoid close interpersonal contact, having at most one friend other than first-degree relatives. The key distinction is that persons with Schizoid Personality Disorder have little or no desire for social relationships and are indifferent to criticism, although individuals with Avoidant Personality Disorder yearn for closeness and acceptance, are upset by their lack of ability to develop relationships, and are very sensitive to criticism.

Even more controversial in recent years is the distinction between Social Phobia and Avoidant Personality Disorder. In both disorders people tend to avoid specific situations due to a fear of humiliation. If the social phobic's fear is circumscribed, such as an isolated fear of public speaking, or a specific fear of eating, drinking, or writing in public, the distinction from Avoidant Personality Disorder is straightforward. In generalized Social Phobia, however, the social phobic may fear most social situations and many of the symptoms overlap with Avoidant Personality Disorder. In *DSM-III* (1980), the diagnosis of Avoidant Personality Disorder specifically precluded a diagnosis of Social Phobia. In *DSM-III-R* (1987), this exclusion was eliminated and it was possible to give both diagnoses of APD and Social Phobia. In a study comparing Social Phobia to Avoidant Personality Disorder, Turner, Beidel, Dancu, and Keys (1986) found that individuals with a diagnosis of Avoidant Personality Disorder were more sensitive interpersonally and had significantly poorer social skills than did the Social Phobia participants. Controversy remains over whether Avoidant Personality Disorder and Social Phobia are really different disorders. Some suggest that APD is simply a more extreme form of Social Phobia (Herbert, Hope, & Bellack, 1992; Holt, Heimberg, & Hope, 1992; Turner, Beidel, & Townsley, 1992).

Avoidant Personality Disorder is more than simply being anxious in social situations. Avoidant individuals maintain their avoidance by actively keeping people at a distance. Although these individuals do not seem as cold as the schizoid, they often are experienced as not being very likable. They are shy, apprehensive, awkward, and uncomfortable in social situations, and seem to actively shrink from interaction. Their speech is generally slow and constrained, with frequent hesitations. Their behavior tends to be highly controlled and tense or lethargic, with a complete lack of spontaneity. Overt expression of emotions is rare. Alden and Capreol (1993) suggest that clients with Avoidant Personality Disorder can be divided into two groups: those in whom distrustful and angry behavior is dominant, and those who are unassertive.

When assessing Avoidant Personality Disorder, some indications to watch for include:

1. a tendency to interpret ambiguous actions as rejection;
2. a strong tendency to avoid situations rather than face the risk of rejection;
3. a strong desire for relationships; and
4. a tendency to keep others at a distance by appearing unlikable.

For example:

> Laura was a 29-year-old secretary who sought treatment for what she described as a "fear of people." She presented with symptoms of Social Phobia as well as Dysthymic Disorder. However, when these symptoms were explored further, it became clear that she had a chronic pattern of avoiding social situations and interpersonal relationships in general since high school. Her one close friend had written Laura a note during the previous year that Laura interpreted as meaning, "Go away." Laura concluded that, "If I ever take down my wall of trust, something bad happens and it goes back up." When Laura came for her first session, she sat in the waiting room in an almost fetal position and did not make eye contact at all with the therapist for several sessions. She reported thoughts such as, "I hate being me," "I'm 29 going on 5," "If I go to the party, I'll feel dumb and won't know what to say," "I'll end up alone, 'cause no one will talk to me." During her evaluation, she constantly made disparaging remarks about herself, criticizing the way she phrased things.

Conceptualization

Individuals with Avoidant Personality Disorder are convinced that they are unacceptable to others and that if they try to develop close relationships, they will be hurt, humiliated, and devastated. They see no other alternative but to protect themselves from the pain of this imminent rejection by avoiding relationships as much as possible. Unfortunately, they still very much want affection and acceptance from others and yearn for close relationships. Thus they are lonely and distressed by their inability to relate comfortably to other people. Millon (1996) describes the Avoidant Personality Disorder as characterized by an "actively detached" coping style. Unlike individuals with Schizoid Personality Disorder who are passively detached from others because of indifference, people with Avoidant Personality Disorder are detached from others because they have made an active and self-protective decision to withdraw from social relationships to avoid intense pain from the defeat and humiliation they anticipate.

Because individuals with Avoidant Personality Disorder expect to be hurt and rejected, they are hypervigilant to any possible signs of rejection and tend to over-interpret innocuous behavior as a threat. They show such strong selective attention to negative cues from others that they do not even notice positive responses from other people. This selective attention, along with their avoidance of social interactions, tends to eliminate any evidence that would disconfirm their fears and their expectation of rejection is maintained.

> Yue was a 21-year-old single male who sought treatment for his extreme social anxiety and depression. He reported automatic thoughts such as, "I'll be inferior," "I won't measure up," and, "Others will judge me harshly." When taking the elevator and walking through the cafeteria as part of *in vivo* exposure with his therapist, Yue kept his head down and did not look at other people at all. When his therapist asked him about this, Yue reported that although he did not actually see the other people, he had a "sense" that they were judging him negatively. When he tried the exposure again, making it a point to look at other people, he found no evidence to support his assumption that the other people were judging him.

The avoidant individual's focus on the potential for rejection and his or her subsequent social detachment have a number of additional dysfunctional side effects. Between their limited social interaction and their strong focus on possible signs of rejection, avoidant individuals have little opportunity to learn from experience with others, to master social skills, and to develop effective interpersonal problem-solving strategies. Also, because they do not spend their time relating to other people, they tend to be preoccupied with their own thoughts and impulses, increasing their estrangement from other people.

The self-protective stance of individuals with Avoidant Personality Disorder is summarized by Millon (1996), "their outlook is therefore a negative one: to avoid pain, to need nothing, to depend on no one, and to deny desire" (p. 265). Their efforts to protect themselves from pain extend beyond social situations; in fact, avoidant individuals often feel so inadequate at coping with distress that they try to avoid confronting their own upsetting thoughts and feelings. The dilemma, however, is that they want to ignore painful thoughts and feelings, yet are so often alone and preoccupied with themselves that the pain is difficult to ignore.

There is a hopelessness that characterizes individuals with Avoidant Personality Disorder. They are so convinced that all relationships will necessarily turn out to be rejecting and painful that they choose not even to try anymore. As uncomfortable as social alienation may be, they perceive it as less distressing than the anguish of rebuff or ridicule. Avoidant individuals also tend to have a strongly negative view of themselves, minimizing their accomplishments and maximizing their shortcomings. A negative view of self tends to confirm their belief that they will be rejected because they do not feel worthy of acceptance. Yue was certain that either he was fated to be the way he was or that there was something terribly, deeply wrong with him, such as a brain tumor.

Individuals with Avoidant Personality Disorder tend to restrict their range of behavior in order to minimize the chance of rejection. The less they do, the less chance they have of being criticized. For example, Laura went to bed at 6 p.m. on any nights when she did not have a specific appointment. She reported that this was a good way to not have to deal with anything or anyone.

Common automatic thoughts of individuals with Avoidant Personality Disorder include: "I'm obviously a loser"; "They'll see how anxious I am and judge/criticize me for it"; "I'm better off just staying home tonight—I'll just be disappointed if I go and don't fit in"; "I'm really a sad, pathetic person without any real friends"; "I don't say anything interesting or original"; "What's the use in going places? I'm going to always be alone anyway"; and "I'd rather live alone than be humiliated again." Common assumptions include: "If anyone knew the real me, they would reject me"; "Being rejected by someone else would be a disaster"; "The only way I can protect myself from the pain of rejection is to keep at a safe distance from others"; "Since I've never had friends, I must not have what it takes to make friends," "If I make a mistake, I'll never live it down," "People can't be trusted to care," "It's easier to remain passive than to be active"; and, "It's safest to sit still and do nothing." These thoughts and beliefs lead to very persistent avoidance of a wide range of interpersonal interactions.

Intervention Strategies and Techniques

One of the main things to remember in the treatment of these individuals is that the process of coming to therapy can be sheer torture to the client with Avoidant Personality Disorder. Having spent a lifetime trying to avoid close relationships with their risks of rejection, they find themselves having to enter a therapeutic relationship that by definition involves sharing information that could lead to rejection. Not surprisingly, avoidant clients are difficult to keep in therapy. Both the therapy itself and the homework present risks of rejection, and so are frightening and uncomfortable.

For this reason, it is crucial for the therapist not to push for intimacy and self-disclosure too quickly, whether within the therapy session or in homework assignments. It is much more effective to allow the client to maintain a safe distance until he or she feels ready to move closer than to pursue him or her. One way to help build the intimacy gradually is to begin with behavioral strategies and to work toward specific goals, helping the individual learn to cope with difficult situations. It is hoped that these behavioral strategies will enhance the client's sense of self-worth and help him or her to cope with anxiety in a non-threatening manner, without the client being required to disclose too much or to get too close to the therapist. At the beginning of therapy it can be quite useful to maintain more distance than usual from these clients. Even if a therapist generally takes an informal approach and uses first names with clients, it may be wiser to introduce oneself by title and address the client formally as well with individuals having an Avoidant Personality Disorder. This should continue until the client gives some indication that he or she would prefer less formality.

Individuals with Avoidant Personality Disorder will often want to terminate therapy during the initial phases of treatment. When they express interest in ending treatment, it is important to use the issue of early termination as an opportunity to identify automatic thoughts and begin to challenge them. Even more common with avoidant clients is a tendency to develop a pattern of canceling appointments or having difficulty in scheduling regular appointments. This is more difficult to confront directly, because clients typically insist that their poor attendance has nothing to do with discomfort with therapy or with their motivation to improve, but is due solely to external factors. In addition, when the therapist points out the pattern of poor attendance, this may be seen as criticism and disapproval (hence rejection) by the therapist. The situation is further complicated by the fact that treatment can be very frustrating to the therapist because progress is so slow. If the therapist is sufficiently frustrated, he or she may become increasingly critical and disapproving and be tempted to agree with the client's desire to terminate and thus allow the therapy to end prematurely. Rather than become increasingly confrontational, the therapist might consider scheduling sessions less frequently in the hopes of reducing the client's anxiety. If attendance continues to be a problem, it may be necessary, first, to help the client find ways to make therapy more comfortable, and second, to discuss the advantages and disadvantages of staying in therapy quite explicitly. The therapist can emphasize that it is the client's choice but that staying in therapy may be the best way to attain his or her goals.

Building trust in the therapeutic relationship is one of the first major hurdles of therapy, because the fears and cognitive distortions common to Avoidant Personality Disorder will occur regularly within the therapy relationship. Tests of the therapist's trustworthiness are a common part of early treatment, but are less dramatic than those common among borderline or antisocial clients. The client carefully observes whether the therapist is going to criticize or disapprove of him or her, but is usually not overtly provocative. Given that these clients tend not to be particularly likable, yet are exquisitely sensitive to indications of rejection, it is important for the therapist to find something he or she can genuinely like about the client. The therapist may not find it easy to empathize with these clients because they are not at all engaging; however, it is crucial to work to see things from the client's point of view.

> Ruth was a 61-year-old housewife who sought treatment for her anxiety. When she first came into therapy, she appeared irritable and distant. Her therapist worked hard to be accepting and was able to empathize with Ruth's fears. It was not until the fifth session that Ruth cautiously confessed that she had fantasies of having an extramarital affair, something that she was ashamed of and had never discussed with anyone before. At the time of this "confession," she watched the therapist intently to see if there were any signs of disapproval. It was even later in the treatment that she admitted to not having graduated from high school, again watching the therapist's reaction closely. It was not until after the therapist passed these "trust tests" that Ruth began to relax a bit in the therapy sessions and appeared less irritable and distant.

No matter how carefully the therapist works to be accepting, the client is still likely to interpret the therapist's behavior as rejecting at times. Therefore, it is important for the therapist to frequently check for thoughts and images in the therapy session, especially when there is any evidence of mood change in the client. Even if the client is not ready to share something as personal as his or her thoughts about the therapist, the therapist should continue to ask about them. This will gradually communicate the message that it is acceptable to have thoughts and feelings about the therapy and the therapist and to discuss these in the session. In order to maximize the possibility of the client sharing his or her concerns about therapy, it can be helpful to phrase questions as if you expect and want to hear some negative reactions. For example, in getting feedback at the end of the session, it is better to ask, "What do you wish had been different in this session?" than the more open-ended, "How did you feel about the session?" Asking the client to fill out a written therapy session evaluation form at the end of each session can also be particularly useful with the avoidant individual. These clients may be more likely to share thoughts and feelings about the sessions in this less personal way than face-to-face where potential rejection would be more obvious and immediate.

In the initial stages of treatment, it is important not to move too quickly to challenge automatic thoughts, because such challenges could be seen as criticism. Only gradually, once the client is engaged in therapy and some trust has been established, would the therapist move to more cognitive interventions to test out some of the individual's expectancies in social situations. If the therapist is careful to be collaborative rather than confrontational and is consistent in the use of guided discovery rather than direct disputation of thoughts, it is less likely that the client will view the cognitive work as criticism.

Because Avoidant Personality Disorder is a chronic and pervasive pattern, these clients may never have learned the basics of social interaction and may therefore need structured social skills training. This would include training in the nonverbal aspects of social interaction (such as smiling, eye contact, posture) and conversational skill training (such as learning to make small talk, active listening). They may also need some basic social education so that they can better interpret other people's behavior.

Work on reducing anxiety can be very helpful to these clients, because they are likely to experience high levels of anxiety when they begin to reverse their patterns of avoidance. The techniques discussed in Chapter 5 can be useful for anxiety management. With such chronic and pervasive patterns of avoidance, avoidant individuals need to be taught to do explicit cost-benefit analyses whenever they are tempted to automatically avoid situations. In doing so, they may learn to make conscious, thoughtful decisions about whether to avoid or not, rather than automatically taking the easy way out.

Although individuals with Avoidant Personality Disorder are socially isolated and afraid of intimacy, they also often believe that if they could only find the right relationship and be guaranteed acceptance, everything would be all right. Interventions directed toward finding ways to enjoy being alone and developing a positive relationship with themselves can be useful in reducing the pressure of finding the right relationship immediately. One way to do this is to have the client schedule a "date" to enjoy an evening alone at least once a week, treating himself or herself as one would treat a special friend (preparing a nice dinner, planning favorite activities, and so on.)

Many avoidant clients arrange their lives in such a way as to avoid unpleasant thoughts and feelings. The use of alcohol is one obvious way to distract oneself, but other less obvious ways include excessive sleep (as in Laura's case), television watching, computer use, overeating, or smoking. This pattern of cognitive avoidance can lead to difficulty doing homework assignments, even those as simple as writing down automatic thoughts or listening to an audiotape of a therapy session. Because even the awareness of their own upsetting thoughts and feelings can be anxiety-provoking to these individuals, it may be necessary to desensitize clients to the experience of their own internal state. Thus, the client might be taught to relax and then to face gradually increasing amounts of introspection. Alternatively, the therapist might slowly increase the periods during which distressing thoughts, images, and feelings are the focus of the therapy session. Imagery can be used during the session to rehearse homework assignments in advance, so that plans can be made to overcome any difficulties that arise when attempting the homework. In order to expose clients fully to the internal experience they have been avoiding, it may be necessary to help them gradually eliminate the behaviors they use to avoid their thoughts and feelings. The tendency to avoid can become so automatic that specific steps must be taught to notice and reverse the avoidance. One useful method is to have the client carry index cards with common avoidant automatic thoughts written on one side and anti-avoidance responses in his or her own words written on the back. Thus, whenever the client has one of the thoughts that typically leads to avoidance, they can review the card quickly and easily.

Although it is important to challenge the underlying assumptions that serve to generate the automatic thoughts, it is fruitless to try to challenge these beliefs early in treatment. The client's hopelessness and his or her belief in the dysfunctional underlying assumptions are typically so strong that verbal challenges are ineffective. Later in therapy, when the client has taken some concrete steps toward his or her goals and has begun to develop some trust in the therapist, attempts to challenge these beliefs are more successful.

> After just a few weeks in therapy, Yue was able to identify the assumption, "Other people must think very highly of me. If they don't, I must be a loser." However, he held this belief so strongly that when his therapist tried to challenge this belief in the therapy session, little headway was made. It was only after he had achieved concrete progress in therapy through activity scheduling to reduce his depression and having success with a variety of exposure homework assignments (e.g., making phone calls to stores, visiting stores, calling the therapist on the phone) that they addressed this basic assumption again. This time, when he was given the assignment of finding ways to challenge this belief at his own pace between therapy sessions, he was able to come up with several good rational responses (listed in Table 10.2). This helped to accelerate his progress on his social anxiety hierarchy and enabled him to take greater risks.

Although the issue of trust is central throughout the treatment with Avoidant Personality Disorder, it is too sensitive an issue to discuss explicitly for quite some time. It is only in the later stages of the therapy that lack of trust can be explicitly identified as an issue that helps to maintain dysfunctional patterns in relationships. Once trust is openly acknowledged as an important issue, developing a continuum of trust can be helpful. For an example of a trust continuum, see the chapter on Paranoid Personality Disorder (Chapter 7). At this point in therapy, the client may be able to acknowledge his or her initial difficulty in trusting the therapist, and

Table 10.2. Yue's Rational Responses

Homework Assignment:
  Come up with rational responses to the belief "Others must think very highly of me, and if they don't,
  I must be a loser."
    (1) This is an example of the distortions of all-or-nothing thinking, jumping to conclusions, and
        labeling.
    (2) Having people think highly of me may be desirable, but what people think doesn't necessarily
        reflect the way things really are.
    (3) If the theory is correct, it would mean that my worth as a human being would change as
        peoples' opinions of me changed. My worth would be determined by the thoughts of others.
    (4) The theory breaks down when you consider that not everybody is going to have the same
        opinions. Some people will think highly of me and some won't. Who's right?
    (5) Because I know myself better than anyone else does, my own opinion of myself should be
        more important than others.

---

the therapeutic relationship can be used as an example of the development of close relationships in general. In fact, once trust is established, the therapeutic relationship can be used as an arena to test a variety of thoughts and beliefs. For example:

> After a few months in therapy, Yue commented that he could not remember anything positive ever happening to him in a relationship and was certain that he had never received a compliment. His selective attention was so strong that he actually had no recollection that, at one point in the treatment, the therapist had disclosed that he really liked Yue. When the therapist reminded him of that session, Yue still could not remember the compliment, but he trusted the therapist enough to believe him. This example was very powerful for Yue, and for the first time in therapy he recognized how he had been selectively focusing on the negative. He was then able to begin to become aware of his selective attention in other relationships besides the therapeutic one.

Once some trust and intimacy have developed in the therapy relationship and the client has achieved greater comfort in superficial social contacts, the risks involved in developing close relationships can be addressed. Ideally, the treatment would continue long enough for some of the social contacts made during *in vivo* exposure assignments to develop the potential for becoming closer friendships. This can be quite threatening to the client, and it often is helpful to explore the advantages and disadvantages of taking the risks involved in moving closer in a relationship. A new set of automatic thoughts and underlying assumptions regarding intimacy may need to be identified and challenged. Dichotomous thinking is common in regards to intimacy, with the client fearing that if he or she gets at all closer to another person, the relationship will automatically become overwhelmingly intense, leading to sex, marriage, or some other frightening prospect. Breaking this process down into steps and outlining a continuum of closeness can be useful. Ultimately, it will be necessary to decatastrophize disapproval and rejection in close relationships as well. It is hoped that by this point in treatment, the client will have developed enough self-efficacy and have had enough success with various types of relationships that he or she is able to entertain the idea that disapproval in a close relationship does not have to be devastating.

After a period of individual treatment, it is useful to move to a group therapy approach so that the client can learn new attitudes and practice new skills in a generally benign and accepting social environment. Group therapy is particularly anxiety-provoking for the client with an Avoidant Personality Disorder, but it can be extremely beneficial.

> Brianna was a 29-year-old businesswoman who inquired about a dating anxiety group that had been publicized. She suffered from acromegaly (giantism) and had long been convinced that she looked grotesque. In addition to her thoughts about her physical appearance, she reported thoughts such as, "I have nothing to say," "Whatever I say, I will look like an idiot," and, "I'll regret this (if I go)." Although the idea of being in group therapy was very anxiety-provoking for her, she was so determined to overcome her problems that she was willing to give it a try. In the first two sessions, she was so anxious that she was virtually unable to speak and she cried in both sessions. Between sessions, she called the group leader expressing her desire to leave the group and asking for reassurance that she should continue. As time went on, however, she was able to use the group to challenge her dysfunctional ideas. The group members were accepting and supportive, she was gradually able to discuss how she had always felt different from other people in her family in many ways, and eventually she was able to discuss her giantism directly.

Conclusion

Many of the outcome studies of cognitive behavioral treatments for Avoidant Personality Disorder conducted thus far are actually studies of Axis I disorders such as Social Phobia or Panic Disorder with Agoraphobia which also measured the effects of Avoidant Personality Disorder on the outcome. Some studies found that the presence of Avoidant Personality Disorder or avoidant traits was a predictor of negative outcome (Chambless *et al.*, 1992; Chambless, Tran, & Glass, 1997; Feske, Perry, Chambless, Renneberg, & Goldstein, 1996; Hoffart, 1994; Scholing & Emmelkamp; 1999). Other studies, however, found that Avoidant Personality Disorder was not predictive of treatment outcome (Brown, Heimberg, & Juster, 1995; Hoffart & Hedley, 1997; Hofmann, Newman, Becker, Taylor, & Roth, 1995; Hope, Herbert, & White, 1995). In fact, some studies found that individuals with Avoidant Personality Disorder made significant positive changes in brief periods of time. Brown *et al.* (1995) found that several participants who received a diagnosis of APD before treatment no longer met criteria for APD after treatment. Hoffart and Hedley (1997) found that between the beginning of treatment and a one-year follow-up, the number of avoidant traits decreased significantly. Interestingly, among the changes during treatment on various symptom and cognitive variables, only change in catastrophic beliefs was significantly related to a reduction in avoidant and dependent traits. The unique effects of Avoidant Personality Disorder may be difficult to discern because of its co-occurrence with depression. Feske *et al.* (1996) found the deleterious effects of Avoidant Personality Disorder on treatment outcome were no longer statistically significant once depression was statistically controlled.

There have been only a few outcome studies that have investigated treatments specifically designed for Avoidant Personality Disorder. Alden (1989) reported encouraging results from a 10-session program for Avoidant Personality Disorder. Coon reported on a case study (1994) examining 22 therapy sessions over 10 months of treatment. This avoidant client's treatment focused on socialization to therapy, goal-setting and basic cognitive restructuring, and work on changing the client's schemas. The client showed improvement on the Beck Depression Inventory and on SUDS ratings of several symptoms both at the end of treatment and at a 3-month follow-up. Renneberg, Goldstein, Phillips, and Chambless (1990) evaluated an intensive group treatment program for Avoidant Personality Disorder that included group systematic desensitization, behavioral rehearsal, and self-image work. Clients participated in 32 hours of group treatment spread over 4 days. Clients showed significant improvement both at posttest and at a 1-year follow-up. The most notable change was on the Fear of Negative Evaluation Scale, where 40% of the sample were improved at posttest.

Stravynski, Marks, & Yule (1982) found that 22 clients diagnosed with Avoidant Personality Disorder improved significantly after 14 sessions of social skills training, with or without the addition of cognitive modification. Both conditions improved significantly and equally, and therapeutic gains were maintained at a 6-month follow-up. A later study by Stravynski, Belisle, Marcouiller, Lavallee, and Elie (1994) found that 14 sessions of social skills training, either in the clinic setting only or with some sessions in real-life situations, led to significant and clinically worthwhile improvement which was maintained at a 3-month follow-up. Here again, there were no significant differences between treatment conditions. Clinically, however, the condition that included real-life exposure had a much higher dropout rate than the condition that was held only in the clinic.

Clearly, much more research is needed. For example, there is not yet enough evidence to determine which specific elements of treatment for Avoidant Personality Disorder are most effective. Although some authors have used the term "socially dysfunctional" as interchangeable with Avoidant Personality Disorder, this personality disorder involves a great deal more than just a lack of social skills or just social anxiety. Therefore, social skills training alone may not be sufficient for treatment. Short-term social skills training has been demonstrated to be effective in improving performance on specific social tasks between sessions for individuals with Avoidant Personality Disorder (Stravynski et al., 1982; Stravynski et al., 1994). However, improvement did not extend to the development of intimate relationships, even after an 18-month follow-up period. The cognitive components of identifying and challenging automatic thoughts and underlying assumptions and a longer course of treatment may well prove to be necessary for the clients to develop the ability to form relationships that are close and intimate, rather than simply less uncomfortable.

Although the data certainly are not yet definitive, it would not be at all surprising if clients with a lifelong pattern of Avoidant Personality Disorder needed a longer course of therapy than did clients with Social Phobia or Panic Disorder alone. Individuals with Avoidant Personality Disorder may turn out to be much more willing to enter a group and more able to make use of group therapy if they have some individual Cognitive Therapy in preparation for the group treatment. The length and intensity of treatment needed, as well as which treatment components are most effective, may depend on the specific treatment goals. Reduction of anxiety and depression may be quite possible with the skilled application of standard short-term cognitive behavioral treatments. Adapting cognitive behavioral treatments to focus more specifically on the issues most relevant to Avoidant Personality Disorder may make it possible to make major, lasting improvements in the ability to form and maintain intimate relationships.

DEPENDENT PERSONALITY DISORDER

The treatment of unassertive clients has been addressed in considerable detail (summarized in Rakos, 1991), but clients with a Dependent Personality Disorder are much more than simply dependent or unassertive. Some clients with Dependent Personality Disorder are so obviously dependent that it is clear from the start that they are going to be difficult. These are the people who call for an initial appointment and then call back every five minutes until their call is returned, leaving the receptionist ready to scream when the therapist gets back from his or her meeting. However, many dependent clients seem deceptively simple at first: They are easy to engage in therapy and are so cooperative that they create the expectation that progress will be quite rapid. They are eager to please and act as if the therapist is wonderful, implicitly giving the message, "Doc, you're so powerful, I know you can help me." This promising start to therapy, however, can add to the therapist's frustration when treatment bogs down. The client remains passive, cannot understand why the therapy is not helping more, clings to therapy, and resists the therapist's attempts to encourage him or her toward greater autonomy. As demonstrated by Turkat and Carlson (1984) in their case study of a client with Dependent Personality Disorder, recognition of the disorder, a comprehensive case formulation, and strategic planning of interventions based on this formulation are likely to make the treatment more effective and less frustrating than symptomatic treatment alone.

Assessment

According to *DSM-IV-TR* (2000), the client with Dependent Personality Disorder shows a "pervasive and excessive need to be taken care of that leads to submissive and clinging behavior and fears of separation" (p. 721, Table 10.3). The differences in criteria between *DSM-IV-TR* and *DSM-III-R* (1987) seem to be primarily those of emphasis and clarification, rather than representing any qualitative changes. Instead of the *DSM-III-R* criterion "allows others to make most of his/her important decisions," *DSM-IV-TR* broadens this to "needs others to assume responsibility for most major areas of his or her life." Also, in *DSM-IV-TR*, the criterion "has difficulty initiating projects or doing things on his or her own," is clarified by the additional specification that this is due to a lack of self-confidence in judgment or abilities rather than a lack of motivation or energy. Similarly, *DSM-IV-TR* clarifies that the individual feels uncomfortable or helpless when alone, adding that this is "because of exaggerated fears of being unable to care for himself or herself."

Table 10.3. *DSM-IV-TR* Diagnostic Criteria for Dependent Personality Disorder

A pervasive and excessive need to be taken care of that leads to submissive and clinging behavior and fears of separation, beginning by early adulthood and present in a variety of contexts, as indicated by five (or more) of the following:

(1) has difficulty making everyday decisions without an excessive amount of advice and reassurance from others

(2) needs others to assume responsibility for most major areas of his or her life

(3) has difficulty expressing disagreement with others because of fear of loss of support or approval.
    Note: Do not include realistic fears of retribution.

(4) has difficulty initiating projects or doing things on his or her own (because of a lack of self-confidence in judgment or abilities rather than a lack of motivation or energy)

(5) goes to excessive lengths to obtain nurturance and support from others, to the point of volunteering to do things that are unpleasant

(6) feels uncomfortable or helpless when alone because of exaggerated fears of being unable to care for himself or herself

(7) urgently seeks another relationship as a source of care and support when a close relationship ends

(8) is unrealistically preoccupied with fears of being left to take care of himself or herself

The criterion "feels devastated or helpless when close relationships end," has been changed to "urgently seek another relationship as a source of care and support when a close relationship ends." The *DSM-III-R* criterion of "is easily hurt by criticism or disapproval" has been dropped completely from *DSM-IV-TR* because it was not seen as being specific to Dependent Personality Disorder.

Common presenting problems for the individual with Dependent Personality Disorder include depression, anxiety, and alcoholism. In assessing Dependent Personality Disorder, it is important to carefully investigate the client's relationship history, with particular attention to his or her responses to the ending of relationships and how other people have said they perceive the client. Careful questioning about how everyday, as well as major, decisions are made can be helpful, as well as information regarding the client's feelings about being alone for extended periods of time. In addition, it can be useful to ask how the client would handle a situation in which he or she disagrees with someone else or is asked to do something unpleasant or demeaning. The therapist's own reactions can sometimes be helpful in diagnosing Dependent Personality Disorder. The therapist may feel tempted to rush in and rescue the client, or the therapist may find him or herself making exceptions for the client without resenting it (as one would with a client who had Borderline Personality Disorder). If either of these reactions occur, the therapist should suspect Dependent Personality Disorder and collect the data necessary to determine if this is the case.

Because clients with a variety of disorders may show dependent features, it is important to differentiate Dependent Personality Disorder from other, superficially similar disorders. For example, whereas clients with either Histrionic Personality Disorder or Dependent Personality Disorder may appear child-like and clinging, clients with Dependent Personality Disorder are less flamboyant, egocentric, and shallow than those with Histrionic Personality Disorder. Agoraphobics may be dependent on other people, but they are dependent in a very specific way: they need someone to go places with them so that they do not have to worry about being alone if they should have a panic attack. Agoraphobics are often much more active in asserting their dependence than individuals with Dependent Personality Disorder, actively demanding that they be accompanied wherever they go. It is possible, of course, for a client to have both Panic Disorder with Agoraphobia and Dependent Personality Disorder. For example:

> Allison fit the criteria for Dependent Personality Disorder very well. She was a 37-year-old homemaker who had stayed with her husband for 18 years, despite the fact that he was alcoholic and she felt she was unable to get what she wanted or needed from him. She allowed him to make decisions for her, tolerating moves even when they were not good for her. This was clearly a long-standing pattern for her in relationships in general, and she acknowledged that she had a tendency to get into dependent relationships. She stated that, "I can't exist without them, even if they are not good for me." Allison felt disgusted with herself, and felt as if she was a failure, incapable, and inadequate. She came into treatment presenting with problems of panic attacks, depression, and avoidance of going virtually anyplace alone.

Conceptualization

The cognitive behavioral conceptualization of Dependent Personality Disorder is relatively straightforward. These clients see themselves as inherently inadequate and helpless, and thus unable to cope with the demands of day-to-day life. They see the world as a cold, lonely, or even dangerous place that they could not possibly handle on their own. Their solution is to try to find someone they view as competent to handle life who is willing to make a trade-off: the dependent individual will give up responsibility and subordinate his or her own needs and desires in exchange for having that person take care of him or her. With Allison, this pattern was obvious by age 13. She always made a point of having a steady boyfriend who she saw as being able to take care of her, even if this meant tolerating substantial abuse.

This "solution" creates two dilemmas for these individuals. First, relying on others to handle problems and make decisions results in their having little opportunity to master and exercise the skills needed for independence. Either they never learn the skills of independent living (e.g., problem solving, decision making) or they do not recognize the skills that they have and therefore do not use them. Second, the idea of being more competent is terrifying, because they believe that if they become less needy they will no longer be taken care of, but still will be unable to cope on their own. Thus, their fear that competence will lead to abandonment impedes any steps toward becoming more capable.

In addition to these dilemmas, the dependency "solution" has several additional disadvantages. First, the individual always has to be very careful to please the other person and avoid conflict for fear of being abandoned and having to fend for himself or herself. Second, the dependent individual may seem so desperate, needy, and clinging, that his or her partner feels overwhelmed. Alternatively, it may become hard to find a willing partner that can meet the dependent individual's needs for any length of time. Finally, if the relationship ends, the individual is almost certain to be devastated and to see no alternative but to find someone new to depend upon. For example, Allison's panic attacks started with the end of a close friendship and she had a serious relapse with the end of a previous therapy, remaining obsessed with her previous therapist even after two years had passed.

Among the most frequent and characteristic automatic thoughts of the individual with Dependent Personality Disorder are, "I can't," "I never would be able to do that," and "I'm much too stupid, weak, ... " Their underlying assumptions include, "I can't survive without someone to take care of me," "I'm too inadequate to handle life on my own," "If my spouse (parent, etc.) left me, I'd fall apart," "If I were more independent, I'd be isolated and alone," and, "Independence means being completely on your own." The primary cognitive distortion in Dependent Personality Disorder is a strong all-or-none thinking in regards to autonomy. In their eyes, either they are helpless and dependent or they are totally independent and alone, and they can see no options in between.

Intervention Strategies and Techniques

The primary goal in therapy with the person with Dependent Personality Disorder is to help him or her learn to gradually become more independent from significant others (including the therapist) and to increase his or her self-confidence and sense of self-efficacy. Millon (1996) points out that, "Neither the therapist nor the client must forget that the ultimate goal is not necessarily complete independence, but rather the flexibility to move between self-reliance and a healthy mutual dependence" (p. 355). However, because these clients typically fear that competence will lead to abandonment, this must be done with considerable delicacy. It is particularly important to pay careful attention to one factor that is too often ignored by cognitive behavioral therapists: the client-therapist relationship. The client's dependent behavior is typically manifested within the therapeutic relationship. This has led some to suggest that humanistic or nondirective approaches may be preferable to more directive, cognitive behavioral approaches which might encourage the client to remain submissive in relation to a dominant therapist (e.g., Millon, 1981). However, if the cognitive behavioral therapist modifies the treatment appropriately, the interactions between the client and the therapist can provide rich behavioral and cognitive data, leading to cognitive behavioral interventions within the session that can have a particularly strong impact on the client due to their immediacy.

Because the individual with Dependent Personality Disorder comes into treatment looking desperately for someone to solve his or her problems, it may be necessary to allow some dependence initially in order to engage the client. However, the therapist needs to continually monitor the status of the relationship, consistently working to gradually wean the client away from that dependence. Collaboration does not need to always be 50:50, and at the beginning of treatment, the therapist may need to do more than half of the work. However, that pattern must change during the course of therapy so that the treatment eventually becomes more clearly the client's own.

Four main stages in the cognitive behavioral treatment of excessive interpersonal dependency have been delineated (Overholser, 1997; Overholser & Fine, 1994). These authors see it as crucial to use sequential steps so that the treatment is adapted to the changing needs of the client. They outline desirable outcomes that clients must achieve in each stage before advancing to the next stage of treatment. They define Stage 1 as that of "Active Guidance." In this stage of treatment, clients are engaged in the therapy, are taught behavioral skills to help them make small but immediate behavioral changes, and are encouraged to commit themselves to make longer-term changes.

Early in treatment, the therapist needs to take an active stance and allow some initial dependence. Cognitive Therapy is always collaborative, but in the treatment of Dependent Personality Disorder, the therapist may need to take a very active role in setting agenda, setting goals, assigning homework, and so on. As is generally the case in Cognitive Therapy, the treatment needs to begin with the setting of clear, mutual goals. However, dependent clients, being passive and lacking initiative, are usually unable to identify relevant treatment goals. This is associated with a reduction in personal responsibility and initiative. An active stance by the therapist can temporarily overcome the client's inertia. This could temporarily foster dependency, but it is often necessary to establish a working alliance and initiate the therapeutic process.

Although it may be obvious to the therapist from the beginning that dependence is the major issue for the client, dependence is rarely the client's presenting problem. In fact, even the use of the words dependence, independence, or autonomy can be quite frightening to the client early therapy. The issue of dependence will become obvious as the treatment progresses, no matter what goals the therapy is working toward. However, it may be most natural and least frightening to the client to let the actual use of the terms come first from the client when he or she is ready to bring them up.

The structured collaborative approach used in Cognitive Therapy encourages the client to play an active role in the therapy. Even setting an agenda can be an exercise in taking more initiative than the dependent individual customarily does. It is common for these clients to try to give all the power in the therapy over to the therapist, responding to questioning about what they want to focus on in the session, with, "Oh, whatever you want." In the first session or two, if these clients have no items to add to the agenda, the therapist can provide a suggested plan and ask if that is acceptable to them. After that, however, it is important to take it one step further and explain that because this is their therapy, they will be expected to make suggestions each session about how they want to spend the time. This can even be included as part of their written homework assignment for the week. By making it clear that the therapist expects them to contribute items to the agenda, continuing to ask at each session even if they repeatedly offer no suggestions, and waiting until they do offer some suggestions before moving on, the therapist may be able to foster some active involvement in the treatment.

It is particularly important to use guided discovery and Socratic questioning when working with clients who have Dependent Personality Disorder. These clients are likely to look to the therapist as "the expert" and hang on to his or her every word. This can be very gratifying for the therapist, who may have spent the rest of the day seeing clients who do not seem to listen. Thus, it can be tempting to just tell these clients exactly what the problem is and what they need to do, thereby taking an authoritarian role in the therapy. These clients do need to get some active guidance and practical suggestions from the therapist in order to get engaged in the treatment; a totally nondirective approach could be too anxiety-provoking for these clients to tolerate for long. However, when the client asks the therapist to tell him or her what to do, the therapist will be more successful using guided discovery and helping the client arrive at his or her own solutions rather than making direct suggestions. Teaching the process of problem solving is much more useful than just giving the client solutions to his or her problems. For example:

> Amanda seemed to look to her therapist to come up with the answers, especially when it came to understanding and explaining her own feelings. She would walk into sessions saying, "I felt depressed and discouraged last week. Why?," fully expecting her therapist to sit down and explain it all to her without any effort on her part. Instead, he would ask her questions about how she had felt, when her feelings had seemed to change, and details of specific thoughts and feelings she had when particularly upset. Through this process of questioning, she was able to arrive at her own increased understanding of what had transpired throughout the week and how her feelings were related to her thoughts.

When planning interventions, it is important to assess to what extent the client actually has skill deficits as opposed to not recognizing or using the coping skills that he or she does possess. It is easy to assume that dependent clients really are as helpless as they present themselves to be; yet often they have many of the skills needed to function independently and successfully, but they simply do not recognize this. When there is a skill deficit, the client can be trained in skills such as assertion (Rakos, 1991), problem solving (Hawton & Kirk, 1989), decision-making (Turkat & Carlson, 1984), and social interaction (Liberman *et al.*, 1989) in order to increase his or her competence. In Allison's case, however, she was already able to be assertive in some situations that she did not perceive as personal (such as when shopping and in her volunteer work). It was in her close interpersonal relationships that she rarely used assertion. Therefore, she did not need to be taught these basic skills, but needed help in learning to apply them to her close interpersonal relationships. This involved looking carefully at the thoughts that were inhibiting her from asserting herself when the relationship was important to her.

High levels of dependency in these individuals can block the awareness and expression of their angry feelings. Assertion training can help these clients become more aware of these feelings, overcome social skills deficits and passive tendencies, and begin to become more independent and self-confident. In doing assertion training with dependent individuals, it is necessary to spend time on explanations, and to start with very small steps. It is important for the therapist to teach both the verbal and nonverbal behaviors that go with appropriate assertion, and to collect data on exactly what the client said and how they said it. It is also crucial to address their fears about what it means to be assertive, because they often see assertion as being terribly aggressive. They also need to learn that it is possible to make a conscious choice to not be assertive at times. It is never safe to assume we know how other people will react to increased assertion on the part of these clients. After all, some of their spouses may have chosen them specifically because they were dependent and unassertive. It can be quite unsettling to a family member to suddenly have a passive, dependent spouse starting to make demands and express opinions. One way to balance the change and to maximize the chance that other people will react positively to these changes is to ask the client to increase the use of both positive as well as negative "I" messages. Thus, for every time the client makes a statement stating a request or expressing a negative emotion, he or she needs to make sure to express a positive emotion or thank the family member.

Dependent clients typically are not capable of dramatic behavior change early in treatment (and in fact that might scare them off). Therefore, it is important to start with small approximations to the final goals. Building a gradual hierarchy of steps toward goals is much more likely to lead to lasting behavior change. As therapy proceeds, progress toward goals can be used as powerful evidence to challenge the dependent person's assumption that he or she is helpless. For example, the process of doing graded exposure to anxiety-provoking situations was an excellent challenge to Allison's belief in her own helplessness. After having worked on following through with guitar lessons for several weeks, Allison was able to generate the rational response of, "Remember last week? No shakes! I played a solo and the teacher said I did very well!" The client does not need to be working on an anxiety hierarchy, however, to collect systematic evidence of competence. Any homework assignment successfully completed can be used as evidence of ability to complete a task. In Stage 1 of treatment the process of stimulus control can be useful. This involves helping the client to identify stimuli that elicit dependent behavior. Once these are identified, these stimuli can be used as cues to encourage the client to use the skills developed in assertiveness training.

Cognitive restructuring can also fit well in the first stage of treatment. In particular, automatic thoughts regarding inadequacy are likely to interfere with trying homework assignments between sessions. These individuals may assume that they do not have the ability to make behavioral changes. As a result, they may not comply with homework assignments between sessions, in the hopes of avoiding failure experiences. Therapists need to emphasize that even attempting to complete the homework is an important initial step toward reducing their distress. Early success experiences strengthen the therapeutic relationship and reduce client resistance. Therefore, thoughts regarding the homework need to be elicited and evaluated very early in treatment. Behavioral experiments in the session can be very useful in challenging some of these ideas.

When the idea of monitoring and challenging automatic thoughts was introduced to one client, she responded with her typical thought of, "I can't do it." Rather than taking an authoritarian role and just plunging forward anyway, the therapist helped her to write a list of the advantages and disadvantages of doing Thought Records. As they explored the pros and cons, the client reported the thought, "I can't comprehend anything written." The therapist was able to set up a behavioral experiment to challenge this thought by pulling a book out of his bookshelf, opening it to a random page, and asking her to read the first sentence aloud. He then asked her to explain to him what the sentence meant. When she was, in fact, able to do this, they were able to write a convincing rational response to her automatic thought, stating that, "It's true that it's *hard* for me to understand some things that are written, but if I work at it I usually can."

Some clients, particularly those who were not initially in serious distress, may be satisfied with the changes made in this first stage of treatment and will lack the motivation to continue making subsequent changes. The therapist can inform

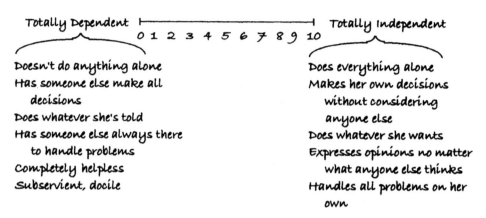

Totally Dependent ├──────────────────────┤ Totally Independent

0 1 2 3 4 5 6 7 8 9 10

Doesn't do anything alone
Has someone else make all
    decisions
Does whatever she's told
Has someone else always there
    to handle problems
Completely helpless
Subservient, docile

Does everything alone
Makes her own decisions
    without considering
    anyone else
Does whatever she wants
Expresses opinions no matter
    what anyone else thinks
Handles all problems on her
    own

FIGURE 10.1. Independence Continuum Drawn by Allison, a Dependent Client.

the client about the potential benefits of making a commitment to working toward additional changes, but needs to respect the client's decision to terminate if he or she chooses to do so. As always, a relapse prevention plan needs to be developed, clearly giving the client permission to return to treatment in the future if he or she decides to work toward further goals.

For clients who choose to continue in treatment, Stage 2 of the treatment outlined by Overholser and Fine (1994) is defined as the enhancement of self-esteem using cognitive techniques. This involves moving beyond the cognitive restructuring of automatic thoughts toward schema change. At this phase of the treatment, it is important to begin to challenge underlying assumptions, such as, "I am inadequate and helpless," "I can't survive without someone to take care of me," "If my spouse (parent, etc.) left me, I'd fall apart," and, "If I were more independent, I'd be isolated and alone."

The dichotomous view of independence is a crucial area to explore. If the client believes that one is either totally dependent and helpless or one is totally independent, isolated, and alone, this belief makes any movement toward autonomy seem like a commitment to complete alienation. Working with the client to draw a continuum from dependence to independence can be very useful, as it was with Allison (Figure 10.1). Seeing that there were many steps between the extremes of total dependence and total independence made it less frightening for her to take small steps toward independence. One illustration that can be useful with clients is that even independent, well-functioning adults still can join the Automobile Club in order to have help available when they need it. Thus, no one needs to be totally independent at all times and it is no disgrace to admit that one might need help from time to time.

At some point in the treatment, these clients will need to explore the belief that if they become more competent they will be abandoned. One useful way to challenge this is by setting up specific behavioral experiments where they behave a bit more competently and observe the reaction from their significant others. Because this type of behavioral experiment involves other people, this truly is an "experiment": neither the client nor the therapist can be certain how it will turn

Daily Record of Automatic Thoughts				
Situation Briefly describe the situation	**Emotions** Rate 0-100%	**Automatic Thoughts** Try to quote thoughts then rate your belief in each thought 1-100%	**Rational Response** Rate degree of belief 0-100%	**Outcome** re-rate emotions
Thinking about HN (previous therapist) and Don (husband)	Sad 90% Angry 75%	1) HN really knew how to comfort me - He'd rub my back and speak quietly and reassuringly. 100% 2) HN really cared for me unlike Don, who doesn't comfort me like I want. 100%	1) He did have a very endearing way about him - it felt good what he did & made me aware of what I want and need. But he may not be the only one who could do that for me. 85% 2) HN didn't love me the way Don does - Don is my real relationship. 100% Don hugged me and rubbed my back when I asked him to and also spoke quietly & reassuringly! He did what I asked and I felt better - He gave me what I wanted! And I could ask! 100%	 Sad 50% Angry 25%

FIGURE 10.2. Allison's Thought Sheet Regarding Her Reactions to Her Husband.

out. Although it may be irrational to believe that one will end up totally abandoned and alone forever if one is assertive, we really do not know if more competence will lead to abandonment by the client's primary significant other or not. Without having even met Allison's husband Cameron, her therapist would have no way of knowing how he would react to changes in Allison. Many people get involved with dependent individuals because they are attracted to that dependency, so it is possible that a spouse, parent, or some other person will react negatively if the client begins to change and become more assertive and independent. The dependent behavior may be actively reinforced by significant others and attempts to change may be punished. However, it is also possible that the spouse will react well to these changes, even if the client is positive that the spouse will react negatively. By starting with small steps, one can usually observe the spouse's reaction without risking enormous upheaval or total abandonment. Allison was certain that her husband would get angry with her if she started to express her feelings and to ask for more support. She did some TRs about this (see Figure 10.2) and eventually built up the nerve to try the behavioral experiment of asking for more support. She was amazed and delighted at his positive reaction and regretted having been too frightened to try this sooner.

In cases where the spouse's reaction to increased assertion is, in fact, negative, it may be necessary to explore other options. Marital or family therapy can often be useful in helping both spouses begin to adjust to the changes and even change together. For example, Jasmine, a 42-year-old mother of two, finally decided to learn to drive after much therapy focusing on other issues. Her husband had been quite supportive up to that point, but suddenly became irritable, procrastinated about taking her to get a learner's permit, and eventually refused to do so. Several marital sessions were required to calm his fears and resolve the crisis. If either the client or the spouse is not willing to pursue conjoint treatment, however, the client may need to explore the advantages and disadvantages of maintaining his or her current approach to relationships.

Whether the person decides to stay in the relationship and work toward change, stay in it and accept it as it is, or get out of the relationship, he or she will eventually need to accept the idea that relationships can and do end. Even if he or she insists that things are wonderful in the dependent relationship, unexpected difficulties are always possible, so no one can absolutely count on another person always being there. Of course, the therapist would not deny that losing an important relationship could be extremely upsetting. The idea is not to convince dependent clients that other people are not important, but to help them to see that they could and would survive the loss of the relationship.

Because maladaptive patterns in interpersonal relationships are a major part of the problem with Dependent Personality Disorder, much time in the therapy usually needs to be spent on dealing with interpersonal relationships. In order to use the therapeutic relationship most effectively as an example of an ongoing pattern of dependent relationships, it is necessary to explicitly encourage the client to explore his or her thoughts and feelings about the therapist. These clients may be so focused on other relationships in their lives that it may not occur to them that thoughts and feelings about the therapist are important, or even appropriate, to discuss. Allison had developed such a dependent relationship with her previous, humanistic therapist (seeing herself as being "madly in love" with him), that she initially had great difficulty dealing with her new cognitive therapist, who happened to be a woman. Through the use of Thought Records (TRs) (see Figure 10.3), she was able to resolve the difficulties she had been having with her new therapist. Furthermore, she was able to come to a better understanding of how her previous therapy relationship had been similar to other relationships in her past, fostering her dependency.

Another important part of paying careful attention to the client-therapist relationship is for the therapist to monitor his or her own thoughts and feelings toward the client. The temptation to rescue this type of client is particularly strong, and it can be very easy to either accept the client's belief in his or her own helplessness or try to rescue the client out of frustration with slow progress. Unfortunately, attempts at rescuing the client are incompatible with the goal of increasing the client's independence and self-sufficiency. For example:

> A resident came to supervision after an initial session with a new client, reporting how terribly distressed and anxious the client was. Only after the session had been discussed at length did the resident acknowledge that he had prescribed anti-anxiety medication, even though there was a policy of not prescribing medications to new clients until after discussing it in supervision. It became clear that he had automatically accepted her view of herself as totally helpless and had felt good at the time that he could be of so much help to this pathetic woman.

Daily Record of Automatic Thoughts				
Situation Briefly describe the situation	**Emotions** Rate 0-100%	**Automatic Thoughts** Try to quote thoughts then rate your belief in each thought 1-100%	**Rational Response** Rate degree of belief 0-100%	**Outcome** re-rate emotions
Thinking of previous therapist (HN) and current therapist (Mrs. P)	Sad 90% Anxious 90%	1) I don't feel like a person to Mrs. P. She always wants to talk about the homework & the program. 2) Mrs. P ignores me outside of sessions, doesn't call me by name. 3) HN made me feel like the most important person in the world for that hour. He relaxed me with his voice & manner & patience.	1) We are not here to get close and dependent. I'm here to learn how to deal with my anxiety & function more effectively in the world. 2) These are valid points - rather than leave, why not discuss these issues and get more of what I want in this relationship? 3) Mrs. P is not HN - I got into a lot of trouble with his approach. I'm not here to make friends. I want to learn to do things for me, not for my therapist.	 Sad 30% Anxious 50%

FIGURE 10.3. Allison's Thought Sheet Regarding Her Reactions to Her Therapist.

Whenever a therapist feels tempted to be more active and less collaborative with a client or to make exceptions, it may be useful for the therapist to write a Thought Record to clarify whether the exception is going to be in the best long-term interests of the client or whether it will serve to foster dependency.

Because these clients are especially prone to developing overly dependent relationships, it is crucial to set clear limits on the extent of the therapist's professional relationship with the client. Allison is certainly not the first client with Dependent Personality Disorder to fall in love with her therapist; in fact, our clinical experience indicates that clients with this disorder are more likely than other clients to develop idealized love relationships with their therapists. These are not the clients with whom to use techniques that involve physical contact or intimate settings, nor is it a good idea to bend one's usual rules of maintaining a professional distance. If the use of *in vivo* exposure necessitates being outside of the office with a client, it is important to be very clear about the goals of the exercise, keep it very professional (for example, to take notes of cognitions and write down anxiety levels at regular intervals), and to minimize "chit-chat."

When issues of noncompliance arise, it is helpful to prompt the client to list the advantages and disadvantages of changing, seriously exploring the disadvantages of change. Rather than the therapist pushing for autonomy, which the client can then work to resist, it is more useful to put the client in the position of convincing the therapist that change is worth the consequences. Sometimes, an exploration of the advantages and disadvantages of changing will reveal that the disadvantages of change outweigh the advantages for a particular client. For example:

> Bianca was a 24-year-old woman who sought treatment for depression. She had always
> been extremely dependent on her mother and never learned to do things on her own. She
> rigidly believed that she could not do anything successfully on her own and was therefore
> terrified to try anything new, certain she would fail miserably. She had gotten married
> the previous May to her high school sweetheart and moved out of state. She immediately
> became very depressed because she felt overwhelmed by the responsibilities of being
> a wife and felt helpless to handle them without her mother. She ruminated about her
> inadequacies and believed she would be fine if she could only be back in her hometown.
> If she became less depressed and learned to accept life away from her hometown, her
> husband would have no incentive to move back. When she acknowledged that her main
> goal was to convince her husband to move back home, it became clear why she had been
> noncompliant in treatment. In fact, her mood improved not in relation to any interventions,
> but when her husband agreed that they could move back within the year.

There may be some good reasons for the dependent person to be ambivalent
about changing. Although the person struggling with feelings of helplessness may
feel that he or she has no power, taking the helpless role can actually be very powerful and reinforcing (as with Bianca), and this can be difficult to give up. If the client
can be helped to identify what would be lost if he or she no longer were as helpless,
it may be possible to find a more constructive way of achieving the same ends.

Impediments to progress in Stage 2 may include the client's difficulty in fully
accepting the validity and usefulness of the techniques. When working on schema
change, clients may say they believe the new idea intellectually but not emotionally.
This is understandable. It takes much time and evidence to fully change a belief. The
person needs to actually try using the new beliefs outside the session to determine
if the new ideas have validity.

Stage 3 of the treatment focuses on promoting autonomy. In this stage, it is
time to begin to reduce dependence on the therapist and other authority figures.
This involves building upon the client's strengthened self-image. Several different
methods can be used at this stage to help promote autonomy. Problem-Solving
Training (discussed in Chapter 8) involves teaching the client systematic steps when
approaching a problem and can be very helpful in decreasing dependence on others.
The therapist and client can collaboratively develop a hierarchy of increasingly
difficult independent actions (Turkat & Carlson, 1984). For example, a hierarchy of
decision-making could range from what type of fruit to have for lunch to decisions
regarding jobs and places to live. Every decision made increases the client's belief
that he or she can do at least some things on his or her own. The self-control
strategies of self-monitoring, self-evaluation, and self-reinforcement can also be
used to teach clients to begin making their own changes. Also, strategies to increase
self-efficacy (summarized in Chapter 5) can be useful at this stage of treatment.

One way to foster the progression from dependence in therapy to independence is to change the structure of therapy itself. Moving the client from individual
therapy to group therapy (preferably with the individual therapist as one of the co-
therapists of the group) can help to reduce the client's dependence on the therapist
and serve to dilute the relationship. In a group setting, the client can still get a great
deal of support, but can begin to derive more support from peers than from the

therapist. This serves as a good first step toward finding even more natural means of support in the client's circle of family and friends. Modeling has been found to help increase independent behavior (Goldstein *et al.*, 1973) and in group therapy, the other clients can serve as models for the development of many skills. In addition, the group therapy setting provides a safe place to practice new skills, such as assertion. After twenty sessions of individual therapy, Allison moved to group therapy and was able to use the group to practice assertion, to practice difficult hierarchy items (such as taking two airplane trips) and eventually to challenge her perfectionism by playing guitar in front of the group.

Stage 4 is the final stage of the treatment for dependency. The focus in Stage 4 is on relapse prevention designed to reduce the likelihood that the client will behave in an excessively dependent manner in the future. Impediments to progress in Stage 4 include the possibility that the client may not see the need for relapse prevention or that the client may be fearful of termination and cling to therapy.

One structural change which helps to facilitate the transition from dependence to independence is the "fading" of sessions by meeting less frequently toward the end of therapy, as discussed in Chapter 1. The concept of terminating therapy can be an extremely threatening one for people with Dependent Personality Disorder, because they are likely to believe that it would be impossible to maintain their progress without the therapist's support. Rather than trying to challenge this belief in the abstract, the process of fading sessions can serve as a behavioral experiment to test out the belief. If sessions are moved to every other week, clients will be able to see how well gains can be maintained over two weeks. If they see that they are able to function well over the two-week period, they may then be able to move to monthly sessions. If a client is not able to maintain progress over a two-week period, then perhaps he or she is not ready to fade the therapy, and it may be appropriate to return to weekly sessions for a while. If clients can be given a great deal of control over the spacing of the sessions, they are likely to feel less threatened and more willing to try some fading, because the choice is not irrevocable. The therapist can fade sessions further and further, offering to meet every month, every three months, or even every six months if they choose. When given this type of free choice, however, clients usually come to realize that if they can go a full month without therapy, they really no longer need to be in treatment. After 14 sessions of group therapy, Allison felt that she had achieved most of her goals and felt ready to begin the process of termination. She moved to meeting every other week for the next six sessions, and then met for one last session after an interval of one month. This type of fading can be very useful for the individual client, but can be disruptive for a group, especially with various clients on different fading schedules. One workable compromise is for the client to end group therapy when he or she feels ready to move toward termination, and then do a limited number of fading sessions individually with one of the group co-therapists. If one is going to try this compromise, it is important to be sure that the client is really ready to move toward termination and is not just using the change in therapy modality as a way to get more individual attention from the therapist (and, hence, more dependency).

Another factor that can make termination easier for the person with Dependent Personality Disorder is the offer of booster sessions when necessary. Whenever terminating therapy with a client, the therapist explains that if the client experiences any difficulties in the future, either with these or other issues, it is a good idea to contact the therapist for one or two booster sessions. Such booster sessions often simply serve to get clients back on the track of doing what they had been doing which had helped in the past. Just knowing that they have the option of contacting the therapist in the future helps to make the transition to termination easier.

There is not much outcome data available on the cognitive behavioral treatment of Dependent Personality Disorder. Turner (1987) found that in a small trial of socially phobic clients, clients with Dependent Personality Disorder responded better to therapist-aided *in vivo* exposure than to self-directed exposure. Similarly, Chambless *et al.* (1992) found that Dependent Personality Disorder was associated with greater decreases in phobic avoidance with treatment by therapist-assisted *in vivo* exposure (plus eclectic psychotherapy) in a two-week intensive treatment programs. However, this was not the case in individual weekly therapy where exposure was usually conducted via homework assignments and treatment was, in general, less structured. This would support the idea that dependent clients benefit, at least initially, from treatment when the sessions are very structured and the therapist is actively involved.

Conclusion

Although treatment of Dependent Personality Disorder can be a slow, arduous process that can be frustrating at times, it can be very rewarding as well. The therapist needs to be realistic about the length of therapy, goals for therapy, and the standards for self-evaluation. With the proper conceptualization and careful strategic planning throughout treatment, however, the therapist may have the opportunity to watch the client blossom into an autonomous adult, providing satisfaction not unlike that of watching a child grow up.

OBSESSIVE–COMPULSIVE PERSONALITY DISORDER

The symptoms of Obsessive–Compulsive Personality Disorder (OCPD) are characteristics that are common in our culture. In fact, Millon (1996; Millon, Davis, Millon, Escovar, & Meagher, 2000) has stated that the compulsive style is common in developed societies because its characteristics are so well suited to societal demands. Unfortunately, problems arise when socially desirable characteristics are taken to an extreme. For example, perseverance and attention to detail generally are valued and functional; however, when carried to an extreme, they result perseveration, inability to grasp "the big picture" and an excessively thorough approach that can be seriously dysfunctional. Because some aspects of compulsive behavior are functional, and perhaps even essential, to success in our society, treatment presents some complications. The compulsive, like the overeater, cannot totally stop performing the problem behaviors. He or she must learn to use his or her compulsivity in a judicious and functional way rather than simply abandoning attention to detail, thoroughness, and persistence.

Assessment

Ashley was an 18-year-old woman who had graduated from high school a few months before. She complained of being depressed for the previous 2½ months and was anhedonic, self-critical, lethargic, and in her "own little world." She had gained 15–20 pounds and was "obsessed" with her weight. She explained that she had planned to go away to college, but had postponed these plans because she was depressed. As a result, she was attending classes at a local college while living at home with her parents and her younger brother. She had held an internship during the summer, but left it early because she felt so badly. Her parents had gone on a trip to Malaysia a few days later, but Ashley called her mother home because she could not tolerate being alone. She had always had one or two close friends, but felt nervous getting to know new people. She had dated for the past 2 years and felt flattered to be asked out, but the boys had never measured up to her standards.

As Ashley described her history, it became clear that she constantly scanned herself and others for mistakes and was intolerant of imperfection wherever she found it. She had held a rigid long-range plan for her life and became extremely anxious when she was not able to follow the plan exactly. Once she had decided that she was not following her "correct" life plan, she panicked and became lost in rumination and indecisiveness as she tried to determine another "correct" path.

The characteristics of OCPD specified by *DSM-IV-TR* (2000) are shown in Table 10.4. Ashley's initial interview gave evidence of perfectionism, indecisiveness, rigidity, inability to relax, and tendency to ruminate. These were quite apparent from the beginning of treatment, as is often the case with such clients.

These qualities of OCPD are characteristic of the individual's long-term functioning and are self-consonant. That is, they are part of the individual's identity and are rarely considered by the client to be the cause of any of the problems that they experience. Unlike the person with Major Depressive Disorder, who complains of

---

TABLE 10.4. *DSM-IV-TR* Criteria for Obsessive–Compulsive Personality Disorder

---

A pervasive pattern of preoccupation with orderliness, perfectionism, and mental and interpersonal control, at the expense of flexibility, openness, and efficiency, beginning by early adulthood and present in a variety of contexts, as indicated by four (or more) of the following:

(1) is preoccupied with details, rules, lists, order, organization, or schedules to the extent that the major point of the activity is lost

(2) shows perfectionism that interferes with task completion (e.g., is unable to complete a project because his or her own overly strict standards are not met)

(3) is excessively devoted to work and productivity to the exclusion of leisure activities and friendships (not accounted for by obvious economic necessity)

(4) is overconscientious, scrupulous, and inflexible about matters of morality, ethics, or values (not accounted for by cultural or religious identification)

(5) is unable to discard worn-out or worthless objects even when they have no sentimental value

(6) is reluctant to delegate tasks or to work with others unless they submit to exactly his or her way of doing things

(7) adopts a miserly spending style toward both self and others; money is viewed as something to be hoarded for future catastrophes

(8) shows rigidity and stubbornness

severe depression, the person with OCPD does not tend to complain of compulsivity. This person may enter therapy complaining of any of a large number of problems–including depression, anxiety, or problems with spouses, children, or co-workers– but rarely recognize the connection between the problem and his or her compulsivity. It is the clinician's job to be alert to the underlying pathology that may be giving rise to the Axis I complaints.

It is important to note the differences between OCPD and Obsessive-Compulsive Disorder. As was discussed in Chapter 5, Obsessive–Compulsive Disorder is characterized by obsessions, compulsions, or both. It can be seen from Table 10.4 that despite the name "Obsessive–Compulsive Personality Disorder," obsessions and compulsions are not symptomatic of OCPD. Although a client may have both disorders, they are separate and distinct problems. The obsessions and compulsions experienced by individuals with Obsessive–Compulsive Disorder are (at least initially) self-dissonant, and are likely to be primary complaints when they enter therapy. Persons with Obsessive–Compulsive Personality Disorder are prone to excessive internal debate and rumination and apparently compulsive behavior such as excessive double-checking of their work. However, these characteristics are typically seen by the client as being signs of appropriate carefulness and thoroughness and are not often considered to be problems. The treatment of Obsessive–Compulsive Disorder has been discussed in Chapter 5; the present chapter will focus on the treatment of OCPD.

Indications of OCPD may be evident even before the initial session. At the first telephone contact with the client, the therapist may find that it takes an inordinately long time to agree on a mutually acceptable appointment time because the client is extremely indecisive yet tries to find the "perfect" meeting time. Even after an appointment time has been agreed upon, the client may call back moments later to change the time. Alternatively, the client may go into excessive detail in a way that the therapist finds it difficult to interrupt or may take an inordinately long time to respond to seemingly straightforward questions because he or she ruminatively considers all possible responses to the question and their relative merit before answering.

The compulsive frequently gravitates toward professions that require focused attention to detail and adherence to rigid procedures such as law or accounting. Choice of leisure activities may be even more suggestive of OCPD than is job choice. It is often difficult for the compulsive to engage in activities purely for the sake of pleasure because they feel as if they are "wasting time." Their television viewing must be "educational", books or magazines must be related to work activities or self-improvement, a day at the pool must include swimming laps or dictating into a tape recorder. The compulsive often experiences anxiety in unstructured situations and therefore tries to plan and organize even leisure activities. Individuals with OCPD often are perfectionistic about unimportant areas of life, spending hours perfecting their appearance before leaving the house, commenting on the clutter on the therapist desk, or actually starting to tidy the therapist's desk or waiting room.

The presenting problems that bring the client to treatment also can be suggestive of OCPD. Common presenting problems include problems with procrastination, difficulty coping with anything that disrupts their rigid routine, thoroughness that results in their being slow and inefficient, difficulty completing tasks, and excessive dissatisfaction with their performance on tasks.

> Ashley, showed many of these characteristics. She had been a chronic procrastinator all through high school but her crisis did not begin until she graduated and found herself entering a new and more demanding stage of life where her habitual means of coping by being more careful and thorough was particularly dysfunctional. She became intensely ruminative and anxious and then became severely depressed and hopeless about her lack of control over her emotional state.

Table 10.5 lists a number of characteristics that can be suggestive of OCPD. As with all personality disorders, the earlier that correct diagnosis can be made,

TABLE 10.5. Possible Indications of Obsessive–Compulsive Personality Disorder

In presenting problems
  Severe procrastination
  Indecision regarding fairly commonplace decisions
  Dissatisfaction with own performance despite others viewing his or her performance as good
  Stress resulting from own standards and own pressure to do well
  Inefficiency, inability to maintain an acceptable level of productivity despite having adequate skills
    and intelligence
  Depression due to inability to live up to own standards

In personal characteristics
  Insists on neatness and thoroughness even when it is unnecessary or counterproductive
  Prefers activities that involve attention to detail and adherence to clear procedures
  Inability to relax or take vacations, leisure time (if any) is occupied with self-improvement or
    productive activities
  Very controlled, little expression of emotion, little spontaneity or humor
  Discomfort with uncertainty or ambiguity
  Strong reactions when plans are disrupted

In interpersonal relationships
  Insists that others do things his or her way, unable to compromise or
  delegate responsibility
  Unable to express warmth, tenderness, affection
  Unempathic, shows little understanding of others' feelings
  Moralistic, judgmental, intolerant of others' views
  Critical of others, unable to give positive feedback
  Sensitive to criticism, defensive when criticized

In therapy
  Goes into excessive or irrelevant detail, digresses
  Talks about others in an impersonal, uninvolved way
  Meticulous, precise appearance and mannerisms
  Criticizes therapist's lack of neatness or begins straightening the therapist's desk
  Unusually stiff and formal
  Interprets mild inquiries or suggestions as criticism

In psychological testing
  Requires an excessive amount of time to complete questionnaires
  Excessively detailed, thorough responses
  Discomfort with ambiguous tasks or with questions where there is no "right" answer
  Discomfort with true-false questions when the item is not completely
  true or completely false

the sooner the treatment plan can be modified to take the presence of an Axis II problem into account.

Conceptualization

Shapiro (1965) described the compulsive style in terms of three basic features. First, he considered the thinking of compulsives to show extreme rigidity. Others frequently consider them to be "dogmatic" or "opinionated." Their attention is intense and sharply focused on one particular detail of a situation at a time. Therefore, they frequently miss the point in social interactions, rarely get "hunches," and are rarely surprised. The second significant feature of the compulsive style, according to Shapiro, is that these people are often absorbed in intensive routine or technical activity. Furthermore, their activity seems to be characterized by a "more or less continuous experience of tense deliberateness, a sense of effort, and of trying" (p. 31). The third feature which Shapiro emphasizes is a "loss of reality." Rather than basing their opinions on a sense of personal conviction or on personal experience, they deduce that something "must be" true or good because it follows from accepted rules or principles.

An understanding of the obsessive–compulsive individual's beliefs and assumptions sheds considerable light on his or her reasons for adhering to extreme forms of normally adaptive strategies, despite the obvious problems. In our conceptualization, based in part on the work of Guidano and Liotti (1983), McFall and Wallersheim (1979), and Pretzer and Hampl (1994), the central assumption in Obsessive–Compulsive Personality Disorder is, "I must avoid mistakes at all costs." The individual believes that, "In each situation there is one right answer or right action," that anything else is a mistake, and that mistakes are intolerable. The individual may partly fear the consequences of making a mistake, but beyond this, there is a strong, unreasoning conviction that mistakes are intolerable even when no serious consequences are likely.

Most of the maladaptive aspects of OCPD are the result of the strategies these individuals use to avoid mistakes. They assume that the best way to avoid making mistakes is to be careful and thorough, to pay attention to details, to try hard, to set high standards for oneself, and to be sure to notice mistakes so that they can be corrected. These strategies can be quite useful in minimizing mistakes and doing a good job on a variety of tasks. However, obsessive–compulsive clients are not willing to simply minimize mistakes; their goal is to eliminate them completely. Each time they do something which is perceived as a mistake, they conclude that the thing to do is to try harder, to pay more attention to details, to be more careful, and so on. Thus, obsessive–compulsives take strategies that often are adaptive and carry them to such extremes that they become counterproductive.

One result of the obsessive–compulsive's belief that mistakes must be avoided is his or her strong desire for both self-control and control over his or her environment. The beliefs, "I must be perfectly in control of my environment as well as of myself," and "loss of control is intolerable," underlie the client's insistence on certainty, predictability, and control over others. Another common result of the assumption that mistakes must be avoided is chronic self-criticism. The beliefs that, "to make a mistake is to be deserving of criticism," and "self-criticism is the way to keep from making the mistake again in the future," can have a big impact. Often the individual with OCPD believes that if he or she is not severely self-critical, he or she is compounding the mistake and will become increasingly imperfect and worthless. For example:

> When Ashley followed her diet perfectly for 11 days, but ate one cookie on day 12, she declared that she had failed, was totally out of control, and was fat and disgusting. When her therapist suggested that her guilt and depression were disproportionate to her "sin," she countered that without guilt she would become increasingly out of control and, ultimately, obese.

Given compulsives' efforts to avoid mistakes and their assumption that there is one right answer or action in each situation, they are highly motivated to find the "right" response and then to adhere rigidly to it. Because of dichotomous thinking, any departure from what is "right" is automatically seen as being "wrong." Therefore, the obsessive–compulsive individual often has little tolerance for beliefs, values, or ways of doing things that differ from his or her own. Not surprisingly, this leads the individual to be uncomfortable with any novel or ambiguous situation in which it is not clear what course of action is "right" and with any situation where there are several perfectly acceptable options rather than one right one.

Interpersonal relationships and interactions which involve strong emotions often do not present easily discernable right answers and, in addition, threaten to distract the obsessive–compulsive from his or her work and to cause "mistakes." Thus, obsessive–compulsives tend to be uncomfortable both with intimate relationships and with strong emotions and to avoid both. Over time, this can result in the individual's developing both relatively poor social skills and limited skill at handling emotions adaptively. This tends to lead to further avoidance for fear of making mistakes in interactions and thus tends to be self-perpetuating.

Another assumption that gives rise to many problems is, "If the perfect course of action is not clear, it is better to do nothing." The compulsive frequently will only make choices or act when he or she is certain which alternative is "right." When faced by uncertainty the compulsive frequently assumes that if one does nothing, one cannot fail, and therefore, one does not risk censure from self or others. The problem with this strategy is obvious when one considers that life often presents situations where none of the alternatives is clearly "right."

Given the obvious problems created by the obsessive–compulsive approach to life, it might seem that these individuals would be relieved to discover that they do not have to avoid all mistakes and can safely relax their standards for themselves. However, they typically are convinced that any deviations from doing things the "right" way will lead to disaster. Consequently, if the therapist simply points out the drawbacks to the client's current approach to life and suggests that some rules or rituals might be modified or abandoned, the compulsive typically becomes quite anxious and envisions disaster. Such interventions are likely to lead to thoughts such as, "I'll become a total failure," "My work will become mediocre," "I'll become a total slob," and so on.

Dichotomous thinking is a cognitive distortion that is common in OCPD. It can be seen in the assumption that any deviation from trying to do things perfectly will lead to total disaster, in the assumption that if one is not in total control, one is out of control, and in the assumption that actions are either right or wrong. These dichotomous views make it difficult to induce the client to change his or her compulsive approach to life and make the pattern quite resistant to spontaneous change.

Although there is little empirical evidence regarding the etiology of Obsessive–Compulsive Personality Disorder, a number of factors are suggested by clinical observation. First, our culture strongly reinforces certain characteristics of this personality style. Children are taught to do a good job by watching for mistakes and correcting them. They often are taught to ruminate about misdeeds when their parents send them to their room to think about the "error of their ways." Sayings such as, "If it's worth doing, it's worth doing well," and "If at first you don't succeed, try, try again," teach an approach to life that the obsessive–compulsive carries to a pathological extreme. Parents and teachers usually respond quite positively to the child who is diligent, obedient, and hard working and adults often devote considerable effort to attempting to inculcate these traits in their children. Second, many obsessive–compulsive individuals report having grown up with a critical, demanding parent who reacted negatively to mistakes, who focused on results rather than effort or intentions, and who did not reward a good but imperfect performance. This history could easily form the basis for a belief that mistakes are intolerable and could lead the individual to emphasize avoiding mistakes rather than striving to achieve. It could also encourage the individual to adopt self-criticism and self-punishment as strategies for eliminating mistakes. Although these two factors are probably not sufficient to completely account for the etiology of this disorder, they frequently appear to play a major role in its development.

Intervention Strategies

Although the individual's intense desire to avoid mistakes appears to be central to OCPD and is an important target for intervention, it is also a major impediment to intervention. The individual's unwillingness to risk mistakes results in a reluctance to experiment with new approaches to problem situations. Even when these individuals are in considerable distress, they frequently fear that the changes their therapist advocates will make the situation worse rather than better. If it were possible to eliminate clients' fear of making mistakes before attempting to induce them to change their behavior, this would greatly simplify treatment. Unfortunately, it is rarely possible to effectively challenge the client's inability to tolerate making mistakes without first inducing the client to change his or her behavior, even though this entails the risk of making mistakes.

The first problem in therapy with an obsessive–compulsive client is simply establishing goals toward which therapist and client can work collaboratively. Once the client's OCPD has been recognized, it seems clear that the client needs to adopt more reasonable standards, to become more accepting of ordinary "mistakes" and shortcomings, etc. However, clients with OCPD are not likely to endorse these goals early in treatment. They usually do not recognize the connection between their avoidance of mistakes and their problems, they believe that avoiding mistakes is imperative, and they believe that relaxing their standards for themselves and accepting ordinary mistakes will lead to their making even more mistakes. In fact, Turkat and Maisto (1985) report approaching the treatment of individuals with OCPD by conducting a careful evaluation, developing an individualized conceptualization of the client's problems, and explaining to each individual why it was important for them to develop the ability to tolerate mistakes. They found that each of the five participants agreed that Turkat and Maisto's conceptualization of their problems made sense and agreed that they needed to develop the ability to tolerate mistakes. However, none of the five participants were willing to continue in treatment beyond that point.

It is important to begin treatment by identifing goals for therapy that are acceptable to the client. The initial goals for therapy will typically not include "tolerating mistakes and coping with them." Often the initial goals involve overcoming problems such as depression, procrastination, or interpersonal problems. For clients who have difficulty specifiying goals for therapy, "increasing my efficiency" may be a promising initial goal that most obsessive–compulsives would endorse wholeheartedly. When the therapist and client jointly work to achieve the client's initial goals there will be many opportunities for the therapist to demonstrate the ways in which an obsessive–compulsive approach is counter-productive and to address the client's fear that any changes to the client's compulsive approach will actually result in their making more mistakes.

The therapist also needs to be aware of the compulsive's rigidity, because this often causes significant problems. The cognitive therapist deals with rigidity in what is, for many, a non-intuitive way, by introducing additional structure. Individuals with Obsessive–Compulsive Personality Disorder, for all their rigidity, lack structure. Their speech and thinking is disorganized, rambling, and tortuous. When faced with multiple tasks, they are frequently overwhelmed because they lack the skills for prioritizing, managing time, and problem solving. An important part of our approach to the treatment of Obsessive-Compulsive Personality Disorder is to help the client become more organized. The structure of cognitive therapy can be used as a model for dealing with problems more effectively. Agenda setting, prioritizing problems, and focusing on one topic at a time are forums for teaching the compulsive to organize his or her life more adaptively. Furthermore, some compulsive clients become caught up in their ruminations during sessions and do not hear or remember portions of what the therapist says. By structuring the session carefully, the tendency to ruminate is reduced. Furthermore, the therapist can provide regular opportunities for the client to respond to therapeutic points or to summarize them. If the client is unable to do so, both therapist and client will know that this issue needs to be addressed. This can help the compulsive to realize the ways in which rumination is counterproductive both in and outside of the therapy session and may help to provide the motivation and skills that enable him or her to control the ruminations.

Because the obsessive-compulsive individual takes normally adaptive strategies to a pathological extreme, it is not necessary to attempt to induce the client to abandon these strategies but rather to help him or her to learn to use them more adaptively. The compulsive client needs to learn to use his or her ability to work diligently and to focus on details in a flexible way that is appropriate to the demands of the situation. If this can be done, these characteristics can turned to his or her advantage. If he or she can also learn appropriate ways to handle situations where a careful, detailed approach is not appropriate, the maladaptive aspects of this disorder can be eliminated.

The rigidity that is such a problem for the obsessive–compulsives in daily life, is likely to be a problem in therapy as well. Client are likely to approach therapy as though avoiding mistakes is essential, and approaching therapy compulsively is seen as the way to do this. Thus, these clients are likely to describe their history in excessive detail. They will also take pains to give the "right" answer rather than accurately describing their thoughts and feelings. Moreover, they will tend to avoid topics and assignments where it is not clear what the "right" answer is. They will also tend to persist rigidly in trying to do therapy in the way they see as "right" rather than complying with the therapist's suggestions. Although these tendencies complicate therapy, they also provide abundant opportunities to address the client's rigidity and underlying fear of making mistakes in the moment rather than simply discussing them in the abstract. Through the process of cognitive therapy, these clients discover that changes in their usual way of doing things can be beneficial rather than leading to disaster. They do this through learning that there is considerable value in foregoing irrelevant detail in their responses, through sticking to an agenda, and through completing a TR even if it is not perfect. By trying these changes within therapy before attempting them in the real world, the clients' fears are reduced and the therapist is available to address the fears as they arise.

In dealing with the obsessive–compulsive's life problems, there are a number of advantages to using a problem-solving approach. This teaches the client to analyze the problem, identify the options available to him or her, to consider the pros and cons of each of the options, and to try the most promising of these in a systematic way. The practical, systematic nature of this approach appeals to the obsessive–compulsive and it is often possible to begin therapy alleviating some of the client's immediate problems without requiring him or her to take major risks. At the same time, it involves an implicit shift to choosing actions based on their likely consequences rather than on rigid ideas of the "right" way to respond. Obsessive–compulsive individuals are notorious for transforming therapy into an abstract intellectual exercise in which they will discuss ideas at length but make few changes outside the therapy session. A problem-solving focus puts the therapist in a good position to work for both behavior change outside the therapy session and attention to emotions within the therapy session rather than allowing therapy to be purely verbal and intellectual.

As with Borderline Personality Disorder, it can be quite useful to attempt to challenge the client's dichotomous thinking early in therapy. The compulsive's dichotomous thinking amplifies his or her rigidity, perfectionism, desire for control, and many other problematic characteristics. If it is possible to help him or her to shift to less dichotomous views in these areas, he or she is likely to become more flexible and subsequent interventions are likely to be easier.

The therapist must address the client's intolerance of mistakes throughout therapy. Initially, the therapist can do this by structuring therapy sessions and homework assignments to minimize the need for the client to risk making mistakes.

However, it will soon be necessary to work to help the client verbalize his or her concerns and to examine the likely consequences of specific mistakes. It will also be necessary to consider whether the actions in question are as risky as the client believes them to be. Later in therapy, it is possible to challenge, in a gentle way, the assumption that mistakes must be avoided at all costs. It is also possible to help the client accept being a fallible human, and to face the interpersonal and emotional situations he or she has avoided due to this fear of mistakes.

Cognitive and Behavioral Techniques

Many individuals with OCPD are chronically tense and it is frequently important to help them find a way to reduce tension and anxiety in adaptive ways. Any form of relaxation can be helpful as long as the client uses it regularly (see Chapter 5). The main problem with any relaxation homework is inducing the obsessive–compulsive client to do it regularly. Relaxation is an alien feeling to many compulsives, and he or she may experience it as being "out of control," and may even panic as a result. Alternatively, he or she may see relaxation as "goofing off" or "wasting time" and feel guilty about taking time for it. Beyond this, the compulsive may fear that he or she will make more mistakes if not constantly tense and vigilant. The therapist must be alert to this problem and address the client's reactions to the relaxation exercises directly if they become a problem.

The thinking of the individual with Obsessive–Compulsive Personality Disorder is often characterized by anxiety-provoking, ruminative thoughts regarding past or future errors, mistakes, and catastrophes. In addition to being upsetting, these ruminations are problematic because they occupy time and attention that the compulsive could otherwise use more constructively. Thus, teaching the client to voluntarily control his or her ruminations through using the "worry time" approach discussed in Chapter 5 can have significant benefits.

It is important to help the client to recognize the differences between constructive, problem-solving thinking and rumination and to appreciate the disadvantages of rumination. This can be done by doing an experiment of having the client intentionally ruminate for a limited period of time and then note the results, which usually include increased anxiety and depression, a feeling of being overwhelmed, and confusion. Then the therapist can assist the client in engaging in problem-solving thinking and compare the results. After the client understands the difference between ruminating and problem solving and has seen that the latter is more beneficial than the former, he or she may be willing to give up rumination entirely. At that point, it is primarily a matter of teaching the client techniques for doing so using the approaches discussed in Chapters 2 and 5. Certain clients, although seeing the need to reduce rumination, may be unwilling to give it up entirely. Often, scheduling a specific, limited time can be very helpful in giving the client control over his or her thinking. For example:

> Ayla was a 45-year-old woman who had left a prestigious position in New York, which she loved, to come to Philadelphia at her husband's request. She had immediately gotten a less fulfilling job and spent much of her time crying about New York and the job she left behind. Her memories of New York, although upsetting, were also very important

to her and she was unwilling to give them up entirely. Her therapist suggested that she schedule her rumination for 7-8 p.m. nightly and limit thoughts of New York to that time. She took to this readily, saying that she was, "on a diet of New York." In very little time, her depression remitted and she began to try to make herself happy in Philadelphia.

Activity Scheduling (see Chapter 2) can be useful in a variety of ways early in therapy. Scheduling pleasurable and mastery activities can raise the mood of depressed clients, scheduling proximal goals can help overcome procrastination, and activity scheduling can also provide structure for dealing with multiple tasks. Furthermore, activity scheduling does not generally require the client to make changes that seem risky. Activity scheduling can be particularly useful when procrastination and inefficiency are caused by the client's feeling overwhelmed by tasks that he or she is not approaching systematically. The obsessive–compulsive who is faced with a number of tasks that need to be completed simultaneously is likely to freeze, not knowing what to do first and believing that he or she must do them all perfectly. For example:

> Sharon needed to find a new job, to cope with an ill parent, and to plan a wedding all in the same month and felt overwhelmed by these tasks. Her therapist first asked her to make a list of the steps needed to accomplish her goals in these three areas. When she had done so, her therapist asked her to make a liberal estimate of the time needed to do each step. She was then to schedule each step onto her Weekly Activity Schedule in addition to allowing appropriate time for socializing and relaxing. The client saw that it really was possible to do everything that absolutely needed to be done and that each subtask was well within her capabilities when taken one at a time. Consequently, she stopped avoiding these problems and started working more effectively.

The TR can be quite useful as a way for clients to identify and challenge their dysfunctional thoughts and cognitive distortions. Beyond this, it is also a way to get more accurate information about what clients actually think and feel in problem situations, as opposed to what they believe they should think and feel. Column 2 (specifying emotions) can be especially helpful in getting these clients to pay attention to feelings. Compulsives usually are both reluctant to express their feelings and unskilled at monitoring and reporting feelings. However, if the client can be persuaded to report some of his or her emotions and if the therapist can demonstrate that this provides useful information, it is possible to induce the client to pay more attention to his or her emotions. The client who does this regularly, will over time become more comfortable with his or her emotions and more skilled at expressing them.

There is, however, one caveat in using the TR with obsessive–compulsive clients. The therapist must take more care in teaching and monitoring the use of the TR with this population than with most others because the compulsive has a tendency to approach this task, as most others, obsessively. Often it takes some effort to persuade the client to complete the TR because of a fear that he or she will not do it "right." A useful strategy is for the therapist to address this fear when the TR is first assigned. This can be done by predicting that the concern will arise and then making it clear that the TR does not have to be done perfectly to be useful.

One common problem encountered once the client is using the TR is that the compulsive will record one or more automatic thoughts, then write a rational response, and then have a "yes, but..." thought that discounts the rational response. Some of these clients will jump back and forth between the automatic thoughts and the rational response columns for several pages. This is precisely the mode of thinking to which they are accustomed. Constantly debating both sides of an issue may be a way of postponing a decision and avoiding the risk of making a mistake by reaching the wrong conclusion. Once this problem has been identified, the therapist can help the client learn to address one side of the issue completely before going on to the next. One approach that often works is for the client to list all possible negative thoughts about a situation before going on to the rational responses, and then to write rational responses that address all aspects of the automatic thoughts. Alternatively, the client can start with one automatic thought and write rational responses to that one thought until it has been exhaustively dealt with before going on to the next thought.

Another common problem in using the TR is that the client may start writing negative thoughts, start ruminating about them, and never actually get to the cognitive restructuring. Not only does this produce no relief, but the client may also end up feeling worse than before doing the assignment. If the client can effectively use worry time or thought-stopping techniques to control his or her tendency to ruminate while listing automatic thoughts, he or she will then be able to complete the TR and get its benefits. If the client cannot stop the ruminations, then it is better to discard the TR for the time being and work on rational responses without it. This can be done by identifying typical automatic thoughts during the therapy session and asking the client to write a one-page essay arguing against the automatic thought. For example:

> The thought that her husband might be having an affair greatly troubled Iris. She accepted the homework assignment of writing an essay detailing all the evidence she could muster that was inconsistent with the idea that he was being unfaithful. This helped her to feel much better and gave her ammunition with which to refute subsequent reoccurrences of her negative thoughts.

Although the process of challenging automatic thoughts can be quite effective with OCPD, the use of self-instruction techniques (Meichenbaum, 1977) can also be useful because the automatic thoughts of the compulsive individual are often quite redundant. The client can readily reduce his or her negative affect, without having to generate the rational responses each time, by developing a set of coping statements and writing them on a 3×5 card. For example:

> Jordan tended to feel overwhelmed at work thinking "There's so much to do. There's no way I can get it all done but I *have* to get it all done." With his therapist's help he made up a card that read: "Slow down and take a deep breath. You can only do one thing at a time. Make a list of what you must do this week. Write each task onto your Activity Schedule. Then begin working." Each time he began feeling overwhelmed, he used this card as a reminder of the coping strategy he wanted to try using.

An important part of Cognitive Therapy with OCPD is the process of identifying the client's underlying assumptions and addressing them as opportunities permit. This becomes an increasingly important focus in the middle and later stages of therapy. As the client increasingly recognizes his or her assumptions about the importance of avoiding mistakes and about the most appropriate ways of doing so, the full range of interventions in Chapters 2 and 3 can be used to challenge the beliefs. However, the process of doing so can be complicated by the therapist's own "blind spots." The assumptions of the obsessive–compulsive are extreme forms of beliefs that are widely held in our culture and which are particularly prevalent among those who pursue graduate education and training in a profession. Thus, many therapists find it difficult to look critically at the obsessive–compulsive's assumptions because they themselves hold milder versions of the same beliefs or because the beliefs seem reasonable and logical to them. For example:

> Dr. Torres was a physician who sought treatment because his attempts to avoid making any mistakes resulted in stress and inefficiency. To his therapist, he said, "Sure, tolerating mistakes is OK for some people, but I can't afford to let any mistakes slip by, people could die." His view seemed quite reasonable to the therapist and the idea that a physician might need to tolerate mistakes seemed strange. However, is it true that only persons who never make any mistakes should be physicians? If so, how many physicians would there be? Fortunately, Dr. Torres and his therapist examined the actual effects of his attempts to insure that he made no mistakes rather than assuming that his "logical" conclusions were true. In practice, Dr. Torres' strategy of constantly double-checking his work, frequently looking things up, and regularly consulting colleagues resulted in his becoming more anxious and in his being quite inefficient. The strategy rarely resulted in his catching mistakes so that he could fix them. Instead, it interfered with his using his skills effectively to the point that it actually increased the risk of his making a serious mistake. As he began to acknowledge that humans are fallible and to accept his own fallibility, he not only became much more relaxed and efficient but the quality of the medical care he provided improved substantially as well.

It is often quite useful to help OCPD clients critically examine their strategies for maximizing their performance and minimizing mistakes because they often hold assumptions that seem reasonable but which are not actually true. Should one always try harder when one encounters difficulty? Redoubling one's efforts can be very effective in some situations, but counterproductive in others. Is it a good idea to set very high standards for oneself? Many persons are surprised that when they switch to setting moderate or even low standards, their motivation and performance improves substantially. Is it a bad idea to take time off to relax in the midst of a busy day? The person may find that a brief relaxation break improves his or her efficiency enough so that he or she is more productive than when he or she toils unceasingly. In examining these assumptions, it is important to use behavioral experiments and look at the evidence rather than simply considering whether the assumption seems logical or reasonable.

Given the compulsive's tendency toward selective abstraction, questions that focus the client's attention on evidence that is incompatible with their assumptions can have considerable impact. An example of this would be, "When is willingness to tolerate mistakes a good thing?" Such questions often lead naturally to attempting to formulate a more adaptive alternative assumption. Clients often assume that the therapist is advocating the opposite of the assumption that is being challenged and is trying to convince him or her that mistakes are wonderful. Actually, it is often quite useful to ask the client to think back over the evidence and observations that have been discussed and to formulate an alternative assumption that seems to be both more realistic and more adaptive.

This sets the stage for considering the advantages and disadvantages of the client's continuing to maintain his or her original underlying assumption versus attempting to act on the alternative assumption. It may not be difficult for the client to see how some of their assumptions might be disadvantageous to them, but it is another matter altogether to induce them to put the alternative assumptions into practice. It is important for the therapist and client to design behavioral experiments to empirically test the actual consequences of living by the alternative assumptions.

OCPD clients often have substantial problems in interpersonal relationships. This is due to the client's tendency to pay little attention to his or her emotions and the emotions of others and to act based on assumptions about how relationships "should" be. Often it is quite helpful to focus the client's attention on the actual impact of his or her actions and statements on others. The "empathy induction" approach discussed in Chapter 8 can be quite useful for this purpose, as can marital, family, or group therapy.

Conclusions

Obsessive–Compulsive Personality Disorder is a challenging but treatable problem. Through patient, collaborative, and systematic application of the techniques and strategies described in this chapter, the dysfunctional aspects of this disorder can be mitigated. An understanding of the dysfunctional worldview of the compulsive helps the therapist provide sympathetic treatment of a frequently unsympathetic character. As was discussed, the structure of Cognitive Therapy provides a model of adaptive functioning as well as being an instrument of change. Although standard cognitive techniques frequently need to be modified and closely monitored in order to avoid being used by the client as an occasion for ruminative thinking, they can be quite helpful. The authors have used this approach extensively in their clinical practice and supervision and have found it to be quite effective. While outcome research is limited, there are a growing number of studies suggesting the usefulness of CBT in mitigating Obsessive–Compulsive Personality Disorder (e.g., Black, Monahan, Wesner, Gabel, & Bowers, 1996; Hardy, Barkham, Shapiro, Stiles, Rees, & Reynolds, 1995; McKay, Neziroglu, Todaro, and Yaryura-Tobias, 1996).

IV

Special Applications of Cognitive Therapy

Cognitive Therapy is most widely known as a treatment approach for adults who are in individual therapy in outpatient settings. However, it can be applied much more broadly. With appropriate modifications it can be used with couples, families, and groups, with children and adolescents as well as adults, and in inpatient, partial hospitalization, and other residential settings.

This section discusses three "special applications" for practitioners in outpatient settings: Cognitive Therapy in groups, Cognitive Therapy with couples, and Cognitive Therapy with children and families. Cognitive Therapy is a vital approach that is constantly developing. The concluding chapter, *The Practice of Cognitive Therapy*, offers suggestions about how to learn more about Cognitive Therapy and how to stay up-to-date on new developments.

11

Cognitive Therapy in Groups

In the preceding chapters of this book, we have discussed the usefulness of individual Cognitive Therapy in the treatment of a wide variety of problems. However, individual therapy is not always available and is not always the preferred method of treatment. Group therapy can reduce the cost of treatment and alleviate long waits for appointments when there are too few therapists to satisfy the demand for individual therapy. Beyond these pragmatic considerations, treatment for some problems may be facilitated by the social contact, interpersonal interaction, and social support that can be a part of group therapy. In these situations, group Cognitive Therapy may be an effective alternative or adjunct to individual treatment.

Historically, many group therapy models have involved doing individual intrapsychic therapy within a group context or they have used a group dynamics approach to focus on interpersonal issues. Lazarus (1968) and Rose (1974) were among the first to describe behavioral or cognitive behavioral approaches to group therapy. Since then, the literature has grown tremendously, with group applications to the treatment of such widely diverse problems as depression, anxiety disorders, eating disorders, dissociative disorders, schizophrenia, and personality disorders (Brown, Comtois, & Linehan, 2002; Hollon & Evans, 1983; Linehan, 1993a).

This chapter will discuss therapy groups led by trained professionals, not self-help groups led by nonprofessionals. While self-help groups can be quite helpful, they can also be dangerous. Unless there is a system in place to assure that the group adheres to the planned treatment approach and stays within appropriate boundaries, there is potential for peer-led groups to develop idiosyncratic beliefs or dysfunctional interactions that can be countertherapeutic. For example, individuals who have been stabilized on appropriate psychotrophic medication have then joined peer-run groups where they were required to quit all medications before being considered "clean and sober." One of the authors is familiar with a peer-run aftercare group where members teach each other novel ways to self-mutilate and how to fake multiple personality disorder. Likewise we know of leaderless obsessive-compulsive disorder support groups where participants acquire new concerns about which to obsess, and depression support groups where a member's expression of suicidal intentions has been terrifying for other participants. These problems are certainly not what the organizers of the groups intended and they seem to be fairly rare, but it is wise to monitor the experiences of clients in peer-led self-help groups. Without a knowledgeable, competent therapist leading the group, there certainly is a chance of problems developing.

Advantages and Disadvantages of Group Cognitive Therapy

When group therapy is appropriate, it can have a number of advantages over individual therapy. Group therapy can be made available at a lower cost to the participant, to the clinic or agency that offers it, and to the insurance company that may reimburse for it. In addition, a number of clients may be treated at one time in group therapy, reducing the suffering and deterioration that may occur if there is a long wait until an individual therapist is available. Beyond these pragmatic advantages, there are some important therapeutic advantages. Groups provide the opportunity for social learning among participants through modeling of skills and techniques. Groups also provide participants with social support and reinforcement of their efforts and achievements by others in the group. Wessler (1983) also points out the value to group participants of seeing that they and their problems are not unique. Groups can also facilitate individual learning through the teaching of others. Furthermore, groups may provide the opportunity for *in vivo* practice of assertion and social skills in a relatively safe setting as well as providing immediate feedback from peers.

Some problems, such as social anxiety, can be dealt with most effectively in a group setting and some exercises, such as Ellis' shame attack technique, can be done in a group setting but not in an individual therapy setting. Group therapy can also be used to prepare for problematic social situations by role-playing in advance of feared events. Group interactions can also elicit specific emotional reactions that can then be dealt with *in vivo*. Groups may provide participants with a broader array of suggestions than individual therapy. Because participants can receive a great deal of feedback about their behavior, distorted beliefs about interpersonal interactions may be more quickly refuted. Furthermore, group members can provide peer pressure that facilitates therapeutic compliance, such as following through on exposure homework or taking medication consistently.

One advantage of group therapy with Panic Disorder, for example, is that it often is easier to get people to accept or deliberately induce panic attacks when they see other clients doing it and benefiting. In a panic group conducted by one of the authors, one participant arrived very excited that she had driven by herself to the group for the first time. Her excitement was so contagious that everyone else in the group set himself or herself a tough exposure task immediately and left to go do it.

Group therapy has disadvantages as well. Group treatment necessarily means that less time will be spent on any particular client's issues than would be the case in individual therapy. Group therapy requires greater management skills on the part of the therapist to maintain structure and avoid being sidetracked. If individuals who are not appropriate are included in the group, the therapy group can be disrupted by a single participant, diminishing its value for all of the participants. Group therapy may not be able to meet the needs of individuals who are in an acute crisis or who cannot conform their behavior to the group's expectations, thus these individuals are likely to require individual therapy before group treatment should be considered. Furthermore, some people are reluctant to tolerate the social anxiety involved in the early stages of group participation and this can inhibit them from attending the group or from participating.

Deciding How to Structure Group Therapy

A number of practical issues need to be addressed in planning a Cognitive Therapy group such as the size of the group, the frequency and length of group sessions, and the duration of the group. These can vary depending on the group's purpose and the needs of the participants. Hollon and Evans (1983, p. 20) recommend 6–12 as the optimal group size. They point out that with fewer than six members, group discussion may fizzle; with more than 12 members it may be difficult to involve everyone at each session. Within this general framework, the more people in the group, the more important it is for the therapist to use handouts and written materials. In individual therapy it is relatively easy to determine whether the client understands the point being made. When many people participate, it is more difficult to determine if everyone has gotten the therapeutic message, therefore the point needs to be reinforced in a variety of ways. A room suitable for holding group therapy should be large enough so that participants can sit comfortably in a circle with enough room for role-playing as well.

One important question is whether the group will be time-limited or open-ended. An open-ended group has the advantage of allowing as much time as is necessary for participants to meet their goals. However, when the time frame is unclear, this makes it harder for the therapist to plan ahead and there is the risk of the group becoming smaller and smaller as group members achieve their goals and leave the group. The relative advantages of each will depend on the purpose of the group and the degree of committment of participants, as well as the therapist's ongoing availability. One compromise is a group that is planned for a limited time interval, perhaps 3 months, with group members having the option of signing up for additional intervals as needed.

Another question is whether the group will be closed to new participants once it has begun or will be open to new members on an ongoing basis. With a closed group, all participants begin the group and, ideally, end at the same time. This allows the group leader to teach the skills and techniques of Cognitive Therapy in a sequential manner to individuals at roughly equivalent skill levels. However, a closed group requires that a sufficient number of appropriate people be available to begin the group at the same time, whereas people who miss the formation of the group may have to wait before a sufficient number has been gathered to begin a new group. With an open group, new participants may be admitted on an ongoing basis. This has the advantage of allowing new participants access to treatment without an undue wait and possibly of keeping group membership at an optimal number by counteracting any possible attrition through replacements. It also gives existing group members the opportunity to demonstrate mastery of skills by teaching them to new members.

In some settings, there is little opportunity for a closed group. Because psychiatric inpatient hospitalization stays have tended to be extremely short in recent years, clients may only have a few days in which to learn Cognitive Therapy skills before being discharged. Therefore, groups held in such settings would almost always need to be open to newly admitted hospital patients. (See Simon (1994) for a description of such an open, inpatient Cognitive Therapy group.)

Muñoz, Ghosh-Ippen, Rao, Le, and Dwyer (2000) have recently developed a compromise solution of "semi-open" groups at the University of California at San Francisco. Their treatment approach consists of three modules covering cognition, behavior, and interpersonal skills for 4 weeks each. New group members are enrolled only at the beginning of a module. As a result, no one must wait longer than 4 weeks to start. Furthermore, if a client wants to stay through an extra module they can do so. Lynn Marcinko (personal communication, February 13, 2002) recently reported that this program has been found to be very helpful at Harbor-UCLA Medical Center for first or second episodes of depression, but was not as effective for those with dysthymia.

Due to the constraints of research designs, outcome research on Cognitive Therapy groups has been conducted almost completely in closed groups, so it is known that they are effective for a wide variety of disorders. The effectiveness of open-ended Cognitive Therapy groups has not been studied to the same extent, however, practical realities require that many groups in the real world be open-ended. The semi-open group described above provides a practical alternative that has some empirical support. Another alternative is to use a "beginner's group" that teaches basic Cognitive Therapy skills in a brief closed group, followed by an open-ended "advanced group" where clients can come and go as needed.

Once the degree of "openness" of the group has been determined, the next question in planning group therapy is whether the group should include only participants with similar problems (a homogeneous group) or whether individuals with a variety of problems should be included (a heterogeneous group). The advantages of a homogeneous group are obvious. Treatment can be organized around one problem, such as social anxiety, or for a particular population, such as women who have recently divorced. Participants who share a particular problem or situation may relate better to each other and be able to be more helpful to each other and, therefore, be more committed to their treatment. Also, with a homogenous group it is easier for the therapist to anticipate which issues will need to be addressed and to select the therapeutic interventions that are most likely to be useful. However, it may be difficult in certain settings to find enough individuals who share the same problem at the same time to allow for a homogeneous group.

It is usually easier to find enough individuals to compose a heterogeneous group. However, without having a problem, or situation that group members all share, it is difficult for the therapist to anticipate which issues will need to be addressed or which interventions will be most useful. In a heterogeneous group, the skills taught would most likely need to be generally relevant to a variety of problems, with less focus on any one individual's specific problem.

Another factor to be considered in planning group therapy is whether the group is to be educational or experiential. Would the purpose of the group be served better through a structured, didactic approach or through a flexible approach that makes use of group interaction and teaches techniques as they are relevant to issues that arise within the group? An educational group can allow for larger group membership and can be planned in advance so that the therapist has homework assignments designed in advance and has handouts ready for participants. However, this approach may be less responsive to participants' issues and may be less engaging for participants. An experiential group can be more flexible and more tailored to clients' changing priorities, but there is a risk of failing to teach some important skills because a less systematic approach is used.

Many Cognitive Therapy group treatments will combine the educational and the experiential, but the relative proportion and timing of the two aspects will need to be appropriate to the goals of the group and will need to be determined by the group leader. For example:

> When starting a new Panic Disorder group, a new therapist was excited about using the group for *in vivo* exposures and planned to spend most sessions at the nearby mall having participants face their fears in a variety of ways. She quickly learned, however, that this was unrealistic. It did not leave enough group time to address the clients' concerns, to teach necessary skills, and to assign and review homework assignments. With further experience, she learned that, for this particular group, exposure sessions once per month maintained the balance needed to keep the participants moving forward without overwhelming them.

Another important question regards how structured the group sessions are to be. Groups range from the completely structured to relatively unstructured. A fully structured course of group therapy may take the participants through each step of the thought record (TR) over the course of several weeks before moving on to another intervention. An unstructured group may rely on the participants to determine the goals and agendas for each group meeting, with the therapist primarily serving as a resource for helping clients meet their goals. Because the structure will strongly influence all other aspects of the group, the leader will want to carefully consider how treatment goals will be affected by greater or lesser degrees of structure.

Finally, the leader will need to decide if the group therapy will be considered an adjunct to individual therapy or a complete course of treatment by itself. The group leader will need to consider the therapeutic requirements of the participants, ethical constraints, as well as his or her willingness to be solely responsible for participants' crises. This may not be a significant issue if the group has been established for a specific purpose such as to teach assertive behavior, but it might be an important factor if the group has been set up to treat Borderline Personality Disorder or victims of abuse. Whenever group and individual therapy are combined, it is necessary for clear guidelines to be spelled out from the beginning as to which issues belong in group and which issues belong in individual therapy. If some group members will be in concurrent individual therapy (whether with a group leader or with a completely different therapist) and others will not be having additional therapy, it is important for the expectations to be clear. Although it can be problematic to try to keep secrets about which group members see which therapists, it also can be disruptive to group cohesion if some group members receive special treatment because of their additional relationship with a group leader or if some members feel excluded when others talk about their individual therapy. It usually is best to keep discussions of individual therapy outside of the group sessions.

GROUP PROCESS

In an excellent chapter on group Cognitive Therapy of depression, White (2000) emphasizes the importance of cohesiveness, task focus, therapist role, and careful selection of participants in developing a successful group therapy experience. He states that the group leader must model active participation and collaboration for group members. He believes strongly that the therapist should encourage everyone to participate at every session. This is more likely to happen when the group leader establishes an environment where individual differences are accepted and participants support each other. He believes that the group leader should rely primarily on guided discovery, as in individual Cognitive Therapy. He also recommends that when the level of focus in the group moves into deeper, core issues, the therapist should refer to "us" or "our" issues, rather than "you" participants or "your" problems (White, 2000).

Wessler and Hankin-Wessler (1989) describe the importance of the therapeutic alliance in group process. They state that the group leader should be seen as trustworthy and accepting of the participants as individuals. They also emphasize the importance of the therapist as a model for the group. They state that this will be enhanced by building warm, empathic relationships with the group members and creating an environment in which the welfare and progress of all participants are seen as essential treatment goals. To be credible, the therapist needs to be perceived by participants as being genuinely interested in helping them.

Although the importance of the therapist's role in promoting a successful group therapy experience is unquestioned, the role of group participants is also crucial. All writers who describe group therapy emphasize the importance of selection of appropriate group participants. White (2000) recommends selecting members who would be expected to benefit from the group as well as to contribute to the experience of the other members. Doing this will generally require at least one session of individual assessment for each prospective participant. Active suicidal ideation is a primary exclusion criterion for most outpatient group therapy (White, 2000). Other reasons for exclusion may include current and untreated chemical dependency or current psychosis unless these are the targets for the group itself. Wessler and Hankin-Wessler (1989) add to the list of exclusion criteria individuals who cannot be expected to participate because of the severity of their Axis I or II pathology, their tendency to dominate discussions, or excessive withdrawal and silence. It is essential for the group leaders to use their clinical judgment (and commonsense) to evaluate whether the mix of participants is likely to work well for each specific group.

It often is logistically difficult to assemble enough participants for a therapy group and group leaders may be tempted to focus primarily on having enough people available for the group to start. However, if this means that they are not careful to judge whether the constitution of the group is appropriate, this can be a major problem. For example, the authors are aware of a group for "dating anxiety" that was conducted as part of a research protocol. Although all the participants met the stated criteria for inclusion, it turned out that 11 of the 12 participants in the group met full criteria for Avoidant Personality Disorder. This turned what had been intended to be a short-term, focused social anxiety group into a painfully quiet group, with the group leaders (and the one participant who did not have an Axis II disorder) struggling to get participants to say anything at all. Although the group ended up being helpful, it would have been much more manageable if there had been more group members who were able to participate actively from the beginning.

Once appropriate group participants have been selected, it is important to take steps to retain these participants within the group. Cohesion, collaboration, and mutual respect clearly promote the comfort and commitment of participants within the group. Assessing the expectations of participants, asking for feedback frequently, and encouraging participants to share any negative reactions to the group is also essential. This may help the therapist to address any dissatisfaction with the group before it becomes problematic and pay extra attention to anyone who is thinking of dropping out.

At the beginning of a therapy group, it is important for expectations to be discussed explicitly with participants and preferably be spelled out in writing. Included in the "rules" for group membership should be guidelines regarding confidentiality, interactions among group members outside of the group, and a discussion of how vital each member's participation is to the entire group. Participants should be asked to make a formal commitment to continue with the group and to agree that, if they do consider leaving at any point, they will come to one final session to discuss this. When members do come to a "final" group session to express their concerns and plans to leave the group, this often leads to an extremely useful session. Sometimes, it becomes clear that other members share their concerns and the group as a whole becomes more useful as a result of the discussion. When a participant does quit despite these strategies, White (2000) emphasizes that it is important to deal with the remaining group members' questions and concerns to achieve closure and maintain the cohesiveness of the group.

It is important to remember that group therapy involves more than simply doing individual therapy with each group member sequentially, giving part of the group time to each participant. This approach may seem simple and straightforward, but has major drawbacks. It fails to make use of the group as a resource and instead treats it more as an assembly line. Furthermore, the group members who are not the focus of the leader will tend to stop paying attention out of boredom if their input is not needed. Hollon and Evans (1983) believe that the ability to be therapeutic with each other provides several important opportunities for group participants. These include providing group members with practice in identifying and testing automatic thoughts, minimizing the distinction between helping and being helped, increasing the chance that someone will be able to generate a helpful option, and showing the participants that they can be effective and rational in dealing with problems. Group members are an important resource and can often play a valuable role in identifying, examining, and testing each other's cognitions. For example:

> Gavin was referred for group Cognitive Therapy by his psychiatrist because of recurring Major Depressive Episodes. He participated in a 10-week Cognitive Therapy group for depression. Although he readily learned how to identify situations, emotions, and automatic thoughts (corresponding to the first three columns of the TR) over the course of the first few weeks of group, he had difficulty generating rational responses. He brought a partially completed TR to group as his homework, but was unable to respond to the automatic thought, "I'm a loser," because he felt it to be completely true. The group leader used this as an opportunity to ask the group participants for help in generating rational responses for Gavin. Because even depressed individuals have a sense of perspective when appraising the self-critical thoughts of other people, they were able to produce the TR shown in Fig. 11.1 below. As a result, the intensity of Gavin's negative emotions and the degree of his belief in his hot thought reduced over the group session. He also had more confidence in the process of rational responding and agreed to accept as his homework for the next session responding to two additional negative thoughts. In addition, because several other group members had similar types of thoughts throughout the week, they observed that helping Gavin come up with rational responses had also helped them to deal with some of their own automatic thoughts.

To take advantage of group process, there are a number of issues that must be addressed and a number of changes that must be made in making the transition from individual to group Cognitive Therapy. These range from the fundamental ground rules of therapy to aspects of the Cognitive Therapy structure that must be altered for use in the group format. At the fundamental level, rules regarding confidentiality are generally quite clear in individual adult therapy. These rules become less distinct as more people are involved in treatment. Hollon and Evans (1983, p. 20) advocate setting ground rules for the group that emphasize respecting the privacy of other group members. Although this does not have the force of law, participants are more likely to comply if they know exactly what is expected of them. Other writers go further and advocate a group contract covering confidentiality (see Upper & Flowers, 1994). Without clear guidelines, group participants have been known to engage in various inappropriate activities, such as sexual behavior, borrowing money from each other, and showing up unexpectedly at each other's residences or workplaces. For the safety and comfort of all participants, ground rules for therapy groups are crucial.

Beyond such fundamental issues, the basic structure of Cognitive Therapy may need to be altered for the group format. Some of these alterations will involve goal setting, agenda setting, and reviewing and setting homework assignments. In individual Cognitive Therapy, each client enters treatment with an idiosyncratic list of goals, some of which are presenting problems and some of which are implicit. The therapist helps the client to make his or her goals explicit and to prioritize his or her goals early in treatment. In group therapy, however, the general goal for treatment may have been determined before any clients actually arrive. If the group has been set up for a specific purpose such as the treatment of depression or social anxiety, for example, the participants would have selected the group because their goals are consistent with the group's stated purpose. It is always the case that participants would have additional personal goals

Situation Briefly describe the situation	Emotion(s) Rate 0-100%	Automatic Thought(s) Rate degree of belief 0-100%	Rational Response Rate degree of belief 0-100%	Outcome Re-rate emotions
George received an unexpected insurance bill.	Panic (90%) Depression (99%) Hopeless (99%)	1) I can't believe it. (80%) 2) I messed up again. (100%) 3) I can't afford this. (100%) 4) I don't know what to do. (90%) 5) This always happens to me. (90%) 6) I'll never get out from under. (95%) 7) At my age, money shouldn't be such a problem. (100%) 8) I can't stand it. (90%) 9) I'm a loser. (100%) [hot thought]	[group generated responses to thought, "I'm a loser."] 8) I can't be a loser because I have not lost 100% of the time; I'm not loser because I have been coping with adversity pretty well lately: I filed for reduced alimony with my ex-wife even thought I'm afraid of my kids' reaction; I've gotten precertified for a mortgage and finally started looking for a condo to buy; I haven't run back to my old girlfriend in spite of fear of being alone; I've been able to work consistently for the past 5 weeks and my concentration has been getting better. (50%)	Panic (10%) Anxiety (50%) Depression (40%) Hopelessness (30%)

FIGURE 11.1. Thought Record Produced in a Group Session.

that go beyond those of the group. For example, one participant in a depression group may need to gain control of her compulsive spending; another may need to deal with a sexual addiction; whereas yet another may need to improve communication with a spouse. Depending on the expected duration of the group and the needs of the participants, the degree to which these individual issues will be pursued will vary. For example, if improved marital communication is on the personal goal list of several of the participants, the leader may choose to address this in more detail than he or she normally would.

The typical agenda for group Cognitive Therapy is similar to that of individual Cognitive Therapy. It might include:

1. Feedback from participants regarding the previous group meeting
2. A review of the previous week's homework
3. The specific issues planned for the group at that meeting
4. A check of the understanding of participants on points made
5. Setting next week's homework and answering any questions or concerns related to carrying out the homework
6. Adjournment

In individual Cognitive Therapy the agenda is usually developed jointly by therapist and client. In group Cognitive Therapy, two different approaches are possible. In some Cognitive Therapy groups, the group leader determines which issues will be addressed in a particular session and the content of therapy sessions may be completely planned in advance. See Table 11.1 for examples of agendas for several sessions of a group developed to teach basic Cognitive Therapy skills.

White (2000) recommends an alternative approach to agenda setting in his excellent chapter on group Cognitive Therapy for depression. He believes that the group members themselves should determine the agenda items for each session. His approach is to ask the group members to work to reach consensus on the best use of their session time. He states that with skillful guidance by the therapist, group members are able to do this effectively. This approach is thought to promote cohesiveness among group members and a sense of personal competence within the depressed participants. Such an approach may make excellent therapeutic sense for ongoing groups, but not for others. In a brief structured group (such as a 5-session fear of flying group), time spent on collaborative goal setting limits the time available for addressing the issues. In longer, less structured groups, there are more options for collaborative goal setting. For example, in an ongoing agoraphobia group led by one of the authors, the group members decided to alter the group agenda once each member had a well-defined hierarchy and the skills needed to work steadily up their hierarchies. Instead of focusing solely on the agoraphobia, the group members decided to spend the first hour of the group reviewing homework and setting new homework, but to focus the second hour on broader topics of general interest. These topics included issues such as assertiveness, dealing with extended family, communicating with spouses, and so on. This change in basic group agenda not only met the members' clinical needs better, it also enhanced group cohesion and gave each group member a stronger sense of self-efficacy.

TABLE 11.1.

Example Group Agendas	
Session 1	Session 2
Introduction to group by therapist	Greet group members
Set agenda	Set agenda
Introduce group members to each other	Elicit and answer questions regarding first
Clarify group rules	session
Socialize to cognitive therapy	Review homework
Elicit examples from group	Teach first three columns of thought record
Provide capsule summaries	Elicit examples from group
Develop Homework Assignments	Provide capsule summaries
Elicit participants' reactions to group	Elicit participants' reactions to group
Adjourn	Adjourn
Session 6	Last Session
Greet group members	Greet group members
Set agenda	Set agenda
Answer any questions	Review Personalized Treatment Manual (PTM)
Review homework	and solicit ideas/contributions from group
Complete thought records using groups' difficult	members
automatic thoughts	Group members identify priorities for continued
Provide capsule summaries	progress
Elicit participants' reactions to group	Provide capsule summaries
Adjourn	Elicit participants' reactions to group
	Adjourn

White (2000) recommends that group sessions begin with group members checking in with each other by sharing important events of the week, especially regarding any changes in their mood and functioning. Participants also share significant aspects of their homework during the first 20 minutes or so of the session. Once agenda items have been decided on, each group should include time spent developing adaptive responses to participants' problems. The group will not conclude until homework has been set for the next week based on what was discussed in session. Hollon and Evans (1983) believe that the therapist should get consensus from participants that everyone will get a chance to bring up at least one or two issues for discussion and that the group will focus on that issue long enough to reach some resolution.

Reviewing and assigning homework is a crucial part of Cognitive Therapy, whether group or individual. However, going through each participant's homework in detail could easily take an entire group meeting. It can take some experience as well as a willingness to be directive to choose the optimal degree of detail in reviewing homework. We recommend making a point of asking each participant something about his or her homework at each session. This reinforces the message that homework is valued and necessary, also allows the participants to get credit for success, and provides the opportunity for participants to help others with their knowledge or by their example. Furthermore, asking for the results of the homework and any problems encountered also helps the therapist identify and resolve obstacles to homework before a participant becomes discouraged and considers leaving the group prematurely.

APPLICATIONS OF GROUP COGNITIVE THERAPY
TO SPECIFIC PROBLEMS

Specific protocols for group Cognitive Therapy have been tested with a wide variety of problems. However, a review of the various group CBT approaches to each disorder is beyond the scope of this chapter. What follows is a sampling of studies in the recent literature regarding the application of group Cognitive Therapy to a variety of common problems and populations. (See Bergin & Garfield (1994) for a more comprehensive review of this literature.)

In general, the group CBT protocols that have been tested use the same conceptualizations and intervention techniques that have been discussed in the chapters on individual Cognitive Therapy for specific problems earlier in this book. Usually the group agenda is planned in advance with interventions and homework assignments preplanned on the basis of prior research and clinical experience. With some problems, such as depression, a psychoeducational approach that only makes limited use of group interaction has been used. With other problems, such as Social Phobia, within group interactions play a greater role in the treatment protocol. Typically, the outcome research has been done with time-limited groups using participants with one specific diagnosis and excluding those with major comorbid conditions such as substance abuse or psychosis. Some critics argue that carefully controlled outcome studies have little relevance to real-world clinical practice where interventions are applied more flexibly with a less carefully selected group of clients. However, when group Cognitive Therapy has been tested under real-world conditions the studies have generally produced the same results as have been found in carefully controlled outcome research (for example, see Arean & Miranda, 1996 and Peterson & Halstead, 1998).

Depression

Group Cognitive Therapy for depression is almost as old as Cognitive Therapy itself. A chapter by Hollon and Shaw (1979) on the subject was included in Aaron Beck's seminal work, *Cognitive Therapy of Depression* (Beck, *et al.*, 1979), more than 25 years ago. Since then, many outcome studies have demonstrated the efficacy of group Cognitive Therapy in the treatment of depression. Hollon and Evans (1983) reviewed the outcome literature existing at that time and concluded that the evidence then in existence favored "a structured, time limited, problem focused approach such as Cognitive Therapy over other alternative group approaches for working with depressed clients" (p. 13). No outcome research since then has called this conclusion into question.

Investigators continue to try to expand knowledge about the parameters that contribute to successful treatment. Peterson and Halstead (1998) replicated Beck's model of Cognitive Therapy in a heterogeneous community setting to test whether one could generalize from the results of carefully controlled outcome research to real-world clinical settings. They provided depression management training over the course of six 2-hour group sessions to 138 clinically depressed clients who had been referred by mental health clinicians. The participants reduced their depression as measured by the BDI by an average of 38%, with 43% reducing their BDI score over 50%. The researchers concluded that group cognitive behavioral therapy (CBT) could be applied effectively in a clinical setting with a heterogeneous client population. Clarke and his colleagues (Clarke *et al.*, 1992) conducted a study to determine if group CBT for depressed adolescents would be more effective if augmented by having their parents participate concurrently in a separate group. Not surprisingly, they found that better outcome was associated with parental involvement in treatment. Rohde and his acolleagues (Rohde, Clarke, Lewinsohn, Seeley, & Kaufman, 2001) examined the impact of comorbidity on cognitive behavioral group treatment for adolescent depression. Although outcomes were worse for participants with certain comorbid problems, their overall conclusion was that the presence of psychiatric comorbidity generally did not contraindicate the use of structured group cognitive behavioral interventions for depressed adolescents. Overall, group Cognitive Therapy appears to be a robust treatment for depression in adults and is a promising treatment approach in adolescents as well.

Social Phobia

It can be argued that group treatment is uniquely suited to those types of anxiety involving fears of social interaction. As discussed in Chapter 5, contemporary Cognitive Therapy for Social Phobia combines cognitive restructuring and *in vivo* exposure. Because effective treatment for anxiety requires exposure to the feared situation, exposure to interactions with others is necessary for the treatment of social anxiety. Group therapy provides an ideal opportunity for doing this. For excellent summaries of the basic techniques of cognitive behavioral group therapy (CBGT) for Social Phobia and the empirical evidence regarding its efficacy see Turk, Fresco, and Heimberg (1999) and Coles, Hart, and Heimberg (2001).

Panic Disorder and Agoraphobia

Much of the initial research into the outcome of cognitive behavioral treatment of these two related problems was conducted in group settings and provides convincing evidence of the efficacy of group treatment with both of these problems (see Craske, Barlow, & Meadows, 2000, pp. 1–9 for a concise summary). Current research continues to explore aspects of group treatment with these two problems. For example, Mitchell (1999) reported the effects of medication alone and medication in combination with CBGT in the treatment of adults with Panic Disorder. A quasiexperimental research design was used to compare posttest anxiety scores of participants who received medication alone and participants who received eight weekly sessions of CBGT in addition to medication. Analysis of a 32-item self-report scale revealed significant differences in posttest anxiety scores between the two groups. Participants who received CBGT in addition to medication had lower posttest anxiety scores than those who received medication alone. Rief, Trenkamp, Auer, and Fichter (2000) compared the usefulness of group CBT for adult clients with Panic Disorder versus clients with Panic Disorder and concurrent Major Depressive

Disorder. Structured interviews and multiple clinical self-rating scales were used in assessments that took place 6 months before treatment, at the beginning and end of treatment, and 1 year later. Their results indicated that before treatment clients with Panic Disorder and comorbid Major Depressive Disorder showed higher levels of both anxiety symptoms and symptoms unrelated to anxiety. The strongest effects of treatment were in reducing avoidance behavior, whereas reduction in catastrophic beliefs was a smaller, but still significant, effect. Although clients with and without comorbid depression reported similar levels of improvement on their self-rating scales, the final assessment showed that the clients with Panic Disorder and comorbid depression were still functioning at a significantly lower level than clients with Panic Disorder alone. This raises the possibility that individuals with Panic Disorder and comorbid depression may need a treatment approach that specifically addresses their depression as well as their Panic Disorder and/or may need a longer duration of treatment.

Specific Phobias

Most of the research into the treatment of specific phobias has been conducted in individual treatment formats and it has been suggested that individual treatment may be preferable for phobias (Craske, Anthony, & Barlow, 1997). However, group Cognitive Therapy has been applied to a number of specific phobias. To date, group treatment does not seem to have important advantages in the treatment of specific phobias aside from possibly reducing the cost of treatment. Craske and her colleagues (1997) argue that it is important to limit the group size and to use a co-therapist, if possible, to give clients sufficient individual attention.

Post Traumatic Stress Disorder

Because some traumatic events such as a war or a major disaster can involve many people and can result in a number of individuals who have developed Post Traumatic Stress Disorder (PTSD) in response to the same events, it is natural to conduct group treatment for PTSD, especially if resources for responding to the event are limited. A number of studies have shown that group treatment can be helpful. For example, Humphreys, Westerink, Giarratano, and Brooks (1999) evaluated the efficacy of a treatment program for chronic PTSD. The treatment combined CBT with pharmacotherapy. Treatment began with 4 weeks of inpatient treatment, and continued with outpatient group and individual follow-up sessions over the next 6 months. The treatment population consisted primarily of Australian Vietnam war veterans. Clients completed a battery of self-report scales on completion of the inpatient stay, and at 6 months, 1 year, and 2 years after discharge from the inpatient program. The results obtained from the 64 male clients showed significant reductions in depression, anxiety, and PTSD symptoms, which were maintained at the 2-year follow-up. Although this study presented encouraging findings for treatment with this difficult population, it did not examine the relative contributions of the inpatient, group, or individual Cognitive Therapy to clients' improvement.

Krakow and his colleagues (Krakow et al., 2001) used group CBT to treat nightmares and insomnia in crime victims with PTSD. Sixty-two participants completed

10 hours of treatment involving imagery rehearsal for nightmares as well as education about sleep hygiene, stimulus control, and sleep restriction for insomnia. Researchers assessed nightmare frequency, sleep quality and impairment, and severity of PTSD, anxiety, and depression before and after the 3-month treatment. On most measures symptoms improved from severe to moderate. However, on measures of anxiety and depression improvement went from the extremely severe range to borderline severe. In this uncontrolled study, improvement in insomnia and nightmares in crime victims was associated with improvement in symptoms of PTSD, anxiety, and depression. However, it appears that a more prolonged or more multi-faceted treatment might produce a better outcome.

Substance Abuse and Addiction

There is a long history of group treatment for addictive disorders but many of the traditional approaches have been based on 12-step models. Cognitive behavioral approaches to treating addictive disorders have evolved over time amidst debate and controversy (see Marlatt, 1983; Wilson, 1987) but show potential for increasing the effectiveness of treatment for substance abuse and addictions (see Monti, Abrams, Kadden, & Cooney, 1989, pp. 170–192 for a concise overview). We will highlight a few studies that illustrate the current status of research into group CBT with a variety of substance-related problems.

Cinciripini and his colleagues (Cinciripini, Cinciripini, Wallfisch, & Haque, 1996) studied the effectiveness of group programs for smoking cessation by comparing CBT alone to CBT plus the nicotine patch. Participants who had been smoking freely stopped smoking on a specific date. Cognitive behavioral therapy prepared them for stopping, whereas behavioral rehearsal prepared them for situations that posed a high risk of their resuming smoking. Stress management and coping strategies for dealing with negative affect were also included in the group training. Although participants who received the patch in addition to CBT were more likely to be abstinent through the 3-month follow-up, both groups actually did quite well (79% abstinent vs. 63%). The participants who did not receive a nicotine patch showed more general distress as well as decreased coping effort. For both groups, there was a tendency for treatment effects to decline over time.

Monti, Abrams, Binkoff, and Zwick (1990) evaluated three social learning approaches to the treatment of alcoholic males. They compared groups that focused on communication skills training alone, communication skills training with family participation, or cognitive behavioral mood management training. They found that all groups showed improvement in their anxiety level and in skills for coping with alcohol-related situations. However, the communication skills training group improved most in skills at coping with high-risk situations and in the ability to relax after role-playing.

A recent study (Echeburua, Baez, & Fernandez-Montalvo, 1996) compared the effectiveness of three therapeutic modalities in the treatment of pathological gambling. Individual stimulus control and exposure with response prevention, group cognitive restructuring, and a combination of both of these strategies was compared to a waiting list group. Interestingly, most treated participants gave up gambling as well as showed improvement in family, social, and psychological functioning.

There was also an improvement in controlling gambling in the control group between the pretreatment and the 6-month follow-up. However, the success rate was higher in the individual treatment compared both to the group and combined treatment, and there was no difference between the combined treatment and the control group. The authors concluded that individual stimulus control and exposure with response prevention was an effective therapy for pathological gambling. However, the results can also be interpreted to mean that when individual treatment is unavailable, group Cognitive Therapy is a plausible alternative.

Psychotic Disorders

Until recently, nonpharmacological treatment of psychotic disorders was mainly focused on increasing compliance with the medication regimen, providing support, and improving social skills. This has changed recently, however, and CBT is now being used to target some of the core symptoms of psychosis as well. A variety of treatment approaches have been proposed. For example, Daniels (1998) describes an approach that she calls Interactive-Behavioral Training for chronic mental illness. It actively combines cognitive behavioral and group process techniques for social impairment and negative symptoms in those suffering from chronic mental illness and debilitating problems. In contrast to this approach, Weingardt and Zeiss (2000) describe an entirely didactic skills training group used on a psychiatric intensive care unit. Training modules in their manualized treatment program cover topics including anger management, communications, drugs and alcohol, relationships, coping with mental illness, and relapse prevention. The interested reader should see Tarrier, Haddock, and Barrowclough (1998) for an overview of recent developments into psychosocial treatments of psychotic disorders, including CBT for psychotic symptoms.

A number of cognitive behavioral group treatment approaches are producing encouraging results. Kingdon and Turkington (1998) describe the use of CBT with a group of 12 clients between the ages of 16 and 65 years, all of whom were diagnosed with schizophrenia. The authors report that preliminary results suggest that the long-term outcome is promising especially when clients were managed from their first psychotic episode. Similarly, Gledhill, Lobban, and Sellwood (1998) describe CBT with a small group of adults with a primary diagnosis of schizophrenia. They report that after the group intervention, all four were less depressed, three had higher self-esteem and greater knowledge of schizophrenia, and two felt better able to cope with their symptoms. Clients reported feeling less isolated and expressed a preference for group treatment over individual therapy.

Halperin, Nathan, Drummond, and Castle (2000) investigated the usefulness of group CBT for social anxiety in schizophrenia. Twenty adult clients with schizophrenia and comorbid social anxiety were assigned to group CBT or a waiting list control group. Results showed that the CBT group improved on outcome measures of social anxiety and avoidance, mood, and quality of life. The control group showed no change in symptomatology. The authors concluded that group-based CBT was effective in treating social anxiety in schizophrenia.

In an ambitious study, Chadwick, Sambrooke, Rasch, and Davies (2000) examined the impact of group CBT on drug resistant auditory hallucinations. They focused on the beliefs of participants in the omnipotence and control in a voice. Twenty-two individuals participated in one of five 8-session CBT groups. Measures of omnipotence, control, process measures, and symptoms of anxiety and depression were completed at assessment, and at the first and last group sessions. The groups achieved a significant reduction in conviction in beliefs in the omnipotence and control in hallucinations. Although the authors report no change in mood as a result of the intervention, they do report that certain participants showed important spontaneous changes in behavior. If these results are maintained over time, they suggest that this treatment may prove to be a useful adjunct to existing interventions for auditory hallucinations.

Anger and Abusive Behavior

While the *DSM* diagnostic system has relatively few diagnostic categories for problems with dysfunctional expressions of anger, these widespread problems have received increasing attention in recent years (see Beck, 1999 for a detailed discussion). Deffenbacher and colleagues (Deffenbacher, Dahlen, Lynch, Morris, Gowensmith, 2000) applied Cognitive Therapy to general anger reduction in college students. A course of nine weekly 1-hour small-group sessions in Cognitive Therapy was compared to a no-treatment control. They found that Cognitive Therapy based on the work of Beck (1999) lowered scores on measures of negative forms of anger expression while enhancing positive forms of anger expression. They report that treatment effect sizes were medium to large for many of the group members and that significantly more Cognitive Therapy participants met an index of clinically significant change as compared to the controls. Reductions of anger and trait anxiety were maintained at the 15-month follow-up. In a second study, Dahlen (2000) compared CBGT to groups that included cognitive restructuring only in the treatment of anger problems. Participants were small groups of undergraduates who reported having anger problems and who scored in the upper quartile on a measure of trait anger. After eight weekly sessions both treatment conditions were found to be effective in reducing anger levels. Saunders (1996) compared cognitive behavioral group treatment and a psychodynamic process group in the treatment of male batterers. Although he did not find overall differences in effectiveness between the two treatments, he did find some interesting interaction effects: men with dependent personalities had better outcomes in the psychodynamic process groups whereas men with antisocial characteristics had better outcomes in the cognitive behavioral groups. Saunders suggests that more effective treatment may occur if treatment is tailored to the offenders' personal characteristics.

Group Cognitive Therapy with Mixed Diagnoses in an Inpatient Setting

Simon (1994) describes an inpatient Cognitive Therapy group in which rapid stabilization during a short inpatient stay was the primary goal. The groups were open-ended, heterogeneous, and process oriented as well as educational. The program provided treatment for severely disturbed nonpsychotic individuals who required hospitalization in spite of ongoing individual psychotherapy and psychiatric medication. Because of pragmatic constraints, most of the members had only a few days in which to overcome their immediate crises and return to the community. This program utilized a workbook and corresponding videotapes developed by Byers *et al.* (1992). The workbook consists of 12 chapters, each of which was designed to teach a particular Cognitive Therapy concept or skill. Participants attended three cognitive groups on each weekday, two of which were process-type CBT groups and one didactic. Most participants attended a parallel partial hospitalization program for 3–15 days after being discharged from the inpatient unit. Thus, the average client attended approximately 40 groups over a 3-week period. Many of the clients were admitted and discharged from inpatient and partial hospital treatment more than once over the course of the program. Thus many patients participated in the Cognitive Therapy groups more than once over the course of treatment. Definitive outcome data on the effectiveness of this program is not available, however, clinical observation indicated that many of these severely disturbed clients were able to learn and use basic cognitive behavioral skills over the course of treatment.

Group Cognitive Therapy with Children

As discussed in Chapter 13, when Cognitive Therapy is applied to children, a number of adjustments are required for accommodating with the child's developmental level. However, several controlled trials suggest that, when delivered in a developmentally sensitive fashion, CBT is an effective and enduring treatment for children and adolescents (see Piacentini and Bergman, 2001). It appears that this conclusion applies for group as well as individual CBT. For example, Toren and colleagues (Toren *et al.*, 2000) examined the use of brief parent–child group therapy for childhood anxiety disorders. Ten sessions of manual-based cognitive behavioral treatment was compared to a waiting-list control group. Children were followed for 3 years after treatment. Although anxiety symptoms decreased significantly during the treatment and follow-up periods, depressive symptoms improved only during the follow-up period. The percentage of children with no diagnosable anxiety disorder was 71% at the end of treatment and 91% at the 3-year follow-up. Interestingly, these researchers found that the children of mothers with an anxiety disorder improved more than children of nonanxious mothers did, even though the anxiety level of the mothers remained stable. Similarly, Utay and Lampe (1995) studied the effectiveness of a group counseling game in reducing social skills deficits in school age children with learning disabilities. The game taught basic cognitive behavioral skills, including self-reinforcement, causal attribution, performance mediation for anxiety and errors, and efficacy and outcome expectations. They found that the group process involved in the game helped improve the social skills of learning disabled children.

Group Cognitive Therapy with Older Adults

Both group and individual Cognitive Therapy have been applied successfully to the treatment of mental health problems in older outpatients (see

Gallagher-Thompson and Thompson, 1996a). Often, the treatment of older adults is complicated by the medical problems and cognitive changes that can come with aging. An interesting study from England (Kunik *et al.*, 2001) evaluated the effectiveness of a single 2-hour session of CBT for elderly clients with chronic obstructive pulmonary disease (COPD). Fifty-six participants took part in a blind randomized controlled clinical trial. One 2-hour session of group CBT designed to reduce symptoms of anxiety included relaxation training, cognitive interventions, and graduated practice, followed by homework and weekly telephone calls for 6 weeks. A comparison group received 2 hours of education regarding COPD followed by weekly calls. When compared with the COPD education group, the CBT group showed decreased depression and anxiety despite the fact that there was no improvement in the physical functioning of the participants. It is extremely encouraging that as little as 2 hours of CBT administered in a group setting is able to reduce anxious and depressive symptoms in this population. Similarly, Kipling, Bailey, and Charlesworth (1999) studied the effectiveness of a CBT group for men with mild to moderate cognitive impairment. Rather than teaching mnemonic strategies to older adults as other studies have done, these authors used CBT to address unhelpful beliefs regarding memory in the three older men (aged 75, 81, and 84 years) with mild to moderate dementia and associated low mood or anxiety. Changes in behavior, cognition, and affect were monitored over the course of the 7-week intervention. Results showed that a group approach to memory loss using a cognitive behavioral model was feasible and may be beneficial for older adults with dementia.

Conclusions

There is a great deal of research showing that group Cognitive Therapy is effective for a wide variety of diagnoses and populations and it has become a staple mode of treatment in many inpatient psychiatric and substance abuse settings. In general, group Cognitive Therapy is effective where individual Cognitive Therapy is, with a few exceptions. Group therapy may not be as helpful as individual therapy with those who are in crisis, those who are too severely disturbed to participate in the group, those who refuse to participate in the group process, or those who require more personal guidance than can be delivered in a group setting (Wessler & Hankin-Wessler, 1989).

At present, it is not possible to give a definitive answer to the questions of whether group or individual Cognitive Therapy is more effective. Some studies have shown that group CBT is superior with certain populations. For example, Steffen, Futterman, & Gallagher-Thompson (1998) found evidence that depressed caregivers were helped more by cognitive behavioral groups than by individual psychotherapy. Scholing and Emmelkamp (1993) found that group Cognitive Therapy treatment was more effective than the *in vivo* exposure condition at a 3 month follow-up and that the group treatment with *in vivo* exposure was more effective than individual treatments at the 18-month follow-up. On the other hand, Dick-Grace (1996) and Pinquart and Soerensen (2001) found that individual

interventions were more effective than group CBT for depressed adults. To complicate matters further, Muris, Mayer, Bartelds, Tierney, and Bogie (2001) and Vollmer
and Blanchard (1998) found that group and individual CBT were equally effective
in treating anxiety symptoms in children and irritable bowel syndrome, respectively. Clearly, further research will be needed to determine when group CBT has
an advantage over individual CBT and vice versa.

12

Cognitive Therapy with Couples

Although living "happily ever after" may still be the conclusion of many children's stories, the reality of marriage[1] is often not so happy or permanent. Statistics show that approximately 50% of marriages in the United States end in divorce and one survey shows that many of the marriages that do not end in divorce appear to be distressed (Baucom, Epstein, Rankin, & Burnett, 1996). Thankfully, couple therapy has been shown to be effective in helping troubled couples and there is a large body of research regarding the functioning of couples and the treatment of couple difficulties (well summarized in Baucom, Shoham, Mueser, Daiuto, & Stickle, 1998; Epstein, 2001; and Epstein & Baucom, 2002).

It can be argued that the area of marital dysfunction is especially appropriate for cognitive intervention because marital satisfaction is the individual's evaluation of his or her marriage, a primarily cognitive variable. Although many factors play a role in how people appraise their marriage, marital satisfaction is essentially an evaluation of how one's current relationship compares with what one believes a relationship should be. Unfortunately, the cognitive nature of marital satisfaction does not mean that cognitive marital therapy is easy. The therapist is faced by all of the complexities encountered in individual therapy plus the interactions between the spouses and the complexity added by interactions with the extended family, friends, and extramarital involvements. Furthermore, instead of seeking treatment at the beginning of their difficulties, many couples wait until their relationship is at serious risk and dysfunctional interactions have become quite ingrained.

The cognitive conceptualization of marital interaction includes all the cognitive components of individual functioning discussed previously (Chapter 1). Each individual has his or her own set of thoughts and beliefs that influence feelings and behavior. In particular, each individual has an assortment of beliefs about relationships, standards for how a marriage "should" be, and interpersonal strategies that can have a major influence on marital interactions. In addition, each person's behavior serves as a stimulus for the other partner (see Figure 12.1). The result is a dynamic pattern of interactions as each partner responds to their interpretations of

---

[1] This chapter focuses primarily on the treatment of the problems of married couples. However, the principles discussed would also apply to therapy with unmarried couples and with homosexual couples.

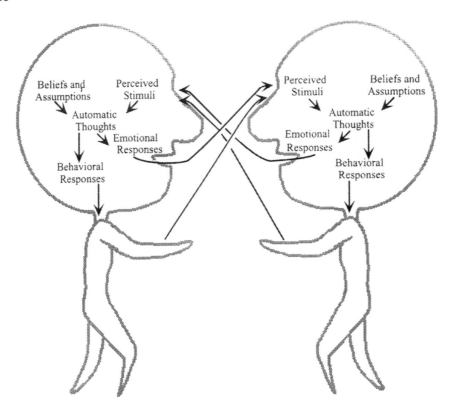

FIGURE 12.1. Basic Cognitive Model of Couple Interaction.

the other's words and actions. Problems can arise due to the effects of dysfunctional beliefs, cognitive distortions, negative automatic thoughts, dysfunctional behavior, and/or dysfunctional interactional patterns. Thus, there are many possible sources of problems and many possible points for intervention.

All of the techniques used in individual Cognitive Therapy (discussed in previous chapters) can be used in couple therapy. In addition, however, the presence of the partner in the session gives the therapist an opportunity to observe interaction patterns, directly test thoughts regarding the partner, and practice negotiating agreements. However, the couple's interactions make marital therapy much more complex than simply doing individual Cognitive Therapy with two people simultaneously.

ASSESSMENT

Just as in individual Cognitive Therapy, Cognitive Therapy with couples begins with an assessment that provides a basis for a cognitive-behavioral conceptualization of the couple and their problems and an initial treatment plan. The overall goals of the assessment are to identify the problems for which the couple is

TABLE 12.1. Information to be Obtained in an Initial Assessment with a Couple

---

Presenting problem
  Nature of problem(s), precipitants, course, couple's understanding of problem, previous attempts at
    dealing with problem.

Current life situation
  Living situation, work, interests and activities, use of leisure time, family relationships, level of
    satisfaction with current life.

Relationship history
  How the couple met, the course of their relationship, previous problems, strengths and weaknesses,
    observation of the couple's interactions over the course of the assessment.

Individual history (of each partner)
  Family history, school/occupational history, social history, legal history, traumatic experiences,
    medical history, psychiatric history, and mental status

Couple's goals for therapy
  Mutual goals, stated clearly and prioritized

Questions and concerns

---

seeking assistance, to identify the factors in the couple's life that contribute to the presenting problems, to clarify whether couples therapy is an appropriate treatment approach, and to identify existing strengths in the couple's relationship that can be used to help resolve the couple's problems (Epstein & Baucom, 2002).

The first assessment decision involves who will be seen for the assessment. One common approach is to see both partners jointly throughout the entire assessment; another is to meet with the couple jointly for the first visit, then to meet individually with each partner, and finally to meet jointly again to discuss the results of the assessment. As with most clinical decisions, there are advantages and disadvantages to each choice. One advantage of meeting with each partner separately is that the therapist can obtain more information about each individual in this format. It also provides a safe environment for discussing sensitive topics such as partner abuse, substance abuse, individual psychopathology, and previous trauma. A disadvantage, however, is that this procedure takes more time and it increases the chance that one or both partners will share information that they do not wish to reveal to their partner. In either case, Epstein & Baucom (2002) recommend obtaining the information shown on Table 12.1.

While the initial assessment is based heavily on the clinical interview and observation of marital interactions during the assessment, a number of self-report questionnaires can provide useful information. See Epstein and Baucom (2002, pp. 217–227) for a discussion of 12 self-report questionnaires that can provide useful information during a couple assessment.

Choosing between Individual, Couple, Group, and Family Therapy

After the assessment, a decision has to be made as to whether to see partners individually, jointly, jointly with the entire family, in group therapy, or in some

TABLE 12.2. Choosing between Individual, Family, Group, and Marital Interventions

Include the whole family in the assessment if possible.
Who plays an active role in the problem(s)?
Who can provide the necessary information?
Who has the power to make the necessary changes?
Whose cooperation do we need? Who is in a position to block the changes if they choose?
Will including this person facilitate change or impede change?
What is/are the goal(s) of therapy?
   To increase family cohesion and interaction
   To strengthen the parents' role in the family
   To increase individuation and autonomy
   ......

combination of the above. See Table 12.2 for a list of factors to consider in choosing between individual, couple, family, and group intervention. This decision often depends on the goals of therapy. If both individuals are primarily interested in improving their relationship, conjoint therapy is likely to be most appropriate and individual therapy alone for the spouses risks increasing strains on the marriage. If work on individual issues is most important, individual therapy may make more sense than marital therapy. If either partner has such severe individual pathology that it would interfere with marital work, that partner may need to be seen individually before marital therapy will be productive.

Individual therapy is not necessarily indicated simply because each of the individuals involved has his or her own problems. Marital intervention can be beneficial for individual problems as well as marital problems. Depression is the primary mental health problem where the idea of using conjoint marital therapy to treat an individual disorder has been studied. Research has found that marital therapy may actually be preferable to individual therapy for maritally discordant couples with a depressed wife. In this case, marital treatment appears to lead to improvement both in the wife's depression and in marital discord whereas individual therapy may lead to improvement in the wife's depression but produce little change in marital discord (Baucom et al., 1998).

When conjoint treatment seems indicated, a common problem is that one spouse says that they want to engage in marital therapy but that their partner refuses to come. When this is the case, it often is useful for the therapist to inquire whether the client has actually asked his or her partner to participate in couple therapy. As strange as it may seem, many clients who report that their partner will not join them in couple therapy have never actually asked the partner whether he or she would be willing to attend. If the client has asked and the partner has refused, it can be useful to have the client to demonstrate how the partner actually was asked. When a spouse has said, "I want you to come so that the therapist can see what a jerk you are," or "You're crazy, you need to see a shrink," it is not terribly surprising if the partner is not eager to attend. The chances of doing couple therapy can be improved if the therapist helps the client practice more diplomatic approaches to inviting their spouse to join in marital therapy. If the partner continues to refuse to attend, the client can be coached in collecting information about the partner's specific objections. Once the specific concerns are understood, it may be possible to find ways to overcome the partner's reluctance.

If, despite the best efforts of the therapist and client, the partner continues to refuse to attend, the therapist may need to work individually with the client rather than pursuing marital therapy. In this situation, it is essential to clarify whether the goal of therapy is to help the client cope with their marital situation, change his or her own behavior, or change the spouse's behavior. It usually is quite difficult for the therapist to work effectively to change the behavior of a spouse who is not participating in the therapy session. Therefore, other goals usually are more promising.

When both individual and couple therapy is needed, the question of whether the therapist should try to do both individual and couple therapy with the same people arises. If a therapist is seeing a client for individual therapy and marital issues arise, should the spouse be invited to join the treatment? Or, if a therapist is seeing a couple for marital therapy and one partner raises individual issues, should the therapist continue to see the couple but, in addition, see one partner individually? This is another clinical question where each option has advantages and disadvantages. One advantage to providing both marital and individual therapy is that moving smoothly from individual to couple therapy can allow for maximal flexibility. The therapist has more information than a new therapist would have, and there is no difficulty coordinating treatment with another therapist who might have an incompatible therapeutic approach. An important disadvantage, however, is that the therapist may have difficulty maintaining an unbiased perspective or may appear biased to one or both of the clients. Also, secrets could be shared in individual sessions that could complicate the couple sessions. In addition, switching from individual to couple sessions and back does change the therapy relationship. It is only viable for a therapist to provide both marital and individual therapy if the pros and cons have been fully discussed and if all of the involved parties (including the therapist) feel comfortable with the idea. The therapist must be careful to anticipate the possible problems and constantly work to maintain a balanced alliance with both individuals. If Axis II problems are present, the therapist may want to be quite cautious about trying to provide both individual and marital therapy.

Establishing a Collaborative Set

The first step in cognitive couple therapy is to establish a collaborative set, an atmosphere conducive to working together (Abrahms, 1983). This can be a major challenge, because many couples come into treatment heavily invested in blaming each other for the problems. To work together effectively, it is important for each individual to accept the idea that he or she plays a role in the problems and to accept the idea that the problems will be resolved only by working together to solve them. Thus, the initial phase of treatment involves careful attention focused on helping partners to switch to a focus on problem solving rather than blaming or retaliating against each other.

Just as individual Cognitive Therapy begins with setting goals for therapy, cognitive couple therapy needs to begin by setting mutual goals. In couple therapy, however, each partner comes into therapy with his or her own goals that are often not clearly articulated and that may not be compatible with their partner's goals. The first step is to get each individual's goals clearly stated. This can begin as a homework assignment, which each partner works on separately between session. Then, the individual goals need to be reframed as mutual goals that are acceptable to both partners. For example, if one of the husband's goals is "I want her to quit nagging about everything," and one of the wife's goals is "I want him to actually do something around the house once in a while," the therapist might suggest "So it sounds like the two of you would like to find a way to agree on what chores are going to be done around the house and to get them done without a lot of nagging."

In developing mutual goals, it is useful to get detailed information about problems and goals, and to focus on specific situations rather than trying to deal with issues in the abstract. For example:

> Brett and Meredith were an unmarried couple who had been living together for the past 3 years. Brett was 42 years old, Meredith was 36 years old, and both had previously been married and divorced. They came into treatment at Meredith's instigation because she was depressed and thought there were problems in the relationship. Brett came along because Meredith asked him to come, but he did not see any point to treatment.
>
> When asked why they were there, Meredith said, "This was really all my idea. Things haven't been going very well at home and I've had a good experience with therapy, so I thought it might be helpful."
>
> When asked why he had come, Brett said, "Well, Meredith gets upset very easily and I certainly don't want her to get depressed again. I don't really think there's anything particularly wrong, but since she gets upset so easily, I figured I'd better go along with her."

It sometimes can require considerable discussion to reach a consensus on goals for therapy, but this important step in the treatment is well worth the effort. After an extended discussion, Meredith and Brett agreed on the goals of: (1) being able to enjoy time together in a way that suited both of them and (2) finding better ways to resolve disagreements and make decisions.

COUNTERACTING NEGATIVE SET

Couples often come into therapy strongly focused on the negative aspects of their partner's behavior. This is understandable because most people find that they tend to automatically focus on the things that are troubling them. However, this can undercut the motivation for therapy, can encourage retaliation rather than collaboration, and can result in there being little reinforcement for small steps toward goals. If it is possible to counteract the negative set, this can improve motivation for therapy, facilitate collaboration, and make it much easier to intervene effectively. There are several ways to bring this about (see Abrahms, 1983).

A useful initial intervention is that the therapist help the couple focus attention on the positives, not just the negatives, in their relationship. A precedent can be set for this in the initial assessment if the therapist asks in detail about what was (and still is) good about the relationship in addition to finding out about the problem areas. In the goal-setting phase of treatment, the therapist can help the couple phrase goals as positives to work toward whenever possible rather than listing problems to eliminate. For example, a goal of, "resolving disagreements peacefully" would have advantages over a goal of, "Not yelling so much." At the beginning of each session, when the therapist asks about how the week went, it can be helpful to ask about positives as well as difficulties. Throughout the course of therapy the therapist can draw attention to realistically positive experiences when they occur.

Especially at the beginning of treatment, the therapist should also consider assigning homework that focuses attention on the positives or attempts to increase the frequency and quality of positive interactions, making sure that the rationale is clear and the clients understand how the homework relates to their goals. Examples of this type of intervention include trying to "catch them being good", trying to do more fun things together, and "caring days" (Stuart, 1980). The idea of "caring days" is to have each partner try to intentionally do at least one nice thing for the other partner each day. If the partners seem at a loss for ideas, each partner could be asked to generate a list of small things that they would personally view as caring and would appreciate receiving from the other. Preferably these would be small acts that would be practical to incorporate into their daily routine. For busy couples, one way to get this exercise off to a fun start is to send the couple to a mall and have them split up and stockpile many small items (greeting cards, small gifts, etc.) that could then be given gradually throughout the following weeks. To increase the focus on the positive, part of the exercise would be for each partner to record not only the caring thing he or she did each day, but also to write down what caring things he or she noticed the partner doing. It is important that any exercises designed to increase positive feelings be set up as experiment, rather than setting up the expectation that they will go smoothly.

Cognitive Interventions

An important intervention in cognitive marital therapy is to help partners identify the cognitions that are related to marital discord, to test the validity or appropriateness of those cognitions, and to modify dysfunctional cognitions (Baucom, Epstein, & LaTaillade, 2002; Beck, 1988; Epstein & Baucom, 2002). As in individual Cognitive Therapy, pinpointing and challenging automatic thoughts can be very useful. Initially, the therapist can ask the couple to describe a situation from the previous week that was upsetting to them, and then elicit the automatic thoughts of each partner. It is much more useful to discuss the thoughts and feelings associated with one specific moment in time than it is to discuss issues in general terms. For example:

> When Brett and Meredith were asked to choose an upsetting time from the prior week to discuss, Meredith mentioned a day when she got home after a long day at work, wanting to talk with Brett. Brett came home and promptly turned on the TV. When asked about how she felt at this time, Meredith reported that she felt sad, angry, and hopeless. When asked what had been running through her mind, she was able to recall thoughts such as,

Situation Briefly describe the situation	Emotion(s) Rate 0-100%	Automatic Thought(s) Try to quote thoughts then rate your belief in each thought 0-100%
Meredith says "Let's go to the Cherry Festival."	Frustrated 80 Annoyed 80 Powerless 60	Why do we have to go to the Cherry festival? 95% I'd rather play golf. 100% I always have to do what she wants. 90%
Morning of festival, Kim says she has to babysit and can't go.	Annoyed 20 Resigned 30	I don't blame her for not wanting to go. 100% There isn't anything I can do about it. 80%
At festival.	Anger 60 Resigned 80	This is boring. 100% This is all Meredith's fault. 80% Why can't she ever just leave me alone? 80%

FIGURE 12.2. Brett's Thought Record.

"He doesn't care about me;" "After all I've done for him, he should care;" and, "There's nothing I can do about it." Although these were her thoughts and feelings at the moment, she didn't say anything to Brett's about wanting to talk and just picked up a book. When Brett was asked about this same event, he said that at the time he had no idea what Meredith was upset. As far as he had known, there was no problem.

Once a specific problematic incident from the previous week has been identified, the couple and the therapist can work together to identify the sequence of events that led up to the problem with an emphasis on the cognitions and behavioral responses that contribute to the problems. Once the couple understands how to pinpoint thoughts, each partner can be sent home to identify his or her own thoughts using a standard thought record (TR) between sessions. They can be asked to write their thoughts whenever they feel upset about the marriage or their partner. It is likely that at times the partners will each write about the same event, but that at other times, only one partner will write about a given event. At first, it is often best if spouses keep their TRs private until they can be discussed in the next marital session to minimize the risk of triggering additional arguments. Later in the treatment, when the partners have been trained to identify, challenge, and discuss thoughts calmly, the partners may share TRs between sessions. For example:

When Brett and Meredith wrote TRs between sessions, they each happened to write about the a local Cherry Festival (Figures 12.2 and 12.3). Both had been upset about the event in different ways. When they were able to discuss the TRs in the couple session, they were each able to get a much clearer understanding of how their thinking led to problems in

Situation Briefly describe the situation	Emotion(s) Rate 0-100%	Automatic Thought(s) Try to quote thoughts then rate your belief in each thought 0-100%
Deciding what to do on the weekend. I say to Brett "Let's go to the Cherry Festival."	Happy 70 Anxious 10 Excited 30	This will give me a chance to get closer to Kim. 90% We'll be together as a family and have a good time together. 95%
Morning of festival, Kim says she has to babysit and can't go.	Hurt 90 Sad 90	She doesn't care about me. 90% She'd go if her mother asked her. 100%
At festival, Brett isn't saying much and doesn't seem to want to do anything.	Hurt 90 Sad 90 Depressed 80	Brett's mad at me. 95% Everything I do comes out wrong. 90% Our relationship isn't going to work out. 80%

FIGURE 12.3. Meredith's Thought Record.

their relationship and their therapists (a co-therapy team) were able to help them identify possible solutions (such as discussing plans in advance, generating rational responses, and being more assertive) that they could test between sessions.

Baucom, Epstein, Sayers, and Sher (1989) discuss five different aspects of cognition that have an impact on marital functioning: selective attention, attributions, expectancies, assumptions, and standards. Each type of cognition can be identified, examined, and challenged in marital Cognitive Therapy when they contribute to marital problems.

Selective Attention

Spouses do not attend equally to all relationship-relevant events, and what they attend to is likely to influence how they feel about the relationship. Once problems have started, selective attention to negative events often occurs and has been called, "the power of negative thinking." Negative thoughts about the partner and the relationship can be generalized into a negative "frame" and perpetuated by selective attention. This negative frame can often be a distortion of what were once considered attractive qualities (sometimes called the "flip–flop factor;" see Abrahms & Spring, 1989). For example:

> Meredith initially saw Brett's calmness as a positive characteristic, but later on, the same behavior seemed like indifference to her. Similarly, Brett originally was attracted to Meredith's energy, and her emotionality made their relationship more exciting. Later in the relationship, however, he complained that she was too volatile and that he found her mood swings to be annoying rather than exciting.

Selective attention can have a major impact on the effectiveness of couple therapy. If partners do not notice positive events that occur in the relationship, gradual changes brought about by therapy may have little effect on marital satisfaction. The interventions designed to create a more collaborative set that were discussed previously can also counteract selective attention to the negative. Even if this intervention has not been used, partners can be asked to keep a log of positive behaviors by their partner on a daily basis or can be taught to reinforce positive behavior as an alternative to focusing on negative behavior.

In the therapy session, the therapist can draw attention to positive behaviors on the part of each partner and can also note when any positives are being ignored. Any shifts in affect during a session can also be an excellent time to inquire regarding automatic thoughts and to bring the positive into focus. Although the TR is often used to examine negative thoughts, it can also be very useful to get partners to notice the times when they felt good about their partner or the relationship and note the automatic thoughts that contribute to more positive feelings.

Attributions

In general, attributions are the cognitions through which people try to explain and evaluate past events. In a relationship, attributions are the conclusions about *why* one's partner does what she or he does, as well as the conclusions one draws about why there are problems in the relationship. These conclusions can make neutral or negative events much more upsetting. For example, when Brett was watching TV instead of talking with Meredith, the fact that Brett was watching TV wasn't nearly as upsetting as Meredith's conclusion that this showed that "He doesn't care about me." Attributions can have a major impact on motivation for change and optimism about overcoming marital problems.

The classic work on the role of attributions in depression is well-known (Abramson, Seligman, & Teasdale, 1978). In their landmark research, these researchers demonstrated that internal, global, and stable attributions about the self can contribute to depression. When there are problems in a relationship, negative internal, global, and stable attributions about the partner can lead to discouragement and anger toward him or her. For example, If one individual is upset because his or her partner came home late, the distress will be more intense if his or her attributions are internal ("It's his fault."), global ("He's always so inconsiderate."), and stable ("He'll never change."). On the other hand, if the partner's attributions are external ("Traffic must have been bad"), specific ("He's considerate in other ways.") and unstable ("He'll try to get home on time in the future."), the upset would be milder. Attributions can also have an important influence on the progress of couple therapy. If one partner notices positive behavior, but makes attributions for the change that discount the importance of the behavior (e.g., "She's only doing that because the therapist said so"), the effect of the positive behavior will be minimized.

The first step in intervening with attributions is to make them explicit. For example:

Brett was in the bathroom and used the last of the toilet paper so he yelled down the hall to ask where the extra toilet paper was. Meredith was offended that he bothered her when she was busy with a phone call especially because the toilet paper was where it was always kept, so she yelled back, "Find it yourself! You should know where it is by now." He yelled back, "I give up, I can't do anything right! Why don't you go ahead and crucify me and get it over with?!" Her response was, "How dare you take that tone with me!" and they didn't talk for the rest of the evening. He read quietly and seemed unconcerned whereas she ruminated about the fight, his previous offenses, and so on. Meredith attributed his not knowing where the toilet paper was to his lack of involvement in the home. "How can he live in the same house for years and not know where we keep the toilet paper!?" She believed that if he cared about the household he would not need to ask. Brett thought that asking her where the toilet paper was to be completely reasonable ("It's easier to ask her than look myself") and concluded that she was acting as she did because she wanted to punish him.

Once problematic attributions have been identified, the partners can be taught to consider other possible explanations and to evaluate the relative validity of their original attribution versus the alternatives. One particularly painful attribution is the attribution of lack of love ("If he cared he wouldn't do that." or "His doing that shows he doesn't love me."). If it is possible to replace attributions of lack of love with more benign attributions, this can be quite helpful.

Expectancies

Although attributions focus on how people explain events that have already occurred, expectancies reflect the individual's attempts to predict what will happen in the future. Expectancies shape behavior in many different situations because individuals typically do not try options that they believe will not work. For example, when Meredith had the expectation, "There's nothing I can do (to make him care)," the result was that she stopped making efforts to please Brett. Unfortunately, if an individual has unrealistically negative expectancies, he or she may not try options that he or she expects to be ineffective but that actually would be effective. If the individual does not try an option, then he or she does not have the opportunity to discover that it actually works.

Expectancies are often based on one partner's perception of the other's behavior during periods of marital discord, and therefore tend to be biased toward the negative. In general, humans attend selectively to information that confirms their expectations and tend to ignore, reject, or discount information that conflicts with their expectations. Therefore, once an individual has a negative expectation regarding the relationship or his or her partner's behavior, the natural tendency is for the negative expectation to persist.

The first step in intervening with expectations is to help clients state them explicitly. Once this has been done, it usually is not difficult to test whether the expectations are realistic either by observing what happens spontaneously in relevant situations or by using behavioral experiments to test whether their partner actually responds the way they expect or not. However, because individuals tend to overlook or discount observations that contradict their preconceptions, it can be important to test expectancies systematically. Otherwise, there is a risk that clients will simply notice experiences that confirm their expectancies and overlook experiences that should disconfirm them.

When an individual has a problematic expectancy that turns out to be realistic, this can provide a good opportunity to work toward more effective problem-solving or to work toward behavior change. For example, suppose that a wife expects "If I ask for what I want, he'll just ignore me" and subsequent observations show that this is indeed the case. The therapist can help the wife explore other ways of getting the response she wants, can help the husband recognize the consequences of ignoring his wife's requests, or can help the couple identify more promising ways for the husband to respond to requests with which he does not wish to comply and test these alternatives in practice. The husband may need to establish a track record of consistently responding to requests before the wife's expectancies will change.

Beliefs and Assumptions

In addition to the dysfunctional beliefs discussed previously in this volume, a number of dysfunctional beliefs about marriage are relatively common and can have a significant impact. For example:

> Meredith held the beliefs that, "If he cared, he'd do what I want without my having to ask," and, "If I do things for someone, he should do the same things for me." Brett held different beliefs, including, "If there's disagreement, the relationship is falling apart," and, "I'm responsible for my partner's feelings." Both sets of beliefs played important roles in their problems.

Assumptions about relationships can effect the process of couple therapy as well. For example, if a spouse believes that relationships cannot change or believes that disagreement is destructive, he or she is unlikely to believe that marital therapy can be effective. Such pessimism about therapy is likely to reduce the extent to which he or she is willing to get involved in the work of the therapy and persist in his or her efforts when the treatment gets difficult.

To intervene with marital beliefs and assumptions, the therapist can use many of the strategies delineated in Chapter 3 regarding schema change. In addition, having the partner present in the session allows the therapist to directly test beliefs in ways that are not an option in individual therapy. For example, it was possible to test Brett's belief disagreement meant that the relationship was falling apart by taking a minor disagreement, having the couple work together to develop a solution that both could live with, and then observing whether this weakened or strengthened their relationship. Many of the common dysfunctional marital beliefs can be tested through behavioral experiments that can be done initially in the session and then tested at home in the real-life situation.

Standards

Standards are the spouse's beliefs about what a good relationship *should* be like and how one's marital partners *should* act. Spouses use their standards as a way of measuring the acceptability of the relationship and of their partner's behavior. Baucom *et al.* (1996) have developed the Inventory of Specific Relationship Standards to measure important relationship standards. Their findings showed that individuals who hold strong relationship-focused standards generally are more satisfied with their marriages. However, they also found that when the partners see their relationship as not meeting their standards, they are more unhappy with the marriage.

The idea that a set of standards can affect a relationship has been formalized in Clifford Sager's concept of "marital contracts" (1976). Sager emphasized the idea that "each partner in a marriage brings to it an individual, unwritten contract, a set of expectations and promises, conscious and unconscious" (p. ix). When people decide to form a relationship, they generally have unspoken expectations that they expect the relationship to fulfill. For example, one of Meredith's unspoken expectations was, "A relationship is where a person can express oneself and get support, no matter what." Brett held the unspoken expectation that, "A relationship is a peaceful place where one can just relax and take it easy." Even though these "marital contracts" may have never been discussed or agreed to, each partner is likely to feel that the other is "breaking the rules" if the relationship does not live up to their unspoken standards.

If the therapist can help each spouse to explicitly state the standards he or she holds for the marriage, the therapist can then use guided discovery to explore whether there are any specific reasons to believe that this is the way it *should* be and can work with the partners to explore the advantages and the disadvantages of continuing to live by this standard. Alternative standards, perhaps ones that are more practical or more acceptable to their partner, can be delineated and the pros and cons of living by the revised standards could be discussed. If the spouses agree on potentially acceptable new standards, they can be tested in the session and, ultimately, at home.

BEHAVIORAL INTERVENTIONS

Cognitions are not the only important factors in a relationship. There also are many behaviors that are necessary to make a relationship work. These include the skills such as communication, assertion, negotiation, and problem solving. Often, cognition and behavior interact in ways that can lead to relationship problems. For example, the more unclear communication is between partners, the easier it is for misinterpretations to occur. In turn, misinterpretations are likely to interfere with effective problem-solving and may generate new problems in the relationship. Dysfunctional cognitions tend to encourage dysfunctional behaviors and negative affect, dysfunctional behaviors and negative affect tend to encourage dysfunctional thoughts, and this all occurs as an on-going cycle of interactions.

The broad range of behavioral interventions can be useful in Cognitive Therapy with couples and extends beyond the scope of this chapter (see Jacobson & Margolin, 1979 for a detailed discussion of behavioral marital therapy). Behavioral techniques can be used both to reduce levels of dysfunctional behavior and to increase the adaptive behaviors that are necessary for a well-functioning relationship. Cognitive Therapy with couples often includes training in communication skills and assertion, training in problem-solving, and using social reinforcement to increase positive interactions.

When behavioral strategies are being used, attention to cognitions can still be helpful. For example, many couples benefit from improving their communication skills, and Gottman's approach (Gottman, Markman, Notarius, & Gonso, 1976) could be used to teach these skills. In addition, it can be useful to identify the cognitions that interfere with communication. These might include expectations regarding the consequences of communicating more clearly ("It won't do any good."), related beliefs ("I shouldn't have to ask."), and attributions ("He won't listen because he doesn't care."). When clients fail to follow through on behavioral assignments or fail to make use of the new skills that they have learned, it can be useful to elicit the automatic thoughts that occur at the point when the individual decides not to follow through on the assignment. It can also be useful to pay attention to the way each partner interprets the results of the assignment.

Just as the concept of acceptance has played an important role in recent developments in the treatment of anxiety disorders (Chapter 5), it has recently received increasing attention in marital therapy. Jacobson and Christensen have developed a variation of cognitive-behavioral marital therapy that adds a focus on acceptance (Christensen, Jacobson, & Babcock, 1995; Jacobson & Christensen, 1996). They advocate two basic strategies for promoting acceptance: tolerance and the use of acceptance to turn problems into vehicles for intimacy. The major techniques they use to promote intimacy-enhancing acceptance are termed "empathic joining around the problem" and "unified detachment from the problem". Empathic joining involves the therapist reformulating the marital problems in terms of common differences between people and understandable emotional reactions to those differences. A special effort is made to underscore the pain that each partner experiences and the efforts, however misdirected, that each makes to accommodate the other. Unified detachment promotes acceptance by encouraging a detached, descriptive, externalized view of the problems. The four primary strategies for promoting tolerance include pointing out the positive features of negative behavior, practicing negative behavior in the therapy session to become desensitized to it, faking negative behavior between sessions (to practice acceptance), and self-care so that spouses can manage better when their partner is unavailable to them.

INTEGRATING COGNITIVE AND SYSTEMS THEORIES

Cognitive-behavioral therapy could be considered a "systems" approach insofar as it emphasizes the interactions between individuals rather than considering each person in isolation. Having a husband who likes to "veg out" when he gets home is not a problem in and of itself, but Meredith's interpreting it as a sign that Brett's didn't care, her withdrawal, and his response to her withdrawal made it a problem in their relationship. Each partner in a couple has a family and personal history that sets the stage for potentially dysfunctional cognitions and behaviors.

Brett and Meredith happened to interact in ways that aggravated their individual problems rather than resolving them.

However, even though cognitive marital therapy addresses the interactions between individuals in the family system, caution is needed when thinking of it as a "systems" approach. The concept of the family as an entity in and of itself makes sense. However, it is crucial not to lose track of which elements are properties of individuals rather than being properties of systems. For example, cognitive therapists recognize that cognitions exist within individuals, not systems. Although members of a couple may share similar beliefs, couples do not have thoughts or beliefs, each individual has his or her own thoughts and beliefs.

Other Issues in Cognitive Marital Therapy

When fear or anxiety interferes with change in one or both partners, it is important to remember that rational responses alone do not eliminate anxiety. It is important to help the individuals "face their fears" in manageable steps within the therapy session or in homework assignments as discussed in Chapter 5.

Angry outbursts on the part of one or both of the spouses are often a problem that needs to be addressed in marital therapy. Although it can be useful to identify the automatic thoughts that elicit the anger and to address any misunderstandings and misinterpretations, it is often more helpful to work with the couple to find more adaptive ways to handle anger before either of them "reaches the exploding point." Often couples attempt to avoid conflict but this can easily have the unintended result of postponing the discussion until one or both of the partners is quite upset. If couples can learn to face conflict before the emotions become too intense and to use their skills in communication and assertion, angry explosions become less frequent and less problematic.

Sometimes couples seek treatment after an extramarital affair. Spring and Spring (1996) present a cognitive approach to helping couples deal with extramarital affairs. Their intervention involves three stages: normalizing the feelings, deciding whether to recommit or not, and rebuilding the relationship. The book is written for the lay person can be used as bibliotherapy in conjunction with couple therapy, with the therapist walking the partners through the process step-by-step.

The Outcome of Cognitive Therapy with Couples

A recent article by Epstein (2001) does an excellent job of summarizing the empirical findings on cognitive-behavioral marital therapy. Many outcome studies have evaluated the effectiveness of the behavioral components of cognitive-behavioral couples therapy, such as communication training, problem-solving training, and behavioral contracting. Reviews and meta-analyses have found that behavioral couple therapy is more effective than waiting list control groups, nonspecific treatments, or placebo control groups. Fewer studies have examined the effects of interventions focused solely on modifying cognitions, and only two published studies (Emmelkamp, van Linden van den Heuvell, Ruephan, Sanderman, Scholing, & Stroink, 1988; Huber & Milstein, 1985) have tested the effectiveness of cognitive interventions unaccompanied by behavioral interventions. These studies found that interventions solely targeting behavior and interventions solely targeting cognitions had comparable effects on self-reported marital adjustment.

Although cognitive therapists have never advocated using cognitive interventions unaccompanied by behavioral interventions, some have argued that there is no need to add cognitive interventions to behavioral marital therapy. The most comprehensive examinations of the relative effectiveness of behavioral interventions versus treatment that included both behavioral and cognitive interventions has been done by Baucom and his colleagues (Baucom & Lester, 1986; Baucom, Sayers, & Sher, 1990) and by Halford, Sanders, and Behrens (1993). The overall finding from these studies was that all treatment groups improved, and that couples were most likely to show improvement on the variables that were the focus of treatment. Neither intervention was superior to the others in improving overall marital adjustment and communication. These findings have at times been interpreted as indicating that adding cognitive interventions to behavioral marital therapy does not increase the effectiveness of couple therapy. However, it is important to note that, to keep the total number of sessions constant across groups, addition of one type of intervention necessitated reducing the number of sessions devoted to the other type of intervention.

The available data suggest that behavioral marital therapy and cognitive marital therapy are both effective and that neither appears to be consistently superior to the other. However, further research is needed into several aspects of cognitive marital therapy. Because behavioral marital therapy and cognitive marital therapy appear to be equally effective overall, research is needed to determine whether matching couples to treatment interventions could enhance the effectiveness of cognitive-behavioral couple therapy. Whisman and Snyder (1997) suggest that existing studies may underestimate the cognitive changes that result from cognitive-behavioral marital therapy because the measures used focus on only a small number of cognitive variables, failing to assess the full range of cognitions important to marital functioning. Research that assesses a broader range of cognitive and behavioral variables would provide a clearer assessment of the effects of cognitive marital therapy. In addition, research is needed to determine whether cognitive interventions are more effective when integrated into a flexible treatment tailored to the needs of individual couples rather than being presented as a skill-building module at a predetermined point in time also would be useful. In clinical practice, cognitive interventions typically are used flexibly and are integrated with other interventions. However, for methodological reasons many research studies implement cognitive interventions as a pre-planned treatment module separate from other interventions. Cognitive-behavioral marital therapy is an effective treatment approach based on a large body of research (see Epstein & Baucom, 2002) but it will be strengthened and refined by additional research.

13

Cognitive Therapy with Children and Adolescents

To some, the idea of doing Cognitive Therapy with children seems absurd: "How are you going to get an 8-year-old to fill out thought records (TRs) and write rational responses?" Others might wonder why a separate discussion of Cognitive Therapy with children and adolescents is needed. After all, don't the principles of Cognitive Therapy apply to children in the same way as they do to adults? The answer to both questions is similar. The general principles of Cognitive Therapy apply to children and adolescents in the same way as they do to adults. However, children and adolescents differ from adults in important ways and significant adjustments are needed if one is to intervene effectively.

Children proceed through a series of stages in cognitive, emotional, moral, and interpersonal development that can influence how they express their thoughts and feelings, what concerns and issues are most important to them, and how they respond to therapeutic interventions. Children, even intelligent and verbal ones, may not have the same skills and capabilities as the average adult. In addition, the family of origin plays a much larger role in the life of children and adolescents than it does in that of the typical adult. Parents often refer the child for treatment and decide whether the child will continue in treatment. They have much more control over the child's life than the therapist does and often are in a position to facilitate or frustrate the therapist's efforts. Finally, the therapist is an adult, not a peer, and this can complicate the therapist–client relationship. If appropriate adjustments are made, Cognitive Therapy can be quite effective with children and adolescents. However, significant adjustments are needed.

ASSESSMENT

It is helpful to note that children and adolescents may be referred for treatment because they *have* a problem, because they *are* a problem, or because an adult *has* a problem *with them*. Many children and adolescents are referred for treatment by parents and teachers who find the child's behavior to be unacceptable but who have been unsuccessful in controlling this behavior. This can occur because the child is engaging in behavior that all would agree is problematic; but it also can occur because the child is engaging in behavior that many would find unremarkable but that the adults in question see as being unacceptable or with which they are unable to cope.

When an adult seeks treatment from a cognitive therapist, we generally proceed with individual therapy without considering whether a different treatment approach is appropriate. However, it is not wise to presume that individual therapy is called for when a child or adolescent is referred for treatment. During the assessment phase, it is important to both develop an understanding of the "identified patient" and to assess whether the situation calls for individual therapy, family therapy, parent training, intervention with the school system, individual therapy for the parent(s), marital therapy for the parents, or a combination of these treatment options. As with adult clients, we need to obtain information about the individual's behavior, thoughts, feelings, and history. In addition, we also need to obtain information about the parents and family, about situations in which the problems occur, and about the family's (and school's) response to the problems. This is most easily done if the parents, and possibly the siblings as well, are included in the initial evaluation. Ideally, the assessment will include all of the individuals who play a significant role in the problems that led to the referral. With young children, much of the initial information is likely to come from the parents, and the assessment may be conducted largely through the therapist meeting with the parents. With older children and adolescents, it can be important for the therapist to both meet with the identified patient alone as well as with the parents and child together because different information may emerge in the two contexts.

Children and adolescents can be diagnosed with most of the problems discussed elsewhere in this volume, and, in addition, they can be diagnosed with a range of problems that usually are first evident in childhood. Discussion of the assessment of each of these disorders is beyond the scope of this chapter. For detailed information regarding the ways in which child development influences assessment of children and adolescents, see Morrison and Anders (1999); for a discussion of structured interviews, behavior rating scales, and methods for assessing a range of specific disorders in children and adolescents, see Shaffer, Lucas, and Richters (1999).

Conceptualization

The basic cognitive processes involved in depression, anxiety, and other disorders function in much the same way in children and adolescents as they do in adults. To a large extent, the cognitive conceptualizations of specific disorders discussed elsewhere in this volume can be applied to children and adolescents. However, adjustments must be made to take the individual's developmental level into account and attention must be paid to the effects of family and peer interactions. Understanding the child's cognitions, emotions, and behaviors provides only a partial understanding of the problems that have resulted in the child's referral to treatment. Family interactions typically play an important role in child and adolescent problems and parents' cognitions can have an important impact on parent–child interactions.

It is often observed that what is annoying to one person may be cherished by another. For example, the active child who challenges adults with questions, socializes with other children instead of paying attention in class, finds the assigned classroom work boring, and moves ahead on his or her own may be seen by one adult as an obstreperous child who should be disciplined whereas another adult may see him or her as a gifted child who should be encouraged. Chapter 12 discussed the ways in which selective attention, attributions, expectancies, assumptions, and standards affect marital interactions and marital satisfaction. It should be obvious that these cognitive factors can have the same effects in parent–child relationships and family interactions. A parent who believes strongly that, "Children should respect their parents," and who sees "respect" as being synonymous with obedience may well see an active, inquisitive child who asks many questions as "disrespectful." If this is the parent's view, he or she is likely to focus selectively on episodes of "disrespect" and to react strongly to them. If the parent responds in a way that is effective in inducing the child to "be more respectful," the problem may subside. However, if the parent's initial attempts are unsuccessful, the stage is set for what has been called the Coercive Behavior Cycle (Barkley, 1997; Barkley, Edwards, & Robin, 1999; see Figure 13.1).

Many parents operate on the assumption that the way to get a child to be good is to punish them for being bad. This strategy is often successful and, when moderate punishment proves to be an effective way to eliminate behavior that the parent finds unacceptable, the situation is not likely to come to professional attention. However, when initial punishments prove to be ineffective, many parents redouble their efforts by being increasingly vigilant for bad behavior and being more vigorous in punishing bad behavior. If more vigorous punishment is effective, the cycle ends and interactions return to normal. However, if more vigorous punishment is ineffective, the cycle continues and becomes more intense. As the parent is increasingly vigilant for bad behavior, he or she is likely to be less attentive to good behavior, to develop an increasingly negative view of the child, and to become increasingly frustrated and angry. The frustration and anger are likely to add to the parent's vigilance for bad behavior and to the intensity of the punishment, without increasing the effectiveness of the punishment. At the same time, the experience of being frequently punished generates anger, resentment, and rebellion on the part of some children, especially if they believe that they are being treated unfairly. At the same time, the parents' frequent remarks about the child's bad behavior accompanied by few comments about good behavior may also result in the child holding an increasingly negative view of himself or herself. The anger, resentment, and rebellion can easily result in an increase in bad behavior whereas the child's negative view of himself or herself and the lack of rewards for good behavior can result in decreasing levels of motivation for good behavior. This Coercive Behavior Cycle can be quite persistent and dysfunctional (Barkley, 1997; Barkley et al., 1999).

Please note that we are not suggesting that discipline is inappropriate or that punishment should never be used as an element of effective discipline. The problem is that when parents engage in a behavior change strategy that proves ineffective,

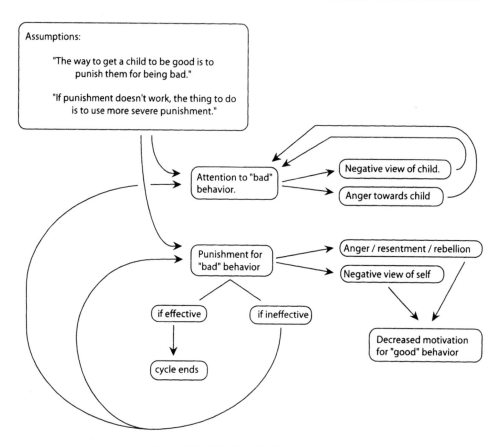

FIGURE 13.1. The Coercive Behavior Cycle.

they often respond by applying the ineffective strategy more persistently and intensely in a way that can be seriously dysfunctional. Alternatively, they may give up and abandon attempts to discipline the child. Unfortunately, either strategy can produce serious problems.

Also, we are not suggesting that the Coercive Behavior Cycle is the only parent–child interaction pattern that can become dysfunctional. Parental fearfulness and overprotection can easily play a role in children's anxiety problems. If parents model pessimistic, self-critical, or aggressive approaches to problem situations, this can have an important influence on the child's development. Likewise, if parents unintentionally reinforce dysfunctional behavior or fail to reinforce adaptive behavior, this can have a significant impact. In short, in conceptualizing the problems presented by children and adolescents who are referred for treatment, we recommend combining the conceptualizations discussed in previous chapters with attention to parent–child interaction patterns. It is not that parents are to blame for their children's problems but that dysfunctional interaction patterns can easily evolve and well-intentioned parents may inadvertently contribute to many problems.

Strategies for Intervention

If the conceptualizations of specific disorders discussed earlier in this volume apply after adjustments are made for the child's developmental level and the influence of family and peers, this implies that some form of intervention focused on modifying the child's cognitions and behavior would be called for. However, if selective attention, attributions, expectancies, assumptions, and standards affect family interactions in much the same way as they affect marital interactions, then family interventions similar to those used with couples (see Chapter 12) would be appropriate. On the other hand, if parent–child interactions play an important role in many problems, this implies that we should work with parents and child together or parents alone to modify those interactions. The first step in developing an effective approach to intervention with children and adolescents is determining whether family intervention, individual therapy, intervention with the parents, or a combination of the above is needed.

Choice of Therapy Format

A number of factors figure into the choice of therapy format (see Table 12.2). If the problems result from poor-parenting skills or ineffective discipline, working with the parents on parenting skills may be sufficient. If destructive parent–child interactions or poor parent–child communication play an important role in the problems, joint sessions with parent(s) and child may be most productive. If the problem is largely a product of the child's thoughts and feelings and is not strongly influenced by interactions within the family, individual therapy for that child may be appropriate. In general, the greater the extent to which the family plays an active role in the problem and the younger the child is, the more likely it is that family therapy or parent training will be needed.

It might seem as though family intervention would be preferred if the problem is primarily "family" in nature and individual therapy would be preferred if the problem is "individual" in nature. However, there are important practical reasons for the family (or other caretakers) to be involved in the therapy even if the child or adolescent has a problem that is primarily individual in nature. After all, parental consent is needed for treatment, the child may not be privy to all of the relevant information, and parents typically provide the transportation and funding that makes therapy possible. A more important reason to involve the family in treatment is that they often have a much stronger influence on the child or adolescent than the therapist does. If the family played a role in the development of the problems and it is not addressed, the therapist is faced with the prospect of trying, in 1 hour a week, to override the effects the family has over the rest of the week. Even if the family played no role in the development of the problems, it provides a potent environment for learning and reinforcement if the parents can be persuaded to actively collaborate with treatment.

Individual therapy without significant parental involvement may be appropriate for older adolescents who are relatively independent of parental influences. However, even when the problems being treated seem to be individual in nature, it can be useful to involve parents in treatment. For example, Cobham, Dadds, and Spence (1998) compared child-focused cognitive-behavioral therapy (CBT) for anxiety disorders with child-focused CBT plus four sessions for parents. These parental sessions included education about the role of the family in childhood anxiety, cognitive restructuring, relaxation training, and contingency management. For anxious children whose parents were not anxious, both treatments were very effective (82.4% and 80% diagnosis-free at the end of treatment). For anxious children whose parents were anxious as well, CBT alone was significantly less effective (38.9% diagnosis free) whereas CBT plus parental involvement was effective (76.5% diagnosis-free). At a 12-month follow-up, the same pattern of results persisted but was no longer statistically significant because the anxious children with anxious parents who received only CBT continued to improve following the conclusion of treatment (59% diagnosis-free at follow-up).

The choice of treatment format can be complicated by the parents' individual problems or problems in the parents' marital relationship. Sometimes the therapist needs to make a difficult clinical decision regarding whom to include in therapy when the situation is far from ideal. For example:

> Jim, aged 14, was referred to an inpatient unit for treatment. The presenting problems were school truancy, suspected drug use (marijuana), "problems at home," and fighting at school. Jim's parents were divorced, but the hospital social worker tried to have them both come in for an appointment to discuss Jim's treatment. Jim lived with his mother as part of the divorce agreement. He rarely saw his father. Jim's mother was unemployed and received SSI disability for a psychiatric disorder. Jim's father was an auto mechanic and lived outside of town in a small auto service station that he owned.
>
> His parents refused to be seen jointly and when the social worker met separately with each parent, she discovered that Jim's mother was schizophrenic and frankly delusional. The mother saw Jim's hospitalization as his being drafted into the army of God. Jim's father was aloof and noncommunicative. The therapist decided to work with Jim and his father but not his mother. Jim's father agreed to have his son live with him as long as Jim helped with household chores and did not "get in the way." This situation was far from ideal but this was the best alternative the therapist could find.

Engaging the Parents

Actively securing the parents' engagement in therapy is quite important. Even if the treatment is going to consist primarily of individual therapy with the child, the parent's consent will be needed for treatment to proceed. If the parents are to play a more important role, their active cooperation will be needed. Securing the parents' engagement typically requires both listening to their concerns and offering information about the nature, goals, focus, and techniques of therapy. By actively encouraging parents (and children) to ask their questions and to express their concerns, the therapist can both avoid problems and model an effective communication style.

Many parents assume that they are being asked to participate in treatment because the therapist believes that the problems are the parent's fault. It can be important to explain that the decision of who to include in therapy is based on choosing the treatment approach that is most likely to be effective, not on deciding who is to blame. Many parents who initially refuse to participate in therapy are willing to do so when they understand that they are not being blamed for the problems and that their participation improves the chance of success.

If the therapist will be meeting individually with the child at times and talking with the parents or family at other times, it is important for everyone involved to understand which communications are confidential and which are not. Otherwise, the child may hesitate to be open with the therapist out of a fear that the therapist will report back to the parents or the parents may feel betrayed when the therapist refuses to betray the child's confidences. With older children and adolescents who are concerned about what the therapist might say to his or her parents, it could be useful to have the child be present or on a second phone whenever the therapist talks with the parents. That way, the child knows whether the therapist is betraying confidences or not.

In working with parents, the clinician must watch for reactions of his or her own that may interfere with therapy. For example:

> Marissa, a doctoral student in clinical psychology reported in supervision that she was very angry at the parents of Alan, an adolescent client of hers. The parents were, in her words, "evil" in demanding a high level of performance in school, on the athletic field, and in the social sphere. When Alan was not elected to a special club in his private school, his parents were angry and disappointed. When confronted and challenged by the therapist, they were quite defensive and stated that election to this club was important to their family and to their "circle." Marissa became quite angry and "explained" to them how their demandingness was inappropriate and reflected narrow, elitist values. Not surprisingly, Alan's parents left the therapy session angry, withdrew Alan from therapy, and wrote a letter complaining to the Clinical Director. In supervision it became clear that Marissa's experiences with her own demanding parents intensified her anger at Alan's parents and interfered with her being able to work with Alan and his parents in a way that was likely to be effective.

Establishing a Collaborative Relationship

It is important to build rapport quickly in working with children and adolescents. Adolescents, in particular, may be quick to judge and may not be willing to give the therapist a second chance. Establishing a collaborative relationship is an important foundation for effective intervention in Cognitive Therapy with children, adolescents, and families just as it is in individual therapy with adults (see Chapter 1 and also Wright & Davis, 1994).

In working to establish a collaborative relationship, it is important for the therapist to adjust his or her vocabulary, metaphors, and examples to be appropriate for the individual's developmental level. However, this does not mean that the therapist should pretend to be a peer. It is a mistake for a middle-aged therapist to pretend to be "cool" when he or she is not. It is better for the therapist to show genuine empathy, respect, and interest and to acknowledge that he or she is no longer young (even though we may hate to admit it). The therapist who is open and honest about what he or she has been told about the child's behavior and shows a genuine interest in hearing the child's side of the story will have greater success in gaining collaboration than one who tries to extract information without revealing what others have said.

In discussing the application of Cognitive Therapy with adolescents, Bedrosian (1981) suggests initiating treatment with an opening such as:

> "Now _____ are concerned with the way things have been going for you, and they feel that there may be a problem that needs attention. It seems like you're not too happy with the way things are going either but you're not sure if you're the one who has the problem and you're not wild about coming in to see me. That makes sense to me.
>
> I can't read minds. All I can do is ask a lot of questions and see if I can find out what's going on and see if I can figure out how to be helpful. I'd like to meet with you two or three more times and maybe meet with your parents too. We'll see how we get along and if there's anything we can work on together."

The intent is for the therapist to communicate that he or she does not necessarily accept the parents' (or the adolescent's) account of the problem, that the adolescent is not necessarily to blame, and that he or she understands and accepts the adolescent's negative feelings about treatment. It is also useful to communicate that therapists do not have special powers but are knowledgeable people who are trying to understand and help, that the therapist will try to work with the adolescent rather than force-feeding therapy to an unwilling participant, and that trying a few sessions of therapy to see what it is like does not mean that the adolescent is making a long-term commitment to therapy.

A collaborative relationship depends on identifying mutually agreeable goals for therapy (see Chapter 1). This is usually a straightforward process when an individual seeks treatment voluntarily but is more complex when the individual enters treatment at the demand of others. Because children and adolescents often enter treatment as parents or teachers think that treatment is necessary, it may take some time and effort to identify goals that are meaningful to the child, which are acceptable to the parents, and which the therapist sees as appropriate. For example:

> Morgan was a 15-year-old girl with a long history of conflict with parents and teachers. Her parents referred her for therapy to "make her behave." Morgan, however, entered therapy with the mind-set that, "Nobody can make me do anything I don't damn well want to!" She denied any distress, blamed all of her problems on parents and teachers, and said that therapy was a pointless waste of time. The therapist first acknowledged Morgan's view that therapy was pointless and expressed the thought that it must be "a pain" to be dragged into therapy against her will. The therapist then proposed that, "If you're going to be stuck meeting with me anyway, it might make sense to see if we can find any way for this to be useful to you." That idea made sense to Morgan but she initially saw no way that therapy could be useful. The therapist proposed several possibilities that did not appeal to Morgan and then suggested, "From what you say, it sounds like your parents are on your back all the time. Would you be interested in seeing if we can find some ways to get your parents off your back?" This possibility appealed to her and provided a basis for working to understand what she could do to "get them off my back." This set the stage for a number of interventions such as helping her anticipate the consequences of her actions and make better choices, improving her impulse control, helping her find better ways to express anger, and helping her better understand her parents' point of view.

A collaborative relationship does not mean that the child or adolescent is in control of the session. In order for therapy to be effective, the therapist must take an active role in the session. Thus, the therapist and the child agree on mutually acceptable goals and on the focus of the session but the therapist decides about the starting and ending times, chooses intervention techniques, maintains the boundaries, and uses contingencies when appropriate.

When family interventions are part of the treatment plan, each member of the family is likely to start with his or her own goals for therapy. For example, the parents may have a goal of getting their son to come home at curfew, the son may have a goal of being allowed to do whatever he wants, and a younger sibling may have a goal of getting everybody to stop fighting. To work collaboratively in family sessions, it is important to develop shared goals that all family members can endorse. Often the therapist needs to take an active role in reframing individual goals in a mutually acceptable way. For example: "So it sounds like the four of you would like to find a way to handle curfew that you all can live with and that eliminates all these arguments. How does that sound as one goal for us to work toward?"

Structuring Therapy in a Way That Suits the Child

Adjustments in the way that therapy is scheduled and structured may be necessary, especially in individual therapy with children and younger adolescents. The average child or adolescent is not accustomed to spending an hour talking face to face with an adult and is not comfortable with the type of face-to-face discussion we customarily use with adult clients. Rather than automatically scheduling a 50-minute session once a week, it may be better to meet for 25-minute sessions twice weekly. Alternatively, it may be helpful to spend part of the time individually with the child and part with parents or family, or to use tasks such as therapeutic board games, drawings, and so on, to facilitate communication.

Many youngsters have difficulty expressing emotions because they have not developed an emotional vocabulary that allows them to describe the full range of positive and negative emotions. Often a child's ability to talk about thoughts and feelings can gradually be improved simply by asking the child to verbally label different emotions (e.g., "When you say you felt 'lousy,' do you mean sad, angry, or scared?"), to describe how he or she feels (e.g., "How does 'sad' feel to you?"), and to differentiate degrees of emotion (e.g., "Think of the saddest you've ever felt.... How did yesterday compare?"). With younger children a chart with drawings of several faces depicting different emotions can be used to help the child label different emotions. However, charts showing dozens of different emotions may be overwhelming for some children.

With young children, play itself can be used as a communication medium. A young child is likely to have difficulty verbalizing his or her thoughts and feelings when asked directly. However, if a stuffed animal (or doll or puppet) is introduced that happens to be in a situation quite similar to the child's situation, the child may well be able to explain what the stuffed animal is thinking or feeling. The therapist then can address the child's dysfunctional thoughts through his or her verbal responses to the animal's concerns and through using animals, dolls, and puppets to role-play alternative responses to problem situations. Although traditional approaches to play therapy tend to assume that play is therapeutic in and of it-self, cognitive-behavioral approaches use play as a communication medium (for an excellent discussion of cognitive-behavioral play therapy see Knell, 1993). With somewhat older children, therapeutic board games can be useful in facilitating communication. However, games that require intense concentration or that divert the child and therapist from focusing on issues relevant to the goals of therapy are likely to be counterproductive.

In using between-session assignments with children and adolescents, it is im-portant to remember that children and adolescents have considerable experience with school homework where the goal is to please the teacher who imposed the assignment without their consent. It is important to maintain a clear distinction be-tween therapeutic assignments and school homework. If children remember that therapeutic tasks are developed with their consent and that the important thing is for the task to be useful to them, they are more likely to follow through on the assignment and they are more likely to find it useful. It can often be useful for parents to be involved in helping children with between-session assignments. In order for parental involvement to be productive, it is important for the parents to understand the rationale behind the assignment, to understand their role in the as-signment, and to refrain from trying to force a reluctant child to do the assignment against his or her will. If therapeutic assignments simply become another occasion for parent–child conflict it is better for the parents not to be involved at all.

COGNITIVE AND BEHAVIORAL TECHNIQUES

A broad range of cognitive and behavioral techniques can be applied with chil-dren and adolescents if appropriate adjustments are made for the child's develop-mental level. Table 13.1 contains suggestions for modifying "standard" cognitive

TABLE 13.1. Making Cognitive Therapy "Child-Friendly"*

Maintain the important components of Cognitive Therapy (a structured and directive approach, collaborative empiricism, guided discovery, identifying and modifying dysfunctional thoughts, and between-session assignments).

Work towards goals that are meaningful to the child.

Communicate genuine interest, understanding, and acceptance.

Be flexible, creative, and playful in applying cognitive and behavioral interventions.

Use a vocabulary suitable for the child's developmental level and use examples and metaphors that the child can relate to.

Simplify interventions as needed and introduce them in manageable steps. Structure treatment so that the child can succeed at each step.

Be gentle in using interventions that increase anxiety. Be sure that the rationale for tolerating increased distress is understood and accepted.

Draw a clear distinction between between-session assignments and homework assignments from school.

Make sure that parents and teachers do not inadvertently reinforce dysfunctional behaviors or punish more adaptive behaviors.

*Adapted from Friedberg et al., 2000.

Table 13.2. Some Cognitive-Behavioral Interventions Used with Children

---

Exposure-based Strategies
  In vivo exposure (usually based on a fear hierarchy)
  Imaginal exposure
  Systematic desensitization (imaginal or *in vivo* exposure paired with relaxation)
  Flooding (imaginal or *in vivo*)

Operant Strategies
  Reinforcement of adaptive behavior and extinction of maladaptive behavior
  Shaping
  Contingency contracting
  Token economy
  (Punishment & aversive conditioning are reserved for seriously maladaptive behavior which must
    be controlled quickly)

Non-operant Behavioral Strategies
  Rehearsal, role-playing
  Behavioral Experiments
  Activity scheduling
  Increasing involvement in activities likely to enhance self-esteem, build self-control, increase peer
    interaction, etc.
  Modeling (filmed, live, participant)

Cognitive Strategies
  Self-instructional training
  Problem-solving training
  Adaptive self-statements

Family-based Strategies
  Training parents in effective discipline, operant strategies, Parent Effectiveness Training, etc.
  Facilitating more effective communication, negotiation, problem-solving, etc.

---

and behavioral techniques for use with children and adolescents. Examples of how these principles have been implemented can be found in Friedberg, Crosby, Friedberg, Rutter, and Knight (2000) and in Dudley (1997).

Interventions Useful in Individual Therapy with Children and Adolescents

Table 13.2 lists some of the more commonly used techniques for Cognitive Therapy with children and adolescents. Ronen's (1995) suggestions regarding which types of intervention are likely to be most promising for a given child are shown in Table 13.3.

The process of identifying and challenging dysfunctional cognitions can be just as valuable for children and adolescents as for adults. However, adjustments need to be made to take the child's developmental level into account. Most children are able to describe their thoughts and feelings in problem situations as long as the therapist remembers to communicate in developmentally appropriate ways. The therapist should simply break the process of identifying dysfunctional thoughts down into small enough steps so that the child is able to succeed at each step and then proceed gradually enough so that the process is not too aversive. However, looking critically at one's own thoughts and developing effective responses

TABLE 13.3. Verbal versus Nonverbal Interventions with Children[*]

Variable	More Appropriate for nonverbal interventions[a]	More Appropriate for verbal interventions[b]
Age	Under 7-years old	From age 10 upward
Cognitive skill level	Less advanced	More advanced
Type of problem	Internalizing, overcontrolled	Externalizing, undercontrolled

[a]Interventions would emphasize play, paint, music, modeling, social reinforcement by therapist, etc., and could include direct environmental interventions.
[b]Interventions would rely more on verbal discussion and verbally-mediated interventions including self-instructional training, adaptive self statements, problem-solving training, etc. Direct environmental interventions would increasingly involve the child in planning and implementing the interventions.
[*]Adapted from Ronen, 1995.

requires relatively advanced thought processes and is likely to be beyond the ability of children and younger adolescents. Instead of expecting children to be able to independently develop "rational responses," the therapist may need to play an active role in developing effective responses to dysfunctional thoughts during the therapy session and then coach the child on how to use those responses between sessions. It can be useful to write the responses that the child finds most helpful on a card that he or she can refer to when a problem situation occurs.

Another alternative that does not require the child to use advanced thought processes is self-instructional training (Meichenbaum, 1977). In this approach, therapist and client plan a sequence of instructions for the individual to follow in problem situations and then practice remembering and following those instructions when problems arise. For example:

> Scott suffered from intense test anxiety whenever he had a math test. He would become anxious the night before the test, would have difficulty sleeping, and would be very anxious during the test. However, his biggest problem was that when he encountered a question that he could not answer, he would persistently try to answer that one question and would not have time to finish the rest of the test. In addition to using many of the interventions discussed in Chapter 5, Scott and his therapist developed a simple set of instructions for him to follow when he encountered a question that he could not answer: "Stop. Take a deep breath and calm down. Go on to the next question. If you can't answer that one, go on until you find a question you can answer. Do all the questions you can answer *then* go back and try the ones you couldn't answer." Next, Scott practiced remembering and following these instructions by imagining a math test being passed out, imagining that there was a question that he could not answer, and imagining himself remembering the instructions and successfully following them. After a week of practice, Scott was successful in following the instructions on an actual test.

When working to increase self-esteem, verbal interventions may be useful. However, it often is easier to increase a child's self-esteem by finding ways for him or her to have the experience of successfully facing challenges. If the child is already achieving some successes but is not receiving much positive feedback, the therapist can call attention to the successes, provide positive feedback himself or herself, can encourage the child to appreciate his or her successes, and can encourage the parents to give genuine positive feedback. If the child is not achieving much success, the therapist can work to identify opportunities for the child to face challenges that are manageable enough that he or she is likely to succeed. Organized sports, youth groups, hobbies, and extracurricular programs can provide good opportunities for this; however, these activities must be chosen carefully as they can also be so demanding that the child is likely to feel like a failure rather than a success. Options that provide a supportive, encouraging environment where progress is noticed and appreciated can be quite useful. Options that provide a critical, demanding environment that punishes mistakes are likely to be counterproductive.

Children and adolescents often benefit from being provided with developmentally appropriate explanations of the problems they are encountering (e.g., "When I'm scared and run away, the fear is worse the next time. If I try it even though I'm scared, it's not as bad as I think and it's less scary next time."). Young clients can also benefit from having the therapist help them think ahead about the consequences of their actions and identify more promising options for dealing with problem situations. Children and adolescents can become better at means–ends thinking and social problem solving through guided practice; but it is important to guide the child through explicitly practicing these skills and applying them in real-life situations. Role-playing problem situations can provide a useful opportunity for the youngster to try out new behaviors in the safety of the therapist's office and get some practice before trying them in real-life situations.

When anxiety interferes with the therapist's efforts to get the child to try new behaviors in real-life situations, it can be important to help the child understand the benefits of facing his or her fears. If the therapist takes a commonplace situation where it is common to experience anxiety and uses guided discovery, it usually is not difficult to help the child realize why it is a good idea to persist despite anxiety. For example:

THERAPIST: Do you have any idea why it would be a good idea to go ahead and try giving your talk in speech class even though it's a little scary?

JOE: I dunno.

THERAPIST: Well imagine a kid (points to empty chair) who is afraid to jump off the high board at the pool. All his friends do it, it looks like fun, but it's scary. What would you say to him?

JOE: Go ahead and do it. You'll get used to it.

THERAPIST: So if you go ahead and do something you're scared of you'll get comfortable with it?

JOE: Yeah. When I was little I was afraid I'd fall off my bicycle and now I ride it all the time.

THERAPIST: Suppose he says, "I want to but it's too scary." What could you suggest to him?

JOE: I dunno.

THERAPIST: Would it help if he started off with the low board and built up to the high board?

JOE: Yeah.

THERAPIST: How would these ideas apply to your speech class?

It can be useful for the therapist to watch for opportunities to model more adaptive behavior throughout the course of therapy. In addition, the therapist can reinforce positive behavior both by noticing it and expressing genuine appreciation and by calling attention to the ways in which the positive behavior produces better results. It can be useful to enlist the school and the parents in modeling and reinforcing the desired behavior as well, if possible.

Interventions Useful in Working with Parents Regarding Their Children's Problems

In working with parents when their child is the "identified patient," it can be quite useful to explore the parent's cognitions. As is the case with marital problems (see Chapter 12), cognitions such as automatic thoughts, expectancies, attributions, unrealistic standards, and dysfunctional interpersonal strategies can play an important role in parent–child interactions. For example:

> Clarise was a single parent with three small children. She sought treatment for her eldest child, Benjamin, who was six. She described Benjamin as "willful" and said that, "He will *not* obey." Benjamin, however, appeared to be a cheerful friendly child who was eager to please. Upon further inquiry, the therapist learned that Clarise believed that Benjamin should remember his chores and do them without reminders from her. She also felt that he should be able to "mind" his younger sisters without becoming frustrated or impatient with them. When he had to be reminded about his chores or had difficulty "minding" his sisters, his mother attributed this to willful disobedience and started to wonder if he had a "bad seed" like his absent father. She seemed not to realize that he actually was remarkable, well-behaved, and responsible for a 6-year-old child. Interventions that focused on helping Clarise to reevaluate her expectations for Benjamin, to develop age-appropriate standards for his behavior, and to increase her attention to his good behavior resolved the problem without any major changes in Benjamin's behavior.

Sometimes parents experience difficulty dealing with behavior problems because they believe that when punishment is ineffective, one should threaten to use increasingly larger punishments. Many parents do not realize that small consequences that are applied consistently are more effective than large consequences that are applied inconsistently. They also may not know that positive consequences for good behavior are usually more effective than negative consequences for bad behavior. In addition, when parents focus on punishing bad behavior, they often fail to pay equal attention to modeling and reinforcing appropriate behavior. Training in more effective parenting, communication, and discipline can be useful to many parents.

When contingency management systems (i.e., systematic application of reinforcers and punishers) are used to help parents deal with behavior problems, it can be useful to involve the child(ren) in the development of the rules and consequences. Children can often be helpful in pointing out problems with proposed rules and in identifying positive and negative consequences that are meaningful to them. Also, children (like adults) are more likely to comply with rules and consequences that they see as reasonable and fair. Older children and adolescents often are less resistant to contingency management systems if they see the proposed rules and consequences as a win-win situation rather than as a way for parents to impose control upon them. For example:

THERAPIST: So the new rule will be, "No TV until your homework is done." How does that sound to everybody?

RYAN: That's just them trying to make me do what they want.

THERAPIST: So it sounds like you feel this is just a way of your parents controlling you.

RYAN: You got it.

THERAPIST: I can see how you wouldn't like that, but let's think this through. From what the five of you have said, it sounds like the current situation is sometimes you do your homework and get to watch TV, sometimes you don't do your homework and get to watch TV, sometimes you do your homework but don't get to watch TV anyway because your Dad is mad about something else, and sometimes there's a big fight and nobody watches TV. Is that about right?

MOM: Yeah. (Others nod)

THERAPIST: (to Ryan) It doesn't sound like you have that much control over whether you watch TV or not. Sometimes you get to watch when you want to and sometimes you don't.

RYAN: (nods)

THERAPIST: If you guys try out the new rule, who's in control of whether you watch TV or not? It seems to me that you'd have a lot of control. If you want to watch TV, all you need to do is get your homework done. If you don't want to watch TV, you don't have to watch it. It seems like you get to decide... and part of the deal is if you do your homework you get to watch TV even if your parents are mad about something else. How does that sound?

RYAN: That's not such a bad deal. (Dad nods)

Often when a therapist is conducting individual therapy with a child or adolescent, the parents can be quite helpful if they are willing to help their child challenge dysfunctional thoughts, practice self-instructions, practice new behaviors, and so on. However, for them to do this effectively, the therapist and the child will need to meet with them to discuss their role, the rationale for the assignment, and how they can be most helpful. Some parents need quite a bit of coaching to be helpful without nagging or being coercive.

Interventions Useful in Cognitive Family Therapy

When Cognitive Therapy is applied in sessions with parents and child or with the entire family, it has much in common with the cognitive approach to couple therapy (see Chapter 12). The therapist has the option of using the interventions that are customarily used in individual therapy but also has the option of directly observing family interactions and working to modify family interactions. In family sessions, it often is more productive to focus directly on modifying family communication and interaction patterns than to spend the time reviewing written assignments.

Once a collaborative relationship has been established and shared goals for family sessions have been developed, it often is useful to begin intervention by facilitating communication and working to increase positive interactions. In many families, misunderstandings persist and problem solving is ineffective due to poor communication between parents and between parents and children. Sometimes improved communication alone results in major improvements. In families that have become enmeshed in the coercive behavior cycle discussed earlier in this chapter, increased attention to positive interactions and an increase in positive communication can be quite useful in decreasing the intensity of this pattern of dysfunctional interactions.

In facilitating communication, the goal is *not* to have the parents treat the children as equals. It is important to reinforce parents' role as the adults in the family and to help them fulfill their parental role effectively whereas simultaneously working to negotiate developmentally appropriate limits for the children. Parents and children can communicate clearly and respect each other's point of view without the parents abandoning their role as decision-makers and disciplinarians. As communication between family members improves, this communication provides a powerful way to address many dysfunctional cognitions. Dysfunctional interpretations of family members' behavior (e.g., "They don't care," or, "They're just doing that to give me a hard time.") often can be addressed effectively if the therapist identifies the dysfunctional cognitions and then "checks them out" by helping each family member involved in the interaction to examine the thoughts and feelings that influences his or her reactions.

It can also be quite useful for the therapist to identify and address dysfunctional interpersonal strategies that play a role in dysfunctional interactions. When a parent feels that being respected by children is essential and believes that the way to be respected is through intimidation, intense conflicts between an intimidating parent and a stubborn child can result. It is possible for the therapist to acknowledge the parent's desire for respect but also help him or her realize that efforts to achieve respect through intimidation are ineffective. If the therapist can then help him or her consider other options for achieving respect, it may be possible to help him or her shift to more promising interpersonal strategies.

One way to help families shift to more adaptive interactions is to adopt a problem-solving approach (Hawton & Kirk, 1989) with the family working together toward a shared goal. The therapist works with the family to help them identify mutually acceptable goals and a range of options for dealing with the problem situations. The therapist then helps them weigh the advantages and disadvantages of the most promising options and to choose an alternative to try. Throughout the problem-solving process there are abundant opportunities for the therapist to facilitate communication, to keep the family focused on working together toward the shared goal, and to address cognitions that interfere with effective problem solving.

In general, changes in family interaction patterns are likely to produce larger and more lasting impacts than changes accomplished in individual therapy with a child. However, family interactions can be complex and difficult to change and not all problems are amenable to family intervention. Often it works well to combine family therapy, individual therapy for the child, and parent training. For an in-depth discussion of CBT with families see Epstein, Schlesinger, and Dryden (1988).

Conclusions

Research into Cognitive Therapy with children and adolescents is less advanced than research into Cognitive Therapy with adults. However, outcome studies have found Cognitive Therapy and related cognitive-behavioral approaches to be effective with a wide range of problems. For example, Cognitive Therapy or closely related approaches have been found to be effective in treating depression in adolescents (Reinecke & Ryan, 1998), childhood Obsessive–Compulsive Disorder (Piacentini, Bergman, Jacobs, McCracken, & Kretchman, 2002), and adolescents with Social Phobia and depression (Hayward, Varady, Albano, Thienemann, Henderson, & Schatzberg, 2000). More research will be needed to determine how to best tailor Cognitive Therapy to the needs of children and adolescents and to test its effectiveness with the full range of problems. However, the available research is quite encouraging.

This chapter has discussed the application of Cognitive Therapy to children and adolescents. Due to space limitations it has not been possible to discuss the treatment of specific disorders in detail. Readers who want to cover this topic in more depth will find that Reinecke, Dattilio and Freeman (1996) cover a wide range of specific disorders whereas Wilkes, Belsher, Rush, Frank, and colleagues (1994) and March (1995) cover the treatment of depression and of anxiety disorders, respectively, in depth.

V

Conclusion

14

The Practice of Cognitive Therapy

Although the principles on which Cognitive Therapy is based are fairly straight-forward, the application of these principles to understanding specific disorders is frequently complex, and the practice of Cognitive Therapy can be quite challenging. The purpose of this concluding chapter is to provide suggestions for assessing and improving your skills in the practice of Cognitive Therapy. Fortunately, there are good options for improving your skill in Cognitive Therapy even if you do not have easy access to a formal training program.

OPTIONS FOR DEVELOPING YOUR SKILL IN COGNITIVE THERAPY

Read Widely

One does not become a skilled cognitive therapist simply by reading a few books, any more than one becomes a skilled psychoanalyst by reading a volume or two of Freud. Despite this, reading is certainly a good idea. Many excellent texts present cognitive-behavioral approaches to treating specific disorders (see Appendix B) and new works appear on a regular basis. For additional recomm-ended readings on many different aspects of Cognitive Therapy, visit the Cognitive Therapy Forum at Behavior On Line (http://www.behavior.net/forums/cognitive/).

Many articles on Cognitive Therapy are published in "mainstream" journals in psychology and psychiatry. In addition, three specialized journals are particu-larly valuable: *Cognitive and Behavioral Practice* is an excellent journal with a strong empirical base that focuses specifically on real-life clinical practice; *The Journal of Cognitive Psychotherapy: An International Quarterly* is oriented toward clinical prac-tice and publishes clinical and theoretical papers as well as empirical papers that are clinically applicable; and *Cognitive Therapy and Research* is a research-oriented journal that publishes many empirical studies as well as a limited number of the-oretical or clinically oriented articles.

Obtain Feedback from Clients

Because there is a limit to the extent to which reading alone can convey skill in the practice of Cognitive Therapy, it is important to make use of other learning options as well. Feedback is important in developing any skill but it is often hard for a therapist to obtain the kind of clear, specific feedback that is needed to identify strengths and pinpoint the areas of therapy in which improvement is needed. Fortunately, a cognitive therapist can obtain valuable feedback about his or her practice of Cognitive Therapy in a variety of ways.

Valuable feedback can come from one's clients. The cognitive approach to therapy advocates soliciting feedback from clients regularly, with the therapist either asking for feedback about today's session toward the end of the session or asking for feedback about the previous session near the beginning of the next session. This feedback lets the therapist know whether he or she is understanding the client and can be particularly valuable in identifying problems in the therapist–client relationship before they disrupt therapy.

To obtain useful feedback, the therapist needs to do more than ask for feedback in an open-ended way (e.g., "How do you feel about the way therapy is going?"). Many clients are hesitant to be assertive with their therapist and are likely to respond with nonspecific positive feedback ("It's fine.") even if they are dissatisfied with some aspects of therapy. It is important for the therapist to explicitly ask for negative feedback (e.g., "Have you noticed any problems?" or "What would you like us to do differently?"). The therapist also needs to respond to negative feedback by taking it seriously, responding nondefensively, and letting the client know that he or she appreciates the client's speaking up.

In addition to soliciting feedback verbally during sessions, the Client's Report of Session Form (Figure 14.1) can be used as well. Although it may seem redundant to use this form if verbal feedback has been requested during the session, the written form has several important advantages. First, some clients who are hesitant to express negative feedback are more willing to communicate it in writing than they are in a face-to-face conversation. Second, this written feedback can be quite useful when reviewing a case over time. Finally, the therapist can obtain useful information about the accuracy of his or her self-perception by completing the Therapist's Report of Session Form (Figure 14.2) and comparing his or her ratings of the session with the client's.

Self-Assessment

By maintaining session notes and reviewing them periodically, the therapist can review a case over time and obtain a clearer view of the process and progress of therapy than is possible on a session-by-session basis. If scores on the Beck Depression Inventory (BDI) or other relevant measures are used weekly to monitor progress, a graph of the client's progress from week to week can be combined with a review of the therapist's notes to identify both problems that arise and interventions that are particularly effective.

A number of Cognitive Therapy rating scales have been developed that can provide a method for assessing the quality of a therapy session and providing this type of feedback (Beck, Rush, et al., 1979, pp. 404–407; Hollon et al., 1988; Young & Beck, 1980). Scales such as these both allow a therapist to assess his or her own performance and allow a supervisor or colleague to provide clear,

1. What did you cover today that is important for you to remember?

2. How well do you feel your therapist understood you today?

   (Rate 0-10, where 10 is their completely understanding you)

3. How much did you feel you could trust your therapist today?

   (Rate 0-10, where 10 is completely trusting your therapist with no reservations)

4. Was there anything that bothered you about therapy today? If so, what was it?

5. Is there anything that you would like to have be different about therapy? If so, what?

6. How much homework had you done for therapy today? How likely are you to do the new

   homework?

8. What do you want to be sure to cover in the next session?

FIGURE 14.1. Client's Report of Session Form.
Source: Adapted from J. Beck, 1995

unambiguous feedback on a therapy session whether observed live or recorded. An up-to-date version of the Cognitive Therapy Scale (CTS) and manual regarding it's use can be found on the Academy of Cognitive Therapy's Web site (http://wwwAcademyofCT.org). The CTS was originally used as a training tool and as a means of assessing the extent to which therapists were adhering to treatment protocols in outcome studies. Vallis, Shaw, and Dobson (1986) studied the psychometric properties of the CTS, and the revised version is designed to remedy the weaknesses and bolster the strengths they observed through greater clarity of description, greater specificity of items, and a more detailed scoring manual.

Cognitive Therapy rating scales can be used most productively if several cautions are kept in mind. When Cognitive Therapy rating scales are used for self-assessment, it is important to make audio or video recordings of the sessions and then to complete the scale while reviewing the recording. It is virtually impossible

1. What did you cover today that is important for the client to remember?

2. How well do you feel that you understood the client today?

    (Rate 0-10, where 10 is completely understanding the client)

3. How much do you feel that the client trusted you today ?

    (Rate 0-10, where 10 is their completely trusting you with no reservations)

4. Was there anything that bothered the client about therapy today? If so, what was it?

5. Is there anything that you would like to have been different about therapy? If so, what?

6. How much homework had the client done for therapy today? How likely are they to do the

    new homework?

8. What do you want to be sure to cover in the next session?

FIGURE 14.2. Therapist's Report of Session Form.

to accurately observe a session while fully participating in it, therefore completing the CTS from memory following a session is not likely to provide much useful feedback. However, if the CTS is completed as one reviews a recording of the session, the feedback can be quite useful. Remember that the aim of these scales is to identify the therapist's specific strengths and weaknesses rather that to provide a global rating of the quality of the therapy session. The information they provide is most useful when raters focus on the specific content of each item and base their ratings on the criteria provided.

One potential problem to be aware of in utilizing the CTS and other Cognitive Therapy rating scales is the "halo effect." When the evaluator perceives a therapist as generally good or generally bad, this can bias the ratings on individual items unless the evaluator makes a point of adhering to the criteria specified for each item. A second potential problem is that some evaluators use their own idiosyncratic notions of what a particular rating means rather than utilizing the operational definitions given with the scale. In order for the ratings to provide useful feedback, the person using the scale must make an effort to remain objective and to adhere to the scale's definitions of ratings. A brief discussion of each of the CTS items are as follows:

1. *Agenda setting.* At the beginning of each Cognitive Therapy session, the therapist and client are expected to jointly establish an agenda that specifies both topics to be addressed during the session and how the time will be allocated. This helps insure that the most pertinent issues are addressed and that the available time is used efficiently (Beck, 1976, pp. 224–300; Beck, Rush, et al., 1979, pp. 77–78, 93–98, 167–208). Some of the most common mistakes observed in agenda setting are as follows: (1) failure to agree on specific problems to focus on, (2) a lack of collaboration in agenda setting, (3) a tendency to skip from problem to problem during the session rather than persistently seeking a satisfactory solution to one problem at a time, (4) failure to adhere to the agreed upon agenda, and (5) rigid adherence to the agenda when it would be more appropriate to modify it. If, later in the session, it becomes clear that the agenda should be modified, changes should be made collaboratively and the rationale for changing the agenda should be stated explicitly.

2. *Feedback.* It is valuable for the therapist to elicit feedback about the previous therapy session at the beginning of each session and to elicit feedback about the current session at the close of each session. He or she should also check periodically during the session to be sure that the client understands the therapist's interventions, formulations, and line of reasoning, and that the therapist has accurately understood the client's main points (Beck, Rush, et al., 1979, pp. 81–84). Many therapists fail to do this or do so only intermittently and superficially, thus allowing misunderstandings or other problems to develop to the point that they disrupt therapy.

3. *Collaboration.* A collaborative approach is central to Cognitive Therapy. It helps insure that the client and therapist have compatible goals at each point in the course of treatment, it minimizes resistance, and it helps prevent misunderstandings between the client and therapist (Beck, 1976, pp. 220–221; Beck, Rush, et al., 1979, pp. 50–54). It is important for the therapist to make active efforts to work with the client without arbitrarily taking control of the session or passively following the client's direction. This requires establishing a comfortable working relationship, striking a balance between being directive on the one hand and allowing the client to make choices and take responsibility on the other, soliciting and respecting the client's input, and explaining the rationale behind the therapist's recommendations and interventions.

4. *Pacing and efficient use of time.* The therapist should maintain sufficient control over the session to insure that the agenda is followed. To achieve this, he or she should limit discussion of peripheral issues or unproductive discussion of major topics, and any unfinished business should be rescheduled (Beck, Rush, et al., 1979, pp. 65–66). The pacing of a session

is quite important. If the therapist belabors a point after the client has already grasped the message or gathers much more data than is necessary before intervening, the session will be slow and inefficient. However, if the therapist moves on rapidly before the client has had an opportunity to integrate a new perspective or intervenes before he or she has gathered enough data, interventions are likely to be ineffective.

5. *Empathy skills.* An important quality of effective therapists is their ability to step into the client's world, understand the way he or she experiences life, and convey this understanding to the client (Beck, Rush, *et al.*, 1979, pp. 47–49). Therapists should be sensitive both to what the client explicitly says and to what the client conveys through tone of voice and nonverbal responses. In addition, they should communicate this understanding by rephrasing or summarizing what the client has said and by reflecting what the client seems to be feeling. The therapist's tone of voice and nonverbal responses should convey a sympathetic understanding of the client's point of view (although the therapist must maintain objectivity toward the client's problems).

6. *Interpersonal effectiveness.* The cognitive therapist should display warmth, concern, confidence, and genuineness in addition to empathy (Beck, Rush, *et al.*, 1979, pp. 45–47, 49–50). He or she should not act in a manner that seems patronizing, condescending, indifferent, or evasive. In the course of questioning the client's point of view, it is important to avoid appearing critical, disapproving, or ridiculing of the client's perspective.

7. *Professionalism.* It is important for the therapist to convey a relaxed confidence and a professional manner without seeming distant or cold. This can serve as a partial antidote for any pessimism or hopelessness the client feels and make it easier for the therapist to take a directive role in therapy and to be convincing in expressing alternative points of view. Professionalism involves acting and dressing the part of the professional while remaining warm and supportive.

8. *Guided discovery.* One of the most basic strategies of Cognitive Therapy is the use of exploration and questioning to help clients see new perspectives rather than debating, persuading, cross–examining, or lecturing (Beck, Rush, *et al.*, 1979, pp. 66–71). This is not to say that the effective cognitive therapist relies solely, or even primarily, on guided discovery in all sessions. There are times when it is important for the therapist to provide information, confront, explain, teach, self-disclose, etc., rather than use questions to guide the client in finding his or her own solutions. The balance between questioning and other modes of intervention depends on the specific problem being dealt with, the particular client, and the point of therapy. However, guided discovery has many advantages. Clients often adopt new perspectives more readily when they come to their own conclusions than when they are persuaded to adopt the therapist's conclusions. In addition, at the same time that the client is gaining a new perspective through guided discovery, he or she is also learning an approach to dealing with problems

that, hopefully, will enable the client to handle problem situations effectively without the therapist's help.

9. *Case conceptualization.* As has been stressed previously, Cognitive Therapy is intended as a strategic approach in which the therapist's conceptualization of the client's problems forms a basis for a systematic approach to intervention (Beck, 1976, pp. 6–131, 233–300 (esp. 257–262); Beck, Rush, *et al.*, 1979, pp. 104–271). Unless the therapist happens to discuss his or her conceptualization with the client in the course of a given session, an observer will not be certain what the therapist's conceptualization is. However, the effects of the therapist's conceptualization (or lack thereof) will be apparent. When the various interventions used during the session seem to "hang together," make sense to the observer, and appear to be "on target," it suggests that the therapist is basing interventions on a coherent understanding of the client's problems. Without a coherent conceptualization to provide a framework to guide intervention, the session is likely to appear disorganized, interventions are likely to appear disconnected, and the session is less likely to be productive.

10. *Focus on key cognitions.* A focus on specific cognitions is clearly central to Cognitive Therapy. Throughout each session, the therapist needs to constantly choose which automatic thoughts, beliefs, attributions, etc., to focus on, which to postpone until a later date, and which to overlook completely. Obviously, session time will be used most productively if the therapist focuses on cognitions that are both important and appropriate for intervention at that point in therapy (Beck, 1976, pp. 6–131, 246–257; Beck, Rush, *et al.*, 1979, pp. 142–152, 163–166, 244–252).

11. *Application of cognitive techniques and behavioral techniques.* A wide range of intervention techniques are available for use in Cognitive Therapy (this volume, Chapter 2; Beck, 1976, pp. 233–300, esp. 257–262; Beck, Rush, *et al.*, 1979, pp. 142–166, 168–206, 345). However, to be effective, these techniques must be used skillfully. Commonly observed problems include the therapist's overlooking promising intervention techniques, overusing a few techniques rather than choosing from a large repertoire of techniques, perseverating with a technique that has proven ineffective rather than trying alternative approaches. Additional problems include attempting to use a technique clinically before having mastered it and failing to integrate individual techniques into a coherent treatment approach.

12. *Homework.* Cognitive Therapy does not occur exclusively within the hour or two per week spent with the therapist. Homework assignments "custom tailored" to help the client test hypotheses, incorporate new perspectives, or experiment with new behavior outside the therapy session are crucial for progress (Beck, Rush, *et al.*, 1979, pp. 272–294). Near the beginning of a typical session, the therapist should review the results of the homework from the previous session and address any problems with noncompliance. Toward the close of the session, the therapist needs to collaboratively develop a new assignment, make sure the rationale for it is clear, and elicit

the client's reactions to it. Commonly observed problems include failing to develop a homework assignment, reviewing the previous assignment superficially (or not at all), and assigning homework rather than developing assignments collaboratively. Other common problems include using assignments that are not sufficiently clear and specific or that are not tailored to the individual client and the goals of therapy at the moment.

Some therapists learning Cognitive Therapy assume that some of the emphasis placed on the "details" of Cognitive Therapy such as agenda setting and soliciting feedback is unnecessary and that all they need to do is master the general concepts and the major techniques. However, the emphasis on these details is based on extensive experience both in the practice of Cognitive Therapy and in the training of therapists. We strongly recommend that therapists master the ability to do Cognitive Therapy "by the book" and exercise caution in modifying the approach to suit their personal preferences. It is certainly true that there is room for improvement in Cognitive Therapy and that some modifications of the approach will do no harm or may even enhance its effectiveness. However, several studies have found that cognitive therapists who adhere to the model (as assessed by the various Cognitive Therapy rating scales) are more effective than those who deviate from it (for example, Luborsky, McLellan, Woody, O'Brian, & Auerbach, 1985).

Formal Training in Cognitive Therapy

Formal workshops and courses in Cognitive Therapy clearly offer much that is difficult to obtain through reading, self-assessment, and client feedback alone. Because it is a relatively new approach, there are many clinicians who are interested in Cognitive Therapy but who did not have access to courses in Cognitive Therapy as part of their graduate education. Training programs in Cognitive Therapy are now much more accessible to practicing therapists than has been the case in the past. At one time, persons interested in training in Cognitive Therapy had no recourse but to travel to Philadelphia to study with A. T. Beck and his colleagues. This training generally consisted of a 1-to 2-year, full-time fellowship that involved seeing clients under supervision, didactic seminars, case discussions, and participation in research. The total number of therapists that can be trained in this intensive and comprehensive manner is, of course, limited; and therapists already in practice would have great difficulty suspending their practices for a year or two to pursue this type of training. Fortunately, there are now Cognitive Therapy programs in many locations across the United States and in Europe and training is offered in many different formats.

Workshops and seminars offer some of the most accessible training in Cognitive Therapy that is available. These are often sponsored by state and regional associations, hospitals, mental health centers, or colleges and universities and are available at a number of national conventions. In particular, the annual convention of the Association for Advancement of Behavior Therapy (AABT) usually offers a number of workshops and preconvention institutes on Cognitive Therapy as well as many papers and symposia that are relevant to Cognitive Therapy. Many workshops last for a single day or less, and thus allow little time for anything but didactic presentations. When longer workshops are offered, they often allow the workshop participants an opportunity to practice the techniques presented in role-plays or other experiential exercises and to discuss clients with whom they are working. The ideal format is for a one- or two-day workshop to be followed by another session a few weeks later so that workshop participants have the opportunity to try the interventions they have learned in practice and then discuss their experiences.

Obviously, a more extended training format has substantial advantages. Several centers in the United States currently offer year-long training programs in Cognitive Therapy that are designed for practicing mental health professionals. These programs generally meet regularly over a period of 10 months and cover the principles of Cognitive Therapy, the application of these principles with a range of disorders, and on-going consultation on clients seen by course participants. The Academy of Cognitive Therapy maintains a listing of training opportunities on their Web site (http://www.AcademyofCT.org) and other information about training opportunities can be found in the Cognitive Therapy Forum at Behavior OnLine (http://www.behavior.net/forums/cognitive).

Supervision in Cognitive Therapy

When expert supervision is available, this is the most effective way to develop skill in the practice of Cognitive Therapy. Several models of supervision have been used in training cognitive therapists. These include (1) the traditional preceptor model in which supervisor and supervisee meet regularly to discuss the supervisee's experiences and problems with clients; (2) an apprenticeship model of training in which the trainee works with a more experienced therapist and gradually takes increasing responsibility for conducting the therapy session as his or her skill grows (Moorey & Burns, 1983); and (3) group supervision (Childress & Burns, 1983).

Whatever the format being used, it is important that the approach to supervision in Cognitive Therapy parallel the approach used in therapy. After the supervisor assesses the trainee's skills and background in Cognitive Therapy, the supervisor and supervisee(s) should agree on mutual goals for supervision and endeavor to work collaboratively and efficiently toward those goals. Practices such as agreeing on an agenda for each supervisory session, emphasizing guided discovery, focusing on specific problem situations, use of "homework assignments," and encouraging explicit feedback are as valuable in supervision as they are in therapy.

It is especially valuable to use more than just verbal discussion in supervision. By reviewing videotapes or audiotapes of therapy sessions or observing live therapy sessions, the supervisor can get a clear picture of exactly what goes on in the therapy session and can use the Cognitive Therapy rating scales discussed earlier to provide valuable feedback. Role-playing of therapist–client interactions with the supervisor or another trainee can give valuable practice in executing interventions and can provide an opportunity to experiment with alternative approaches to a particular problem. By reversing roles so that the supervisee plays the client and the supervisor plays the therapist, supervisees can learn from the therapist's example as well as gaining insight into the client's perspective. Finally, by framing conceptualizations of clients as hypotheses to be tested in subsequent therapy sessions, the supervisor and supervisee frequently can replace theoretical debates with data collection and avoid being misled by preconceptions.

It is important for supervisor not to focus solely on conceptualizations and intervention techniques. The supervisor must be alert for therapeutic "blind spots" that the supervisee may have. The use of audio and video recordings or direct observation of therapy sessions is invaluable for this purpose, because the clinician's blind spots may not be apparent from his or her description of the session. Although the supervisor–supervisee relationship should not become psychotherapeutic, it may well be necessary to help the supervisee address some of his or her dysfunctional thoughts or beliefs to overcome difficulties with certain problems or types of clients. Although supervision may well be personally beneficial for the trainee, there is a major difference between supervision and therapy. The goal in supervision is to develop the trainee's skills in therapy, and his or her personal problems need to be addressed only insofar as they interfere with his or her being an effective therapist.

Workshops and courses in Cognitive Therapy are available in many areas, but supervised experience may be more difficult to obtain if one does not live near an established Cognitive Therapy program. Readers who are interested in locating individuals who are qualified to provide supervision in Cognitive Therapy may want to consult the referral directory of the Academy of Cognitive Therapy (http://www.AcademyofCT.org).

Another valuable, but underutilized, option for developing skill in Cognitive Therapy is a regularly scheduled consultation group consisting of peers who are also interested in improving their skills in Cognitive Therapy. Although it might seem at first glance that consultation with peers who are no more expert than oneself would have little to offer, one does not have to be a superior player to be an excellent coach. Nonexpert peers can offer each other valuable feedback and support, particularly if audiotapes or videotapes of therapy sessions are reviewed using one of the Cognitive Therapy rating scales. It is important for consultation groups to collaboratively set an agenda, to regularly elicit feedback from all group members, and to establish an atmosphere of mutual respect and openness to criticism. Time spent in presenting detailed case histories or in abstract theoretical discussions often is minimally productive. Groups generally find it much more useful to make sure that the goal of each discussion is clear, to present background information concisely, to focus on specific therapist–client interactions or problem situations, and to use videotapes and role-plays when possible.

Extramural Training

One response to the limited availability of training and supervision in Cognitive Therapy has been the development of extramural training programs. This involves the participants coming to a center that offers such training for an initial workshop, and for three or four weekend workshops throughout the year. Between workshops each participant submits a weekly video or audiotape of a therapy session by mail for supervision. The supervisor evaluates the tapes and supervision sessions are conducted by phone. This provides training and supervision in areas where neither is readily available. The most widely known extramural training program is offered by the Beck Institute (http://www.BeckInstitute.org).

Distance Education

The growth of the Internet is likely to expand the availability of training in Cognitive Therapy in coming years. However, distance education in Cognitive Therapy is not yet well developed. Organizations such as the Cleveland Center for Cognitive Therapy[1] offer training over videoconferencing links for organizations but the expense involved makes this impractical for individuals who are seeking training. Educational materials on videotape or audiotape are offered by a number of organizations including the Center for Cognitive Therapy in Huntington Beach, CA[2], the Atlanta Center for Cognitive Therapy[3], and the Obsessive–Compulsive Foundation[4]. At present, the distance education options that are available do not yet provide the individual practitioner with an opportunity that is equivalent to enrolling in an intensive training program. However, some excellent materials are available and additional developments in distance education are anticipated.

Information, Resources, and Discussion via the Internet

A wide variety of resources for cognitive therapists are available over the Internet and even more are likely to be available in the future. However, because the Internet is noted for its rapid rate of change, it is difficult to make concrete recommendations without running the risk that the recommendations will be out of date before this volume appears in print. A good starting point for those interested in locating useful resources on the Internet is *The Insider's Guide to Mental Health Resources Online* (Grohol, 1997), which provides a very good overview of available resources and which stays up-to-date through an accompanying Web site.

Several professional associations maintain useful Web sites. The Academy of Cognitive Therapy's Web site (http:///www.AcademyofCT.org) was mentioned earlier as a source of information about training in Cognitive Therapy. It also provides information about obtaining certification in Cognitive Therapy, locating

---

[1] Cleveland Center for Cognitive Therapy, 24400 Highpoint Road, Suite 9, Beachwood, OH 44122. http://www.BehavioralHealthAssoc.com/About_BHA/Educational_Programs/educational_programs.html

[2] The Center for Cognitive Therapy, 22022 Hula Circle, Huntington Beach, CA 92646 http://www.padesky.com/

[3] Atlanta Center for Cognitive Therapy, 1772 Century Boulevard, Atlanta, GA 30345. http://www.cognitiveatlanta.com/

[4] Obsessive–Compulsive Foundation, Inc., 337 Notch Hill Road, North Branford, CT 06471. http://www.ocfoundation.org/

cognitive therapists in your area, and links to other resources. Despite its name, the Association for Advancement of Behavior Therapy is largely cognitive-behavioral in orientation and its Web site (http://www.aabt.org) provides useful information about training opportunities, locating cognitive-behavioral therapists in your area, client-education materials, and links to other resources. The International Association for Cognitive Psychotherapy's Web site (http://iacp.asu.edu/) also includes links to useful resources with a more international focus.

The Cognitive Therapy Forum at Behavior OnLine provides a lively discussion of topics related to Cognitive Therapy that is free and open to all mental health professionals and graduate students. This site includes information about new developments in Cognitive Therapy, discussions of clinical and theoretical issues, and links to other resources on the Internet. It also provides an opportunity to ask questions about any aspect of Cognitive Therapy. The Cognitive Therapy Forum can be found at http://www.behavior.net/forums/cognitive/

Conclusions

For both the experienced clinician and the neophyte, the task of developing skill in the practice of Cognitive Therapy is easier when formal training and expert supervision are available. However, if a therapist is receptive to feedback from clients, assesses his or her own performance on a regular basis, and takes advantage of opportunities for peer consultation, those without access to formal training programs can master the skills as well. It is important to remember that skill in Cognitive Therapy is not a static entity that is permanently ingrained once it has been obtained. It is incumbent upon even the most skilled therapist to periodically assess his or her performance, to consult with colleagues regularly, and to keep abreast of new developments in this rapidly developing field.

Appendix A
Clinician's Initial Evaluation

Therapist:_____

Date:_____

Name:_____ DOB:_____ Age:_____ Sex:_____

Address:_____ Phone: (H)_____

_____ (W)_____

In Case of Emergency:_____ Phone(s):_____

I. Primary Presenting Problem(s)
  1. Nature of current problem/symptoms
    1. When and where does the problem occur, when and where is it most severe?
    2. What thoughts, images, and emotions are experienced at these times?
    3. When did the problem start? Were there any precipitants? How has the problem progressed?
    4. Have similar problems occurred previously?
    5. Why seek help now?
  2. What is your understanding of why you have this problem and what needs to be done about it?
  3. What have you done to help yourself, how well has it worked?

II. Other Presenting Problems (What other problems do you currently have?)
  1. Nature of current problem/symptoms
    1. When and where does the problem occur, when and where is it most severe?
    2. What thoughts, images, and emotions are experienced at these times?
    3. When did the problem start? Were there any precipitants? How has the problem progressed?
    4. Have similar problems occurred previously?
    5. Why seek help now?

Problem #2	Problem #3	Problem #4

III. Depression/Suicidality/Homicidality
   1. (If the client hasn't mentioned depression) With the problems you've described, have you been feeling depressed?
   2. Have you ever had any thoughts of harming yourself or others?
   3. (If so) Have you made any plans? Any attempts? Do you have any thoughts of suicide currently?

IV. Current Life Situation
   1. With whom are you currently living? How is that going currently?
   2. Can you describe what you do on a typical weekday, starting from the time you get up?
   3. How do you spend your weekends? Has this changed since your present difficulties began?
   4. (If work or school) Where do you work/go to school? How is that going?
   5. Do you have any other interests or activities?
   6. How are you getting along with people?
       1. Do you have friends? Any close friends you can really talk to? How often do you see them?
       2. How do people generally seem to feel about you?
       3. (If unmarried) Are you dating anyone currently? How do you feel it is going?
       4. (If married) How would you describe your relationship with your spouse?
       5. (If client has children) How are things going with your children?

V. Developmental History
   1. What was growing up like for you?
   2. Where did you grow up?
   3. How many brothers and sisters did you have? Where did you fit in?
   4. What was your father like as you were growing up?
   5. What was your mother like as you were growing up?
   6. How did your parents seem to get along with each other?
   7. Were there other adults who played an important role in your life?
   8. Was religion an important part of your upbringing?

9. Were there any major events in your childhood?
10. Have you had any traumatic experiences?
11. How did school go for you?
12. How did you get along with other kids?
13. Were you ever in trouble with police or school authorities?

VI. Relationship/Sexual History
1. When did you start dating? How did dating go for you?
2. How many serious relationships have you had? Can you describe the most significant ones?
3. (If married or cohabiting) How did you meet your partner? How would you describe him/her?
4. How would you describe your relationship with him/her? (If cohabiting) Why have you and your partner chosen not to marry?
5. Have you been married before? (If so) How would you describe your relationship with your ex? What led to the end of that relationship? When did it end?
6. (If client has been married) Have you had any extramarital sexual experiences? If so, under what conditions did this occur? How do you feel about this?
7. Do you have any relationship concerns? Any sexual concerns?
    If relevant
    1. Have you had any relationship problems or sexual problems in the past?
    2. At what age did you first have sex? How was this first experience for you? How would you describe past sexual relationships?
    3. How is (are) your sexual relationship currently? Is there anything you'd like to be different? Have you ever had any form of sexual problem? How often do you and your partner have orgasm?
    4. Has your sexual activity ever resulted in pregnancy besides the children listed? (if so) What was the outcome?
    5. Have you ever been sexually abused, molested, or raped?
    6. Have you had any homosexual experiences? Have you ever been interested in them or worried about that?

VII. Occupational History
1. How far did you go in school?
2. What did you do after that?

Dates	Job Description	Employer	Reasons for Leaving

VIII. Medical History
1. When was your most recent checkup? (If over a year) Are you willing to get a checkup?

2. Who is your family doctor? Is it ok for me to request your medical records?
3. What medical problems do you have currently? What medications are you taking currently?
4. Have you had any significant medical problems in the past? Were there any lasting consequences?
5. Do you have any allergies? (If they don't specify) Are you allergic to any medications?
6. Do you smoke cigarettes?
7. How much caffeine do you drink?
8. How much alcohol do you drink? Do you see this as a problem?
9. Do you use any drugs?
10. Have you had problems with alcohol or drugs in the past?
11. Is there any family history of psychological or emotional problems? Drug or alcohol problems?

IX. Psychiatric History
  1. Have you received any psychotherapy or counseling before?

			What was helpful/	
From whom?	When?	For what?	unhelpful about it?	How did it end?

  2. Have you ever been hospitalized for an emotional problem?

			What was helpful/	
Where?	When?	For what?	unhelpful about it?	How did it end?

  3. Have you ever taken medication for an emotional problem?

ANTIDEPRESSANTS A—SSRI's	ANXIOLYTICS and HYPNOTICS A—Benzodiazepines	ANTIPSYCHOTICS A—Antiparkinsonians
Luvox (Fluvoxamine)	Ativan (Lorazepam)	Akineton (Biperiden)
Paxil (Paroxetine)	Dalmane (Flurazepam)	Artane, Tremin
Prozac (Fluoxetine)	Doral (Quazepam)	(Trihexphenidyl)
Zoloft (Sertraline)	Halcion (Triazolam)	Cogentin (Benztropine)
	Klonopin (Clonazepam)	Symmetral (Amantadine)
B—Cyclic compounds	Librium (Chlordiazepoxide)	
Anafranil (Clomipramine)	ProSom (Estazolam)	B—Antipsychotics
Asendin (Amoxapine)	Restoril (Temazepam)	Clozaril (Clozapine)
Elavil (Amitriptyline)	Serax (Oxazepam)	Haldol (Haloperidol)

Ludiomil (Maprotiline)
Norpramin (Desipramine)
Pamelor (Nortriptyline)
Sinequan, Adapin (Doxepin)
Surmontil (Trimipramine)
Tofranil (Imipramine)
Vivactil (Protriptyline)

C—MAO inhibitors
Nardil (Phenelzine)
Parnate (Tranylcypromine)

D—Others
Desyrel (Trazodone)
Effexor (Venlafaxine)
Serzone (Nefazodone)
Wellbutrin (Bupropion)

BETA BLOCKERS
Inderal (Propanolol)
Lopressor (Metopolol)
Corgad, Lorzide (Nadolol)
Tenormin (Atenolol)

Tranxene (Clorazepate)
Valium (Diazepam)
Versed (Midazolam)
Xanax (Alprazolam)

B—Nonbenzodiazepines
Ambion (Zolpidem)
BuSpar (Buspirone)
Equanil (Meprobamate)
Miltown (Meprobamate)

C—Antihistamines
Benadryl
  (Dyphenhydramine HCl)
Vistaril (Hydroxyzine HCl)

MOOD STABILIZERS
A—Anticonvulsants
Depakene (Valproic Acid)
Depakote (Divalproex
  Sodium)
Tegretol (Carbamazepine)

B—Lithium
Eskalith, Lithonate, Lithotabs
  (Lithium Carbonate)
Lithobid, Eskalith CR (Lithium
  Carbonate, Slow Release)
Cibalith-S (Lithium
  Citrate Syrup)

Inapsine-injection only
  (Droperidol)
Loxitane (Loxapine)
Mellaril (Thioridazine)
Moban (Molindone)
Navane (Thiothixene)
Orap (Pimozide)
Prolixin Permitil
  (Fluphenazine)
Risperdal (Risperidone)
Serentil (Mesoridazine)
Stelazine (Trifluoperazine)
Thorazine (Chlorpromazine)
Trilafon (Perphenazine)

PSYCHOSTIMULANTS
Cylert (Pemoline)
Dexedrine
  (Dextroamphetamine)
Ritalin (Methylphenidate)

OTHER DRUGS
Antabuse (Disulfiram)
Catapres (Clonidine)
Calan, Calan SR, Isoptin,
  Verelan (Verapamil)
Revia (Naltrexone)
Cognex (Tacrine)
Triavil (Amitriptyline +
  Perphenazine)
Others (specify)

4. Electro Convulsive Therapy

Who prescribed it?	When?	For what?	What was helpful/ unhelpful about it?	How did it end?
#1				
#2				
#3				
#4				
#5				
#6				

X. Client's Expectations
1. What do you want out of therapy? What is your image of what therapy is like? Is there anything about therapy that you think will be difficult or uncomfortable for you? What might interfere? What questions do you have?

XI. Mental Status

Appearance
❑Normal
Dress:

Speech
❑Normal
❑Reduced amount

Motor Activity
❑Normal
❑Agitated

❏Meticulous
❏Unkempt
❏Poor hygiene
❏Eccentric/Unusual
❏Seductive
❏Other

Facial Expression:
❏Expressionless
❏Sad expression
❏Tense/Worried
❏Angry/Hostile
❏Avoids eye contact
❏Other

Interview Behavior

❏Normal/cooperative
❏Depressed/Retarded
❏Withdrawn
❏Apathetic/Passive
❏Dependent
❏Ingratiating
❏Naive
❏Dramatic
❏Seductive
❏Coercive/Manipulative
❏Demanding
❏Uncooperative
❏Negativistic
❏Angry/Hostile
❏Suspicious
❏Sensitive
❏Evasive
❏Guarded/Defensive
❏Ill at ease
❏Silly
❏Other

❏Slow
❏Soft
❏Mute
❏Loud
❏Excessive amount
❏Pressured speech
❏Slurred
❏Stuttering
❏Hesitant
❏Monotone
❏Other

Flow of Thought

❏Normal
❏Blocking
❏Circumstantial
❏Tangential
❏Perseveration
❏Confabulation
❏Flight of Ideas
❏Loose Associations
❏Indecisive
❏Distractible
❏Incoherent
❏Other

Mood and Affect

❏Normal
❏Anxious
❏Terrified
❏Depressed
❏Despairing
❏Guilty
❏Angry/Irritable
❏Elevated mood
❏Flat affect
❏Inappropriate affect
❏Other

❏Retarded
❏Mannerisms
❏Tics
❏Tremor
❏Peculiar posture
❏Unusual gait
❏Other

Content of Thought

❏Normal
❏Hopelessness
❏Worthlessness
❏Suicidal ideation
❏Feels persecuted
❏Blames others
❏Homicidal ideation
❏Preoccupations:
❏Obsessions:
❏Delusions:
❏Other

Perception

❏Normal
❏Depersonalization
❏Derealization
❏Auditory hallucinations
❏Visual hallucinations
❏Illusions
❏Other

Cognitive Functioning

❏Normal
❏Orientation impaired
❏Inability to concentrate
❏Poor recent memory
❏Poor remote memory
❏Poor judgment
❏Poor insight
❏Poor abstract thinking
❏Paucity of knowledge
❏Poor vocabulary
❏Other

XII. Diagnosis

Axis I_____   #_____

Axis II_____   #_____

Axis III_____

Axis IV_____

Axis V _____

_____   _____

Clinician (with Degree)   Date

Appendix B
Treating a Broad Range of Axis I Disorders

Cognitive Therapy can be used effectively in treating many different Axis I disorders. However, the treatment approach needs to be modified on the basis of the diagnosis and an individualized conceptualization of each case. A detailed discussion of the modifications to Cognitive Therapy for the treatment of each of the Axis I disorders is beyond the scope of this book. However, a brief summary of some of the treatment variations and references for further study are given below. This is not intended to be an exhaustive list of references, but, rather, a sampling of the available resources on Cognitive Therapy with disorders not covered elsewhere in this book. For information on disorders not listed here, check the Cognitive Therapy forum at Behavior OnLine at http://www.behavior.net/forums/cognitive/.

Schizophrenia and Other Psychotic Disorders

In treating Schizophrenia and other psychotic disorders, Cognitive Therapy is used in combination with pharmacotherapy, *not* as an alternative to medication. Symptoms of Schizophrenia are effectively treated by neuroleptic medication in 50–75% of clients. Thus, there are a significant number of clients where medication alone is insufficient. Cognitive Therapy can be used to improve clients' compliance with a medication regimen, to help them recognize their symptoms and cope more effectively with them, to improve social problem solving and stress management, and to treat comorbid problems such as anxiety and depression. Even cognitive behavioral techniques aimed at the modification of delusions have been the subject of increasing research. Though the database is limited, recent controlled studies show that Cognitive Therapy is of demonstrable benefit to many schizophrenic clients. Cognitive-behavioral interventions are of great significance because of their potential to reduce the costs associated with inpatient treatment and to improve the clients' quality of life.

References

Chadwick, P. D. J., & Lower, C. F. (1994). A cognitive approach to measuring and modifying delusions. *Behaviour Research and Therapy, 32*, 355–367.

Eimer, B. N., & Freeman, A. (1992). The schizophrenic patient. In A. Freeman & F. M. Dattilio (Eds.), *Comprehensive casebook of cognitive therapy* (pp. 231–240). New York: Plenum.

Fowler, D., Garety, P., & Kuipers, E. (1995). *Cognitive behaviour therapy for psychosis.* Chichester: Wiley.

Haddock, G., & Slade, P. D. (1996). *Cognitive-behavioural interventions with psychotic disorders.* London: Routledge.

Hall, J. (1989). Chronic psychiatric handicaps. In K. Hawton, P. M. Salkovskis, J. Kirk, & D. M. Clark. *Cognitive behavior therapy for psychiatric problems: A practical guide* (pp. 315–338). Oxford: Oxford University Press.

Kingdon, D., & Turkington, D. (1994). *Cognitive-behavioural therapy of schizophrenia.* Howve, Sussex: Lawrence Erlbaum.

Nelson, H. (1997). *Cognitive behavioural therapy with schizophrenia: A practice manual.* Cheltenham: Stanley Thornes.

Perris, C. (1989). *Cognitive therapy with schizophrenic patients.* New York: Guilford.

Perris, C., & McGorry, P. D. (Eds.), (1998). *Cognitive psychotherapy of psychotic and personality disorders: Handbook of theory and practice.* New York: John Wiley.

Perris, C., Nordstrom, G., & Troeng, L. (1992). Schizophrenic disorders. In A. Freeman & F. M. Dattilio (Eds.), *Comprehensive casebook of cognitive therapy* (pp. 313–330). New York: Plenum.

Roth, A., & Fonagy, P. (1996). *What works for whom? A critical review of psychotherapy research.* New York: Guildford.

Sensky, T., Turkington, D., Kingdon, D., Scott, J.L., Siddle, R., O'Carroll, M., et al. (2000). A randomized controlled trial of cognitive-behavioral therapy for persistent symptoms in schizophrenia resistant to medication. *Archives of General Psychiatry, 57*, 165–172.

BIPOLAR DISORDER

There is a consensus among cognitive therapists that appropriate mood-stabilizing medication is necessary to enable effective psychotherapy with Bipolar Disorder. When used in combination with medication, Cognitive Therapy emphasizes early identification of hypomanic and depressive episodes; strategies for dealing with these episodes; regulation of the client's sleeping, eating, and activity levels; reduction of the client's vulnerability and exposure to triggering situations; and enhancement of medication compliance.

It is difficult to assess how much psychosocial therapy adds to pharmacological interventions because the research base is small. However, the available research is encouraging. Evidence suggests some benefit from psychological interventions, particularly in increasing adherence to medication regimens, decreasing symptoms of mania and depression, and reducing the need for hospitalization.

References

Basco, M. R., & Rush, A. J. (1996). *Cognitive-behavioral therapy for bipolar disorder.* New York: Guilford.

Henin, A., Otto, M. W., & Reilly-Harrington, N. A. (2001). Introducing flexibility in manualized treatments: Application of recommended strategies to the cognitive-behavioral treatment of bipolar disorder. *Cognitive and Behavioral Practice, 8*, 317–328.

Lam, D. H., Bright, J., Jones, S., Hayward, P., Schuck, N., Chisolm, D., et al. (2000). Cognitive therapy for bipolar disorder—A pilot study of relapse prevention. *Cognitive Therapy and Research, 24*, 503–520.

Newman, C. F., Leahy, R. L., Beck, A. T., Reilly-Harrington, N. A., & Gyulai, L. *Bipolar disorder: A cognitive therapy approach*. Washington, DC: American Psychological Association.

Palmer, A. G., William, H., & Adams, M. (1995). CBT in a group format for bipolar affective disorder. *Behavioral and Cognitive Psychotherapy, 23*, 153–168.

Scott, J. (1996). Cognitive therapy for clients with bipolar disorder. *Cognitive and Behavioral Practice, 3*, 29–51.

Zaretsky, A. E., Segal, Z. V., & Gemar, M. (1999). Cognitive therapy for bipolar depression: A pilot study. *Canadian Journal of Psychiatry, 44*, 491–494.

SOMATOFORM DISORDERS

Clients who have physical symptoms that are not fully explained by a diagnosable medical condition may have a Somatoform Disorder. In *DSM-IV-TR* (2000), these include Somatization Disorder, Undifferentiated Somatoform Disorder, Conversion Disorder, Pain Disorder, Hypochondriasis, Body Dysmorphic Disorder, and Somatoform Disorder Not Otherwise Specified. Paul Salkovskis has done a great deal of research on cognitive behavioral approaches to these disorders. In his conceptualization of Somatoform Disorders, clients have a distorted or unrealistic belief that their bodily functioning is, or is going to be, impaired and this belief leads to anxiety. This belief is based on their observations of their body, which further convince them that their fears are true. The reaction to this perceived impairment can include changes in mood, cognitions, behavior, and physiological functioning. Difficulties that may originally have had a physical causation may later be maintained by psychological factors.

Treatment for Somatoform Disorders may include changes in medication, physical aids, diet, and lifestyle as well as changing beliefs about the nature and consequences of the somatic concerns. Changes may also need to be made in behaviors directly related to the physical problems as well as in the reduction of reassurance-seeking behaviors. In addition, coping strategies used for stress management and the reduction of anxiety can be helpful.

References

Allen, L. A. (2000). Short-term therapy for somatization disorder: A cognitive behavioral approach. *Journal of Cognitive Psychotherapy, 14*, 373–380.

Allen, L. A., Woolfolk, R. L., Lehrer, P. M., Gara, M. A., & Escobar, J. I. (2001). Cognitive behavior therapy for somatization disorder: A preliminary investigation. *Journal of Behavior Therapy and Experimental Psychiatry, 32*, 53–62.

Cash, T. F. (1997). *The body image workbook: An 8-step program for learning to like your looks*. Oakland, CA: New Harbinger.

Eimer, B. N. (1992). The treatment of chronic pain. In A. Freeman & F. M. Dattilio (Eds.), *Comprehensive casebook of cognitive therapy* (pp. 361–372). New York: Plenum.

Kroenke, K., & Swindle, R. (2000). Cognitive-behavioral therapy for somatization and symptom syndromes: A critical review of controlled clinical trials. *Psychotherapy and Psychosomatics, 69*, 205–215.

Salkovskis, P. M. (1989). Somatic problems. In K. Hawton, P.M. Salkovskis, J. Kirk, & D. M. Clark (Eds.), *Cognitive behavior therapy for psychiatric problems: A practical guide* (pp. 235–276). Oxford: Oxford University Press.

Veale, D., Gournay, D., Dryden, W., Boocock, A., Shah, F., Willson, R., et al. (1996). Body dysmorphic disorder. A cognitive behavioural model and pilot randomised controlled trial. *Behaviour Research and Therapy, 34*, 717–279.

Sexual and Gender Identity Disorders

The outcomes for treatments of sexual dysfunction are highly variable, both across different classes and subtypes of dysfunction and within disorders, presumably because of unmeasured aspects of comorbidity. The outcomes from uncontrolled studies should be viewed with caution in light of the relatively high rates of spontaneous remission for erectile dysfunction, and the known situational specificity of other disorders. It is unclear whether marital therapy is always indicated before sex therapy in couples with problematic relationships, although clinical judgment often suggests this to be an appropriate strategy. There has been very little research examining the relative importance of widely accepted elements of sex therapy.

References

Hawton, K. (1989). Sexual dysfunction. In K. Hawton, P. M. Salkovskis, J. Kirk & D. M. Clark (Eds.), *Cognitive behavior therapy for psychiatric problems: A practical guide* (pp. 370–405). Oxford: Oxford University Press.

McCabe, M. P. (2001). Evaluation of a cognitive behavior therapy program for people with sexual dysfunction. *Journal of Sex and Marital Therapy, 27*, 259–271.

Metz, M. E., & Pryor, J. L. (2000). Premature ejaculation: A psychophysiological approach for assessment and management. *Journal of Sex and Marital Therapy, 26*, 293–320.

Sbrocco, T., & Barlow, D. H. (1996). Conceptualizing the cognitive component of sexual arousal: Implications for sexuality research and treatment. In P. Salkovskis (Ed.), *Frontiers of cognitive therapy* (pp. 419–449). New York: Guilford.

Trudel, G., Marchand, A., Ravart, M., Aubin, S., Turgeon, L., & Fortier, P. (2001). The effect of a cognitive-behavioral group treatment program on hypoactive sexual desire in women. *Sexual and Relationship Therapy, 16*, 145–164.

Eating Disorders

Cognitive Therapy emphasizes the restructuring of dysfunctional beliefs about food, weight, and one's self (particularly in regard to body image and self-worth). There is a striking lack of systematic investigation of the efficacy of behavioral and cognitive behavioral methods for anorexia. The effectiveness of cognitive behavior therapy for bulimia nervosa is better supported, although evidence is still limited. Exposure and response prevention strategies alone seem to be of little benefit with eating disorders. Dietary education, advice, and monitoring of food intake appear to be important components of treatment effectiveness. Cognitive-behavioral therapy incorporating these and other methods (i.e., addressing dysfunctional attitudes toward eating and reestablishment of control over-eating) are effective for two-thirds of clients, although they ensure symptom-free status in only one-third of cases. The techniques of cognitive behavior therapy are improving, and more recent studies are showing greater impact. Longer length of therapy (6 months rather than 12 sessions) appears to be associated with better outcome.

References

Allen, H. N., & Craighead, L. W. (1999). Appetite monitoring in the treatment of binge eating disorder. *Behavior Therapy, 30,* 253–272.

Fairburn, C., & Cooper, P. (1989). Eating disorders. In K. Hawton, P. M. Salkovskis, J. Kirk & D. M. Clark. (Eds.), *Cognitive behavior therapy for psychiatric problems: A practical guide* (pp. 277–314). Oxford: Oxford University Press.

Garner, D. (1992). Bulimia Nervosa. In A. Freeman & F. M. Dattilio (Eds.), *Comprehensive casebook of cognitive therapy* (pp. 169–176). New York: Plenum.

Garner, D. M., & Bemis, K. M. (1982). A cognitive-behavioral approach to anorexia nervosa. *Cognitive Therapy and Research, 6,* 123–150.

Garner, D. M., Fairburn, C. G., & Davis, R. (1987). Cognitive-behavioral treatment of bulimia nervosa. *Behavior Modification, 11,* 398–431.

Karfgin, A., & Roth, D. (1992). Obesity. In A. Freeman & F. M. Dattilio (Eds.), *Comprehensive casebook of cognitive therapy* (pp. 177–184). New York: Plenum.

Vitousek, K. M. (1996). The current status of cognitive-behavioral models of anorexia nervosa and bulimia nervosa. In P. Salkovskis (Ed.), *Frontiers of cognitive therapy* (pp. 383–418). New York: Guilford.

Sleep Disorders

Approaches used in the treatment of insomnia include relaxation methods, techniques for enhancing the connection between sleep and bed, education about sleep, careful monitoring of sleep medications, and cognitive-behavioral therapy. The individual's expectations regarding sleep are very important in the treatment of sleep disorders. Individuals who believe that something is wrong unless they are getting 8 hours of sleep a night are very likely to be dissatisfied with their sleep, even though their sleep patterns may not be abnormal compared to other people of the same age.

References

Edinger, J. D., Wohlgemuth, W. K., Radtke, R. A., Marsh, G. R., & Guillian, R. E. (2001). Cognitive-behavioral therapy for treatment of chronic primary insomnia: A randomized controlled trial. *Journal of the American Medical Association, 285,* 1856–1864.

Espie, C. A., Inglis, S. J., Tessier, S., & Harvey, L. (2001). The clinical effectiveness of cognitive behaviour therapy for chronic insomnia: Implementation and evaluation of a sleep clinic in general medical practice. *Behaviour Research and Therapy, 39,* 45–60.

Morin, C. M., Kowatch, R. A., Barry, T., & Walton, E. (1993). Cognitive-behavior therapy for late-life insomnia. *Journal of Consulting and Clinical Psychology, 61,* 137–146.

Sloan, E. P., Hauri, P., Bootzin, R., Morin, C., Stevenson, M., & Shapiro, C. M. (1993). The nuts and bolts of behavioral therapy for insomnia. *Journal of Psychosomatic Research, 37,* 19–37.

Adjustment Disorders

Adjustment disorders often include symptoms of many different disorders. Although some assume that adjustment disorders are harmless because they tend to be transitory, the emotional symptoms of adjustment disorders can be just as intense and potentially dangerous to a client as in other Axis I disorders. It is true that the likelihood of spontaneous improvement is usually greater given the identifiable stressors and the short period of time between precipitating events and psychological symptoms, but the intensity of the reaction to distressing circumstances cannot be predicted from the apparent severity of the situation. Although belief systems may play some role in these disorders, it is more likely that a client's adaptive abilities are only temporarily malfunctioning due to the trauma of recent events; and short-term intervention may be all that is necessary.

References

Gallagher-Thompson, D., & Thompson, L. W. (1996b). Bereavement and adjustment disorders. In E. W. Busse & D. G. Blazer (Eds.), *Textbook of geriatric psychiatry* (2nd ed.). Washington, DC: American Psychiatric Association.

Gilson, M. (1992). An adjustment disorder. In A. Freeman & F. M. Dattilio (Eds.), *Comprehensive casebook of cognitive therapy* (pp. 107–116). New York: Plenum.

Moorey, S. (1996). When bad things happen to rational people: Cognitive therapy in adverse life circumstances. In P. Salkovskis (Ed.), *Frontiers of cognitive therapy* (pp. 450–469). New York: Guilford.

References

Abrahms, J. L. (1983). Cognitive-behavioral strategies to induce and enhance a collaborative set in distressed couples. In A. Freeman (Ed.), *Cognitive therapy with couples and groups* (pp. 125–155). New York: Plenum.

Abrahms, J. L., & Spring, M. (1989). The flip-flop factor. *International Cognitive Therapy Newsletter, 5* (10), 1, 7–8.

Abramson, L. Y., Seligman, M. E., & Teasdale, J. D. (1978). Learned helplessness in humans: Critique and reformulation. *Journal of Abnormal Psychology, 87*, 49–74.

Akhtar, S. (1986). Differentiating schizoid and avoidant personality disorders [letter to the editor]. *American Journal of Psychiatry, 143*, 1060–1061.

Alberti, R., & Emmons, M. (2001). *Your perfect right: Assertiveness and equality in your life and relationships* (8th ed.). Atascadero, CA: Impact Publishers.

Alden, L. (1989). Short-term structured treatment for avoidant personality disorder. *Journal of Consulting and Clinical Psychology, 57*, 756–764.

Alden, L. E., & Capreol, M. J. (1993). Avoidant personality disorder: Interpersonal problems as predictors of treatment response. *Behavior Therapy, 24*, 357–376.

Allen, D. W. (1977). Basic treatment issues. In M. J. Horowitz (Ed.), *Hysterical personality* (pp. 283–328). New York: Jason Aronson.

Allen, H. N., & Craighead, L. W. (1999). Appetite monitoring in the treatment of binge eating disorder. *Behavior Therapy, 30*, 253–272.

Allen, J. P., & Columbus, C. (1995). *Assessing alcohol problems: A guide for clinicians and researchers* NIH Publication No. 95-3745. Bethesda, MD: National Institute on Alcohol Abuse and Alcoholism.

Allen, L. A. (2000). Short-term therapy for somatization disorder: A cognitive behavioral approach. *Journal of Cognitive Psychotherapy, 14*, 373–380.

Allen, L. A., Woolfolk, R. L., Lehrer, P. M., Gara, M. A., & Escobar, J. I. (2001). Cognitive behavior therapy for somatization disorder: A preliminary investigation. *Journal of Behavior Therapy and Experimental Psychiatry, 32*, 53–62.

Alsop, S., & Saunders, B. (1989). Relapse and alcohol problems. In M. Gossop (Ed.), *Relapse and addictive behavior* (pp. 11–40). London: Tavistok/Routledge.

American Psychiatric Association. (1980). *Diagnostic and statistical manual of mental disorders* (3rd ed.). Washington, DC: Author.

American Psychiatric Association. (1987). *Diagnostic and statistical manual of mental disorders* (3rd ed., rev.). Washington, DC: Author.

American Psychiatric Association. (1994). *Diagnostic and statistical manual of mental disorders* (4th ed.). Washington, DC: Author.

American Psychiatric Association. (2000). *Diagnostic and statistical manual of mental disorders* (4th ed., text rev.). Washington, DC: Author.

American Psychiatric Association. (2003). *Practice guideline for the treatment of patients with borderline personality disorder*. Retrieved March 25, 2003, from http://www.psych.org/clin_res/borderline.index.cfm

Antony, M. M., & Swinson, R. P. (2000). *Phobic disorders and panic in adults: A guide to assessment and treatment*. Washington, DC: American Psychological Association.

Arean, P. & Miranda, J. (1996). The treatment of depression in elderly primary care patients: A naturalistic study. *Journal of Clinical Geropsychology*, 2, 153–160.

Arnkoff, D. B., & Glass, C. R. (1982). Clinical cognitive constructs: Examination, evaluation, and elaboration. In P. Kendall (Ed.), *Advances in cognitive-behavioral research and therapy* (Vol. 1, pp. 1–34). New York: Academic Press.

Arntz, A. (1994). Treatment of borderline personality disorder: A challenge for cognitive-behavioural therapy. *Behaviour Research and Therapy*, 32, 419–430.

Arntz, A. (1999). Do personality disorders exist? On the validity of the concept and its cognitive-behavioral formulation and treatment. *Behaviour Research and Therapy*, 37, S97–S134.

Arntz, A., Roos, D., & Dreessen, L. (1999). Assumptions in borderline personality disorder: Specificity, stability and relationship with etiological factors. *Behaviour Research and Therapy*, 37, 545–557.

Bandura, A. (1977). *Social learning theory*. Englewood Cliffs, NJ: Prentice Hall.

Barkley, R. (1997). *Defiant children: A clinician's manual for assessment and parent training*, (2nd ed.). New York: Guilford.

Barkley, R., Edwards, G. H., & Robin, A. L. (1999). *Defiant teens: A clinician's manual for assessment and family intervention* (2nd ed.). New York: Guilford.

Barlow, D. (2002). *Anxiety and its disorders: The nature and treatment of anxiety and panic* (2nd ed.). New York: Guilford.

Barlow, D. H., & Craske, M. G. (2000). *Mastery of your anxiety and panic* (3rd ed.). San Antonio, TX: Graywind/The Psychological Corporation.

Barlow, D. H., Gorman, J. M., Shear, M. K., & Woods, S. W. (2000). Cognitive-behavioral therapy, imipramine, or their combination for panic disorder: A randomized controlled trial. *Journal of the American Medical Association*, 283, 2529–2536.

Barlow, D. H., & Waddell, M. T. (1985). Agoraphobia. In D. H. Barlow (Ed.), *Clinical handbook of psychological disorders: A step-by-step treatment manual* (pp. 1–68). New York: Guilford.

Baron, M., Gruen, R., Asnis, L., & Kane, J. (1983). Age-of-onset in schizophrenia and schizotypal disorders. *Neuropsychobiology*, 10, 199–204.

Barrios, B. A., & Shigatomi, C. (1980). Coping skills training for the management of anxiety: A critical review. *Behavior Therapy*, 10, 491–522.

Basco, M. R., & Rush, A. J. (1996). *Cognitive-behavioral therapy for bipolar disorder*. New York: Guilford.

Baucom, D. H., Epstein, N., & LaTaillade, J. J. (2002). Cognitive-behavioral couple therapy. In A. S. Gurman & N. S. Jacobson (Eds.), *Clinical handbook of couple therapy* (3rd ed., pp. 26–58). New York: Guilford.

Baucom, D. H., Epstein, N., Rankin, L. A., & Burnett, C. K. (1996). Assessing relationship standards: The Inventory of Specific Relationship Standards. *Journal of Family Psychology*, 10, 72–88.

Baucom, D. H., Epstein, N., Sayers, S., & Sher, T. G. (1989). The role of cognitions in marital relationships: Definitional, methodological, and conceptual issues. *Journal of Consulting and Clinical psychology*, 57, 31–38.

Baucom, D. H., & Lester, G. W. (1986). The usefulness of cognitive restructuring as an adjunct to behavioral marital therapy. *Behavior Therapy*, 17, 385–403.

Baucom, D. H., Sayers, L. S., & Sher, T. G. (1990). Supplementing behavioral marital therapy with cognitive restructuring and emotional expressiveness training: An outcome investigation. *Journal of Consulting and Clinical Psychology*, 58, 636–645.

Baucom, D. H., Shoham, V., Mueser, K. T., Daiuto, A. D., & Stickle, T. R. (1998). Empirically supported couple and family interventions for marital distress and adult mental health problems. *Journal of Consulting and Clinical Psychology*, 66, 53–88.

Bauer, S. F., Hunt, H. F., Gould, M., & Goldstein, E. G. (1980). Borderline personality organization, structural diagnosis and the structural interview: A pilot study of interview analysis. *Psychiatry*, 43, 224–233.

Beck, A. T. (1970). The role of fantasies in psychotherapy and psychopathology. *Journal of Nervous and Mental Disease*, 150, 3–17.

Beck, A. T. (1972). *Depression: Causes and treatment*. Philadelphia: University of Pennsylvania Press.

Beck, A. T. (1976). *Cognitive therapy and the emotional disorders*. New York: International Universities Press.

Beck, A. T. (1988). *Love is never enough: How couples can overcome misunderstandings, resolve conflicts, and solve relationship problems through cognitive therapy*. New York: Harper & Row.

Beck, A. T. (1999). *Prisoners of hate: The cognitive basis of anger, hostility, and violence*. New York: Harper/Collins.

Beck, A. T., Butler, A. C., Brown, G. K., Dahlsgaard, K. K., Newman, C. F., & Beck, J. S. (2001). Dysfunctional beliefs discriminate personality disorders. *Behaviour Research and Therapy, 39* (10), 1213–1225.

Beck, A. T., & Emery, G. (1985). *Anxiety disorders and phobias: A cognitive perspective*. New York: Basic Books.

Beck, A. T., Freeman, A., Davis, D., Pretzer, J., Fleming, B., Artz, A., Butler, A., Fusco, G., Simon, K. M., et al. (2003). *Cognitive therapy of personality disorders* (2nd ed.). New York: Guilford.

Beck, A. T., Freeman, A., Pretzer, J., Davis, D. D., Fleming, B., Ottaviani, R., Beck, J., Simon, K. M., et al. (1990). *Cognitive therapy of personality disorders*. New York: Guilford.

Beck, A. T., Kovacs, M., & Weissman, A. (1975). Hopelessness and suicidal behavior: An overview. *Journal of the American Medical Association, 234*, 1146–1149.

Beck, A. T., Kovacs, M., & Weissman, A. (1979). Assessment of suicidal intention: The Scale of Suicidal Ideation. *Journal of Consulting and Clinical Psychology, 47*, 343–352.

Beck, A. T., Laude, R., & Bohnert, M. (1974). Ideational components of anxiety neurosis. *Archives of General Psychiatry, 31*, 319–325.

Beck, A. T., Rush, A. J., Shaw, B. F., & Emery, G. (1979). *Cognitive therapy of depression*. New York: Guilford.

Beck, A. T., Steer, R. A., Kovacs, M., & Garrison, B. (1985). Hopelessness and eventual suicide: A 10-year prospective study of patients hospitalized with suicide ideation. *American Journal of Psychiatry, 142*, 559–563.

Beck, A. T., Wright, F. D., Newman, C. F., & Liese, B. S. (1993). *Cognitive therapy of substance abuse*. New York: Guilford.

Beck, J. S. (1995). *Cognitive therapy: Basics and beyond*. New York: Guilford.

Bedrosian, R. C. (1981). The application of cognitive therapy techniques with adolescents. In G. Emery, S. D. Hollon & R. C. Bedrosian (Eds.), *New directions in cognitive therapy: A casebook* (pp. 68–83). New York: Guilford.

Bedrosian, R. C., & Bozicas, G. D. (1994). *Treating family of origin problems: A cognitive approach*. New York: Guilford.

Bellack, A., & Hersen, M. (Eds.). (1985). *Dictionary of behavior therapy techniques*. New York: Pergamon.

Benson, H. (1975). *The relaxation response*. New York: Morrow.

Bergin, A. E., & Garfield, S. L. (Eds.). (1994). *Handbook of psychotherapy and behavior change* (4th ed.). New York: John Wiley.

Bernstein, D. A., & Borkovec, T. D. (1976). *Progressive relaxation training: A manual for the helping professionals*. Champaign, IL.: Research Press.

Bernstein, D. A., Borkovec, T. D., & Hazlett-Stevens, H. (2000). *New directions in progressive relaxation training: A guidebook for helping professionals*. Westport, CT: Praeger.

Bird, J. (1979). The behavioural treatment of hysteria. *British Journal of Psychiatry, 134*, 129–137.

Black, D. W., Monahan, P., Wesner, R., Gabel, J., and Bowers, W. (1996). The effect of fluvoxamine, cognitive therapy, and placebo on abnormal personality traits in 44 patients with panic disorder. *Journal of Personality Disorders, 10* (2), 185–194.

Borkovec, T. D., & Costello, E. (1993). Efficacy of applied relaxation and cognitive-behavioral therapy in the treatment of generalized anxiety disorder. *Journal of Consulting and Clinical Psychology, 61*, 611–619.

Bourne, E. (1995). *The anxiety and phobia workbook* (2nd ed.). Oakland, CA: New Harbinger.

Bower, G. H. (1981). Mood and memory. *American Psychologist, 36*, 293–300.

Bower, S. A., & Bower, G. H. (1976). *Asserting yourself: A practical guide for practical change*. Reading, MA: Addison-Wesley.

Boyd, J. H. (1986). Use of mental health services for the treatment of panic disorder. *American Journal of Psychiatry, 143*, 1569–1574.

Brown, E. J., Heimberg, R. G., & Juster, H. R. (1995). Social phobia subtype and avoidant personality disorder: Effect on severity of social phobia, impairment, and outcome of cognitive behavioral treatment. *Behavior Therapy, 26,* 467–486.

Brown, G. K., Newman, C. F., Charlesworth, S. E., Crits-Cristoph, P. & Beck, A. T. (in press). An open clinical trial of cognitive therapy for borderline personality disorder. *Journal of Personality Disorders.*

Brown, M. Z, Comtois, K. A, & Linehan, M. M. (2002). Reasons for suicide attempts and nonsuicidal self-injury in women with borderline personality disorder. *Journal of Abnormal Psychology, 111* (1), 198–202.

Brown, N. (1998). Hypnosis in the treatment of severe anxiety. *Australian Journal of Clinical and Experimental Hypnosis, 26* (2), 138–145.

Burns, D. D. (1999a). *Feeling good: The new mood therapy* (Rev. ed.). New York: Avon.

Burns, D. D. (1999b). *The feeling good handbook* (Rev. ed). New York: Plume.

Butler, A. C., & Beck, J. S. (2000). Cognitive therapy outcomes: A review of meta-analyses. *Journal of the Norwegian Psychological Association, 37,* 1–9. Available from The Beck Institute, Bala Cynwyd, PA.

Byers, S. B., Morse, M., & Nackoul, K. (1992). *Cognitive principles and techniques: Video series with workbook (adult).* Available from Creative Cognitive Productions, 2118 Central, S. E., #46, Albuquerque, NM 87106.

Campbell, R. J. (1981). *Psychiatric dictionary* (5th ed.). New York: Oxford University Press.

Carlson, C. R., & Bernstein, D. A. (1995). Relaxation skills training: Abbreviated progressive relaxation. In W. O'Donohue & L. Krasner (Eds.), *Handbook of psychological skills training: Clinical techniques and applications* (pp. 20–35). Needham Heights, MA: Allyn & Bacon.

Carney, F. L. (1986). Residential treatment programs for antisocial personality disorders. In W. H. Reid (Ed.), *The treatment of antisocial syndromes* (pp. 64–75). New York: Van Nostrand Reinhold.

Cash, T. F. (1997). *The body image workbook: An 8-step program for learning to like your looks.* Oakland, CA: New Harbinger.

Chadwick, P., Sambrooke, S., Rasch, S., & Davies, E. (2000). Challenging the omnipotence of voices: Group cognitive behavior therapy for voices. *Behaviour Research and Therapy, 38* (10), 993–1003.

Chadwick, P. D. J., & Lower, C. F. (1994). A cognitive approach to measuring and modifying delusions. *Behaviour Research and Therapy, 32,* 355–367.

Chambless, D. L., Renneberg, B., Goldstein, A., & Gracely, E. J. (1992). MCMI-diagnosed personality disorders among agoraphobic outpatients: Prevalence and relationship to severity and treatment outcome. *Journal of Anxiety Disorders, 6,* 193–211.

Chambless, D. L., Tran, G. Q., & Glass, C. R. (1997). Predictors of response to cognitive-behavioral group therapy for social phobia. *Journal of Anxiety Disorders, 11,* 221–240.

Childress, A. R., & Burns, D. D. (1983). The group supervision model in cognitive therapy training. In A. Freeman (Ed.), *Cognitive therapy with couples and groups* (pp. 323–335). New York: Plenum.

Christensen, A., Jacobson, N. S., & Babcock, J. C. (1995). Integrative Behavioral Couple Therapy. In N. S. Jacobson & A. S. Gurman (Eds.), *Clinical handbook of couple therapy.* (2nd ed., pp. 31–64). New York: Guilford.

Cinciripini, P. M., Cinciripini, L. G., Wallfisch, A., & Haque, W. (1996). Behavior therapy and the transdermal nicotine patch: Effects on cessation outcome, affect, and coping. *Journal of Consulting and Clinical Psychology, 64* (2), 314–323.

Clark, D. M. (1986). A cognitive approach to panic. *Behaviour Research and Therapy, 24,* 461–470.

Clarke, G., Hops, H., Lewinsohn, P. M., Andrews, J., Seeley, J. R., & Williams, J. (1992). Cognitive-behavioral group treatment of adolescent depression: Prediction of outcome. *Behavior Therapy, 23* (3), 341–354.

Clarkin, J. F., Widiger, T. A., Frances, A., Hurt, S. W., & Gilmore, M. (1983). Prototypic typology and the borderline personality disorder. *Journal of Abnormal Psychology, 93,* 263–275.

Cleckley, H. (1976). *The mask of sanity.* St. Louis: Mosby.

Cobham, V. E., Dadds, M. R., & Spence, S. H. (1998). The role of parental anxiety in the treatment of childhood anxiety. *Journal of Consulting and Clinical Psychology, 66,* 893–905.

Coché, E. (1987). Problem-solving training: A cognitive group therapy modality. In A. Freeman & V. Greenwood (Eds.), *Cognitive therapy: Applications in psychiatric and medical settings* (pp. 83–102). New York: Human Sciences Press.

Colby, K. M. (1981). Modeling a paranoid mind. *The Behavioral and Brain Sciences, 4,* 515–560.

Colby, K. M., Faught, W. S., & Parkinson, R. C. (1979). Cognitive therapy of paranoid conditions: Heuristic suggestions based on a computer simulation model. *Cognitive Therapy and Research, 3,* 5–60.

Coles, M. E., Hart, T. A., & Heimberg, R. G. (2001). Cognitive-behavioral group treatment for social phobia. In W. R. Crozier & L. E. Alden (Eds.), *International handbook of social anxiety: Concepts, research and interventions relating to the self and shyness* (pp. 449–469). New York: John Wiley.

Coon, D. W. (1994). Cognitive-behavioral interventions with avoidant personality: A single case study. *Journal of Cognitive Psychotherapy: An International Quarterly, 8,* 243–253.

Craighead, W. E., Kimball, W. H., & Rehak, P. J. (1979). Mood changes, physiological responses, and self-statements during social rejection imagery. *Journal of Consulting and Clinical Psychology, 47,* 385–396.

Craske, M. G., Antony, M. M., & Barlow, D. H. (1997). *Mastery of your specific phobia: Therapist guide.* San Antonio, TX: The Psychological Corporation.

Craske, M. G., Barlow, D. H., & Meadows, E. A. (2000). *Mastery of your anxiety and panic, third ed. (MAP-3): Therapist guide for anxiety, panic, and agoraphobia.* San Antonio, TX: The Psychological Corporation.

Dahlen, E. R. (2000). A partial component-analysis of Beck's cognitive therapy for the treatment of general anger. *Dissertation Abstracts International: Section B: The Sciences and Engineering, 60* (8-B), 4213.

Daniels, L. (1998). A group cognitive-behavioral and process-oriented approach to treating the social impairment and negative symptoms associated with chronic mental illness. *Journal of Psychotherapy Practice and Research, 7* (2), 167–176.

Davidson, P. R., & Parker, K. C. H. (2001). Eye movement desensitization and reprocessing (EMDR): A meta analysis. *Journal of Consulting and Clinical Psychology, 69,* 305–316.

Davidson, K. M., & Tyrer, P. (1996). Cognitive therapy for antisocial and borderline personality disorders: Single case study series. *British Journal of Clinical Psychology, 35,* 413–429.

Davis, M., Eshelman, E. R., & McKay, M. (2000). *The relaxation and stress reduction workbook* (5th ed.). Oakland, CA: New Harbinger.

Deffenbacher, J. L., Dahlen, E. R., Lynch, R. S., Morris, C. D., & Gowensmith, W. N. (2000). An application of Beck's cognitive therapy to general anger reduction. *Cognitive Therapy and Research, 24* (6), 689–697.

Deffenbacher, J. L., Zwemer, W. A., Whisman, M. A., Hill, R. A., & Sloan, R. D. (1986). Irrational beliefs and anxiety. *Cognitive Therapy and Research, 10,* 281–292.

DeRubeis, R. J., & Crits-Cristoph, P. (1998). Empirically supported individual and group psychological treatments for adult mental disorders. *Journal of Consulting and Clinical Psychology, 66,* 37–52.

Devilly, G. J., & Spence, S. H. (1999). The relative efficacy and treatment distress of EMDR and a cognitive behavioral trauma treatment protocol in the amelioration of post traumatic stress disorder. *Journal of Anxiety Disorders, 13,* 131–158.

Diaferia, G., Sciuto, G., Perna, G., Bernardeschi, L., Battaglia, M., Rusmini, S., et al. (1993). *DSM-III-R* personality disorders in panic disorder. *Journal of Anxiety Disorders, 7,* 153–161.

Dick-Grace, J. E. (1996). Cognitive therapy with depressed, female outpatients in individual, couple, and group treatment modalities: An evaluation. *Dissertation Abstracts International Section A: Humanities and Social Sciences, 56* (7-A), 2871.

Dobson, K. S., & Pusch, D. (1993). Toward a definition of the conceptual and empirical boundaries of cognitive therapy. *Australian Psychologist, 28,* 137–144.

Dryden, W. (1984). Rational-emotive therapy and cognitive therapy: A critical comparison. In M. A. Reda, & M. J. Mahoney (Eds.), *Cognitive psychotherapies: Recent developments in theory, research, and practice* (pp. 81–99). Cambridge, MA: Ballinger.

Dudley, C. D. (1997). *Treating depressed children: A therapeutic manual of cognitive behavioral interventions.* Oakland, CA: New Harbinger.

DuPont, R. L., Spencer, E. D., & DuPont, C. M. (1998). *The anxiety cure: An eight-step program for getting well.* New York: John Wiley.

Dushe, D. M., Hurt, M. L., & Schroeder, H. (1983). Self-statement modification with adults: A meta-analysis. *Psychological Bulletin, 94,* 408–442.

Echeburua, E., Baez, C., & Fernandez-Montalvo, J. (1996). Comparative effectiveness of three therapeutic modalities in the psychological treatment of pathological gambling: Long term outcome. *Behavioural and Cognitive Psychotherapy, 24* (1), 51–72.

Edinger, J. D., Wohlgemuth, W. K., Radtke, R. A., Marsh, G. R., & Guillian, R. E. (2001). Cognitive behavioral therapy for treatment of chronic primary insomnia: A randomized controlled trial. *Journal of the American Medical Association, 285,* 1856–1864.

Eich, J. E. (1977). State-dependent retrieval of information in human episodic memory. In I. M. Birnbaum & E. S. Parker (Eds.), *Alcohol and human memory* (pp. 141–157). New York: Erlbaum.

Eidelson, R. J., & Epstein, N. (1982). Cognition and relationship maladjustment: Development of a measure of dysfunctional relational beliefs. *Journal of Consulting and Clinical Psychology, 50,* 715–720.

Eimer, B. N. (1992). The treatment of chronic pain. In A. Freeman & F. M. Dattilio (Eds.), *Comprehensive casebook of cognitive therapy* (pp. 361–372). New York: Plenum.

Eimer, B. N., & Freeman, A. (1992). The schizophrenic patient. In A. Freeman & F. M. Dattilio (Eds.), *Comprehensive casebook of cognitive therapy* (pp. 231–240). New York: Plenum.

Elliot, A. J., & Devine, P. G. (1994). On the motivational nature of cognitive dissonance: Dissonance as psychological discomfort. *Journal of Personality and Social Psychology, 67,* 382–394.

Ellis, A. (1990). How to deal with your most difficult client—you. In W. Dryden (Ed.), *The essential Albert Ellis: Seminal writings on psychotherapy* (pp. 300–311). New York: Springer.

Ellis, A. (2002). *Overcoming resistance: A rational emotive behavior therapy integrated approach* (2nd ed.). New York: Springer.

Ellis, A., & Becker, I. (1982). *A guide to personal happiness.* North Hollywood, CA: Wilshire.

Ellis, A., & Greiger, R. (1977). *Handbook of rational-emotive therapy.* New York: Springer.

Ellis, A., Young, J., & Lockwood, G. (1987). Cognitive therapy and rational-emotive therapy: A dialogue. *Journal of Cognitive Psychotherapy: An International Quarterly, 1,* 205–256.

Ellis, H. (1898). Auto-eroticism: A psychological study. *Alienist and Neurologist, 19,* 260–299.

Emmelkamp, P. M. G., van Linden van den Heuvell, C., Ruephan, M., Sanderman, R., Scholing, A., & Stroink, F. (1988). Cognitive and behavioral interventions: A comparative evaluation with clinically distressed couples. *Journal of Family Psychology, 1,* 365–377.

Epstein, N. (2001). Cognitive-behavioral therapy with couples: Empirical status. *Journal of Cognitive Psychotherapy: An International Quarterly, 15,* 299–310.

Epstein, N. B., & Baucom, D. H. (2002). *Enhanced cognitive-behavioral therapy for couples: A contextual approach.* Washington, DC: American Psychological Association.

Epstein, N., & Eidelson, R. J. (1981). Unrealistic beliefs of clinical couples: Their relationship to expectations, goals and satisfaction. *American Journal of Family Therapy, 9,* 13–22.

Epstein, N., Schlesinger, S. E., & Dryden, W. (1988). *Cognitive behavior therapy with families.* New York: Brunner/Mazel.

Ericsson, K. A., & Simon, H. A. (1980). Verbal reports as data. *Psychological Review, 87,* 215–251.

Espie, C. A., Inglis, S. J., Tessier, S., & Harvey, L. (2001). The clinical effectiveness of cognitive behaviour therapy for chronic insomnia: Implementation and evaluation of a sleep clinic in general medical practice. *Behaviour Research and Therapy, 39,* 45–60.

Fairburn, C., & Cooper, P. (1989). Eating disorders. In K. Hawton, P. M. Salkovskis, J. Kirk, & D. M. Clark (Eds.), *Cognitive behavior therapy for psychiatric problems: A practical guide* (pp. 277–314). Oxford: Oxford University Press.

Farrell, J. M., & Shaw, I. A. (1994). Emotion awareness training: a prerequisite to effective cognitive-behavioral treatment of borderline personality disorder. *Cognitive and Behavioral Practice, 1,* 71–91.

Federal Bureau of Prisons (2000). *Clinical practice guidelines: Detoxification of chemically dependent inmates.* Retrieved March 24, 2003, from http://www.nicic.org/pubs/2000/016554.pdf

Feske, U., Perry, K. J., Chambless, D. L., Renneberg, B., & Goldstein, A. J. (1996). Avoidant personality disorder as a predictor for treatment outcome among generalized social phobics. *Journal of Personality Disorders, 10,* 174–184.

Festinger, L. (1957). *A theory of cognitive dissonance.* Evanston, IL: Row, Peterson.

Foa, E. B., & Kozak, M. J. (1996). Psychological treatment for obsessive-compulsive disorder. In M. R. Mavissakalian & R. F. Prien (Eds.), *Long-term treatments of anxiety disorders* (pp. 285–309). Washington, DC: American Psychiatric Press.

Foa, E. B., & Rothbaum, B. O. (1998). *Treating the trauma of rape: Cognitive-behavioral therapy for PTSD.* New York: Guilford.

Foa, E. B., Steketee, G., Grayson, J. B., Turner, R. M., & Latimer, P. (1984). Deliberate exposure and blocking of obsessive-compulsive rituals: Immediate and long term effects. *Behavior Therapy, 15,* 450–472.

Foa, E. B., Steketee, G., & Milby, J. B. (1980). Differential effects of exposure and response prevention in obsessive-compulsive washers. *Journal of Consulting and Clinical Psychology, 48,* 71–79.

Fossel, R. V., & Wright, J. H. (1999). Targeting core beliefs in treating borderline personality disorder: The case of Anna. *Cognitive and Behavioral Practice, 6,* 54–60.

Fowler, D., Garety, P., & Kuipers, E. (1995). *Cognitive behaviour therapy for psychosis.* Chichester, UK: Wiley.

Franklin, M. E., Jaycox, L. H., & Foa, E. B. (1999). Social skills training. In M. Hersen & A. S. Bellack (Eds.), *Handbook of comparative interventions for adult disorders* (2nd ed., pp. 317–339). New York: John Wiley.

Frazee, H. E. (1953). Children who later become schizophrenic. *Smith College Studies in Social Work, XXIII,* 125–149.

Freeman, A., Epstein, N., & Simon, K. M. (1986). *Depression in the family.* New York: Haworth.

Freeman, A., Pretzer, J., Fleming, B., & Simon, K. M. (1990). *Clinical applications of cognitive therapy.* New York: Plenum.

Freeman, A., & White, D. (1989). Cognitive therapy of suicide. In A. Freeman, K. M. Simon, H. Arkowitz, & L. Beutler (Eds.), *Comprehensive Handbook of cognitive therapy* (pp. 321–346). New York: Plenum.

Freeston, M. H., Ladouceur, R., Gagnon, F., Thibodeau, N., Rheaume, J., Letarte, H., et al. (1997). Cognitive-behavioral treatment of obsessive thoughts: A controlled study. *Journal of Consulting and Clinical Psychology, 65,* 405–413.

Freud, S. (1914). On narcissism: An introduction. In J. Strachey (Ed.), *The standard edition of the complete works of Sigmund Freud* (Vol. 14, pp. 69–102). London: Hogarth Press.

Friedberg, R. D., Crosby, L. E., Friedberg, B. A., Rutter, J. G., & Knight, K. R. (2000). Making cognitive behavioral therapy user-friendly to children. *Cognitive and Behavioral Practice, 6,* 189–200.

Frosch, J. P. (1964). The psychotic character: Clinical psychiatric considerations. *Psychiatric Quarterly, 38,* 81–96.

Frosch, J. P. (1983). *Personality disorders.* Washington, DC: American Psychiatric Association Press.

Gallagher-Thompson, D., & Thompson, L. W. (1996a). Applying cognitive-behavioral therapy to the psychological problems of later life. In S. H. Zarit & B. G. Knight (Eds.), *A guide to psychotherapy and aging: Effective clinical interventions in a life-stage context* (pp. 61–82). Washington, DC: American Psychological Association.

Gallagher-Thompson, D., & Thompson, L. W. (1996b). Bereavement and adjustment disorders. In E. W. Busse & D. G. Blazer (Eds.), *Textbook of geriatric psychiatry* (2nd ed., pp. 313–328). Washington, DC: American Psychiatric Association.

Garner, D. (1992). Bulimia nervosa. In A. Freeman & F. M. Dattilio (Eds.), *Comprehensive casebook of cognitive therapy* (pp. 169–176). New York: Plenum.

Garner, D. M., & Bemis, K. M. (1982). A cognitive-behavioral approach to anorexia nervosa. *Cognitive Therapy and Research, 6,* 123–150.

Garner, D. M., Fairburn, C. G., & Davis, R. (1987). Cognitive-behavioral treatment of bulimia nervosa. *Behavior Modification, 11,* 398–431.

Gilson, M. (1992). An adjustment disorder. In A. Freeman & F. M. Dattilio (Eds.), *Comprehensive casebook of cognitive therapy* (pp. 107–116). New York: Plenum.

Gittleman-Klein, R., & Klein, D. (1969). Premorbid asocial adjustment and prognosis in schizophrenia. *Journal of Psychiatric Research, 7,* 35–53.

Glass, C. R., & Arnkoff, D. B. (1982). Think cognitively: Selected issues in cognitive assessment and therapy. In P. Kendall (Ed.), *Advances in cognitive-behavioral research and therapy* (Vol. 1, pp. 35–71). New York: Academic Press.

Gledhill, A., Lobban, F., & Sellwood, W. (1998). Group CBT for people with schizophrenia: A preliminary evaluation. *Behavioural and Cognitive Psychotherapy, 26* (1), 63–75.

Goldsmith, J. B., & McFall, R. M. (1975). Development and evaluation of an interpsersonal skill-training program for psychiatric inpatients. *Journal of Abnormal Psychology, 84,* 51-58.

Goldstein, A. J., & Chambless, D. A. (1978). A reanalysis of agoraphobia. *Behavior Therapy, 9,* 47–59.

Goldstein, A. P., Martens, J., Hubben, J., Van Belle, H. A., Schaaf, W., Wirsma, H., et al. (1973). The use of modeling to increase independent behavior. *Behavior Research and Therapy, 11,* 31–42.

Gottman, J., Markman, H., Notarius, C., & Gonso, J. (1976). *A couple's guide to communication.* Champaign, IL: Research Press.

Greenberger, D., & Padesky, C. A. (1995). *Mind over mood: A step-by-step cognitive therapy treatment manual.* New York: Guilford.

Grieger, R. M., & Boyd, J. D. (1980). *Rational emotive therapy: A skills based approach.* New York: Van Nostrand Reinhold.

Grinker, R. R., Werble, B., & Drye, R. C. (1968). *The borderline syndrome.* New York: Basic Books.

Grohol, J. M. (1997). *The insider's guide to mental health resources online.* New York: Guilford.

Guidano, V. F., & Liotti, G. (1983). *Cognitive processes and the emotional disorders.* New York: Guilford.

Guntrip, H. (1969). *Schizoid phenomena, object relations and the self.* New York: International Universities Press.

Haber, D. L. (1995). Self-hypnotic and cognitive-behavioral techniques for inpatients. *International Journal of Mental Health, 23* (4), 44–52.

Haddock, G., & Slade, P. D. (1996). *Cognitive-behavioural interventions with psychotic disorders.* London: Routledge.

Hale, W. C. (1998). *Pocket thought record.* (Available from the Cleveland Center for Cognitive Therapy, 24400 Highpoint Road, Suite 9, Beachwood, OH 44122).

Halford, W. K., Sanders, M. R., & Behrens, B. C. (1993). A comparison of the generalization of behavioral marital therapy and enhanced behavioral marital therapy. *Journal of Consulting and Clinical Psychology, 61,* 51–60.

Hall, J. (1989). Chronic psychiatric handicaps. In K. Hawton, P. M. Salkovskis, J. Kirk, & D. M. Clark (Eds.), *Cognitive behavior therapy for psychiatric problems: A practical guide* (pp. 315–338). Oxford: Oxford University Press.

Halleck, S. L. (1967). Hysterical personality traits. *Archives of General Psychiatry, 6,* 750–757.

Halperin, S., Nathan, P., Drummond, P., & Castle, D. (2000). A cognitive-behavioural, group-based intervention for social anxiety in schizophrenia. *Australian and New Zealand Journal of Psychiatry, 34* (5), 809–813.

Hamilton, N. G., Green, H. J., Mech, A. W., Brand, A. A., Wong, N., & Coyne, L. (1984). Borderline personality: *DSM-III-R* versus a previous usage. *Bulletin of the Menninger Clinic, 48,* 540–543.

Hamner, T., & Turner, P. (1985). *Parenting in contemporary society.* Englewood Cliffs, NJ: Prentice Hall.

Hardy, G. E., Barkham, M., Shapiro, D. A., Stiles, W. B., Rees, A., & Reynolds, S. (1995). Impact of Cluster C personality disorders on outcomes of contrasting brief psychotherapies for depression. *Journal of Consulting and Clinical Psychology, 63* (6), 997–1004.

Hare, R. D. (1970). *Psychopathy: Theory and research.* New York: John Wiley.

Hare, R. D. (1991). *The Hare Psychopathy Checklist—Revised.* Toronto: Multi-Health Systems.

Harlow, H. F. (1971). *Learning to love.* San Francisco: Albion.

Hawton, K. (1989). Sexual dysfunction. In K. Hawton, P. M. Salkovskis, J. Kirk, & D. M. Clark (Eds.), *Cognitive behavior therapy for psychiatric problems: A practical guide* (pp. 370–405). Oxford: Oxford University Press.

Hawton, K., & Kirk, J. (1989). Problem-solving. In K. Hawton, P. Salkovskis, J. Kirk, & D. M. Clark (Eds.), *Cognitive behavior therapy for psychiatric problems* (pp. 406–426). Oxford: Oxford University Press.

Hayward, C., Varady, S., Albano, A., Thienemann, M. A., Henderson, L., & Schatzberg, A. F. (2000). Cognitive-behavioral group therapy for social phobia in female adolescents: Results of a pilot study. *Journal of the American Academy of Child and Adolescent Psychiatry, 39,* 721–726.

Heimberg, R. G., Liebowitz, M. R., Hope, D. A., & Schneier, F. R. (1995). *Social phobia: Diagnosis, assessment, and treatment.* New York: Guilford.

Henin, A., Otto, M. W., & Reilly-Harrington, N. A. (2001). Introducing flexibility in manualized treatments: Application of recommended strategies to the cognitive-behavioral treatment of bipolar disorder. *Cognitive and Behavioral Practice, 8,* 317–328.

Herbert, J. D., Hope, D. A., & Bellack, A. S. (1992). Validity of the distinction between generalized social phobia and avoidant personality disorder. *Journal of Abnormal Psychology, 101,* 332–339.

Hersen, M. (2002). *Clinical behavior therapy: Adults and children.* New York: John Wiley.

Hill, A. B. (1976). Methodological problems in the use of factor analysis: A critical review of the experimental evidence for the anal character. *British Journal of Medical Psychology, 49,* 145–159.

Hoch, P., & Polatin, P. (1949). Pseudoneurotic forms of schizophrenia. *Psychiatric Quarterly, 23,* 248–276.

Hoffart, A. (1994). State and personality in agoraphobic patients. *Journal of Personality Disorders, 8,* 333–341.

Hoffart, A., & Hedley, L. M. (1997). Personality traits among panic disorder with agoraphobia patients before and after symptom-focused treatment. *Journal of Anxiety Disorders, 11,* 77–87.

Hofmann, S. G., Newman, M. G., Becker, E., Taylor, C. B., & Roth, W. T. (1995). Social phobia with and without avoidant personality disorder: Preliminary behavior therapy outcome findings. *Journal of Anxiety Disorders, 9,* 427–438.

Hoffman, N. G., Halikas, J. A., Mee-Lee, D., & Weedman, R. D. (1991). *Patient placement criteria for the treatment of psychoactive substance use disorders.* Chevy Chase, MD: American Society of Addiction Medicine.

Hollon, S. D., & Evans, M. D. (1983). Cognitive therapy for depression in a group format. In A. Freeman (Ed.), *Cognitive therapy with couples and groups,* (pp. 11–41). NY: Plenum.

Hollon, S. D., Evans, M. D., Auerbach, A., DeRubeis, R. J., Elkin, I., Lowery, A., et al. (1988). *Development of a system for rating therapies for depression: Differentiating cognitive therapy, interpersonal therapy, and clinical management pharmacotherapy.* Unpublished manuscript, University of Minnesota, Twin Cities Campus.

Hollon, S. D., & Shaw, B. F. (1979). Group cognitive therapy for depression. In A. T. Beck, B. F. Rush, A. J. Shaw, & G. Emery (Eds.), *Cognitive therapy of depression: A treatment manual* (pp. 328–353). New York: Guilford.

Holmes, T. H., & Rahe, R. H. (1967). The Social Readjustment Rating Scale. *Journal of Psychosomatic Research, 11* (2) 213–218.

Holt, C. S., Heimberg, R. G., & Hope, D. A. (1992). Avoidant personality disorder and the generalized subtype of social phobia. *Journal of Abnormal Psychology, 101,* 318–325.

Holtzworth-Munroe, A., Smutzler, N., & Sandin, E. (1997a). A brief review of the research on husband violence: Part I. Maritally violent versus nonviolent men. *Aggression and Violent Behavior, 2,* 65–99.

Holtzworth-Munroe, A., Smutzler, N., & Sandin, E. (1997b). A brief review of the research on husband violence: Part II. The psychological effects of husband violence on battered women and their children. *Aggression and Violent Behavior, 2,* 179–213.

Holtzworth-Munroe, A., Smutzler, N., & Sandin, E. (1997c). A brief review of the research on husband violence: Part III. Sociodemographic factors, relationship factors, and differing consequences of husband and wife violence. *Aggression and Violent Behavior, 2,* 285–307.

Hope, D. A., & Heimberg, R. G. (1993). Social phobia and social anxiety. In D. H. Barlow (Ed.), *Handbook of psychological disorders* (2nd ed., pp. 99–136). New York: Guilford.

Hope, D. A., Herbert, J. D., & White, C. (1995). Diagnostic subtype, avoidant personality disorder, and efficacy of cognitive-behavioral group therapy for social phobia. *Cognitive Therapy and Research, 19,* 399–417.

Huber, C. H, & Milstein, B. (1985). Cognitive restructuring and a collaborative set in couples' work. *American Journal of Family Therapy, 13* (2), 17–27.

Humphreys, L., Westerink, J., Giarratano, L., & Brooks, R. (1999). An intensive treatment program for chronic posttraumatic stress disorder: 2-year outcome data. *Australian and New Zealand Journal of Psychiatry, 33,* 848–854.

Ingram, R. E., & Wisnicki, K. S. (1991). Cognition in depression. In P. A. Magaro (Ed.), *Cognitive bases of mental disorders* (pp. 187–230). Newbury Park, CA: Sage.

Institute of Medicine (1987). *Causes and consequences of alcohol problems.* Washington, D. C.: National Academy Press.

Jacobson, N. S., & Christensen, A. (1996). *Integrative couple therapy: Promoting acceptance and change.* New York: Norton.

Jacobson, N. S., & Margolin, G. (1979). *Marital therapy: Strategies based on social learning and behavior exchange principles.* New York: Brunner/Mazel.

Jones, L., & River, E. (1997). Current uses of imagery in cognitive and behavioral therapies. In L. VandeCreek, S. Knapp, et al. (Eds.), *Innovations in clinical practice: A source book* (Vol. 15, pp. 423–439). Sarasota, FL: Professional Resource Press.

Karfgin, A., & Roth, D. (1992). Obesity. In A. Freeman & F. M. Dattilio (Eds.), *Comprehensive casebook of cognitive therapy* (pp. 177–184). New York: Plenum.

Kass, D. J., Silvers, F. M., & Abrams, G. M. (1972). Behavioral group treatment of hysteria. *Archives of General Psychiatry, 26,* 42–50.

Kelley, G. (1955). *The psychology of personal constructs.* New York: Norton.

Kendall, P. C. (1981). Assessment and cognitive-behavioral interventions: Purposes, proposals, and problems. In P. C. Kendall & S. D. Hollon (Eds.), *Assessment strategies for cognitive behavioral interventions* (pp. 1–12). New York: Academic Press.

Kendall, P. C., & Hollon, S. D. (Eds.). (1981). *Assessment strategies for cognitive behavioral interventions.* New York: Academic Press.

Kendall, P. C., & Korgeski, G. P. (1979). Assessment and cognitive-behavioral interventions. *Cognitive Research and Therapy, 3,* 1–21.

Kendler, K. S., & Gruenberg, A. M. (1982). Genetic relationship between paranoid personality disorder and the "schizophrenic spectrum" disorders. *American Journal of Psychiatry, 139,* 1185–1186.

Kendler, K. S., Gruenberg, A. M., & Strauss, J. S. (1981). The relationship between schizotypal personality disorder and schizophrenia. *Archives of General Psychiatry, 38,* 982–984.

Kernberg, O. F. (1967). Borderline personality organization. *Journal of the American Psychoanalytic Association, 15,* 641–685.

Kernberg, O. F. (1970). Factors in the treatment of narcissistic personalities. *Journal of the American Psychoanalytic Association, 18,* 52–85.

Kernberg, O. F. (1975). Borderline conditions and pathological narcissism. New York: Jason Aronson.

Kernberg, O. F. (1977). Structural change and its impediments. In P. Hartocollis (Ed.), *Borderline personality disorders: The concept, the syndrome, the patient* (pp. 275–306). New York: International Universities Press.

Kety, S. S., Rosenthal, D., Wender, P. H., & Schulsinger, F. (1968). Mental illness in the biological and adoptive families of adopted schizophrenics. In D. Rosenthal & S. S. Kety (Eds.), *Transmission of schizophrenia* (pp. 345–362). Oxford: Pergamon.

Kinderman, P., & Bental, R. P. (1997). Attribution therapy for paranoid delusions: A case study. *Behavioural and Cognitive Psychotherapy, 25,* 269–280.

Kingdon, D., & Turkington, D. (1994). *Cognitive-behavioural therapy of schizophrenia.* Howve, Sussex: Lawrence Erlbaum.

Kingdon, D., & Turkington, D. (1998). Cognitive behaviour therapy of schizophrenia. In T. Wykes, N. Tarrier, & S. Lewis (Eds.), *Outcome and innovation in psychological treatment of schizophrenia,* (pp. 59–79). Chichester, UK: Wiley.

Kipling, T., Bailey, M., & Charlesworth, G. (1999). The feasibility of a cognitive behavioral therapy group for men with mild/moderate cognitive impairment. *Behavioural and Cognitive Psychotherapy, 27*(2), 189–193.

Knell, S. M. (1993). *Cognitive-behavioral play therapy.* Northvale, NJ: Aronson.

Kohut, H. (1968). The psychoanalytic treatment of narcissistic personality disorders. *Psychoanalytic Study of the Child, 23,* 86–113.

Kohut, H. (1971). *The analysis of the self.* New York: International Universities Press.

Kolb, L. C. (1968). *Noyes' clinical psychiatry* (7th ed., p. 86). Philadelphia: W. B. Saunders.

Koons, C. R., Robins, C. J., Tweed, J. L., Lynch, T. R., Gonzalez, A. M., Morse, J. Q., et al. (2001). Efficacy of dialectical behavior therapy in women with borderline personality disorder. *Behavior Therapy, 32,* 371–390.

Kozak, M. J., & Foa, E. B. (1997). *Mastery of obsessive-compulsive disorder: A cognitive-behavioral approach.* New York: Graywind.

Kraepelin, E. (1913). *Psychiatrie: Ein lehrbuch* (8th ed., Vol. 3). Leipzig: Barth.

Krakow, B., Johnston, L., Melendrez, D., Hollifield, M., Warner, T. D., Chavez-Kennedy, D., et al. (2001). An open-label trial of evidence-based cognitive behavior therapy for nightmares and insomnia in crime victims with PTSD. *American Journal of Psychiatry, 158* (12), 2043–2047.

Kretschmer, E. (1936). *Physique and character.* London: Routledge & Kegan Paul.

Kristiansson, M. (1995). Incurable psychopaths? *Bulletin of the American Academy of Psychiatry and the Law, 23,* 555–562.

Kroenke, K., & Swindle, R. (2000). Cognitive-behavioral therapy for somatization and symptom syndromes: A critical review of controlled clinical trials. *Psychotherapy and Psychosomatics, 69,* 205–215.

Kunik, M. E., Braun, U., Stanley, M. A., Wristers, K., Molinari, V., Stoebner, D., et al. (2001). One session cognitive behavioural therapy for elderly patients with chronic obstructive pulmonary disease. *Psychological Medicine, 31* (4), 717–723.

Kuyken, W. (1999). A developmental psychopathology approach. *Cognitive and Behavioral Practice, 6,* 78–83.

Ladouceur, R., Dugas, M. J., Freeston, M. H., Leger, E., Gagnon, F., & Thibodeau, N. (2000). Efficacy of a cognitive-behavioral treatment for generalized anxiety disorder: Evaluation in a controlled clinical trial. *Journal of Consulting and Clinical Psychology, 68,* 957–964.

Lam, D. H., Bright, J., Jones, S., Hayward, P., Schuck, N., Chisolm, D., et al. (2000). Cognitive therapy for bipolar disorder—A pilot study of relapse prevention. *Cognitive Therapy and Research, 24,* 503–520.

Layden, M. A., Newman, C. F., Freeman, A., & Morse, S. B. (1993). *Cognitive therapy of borderline personality disorder.* Needham Heights, MA: Allyn & Bacon.

Lazare, A., Klerman, G. L., & Armor, D. J. (1966). Oral, obsessive, and hysterical personality patterns. *Archives of General Psychiatry, 14,* 624–630.

Lazarus R. S. (1968). Emotions and adaptation: Conceptual and empirical relations. *Nebraska Symposium on Motivation, 16,* 175–266.

Leahy, R. L. (2003). *Cognitive therapy techniques: A practitioner's guide.* New York: Guilford.

Lester, D. (1983). *Why people kill themselves.* Springfield, IL: Charles C. Thomas.

Liberman, R., De Risis, W., & Mueser, K. (1989). *Social skills training for psychiatric patients.* New York: Pergamon.

Linehan, M. M. (1977). Issues in behavioral interviewing. In J. D. Cone & R. P. Hawkins (Eds.), *Behavioral assessment: New directions in clinical psychology* (pp. 30–51). New York: Bruner/Mazel.

Linehan, M. M. (1993a). *Cognitive-behavioral treatment of borderline personality disorder.* New York: Guilford.

Linehan, M. M. (1993b). *Skill training manual for treating borderline personality disorder.* New York: Guilford.

Linehan, M. M., Armstrong, H. E., Suarez, A., Allmon, D., & Heard, H. L. (1991). Cognitive-behavioral treatment of chronically parasuicidal borderline patients. *Archives of General Psychiatry, 48,* 1060–1064.

Linehan, M. M., Heard, H. L., & Armstrong, H. E. (1993). Naturalistic follow-up of a behavioral treatment for chronically parasuicidal borderline patients. *Archives of General Psychiatry, 50,* 971–974.

Linehan, M. M., Tutek, D. A., Heard, H. L., & Armstrong, H. E. (1994). Interpersonal outcome of cognitive behavioral treatment for chronically suicidal borderline patients. *American Journal of Psychiatry, 151,* 1771–1776.

Livesley, W. J., West, M., & Tanney, A. (1985). Historical comment on *DSM-III* schizoid and avoidant personality disorders. *American Journal of Psychiatry, 42,* 1344–1347.

Livesley, W. J., West, M., & Tanney, A. (1986a). Dr. Livesley and associates reply. *American Journal of Psychiatry, 143,* 1062–1063.

Livesley, W. J., West, M., & Tanney, A. (1986b). "Schizoid and avoidant personality disorders in *DSM-III*": Dr. Livesley and associates reply. *American Journal of Psychiatry, 143,* 1322–1323.

Longabaugh, R., & Eldred, S. H. (1973). Premorbid adjustments, schizoid personality and onset of illness as predictors of post-hospitalization functioning. *Journal of Psychiatric Research, 10,* 19–29.

Luborsky, L., McLellan, A. T., Woody, G. E., O'Brien, C. P., & Auerbach, A. (1985). Therapist success and its determinants. *Archives of General Psychiatry, 42,* 602–611.

MacKinnon, R. A., & Michaels, R. (1971). *The psychiatric interview in clinical practice* (pp. 110–146). Philadelphia: W. B. Saunders.

Mahoney, M. J. (1977). Some applied issues in self-monitoring. In J. D. Cone & R. P. Hawkins (Eds.), *Behavioral assessment: New directions in clinical psychology* (pp. 245–254). New York: Bruner/Mazel.

Maier, W., Lichtermann, D., Minges, J., & Heun, R. (1994). Personality disorders among the relatives of schizophrenia patients. *Schizophrenia Bulletin, 20,* 481–493.

Malmquist, C. P. (1971). Hysteria in childhood. *Postgraduate Medicine, 50,* 112–117.

March, J. S. (1995). *Anxiety disorders in children and adolescents.* New York: Guilford.

March, J. S., Frances, A., Carpenter, D., & Kahn, D. A. (Eds.). (1997). The expert consensus guidelines series: Treatment of obsessive-compulsive disorder. *Journal of Clinical Psychiatry, 58* (Suppl. 4), 1–73.

Marlatt, G. A. (1983). The controlled drinking controversy. *American Psychologist, 38*, 1097–1110.

Marlatt, G. A., & Gordon, J. R. (1985). *Relapse prevention*. New York: Guilford.

Marshall, W. L., & Barbaree, H. E. (1984). Disorders of personality, impulse, and adjustment. In S. M. Turner & M. Hersen (Eds.), *Adult psychopathology and diagnosis* (pp. 406–449). New York: John Wiley.

Masterson, J. F. (1978). *New perspectives on psychotherapy of the borderline adult.* New York: Brunner/Mazel.

Masterson, J. F. (April, 1982). *Borderline and narcissistic disorders: An integrated developmental approach.* Workshop presented at Adelphi University, Garden City, New York.

Matthews, W. M., & Reid, W. H. (1986). A wilderness experience treatment program for offenders. In W. H. Reid (Ed.), *The treatment of antisocial syndromes* (pp. 247–258). New York: Van Nostrand Reinhold.

Mays, D. T. (1985). Behavior therapy with borderline personality disorders: One clinician's perspective. In D. T. Mays & C. M. Franks (Eds.), *Negative outcome in psychotherapy and what to do about it* (pp. 301–311). New York: Springer.

Mays, D. T., & Franks, C. M. (Eds.). (1985). *Negative outcome in psychotherapy and what to do about it.* New York: Springer.

McCabe, M. P. (2001). Evaluation of a cognitive behavior therapy program for people with sexual dysfunction. *Journal of Sex and Marital Therapy, 27*, 259–271.

McFall, M. E., & Wallersheim, J. P. (1979). Obsessive-compulsive neurosis: A cognitive-behavioral formulation and approach to treatment. *Cognitive Therapy and Research, 3*, 333–348.

McKay, D., Neziroglu, F., Todaro, J., and Yaryura-Tobias, J. A. (1996). Changes in personality disorders following behavior therapy for obsessive-compulsive disorder. *Journal of Anxiety Disorders, 10* (1), 47–57.

McKay, M., Davis, M., & Fanning, P. (1999). *Thoughts & feelings: Taking control of your moods and your life.* New York: MJF Books.

McMullin, R. E. (1986). *Handbook of cognitive therapy techniques.* New York: Norton.

Meichenbaum, D. (1977). *Cognitive-behavior modification: An integrative approach.* New York: Plenum.

Meichenbaum, D., & Fong, G. T. (1993). How individuals control their own minds: A constructive narrative perspective. In D. M. Wegner & J. W. Pennebaker (Eds.), *Handbook of mental control* (pp. 473–490). Upper Saddle River, NJ: Prentice Hall.

Meichenbaum, D., & Turk, D. C. (1987). *Facilitating treatment adherence: A practitioner's guidebook.* New York: Plenum.

Mellsop, G. W. (1972). Psychiatric patients seen as children and adults: Childhood predictors of adult illness. *Journal of Child Psychological Psychiatry, 13*, 91–101.

Mellsop, G. W. (1973). Adult psychiatric patients on whom information during childhood is missing. *British Journal of Psychiatry, 123*, 703–710.

Merluzzi, T. V., Glass, C. R., & Genest, M. (1981). *Cognitive assessment.* New York: Guilford.

Metz, M. E., & Pryor, J. L. (2000). Premature ejaculation: A psychophysiological approach for assessment and management. *Journal of Sex and Marital Therapy, 26*, 293–320.

Michelson, L. (1987). Cognitive-behavioral assessment and treatment of agoraphobia. In L. Michelson and L. M. Ascher (Eds.), *Anxiety and stress disorders: Cognitive-behavioral assessment and treatment* (pp. 213–279). New York: Guilford.

Miller, R. C., & Berman, J. S. (1983). The efficacy of cognitive behavior therapies: A quantitative review of the research evidence. *Psychological Bulletin, 94*, 39–53.

Miller, W. R., & Brown, S. A. (1997). Why psychologists should treat alcohol and drug problems. *American Psychologist, 52*, 1269–1279.

Miller, W. R. & Rollnick, S. (1991). *Motivational interviewing: Preparing people to change addictive behavior.* New York: Guilford.

Miller, W., Rollnick, S., Conforti, K., & Miller, W. R. (2002). *Motivational interviewing* (2nd ed.). New York: Guilford.

Millon, T. (1969). *Modern psychopathology: A biosocial approach to maladaptive learning and functioning.* Philadelphia: W. B. Saunders.

Millon, T. (1981). *Disorders of personality: DSM-III-R: Axis II.* New York: John Wiley.

Millon, T. (1986a). *DSM-III* distinction between Schizoid and Avoidant Personality Disorders [letter to the editor]. *Canadian Journal of Psychiatry, 31*, 600–700.

Millon, T. (1986b). Schizoid and avoidant personality disorders in *DSM-III*. *American Journal of Psychiatry, 143*, 1321–1322.

Millon, T. (with Davis, R. D.). (1996). *Disorders of personality: DSM-IV-TR and beyond* (2nd ed.). New York: John Wiley.

Millon, T., Davis, R. D., & Millon, C. (1996). *The Millon clinical multiaxial inventory—III manual*. Minnetonka, MN: National Computer System.

Millon, T., Davis, R., Millon, C., Escovar, L., & Meagher, S. (2000). *Personality disorders in modern life*. New York: John Wiley.

Millon, T., Simonsen, E., Birket-Smith, M., & Davis, R. D. (Eds.) (1998). *Psychopathy: Antisocial, criminal, and violent behavior*. New York: Guilford.

Mitchell, C. G. (1999). Treating anxiety in a managed care setting: A controlled comparison of medication alone versus medication plus cognitive-behavioral group therapy. *Research on Social Work Practice, 9* (2), 188–200.

Mizes, J. S., Landolf-Fritsche, B., & Grossman-McKee, D. (1987). Patterns of distorted cognitions in phobic disorders: An investigation of clinically severe simple phobics, social phobics, and agoraphobics. *Cognitive Therapy and Research, 11*, 583–592.

Monti, P. M., Abrams, D. B., Binkoff, J. A., & Zwick, W. R. (1990). Communication skills training, communication skills training with family and cognitive behavioral mood management training for alcoholics. *Journal of Studies on Alcohol, 51* (3), 263–270.

Monti, P. M., Abrams, D. B., Kadden, R. M., & Cooney, N. L. (1989). *Treating alcohol dependence*. New York: Guilford.

Moorey, S. (1996). When bad things happen to rational people: Cognitive therapy in adverse life circumstances. In P. Salkovskis (Ed.), *Frontiers of cognitive therapy* (pp. 450–469). New York: Guilford.

Moorey, S., & Burns, D. D. (1983). The apprenticeship model: Training in cognitive therapy by participation. In A. Freeman (Ed.), *Cognitive therapy with couples and groups* (pp. 303–322). New York: Plenum.

Morin, C. M., Kowatch, R. A., Barry, T., & Walton, E. (1993). Cognitive-behavior therapy for late-life insomnia. *Journal of Consulting and Clinical Psychology, 61*, 137–146.

Morris, D. P., Soroker, E., & Burruss, G. (1954). Follow-up studies of shy, withdrawn children: I. Evaluation of later adjustment. *American Journal of Orthopsychiatry, 24*, 743–754.

Morrison, J., & Anders, T. F. (1999). *Interviewing children and adolescents: Skills and strategies for effective DSM-IV diagnosis*. New York: Guilford.

Muñoz, R. F., Ghosh-Ippen, C., Rao, S., Le, H. L., & Dwyer, E. V. (2000). *Manual for group cognitive behavioral therapy of major depression: A reality management approach*. [Participant Manual and Instructor's Manual]. Available from the author, University of California, San Francisco, Department of Psychiatry, San Francisco General Hospital, 1001 Potrero Avenue, Suite 7M, San Francisco, CA 94110.

Muris, P., Mayer, B., Bartelds, E., Tierney, S., & Bogie, N. (2001). The revised version of the Screen for Child Anxiety Related Emotional Disorders (SCARED-R): Treatment sensitivity in an early intervention trial for childhood anxiety disorders. *British Journal of Clinical Psychology, 40* (3), 323–336.

Nacke, P. (1899). Die sexuellen perversitaten in der irrenanstalt. *Psychiatrische en Neurologische Bladen, 3*, 20–30.

Nauth, L. (1998). The problem is crime. *The Behavior Therapist, 21*, 93–94.

Needleman, L. D. (1999). *Cognitive case conceptualization: A guidebook for practitioners*. Mahwah, New Jersey: Lawrence Erlbaum.

Nestadt, G., Hanfelt, J., Liang, K. Y., Lamacz, M., Wolyniec, P., & Pulver, A. E. (1994). An evaluation of the structure of schizophrenia spectrum persnality disorders. *Journal of Personality Disorders, 8*, 288–298.

Nelson, H. (1997). *Cognitive behavioural therapy with schizophrenia: A practice manual*. Cheltenham: Stanley Thornes.

Newman, C. (1999). The case of Anna: Addressing three special problems in treatment. *Cognitive and Behavioral Practice, 6*, 84–91.

Newman, C. F., Leahy, R. L., Beck, A. T., Reilly-Harrington, N. A., & Gyulai, L. *Bipolar disorder: A cognitive therapy approach*. Washington, DC: American Psychological Association.

Nezu, A. (1998). Just the FACTS . . .. *The Behavior Therapist, 21,* 57–59.

Nisbett, R. E., & Wilson, T. D. (1977). Telling more than we can know: Verbal reports on mental processes. *Psychological Review, 84,* 231–259.

Norton, G. R., Harrison, B., Hauch, J., & Rhodes, L. (1985). Characteristics of people with infrequent panic attacks. *Journal of Abnormal Psychology, 94,* 216–221.

Otto, M. W., Pollack, M. H., & Sabatino, S. A. (1996). Maintenance of remission following cognitive behavior therapy for panic disorder: Possible deleterious effects of concurrent medication treatment. *Behavior Therapy, 27,* 473–482.

Overholser, J. C. (1997). Treatment of excessive interpersonal dependency: A cognitive-behavioral model. *Journal of Contemporary Psychotherapy, 27,* 283–301.

Overholser, J. C., & Fine, M. A. (1994). Cognitive-behavioral treatment of excessive interpersonal dependency: A four-stage psychotherapy model. *Journal of Cognitive Psychotherapy, 8,* 55–70.

Padesky, C. A. (1994). Schema change processes in cognitive therapy. *Clinical Psychology and Psychotherapy, 1* (5), 267–278.

Padesky, C. A., & Greenberger, D. (1995). *Clinician's guide to mind over mood.* New York: Guilford.

Palmer, A. G., William, H., & Adams, M. (1995). CBT in a group format for bipolar affective disorder. *Behavioral and Cognitive Psychotherapy, 23,* 153–168.

Patterson, W. M., Dohn, H. H., Bird, J., & Patterson, G. A. (1983). Evaluation of suicidal patients: The SAD PERSONS scale. *Psychosomatics, 24,* 343–349.

Pattison, E. M. (1979). The selection of treatment modalities for the alcoholic patient. In J. H. Mendelson & N. K. Mello (Eds.), *The diagnosis and treatment of alcoholism* (pp. 125–227). New York: McGraw-Hill.

Perris, C. (1989). *Cognitive therapy with schizophrenic patients.* New York: Guilford.

Perris, C., & McGorry, P. D. (Eds.). (1998). *Cognitive psychotherapy of psychotic and personality disorders: Handbook of theory and practice.* New York: John Wiley.

Perris, C., Nordstrom, G., & Troeng, L. (1992). Schizophrenic disorders. In A. Freeman & F. M. Dattilio (Eds.), *Comprehensive casebook of cognitive therapy* (pp. 313–330). New York: Plenum.

Persons, J. D. (1989). *Cognitive therapy in practice: A case formulation approach.* New York: W. W. Norton.

Persons, J. B., Burns, D. D., & Perloff, J. M. (1988). Predictors of dropout and outcome in cognitive therapy for depression in a private practice setting. *Cognitive Therapy and Research, 12,* 557–575.

Persons, J. B., & Miranda, J. (2002). Treating dysfunctional beliefs: Implications of the mood-state hypothesis. In R. L. Leahy & E. T. Dowd (Eds.), *Clinical advances in cognitive psychotherapy: Theory and application* (pp. 62–74). New York: Springer.

Peterson, A. L., & Halstead, T. S. (1998). Group cognitive behavior therapy for depression in a community setting: A clinical replication series. *Behavior Therapy, 29 (1),* 3–18.

Peterson, R. J. (2000). *The assertiveness workbook: How to express your ideas and stand up for yourself at work and in relationships.* Oakland, CA: New Harbinger.

Pfohl, B. (1991). Histrionic personality disorder: A review of available data and recommendations for DSM-IV. *Journal of Personality Disorders, 5,* 150–166.

Piacentini, J., & Bergman, R. L. (2001). Developmental issues in cognitive therapy for childhood anxiety disorders. *Journal of Cognitive Psychotherapy, 15* (3), 165–182.

Piacentini, J., Bergman, R. L., Jacobs, C., McCracken, J. T., & Kretchman, J. (2002). Open trial of cognitive behavior therapy for childhood obsessive-compulsive disorder. *Journal of Anxiety Disorders, 16,* 207–219.

Pinquart, M., & Soerensen, S. (2001). How effective are psychotherapeutic and other psychosocial interventions with older adults? A meta-analysis. *Journal of Mental Health and Aging, 7* (2), 207–243.

Pretzer, J. L. (1983, August). *Borderline personality disorder: Too complex for cognitive-behavioral approaches?* Paper presented at the meeting of the American Psychological Association, Anaheim, CA. (ERIC Document Reproduction Service No. ED 243 007).

Pretzer, J. L. (1998). Cognitive-behavioral approaches to the treatment of personality disorders. In C. Perris & P. D. McGorry (Eds.), *Cognitive psychotherapy of psychotic and personality disorders: Handbook of theory and practice* (pp. 269–291). New York: John Wiley.

Pretzer, J. L., & Beck, A. T. (1996). A cognitive theory of personality disorders. In J. F. Clarkin & M. F. Lenzenweger (Eds.), *Major theories of personality disorder* (pp. 36–105). New York: Guilford.

Pretzer, J., & Hampl, S. (1994). Cognitive behavioural treatment of obsessive compulsive personality disorder. *Clinical Psychology and Psychotherapy, 1* (5), 298–307.

Prochaska, J. O., & DiClemente, C. C. (1982). Transtheoretical therapy: Toward a more integrative model of change. *Psychotherapy: Theory, Research, and Practice, 20*, 161–173.

Prochaska, J. O., DiClemente, C. C., & Norcross, J. C. (1992). In search of how people change: Applications to addictive behaviors. *American Psychologist, 47*, 1102–1114.

Rado, S. (1956). Dynamics and classification of disordered behavior. In S. Rado, *Psychoanalysis of behavior* (pp. 268–285). Oxford: Grune and Stratton.

Rakos, R. F. (1991). *Assertive behavior: Theory, research, and training.* New York: Routledge.

Ramsay, J. R. (1999). A life of quiet desperation: The case example of Anna. *Cognitive and Behavioral Practice, 6*, 73–77.

Ratto, C. L., & Capitano, D. L. (1999). New directions for cognitive therapy: A schema-focused approach. *Cognitive and Behavioral Practice, 6*, 68–73.

Reich, J., & Noyes, R. (1986). "Historical comment on *DSM-III* schizoid and avoidant personality disorder": Comment. *American Journal of Psychiatry, 42*, 1062.

Reid, W. H., & Solomon, G. F. (1986). Community-based offender programs. In W. H. Reid (Ed.), *The treatment of antisocial syndromes* (pp. 76–94). New York: Van Nostrand Reinhold.

Reinecke, M. A., Dattilio, F. M., & Freeman, A. (Eds.). (1996). *Cognitive therapy with children and adolescents: A casebook for clinical practice.* New York: Guilford.

Reinecke, M. A., & Ryan, N. E. (1998). Cognitive-behavioral therapy of depression and depressive symptoms during adolescence: A review and meta-analysis. *Journal of the American Academy of Child and Adolescent Psychiatry, 37*, 26–34.

Renneberg, B., Goldstein, A. J., Phillips, D., & Chambless, D. L. (1990). Intensive behavioral group treatment of avoidant personality disorder. *Behavior Therapy, 21*, 363–377.

Resick, P. A., & Schnicke, M. K. (1992). Cognitive Processing Therapy for sexual assault victims. *Journal of Consulting and Clinical Psychology, 60*, 748–756.

Rice, M. E. (1997). Violent offender research and implications for the criminal justice system. *American Psychologist, 52*, 414–423.

Rief, W., Trenkamp, S., Auer, C., & Fichter, M. M. (2000). Cognitive behavior therapy in panic disorder and comorbid major depression. *Psychotherapy and Psychosomatics, 69*, 70–78.

Robins, E., Gassner, S., Kayes, J., Wilkinson, R. H., Jr., & Murphy, G. E. (1959). The communication of suicidal intent: A study of 134 consecutive cases of successful (completed) suicide. *American Journal of Psychiatry, 115*, 724–733.

Roff, J. D., Knight, R., & Wertheim, E. (1976). A factor analytic study of childhood symptoms antecedent to schizophrenia. *Journal of Abnormal Psychology, 85*, 543–549.

Rohde, P., Clarke, G. N., Lewinsohn, P. M., Seeley, J. R., & Kaufman, N. K. (2001). Impact of comorbidity on a cognitive-behavioral group treatment for adolescent depression. *Journal of the American Academy of Child and Adolescent Psychiatry, 40*, 795–802.

Ronen, T. (1995). From what kind of self-control can children benefit? *Journal of Cognitive Psychotherapy: An International Quarterly, 9*, 45–61.

Rose, S. D. (1974). Training parents in groups as behavior modifiers of their mentally retarded children. *Journal of Behavior Therapy and Experimental Psychiatry. 5* (2), 135–140.

Roth, A., & Fonagy, P. (1996). *What works for whom? A critical review of psychotherapy research.* New York: Guilford.

Rothbaum, B. O., & Hodges, L. F. (1999). The use of virtual reality exposure in the treatment of anxiety disorders. *Behavior Modification, 23*, 507–525.

Rothbaum, B. O., Hodges, L. F., Kooper, R., Opdyke, D., Williford, J. S. & North, M. (1995). Effectiveness of computer-generated (virtual reality) graded exposure in the treatment of acrophobia. *American Journal of Psychiatry, 152*, 626–628.

Rothbaum, B. O., Meadows, E. A., Resick, P., & Foy, D. W. (2000). Cognitive-behavioral therapy. In E. B. Foa, T. M. Keane, & M. J. Friedman (Eds.), *Effective treatments for PTSD* (pp. 60–83). New York: Guilford.

Ruegg, R., & Frances, A. (1995). New research in personality disorders. *Journal of Personality Disorders, 9*, 1–48.

Rush, A. J., & Shaw, B. F. (1983). Failures in treating depression by cognitive therapy. In E. B. Foa & P. G. M. Emmelkamp (Eds.), *Failures in behavior therapy* (pp. 217–228). New York: John Wiley.

Rutter, M. L. (1997). Nature-nurture integration: The example of antisocial behavior. *American Psychologist, 52,* 390–398.

Sager, C. J. (1976). *Marriage contracts and couple therapy: Hidden forces in intimate relationships.* New York: Brunner/Mazel.

Salkovskis, P. M. (1985). Obsessional compulsive problems: A cognitive behavioral analysis. *Behaviour Research and Therapy, 23,* 571–583.

Salkovskis, P. M. (1989). Somatic problems. In K. Hawton, P. M. Salkovskis, J. Kirk, & D. M. Clark (Eds.), *Cognitive behavior therapy for psychiatric problems: A practical guide* (pp. 235–276). Oxford: Oxford University Press.

Sanderson, W. C., Beck, A. T., & McGinn, L. K. (1994). Cognitive therapy for generalized anxiety disorder: Significance of comorbid personality disorders. *Journal of Cognitive Psychotherapy: An International Quarterly, 8,* 13–18.

Saunders, D. G. (1996). Feminist-cognitive-behavioral and process-psychodynamic treatments for men who batter: Interaction of abuser traits and treatment models. *Violence and Victims, 11* (4), 393–414.

Sbrocco, T., & Barlow, D. H. (1996). Conceptualizing the cognitive component of sexual arousal: Implications for sexuality research and treatment. In P. Salkovskis (Ed.), *Frontiers of cognitive therapy* (pp. 419–449). New York: Guilford.

Scholing, A., & Emmelkamp, P. M. G. (1993). Exposure with and without cognitive therapy for generalized social phobia: Effects of individual and group treatment. *Behaviour Research and Therapy, 31* (7), 667–681.

Scholing, A., & Emmelkamp, P. M. G. (1996). Treatment of generalized social phobia: Results at long-term follow-up. *Behaviour Research and Therapy, 34* (5,6), 447–452.

Scholing, A., & Emmelkamp, P. M. G. (1999). Prediction of treatment outcome in social phobia: A cross validation. *Behaviour Research and Therapy, 37,* 659–670.

Schuckit, M. A. (1979). Treatment of alcoholism in office and outpatient settings. In J. H. Mendelson & N. K. Mello (Eds.), *The diagnosis and treatment of alcoholism* (pp. 229–255). New York: McGraw-Hill.

Schwartz, R. M., & Gottman, J. M. (1976). Toward a task analysis of assertive behavior. *Journal of Consulting and Clinical Psychology, 44,* 910–920.

Sciuto, G., Diaferia, G., Battaglia, M., Perna, G. P., Gabriele, A., & Bellodi, L. (1991). *DSM-III-R* personality disorders in panic and obsessive compulsive disorder: A comparison study. *Comprehensive Psychiatry, 32,* 450–457.

Scott, E. M. (1986). "Historical comment on *DSM-III* schizoid and avoidant personality disorders": Comment. *American Journal of Psychiatry, 42,* 1062.

Scott, J. (1996). Cognitive therapy for clients with bipolar disorder. *Cognitive and Behavioral Practice, 3,* 29–51.

Seligman, M. E. P. (1975). *Helplessness: On depression, development, and death.* San Francisco: Freeman.

Sensky, T., Turkington, D., Kingdon, D., Scott, J. L., Siddle, R., O'Carroll, M., et al. (2000). A randomized controlled trial of cognitive-behavioral therapy for persistent symptoms in schizophrenia resistant to medication. *Archives of General Psychiatry, 57,* 165–172.

Shaffer, D., Lucas, C. P., & Richters, J. E. (Eds.). (1999). *Diagnostic assessment in child and adolescent psychopathology.* New York: Guilford.

Shapiro, D. (1965). *Neurotic styles.* New York: Basic Books.

Shapiro, F. (1995). *Eye movement desensitization and reprocessing: Basic principles, protocols, and procedures.* New York: Guilford.

Shaw, B. F., Vallis, T. M., & McCabe, S. B. (1985). The assessment of the severity and symptom patterns in depression. In E. E. Beckham & W. R. Leher (Eds.), *Handbook of depression* (pp. 372–407). Homewood, IL: Dorsey.

Siever, L. J. (1981). Schizoid and schizotypal personality disorders. In J. R. Lion (Ed.), *Personality disorders: Diagnosis and management* (pp. 32–64). Baltimore: William and Wilkens.

Siever, L. J., & Davis, K. L. (1991). A psychobiological perspective on the personality disorders. *American Journal of Psychiatry, 148,* 1647–1658.

Simon, K. M. (1994). A rapid stabilization cognitive group therapy programme for psychiatric inpatients. *Clinical Psychology and Psychotherapy, 1,* 286–297.

Simon, K. M, & Fleming, B. M. (1985). Beck's cognitive therapy of depression: Treatment and outcome. In R. M. Turner & L. M. Ascher (Eds.), *Evaluating behavior therapy outcome* (pp. 146–179). New York: Springer.

Sloan, E. P., Hauri, P., Bootzin, R., Morin, C., Stevenson, M. & Shapiro, C. M. (1993). The nuts and bolts of behavioral therapy for insomnia. *Journal of Psychosomatic Research, 37*, 19–37.

Sobell, M. B., & Sobell, L. A. (1993). *Problem drinkers: Guided self-change treatment.* New York: Guilford.

Solomon, K. E., & Annis, H. M. (1990). Outcome and efficacy expectancy in the prediction of post-treatment drinking behavior. *British Journal of Addiction, 85*, 659–665.

Somers, J. M., & Marlatt, G. A. (1992). Alcohol problems. In P. H. Wilson (Ed.), *Principles and practice of relapse prevention* (pp. 23–42). New York: Guilford.

Spivack, G., & Shure, M. B. (1974). *Social adjustment of young children: A cognitive approach to solving real-life problems.* San Francisco: Jossey-Bass.

Spring, J. A., & Spring, M. (1996). *After the affair: Healing the pain and rebuilding trust when a partner has been unfaithful.* New York: Harper Collins.

Stampfl, T. G., & Levis, D. J. (1967). Essential of implosive therapy: A learning based psychodynamic behavior therapy. *Journal of Abnormal Psychology, 72*, 496–503.

Stasiewicz, P. R., Carey, K. B., Bradizza, C. M., & Maisto, S. A. (1996). Behavioral assessment of substance abuse with co-occurring psychiatric disorder. *Cognitive and Behavioral Practice, 3*, 91–105.

Steffen, A. M., Futterman, A., & Gallagher-Thompson, D. (1998). Depressed caregivers: Comparative outcomes of two interventions. *Clinical Gerontologist, 19* (4), 3–15.

Stein, D. J., & Hollander, E. (2002). *Textbook of anxiety disorders.* Washington, DC: American Psychiatric Association.

Steketee, G., & Foa, E. B. (1985). Obsessive-compulsive disorder. In D. H. Barlow (Ed.), *Clinical handbook of psychological disorders: A step-by-step treatment manual* (pp. 69–144). New York: Guilford.

Steketee, G., Foa, E. G., & Grayson, J. B. (1982). Recent advances in the treatment of obsessive-compulsives. *Archives of General Psychiatry, 39*, 1365–1371.

Steketee, G., Pigott, T. A., & Schemmel, T. (1999). *Obsessive compulsive disorder: The latest assessment and treatment strategies.* Kansas City, MO: Compact Clinicals.

St. Onge, S. (1995). Systematic desensitization. In M. Ballou (Ed.), *Psychological interventions: A guide to strategies* (pp. 95–115). Westport, CT: Praeger.

Stravynski, A., Belisle, M., Marcouiller, M., Lavallee, Y., & Elie, R. (1994). The treatment of avoidant personality disorder by social skills training in the clinic or real-life settings. *Canadian Journal of Psychiatry, 39*, 377–383.

Stravynski, A., Lamontagne, Y., & Lavallee, Y. (1986). Clinical phobias and avoidant personality disorder among alcoholics admitted to an alcoholism rehabilitation setting. *Canadian Journal of Psychiatry, 31*, 714–718.

Stravynski, A., Marks, I., & Yule, W. (1982). Social skills problems in neurotic outpatients: Social skills training with and without cognitive modification. *Archives of General Psychiatry, 39*, 1378–1385.

Stuart, R. B. (1980). *Helping couples change: A social learning approach to marital therapy.* New York: Guilford.

Tarrier, N., Haddock, G., & Barrowclough, C. (1998). Training and dissemination: Research to practice in innovative psychosocial treatments of schizophrenia. In T. Wykes, N. Tarrier, & S. Lewis (Eds.), *Outcome and innovation in psychological treatment of schizophrenia* (pp. 215–236). Chichester, UK: Wiley.

Toren, P., Wolmer, L., Rosental, B., Eldar, S., Koren, S., Lask, M., et al. (2000). Case series: Brief parent-child group therapy for childhood anxiety disorders using a manual-based cognitive-behavioral technique. *Journal of the American Academy of Child and Adolescent Psychiatry, 39* (10), 1309–1312.

Torgerson, S. (1980). The oral, obsessive and hysterical personality syndromes. *Archives of General Psychiatry, 37*, 1272–1277.

Trudel, G., Marchand, A., Ravart, M., Aubin, S., Turgeon, L., & Fortier, P. (2001). The effect of a cognitive-behavioral group treatment program on hypoactive sexual desire in women. *Sexual and Relationship Therapy, 16*, 145–164.

Turk, C. L., Fresco, D. M., & Heimberg, R. G. (1999). Cognitive behavior therapy. In M. Hersen & A. S. Bellack (Eds.), *Handbook of comparative interventions for adult disorders* (2nd ed., pp. 287–316). New York: John Wiley.

Turk, C. L., Heimberg, R. G., & Hope, D. A. (2001). Social anxiety disorder. In D. H. Barlow (Ed.), *Clinical handbook of psychological disorders: A step-by-step treatment manual,* (3rd ed., pp. 114–153). New York: Guilford.

Turkat, I. D. (1990). *The personality disorders: A psychological approach to clinical management.* New York: Pergamon.

Turkat, I. D., & Carlson, C. R. (1984). Data-based versus symptomatic formulation of treatment: The case of a dependent personality. *Journal of Behavioral Therapy and Experimental Psychiatry, 15*,153–160.

Turkat, I. D., & Maisto, S. A. (1985). Personality disorders: Application of the experimental method to the formulation and modification of personality disorders. In D. H. Barlow (Ed.), *Clinical handbook of psychological disorders* (pp. 502–570). New York: Guilford.

Turner, R. M. (1987). The effects of personality disorder diagnosis on the outcome of social anxiety symptom reduction. *Journal of Personality Disorders, 1,* 136–143.

Turner, R. M. (1989). Case study evaluations of a bio-cognitive-behavoral approach for the treatment of borderline personality disorder. *Behavior Therapy, 20,* 477–489.

Turner, S. M., Beidel, D. C., Dancu, C.V., & Keys, D. J. (1986). Psychopathology of social phobia and comparison to avoidant personality disorders. *Journal of Abnormal Psychology, 95,* 389–394.

Turner, S. M., Beidel, D. C., & Townsley, R. M. (1992). Social phobia: A comparison of specific and generalized subtypes and avoidant personality. *Journal of Abnormal Psychology, 101,* 326–331.

Upper, D., & Flowers, J. V. (1994). Behavioral group therapy in rehabilitation settings. In J. R. Bedell (Ed.), *Psychological assessment and treatment of persons with severe mental disorders* (pp. 191–214). Philadelphia: Taylor & Francis.

Utay, J. M., & Lampe, R. E. (1995). Use of a group game to enhance social skills of children with learning disabilities. Special Issue: Group process considerations for inclusion of people with disabilities. *Journal for Specialists in Group Work, 20* (2), 114–120.

Vallis, T. M., Shaw, B. F., & Dobson, K. S. (1986). The Cognitive Therapy Scale: Psychometric properties. *Journal of Consulting and Clinical Psychology, 54,* 381–385.

van Oppen, P., de Haan, E., van Balkom, A. J. L. M., Spinohoven, P., Hoogduin, K., & van Dyck, R. (1995). Cognitive therapy and exposure in vivo in the treatment of obsessive compulsive disorder. *Behaviour Research and Therapy, 33,* 379–390.

Veale, D., Gournay, D., Dryden, W., Boocock, A., Shah, F., Willson, R., et al. (1996). Body dysmorphic disorder. A cognitive behavioural model and pilot randomised controlled trial. *Behaviour Research and Therapy, 34,* 717–279.

Veen, G., & Arntz, A. (2000). Multidimensional dichotomous thinking characterizes borderline personality disorder. *Cognitive Therapy and Research, 24,* 23–45.

Vieth, I. (1977). Four thousand years of hysteria. In M. J. Horowitz (Ed.), *Hysterical personality* (pp. 7–93). New York: Jason Aronson.

Vitousek, K. M. (1996). The current status of cognitive-behavioral models of anorexia nervosa and bulimia nervosa. In P. Salkovskis (Ed.), *Frontiers of cognitive therapy* (pp. 383–418). New York: Guilford.

Vollmer, A., & Blanchard, E. B. (1998). Controlled comparison of individual versus group cognitive therapy for irritable bowel syndrome. *Behavior Therapy, 29* (1), 9–33.

Weekes, C. (1969). *Hope and help for your nerves.* New York: Hawthorn Books.

Weingardt, K. R., & Zeiss, R. A. (2000). Skills training groups on a psychiatric intensive care unit: A guide for group leaders. *Cognitive and Behavioral Practice, 7,* 385–394.

Weintraub, W. (1981). Compulsive and paranoid personalities. In J. R. Lion (Ed.), *Personality disorders: Diagnosis and management* (pp. 163–181). Baltimore: Williams and Wilkins.

Weishaar, M. (1993). *Aaron T. Beck.* Thousand Oaks, CA: Sage.

Weissman, A. (1979). The Dysfunctional Attitude Scale: A validation study. *Dissertation Abstracts International, 40,* 1389–1390B. (University Microfilm No.79-19, 533).

Weissman, A. N., & Beck, A. T. (1978, November). *Development and validation of the Dysfunctional Attitude Scale: A preliminary investigation.* Paper presented at the Annual Meeting of the American Educational Research Association, Toronto.

Weissman, M. M. (1993). The epidemiology of personality disorders: A 1990 update. *Journal of Personality Disorders, 7* (Suppl. 1), 44–62.

Welch, B. L. (2000). Borderline patients: Danger ahead. Interview published in *Insight: Safeguarding psychologists against liability risks.* Simsbury, CT: American Professional Agency.

Wessler, R. L. (1983). Rational-emotive therapy in groups. In A. Freeman (Ed.), *Cognitive therapy with couples and groups* (pp. 43–65). New York: Plenum.

Wessler, R. L., & Hankin-Wessler, S. (1989). Cognitive group therapy. In A. Freeman, K. M. Simon, L. E. Beutler, & H. Arkowitz (Eds.), *Comprehensive handbook of cognitive therapy* (pp. 559–581). New York: Plenum.

Wessler, R. A., & Wessler, R. L. (1980). *The principles and practices of rational-emotive therapy*. San Francisco: Jossy-Bass.

Westra, H. A., & Stewart, S. H. (1998). Cognitive behavioural therapy and pharmacotherapy: Complementary or contradictory approaches to the treatment of anxiety? *Clinical Psychology Review, 18*, 307–340.

Westra, H. A., Stewart, S. H., & Conrad, B. E. (2002). Naturalistic manner of benzodiazepine use and cognitive behavioral therapy outcome in panic disorder with agoraphobia. *Journal of Anxiety Disorders, 16*, 233–246.

Whisman, M. A., & Snyder, D. K. (1997). Evaluating and improving the efficacy of conjoint couple therapy. In W. K. Halford & H. J. Markman (Eds.), *Clinical handbook of marriage and couples interventions* (pp. 679–694). Chichester, UK: Wiley.

White, J. R. (2000). Depression. In J. R. White & A. Freeman (Eds.), *Cognitive-behavioral group therapy for specific problems and populations* (pp. 29–61). Washington, DC: American Psychological Association.

White, P. (1980). Limitations on verbal reports of internal events: A refutation of Nisbett and Wilson and of Bem. *Psychological Review, 87*, 105–112.

Wilkes, T. C. R., Belsher, G., Rush, A. J., Frank, E., and associates. (1994). *Cognitive therapy for depressed adolescents*. New York: Guilford.

Wilson, G. T. (1987). Cognitive studies in alcoholism. *Journal of Consulting and Clinical Psychology, 55*, 325–331.

Wilson, R. R. (1996). Imaginal desensitization and relaxation training. In C. G. Lindemann (Ed.), *Handbook of the treatment of the anxiety disorders* (2nd ed., pp. 263–290). Northvale, NJ: Aronson.

Wolpe, J. (1958). *Psychotherapy by reciprocal inhibition*. Stanford, CA: Stanford University Press.

Wolpe, J., & Lang, P. J. (1969). *Fear survey schedule*. San Diego: Educational and Industrial Testing Service.

Woody, G. E., McLellan, A. T., Luborsky, L., & O'Brien, C. P. (1985) Sociopathy and psychotherapy outcome. *Archives of General Psychiatry, 42*, 1081–1086.

Woolson, A. M., & Swanson, M. G. (1972). The second time around: Psychotherapy with the "hysterical woman." *Psychotherapy: Theory, Research and Practice, 9*, 168–175.

Wright, J. H. (1987). Cognitive Therapy and medication as combined treatment. In A. Freeman & V. Greenwood (Eds.), *Cognitive therapy: Applications in psychiatric and medical settings* (pp. 36–50). New York: Human Sciences Press.

Wright, J. H., & Davis, D. D. (1994). The therapeutic relationship in cognitive-behavioral therapy: Patient perceptions and therapist responses. *Cognitive and Behavioral Practice, 1*, 25–45.

Wright, J. H., Thase, M. E., Beck, A. T., & Ludgate, J. W. (Eds.). (1993). *Cognitive therapy with inpatients*. New York: Guilford.

Young, J. E. (1994). *Cognitive therapy for personality disorders: A schema-focused approach* (Rev. ed.). Sarasota, FL: Professional Resource Press.

Young, J., & Beck, A. T. (1980). *Cognitive Therapy Scale rating manual*. Unpublished manuscript, Philadelphia, PA.

Young, J. E., & Lindemann, M. (2002). An intrgrative schema focused model for personality disorders. In E. T. Dowd & R. Leahy (Eds.), *Clinical advances in cognitive psychotherapy: Theory and application* (pp. 93–109). New York: Springer.

Zaretsky, A. E., Segal, Z. V., & Gemar, M. (1999). Cognitive therapy for bipolar depression: A pilot study. *Canadian Journal of Psychiatry, 44*, 491–494.

Zohar, J., Insel, T., & Rasmussen, S. (1991). *The psychobiology of obsessive-compulsive disorder*. New York: Springer.

Zwemer, W. A., & Deffenbacher, J. L. (1984). Irrational beliefs, anger and anxiety. *Journal of Counseling Psychology, 31*, 391–393.

INDEX

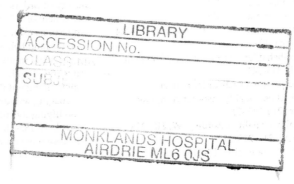
LIBRARY
ACCESSION No.
CLASS
SUBJ
MONKLANDS HOSPITAL
AIRDRIE ML6 0JS

Lightning Source UK Ltd.
Milton Keynes UK
24 March 2010

151787UK00007B/5/A

9 780306 484629